The Last and Greatest Art

The Last and Greatest Art

Some Unpublished Poetical Manuscripts
of
Alexander Pope

Transcribed and Edited by
Maynard Mack

Newark
University of Delaware Press
London and Toronto: Associated University Presses

Associated University Presses, Inc.
440 Forsgate Drive
Cranbury, NJ 08512

Associated University Presses
25 Sicilian Avenue
London WC1A 2QH, England

Associated University Presses
2133 Royal Windsor Drive
Unit 1
Mississauga, Ontario, Canada

Library of Congress Cataloging in Publication Data

Pope, Alexander, 1688–1744.
The last and greatest art.

Bibliography: p.
1. Pope, Alexander, 1688–1744—Manuscripts—Facsimiles. I. Mack, Maynard, 1909– II. Title.
PR3622.M3 1982 821′.5 82-4772
ISBN 0-87413-183-9 AACR2

Printed in the United States of America

Contents

Abbreviations

Correspondence: *Correspondence of Alexander Pope,* ed. George Sherburn, 5 vols. (Oxford: Clarendon Press, 1956).

Griffith: R. H. Griffith, *Alexander Pope: A Bibliography* (Austin, Tex.: University of Texas Press, 1922–27).

Spence: Joseph Spence, *Observations, Anecdotes, and Characters of Books and Men,* ed. J. M. Osborn, 2 vols. (Oxford: Clarendon Press, 1966).

TE: *The Twickenham Edition of the Poems of Alexander Pope* 11 vols. (London: Methuen; New Haven, Conn.: Yale University Press, 1938–61).

TS: Transcripts facing the photographic reproductions of the manuscripts in this volume.

Preface

THIS VOLUME IS in some respects an extended footnote or appendix to the second of my Northcliffe lectures, now published in *Collected in Himself: Essays Critical, Biographical, and Bibliographical on Pope and Some of His Contemporaries.* It contains photographic reproductions and transcripts of those longer poems of Pope's that have not hitherto been reproduced, or not reproduced in full, or at least not made available for general circulation: the *Pastorals* and the accompanying *Discourse on Pastoral Poetry, Sapho to Phaon,* the *Epistle to Jervas,* the *Epistle to Burlington, The First Satire of the Second Book of Horace Imitated* (addressed to Fortescue), the *Essay on Man* (two manuscripts), and the *Epistle to Dr. Arbuthnot.* I also give the collations made by Jonathan Richardson, Jr., from the lost manuscripts of the early *Dunciad.* More explicit information about these and about the manuscript texts generally will be found in the introduction to this volume and in the headnotes with which the individual texts are prefaced. I hope to say more about some of these matters in the biography on which I am presently engaged.

For permission to reproduce the manuscripts in this volume, I offer warm thanks to Arthur A. Houghton, Jr., the British Library, the Houghton Library of Harvard University, the Henry E. Huntington Library, the New York Public Library, the Pierpont Morgan Library, and the Beinecke Library of Yale University. For many kindnesses along the way, I wish to thank also William H. Bond, director of the Houghton Library; Charles Ryskamp, director of the Morgan Library; and Verlyn Klinkenborg of its staff; Daniel H. Woodward, librarian of the Huntington Library; and James Thorpe, its director; Lola Szladits *(prima semper inter pares)* curator of the Berg Collection of the New York Public Library; the late T. S. Wragge, keeper of the Devonshire Collections, Chatsworth; and Marjorie G. Wynne, research librarian of the Beinecke Library, and Stephen R. Parks, curator of its Osborn Collection. To the editors of *The Scriblerian,* especially Peter Tasch, I also owe much.

I am indebted to my own university for a fellowship in 1961–62 that enabled me to begin the work represented here, and to the National Endowment for the Humanities and the Henry E. Huntington Library for similar aid during 1979–80, enabling me to complete it. I have a further debt to the American Council of Learned Societies for a grant underwriting a portion of the photographic and clerical costs incurred in the preparation of this volume for the press.

In that same complicated task, I have benefited from the skilled help of Deborah Knuth, Grace Michel, Elizabeth Reynolds, and Peter Wallace. My deepest obligation however, is to Annetta Boyett, a distinguished assistant of long standing and a vigilant friend. To her I offer this volume with admiration and affection.

New Haven, Connecticut M. M.

For
Annetta Boyett
Without Whose Gallant Assistance This Book Could Not Have Been Completed

*General Introduction**

1

THIS VOLUME OF MANUSCRIPTS and transcripts represents the attainable and certainly the most useful part of what was once intended to be a collection of the entire canon of Pope's surviving poetical manuscripts apart from the translations of Homer.[1] This was without doubt a reckless ambition and (the gods having their usual way with overreachers) became dramatically more so as three of the important manuscripts were made available separately by Professors R. M. Schmitz of Washington University, Saint Louis, and Earl R. Wasserman of Johns Hopkins University,[2] and the costs of photography and printing, especially during the seventies, soared.

These considerations have made it expedient to gather into the present collection only manuscripts not previously published, and, among these, only those of substantial poems.[3] What now remains of the earlier project has proved to be quite sufficiently bulky and costly in its own right; and if used with the work of Professors Schmitz and Wasserman, and with volume 6 of the Twickenham Edition (hereafter cited as *TE*), which preserves manuscript variants for a considerable number of the short poems, it can serve many of the purposes proposed for the original plan. It can at any rate allow students of Pope—or of autography, calligraphy, graphology, or simply eighteenth-century culture generally—to rove widely and easily among the working papers (first jottings as well as final revisions, immediate inspirations as well as long labors of the file, allusions suppressed because too daring, locutions excised because too racy) of one of the great revisers of all time.

Pope's autograph manuscripts are presented here in photographs and transcripts on facing pages. The transcript of each autograph page was made on a wide-carriage typewriter, then reduced and photographed, rather than set in type by a compositor. This procedure affords far less flexibility than composition because the size of letters and spacings is fixed; and this means, in turn, that the position of any given passage in the transcript page may differ more than is desirable from its position in the accompanying photograph. But these disadvantages, it has seemed to me, are offset by reductions in cost and also by some reduction in the multiplying of errors since transference from copy to printer's proofs becomes unnecessary.

2

The scrupulous editor of Newton's *Mathematical Papers* has lately reminded us that a wholly accurate text of any body of manuscripts is a literary fiction.[4] Certainly I have found this true in my case. Sometimes one fails altogether to decipher the cramped or blotted letters of an insertion or of the word or phrase it replaces. Sometimes, after prolonged effort, one imagines one has the passage right only to discover on the ninth or ninety-ninth perusal that one has slightly, or even grievously, misread it. I am confident that errors of this kind will have escaped me, perhaps many. There is also the crucial role of serendipity. As everyone who has worked with manuscripts knows, one may stare at a crabbed or blotted line for hours in vain, and then, on another occasion, or in a sharper light, or, perhaps more important, in a changed mood or engaged by a different stream of consciousness, one will suddenly detect a shape in the shapeless and consequently a meaning. Close readers of these pages will now and then, I fear (I hope no oftener than now and then), enjoy the satisfaction of recapturing what I have had to omit or have made a poor guess at. In that event, happy man be their dole, say I, and pass the Falernian! The point to be taken is that, for all the labor and care that have gone into them, these transcriptions cannot pretend to be "definitive." They are offered instead as a reasonably reliable resource toward making sense of a body of manuscripts whose worst pages are probably as difficult to make out as those of any autograph known.

To the extent possible with typescript, the transcript page imitates the manuscript page. Pope's cancels, carets, glosses, numerals, large bracketings (as well as his smaller brackets both round and square) are retained. Doubtful readings and failures to decipher are signalized by pointed brackets, as are other editorial intrusions. A straight line enclosed in pointed brackets signifies material so well canceled by the poet that I have been unable to reconstruct it.

*In all quotations in the following introductions, raised letters have been lowered, and the period normally used in Pope's time beneath terminal raised letters [e.g. y^{n}] has been retained in lowering them. Quotations with authorial revisions or insertions have been reproduced according to the procedures specified for the *Dunciad* collations (pp. 97–98) except when doing so would obscure the point being made. Editorial matter in Notes to the Transcripts appears in italic.

Manuscript features not imitable by type—e.g., alteration of one word into another, or overwritings of one word by another—are reported in notes at the end of each particular transcript. In these cases, I have placed in the transcript text the reading that I believe was intended to take precedence and have recorded the other or others in the notes.

When, in Pope's successive revisions, the relationships of phrases to each other, or of parts of lines to other parts, have become intolerably scrambled or obscure, I have sometimes been obliged to reposition the materials on the transcript page (as compared with the manuscript) so as to elucidate what I take to be the poet's intention.

3

The collative readings from the two early *Dunciad* manuscripts set down by Jonathan Richardson, Jr., are another story. As a note by Pope testifies in each case, Richardson has preserved the readings of the "first" *Dunciad* manuscript in a copy of the *Dunciad* of 1728, and those of the "second" *Dunciad* manuscript in a copy of the edition published in 1736. [These, like the transcripts, I have chosen to present in photographed typescript]. The choice is dictated partly by the economic considerations mentioned earlier—photographs with transcripts would have extended this volume by more than three hundred very expensive pages—but also by the reflection that Richardson's notation of the manuscript readings in a printed text represents, inevitably, his own personal rationalization of the original pages rather than the original pages themselves with all their luxuriant growth and undergrowth. What is valuable in his work is the content, and that content, I am convinced, can be communicated with as much clarity and conciseness as can be hoped for in these matters by the means employed below, a full account of which is given here in the *Dunciad* introduction.

In a few other instances in this volume, I have also printed from a contemporary manuscript without providing accompanying photographs. The archives of Mapledurham House, home of Pope's friends the Blount sisters, preserve a few fragments of paper, torn from larger sheets, on which an unidentified hand has set down small groups of couplets belonging to the *Epistle to Burlington*, the *Epistle to Bathurst*, and the *Epistle to Fortescue* (*Imit. Hor.* Sat. II. i), but not unmistakably related to any particular compositional stage of these poems. These I have printed at appropriate points below. The only other text excluded from photographic reproduction is a contemporary transcript of the *Epistle to Burlington*, preserved today at Chatsworth. Since it is not an autograph and is a fair copy, little is gained from a photograph; yet it warrants publication with the autograph fragments because it contains the completed poem, and contains it in a text intermediate between that of the autograph and that of the first printed edition.

4

In his brilliant samplings down the centuries from the manuscripts of poets writing in English, P. J. Croft takes for his motto Keats's compelling phrase, "This warm scribe my hand." The phrase evokes vividly, as Mr. Croft remarks, "the living immediacy of all such texts as those here represented."[5] From looking intently at a poet's manuscripts as he composes, or even as he copies fair, impressions of mind and personality arise—subjective partly in the viewer, no doubt, like the impressions that arise from faces, yet perhaps answering to something in the object viewed that is real though not readily stated in words. What emanates in this way from Pope's papers, it seems to me (if I may make a partly fanciful effort to describe it), is not alone the "innate elegance" that Mr. Croft ascribes to his hand[6] but an exhilarating realism about the nature of art, incorporated and made visible in the very appearance of a typical page. For Pope's typical manuscript page is blessedly free of modernist cant about the sanctity of the artistic *moi* and the inviolability of that *moi*'s expressive effort. His practice reflects instead a poetic in which the poem is assumed to be a process of exploration and discovery, the poet's individual sensibility acting and reacting with the common language of men and the common symbolic language of mankind to produce a structure that is responsive to all three of these centers of poetic energy, but is at the same time available and gratifying to other readers, and, though determinate in the sense of having shape, remains capable of change and growth without loss of identity. Poetry, in what seems to be Pope's conception of it, is not history, but a form of action within history that has a history: his completed poem presents itself not as a species of Scripture or Revelation, but as a configuration of elements arranged in dramatic and dynamic poise by an entirely human wit that is ever susceptible to second (and even third) thoughts.

Thus *Windsor Forest* begins, so far as we know, in 1704–8 as a simple pastoral/georgic[7] and ends in 1713, having incorporated the imminent Peace of Utrecht, as a great idealizing myth about the English nation, past, present, and future. *The Rape of the Lock*, a tour de force when it was published in two cantos in 1712—"merum sal," Addison is reported to have said[8]—widened its sweep measurably when republished in 1714 in five (complete with sylphs), and added further to its resonances when, in 1717, Clarissa's speech imitating Sarpedon's was smoothed into place. The manuscripts of the *Essay on Man* testify that the poet first judged his poem to be complete in one epistle, then in two, then—by what seems to have been for a time a settled judgment—in three, and finally in four. As for the *Dunciad*, a poem that like the *Faerie Queene* we have barely begun to assimilate, its record of expansion is notorious: the slim volume of 1728, the *Variorum* of 1729, the *New Dunciad* of 1742, the four-book *Dunciad* of 1743—with other less distinctive states between. Throughout his career, the typical Pope poem is a work-in-progress. States of provisional wholeness and balance occur along the way, some more inclusive than others but each conceivable as an end stage; and the one at which the poet finally rests, though in most cases recognizably superior, never declares itself to be definitive in any absolute sense. Subtractions and accretions remain imaginable.

Looked at in this light, which it must be recalled is only partly fanciful, a leaf from Pope's work-table may be read in some measure as an epitome of his career. Always there is the stately processional of perceived intent coursing in a firm column down one side of the page. Always nearby there are the dance and play of new perceptions spinning off, developing their own fields of force, some wandering afield to die upon the margins or possibly to be revived in later contexts, others colliding, warring, at last fusing with the original column, altering its direction, sometimes causing it to disintegrate altogether. Then, once more, on a fresh page, now perhaps appreciably transformed, the onward march reasserts itself, only to strike out new clouds of fancy till the process of assimilation has to begin anew.

On some such pattern, perhaps, all good poems are made. That it is certainly the pattern on which many of Pope's were made the remainder of this volume will show.

NOTES

1. The Homer manuscripts were at that time in process of being collated and edited by Dr. Hans-Joachim Zimmermann of Heidelberg University, but the pressure of other duties has since forced Dr. Zimmermann to give up this project. For a pioneering survey and register of the existing autograph manuscripts of the original poems, see John Butt, "Pope's Poetical Manuscripts," in *Proceedings of the British Academy* 40 (1954): 23–39. (This is somewhat expanded in my recent volume entitled *Collected in Himself: Essays Critical, Biographical, and Bibliographical on Pope and Some of His Contemporaries* [Newark, Del.: University of Delaware Press, 1982]. Further commentary will be found in George Sherburn's "Pope at Work," in *Essays on the Eighteenth Century Presented to David Nichol Smith* (Oxford: Clarendon Press, 1945). Existing autographs of the longer poems are reproduced photographically in this volume and in the four volumes cited below in notes 2–3. Autograph and contemporary transcript variants for the shorter poems are recorded among the printed variants in *TE,* 6. See in addition *TE,* 10: Appendix C; D. M. Knight, "The Development of Pope's *Iliad* Preface: A Study of the Manuscript," *Modern Language Quarterly* 16 (1955): 237–46; and H.-J. Zimmermann, "Bemerkungen zum Manuskript and Text von Popes *Brutus,*" *Archiv* 199 (1962): 100–106.

Transcripts have been published of the three surviving manuscripts of Pope's prose: the *Preface* to the *Iliad* and the *Postscript* to the *Odyssey,* in *TE,* 10: appendices A, B; and the Preface to the *Works* of 1717 in *Augustan Worlds,* ed. J. C. Hilson, M. M. B. Jones and J. R. Watson (Leicester: Leicester University Press, 1978), pp. 85–106.

2. R. M. Schmitz, *Pope's Windsor Forest 1712: A Study of the Washington University Holograph* (St. Louis, Mo.: Washington University Press, 1952); *Pope's Essay on Criticism 1709: A Study of the Bodleian Manuscript Text, with Facsimiles, Transcripts and Variants* (St. Louis, Mo.: Washington University Press, 1962); E. R. Wasserman, *Pope's Epistle to Bathurst: A Critical Reading with an Edition of the Manuscripts* (Baltimore, Md.: The Johns Hopkins Press, 1960). To Professor Schmitz we owe the rediscovery of the *Windsor Forest* manuscript, long thought to be lost.

At an earlier time these presses and individuals graciously agreed to allow me to appropriate their work for this volume; but in the light of the economic realities of the late 70s and early 80s, already mentioned, this appeared in the end a wasteful and reckless proceeding. I want to express my thanks, however, for the generosity shown me.

3. Included in this volume are the autograph manuscripts of the *Pastorals,* with the introductory prose "Essay on Pastoral" (1709), *Sapho to Phaon* (1712), the *Epistle to Jervas* (1717), the *Epistle to Burlington,* incomplete (1731), the *Epistle to Fortescue* (1733), the *Essay on Man,* (two manuscripts: 1733–34), and the *Epistle to Arbuthnot* (1735). Also included, but in type only and not in photographs, are the Richardson collations of two *Dunciad* manuscripts (I suspect that the manuscripts themselves were destroyed as were apparently those of the later *Dunciads*) and an important transcript of the *Epistle to Burlington.* Apart from these and the three poems published by Professors Schmitz and Wasserman, no others of Pope's longer poetical works are now known to survive in manuscript, despite the fact that the manuscript of the *Epistle to a Lady* (1735) is recorded as late as 1887. (The dates in parentheses are those of publication).

Though the manuscripts of the *Essay on Man* have been previously reproduced photographically in *An Essay on Man: Reproductions of the Manuscripts in the Pierpont Morgan Library and the Houghton Library with the Printed Text of the Original Edition* (Oxford: Printed for Presentation to the Members of the Roxburgh Club, 1962), the scarcity of this volume, together with the fact that the photographs are not accompanied by transcripts, without which many pages remain largely impenetrable, has seemed to me to warrant their reappearance here.

4. D. T. Whiteside, *the Mathematical Papers of Isaac Newton* (Cambridge: Cambridge University Press, (1967), 1:x–xi.

5. *Autograph Poetry in the English Language: Facsimiles of Original Manuscripts from the Fourteenth to the Twentieth Century,* 2 vols. (London: Cassell, 1973), 1:xx.

6. Ibid., 1:70.

7. See *TE,* 1:125–27.

8. By Warburton in his edition of Pope's *Works* (1751), 4: 26 n.

The Pastorals

INTRODUCTION

THE MANUSCRIPT OF POPE'S *Pastorals* survives today in a small leather-bound volume measuring 20 by 13 cm (internal measurement, 19.4 by 12.5 cm).[1] It is protected by front and rear flyleaves together with twelve binder's leaves, six preceding and six following. The first binder's leaf (verso blank) carries on its recto the statement:

> This first copy of the Pastorals of Mr. Pope in his own fine hand writing, was given to Thomas Brand Hollis Esqr. by Mr. Wm: Gregson, nephew of the late Jonathan Richardson Junr.
> Transcribed from the hand writing of T. B. H. by me J. D. Nov. 20. 1805.

To this is added immediately below:

> This MS. was bound in Septr. 1812. The above Meñdum again transcribed Sept. 25. 1812. J. D.

"J. D." presumably stands for John Disney (1746–1816), a Unitarian clergyman to whom Thomas Brand Hollis in 1808 bequeathed his estates and (apparently somewhat before) donated the manuscript of the *Pastorals.* In acknowledgment, Disney published *Memoirs of Thomas Brand Hollis,* also in 1808.

The second binder's leaf, rector and verso, is occupied by a later note in the same hand dated 31 December 1813, which begins "Alexander Pope was born May 22, 1688. died May 30. 1744. Aged 56," and then introduces a quotation from Johnson's *Life* of Pope about his learning to write a fine hand by copying books, two quotations from the same source about his *Pastorals,* and a reference to William Lisle Bowles's account of similar matters in the first volume of his edition of Pope's *Works* (1806). A further comment on the poet's calligraphy, this time in a different hand and quoted from William Roscoe's edition of the *Works* (1824), occupies the recto (verso blank) of the third binder's leaf. All other binder's leaves are blank.

The manuscript itself contains twenty leaves. Following the cover leaf, with the inscriptions recorded below, "An Essay on Pastoral" occupies leaves 2 through 5; 6 is blank (as if reserved in advance for the conclusion of the essay, which breaks off with the catchword "Whence" at the foot of leaf 5v); and the four poems of just under 100 lines each take up the rest: "Spring," "Summer," "Autumn," "Winter." These, much revised, were to make their published appearance somewhat earlier than the "Essay," in the sixth and final volume of the series of miscellanies then still associated with Dryden: *Poetical Miscellanies, The Sixth Part,* published by Jacob Tonson in 1709. The revised "Essay" would first appear in Pope's *Works* of 1717 under the title "A Discourse on Pastoral."

Among Pope's extant autographs, this manuscript is easily the handsomest. Prose and verse alike are set down in the poet's finest italic printing hand, with running heads, titles framed between single and double rules, footnotes to the prose fenced off below a single rule, and proper names formed in roman in the otherwise italic text: conventions designed to convey the impression that one has in one's hands an exquisitely printed book. For such pains there were doubtless reasons. One, obviously, would have been a young author's natural pride in a first major undertaking brought to a happy close. Another, it seems clear, was concern for a suitable dress in which to circulate the new work among the growing circle of writers, litterateurs, and men of affairs whose respect his talents had already begun to win. All his life, Pope would follow the practice of submitting his verses to the criticism of friends. Now, all the more for his being a fledgling poet about to take first wing, it was important to him to solicit objections, make improvements, and, if possible, receive the imprimatur of seasoned critics.[2]

An autograph note on the manuscript's cover leaf (verso) offers the following biographical and bibliographical information:

> Mem. This Copy is that wch past thro ye / hands of Mr Walsh, Mr Congreve, Mr Main- / waring, Dr Garth, Mr Granville, Mr / Southern, Sr H. Sheers, Sr W. Trumbull, / Ld. Halifax, Ld. Wharton, Marq. of Dorchestr., / D. of Bucks. &c. Only ye 3rd Eclog was / written since some of these saw ye other 3. / wch were written as they here stand wth. / ye Essay, anno 1704. — Aetat. meae, 16.
>
> The Alterations from this copy were upon / ye Objections of some of these, or my own.[3]

The date of this memorandum is not easy to assign. The handwriting looks to be later than that of the manuscript texts, as the Twickenham editors have noted,[4] and the content of the note would fit nicely into that period of the mid-1730s when Pope was beginning to issue his poems in small octavo editions, where variant readings from the manuscripts were frequently salted in among the footnotes.[5] On the other hand, a certain air of contingency in the information given, together with the manner in which some of these early judges are denominated, makes a late date improbable. Would Pope, after 1711, when George Granville became Baron Lansdowne as one of the "Peers for the Peace," have named him Mr. Granville? On similar grounds, after 1715, when the Marquess of Dorchester became Duke of Kingston, would Pope have miscalled him marquess? Is it likely, moreover, that this throng of names, several of them belonging to persons with whom he had no recorded later associations, would linger in his mind with such unblemished heterogeneity for any length of years? To my mind, though certainty is impossible, Pope's testimony has the ring of something set down in a flush of youthful self-gratulation probably not too long after the manuscript had completed the rounds described.

As for the manuscript itself, the likeliest range of dates is probably 1704–6, though there is nothing inherently wrong with Pope's explicit date of 1704. Already by April 1705, Walsh, and also Wycherley, whose name is oddly missing from Pope's list of connoisseurs,[6] have looked over "Papers" that Pope will identify, when he publishes their letters to him, as "Mr. Pope's *Pastorals*."[7] These may, of course, have consisted of loose papers antecedent to this manuscript, but it is worth noting that the "Essay"—in some ways, a more remarkable document for a sixteen-year-old to have produced than the poems—is already present.[8] Granville, too, the future Lord Lansdowne, in an undated letter to an unidentified "Harry," in which he describes Pope as "not above Seventeen or Eighteen" (and thus establishes for his letter an approximate date of 1705–6), has seen both the poems and the poet, and is eager to introduce him, along with Wycherley, to his correspondent on any day the correspondent cares to name.[9] By 20 April 1706, shortly before Pope's eighteenth birthday, the manuscript has reached Congreve's hands and has been shown to Tonson, who solicits it for publication.[10]

Internal evidence also supports an early date. In "Spring" as set down in the manuscript, Strephon's riddle carries an allusion to the great victory at Blenheim on 13 August 1704, when the Stuart "Thistle" of Queen Anne (who was further associated with this emblem through having revived the Order of the Thistle in 1703) triumphed over the "Lily" of Louis XIV and France:

> Say, Daphnis, say, what Region canst thou find,
> In which by Thistles, Lilies are outshin'd?
> (TS, 9 "Spring," ll. 25, 27)[11]

As time wore on, and the freshness along with the intelligibility of this first allusion waned, Pope conflated it with a more current reference to the Union of England and Scotland (this took place on 1 May 1707, though it had been in the news for more than a year) and the consequent changes in the royal arms. These thereafter were to show the arms of England and Scotland (not as formerly, those of England and France) impaled in the important first and fourth quarters, with the French fleur-de-lys relegated to the less important second.[12] Hence The new allusion in "Spring" brought together fields pastoral and fields martial with fields armorial:

> Nay, tell me first in what more happy Fields,
> The Thistle springs, to which the Lilly yields?
> (*TE*, "Spring," ll. 89–90)

The updating of the allusion suggests that the original passage (and presumably the manuscript in which it was set down) can hardly have been composed later than 1706 and may have been made, just as Pope claims, in the actual year of Blenheim, 1704.

The one exception, as the memorandum acknowledges, is "Autumn." In the manuscript, this has had to be shoe-horned into a space reserved for it that proved too small. The pages of the other three *Pastorals* in this manuscript never carry more than sixteen of Pope's exquisitely formed lines, whereas the last two pages of "Autumn," to which for some reason only six pages are allocated as against seven for each of the other poems, are obliged to accommodate, respectively, eighteen and twenty. On such slim evidence as we have, the insertion is probably to be ascribed to the last months of 1706. Writing to Pope on 9 September of that year, Walsh notes that he has not yet seen the third *Pastoral* but expects it will be finished by the time he comes to town for the opening of parliament[13]—this would have been November. One may reasonably suspect, then, that "Autumn" was in place in its cramped quarters by the close of 1706.

As always, however, Pope continued to tinker with his work, sending Walsh in due course four pages of proposals for revision,[14] apparently in response, as he puts it in the Memorandum, to "the Objections of some of these, or my own." The presence of the new version of the Thistle/Lily conceit among these propsals suggests that they may have been drawn up and sent to Walsh in the late spring of 1707. That summer, Pope also undertook what his elderly mentor Sir William Trumbull called "a dreadful long journey into Worcestershire" to stay with Walsh.[15] Possibly during this visit some or all of the many changes were made that appear neither in the manuscript nor in the four pages of proposals but only in the printed edition. Words, lines, and whole passages are excised, added, rearranged, or shifted to new positions (even the names of participants are altered)[16] in what we can now recognize, with the aid of these manuscripts and the Twickenham edition, to have been a continuing process of revision, not merely for the *Pastorals* but for all of Pope's poetry, never wholly abandoned while he lived.

NOTES

1. I am deeply grateful to Arthur A. Houghton, Jr. *(amicorum Musarum facile princeps),* for having allowed me to publish this manuscript in *The Scriblerian* (12 [1980]: 85–161) in advance of the sale of the second portion of his library at Christie's in June 1980. It is here republished from that source. A version of the present introduction was also printed with the manuscript in the *Scriblerian.*

2. Even at this early stage (partly no doubt from diffidence but partly also, one suspects, from the acute sense of audience that stayed with him all his life, Pope seeks the approval of a small but prestigious company of readers before facing the hypercritics of the coffee houses. This aspect of his "business" sense is splendidly illuminated in David Foxon's magisterial *Pope and the Eighteenth-Century Book-Trade* (forthcoming).

3. One need not suppose that Pope knew all of these men personally. The manuscript of a precocious new poet was easily passed from one writer or nobleman to another, who might look it over and register an opinion without meeting the author.

4. *TE,* 1:38.

5. Volume 1 containing the *Pastorals* was published in 1736.

6. This might result from the sort of oversight of which we all are capable in forgetting to set down a fact or name most material to the case in hand; or it might, conceivably, indicate a momentary cooling in the relationship of the two, which was occasionally somewhat perplexed by Wycherley's desire to submit his verses to Pope's revision without quite wishing them to be revised. In either case, it seems to me additional evidence that Pope's memorandum belongs early rather than late. The omission of Wycherley's name was rectified in a note to the first printed edition in 1709. On Pope's varying lists of early supporters, see Spence's *Observations, Anecdotes, and Characters of Books and Men,* ed. J. M. Osborn, 2 vols. (Oxford: Clarendon Press, 1956), 2:616–18; hereafter referred to as Spence.

7. Wycherley to Pope, 7 April 1705, and Walsh to Wycherley, 20 April 1705 (*Correspondence,* 1:6–7). It is only Walsh's allusion to "Papers" that Pope glosses in his own editions of his correspondence as referring to the *Pastorals;* but it seems plausible that at this date Wycherley's allusion is to the same work. Though Pope's own editions are the only authority for these letters and he rather liked to stress his precocity, other evidence shows that his statements are not far off the truth.

8. In the April letter to Wycherley, Walsh calls it "very judicious and very learned."

9. *The Genuine Works in Verse and Prose of the Right Honorable George Granville, Lord Lansdowne* (1732), 1:436–37. I suspect that Granville's "Harry" is Pope's "Sr. H. Sheers" (Sir Henry Sheers, engineer and author, d. 1710); that the proposed introductions took place with possibly a loan of the manuscript to the new acquaintance; and that in this way Sheers' name reaches the list.

10. Tonson to Pope, 20 April 1706 (*Correspondence,* 1:17). Tonson's statement that he has seen "a pastoral of yours" can mean that he was shown but one of the (at the time only three) *Pastorals* completed; but it can as easily mean "a pastoral work of yours." As such—a plainly soon-to-be-completed work celebrating four seasons—it might more plausibly earn its description in Tonson's letter as a "Poem for the Press" than if he had seen a single poem celebrating a single season, standing alone.

11. Readers were helped to solve the riddle by the immediately succeeding Stuart reference—to the oak in whose branches Charles II is said to have harbored from his pursuers: "A wondrous Tree, that sacred Monarchs bears."

12. On this whole matter see the excellent discussion in *TE,* 1:39–41. For the suggestion that Strephon's riddle might be read as a covert tribute to James II and the Stuart line, see J. M. Aden, *Pope's Once and Future Kings: Satire and Politics in the Early Career* (Knoxville, Tenn.: University of Tennessee Press, 1978), pp. 62–63.

13. *Correspondence,* 1:22.

14. These follow the manuscript of the *Pastorals* in this volume.

15. Trumbull to his nephew Ralph Bridges, 5 August 1707, in Sherburn's "New Anecdotes about Alexander Pope," *Notes and Queries,* n.s. 5 (1958): 347.

16. In "Spring," Strephon's beloved Sylvia changes to Delia and Daphnis's Amaryllis to Sylvia. In "Summer" the Amaryllis for whom Alexis pines becomes a she without a name. The friend whose loss "Autumn's" Aegon laments changes in the printed text from Phillis to Doris. "Winter's" Meliboeus is replaced by Lycidas.

119.

First. Copy
of the
Pastoralls.

7

<Cover leaf, recto>

WG.

First Copy

of the

Pastoralls.

Mem: This Copy is that wch past thro ye hands of Mr Walsh, Mr Congreve, Mr Mainwaring, Dr. Garth, Mr Granville, Mr Southern, Sr H. Sheers, Sr W. Trumbull, Ld Halifax, Ld Wharton, Marq. of Dorchestr. D. of Bucks. &c. Only ye 3rd Eclog was written since some of these saw ye other 3. wch were written as they here stand wth ye Essay, anno 1704. — Ætat. meæ, 16.

The Alterations from this Copy were upon ye Objections of some of these, or my own.

AN

ESSAY

ON

PASTORAL.

THE original of Poesie is attributed to that Age of Innocence which succeeded the Creation of the World. And as the Feeding of Flocks ~~appears~~ seems to have been the first Employment of Mankind; the most ancient sort of Poetry was probably Pastoral.(a) It is natural to imagine, that the Leisure of those ancient Shepherds requir'd some Diversion; & none was so proper to that Solitary Life as Singing. These Songs were adapted to their present Circumstances; &

(a) Fontanelle's Discourse of Pastorals.

in

Mem: This Copy is that wch past thro ye hands of Mr Walsh, Mr Congreve, Mr Mainwaring, Dr. Garth, Mr Granville, Mr Southern, Sr H. Sheers, Sr W. Trumbull, Ld Halifax, Ld Wharton, Marq. of Dorchest^{r} D. of Bucks. &c. Only ye 3rd Eclog was written since some of these saw ye other 3. wch were written as they here stand wth ye Essay, anno 1704. -- AEtat. meae, 16.

The Alterations from this Copy were upon ye Objections of some of these, or my own.

AN ESSAY ON PASTORAL.

The Original *of Poesie is attributed to that Age of Innocence which succeeded the Creation of the World. And as the Feeding of Flocks* ~~*appears*~~ *seems to have been the first Employment of Mankind; the most ancient sort of Poetry was probably* Pastoral. (a) *It is natural to imagine, that the* Leisure *of those ancient* Shepherds *requir'd some Diversion; & none was so proper to that* Solitary Life *as singing. These Songs were adapted to their present Circumstances; &*

(a) Fontanelle's *Discourse of Pastorals.*

in

in these they took occasion to celebrate their owne Felicity. From hence a Poem *was invented, and afterwards improv'd to a perfect Image of that happy Time: which by infusing into us an Esteem for the Virtues of a former Age, might recommend the same to the present. And since the Life of a* Shepherd *was attended with most* Tranquillity, *the Poets retain'd their Persons, from whom it receiv'd the Name of* Pastoral.

A Pastoral *is an* Imitation *of the* Action *of a* Shepherd, *or* One consideed under that Character. *The* Form *of this* Imitation *is Dramatick, Narrative, or Mixt.* (b) *The* Fable *simple.* (c) *The* Manners *not too polite, nor yet too rustic: In Order to a just Preservation of which, they are represented according to the Genius of the Golden Age.* (d) *Conformable to the Manners, the* Thoughts *are plain and pure; yet admit a little Quickness and Passion, but that short and flowing. The* Expression *humble, yet as pure as the Language will afford: neat, but not exquisit; easy, but yet lively. In short, the Fable, Manners, Thoughts, and Expressions, are full of the greatest* Simplicity *in Nature.*

(b) Heinsius, *Not. in* Theocr. Idyll.

(c) Hor. Ar. Poet. *vers.* 23.
Denique sit, quod vis, simplex duntaxat, & unum.

(d) Rapin, *de Carm. pastor.* p. 2.

The

The compleat Character *of this Poem consists in* Simplicity, Brevity, *and* Delicacy: *the two first of which render an Eclogue* Natural, *and the last* Delightfull.

If we design to copy Nature, *it may be useful to take this Consideration along with us; that* Pastoral *properly belongs to the* Golden Age. *So that we are not to describe our Shepherds as Shepherds at this Day really are; but as they may be conceiv'd then to have been; wn. a Notion of Quality was annex'd to the Name, and the best of Men follow'd that Employment. To carry this Resemblance yet farther, it wou'd not be amiss to give the Shepherds some Skill in* Astrology *(Astronomy), as far as it may be useful to that sort of Life. And an Air of* Piety to the Gods, *which is so visibly diffus'd thro' all the Works of Antiquity, shou'd shine throughout the Poem.* (f) *Above all, a* Pastoral *ought to preserve some Relish of the* Ancient Way *of Writing. For which Reason the* Connexions *shou'd be loose; the* Narrations *and* Descriptions *little; and the* Periods *short.* (g) *Yet it is not sufficient that the Sen-*

(f) *Preface to the* Pastorals *in* Dryd. Virg.

(g) Rapin, *Reflexions sur l'Art Poet. d'Arist.* p. 2. *refl.* 27.

ten-

in these they took occasion to celebrate their owne Felicity. From hence a **Poem** *was invented, and afterwards improv'd to a perfect Image of that happy Time: which by infusing into us an Esteem for the Virtues of a former Age, might recommend the same to the present. And since the Life of a* **Shepherd** *was attended with most* **Tranquillity,** *the Poets retain'd their Persons, from whom it receiv'd the name of Pastoral.*

A **Pastoral** *is an* **Imitation** *of the* **Action** *of a* **Shepherd,** *or* **One considred under that Character.** *The* **Form** *of this* **Imitation** *is Dramatick, Narrative, or Mixt.* (b) *The* **Fable** *simple.* (c) *The* **Manners** *not ^too polite, nor yet too rustic: In Order to a just Preservation of which, they are represented according to the Genius of the Golden Age.* (d) *Conformable to the Manners, the* **Thoughts** *are plain and pure; yet admit a little Quickness and Passion, but that short and flowing. The* **Expression** *humble, yet as pure as the Language will afford: neat, but not exquisit; easy, but yet lively. In short, the Fable, Manners, Thoughts, and Expressions, are full of the greatest* **Simplicity** *in Nature.*

(b) **Heinsius,** *Not. in* **Theocr. Idyll.**

(c) **Hor. Ar. Poet.** *vers.* 23.
Denique sit, quod vis, simplex duntaxat, & unum.

(d) **Rapin,** *de Carm. pastor.* p^{t} 2.

The

The Compleat **Character** *of this Poem consists in* **Simplicity, Brevity,** *and* **Delicacy:** *the two first of which render an Eclogue* **Natural,** *and the last* **Delightfull.**

If we design to copy **Nature,** *it may be useful to take this Consideration along with us; that* **Pastoral** *properly belongs to the* **Golden Age.** *So that we are not to describe our Shepherds as Shepherds at this Day really are; but as they may be conceiv'd then to have been; w^{n} a Notion of Quality was annex'd to the Name, and the best of Men follow'd that Employment. To carry this Resemblance yet farther, it wou'd not be amiss to give the Shepherds.* *Astronomy* *some Skill in Astrology, as far as it may be useful to that sort of Life. And an Air of* **Piety** *to the* **Gods,** *which is so visibly diffus'd thro' all the Works of Antiquity, shou'd shine throughout the Poem.* (f) *Above all, a* **Pastoral** *ought to preserve some Relish of the* **Ancient Way** *of Writing. For which Reason the* **Connexions** *shou'd be loose; the* **Narrations** *and* **Descriptions** *little; and the* **Periods** *short.* (g) *Yet it is not sufficient that the* **Sen-**

(f) **Preface** *to the* **Pastorals** *in* **Dryd. Virg.**

(g) **Rapin,** *Reflexions sur l'Art Poet. d'Arist. p.2. refl. 27.*

ten-

Essay on Pastoral.

tences, only be brief; the whole Eclogue shou'd be so too. For we cannot suppose Poetry in those days to have been the Business of Men, but their Recreation us'd at vacant Hours. But with a Respect to the present Age, nothing more conduces to make these Composures natural, than when some **Knowledge** in **Rural Affairs** is discover'd. (i) This may be made appear rather done by Chance than on Design, and sometimes is best shown by **Inference**: Lest by too much Study to seem **Natural**, we Destroy the **Delight**. For what is inviting in this Poetry, proceeds not so much from the **Idea of a Country** Life it self, as from that of its Tranquillity.

We must therefore use some **Illusion** to render a **Pastoral, Delightfull**: And this consists in exposing the best Side only of a Shepherds Life, and in concealing its Miseries.(k) Nor is it enough to introduce **Shepherds** discoursing together, but a Regard must be had to the **Subject**. First, that it contain some particular Beauty in it self, and secondly, that it be **different** in every Eclogue. Besides, in evry one of them, a design'd **Scene** or **Prospect** is to be presented to our Eyes;

(i) Preface to Virg. Past. in Dryd. Virg.
(k) Fontanelle's *Discourse* of Pastorals.

which

Essay on Pastoral.

which shou'd also charm by its Variety. (l) ∴ This Grace is obtain'd, in a great Degree, by frequent Comparisons, drawn from the most agreable Objects in the Country: by Interrogations to Things inanimate, in which the **Delicacy of Pastoral** is chiefly compriz'd: by beautiful Digressions, but those short: sometimes by enlarging a little on Circumstances: And lastly, by elegant Turns on the Words; which render the Numbers extreamly sweet and pleasing. As for the Numbers themselves, they are properly of the **Heroick** Measure; but the smoothest, the most easy, and flowing imaginable. (m)

It is by Rules like these, which are but Nature reduc'd to Method, that we ought to judge of **Pastoral**: And since the Instructions giv'n for any Art, are to be deliver'd as that Art is in perfection, they must be deriv'd from those in whom it is generally acknowledg'd so to be. 'Tis therefore from the Practise of **Theocritus** and **Virgil**, (the only uncontested Authors of **Pastoral**) that the Criticks have drawn these ~~useful~~ Notions concerning it. Perhaps a Word of those Poets in this place may not be impertinent.

(l) *See the forementioned* Preface.
(m) Rapin, *de Carm. Pastor.* Pt. 3.

Theotences only be brief; the whole Eclogue shou'd be so too. For we cannot suppose Poetry in those days to have been the Business of Men, but their Recreation us'd at vacant Hours. But with a Respect to the present Age, nothing more conduces to make these Composures natural, than when some Knowledge in Rural Affairs is discover'd. (i) This may be made appear rather done by Chance than on Design, and sometimes is best shown by Inference: Lest by too much Study to seem Natural, we Destroy the Delight. For what is inviting in this Poetry, proceeds not so much from the Idea of a Country Life it self, as from that of its Tranquillity.

We must therefore use some Illusion to render a Pastoral, Delightfull: And this consists in exposing the best Side only of a Shepherds Life, and in concealing its Miseries. (k) Nor is it enough to introduce Shepherds discoursing together, but a Regard must be had to the Subject. First, that it contain some particular Beauty in it self, and secondly, that it be different in every Eclogue. Besides, in ev'ry one of them, a design'd Scene or Prospect is to be presented to our Eyes;

(i) Preface to Virg. Past. in Dryd. Virg.

(k) Fontanelle's Discourse of Pastorals.

which

which shou'd also charm by its Variety. (1)

∴ This Grace is obtain'd, in a great Degree, by frequent Comparisons, drawn from the most agreable Objects in the Country: by Interrogations to Things inanimate, in which the Delicacy of Pastoral is chiefly compriz'd: by beautiful Digressions, but those short: sometimes by enlarging a little on Circumstances: And lastly, by elegant Turns on the Words; which render the Numbers extreamly sweet and pleasing. As for the Numbers themselves, they are properly of the Heroick Measure; but the smoothest, the most easy, and flowing imaginable. (m)

It is by Rules like these, which are but Nature reduc'd to Method, that we ought to judge of Pastoral. And since the Instructions giv'n for any Art, are to be deliver'd as that Art is in perfection, they must be deriv'd from those in whom it is generally acknowledg'd so to be. Tis therefore from the Practise of Theocritus and Virgil, (the only uncontested Authors of Pastoral) that the Criticks have draw̃ these ~~useful~~ Notions concerning it. Perhaps a Word of those Poets in this place may not be impertinent.

(1) See the foremention'd Preface.

(m) Rapin, de Carm. Pastor. Pt.3.

Theo-

Essay on Pastoral.

Theocritus excells all Others, in Nature and Simplicity. The Subjects of his Idyllia are purely Pastoral; but he is not so exact in the Persons, having introduc'd * Reapers and Fishermen among his Shepherds. He is apt to be long in his Descriptions, of which that of ye Cup in the first Idyll is a remarkable Instance. In the Manners he seems a little defective, for his Swains are sometimes abusive and immodest, and perhaps too much inclining to Rusticity.†

But 'Tis enough that all others learnt their Excellences from him; and that his Dialect alone has a secret Charm in it, which no other could ever attain.

Virgil is certainly the Copy, but then he is such an one as equalls his Original: × In all points where Judgment has the principal Part, he is much superior to his Master. Tho' some of his Subjects are not Pastoral in themselves, but only appear to be such, they have a wonderfull Variety in them, which the Greek was ~~utterly~~ a Stranger to. * He exceeds him in Regularity and Brevity, and is perfect in the Manners. And falls short of him in nothing, but Simplicity

* ΘΕΡΙΣΤΑΙ, Idyl. 10. And ἉΛΙΕΙΣ, Idyl. 21.
† Idyl. 4, & 5.
× Rapin Reflex. on Arist. p. 2. refl. 27.
* Preface to the Eclogues in Dryd. Virg.

Essay on Pastoral.

city and Propriety of Style: The first of which was the Fault of his Age, and the last of his Language.

Among the Moderns, their Success has been greatest, who have most endeavor'd to make these Ancients their Pattern. The most considerable Genius appears in the Famous Tasso, and our Spencer. Tasso in his Amintas is said to have as far excell'd all the Pastoral Poets of his Nation, as in his Jerusalem he has outdone the Epicks. But as this Piece was the Original of a new sort of Poem, the Pastoral Comedy, in Italy, it cannot so well be thought a Copy of ye Ancients. ~~I shall then proceed to~~ Spencer's ~~whole~~ Kalender, in Mr. Dryden's Opinion, is the most compleat Work of this sort, which any Nation has produc'd ever since the Time of Virgil. (n) Not but that he seems imperfect in some few points; His Eclogues are generally too long, Some of them contain two hundred Lines, and others considerably exceed that Number. He has emploid the Lyric Measure, which is contrary to the Practise of the Ancients. His Stanza is not still the same, nor always well chosen. This last may be the Reason his Expression is not often concise enough: For the Tetrastic has obliged him to spin out his Sense to the Compass of

(n) Dedication to Virgil's Eclogs.

Theocritus *excells all Others, in Nature and Simplicity. The Subjects of his* **Idyllia** *are purely Pastoral; but he is not so exact in the Persons, having introduc'd* Reapers and Fishermen among his Shepherds. He is apt to be long in his* <u>*Descriptions*</u>*, of which that of* y^e <u>Cup</u> *in the first Idyll is a remarkable Instance. In the* <u>*Manners*</u> *he seems a little defective, for his Swains are sometimes abusive and immodest, and perhaps too much inclining to* **Rusticity.**+ *But* *'Tis enough that all others learnt their Excellences from him; and that his Dialect alone has a secret Charm in it, which no other could ever attain.*

Italic. (beside line 6)
Italic. (beside line 8)

Virgil *is certainly the* **Copy,** *but then he is such an one as equalls his Original.*x *In all points where*x <u>*Judgment*</u> *has the principal Part, he is much superior to his Master. Tho' some of his Subjects are not Pastoral in themselves, but only appear to be such, they have a wonderfull* <u>*Variety*</u> *in them, which the* **Greek** *was* ~~*utterly*~~ *a Stranger to.** *He exceeds him in*ˆ <u>*Regularity*</u> *and*ˆ <u>*Brevity*</u>*,* <u>*and is perfect in the Manners*</u>*. And falls short of him in nothing, but Simpli-*

he is$^{n<t>}$
in his

Italick. (beside line 28)
Italic. (beside line 36)
Italic. (beside line 40)

* ΘΕΡΙΣΤΑΙ *Idyl.10. And,* ʽΑΛΙΕΙΣ *Idyl.21.*

+ *Idyl. 4, & 5.*

x **Rapin** *Reflex. on Arist.* p^t *2. ref. 27.*

* *Preface to the Eclogues in* **Dryd.** *Virg.*

city

city and Propriety of Style: The first of which was the Fault of his **Age,** *and the last of his* **Language.**

Among the Moderns, their Success has been greatest, who have most endeavor'd to make these Ancients their Pattern. The most considerable Genius appears in the Famous **Tasso,** *and our* **Spencer. Tasso** *in his* **Aminta** *is said to have as far excell'd all the Pastoral Poets of his Nation, as in his* **Jerusalem** *he has outdone the* **Epicks.** *But as this Piece was the Original of a new sort of Poem, the Pastoral Comedy, in* **Italy,** *it cannot so well be thought a Copy of* y^e **Ancients.** ~~*I shall then proceed to*~~ | **Spencer's** ~~*whose*~~ **Kalender,** *in Mr.* **Dryden's** *Opinion, is the most compleat Work of this sort, which any Nation has produc'd ever since the Time of* **Virgil.** *(n) Not but that he seems imperfect in some few points; His* **Eclogues** *are generally too long, Some of 'em contain two hundred Lines, and others considerably exceed that Number. He has emploid the* **Lyric** *Measure, which is contrary to the Practice of the Ancients. His* **Stanza** *is not still the same, nor always well chosen. This last may be the Reason his Expression is not often concise enough: For the* **Tetrastic** *has obligd him to spin out his Sense to the Compass*

(n) **Dedication** *to* **Virgil's** *Eclogs.*

of

Essay on Pastoral.

of four Lines, which had been more closely con-fin'd in the Couplet.

For the Manners, Thoughts, and Characters, he comes near to Theocritus himself; tho' not-withstanding all the Care he has taken, he is certainly inferior in his Dialect. The Additiō he has made of a Kalendar to his Eclogues, is beautiful in the highest Degree. For by this, besides the general Moral of Innocence and Simplicity, which is common to other Authors, he has One peculiar to himself. He compares the Life of Man to the several Seasons, and at once exposes to his Readers a View of the Great and Little Worlds, in their various Aspects and Conditions.

'Twas from hence I took my first Design of the following Eclogues. For looking upon Spēcer as the Father of English Pastoral, I thought my self unworthy to be esteem'd even the meanest of his Sons, unless I bore some Resemblance of him. But as it happens with degenerate Ofspring, not only to recede from yͤ Virtues, but dwindle from the Bulk of their Ancestors; So I have copy'd Spencer in Mini-ature, and reduc'd his Twelve Months into Four Seasons. For his Choice of the former, has either oblig'd him to repeat the same Des-cription for three' Months together; or, when it was exhausted before, entirely to Omit it.

Whence

Essay *on* Pastoral

*of four Lines, which had <u>been</u> <u>more</u> <u>closely</u> con-
fin'd in the Couplet.*

*For the Manners, Thoughts, and Characters,
he* comes near *to* Theocritus *himself; tho' not-
withstanding all the Care he has taken, he is
certainly inferior in his Dialect. The Additiõ
he has made of a Kalendar to his Eclogues, is
beautiful in the highest Degree. For by this,
besides the general Moral of Innocence and
Simplicity, which is common to other Authors,
he has One peculiar to himself. He compares
the Life of Man to the several Seasons, and
at once exposes to his Readers a View of the
Great and Little Worlds, in their various
Aspects and Conditions.*

*'Twas from hence I took my first Design of
But I have copied--
the following Eclogues. For looking upon* Spẽ-
cer *as the Father of English Pastoral, I
thought myself unworthy to be esteem'd even
the meanest of his Sons, unless I bore some
Resemblance of him. But as it happens with
degenerate Offspring, not only to recede from yᵉ
to
Virtues, but ‸ dwindle from the Bulk of their
—Eclogs. But
Ancestors; So I have copy'd* Spencer *in* Mini-
ature, *and reduc'd his Twelve* Months *into
Four* Seasons. *For his Choice of the former,
has <u>either</u> <u>oblig'd</u> <u>him</u> to repeat the same Description*[8] *for three' Months together; or, when
it was exhausted before, entirely to Omit it.*

Whence

SPRING:

The First Pastorall;

OR

DAMON.

FIrst in these Fields I sing the Sylvan Strains,
Nor blush to sport on Windsor's peaceful Plains:
Fair Thames flow gently from thy sacred Spring
While on thy Banks Sicilian Muses sing;
Let Vernal Airs thro' trembling Osiers play,
And Albion's Cliffs resound the Rural Lay.

Daphnis and Strephon led their Flocks along,
Both fam'd for Love, and both renown'd in Song;

Fresh

S P R I N G :

The First Pastorall;

OR

D A M O N.

· *First in these Fields I sing the Sylvan Strains,*
Nor blush to sport on Windsor's *peaceful Plains:*
Fair Thames *flow gently from thy sacred Spring*
While on thy Banks Sicilian *Muses sing;*
Let Vernal Airs thro' trembling Osiers play,
And Albion's *Cliffs resound the Rural Lay.*

Daphnis *and* Strephon *led their Flocks along,*
· *Both fam'd for Love, and both renown'd in Song;*

Fresh

SPRING.

Freſh as the Morn, and as the Seaſon fair,
In flow'ry Plains they fed their fleecy Care;
And while Aurora gilds the Mountains Side,
Thus Daphnis ſpoke, and Strephon thus reply'd.

Daphnis.

Hear how the ~~Larks~~ Birds, on ev'ry bloomy Spray,
With joyous Muſick wake the dawning Day;
Why ſit we mute, when early ~~Turtles~~ Linnets ſing,
When warbling Philomel ſalutes the Spring?
Why ſit we ſad, when Phoſphor ſhines ſo clear,
And laviſh Nature paints the Purple Year?

Strephon.

Sing then, and Damon ſhall attend the Strain,
Where yon' ſlow Oxen turn the furrow'd Plain;
There the pale Primroſe and the Vi'let grow;
There Weſtern Winds on Beds of Roſes blow:
I'l ſtake my Lamb, that near ~~the fountain~~ plays,
And his own Image from the Bank ſurveys.

Daph.

The First Paſtoral.

Daphnis.

And I this Bowl, where wanton Ivy twines,
And Cluſters lurk beneath the curling Vines:
Four Figures riſing from the Work appear,
The various Seaſons of the rowling Year;
And what is That, which binds the Radiant Sky,
Where twelve fair Signs in beauteous Order lie?

Damon.

Then ſing by turns, by turns the Muſes ſing;
Now Hawthorns bloſsome, now the Daiſies ſpring,
Now Leaves the Trees, and Flow'rs adorn the Ground;
Begin, the Vales ſhall echo to the Sound.

Strephon.

Ye Fountain Nymphs, propitious to the Swain,
Now grant me Phœbus or Alexis Strain:
My faireſt Bull ſhall at your Altars ſtand,
With butting Horns, and Heels yſpurn the Sand.

Daph.

SPRING.

Fresh as the Morn, and as the Season fair,
In flow'ry Plains they fed their fleecy Care;
And while Aurora gilds the Mountains Side,
Thus Daphnis spoke, and Strephon thus reply'd.

Daphnis

Birds
Hear how the ~~Larks~~, on ev'ry bloomy Spray,
With joyous Musick wake the dawning Day;
Linnets
Why sit we mute, when early ~~Turtles~~ sing,
When warbling Philomel salutes the Spring?
Why sit we sad, when Phosphor shines so clear,
And lavish Nature paints the Purple Year?

Strephon

Sing then, and Damon shall attend the Strain,
· Where yon' slow Oxen turn the furrow'd Plain;
There the pale Primrose and the Vi'let grow;
· There Western Winds on Beds of Roses blow:
I'l stake my Lamb, that near the fountain plays,
And his own Image from the Bank surveys.

Daph.

The First Pastoral.

Daphnis.

And I this Bowl, where wanton Ivy twines,
And Clusters lurk beneath the curling Vines:
Four Figures rising from the Work appear,
The various Seasons of the rowling Year;
And what is That, which binds the Radiant Sky,
Where twelve fair Signs in beauteous Order lie?

Damon.

Then sing by turns, by turns the Muses sing;
Now Hawthorns blossome, now the Daisies spring,
· Now Leaves the Trees, and Flow'rs adorn the Ground;
Begin, the Vales shall echo to the Sound.

Strephon.

· Ye Fountain Nymphs, propitious to the Swain,
Now grant me Phaebus or Alexis Strain:
My fairest Bull shall at your Altars stand,
With butting Horns, and Heels y^{t} spurn the Sand.

Daph.

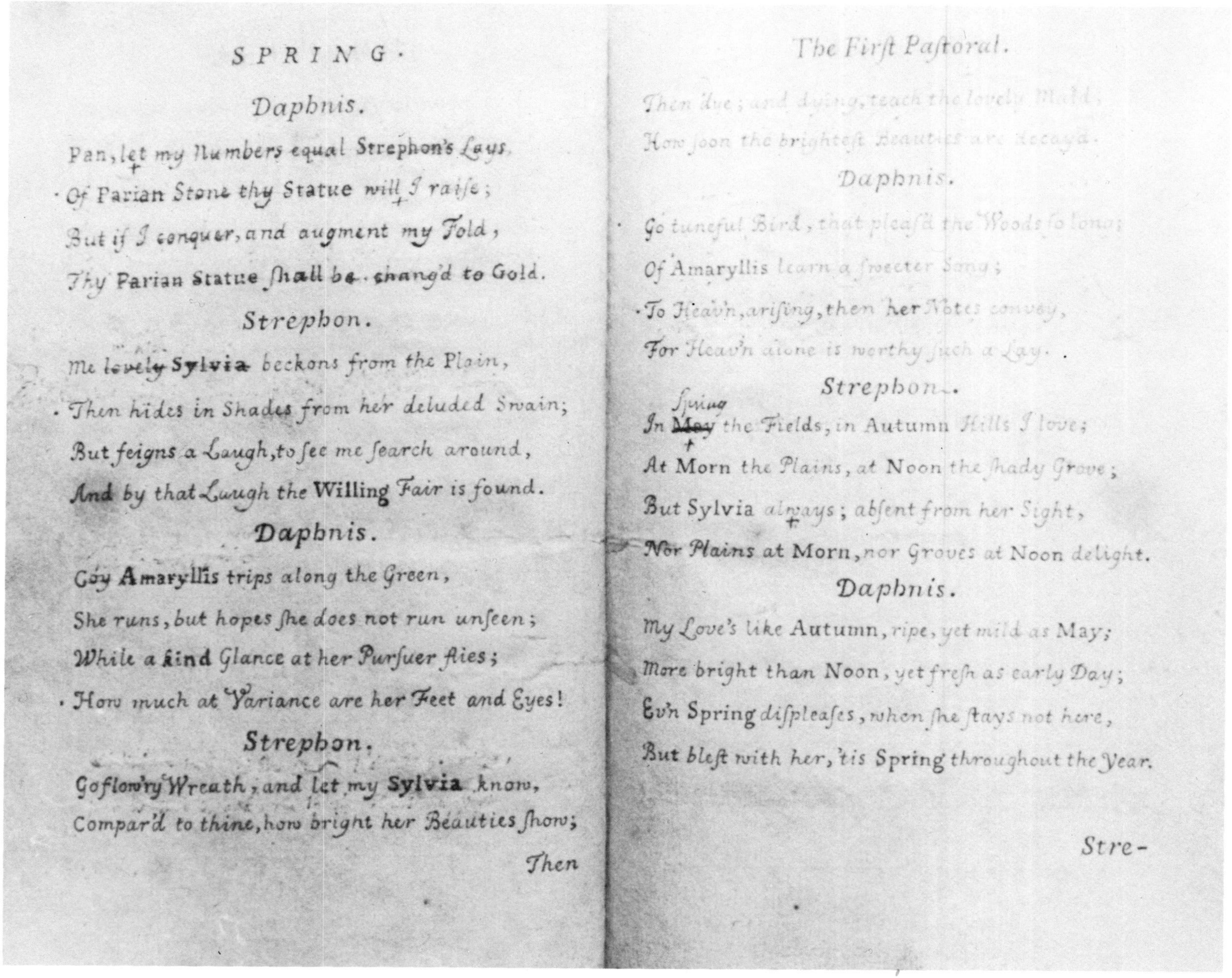

SPRING.

Daphnis.

Pan, let my Numbers equal Strephon's Lays,
Of Parian Stone thy Statue will I raise;
But if I conquer, and augment my Fold,
Thy Parian Statue shall ~~be~~ chang'd to Gold.

Strephon.

Me ~~lovely~~ Sylvia beckons from the Plain,
Then hides in Shades from her deluded Swain;
But feigns a Laugh, to see me search around,
And by that Laugh the Willing Fair is found.

Daphnis.

Coy Amaryllis trips along the Green,
She runs, but hopes she does not run unseen;
While a kind Glance at her Pursuer flies;
How much at Variance are her Feet and Eyes!

Strephon.

Go flow'ry Wreath, and let my Sylvia know,
Compar'd to thine, how bright her Beauties show;
Then

The First Pastoral.

Then die; and dying, teach the lovely Maid,
How soon the brightest Beauties are decay'd.

Daphnis.

Go tuneful Bird, that pleas'd the Woods so long;
Of Amaryllis learn a sweeter Song;
To Heav'n, arising, then her Notes convey,
For Heav'n alone is worthy such a Lay.

Strephon.

In ~~May~~ Spring the Fields, in Autumn Hills I love;
At Morn the Plains, at Noon the shady Grove;
But Sylvia always; absent from her Sight,
Nor Plains at Morn, nor Groves at Noon delight.

Daphnis.

My Love's like Autumn, ripe, yet mild as May;
More bright than Noon, yet fresh as early Day;
Ev'n Spring displeases, when she stays not here,
But blest with her, 'tis Spring throughout the Year.

Stre-

S P R I N G .

Daphnis.

Pan, let my Numbers equal Strephon's Lays,
Of Parian Stone thy Statue will I raise;
But if I conquer, and augment my Fold,
Thy Parian Statue shall be chang'd to Gold.

Strephon.

Me lovely Sylvia beckons from the Plain,
Then hides in Shades from her deluded Swain;
But feigns a Laugh, to see me search around,
And by that Laugh the Willing Fair is found.

Daphnis.

Coy Amaryllis trips along the Green,
She runs, but hopes she does not run unseen;
While a kind Glance at her Pursuer flies;
How much at Variance are her Feet and Eyes!

Strephon.

Go flow'ry Wreath, and let my Sylvia know,
Compar'd to thine, how bright her Beauties show;

Then

The First Pastoral.

Then dye; and dying, teach the lovely Maid,
How soon the brightest Beauties are decay'd.

Daphnis.

Go tuneful Bird, that pleas'd the Woods so long;
Of Amaryllis learn a sweeter Song;
To Heav'n, arising, then her Notes convey,
For Heav'n alone is worthy such a Lay.

Strephon.

In ~~May~~ Spring the Fields, in Autumn Hills I love;
At Morn the Plains, at Noon the shady Grove;
But Sylvia always; absent from her Sight,
Nor Plains at Morn, nor Groves at Noon delight.

Daphnis.

My Love's like Autumn, ripe, yet mild as May;
More bright than Noon, yet fresh as early Day;
Ev'n Spring displeases, when she stays not here,
But blest with her, 'tis Spring throughout the Year.

Stre-

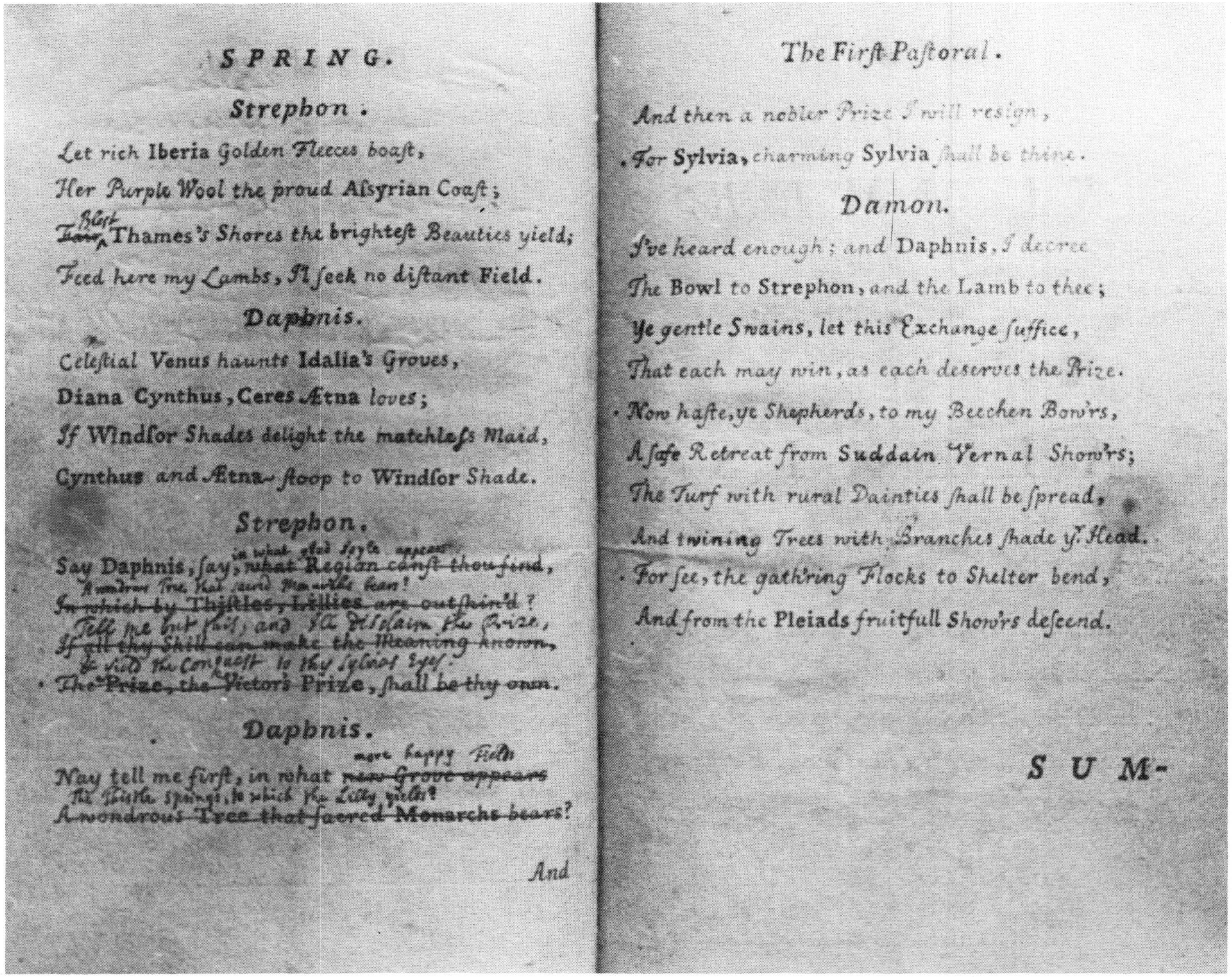

SPRING.

Strephon.

Let rich Iberia Golden Fleeces boast,
Her Purple Wool the proud Assyrian Coast;
~~Fair~~ Blest Thames's Shores the brightest Beauties yield;
Feed here my Lambs, I'll seek no distant Field.

Daphnis.

Celestial Venus haunts Idalia's Groves,
Diana Cynthus, Ceres Ætna loves;
If Windsor Shades delight the matchless Maid,
Cynthus and Ætna ~~must~~ stoop to Windsor Shade.

Strephon.

in what glad Soyle appears
Say Daphnis, say, ~~what Region canst thou find,~~
A wondrous Tree that sacred Monarchs bears!
~~In which by Thistles, Lillies are outshin'd?~~
Tell me but this, and I'll disclaim the Prize,
~~If all thy Skill can make the Meaning known,~~
& yield the Conquest to thy Sylvia's Eyes.
~~The Prize, the Victor's Prize, shall be thy own.~~

Daphnis.

more happy Fields
Nay tell me first, in what ~~new Grove appears~~
The Thistle springs, to which the Lilly yields?
~~A wondrous Tree that sacred Monarchs bears?~~

And

The First Pastoral.

And then a nobler Prize I will resign,
For Sylvia, charming Sylvia shall be thine.

Damon.

I've heard enough; and Daphnis, I decree
The Bowl to Strephon, and the Lamb to thee;
Ye gentle Swains, let this Exchange suffice,
That each may win, as each deserves the Prize.
Now haste, ye Shepherds, to my Beechen Bow'rs,
A safe Retreat from Suddain Vernal Show'rs;
The Turf with rural Dainties shall be spread,
And twining Trees with Branches shade y^r Head.
For see, the gath'ring Flocks to Shelter bend,
And from the Pleiads fruitfull Show'rs descend.

SUM-

S P R I N G .

Strephon.

Let rich Iberia Golden Fleeces boast,
Her Purple Wool the proud Assyrian Coast;
Blest
~~Fair~~ ^ Thames's Shores the brightest Beauties yield;
Feed here my Lambs, I'l seek no distant Field.

Daphnis.

Celestial Venus haunts Idalia's Groves,
Diana Cynthus, Ceres AEtna loves;
If Windsor Shades delight the matchless Maid,
Cynthus and AEtna stoop to Windsor Shade.

Strephon.

in what glad Soyle appears
Say Daphnis, say, ~~what Region canst thou find,~~
A wondrous Tree that sacred Monarchs bears?
~~In which by Thistles, Lillies are outshin'd~~
Tell me but this, and I'll disclaim the Prize,
~~If all thy Skill can make the Meaning known,~~
& yield the Conquest to thy Sylvias Eyes.
· ~~The Prize, the Victor's Prize, shall be thy own.~~

Daphnis.

more happy Fields
Nay tell me first, in what ~~new Grove appears~~
The Thistle springs, to which the Lilly yields?
~~A wondrous Tree that sacred Monarchs bears~~?

And

The First Pastoral

And then a nobler Prize I will resign,
· For Sylvia, charming Sylvia shall be thine.

Damon.

I've heard enough; and Daphnis, I decree
The Bowl to Strephon, and the Lamb to thee;
Ye gentle Swains, let this Exchange suffice,
That each may win, as each deserves the Prize.
· Now haste, ye Shepherds, to my Beechen Bow'rs,
A safe Retreat from Suddain Vernal Show'rs;
The Turf with rural Dainties shall be spread,
And twining Trees with Branches shade y.r Head.
· For see, the gath'ring Flocks to Shelter bend,
And from the Pleiads fruitfull Show'rs descend.

S U M -

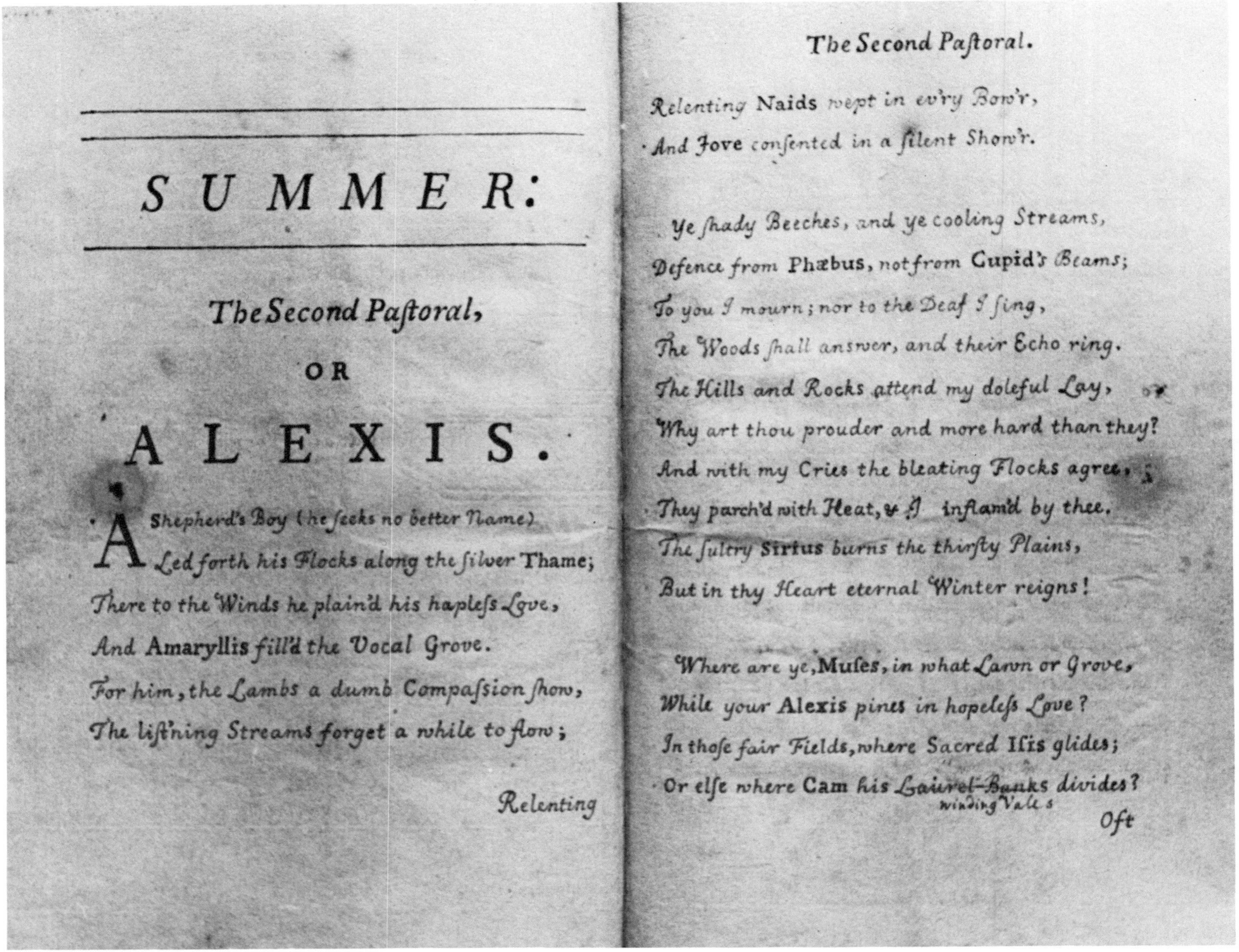

SUMMER:

The Second Pastoral,

OR

ALEXIS.

A Shepherd's Boy (he seeks no better Name)
Led forth his Flocks along the silver Thame;
There to the Winds he plain'd his hapless Love,
And Amaryllis fill'd the Vocal Grove.
For him, the Lambs a dumb Compassion show,
The list'ning Streams forget a while to flow;

Relenting

The Second Pastoral.

Relenting Naids wept in ev'ry Bow'r,
And Jove consented in a silent Show'r.

Ye shady Beeches, and ye cooling Streams,
Defence from Phœbus, not from Cupid's Beams;
To you I mourn; nor to the Deaf I sing,
The Woods shall answer, and their Echo ring.
The Hills and Rocks attend my doleful Lay,
Why art thou prouder and more hard than they?
And with my Cries the bleating Flocks agree,
They parch'd with Heat, & I inflam'd by thee.
The sultry Sirius burns the thirsty Plains,
But in thy Heart eternal Winter reigns!

Where are ye, Muses, in what Lawn or Grove,
While your Alexis pines in hopeless Love?
In those fair Fields, where Sacred Isis glides;
Or else where Cam his ~~Laurel-Banks~~ winding Vales divides?

Oft

S U M M E R :

The Second Pastoral,

OR

A L E X I S .

· *A Shepherd's Boy (he seeks no better Name)*
Led forth his Flocks along the silver **Thame;**
There to the Winds he plain'd his hapless Love,
And **Amaryllis** *fill'd the Vocal Grove.*
For him, the Lambs a dumb Compassion show,
The list'ning Streams forget a while to flow;

Relenting

The Second Pastoral.

Relenting **Naids** *wept in ev'ry Bow'r,*
· *And* **Jove** *consented in a silent Show'r.*

Ye shady Beeches, and ye cooling Streams,
Defence from **Phæbus**, *not from* **Cupid's** *Beams;*
To you I mourn; nor to the Deaf I sing,
The Woods shall answer, and their Echo ring.
The Hills and Rocks attend my doleful Lay,
Why art thou prouder and more hard than they?
And with my Cries the bleating Flocks agree,
· *They parch'd with Heat, & I inflam'd by thee.*
The sultry **Sirius** *burns the thirsty Plains,*
· *But in thy Heart eternal Winter reigns!*

Where are ye, **Muses**, *in what Lawn or Grove,*
While your **Alexis** *pines in hopeless Love?*
In those fair Fields, where Sacred **Isis** *glides;*
· *Or else where Cam his ~~Laurel-Banks~~ divides?*
winding Vales

Oft

SUMMER.

Oft'in the Spring I caſt a careful View,
And rival'd **Daphnis**, if the Glaſs be true;
But now thoſe **Graces** meet my Eyes no more,
I ſhun the Fountains which I ſought before.
Once I was ſkill'd in ev'ry Herb that grew,
And ev'ry Plant that drinks the Morning Dew;
Ah wretched Shepherd, what avails thy Art,
To cure thy Lambs, but not to heal thy Heart!

Let those who liſt attend the Rural Care,
Feed fairer Flocks, or richer Fleeces ſhare;
But nigh that Mountain let me tune my Lays,
Embrace my **Love**, and bind my Brows with Bays.
Of ſlender Reeds a tuneful Flute I have,
The tuneful Flute, which dying **Colin** gave;
And ſaid, **Alexis**, take this Pipe, the ſame
That taught the Groves my **Roſalinda's** Name.

But

The Second Paſtoral.

But ſoon the Reeds ſhall hang on yonder Tree,
If once their Muſic ſounds not ſweet to thee.
Oh were I made by some transforming Pow'r
Some pitying God command me to be made
The Captive Bird that sings within thy Bow'r!
The **Bird** that ſings within thy ſecret Shade!
Then might my Voice thy willing Ear employ,
And I thoſe Kiſſes, he receives, enjoy!

And yet my Numbers pleaſe the Sylvan Throng;
Rough **Satyrs** dance, and **Pan** attends the Song;
And **Nymphs**, forſaking ev'ry Cave and Spring,
Of Fruits and Turtles rural Preſents bring:
Ah wanton **Nymphs**, your rural Gifts are vain;
My **Amaryllis** wins them all again!
For you the Swains their choiceſt Flow'rs deſign,
And in one Garland all their Beauties joyn:
Accept a Wreath which you deſerve alone,
In whom all Beauties are combin'd in One.

Nor

<11a>

S U M M E R .

Oft' in the Spring I cast a careful View,
And rival'd Daphnis, *if the Glass be true;*
But now those Graces meet my Eyes no more,
I shun the Fountains which I sought before.
Once I was skill'd in ev'ry Herb that grew,
And ev'ry Plant that drinks the Morning Dew;
Ah wretched Shepherd, what avails thy Art,
To cure thy Lambs, but not to heal thy Heart!

Let those who list attend the Rural Care,
Feed fairer Flocks, or richer Fleeces share;
But nigh ~~this~~ that Mountain let me tune my Lays,
Embrace my Love, and bind my Brows with Bays.
Of slender Reeds a tuneful Flute I have,
The tuneful Flute, which dying Colin *gave;*
And said, Alexis, take this Pipe, the same
That taught the Groves my Rosalinda's *Name.*

But

<11b>

The Second Pastoral.

But soon the Reeds shall hang on yonder Tree,
If once their Music sounds not sweet to thee.
Oh were I made by some transforming Pow'r
Some pitying God command me to be made
The Captive Bird that sings within thy Bow'r!
The Bird that sings within thy secret Shade:
· *Then might my Voice thy willing Ear employ,*
And I those Kisses, he receives, enjoy!

And yet my Numbers please the Sylvan Throng;
Rough Satyrs *dance, and* Pan *attends the Song;*
And Nymphs, *forsaking ev'ry Cave and Spring,*
Of Fruits and Turtles rural Presents bring:
Ah wanton Nymphs, *your rural Gifts are vain;*
My Amaryllis *wins them all again!*
For you the Swains their choicest Flow'rs design,
And in one Garland all their Beauties joyn:
Accept a Wreath which you deserve alone,
In whom all Beauties are combin'd in One.

Nor

SUMMER.

Nor scorn a Shepherd; Heav'ns Immortal Pow'rs
For Sylvan Scenes have left their blissful Bow'rs;
In Woods ~~fair~~ bright Venus with Adonis stray'd,
And chast Diana haunts the Forest Shade.
Oh deign a while to bless our humble Seats,
Our mossie Fountains, and our Green Retreats.
This harmless Grove no lurking Viper hides,
But ~~Love the Serpent in my Breast~~ in my Breast the Serpent Love abides.
dele. ~~Here Tereus mourns, and Itys tells his Pain;~~
~~Of Progne they, and I of you complain.~~
Here Bees from Blossomes sip the rosie Dew,
But your Alexis knows no Sweet but You.

Come lovely Maid, and crown the silent Hours,
When Swains from Shearing seek their nightly Bow'rs;
When weary Reapers leave the sultry Field,
And crown'd with Corn, their Thanks to Ceres yield.

While

The Second Pastoral.

While to the Groves your Presence you deny,
Our Flow'rs are faded, and our Floods are dry;
Tho' with'ring Herbs lay dying on the Plain,
At your Return, they shall be green again.
In shady Forests I may waste my Days,
Invoke the Muses, and proclaim your Praise;
Your Praise in Songs the Birds to Heav'n shall bear,
And Wolves grow milder when the Sound they hear.
Such magick Musick dwells within your Name,
The Voice of Orpheus no such pow'r cou'd claim;
Had You then liv'd, when he the Forests drew,
The Trees and Orpheus both had follow'd You.

But see, the Southing Sun displays his Beams;
See Tity'rus leads his Herd to Silver Streams;
To closer Shades the panting Flocks remove;
Ye Gods! and is there no Relief for Love?

But

S U M M E R .

Nor scorn a Shepherd; Heav'ns Immortal Pow'rs
For Sylvan Scenes have left their blissful Bow'rs;
bright
• *In Woods* ~~*fair*~~ Venus *with* Adonis *stray'd,*
And chast Diana *haunts the Forest Shade.*
Oh deign a while to bless our humble Seats,
Our mossie Fountains, and our Green Retreats.
This harmless Grove no lurking Viper hides,
in my Breast the Serpent Love
• *But* ~~*Love the Serpent in my Breast*~~ *abides.*
dele. ~~*Here* Tereus *mourns, and* Itys *tells his Pain*~~;
~~*Of* Progne *they, and I of you complain*~~.
Here Bees from Blossomes sip the rosie Dew,
But your Alexis *knows no Sweet but You.*

Come lovely Maid, and crown the silent Hours,
When Swains from Shearing *seek their nightly Bow'rs;*
When weary Reapers *leave the sultry Field,*
And crown'd with Corn, *their Thanks to* Ceres *yield.*
While

The Second Pastoral.

• *While to the Groves your Presence you deny,*
Our Flow'rs are faded, and our Floods are dry;
x *Tho' with'ring Herbs lay dying on the Plain,*
At your Return, they shall be green again.
In shady Forests I may waste my Days,
Invoke the Muses, and proclaim your Praise;
• *Your Praise in Songs the Birds to Heav'n shall bear,*
And Wolves grow milder when the Sound they hear.
• *Such magick Musick dwells within your* Name,
The Voice of Orpheus *no such pow'r cou'd claim;*
• *Had You then liv'd, when he the Forests drew,*
The Trees and Orpheus *both had follow'd You.*

But see, the Southing Sun displays his Beams;
See Tity'rus *leads his Herd to Silver Streams;*
To closer Shades the panting Flocks remove;
Ye Gods! and is there no Relief for Love?
But

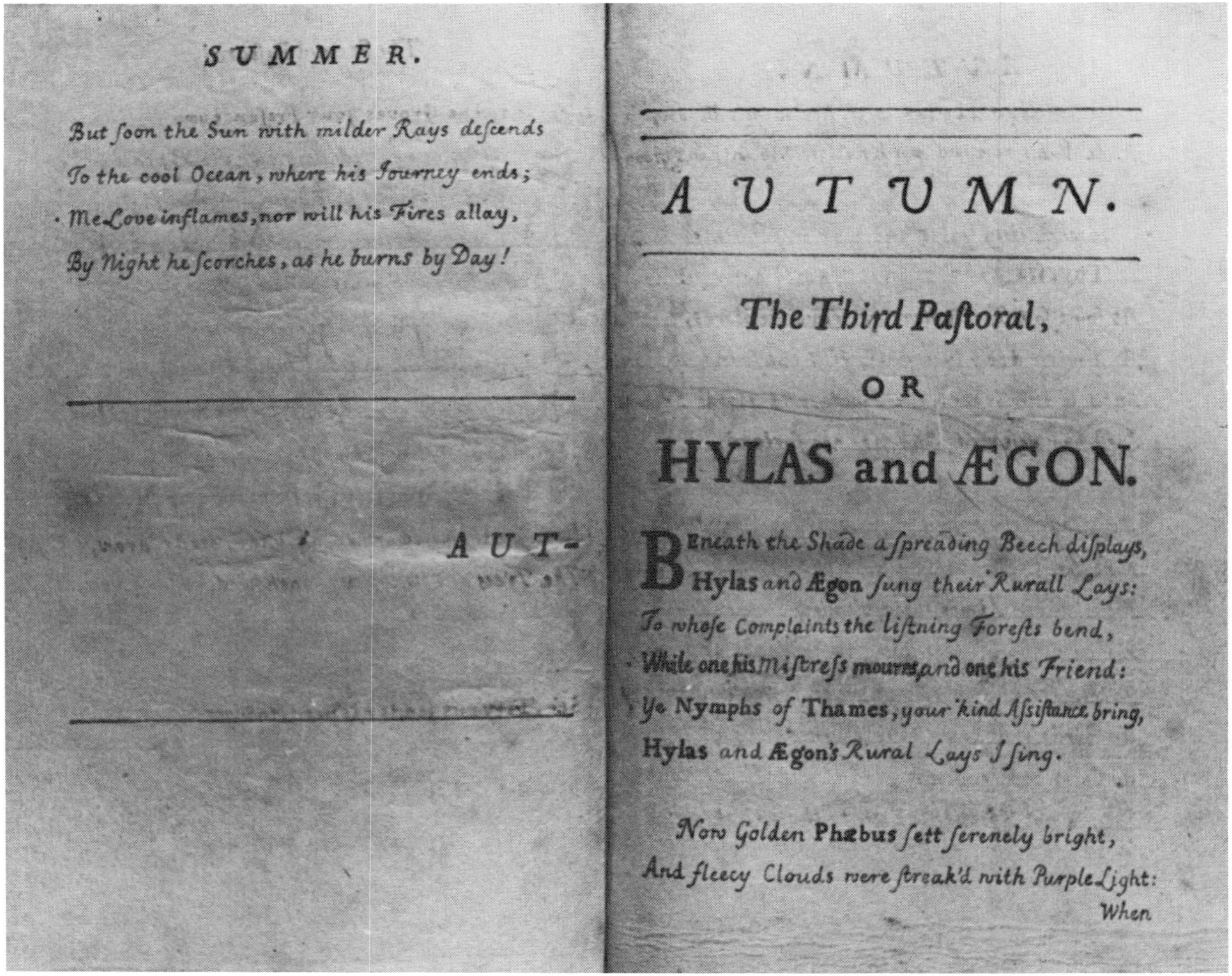

SUMMER.

But ſoon the Sun with milder Rays deſcends
To the cool Ocean, where his Journey ends;
Me Love inflames, nor will his Fires allay,
By Night he ſcorches, as he burns by Day!

AUT-

AUTUMN.

The Third Paſtoral,

OR

HYLAS and ÆGON.

Beneath the Shade a ſpreading Beech diſplays,
Hylas and **Ægon** ſung their Rurall Lays:
To whoſe Complaints the liſtning Foreſts bend,
While one his Miſtreſs mourns, and one his Friend:
Ye Nymphs of **Thames**, your kind Aſſiſtance bring,
Hylas and **Ægon's** Rural Lays I ſing.

Now Golden **Phæbus** ſett ſerenely bright,
And fleecy Clouds were ſtreak'd with Purple Light:
When

S U M M E R .

But soon the Sun with milder Rays descends
To the cool Ocean, where his Journey ends;
• *Me Love inflames, nor will his Fires allay,*
By Night he scorches, as he burns by Day!

A U T -

A U T U M N .

The Third Pastoral,

o r

HYLAS and AEGON.

Beneath the Shade a spreading Beech displays,
Hylas *and* AEgon *sung their Rurall Lays:*
To whose Complaints the listning Forests bend,
• *While one his Mistress mourns, and one his Friend:*
• *Ye* Nymphs *of* Thames, *your kind Assistance bring,*
Hylas *and* Aegon's *Rural Lays I sing.*

Now Golden Phaebus *sett serenely bright,*
And fleecy Clouds were streak'd with Purple Light:

When

AUTUMN,

When tunefull **Hylas** *with Melodious Moan,*
Made Vales resound and hollow Mountains groan.

Go whispring Gales and bear my Plaints away;
To **Thyrsis** *Ear the tender Notes convey:*
As some sad Turtle her lost Love deplores,
And with deep Murmurs fills the sounding Shores;
Thus to the Groves, the Fields, and Floods I mourn,
Like her deserted, and like her forlorn.

Go whispring Gales and bear my Plaints along:
For him the Feather'd Quires neglect their Song,
For him the Limes their pleasing Shades deny,
For him the Lillies hang their Heads and die.
Ye Flow'rs that languish when forsook by Spring,
Ye Birds that cease when Summer's past to sing,
Ye Trees that fade when Autumn Heats remove,
Say, is not Absence Death to those that love?

Go

The Third Pastoral.

Go whispring Gales and bear my Plaints away:
Curst be the Fields that cause my **Thyrsis** *Stay!*
Fade ev'ry Blossome, wither ev'ry Tree,
Die ev'ry Flow'r, and perish all—but he.
What have I said?—Where e're my Friend remains,
Let Flow'rs and Blossoms purple all the Plains:
Let opening Roses knotted Oaks adorn,
And liquid Amber drop from ev'ry Thorn.

Go whispring Gales and bear my Plaints along:
The Birds shall cease to tune their Ev'ning Song,
The Winds to breath, the waving Woods to move,
And Streams to murmur, e'er I cease to love.
With him thro' **Lybia's** *burning Plains I'll go,*
On **Alpine** *Mountains tread th' Eternal Snow;*
Yet feel no Heat **but** *what our Loves impart,*
And dread no Coldness but in **Thyrsis** *Heart.*

Go

<14a>

A U T U M N ,

When tunefull Hylas with Melodious Moan,
Made Vales resound and hollow Mountains groan.

Go whispring Gales and bear my Plaints away;
To Thyrsis Ear the tender Notes convey:
As some sad Turtle her lost Love deplores,
And with deep Murmurs fills the sounding Shores;
Thus to the Groves, the Fields, and Floods I mourn,
Like her deserted, and like her forlorn.

Go whispring Gales and bear my Plaints along;
For him the Feather'd Quires neglect their Song,
For him the Limes their pleasing Shades deny,
For him the Lillies hang their Heads and die.
Ye Flow'rs that languish when forsook by Spring,
Ye Birds that cease when Summer's past to sing,
Ye Trees that fade when Autumn Heats remove,
Say, is not Absence Death to those that love?

Go

<14b>

The Third Pastoral.

Go whispring Gales and bear my Plaints away:
Curst be the Fields that cause my Thyrsis Stay!
Fade ev'ry Blossome, wither ev'ry Tree,
Die ev'ry Flow'r, and perish all--but he.
What have I said? -- Where e're my Friend remains,
Let Flow'rs and Blossoms purple all the Plains:
Let opening Roses knotted Oaks adorn,
And liquid Amber drop from ev'ry Thorn.

Go whispring Gales and bear my Plaints along:
The Birds shall cease to tune their Ev'ning Song,
The Winds to breath, the waving Woods to move,
And Streams to murmur, e'er I cease to love.
With him thro' Lybia's burning Plains I'll go,
On Alpine Mountains tread th' Eternal Snow;
Yet feel no Heat but what our Loves impart,
And dread no Coldness but in Thyrsis Heart.

Go

AUTUMN,

Go whiſpring Gales and bear my Plaints away:
Come Thyrſis, come, ah why this long Delay?
Not bubling Fountains to the thirſty Swain,
Not balmy Sleep to Lab'rers ſpent with Pain,
Not Show'rs to Larks, or Sunſhine to the Bee,
Are half so charming as thy Sight to me.
But ſee, my Thyrſis comes! now ceaſe my Song,
And cease, ye Gales, to bear my Plaints along.

Next Ægon ſung, and Windſor Groves admir'd;
Rehearse, ye Muſes, what yourſelves inſpir'd.

Resound ye Hills, resound my mournful Strain:
Of perjur'd Phillis, dying I'll complain:
While lab'ring Oxen, tir'd with Toil and Heat,
In their looſe Traces from the Field retreat;
While curling Smokes from Village Tops are ſeen,
And the fleet Shades fly gliding o'er the Green.

The Third Paſtoral.

Resound ye Hills, resound my mournful Lay:
Beneath this Poplar oft we paſt the Day.
Oft on this Rind I carv'd her am'rous Vows,
While She with Garlands hung the bending Boughs:
The Garlands fade, the Vows are worn away;
So dies her Love, and so my Hopes decay.

Resound ye Hills, resound my mournful Strain:
Now bright Arcturus glads the teeming Grain;
Now Golden Fruits on loaded Branches ſhine,
And grateful Cluſters ſwell with floods of Wine;
Now bluſhing Berries paint the ~~Yellow~~ flowing Grove,
Just Gods! ſhall all things yield Returns but Love?

Resound ye Hills, resound my mournful Lay:
The Shepherds cry, Thy Flocks are left to ſtray:
Ah what avails it me my Flocks to keep,
Who loſt my Heart while I preſerv'd my Sheep!
Pan comes & aſks, what Magick works my Smart,
Or what ill Eyes malignant Glances dart?

<15a>

A U T U M N .

Go whispring Gales and bear my Plaints away:
Come **Thyrsis**, *come, ah why this long Delay?*
Not bubling Fountains to the thirsty Swain,
Not balmy Sleep to Lab'rers spent with Pain,
• *Not Show'rs to Larks, or Sunshine to the Bee,*
Are half so charming as thy Sight to me.
But see, my **Thyrsis** *comes! now cease my Song,*
And cease, ye Gales, to bear my Plaints along.

• *Next* **AEgon** *sung, and* **Windsor** *Groves admir'd;*
Rehearse, ye **Muses**, *what yourselves inspir'd.*

Resound ye Hills, resound my mournful Strain:
Of perjur'd **Phillis**, *dying I'll complain:*
While lab'ring Oxen, tir'd with Toil and Heat,
In their loose Traces from the Field retreat;
While curling Smokes from Village Tops are seen,
• *And the fleet Shades fly gliding o'er the Green.*

<15b>

The Third Pastoral

Resound ye Hills, resound my mournful Lay:
Beneath this Poplar oft we past the Day.
Oft on this Rind I carv'd her am'rous Vows,
While she with Garlands hung the bending Boughs:
The Garlands fade, the Vows are worn away;
So dies her Love, and so my Hopes decay.

Resound ye Hills, resound my mournful Strain:
Now bright **Arcturus** *glads the teeming Grain;*
Now Golden Fruits on loaded Branches shine,
And grateful Clusters swell with floods of Wine;
-lowing
Now blushing Berries paint the Yellow Grove,
• *Just Gods! shall all things yield Returns but Love?*

Resound ye Hills, resound my mournful Lay:
The Shepherds cry, Thy Flocks are left to stray:
Ah what avails it me my Flocks to keep,
Who lost my Heart while I preserv'd my Sheep!
Pan *comes & asks, what Magick works my Smart,*
Or what ill Eyes malignant Glances dart?

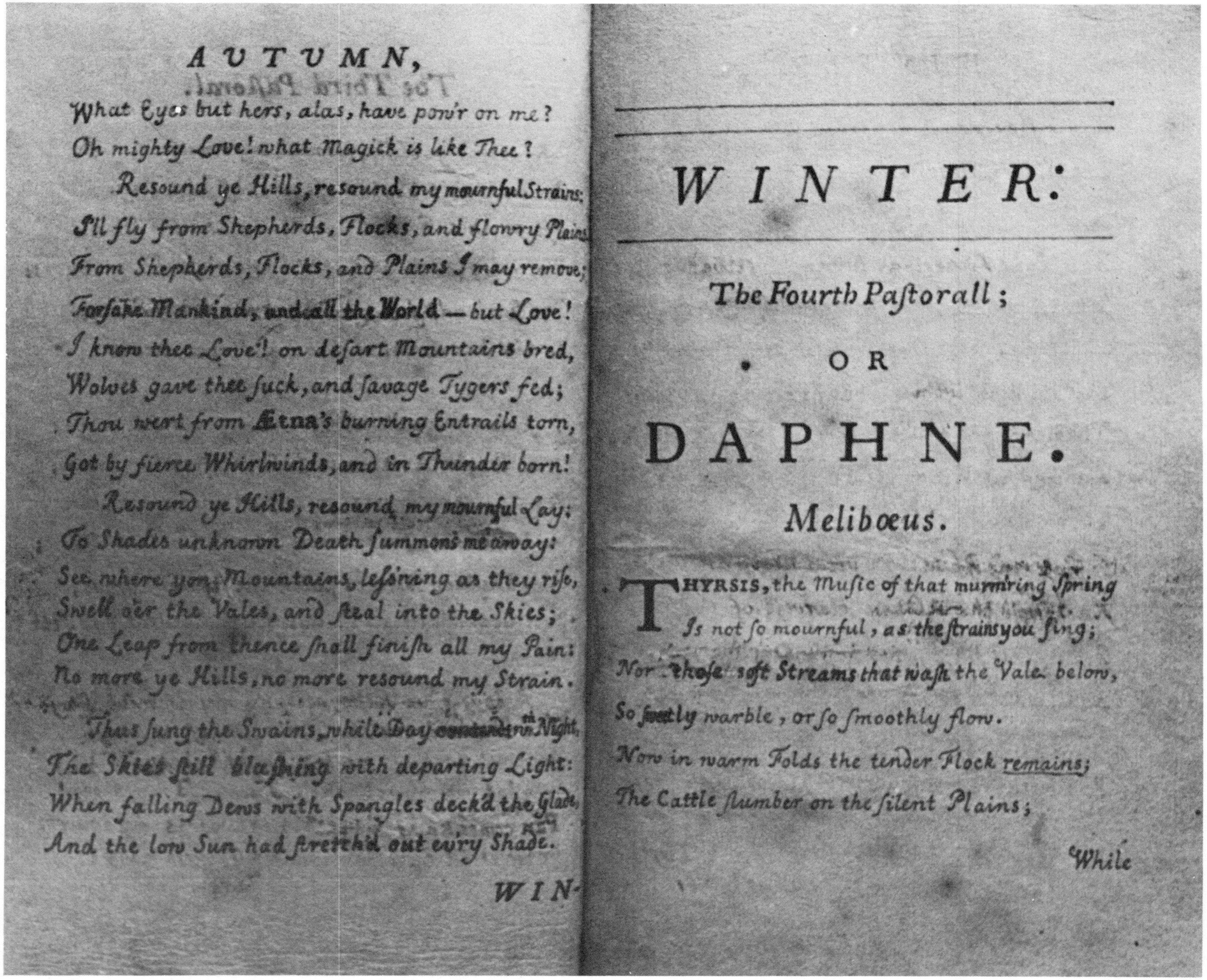

AUTUMN,

What Eyes but hers, alas, have pow'r on me?
Oh mighty Love! what Magick is like Thee?
Resound ye Hills, resound my mournful Strains;
I'll fly from Shepherds, Flocks, and flow'ry Plains.
From Shepherds, Flocks, and Plains I may remove,
Forsake Mankind, and all the World — but Love!
I know thee Love! on desart Mountains bred,
Wolves gave thee suck, and savage Tygers fed;
Thou wert from Ætna's burning Entrails torn,
Got by fierce Whirlwinds, and in Thunder born!
Resound ye Hills, resound my mournful Lay;
To Shades unknown Death summons me away:
See, where yon Mountains, less'ning as they rise,
Swell o'er the Vales, and steal into the Skies;
One Leap from thence shall finish all my Pain:
No more ye Hills, no more resound my Strain.
Thus sung the Swains, while Day contended with Night,
The Skies still blushing with departing Light:
When falling Dews with Spangles deck'd the Glade,
And the low Sun had stretch'd out ev'ry Shade.

WIN-

WINTER:

The Fourth Pastorall;

OR

DAPHNE.

Meliboeus.

THYRSIS, *the Music of that murm'ring Spring*
Is not so mournful, as the strains you sing;
Nor those soft Streams that wash the Vale below,
So sweetly warble, or so smoothly flow.
Now in warm Folds the tender Flock remains;
The Cattle slumber on the silent Plains;

While

A U T U M N,

What Eyes but hers, alas, have pow'r on me?
Oh mighty Love! what Magick is like Thee?
Resound ye Hills, resound my mournful Strains:
I'll fly from Shepherds, Flocks, and flowry Plains.
From Shepherds, Flocks, and Plains I may remove;
Forsake Mankind, and all the World--but Love!
I know thee Love! on desart Mountains bred,
Wolves gave thee suck, and savage Tygers fed;
Thou wert from Aetna's *burning Entrails torn,*
Got by fierce Whirlwinds, and in Thunder born!
Resound ye Hills, resound, my mournful Lay:
To Shades unknown Death summons me away:
See where yon Mountains, less'ning as they rise,
Swell o'er the Vales, and steal into the Skies;
One Leap from thence shall finish all my Pain:
No more ye Hills, no more resound my Strain.

Thus sung the Swains, while Day contends w[th] *Night,*
The Skies still blushing with departing Light:
When falling Dews with Spangles deck'd the Glade,
And the low Sun had stretch'd out ev'ry Shade.

W I N-

W I N T E R:

The Fourth Pastorall;

O R

D A P H N E.

Meliboeus.

Thyrsis, *the Music of that murm'ring Spring*
Is not so mournful, as the strains you sing;
Nor those soft Streams that wash the Vale below,
So sweetly warble, or so smoothly flow.
Now in warm Folds the tender Flock <u>*remains;*</u>
The Cattle slumber on the silent Plains;

While

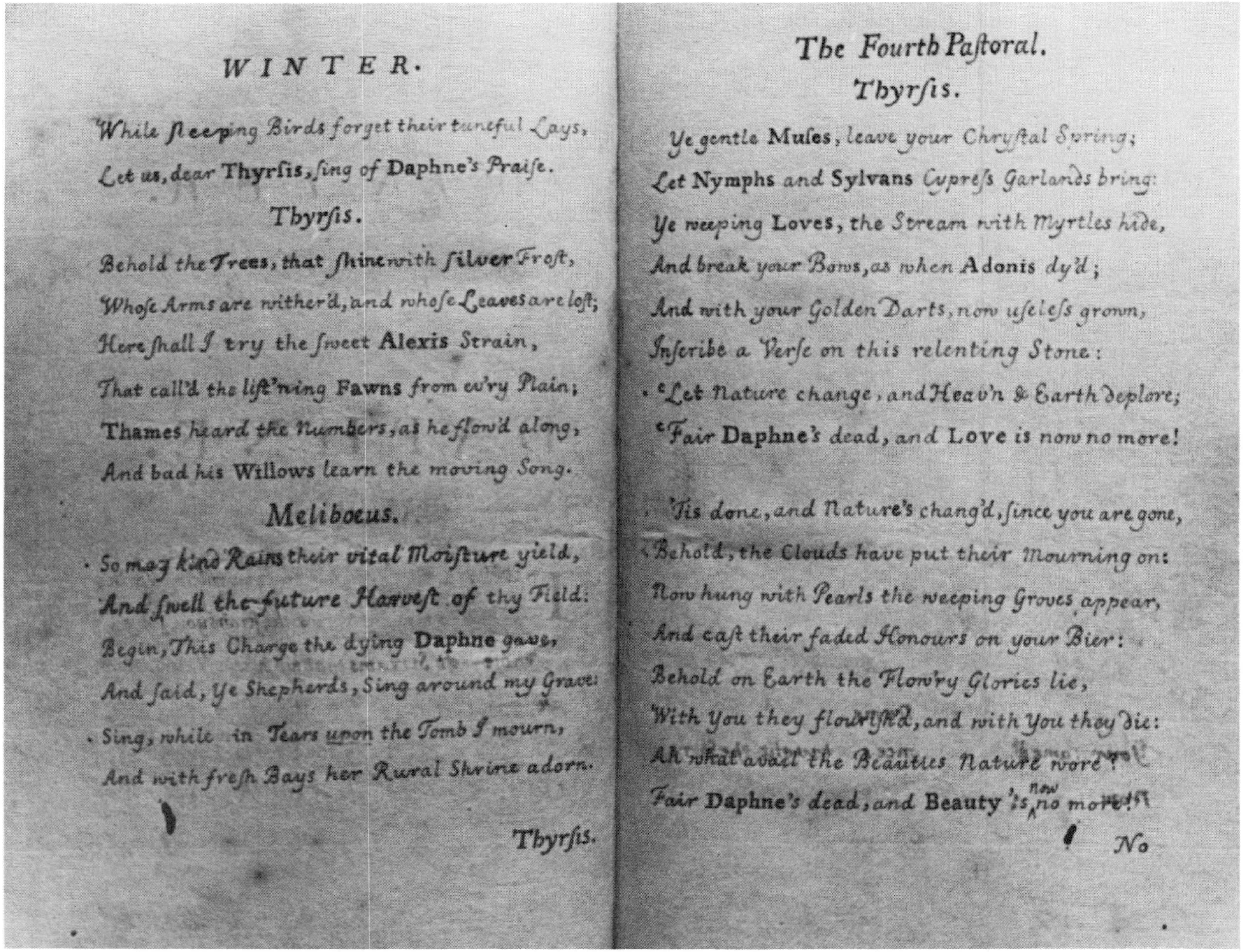

WINTER.

While ſleeping Birds forget their tuneful Lays,
Let us, dear Thyrſis, ſing of Daphne's Praiſe.

Thyrſis.

Behold the Trees, that ſhine with ſilver Froſt,
Whoſe Arms are wither'd, and whoſe Leaves are loſt;
Here ſhall I try the ſweet Alexis Strain,
That call'd the liſt'ning Fawns from ev'ry Plain;
Thames heard the Numbers, as he flow'd along,
And bad his Willows learn the moving Song.

Meliboeus.

So may kind Rains their vital Moiſture yield,
And ſwell the future Harveſt of thy Field:
Begin, This Charge the dying Daphne gave,
And ſaid, Ye Shepherds, Sing around my Grave:
Sing, while in Tears upon the Tomb I mourn,
And with freſh Bays her Rural Shrine adorn.

Thyrſis.

The Fourth Paſtoral.

Thyrſis.

Ye gentle Muſes, leave your Chryſtal Spring;
Let Nymphs and Sylvans Cypreſs Garlands bring:
Ye weeping Loves, the Stream with Myrtles hide,
And break your Bows, as when Adonis dy'd;
And with your Golden Darts, now uſeleſs grown,
Inſcribe a Verſe on this relenting Stone:
"Let Nature change, and Heav'n & Earth deplore;
"Fair Daphne's dead, and Love is now no more!

'Tis done, and Nature's chang'd, ſince you are gone,
Behold, the Clouds have put their Mourning on:
Now hung with Pearls the weeping Groves appear,
And caſt their faded Honours on your Bier:
Behold on Earth the Flow'ry Glories lie,
With You they flouriſh'd, and with You they die:
Ah what avail the Beauties Nature wore?
Fair Daphne's dead, and Beauty 'is now no more!

No

W I N T E R .

While sleeping Birds forget their tuneful Lays,
Let us, dear Thyrsis, sing of Daphne's Praise.

Thyrsis

Behold the Trees, that shine with silver Frost,
Whose Arms are wither'd, and whose Leaves are lost;
Here shall I try the sweet Alexis Strain,
That call'd the list'ning Fawns from ev'ry Plain;
Thames heard the Numbers, as he flow'd along,
And bad his Willows learn the moving Song.

Meliboeus

· So may kind Rains their vital Moisture yield,
And swell the future Harvest of thy Field:
Begin, This Charge the dying Daphne gave,
And said, Ye Shepherds, Sing around my Grave:
· Sing, while in Tears upon the Tomb I mourn,
And with fresh Bays her Rural Shrine adorn.

Thyrsis.

The Fourth Pastoral

Thyrsis.

Ye gentle Muses, leave your Chrystal Spring;
Let Nymphs and Sylvans Cypress Garlands bring;
Ye weeping Loves, the Stream with Myrtles hide,
And break your Bows, as when Adonis dy'd;
And with your Golden Darts, now useless grown,
Inscribe a Verse on this relenting Stone:
· 'Let Nature change, and Heav'n & Earth deplore;
'Fair Daphne's dead, and Love is now no more!

'Tis done, and Nature's chang'd, since you are gone,
Behold, the Clouds have put their Mourning on:
Now hung with Pearls the weeping Groves appear,
And cast their faded Honours on your Bier:
Behold on Earth the Flow'ry Glories lie,
With you they flourish'd and with You they die:
Ah what avail the Beauties Nature wore?
Fair Daphne's dead, and Beauty' is ^now no more!

No

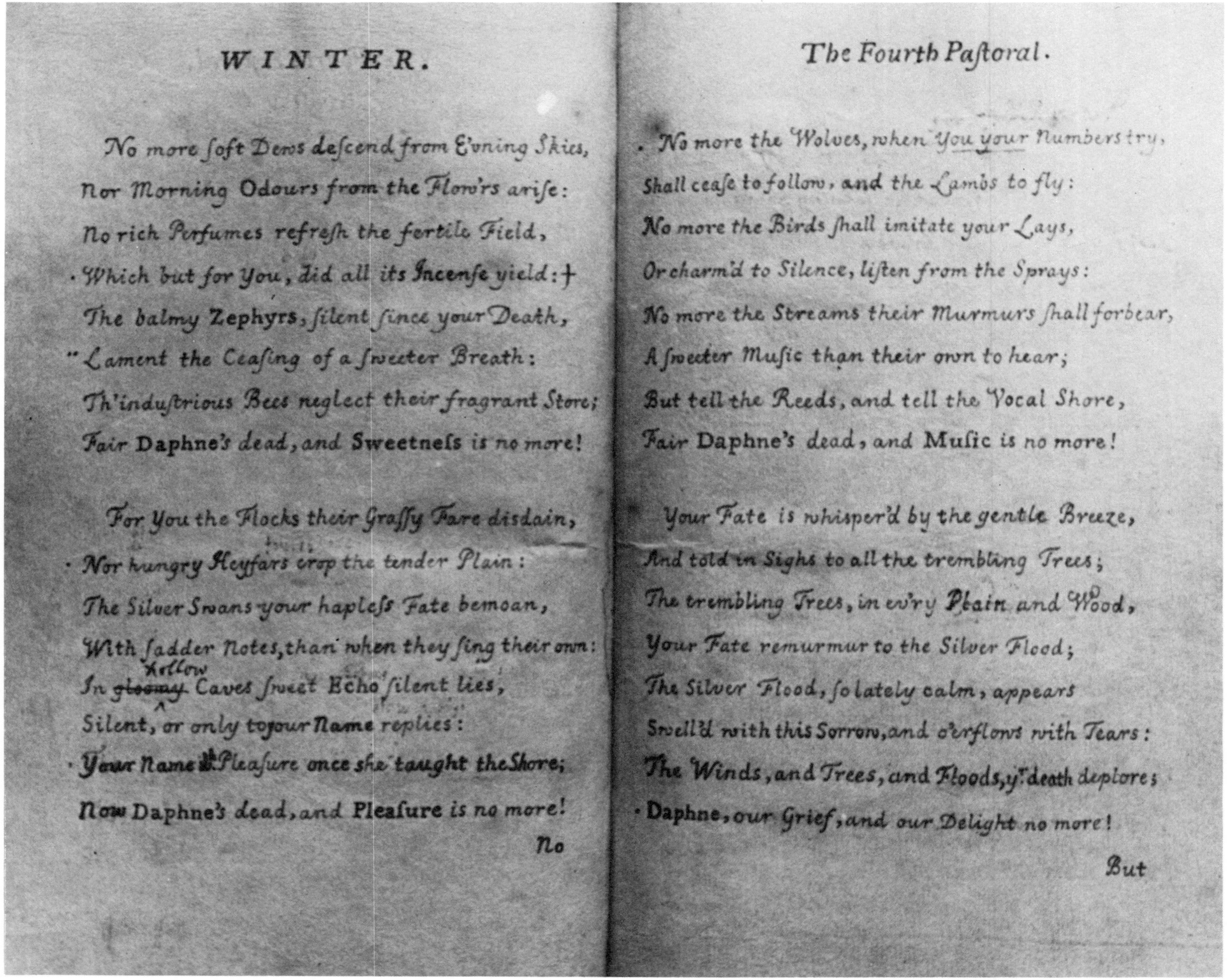

WINTER.

No more ſoft Dews deſcend from E'vning Skies,
Nor Morning Odours from the Flow'rs ariſe:
No rich Perfumes refreſh the fertile Field,
· Which but for You, did all its Incenſe yield: †
The balmy Zephyrs, ſilent ſince your Death,
" Lament the Ceaſing of a ſweeter Breath:
Th'induſtrious Bees neglect their fragrant Store;
Fair Daphne's dead, and Sweetneſs is no more!

For You the Flocks their Graſſy Fare diſdain,
· Nor hungry Heyfars crop the tender Plain:
The Silver Swans your hapleſs Fate bemoan,
With ſadder Notes, than when they ſing their own:
In ~~gloomy~~ hollow Caves ſweet Echo ſilent lies,
Silent, or only to your Name replies:
· Your Name wth Pleaſure once she taught the Shore;
Now Daphne's dead, and Pleaſure is no more!
No

The Fourth Paſtoral.

· No more the Wolves, when You your Numbers try,
Shall ceaſe to follow, and the Lambs to fly:
No more the Birds ſhall imitate your Lays,
Or charm'd to Silence, liſten from the Sprays:
No more the Streams their Murmurs ſhall forbear,
A ſweeter Muſic than their own to hear;
But tell the Reeds, and tell the Vocal Shore,
Fair Daphne's dead, and Muſic is no more!

Your Fate is whisper'd by the gentle Breeze,
And told in Sighs to all the trembling Trees;
The trembling Trees, in ev'ry Plain and Wood,
Your Fate remurmur to the Silver Flood;
The Silver Flood, ſo lately calm, appears
Swell'd with this Sorrow, and o'erflows with Tears:
The Winds, and Trees, and Floods, y^t death deplore;
· Daphne, our Grief, and our Delight no more!
But

<18a>

W I N T E R .

No more soft Dews descend from E'vning Skies,
Nor Morning Odours from the Flow'rs arise:
No rich Perfumes refresh the fertile Field,
• Which but for You, did all its Incense yield: †
The balmy Zephyrs, silent since your Death,
•• Lament the Ceasing of a sweeter Breath:
Th' industrious Bees neglect their fragrant Store;
Fair Daphne's dead, and Sweetness is no more!

For You the Flocks their Grassy Fare disdain,
• Nor hungry Heyfars crop the tender Plain:
The Silver Swans your hapless Fate bemoan,
With sadder Notes, than when they sing their own:
In ~~gloomy~~ hollow Caves sweet Echo silent lies,
Silent, or only to your Name replies:
• Your Name wth Pleasure once she taught the Shore;
Now Daphne's dead, and Pleasure is no more!

No

<18b>

The Fourth Pastoral.

• No more the Wolves, when <u>You</u> <u>your</u> Numbers try,
Shall cease to follow, and the Lambs to fly:
No more the Birds shall imitate your Lays,
Or charm'd to Silence, listen from the Sprays:
No more the Streams their Murmurs shall forbear,
A sweeter Music than their own to hear;
But tell the Reeds, and tell the Vocal Shore,
Fair Daphne's dead, and Music is no more!

Your Fate is whisper'd by the gentle Breeze,
And told in Sighs to all the trembling Trees;
The trembling Trees, in ev'ry Plain and Wood,
Your Fate remurmur to the Silver Flood;
The Silver Flood, so lately calm, appears
Swell'd with this Sorrow, and o'erflows with Tears:
The Winds, and Trees, and Floods, y^{r}. death deplore;
• Daphne, our Grief, and our Delight no more!

But

WINTER.

∴ But see where Daphne wondring mounts on high,
Above the Clouds, above the Starry Sky:
Eternal Beauties grace the shining Scene,
Fields ever fresh, and Groves for ever green.
There, while You rest in Amarantine Bow'rs,
Or from those Meads select unfading Flow'rs,
Behold us kindly, who your Name implore,
Daphne, our Goddess, and our Grief no more!

Meliboeus.

Thy Songs, dear Thyrsis, more delight my Mind,
Than the soft musick of the breathing Wind;
Or whisp'ring Groves, when some expiring Breeze
Pants on the Leaves, and trembles in the Trees!
· When teeming Ewes increase my fleecy Breed, 2
To Thee, bright Daphne, oft' a Lamb shall bleed. 1
While Vapours rise, and driving Snows descend,
Thy Honor, Name, and Praise, shall never end!

Thyrsis.

The Fourth Pastoral.

Thyrsis.

But see, Orion sheds unwholesome Dews,
Arise, the Pines a noxious Shade diffuse;
Sharp Boreas blows, & Nature feels Decay;
Time conquers all, and we must Time obey!
· Adieu ye Rivers, Plains, and conscious Groves;
Adieu ye Shepherd's rural Lays, and Loves;
Adieu my Flock; farewell ye Sylvan Crew;
Daphne farewell; and all the World adieu!

The End of the Pastorals.

W I N T E R .

see where Daphne wondring mounts on high,
∴ *But*
Above the Clouds, above the Starry Sky:
Eternal Beauties grace the shining Scene,
Fields ever fresh, and Groves for ever green.
There, while You rest in **Amarantine** *Bow'rs,*
Or from those Meads select unfading Flow'rs,
Behold us kindly, who your Name implore,
Daphne, *our Goddess, and our Grief no more!*

Meliboeus.

Thy Songs, dear **Thyrsis**, *more delight my Mind,*
Musick
Than the soft of the breathing Wind;
Or whisp'ring Groves, when some expiring Breeze
Pants on the Leaves, and trembles in the Trees!
• *When teeming Ewes increase my fleecy Breed,* 2
To Thee, bright **Daphne**, *oft' a Lamb shall bleed.* 1
While Vapours rise, and driving Snows descend,
Thy Honor, Name, and Praise, shall never end!

Thyrsis.

The Fourth Pastoral.

Thyrsis.

But see, **Orion** *sheds unwholesome Dews,*
Arise, the Pines a noxious Shade diffuse;
Sharp **Boreas** *blows, & Nature feels Decay;*
Time conquers all, and we must Time obey!
• *Adieu ye Rivers, Plains, and conscious Groves;*
Adieu ye Shepherd's rural Lays, and Loves;
Adieu my Flocks, farewell ye Sylvan Crew;
Daphne *farewell; and all the World adieu!*

The End of the **Pastorals**.

421

Mr. Pope's Pastorals

Alterations to the Pastoralls:
(The Solutions of the Queries are written by Mr. Walsh.)

Past. 1. lin. 1. First in these Fields I sing the Sylvan Strains,
Nor blush to sport on Windsor's peaceful Plains;
Fair Thames flow gently from thy sacred Spring,
While on thy Banks Sicilian Muses sing.

Objection. That the Letter is hunted too much — Sing the Sylvan — Peaceful Plains — and that the word Sing is us'd two lines after, Sicilian Muses sing.

Alteration. First in these Fields I try the Sylvan Strains,
Nor blush to sport on Windsor's happy Plains. &c.

Quere. ~~If~~ Try be not properer in relation to First; as, we first attempt a thing; and more modest? and if Happy be not more than Peaceful?
Try is better than sing — Happy does not sound right, ye first Syllable being short, perhaps you may finde a better word than Peacefull or Flowry

---

Past. 1. lin. 23. I'll take my Lamb that near the Fountain plays,
And his own Image from the Brink surveys.
Or, And from the Brink his dancing Shade surveys.
Quere. Which of these 2 lines is better? The second

Past. 1. lin. 43. Me lovely Chloris beckons from the Plain,
Then hides in Shades from her deluded Swain;
But feigns a Laugh to see me search around,
And by that Laugh the willing Fair is found.

Objection. That hides without the Accusative herself is not good English, and that from her deluded Swain is needless.

Alteration. Me wanton Chloris beckons from the Plain,
Then hid in Shades, eludes her eager Swain; &c.

Quere. If wanton be more significant than lovely: If Eludes be properer in this case than deluded: If eager be an expressive Epithet to the Swain who searches for his mistress? Wanton applyd to a woman is equivocal & therefore not proper — Elude is properer than delude. Eager is very well
Past.

Alterations to the Pastoralls:

(The Solutions of the Queries are written by Mr. Walsh.)

Past.1.lin.1.

First in these Fields I *sing* the Sylvan Strains,
Nor blush to sport on Windsor's *peaceful* Plains;
Fair Thames Flow gently from thy sacred Spring,
While on thy Banks Sicilian Muses *sing*.

Objection. That the Letter is hunted too much -- Sing the Sylvan -- Peaceful Plains -- and that the word *Sing* is us'd two lines after, Sicilian Muses Sing.

Alteration.

First in these Fields I *try* the Sylvan Strains,
Nor blush to sport on Windsor's *happy* Plains. &c.

Quere. If *Try* be not properer in relation to First; as, we first attempt a thing; and more modest? and if *Happy* be not more than *Peaceful*?
Try is better than sing -- *Happy* does not sound right, ye first Syllable being short, perhaps you may find a better word than Peaceful as Flowry

Past.1.lin.23.

I'll stake my Lamb that near the Fountain plays,
And *his own Image* from the Brink surveys.
∴ Or, And from the Brink *his dancing Shade* surveys.

Quere. Which of these 2 lines is better? The second

Past.1.lin.43.

Me *lovely* Chloris beckons from the Plain,
Then *hides* in Shades *from her deluded Swain*;
But feigns a Laugh to see me search around,
And by that Laugh the willing Fair is found.

Objection. That *hides* without the Accusative *herself* is not good English, and that *from her deluded Swain* is needless.

Alteration.

Me *wanton* Chloris beckons from the Plain,
Then *hid* in Shades, *eludes her eager Swain*; &c.

Quere. If *wanton* be more significant than *lovely*: If *Eludes* be properer in this case than *deluded*: If *eager* be an expressive Epithet to the Swain who searches for his Mistress? -- Wanton apply'd to a woman is equivocal & therefore not proper--Eludes is properer than deluded. Eager is very well

Past.

Past. 1. lin. 57. If Sylvia smile, she brightens all the Shore,
The Sun's outshin'd, and Nature charms no more.

Whether to say the Sun is outshin'd, be too bold & Hyperbolical? (For Portrait any of these Alterations)
Quere. If it shou'd be soften'd with seems; Do you approve

If Sylvia smile, she brightens all the Shore,
All Nature seems outshin'd, and charms no more.
Quere which of these three? { Or, Light seems outshin'd, and Nature charms no more.
Or, And vanquish'd Nature seems to shine no more.
The last of these I like best

Past. 1. lin. 81. Nay tell me first what Region canst thou find,
In which by Thistles Lillies are outshin'd?
Or, Nay tell me first in what× more happy Fields
The Thistle springs to which the Lilly yields?
× This Epithet refers to something going before.

Quere. Which of these Couplets are better express'd and better Numbers? and whether it's better here to use Thistle or Thistles, Lilly or Lillies, Singular or Plural? (Alluding to ye Arms of Scotland & France)
The second Couplet is best; & singular, I think better than Plural

---

Past. 2. lin. 1. A Shepherd's Boy (he seeks no better Name)
Led forth his Flocks along the silver Thame.
Objection. against the Parenthesis (he seeks no better name)
Quere. Wou'd it be any thing better to say
A Shepherd's Boy (who sung for Love, not Fame)
Or, A Shepherd's Boy, who fed an Am'rous Flame,
Led forth his Flocks along the silver Thame.
Quere which of all these is best, or are none of them good?
The first is Spenser's way, & I think better than the other.

Past. 2. lin. 7. Relenting Naïads wept in ev'ry Bow'r,
And Jove consented in a silent Show'r.
Objection. That the Naïads weeping in Bowers is not so proper being Water Nymphs. and that the word consented is doubted by some to whom I have shown these verses.
Alteration

Past.1.lin.57.

If Sylvia smile, she brightens all the Shore,
The Sun's outshin'd, and Nature charms no more.

Quere.

Whether to say the Sun is outshin'd, ~~is~~ be too bold & Hyperbolical? (For Pastoral it is) If it shou'd ~~not~~ be soften'd with seems; Do you approve any of these Alterations)

If Sylvia smile, she brightens all the Shore,

Quere which of these three?

All Nature seems outshind, and charms no more.
or, Light seems outshind, and Nature charms no more.
Or, And vanquishd Nature seems to shine no more.

The last of these I like best

Past.1.lin.81.

Nay tell me first what Region canst thou find,
In which by Thistles Lillies are outshin'd?
Or, Nay tell me first in what x more happy Fields
The Thistle springs to which the Lilly yields?

xThis Epithet refers to something going before.

Quere.

Which of these Couplets are better express'd and better Numbers? and whether it's better here to use Thistle or Thistles, Lilly or Lillies, Singular or Plural? (Alluding to ye Arms of Scotland & France)

The second Couplet is best; & singular, I think better than Plural

Past.2.lin.1.

A Shepherds Boy (he seeks no better Name)
Led forth his Flocks along the silver Thame.

Objection.

against the Parenthesis (he seeks no better Name)

Quere.

Wou'd it be anything better to say (he loves that humble Name) or thus:

A Shepherds Boy, (who sung for Love, not Fame)
or, A Shepherds Boy, who fed an Am'rous Flame,
Led forth his Flocks along the silver Thame.

Quere which of all these is best, or are none of them good?

The first is Spensers way, & I think better than the others.

Past.2.lin.7.

Relenting Naïads wept in ev'ry Bow'r,
And Jove consented in a silent Show'r.

Objection.

That the Naïads weeping in Bowers is not so proper being Water Nymphs. and that the word consented is doubted by some to whom I have shown these verses.

Alteration

Alteration. The Naiads wept in ev'ry watry Bow'r,
And Jove relented in a silent Show'r.

Quere. Which of these Couplets you like best? — ~~The First~~ upon ye second thoughts I think the second is best.

Past. 2. lin. 35. Of slender Reeds a tuneful Flute I have,
The tuneful Flute which dying Colin gave.

Objection: That the first line is too much transpos'd from the natural Order of ye words: and that the Rhyme is unharmonious.

Alteration. That Flute is mine which Colin's tuneful Breath
Inspir'd when living, and bequeath'd in Death.

Quere. Which of these is best? — The second

Past. 2. lin. 41. Some pitying God permit me to be made
The Bird that sings beneath thy Mirtle Shade:
Then might my Voice thy listning Ears employ,
& I those Kisses he receives, enjoy.

Or, Oh, were I made by some transforming Pow'r
The Captive Bird that sings within thy Bow'r! Then might — &c.

The Epithet Captive seems necessary to explain the Thought, on account of those Kisses in ye last line. Quere. If these be better than the other? The second are best, for tis not enough to permitt you to bee made, but to make you

---

Past 2. lin. 67. Oh deign to grace our happy rural Seats,
Our mossy Fountains, and our Green Retreats:
While you y^r Presence to the Groves deny,
Our flow'rs are faded, and our Brooks are dry;
Tho' withring Herbs lay dying on the Plain,
At y^r Return they shall be green again.

Or, Oh deign to grace our happy Rural Seats,
Our mossy Fountains, & our green Retreats:
× Winds, where you walk, shall gently fann the Glade,
Trees, where you sit, shall crowd into a Shade,
× Flow'rs, where you tread, in painted Pride shall rise,
And all things flourish where you turn your Eyes!

× Or,
Where'er you walk,
fresh Gales shall fann ye Glade,

× or
where'er you tread, the purple flow'rs shall rise,

Quere. Which of these you like better?
The second, with the alterations on ye side

Alteration.

The Naïads wept in ev'ry watry Bow'r,
And Jove relented in a silent Show'r.

Quere

Which of these Couplets you like best? —— ~~The First~~ Upon ye second thoughts I think the second is best.

Past.2.lin.35.

Of slender Reeds a tuneful Flute I have,
The tuneful Flute which dying Colin gave.

Objection.

That the first line is too much transpos'd from the natural Order of ye words: and that the Rhyme is unharmonious.

Alteration.

That Flute is mine which Colin's tuneful Breath
Inspir'd when living, and bequeath'd in Death.

Quere.

Which of these is best? —— The second

Past.2.lin.41.

Some pitying God permit me to be made
The Bird that sings beneath thy Mirtle Shade:
Then might my Voice thy listning Ears employ,
& I those Kisses he receives, enjoy.

Or, Oh, were I made by some transforming Pow'r
The Captive Bird that sings within thy Bow'r! Then might —— &c.

The Epithet Captive seems necessary to explain the Thought, on account of those Kisses in ye last line.

Quere.

If these be better than the other? The second are best, for tis ^{not}enough to permitt you to bee made, but to make you

Past.2.lin.67.

Oh deign to grace our happy rural Seats,
Our mossy Fountains, and our Green Retreats:
While you y^{r} Presence to the Groves deny,
Our flow'rs are faded, and our Brooks are dry;
Tho' withring Herbs lay dying on the Plain,
At y^{r} Return they shall be green again.

Or, Oh deign to grace our happy Rural Seats,
Our mossy Fountains, & our green Retreats:
x Winds, where you walk, shall gently fann the Glade,
Trees, where you sit, shall crowd into a Shade,
x Flow'rs, where you tread, in painted Pride shall rise,
And all things flourish where you turn your Eyes!

x Or,
Where'er you walk,
fresh Gales shall fann ye
Glade,
x or
Where'er you tread, the
purple flow'rs shall
rise,

Quere.

Which of these you like better?

The second, with the alterations on ye side.

Past. 4. lin. 5. Now in warm folds the tender Flock remains,
The Cattle slumber on the silent Plains,
While sleeping Birds forget their tuneful Lays,
Let us, dear Thyrsis, sing in Delia's Praise.
(Daphne's written above "Delia's")

Objection to the word remains:
I do not know whether these following be better or no, & desire yr opinion.

Now while the Groves in Cynthia's Beams are drest,
And folded Flocks on their soft Fleeces rest;
While sleeping Birds —

Or, While Cynthia tips with silver all the Groves; | or, While the bright moon wth silver tips ye gro[ves]
And scarce the Winds the topmost Branches move; &c. I think ye last best but might not
(written below: not a breeze / quivering / moves / even yt be mended)

Past. 4. lin. 29. Tis done, and Nature's chang'd since you are gone,
Behold the Clouds have put their Mourning on.

Or, Tis done, and Nature's various Charms decay,
See sable Clouds eclypse the chearful Day.

Quere, which of these is the better? — Clouds put on mourning is too conceited for Pastoral. the second is better & the third in the dark I like better than sable

---

Past. 4. lin. 39. No rich Perfumes refresh the fruitful Field,
Which, but for you, did all its Incense yield.
(for yr sake written below "for you")

Quere, will the second line be better'd by being altred thus?
No rich Perfumes refresh the fruitful field,
Nor fragrant Herbs their native Incense yield.
The second is better

Pas. 3. lin. 91. Thus sung the Swains, while Day yet strove with Night,
And Heav'n yet ×languish'd with departing light; × Quere, if languish be a proper word?
When falling Dews with Spangles deck'd the Glade, — Not very proper
And the low Sun had lengthen'd evry Shade.

Objection. That to mention the Sunsett after Twilight (Day yet strove wth Night) is improper, Is the following Alteration any thing better?
Thus sung the Swains while Day yet strove wth Night,
The Sky still blushing wth departing light;
When falling Dews with Spangles deck'd the Glade,
And the brown Evening lengthen'd evry Shade.

Tis not ye Evening but ye Sun being low yt lengthens ye Shades. otherwise ye second pleases me best.

Past.4.lin.5.

Now in warm folds the tender Flock <u>remains</u>,
The Cattle slumber on the silent Plains,
While sleeping Birds forget their tuneful lays,
Daphne's
Let us, dear Thyrsis, sing in Delias Praise.

Objection to the word <u>remains</u>:
I do not know whether these following be better or no, & desire y^r opinion.

Now while the Groves in Cynthia's Beams are drest,
And folded Flocks on their soft Fleeces rest;
While sleeping Birds ——

Or, While Cynthia tips with silver all the Grove^s
And scarce the Winds the topmost Branches move; & c.
not a Breeze quiv'ring moves

Or, While the bright Moon wth silver tips ye Gro<ve>
I think ye last best but might not even y^t bee mended?

Past.4.lin.29.

Tis done, and Nature's chang'd since you are gone,
Behold the clouds have put their Mourning on.
Or, Tis done, and Nature's various Charms decay,
See sable Clouds eclypse the chearful Day.

Quere, Which of these is the better? —— Clouds put in mourning is too conceited for Pastoral: the second is better & the thick or the dark I like better than sable

Past.4.lin.39.

No rich Perfumes refresh the fruitful Field,
Which, but for you, did all its Incense yield.
for y^r sake

Quere, Will the second line be better'd by being altred thus?

No rich Perfumes refresh the fruitful field,
Nor fragrant Herbs their native Incense yield.

The second is better

Pas.3.lin.91.

Thus sung the Swains, while Day yet strove with Night,
And Heav'n yet x<u>languish'd</u> with departing light;
When falling Dews with Spangles deck'd the Glade,
And the <u>low Sun</u> had lengthend ev'ry Shade.

x Quere, if languish be a proper word?
x Not very proper

Objection. That to mention the <u>Sunsett</u> after Twilight (Day yet strove wth Night) is improper, Is the following Alteration any thing better?

Thus sung the Swains while Day yet strove w^{th}: Night,
The Sky still blushing wth departing light;
When falling Dews with Spangles deck'd the Glade,
And the <u>brown Evening</u> lengthen'd evry Shade.

Tis not ye Evening but ye Suns being low y^t lengthens ye Shades. otherwise ye second pleases mee best.

The Pastorals

NOTES TO THE TRANSCRIPTS

IN INTERPRETING THE TRANSCRIPTS of the *Pastorals* and these notes, it is important to observe that a crowding of words in Pope's manuscript line does not *invariably* point to an erasure and a new insertion. In some instances, the poet either left a blank space to be filled (which then proved too small) or miscalculated in copying fair from his draft. In lines 23–24, for instance, on page 2a (a and b in these pages refer to the left-hand and right-hand columns in the manuscript and transcript), "but . . . easy" is cramped into a space too narrow, but there is no sign of an erasure. On the other hand, in line 8 on that page, "retain'd" is fitted into a space too large, with again no evidence of erasure.

The frequency of erased insertions is, however, noteworthy. It may suggest not only the gradual accumulation of new readings to meet his own and his friends' second thoughts, but also at some point (perhaps not till the '30s when he began to use "variations" from his manuscripts as notes to his printed texts) a decision to restore the manuscript of the *Pastorals* closer to its pristine state by eliminating most of the insertions. Some of these were possibly in the handwritings of his friends: see, for example, page 12b, line 3, and page 14b, line 18. The meaning of the dot placed before certain verses is unclear. It does not always indicate an erasure. Perhaps it indicates that something in the line has been queried.

Page:Line	
3a:18	We . . . therefore *overwrites an erased word or words.*
4a:24–26	but . . . equalls *apparently overwrites an erasure,* equalls *probably replacing* to equall.
4a:24	*From* Virgil *a second* l *has been erased.*
4b:8	is said *overwrites an erased word, possibly* has.
5a:23	Offspring *in the transcript is an error for* Ofspring *in the manuscript.*
6b:6	'd *has been erased after* blush.
7a:14	Linnets *overwrites an erased word.*
7a:17	*The second* o *of* Phosphor *overwrites* e.
7b:18	*Above and below* Strephon *two inserted lines have been erased, the first possibly beginning* Inspire me, Phoebus *(as in TE, 1:65).*

Page:Line	
7b:20	*Below this line an inserted line has been erased.*
8a:3–6	*Above each of these lines, a line has been erased.*
8a:9	wanton Chloris *has been inserted and erased above* lovely Sylvia.
8a:10	*Above this line* Then hid in Shades eludes her eager Swain *(see* Alterations, *p. 20, l. 20) has been inserted and erased. In the left margin beside this and the preceding line words have been erased, and the paper torn and repaired.*
8a:27, 29	*Above each of these lines a line has been erased.*
8b:3–4, 7–10	*Above each of these lines a line has been erased.*
9b:20	twining *may overwrite an erasure; above* with Branches, *a word has been erased, possibly* twining; *in the margin to right of this line, something has been erased.*
10b:12	parch'd . . . I *seems to overwrite an erasure.*
10b:18	*Above* Laurel-Banks, *something has been erased.*
11a:4	*Above* meet *a word has been erased.*
11a:11	*Above the final four words, an insertion has been erased, possibly* not heed thy <?> smart.
11a:20, 22	*Above each of these lines, a line has been erased, as follows* (Alterations, *p. 22, ll. 9–10*): "That Flute is mine which Colin's tuneful Breath / Inspir'd when living and bequeath'd in Death."
11b:3	*Above* sounds not sweet, *something has been erased.*
11b:9	listning *has been inserted and erased above* willing.
11b:13	attends *may overwrite an erasure and has above it an erased word.*
11b:14	*Above* And *an insertion has been erased, possibly* The.
11b:17	The *has been inserted above* Ah *and then erased. Above* your . . . vain *an insertion has been erased, possibly* prefer their Gifts in. *Below this line,* On you their Gifts are all bestowed again *(as in TE, 1:76) has been inserted and erased.*
11b:21	*Above* choicest *an insertion has been erased, probably* fairest.

Page:Line	
12a:9	Grace *has been inserted and erased above* bless.
12a:13	*Above* lurking *an insertion has been erased, possibly* latent.
12a:19	Blossomes *appears to overwrite an erasure.*
12a:22	bless *has been inserted and erased above* crown.
12b:2, 3, 4, 6	*Above each of these lines, a line has been erased.*
12b:3	*In the margin to right of this line,* Rivers *has been inserted, in pencil, in a hand not Pope's.*
12b:10	*Above* proclaim, *an insertion has been erased, probably* resound.
12b:16–19	*Above each of these lines, a line has been erased.*
12b:19	*It is possible that the whole of this line overwrites another.*
13b:12	While one his, mourns, *and* one his *overwrite erasures.*
14a:10	*Above this line,* unheard, unpityd, friendless, and forlorn *has been erased.*
14a:16	*Above* forsook, *an insertion has been erased, possibly* betray'd.
14b:5	*The underscoring is in pencil and may not be Pope's.*
14b:18	Rigor *has been inserted, in pencil, below* Coldness, *in a hand not Pope's.*
15a:18	spent *has been inserted and erased above* tir'd.
15b:13	*The* -lowing *inserted above the* low *of* Yellow *in l. 14 is in a hand that I believe is not Pope's.*
15b:21	*Above* the Shepherds *an insertion has been erased, probably* The Sheppards *and clearly not in Pope's hand.* Shepherds *overwrites an erasure. Above* to stray, *an insertion has been erased, probably* a prey.
15b:26	*An insertion above the first four words has been erased, probably* Pan came & askt.

Page:Line	
16a:7	Forsake . . . World *overwrites an erasure.*
16a:16–17	*In the margin to left of these lines, something has been erased and the paper perforated by it.*
16a:16	*Above* Death . . . away *an insertion has been erased.*
16a:23	*Above* Skies *an insertion has been erased, possibly* Heavn.
16a:25	*Above* stretch'd *a word has been erased.*
16b:17, 18	murm'ring Spring *and* as . . . sing *overwrite erasures.*
16b:19	those . . . wash *overwrites an erasure; above* those *an inserted word has been erased.*
16b:20	sweetly *overwrites an erasure.*
17a:20, 21	may . . . Moisture *and* And . . . of *may overwrite erasures.*
17b:26	*The apostrophe was inserted later and the* i *of* is *partly erased.*
18a:11	*Above* Heyfars crop *an insertion of two words has been erased, of which the second is* graze.
18a:15, 17	Echos *has been erased above* Echo, *as has a now illegible word above* lies; *above* name replies, *an insertion has been erased, possibly* slow reply.
18a:19	Your *overwrites an illegible word, possibly* Thy.
18b:2	*Above the last four words, an insertion has been erased.*
18b:12	Plain *overwrites an erasure.*
19a:3	*All of this line except* But *has been erased.*
19a:15	*The erased word is* Whisper.
19a:16	*Above* whisp'ring, *an insertion has been erased, probably* murm'ring.
19a:22	never end *is faintly underscored in pencil.*
19b:8	*Above* Rivers . . . conscious, *an insertion has been erased.*
21:4	Whether *overwrites* Objection, That.
21:6	Do *overwrites* Qu. (if .

Sapho to Phaon

Introduction

THE MANUSCRIPT OF *Sapho to Phaon* is (apart from the Homer manuscripts) the only surviving autograph of a substantial translated work.[1] Its text falls late, however, in the sequence that leads from the original language to English, showing, for Pope, a remarkably small number of differences from the first published text, which appeared in 1712 in the eighth edition of Tonson's highly successful *Ovid's Epistles . . . By Several Hands*[2]. This collection had contained from its beginnings in 1680 a translation of *Sapho to Phaon* (the fifteenth of Ovid's *Heroides*) by one of the mob of gentlemen who wrote with ease, Sir Carr Scrope; but for the 1712 edition—so a note of Tonson's informs us—an entire new translation of the epistle had been commissioned because Scrope's was abbreviated and incomplete. "The Author [of the new translation]," Tonson continues, "will have me acquaint the Reader, that it was undertaken on that account only, and not out of any suppos'd defect in what that Gentleman had done." Pope evidently wishes not to offend an audience that he knows will consist in large part of gentlemen amateurs like Scrope himself.

The manuscript (at the Pierpont Morgan Library) contains seven pages and a cover page, measuring approximately 7½ by 11¾ inches. On the cover page, a note in Pope's hand says: "Written in 1707." This can hardly be the date of the commission from Tonson that the translation fulfilled, but it may easily be the date of a first working draft of the poem made during the years when Pope was educating himself by imitating the Roman and English poets. Word that he had such a work by him, or, conversely, that Tonson was looking for a new translation of no. XV, can have reached either man by direct inquiry—for they were now acquaintances—or through report of friends, and so have precipitated Pope's preparation of the manuscript we now have—in (we may guess) 1711.[3]

The manuscript obviously began its career as a fair copy, set down in a hand almost as exquisite as that of the *Pastorals,* and intended like them to be passed about for criticism. One of Pope's readers was apparently consulted by word of mouth, and his opinions are registered marginally by Pope himself—on page 1, for example: "X woud al / ter to—standing Corn / By rapid Winds ye sprading[4] flames are born" (TS, 19–22); or again: "X thinks mine best" (TS, 26–27). Another reader entered a running response to the translation, in Latin, along the right-hand margin, comparing it with Scrope's and, occasionally, calling attention to departures from the original.[5] A good deal of his commentary consists simply of approving or disapproving exclamations, such as "Benè," "Bellè," "Pulchrè" or "jejunè," "haud liquet," and "Paraphrasis nimia." Where the judgments were less than favorable, the poet has gone to work to improve matters and the copy has ceased to be fair copy.

Though the author of this running commentary cannot surely be identified, one may reasonably guess that he is Pope's early friend Henry Cromwell, litterateur and man-about-town, with whom he corresponded for some years. Cromwell, we know, made comments of exactly this kind when Pope sent his translation of Statius for review in 1709.[6] Moreover, though the evidence now to follow is highly speculative, the rowdy epigram Pope jotted on the cover page of the manuscript (below, TS, 1; first published by D. C. Jenkins in *The Scriblerian* 8 (1976): 77–78) could and perhaps does concern Cromwell, who, when Pope knew him, *seems* to have been keeping at least one mistress,[7] and who divided his time nearly equally, if we may judge from his letters to Pope and Pope's to him, between Latin learning and womanizing. The name Gellius used in the epigram could easily apply to Cromwell because he seems to have fancied collectors of learned lumber like Macrobius and Aulus Gellius[8] and in his enthusiasm for fine points of grammar somewhat resembles theirs. What Pope thought of Gellius we may gather from the role assigned to him in Dr. Richard Bentley's select curriculum for petrifying geniuses in *Dunciad* IV, and Pope's contemptuous note at that place: "a minute critic"—which is to say, a collector and preserver of critical minutiae.[9]

All this fits with what we know of Henry Cromwell, and the recording of the epigram, if it is aimed at Cromwell, on this sheet of manuscript may hint a connection in Pope's mind between "Gellius" and the marginal commentator, and hence at his identity. Or again it may not: it is important to recall in these matters that speculation is not knowledge.[10]

NOTES

1. The manuscript is discussed in *TE,* 1:340–42.

2. The *Spectator* of 18 March announces it as lately published.

3. Though the manuscript is too much overwritten and doubtless too personal to have been sent to the printer for copy, Pope must have regarded its text as all but final, since he has used the left margin to reckon up page-breaks when the verses are set in type.

4. Probably a phonetic spelling like Pope's "Heyfars" in "Winter" (*Pastorals,* 18a:11).

5. In the notes to the transcripts, the latter are referred to line numbers in the Latin text.

6. Pope to Cromwell, 10 June 1709 (*Correspondence,* 1:63).

7. If so, she was perhaps Elizabeth Thomas, the "Sappho" who later sold Pope's letters, which Cromwell had bestowed on her as a (parting?) gift, to Curll. The other "Maid" of the epigram was possibly his housekeeper—"the lady Isabella," as Pope calls her (see following note).

8. Pope to Cromwell, 10 May 1711 (*Correspondence,* 1:116): ". . . and let the lady Isabella"—see above, n. 7—"put your Macrobius & A. Gellius somewhere out of your way, for a Month of so." This is in preparation for his visiting Pope at Binfield.

9. See *Dunciad,* IV:230–32:

> Be sure I give them Fragments, not a Meal;
> What Gellius or Stobaeus hash'd before,
> Or chew'd by blind old Scholiasts o'er and o'er.

In the years when he was seeing Cromwell, Pope's opinion seems to have been much the same. Among the purveyors of critic-learning he will have to master in translating Homer, Gellius is "worse than 'em all." Pope to Parnell [25 May or 1 June 1714] (*Correspondence,* 1:225).

10. If the epigram *does* concern Cromwell, and is Pope's (rather than a current one he has simply jotted down), it may be the bitter fruit of Pope's conflicts with Dennis, of whom Cromwell seems to have been a longtime friend and admirer. Cromwell may have tacitly resented Pope's singling out the aging critic for ridicule in the *Essay on Criticism,* and Pope may have felt that Cromwell could have intervened to allay the savage fury of Dennis's attack on his crippled person, in *Reflections Critical and Satyrical, upon a Late Rhapsody, call'd An Essay upon Criticism.* But this too is guesswork, as is the tempting thesis that the "Gentleman" in Pope's satiric reply to Dennis's attack (*The Narrative of Dr. Robert Norris,* 1713), who praises Dennis's "sound Intellectuals, and unerring Judgment," represents Cromwell—ever engaged in defending his irascible friend.

~~Errata in ye Verses to Ovid~~ Epig:

Poor Gellius keeps, or rather starves two Maids,
Seldome he feeds, but often f—s ye Jades,
He stops one Mouth that t'other may not mutter,
So what they want in Bread, they have in Butter.

Sapho to Phaon.

Written first 1707.

~~Errata in ye Notes to Ovids -~~

Epig:

Poor Gellius keeps, or rather starves two Maids,
Seldome he feeds, but often f——s ye Jades.
He stops one Mouth that tother may not mutter,
So what they want in Bread, they have in Butter.

Sapho to Phaon.

Written first 1707

1

Sapho to Phaon:

Wholly Translated.

Say lovely Youth that dost my Heart command,
Can Phaon's Eyes forget his Sapho's Hand?
Must then her Name the wretched Writer prove,
To thy Remembrance lost, as to thy Love? - - - - | Paraphr:
Ask not the cause that I new Numbers chuse,
The Lute neglected and the Lyric Muse; | Bene
Love taught my Tears in sadder notes to flow,
And tun'd my Heart to Elegies of Woe.
I burn, I burn, as when fierce Whirlwinds raise
The spreading Flames, and crackling Harvests blaze | Bene, at melius Scrop.
Phaon to Ætna's scorching Fields retires,
1\. While I consume with more than Ætna's Fires.
No more my Soul a Charm in Musick finds,
Musick has Charms alone for peaceful Minds. | Pulchre - at recitius Scrop.
2\. No more The Lesbian Dames my Passion move,
Once the dear Objects of my guilty Love; | Bene
[illegible]
Oh Youth ungrateful to a Flame like mine! - Tautologie
Whom wou'd not all those blooming Charms surprize,
Those heav'nly Looks, and dear deluding Eyes? - Pulchrè
The Harp and Bow wou'd you like Phœbus bear,
A brighter Phœbus, Phaon might appear;
Wou'd you with Ivy wreath your flowing Hair,
Not Bacchus self with Phaon cou'd compare; | Benè
Yet Phœbus lov'd, and Bacchus felt the Flame;
One Daphne warm'd, and one the Cretan Dame;
Nymphs that in Verse no more cou'd rival me,
2\. Than ev'n those Gods contend in Charms with thee. - Paraphr: pulchra.
The Muses teach me all their softest Lays,
And the wide World resounds with Sapho's Praise. | Pulchrè
Tho' great Alcæus more sublimely sings,
And strikes with bolder Rage the sounding Strings; | Pulchra Paraphrasis
No less Renown attends the moving Lyre,
Which Cupid tunes, and Venus does inspire.

To

Sapho to Phaon:
Wholly Translated.

+stet
∴ Say lovely Youth that dost my Heart command, my Heart.
Can Phaon's Eyes forget his Sapho's Hand? Bene +likes <the. is ll> best.
Must then her Name the wretched Writer prove,
To thy Remembrance lost, as to thy Love? Paraphr.
Ask not the cause that I new Numbers chuse,
The Lute neglected and the Lyric Muse, ~~The Lute neglec-ted & ye Lyric Muse~~
~~These mournful Numbers suit a mournful Muse;~~ Bene
+Love taught my Tears in sadder notes to flow, ~~Lyricis. Barbitos perperam omissa~~
And tun'd my Heart to+Elegies of Woe.
I burn, I burn, as when fierce Whirlwinds raise by Whirlwinds born
The spreading Flames, +and crackling Harvests blaze. The spreading flames ~~involve~~ ye standing corn
Bene, at melius Scroop ni fallor +woud alter to—standing corn
scorching
Phaon to +AEtna's ~~distant~~ Fields retires,
~~Sapho~~ ~~<in>~~
1. ~~Me, Love~~ consume~~s~~ with more than AEtna's Fires. By rapid ~~Whirl~~Winds ye spreading/~~fierce~~/Flames are born
While I
No more my Soul a Charm in Musick finds, Pulchrè— at rectius Scroop +thinks mine best
Musick has Charms alone for peaceful Minds.
2 No more ~~2~~ The Lesbian Dames ~~no more~~ my Passion move, Benè
~~a guiltier~~
Once the dear Objects of my guilty Love.
<Love can st>
Soft scenes of Solitude no more ~~I fly for ease~~ can please, ~~Thou only thou of all my boast~~
~~No more I sigh for Amythone's Charms,~~ ~~Anactorie~~ ~~But all my Cares on thee <unkind> is are cast~~
1
~~They <fan the><blank> soothe the dear Disease.~~ Love enters there, & I'm my own Disease.
~~No more I melt in Athys circling Arms,~~ ~~Ah! rimis Lascivè innuat~~ ~~Licet se esse Tribade~~m non ~~tamen profitetur~~
3 This once divided Heart ~~is All other Loves are lost in only thine~~
3 All other Loves are lost ~~All other Loves are lost in thine alone,~~ in only thine, +
Ah youth ungrateful to a ~~Love~~ like mine! ~~Tautologie~~
Flame ~~dum~~ < >
~~This once-divided Heart is all thy own.~~ ~~tè improbè i.e. ingratè omitten~~
all those blooming Charms
Whom wou'd not ~~that resistless Youth~~ surprize, ~~Who woud not all yt blooming youth~~ — ~~Well might those Charms my tender Soul sur~~
Those heav'nly Looks, and dear deluding Eyes? —Pulchrè
The Harp and Bow woud you like Phoebus bear, Benè
A brighter Phoebus, Phaon might appear:
Wou'd you with Ivy wreath your flowing Hair,
Not Bacchus self with Phaon cou'd compare.
Yet Phoebus lov'd, and Bacchus felt the Flame; Benè
One Daphne warm'd, and one the Cretan Dame:
Nymphs that in Verse no more cou'd rival me,
2. Than ev'n those Gods contend in Charms with thee. Paraphr. pulchra.
all
The Muses teach me+ ^ their softest Lays, Pulchrè
And the wide World resounds with Sapho's Praise:
Tho' great Alcaeus more sublimely sings,
And strikes with bolder Rage the sounding Strings; Pulchra Paraphrasis—
No less Renown attends the moving Lyre
Which Cupid tunes, and Venus does inspire.

To

2

To me what Nature has in Charms deny'd,
Is well by Wit's more lasting Charms supply'd.
Tho' short my Stature, yet my name extends
To Heav'n itself and Earths extreamest Ends.
Brown as I am, an Ethiopian Dame
Inspir'd young Perseus with a gen'rous flame
Turtles and Doves of diff'ring Hues unite,
And glossie Jett is pair'd with shining White.
If to no Charms thou wilt thy Heart resign,
But such as merit, such as equal thine,
By none alas! by none thou canst be mov'd,
3. Phaon alone by Phaon must be lov'd!
Yet once thy Sapho cou'd thy Cares employ,
Once in her arms you center'd all yr Joy:
Still all those joys to my Remembrance move,
For oh! how vast a Memory has Love!
My Musick then you cou'd for ever hear,
And all my Words were Musick to your Ear.
Kisses you snatch'd, & stop'd my charming Tongue,
And found my Kisses sweeter than my Song.
In all I pleas'd; but most, in what was best;
And the last Joy was dearer than the rest.
Then with each Word, each Glance, each Motion fir'd,
You still enjoy'd, and yet you still desir'd;
Till all dissolving in the Trance we lay,
And in tumultuous Raptures dy'd away.
The fair Sicilians now thy Soul inflame;
Why was I born, ye Gods, a Lesbian Dame?
But ah beware, Sicilian Nymphs! nor boast
4. That wandring Heart which I so lately lost;
Nor be with all those tempting words abus'd,
Those tempting words were all to Sapho us'd.
And you that rule Sicilia's happy Plains,
Have pity, Venus, on yr Poet's Pains!
Shall Fortune still in one sad Tenor run,
And still increase the Woes so soon begun?
Enur'd to Sorrows from my tender Years,
My Parent's Ashes drank my early Tears.
~~My ruin'd Brother trades from Shore to Shore,~~
~~And gains as basely as he lost before:~~
My Brother next, neglecting Wealth and Fame,
Ignobly burn'd in a destructive flame:

Pulchrè
Pulchrè
Pulchrè non rectè
Magis Poeticè quam Scroop
minus ad rem etiam et Scroop.
melius Scroop.
Pulchrè
Paraph: ut et Scroop
Bellè etiā Scroop
Bellè etiam Scroop
Melius Scroop
minus rectè
Pulchrè
remittite minus rectè
Pulchre
rectè melius quam Scroop
Benè
Benè
Pulchrè
Bene.
2 priores versus Scroop Pulcherrimi
Beware

41 49

To me what Nature has in Charms deny'd,

Is well by Wit's more lasting Charms supply'd.

~~yet~~ yet my name extends

Tho' short my Stature, ~~my Immortal Name~~

itself and Earth's extreamest Ends.

To Heav'n ~~extends, and thro' the Globe my Fame.~~

an Ethiopian Dame

---- Brown as I am, ~~the beauteous AEthiop mov'd~~

Inspir'd young Perseus with a gen'rous flame

--- ~~Great Perseus heart; he saw, admir'd, and lov'd.~~

Turtles and Doves of diff'ring Hues unite,

And glossie Jett is pair'd with shining White.

If to no Charms thou wilt thy Heart resign,

But such as merit, such as equal thine,

By none alas! by none thou canst be mov'd,

3. Phaon alone by Phaon must be lov'd!

thy Sapho coud thy cares employ,

Yet once ~~ev'n I, neglected I, had Charms,~~

in her arms you centerd all y[r] ~~her~~ Joy.

~~There was a Time when~~ ~~Sapho yet had charms~~ Once ~~all thy joys were centered in these Arms:~~

Still all those joys to my remembrance move,

For oh! how vast a Memory has Love!

My Musick then you cou'd for ever hear,

And all my Words were Musick to your Ear.

Kisses you snatch'd, & stop'd my Charming Tongue,

And found my Kisses sweeter than my Song.

~~Then urg'd by those to <blank> Joys you prest,~~

In All I pleas'd; but most, in what was best;

~~Still~~

And the last Joy was dearer than the rest.

Then with each Word, each Glance, each Motion fir'd,

You still enjoy'd, and yet you still desir'd;

~~and both entranced~~

~~Both warm'd at once, at once entranc'd we lay,~~

Till all dissolving in the Trance we lay,

And in tumultuous Raptures dy'd away.

The fair Sicilians now thy Soul inflame;

Why was I born, ye Gods, a Lesbian Dame?

But ah beware, Sicilian Nymphs,

~~Ye fair Sicilians, ah be warn'd,~~ nor boast

4. That wandring Heart which I so latelv lost;

~~by~~ ~~his~~

Nor be with all those tempting words abus'd,

<4> Those tempting words were all to Sapho+ us'd.

And you that rule Sicilia's happy Plains,

Have pity, Venus, on y[r] Poet's Pains!

Shall Fortune still in one sad Tenor run,

~~she~~ so ~~so soon~~ soon

And still increase the Woes ~~it has~~ begun?

Enur'd to Sorrows from my tender Years,

My Parent's Ashes drank my early Tears.

~~Quere si~~ ~~My ruin'd Brother trades from Shore to Shore,~~

~~delenda?~~ ~~And gains, as basely as he lost before:~~

~~He hates his Sister for a Sister's Care,~~

~~Me too he hates, advis'd by me in vain,~~

~~So unsuccessful 'tis to be sincere!~~

~~So fatal 'tis to be sincere and plain!~~

My Brother next, neglecting Wealth and Fame,

Ignobly burn'd in a destructive flame:

An

~~exprimantur oportet~~

~~si difficilis~~

—pulchrè

Though short my stature, yet my Name extends

Pulchrè To Heavn itself, and Earths extremest ends.

minus placent-- ~~an Ethiopian Dame~~

~~Taught Perseus wth a genrous flame~~

~~Breast to feel a genrous~~

Pulchrè non rectè

Magis Poeticè quam Scroop

~~<once>~~

~~yet < > neglected Sapho~~

~~sure <had charms>~~

minus ad rem etiam et Scroop

—melius Scroop

—Pulchrè

Paraph: ut et Scroop

Bellè—etiã Scroop

Bellè—etiam Scroop

Melius Scroop

<~~Till all dissolving in~~

~~ye trance we lay~~

~~& in tumultuous Raptures~~

~~dyd away~~.>

—nova praeda— minus rectè

—Pulchrè

—remittite—minus recte

—Pulchre

rectè—melius quam Scroop

~~have all to me been usd~~

Benè

Benè

Pulchrè

~~My brother next neglecting Wealth and Fame~~

~~Ignobly burnd in <u>niversal Shame>~~

~~haut liquet~~

Bene

2 priores versus Scroop Pulcherrimi

Beware—

An infant Daughter late my Griefs increas'd,
And all a Mother's Cares distract my Breast.
Alas, What more cou'd Fate it self impose,
But Thee, the last and greatest of my Woes?
No more my Robes in waving Purple flow,
Nor on my Hand the sparkling Diamonds glow;
No more my Locks in Ringlets curl'd diffuse
5. The costly Sweetness of Arabian Dews,
Nor Braids of Gold the vary'd Tresses bind,
That fly disorder'd to the wanton Wind.
For whom shou'd Sapho use such Arts as these?
He's gone, whom only she desir'd to please!
Cupid's light Darts my tender Bosome move;
Still is there cause for Sapho still to love:
So from my Birth the Sisters fix'd my doom,
And gave to Venus all my Life to come;
By Charms like thine which all my Soul have won,
Who might not, ah! who wou'd not be undone?
For those, Aurora Cephalus might scorn,
And with fresh Blushes paint the conscious Morn;
For those, might Cynthia lengthen Phaon's Sleep,
And bid Endymion nightly tend his Sheep;
Venus for those had rapt thee to the Skies,
6. But Mars on thee might look with Venus' Eyes.
O scarce a Youth, yet scarce a tender Boy!
O useful Time for Lovers to employ!
Pride of thy Age, and Glory of thy Race!
Come to these Arms, and melt in this Embrace!
The Vows you never will return, receive;
And take at least the Love you wilt not give.
See while I write, my Words are lost in Tears!
The less my Sense, the more my Love appears.
Sure 'twas not much to bid one kind Adieu,
(At least to feign was never hard to you)
Farewell my Lesbian Love! you might have said,
Or coldly thus, Farewell oh Lesbian Maid!
No Tear did you, no parting Kiss receive;
Nor knew I then how much I was to grieve.
No Gift on thee thy Sapho cou'd confer,
And Wrongs and Woes were all you left with her.
No Charge I gave you, and no Charge cou'd give,
7. But this; Be mindful of our Loves, and live!

Benè — minus placent — likes em — rectè — recte — Pulchre — Tres versus — Scroop minus placent — Benè — melius quam Scroop — Pulchre — Benè
Or while my Muse in melting notes complains,
My Heart relents, & answers to my Strains;
Pulchriti magis placent — Haud liquet — Bellè — Recte — Benè — Bellè — Scroop — melius hic — pulchre — the Parenthesis is an interpolation — Pulchre — Optime — melius quam Scroop — recte — jejune — still express — Pulchre — Melius Scroop — Now

<3>

An infant Daughter late my Griefs increas'd,
And all a Mother's Cares distract my Breast. — Benè
~~An Infant now my hapless Fortune shares,~~
~~And this sad Breast feels all a Mother's Cares.~~

more
Alas, What ~~<heavier Ill>~~ cou'd Fate it self impose, — minus placent— ~~complaint~~ +likes 'em.
~~<5>~~ But Thee, the last and greatest of my Woes?
No more my Robes in waving Purple flow, +
Nor on my Hand the sparkling Diamonds glow; —rectè

in Ringlets curl'd
No more my Locks ~~by Zephyrs fann'd,~~ diffuse — ~~bound~~ ~~Nor shake my Locks in golden circles~~ ~~Nor wide diffuse Arabian sweets aroũd~~
5. The costly Sweetness of Arabian Dews, —recte
Nor Braids of Gold the vary'd Tresses bind, — ~~For whom~~
That fly disorder'd to the wanton Wind. — <2> Tres versus Pulchre — Scroop minus placent
For whom shou'd Sapho+ use such Arts as these?
He's gone, whom only she desir'd to please! — Benè — melius quam Scroop

Cupid's light Darts my tender Bosome move,
~~My tender Heart the slightest Darts can move;~~ +
Still is there cause for Sapho still to love: — Pulchre

~~Or~~ Sisters ~~Fates so~~
So ~~So~~ from my Birth the ~~Sisters~~ fix'd my Doom, — Benè ~~<So from my>~~ + ~~likes~~ ~~stet~~
And gave to Venus all my Life to come;
~~Or taught to feel what first my Muse did feign,~~ — Or while my Muse in melting notes complains
~~My <blank> Heart beats Measure to my Strain~~ — My Heart relents, & answers to my Strains — Pulchrè Hi magis placent ~~haud liquet~~

thine
By Charms like ~~those~~ which all my Soul have won,
Who might not, ah! who would not be undone?
~~Alas! who might not, wou'd not be undone?~~
For those, Aurora Cephalus might scorn,
And with fresh Blushes paint the conscious Morn; — Bellè
For those, might Cynthia lengthen Phaon's Sleep, —Recte

bid
And ~~let~~ Endymion nightly tend his Sheep;
Venus for those had rapt thee to the Skies,
6. But Mars on thee might look with Venus' Eyes. — Benè
O scarce a Youth, yet scarce a tender Boy!
O+ useful Time for Lovers to+ employ!
Pride of thy Age, and Glory of thy Race! — Bellè
Come to these Arms, and melt in this Embrace!
The Vows thou never wilt return, receive,
\+ ~~Thy Love I ask not to forsaken me~~
And take ~~beg~~ at least the Love thou wilt not give.
~~All that I ask is but to doat on thee.~~ — Scroop melius ⟷ hic ⟷

my
See while I write ~~and weep; see~~ Words are lost in Tears!
The less my Sense, the more my Love appears. — pulchrè Bella pa-raphrasis

bid
Sure 'twas not much to ~~give~~ one kind Adieu,
~~not so~~
(At least to feign was never hard to you) — The Parenthesis is an —interpolatio ~~<melius>~~ ~~rectè~~
Farewell my Lesbian Love! you might have said, — Pulchrè

coldly
Or thus, ~~at least~~: Farewell oh Lesbian Maid!
you
No Tear did~~st thou~~, no parting Kiss receive; —Optimè
Nor knew I then how much I was to grieve. — melius quã Scroop

No Gift on thee thy Sapho coud confer,
No Pledge you left me, faithless and unkind! — ~~no Gift on thee thy Sapho coud confer, & Wrongs & Woes~~ recte

And Wrongs and Woes were all you left with her.
Nothing wth me, but Wrongs, was left behind. — jejunè fla<t> & ill Expres<t>

you,
No Charge I gave ~~thee,~~ and no Charge cou'd give, — Pulchrè
7. But this; Be mindful of our Loves, and live! — Melius qu<am> ~~<omittit>~~ Scroop

Now

4

Now by the Nine, the Pow'rs ador'd by me,
And Love, the God that ever waits on thee;
When first I heard (from whom I hardly knew)
That you were fled, and all my Joys with you,
Like some sad Statue, speechless, pale, I stood; Grief chill'd my breast, & stop'd my
~~[illegible]~~; curdled all my blood
freezing
No Sigh to rise, no Tear had pow'r to flow;
Fix'd in a stupid Lethargy of Woe.
But when its way th' impetuous Passion found, ~~[illegible] Passage~~
I rend my Tresses, and my Breast I wound;
I rave, then weep; I curse, & then complain;
Now swell to Rage, now melt in Tears again.
Not fiercer Pangs distract the mournful Dame,
Whose only Infant feeds the Fun'ral Flame.
My scornful Brother with a Smile ~~[illegible]~~ appears,
Insults my Woes, ~~[illegible]~~ and triumphs in my Tears,
His hated Image ever haunts my eyes,
(8.) And Why this Grief? thy Daughter lives, he cries.
Stung with my Love, and furious with Despair,
All torn my Garments, and my ~~[illegible]~~ Bosome bare,
My Woes, thy Crimes, I to the World proclaim;
Such inconsistent Things are Love and Shame!
Phaon ~~[illegible]~~ all my Care and my Delight,
~~[illegible]~~
My Dayly Longing, and my Dream by Night.
~~[illegible]~~:
O Night more pleasing than the brightest Day,
When Fancy gives what Absence takes away,
And drest in all its visionary Charms,
Restores my fair Deserter to my Arms!
Then round your Neck in wanton wreaths I twine; ~~thy~~ ~~[illegible]~~
Then you, methinks, as fondly circle mine:
del. ~~Thy Kisses, then, thy Words my Soul indear;~~
~~Glow on my Lips, and murmur in my Ear:~~
A thousand tender Words, I hear and speak;
A thousand melting Kisses, give, and take!
Then fiercer Joys — I blush to mention these
Yet while I blush, confess ~~[illegible]~~ how much they please!
But when, with Day, the sweet Delusions fly,
(9.) And all things wake to Life and Joy, but I;
As if once more forsaken, I complain,
~~[illegible]~~
And close my Eyes, to dream of you again; ~~[illegible]~~
~~[illegible]~~
~~[illegible]~~ Then frantic rise, & like some Fury rove
Thro' lonely Plains, and thro' the silent Grove;
As if the silent Grove, and lonely Plains,
That knew my Pleasures, coud relieve my Pains.
~~[illegible]~~

Margin notes: Pulchre — Hic — Cuncta — magis Poetice — Astrictus fere — Scroop — Pulchre — melius quam Scroop — Bene — Bella parapphrasis — Scroop fere melius precre — Recte — Pulchra Amplificatio et recte — Pulchrum Epiphonema et recte — Pulchre — Paraphrasis — Pulchre — Pulcherrime — longe praestas Scroop meo judicio — At Scroop hic — (Paraphrasis nimia et error, ne abeo.) — praestat. — Pulchre

47

<4>

Now by the Nine, the Pow'rs ador'd by me, — Pulchre

And Love, the God that ever waits on thee;

When first I heard (from whom I hardly knew) — Haec < >

That you were fled, and all my joys with you, — Cuncta

Like some sad Statue, speechless, pale, I stood; Grief chilld my breast & stopd m y m — magis Poeticè ~~Grief <child my breast>~~ <——>

~~A sudden~~ ~~deadly~~ ~~Damp crept cold along my Blood;~~ curdled all my blood — Astrictū frigore <——> ~~<Damp>~~ quam Scroop.

No Sigh to rise, no Tear had pow'r to flow; freezing

Fix'd in a stupid Lethargy of Woe. < > < >

But when ~~impetuous Grief its Passage~~ its way th' impetuous Passion found, — Pulchrè--

I rend my Tresses, and my Breast I wound; — melius quā Scroop Benè--

I rave, then weep; I curse, & then complain; <sigh>

Now swell to Rage, now melt in Tears again. — Bella paraphrasis

Not fiercer Pangs distract the mournful Dame,

Whose only ~~Offspring~~ Infant feeds the Fun'ral Flame. — Scroop ferè melius/ rectè

~~My scornful Brother with a Frown~~ My scornful Brother with a smile appears,

~~Insults my Rage~~ Insults my Woes, and triumphs in my Tears. — Rectè

His hated Image ever haunts my eyes,

(8.) And Why this Grief? thy Daughter lives, he cries.

Stung with my Love, and furious with Despair, — Pulchra Amplificatio -- et recta

~~My Robes all torn, my wounded~~ All torn my Garments, and my Bosome bare,

My Woes, thy Crimes, I to the World proclaim;

~~What~~ Such inconsistent Things are Love and Shame! — Pulchrum epiphonema -- et rectum

< > < > Phaon is ~~<Tis thou art>~~ Tis thou art all my Care and my Delight,

~~Thou art, at once, my Anguish and Delight;~~

My Dayly Longing, and my Dream by Night.

~~Care of my Day, and Phantome of my Night:~~

O Night more pleasing than the brightest Day, — Pulchre

When Fancy gives what Absence takes away;

And drest in all its visionary Charms,

Restores my fair Deserter to my Arms! — Paraphrasis

Then round ~~thy~~ your Neck in ~~Am'rous Folds~~ w^th ~~longing~~ wanton Wreaths, I twine; — Pulchrè

Then you, methinks, as fondly circle mine:

~~Thy Kisses, then, thy Words my Soul indear;~~ — quaere si delend. del. ~~Non liquet~~ ~~+likes these 2~~

~~Glow on my Lips, and murmur in my Ear:~~

A thousand tender Words, I hear and speak;

A thousand melting Kisses, give, and take!

Then fiercer Joys -- ~~<alas>~~ I blush to mention these — Pulcherrimè

~~I blush, yet blushing, own~~ Yet while I blush, confess how much they please! — longè praestas Scroop--meo judicio

But when, with Day, the sweet Delusions fly,

(9.) And all things wake to Life and Joy, but I; — At Scroop hic--

~~I dread the Light of cruel Heav'n to view,~~ As if once more forsaken, I complain, — ~~After this 3.rd line put in ye sense of y^e~~ <——>

And close my Eyes, ~~again~~ ~~once more~~ to dream of you; again. — ~~by thee forsaken I complain~~ ~~As if thyself forsook me once again~~ <——> ~~to dream of thee~~ — (Paraphrasis nimia et vereor, ne abire.)

~~The charming Phantom flies, and I complain,~~

~~Then <then> like some raging Bacchanal I rove,~~ Then frantic rise, & like some Fury rove — --praestat: ni fallor

<4a>

Thro' lonely Plains, and thro' the ~~conscious~~ silent Grove;

As if the silent Grove, and lonely Plains, — Pulchrè

That knew my Pleasures, cou'd relieve my Pains.

~~As if, once more forsaken, I complain,~~

~~And close my eyes, to dream of you again.~~ I

~~Then frantic rise, & like some Fury rove~~

I view the Grotto, once the Scene of Love;
The Rocks around, the hanging Roofs above;
Which charm'd me more, with native Moss o'ergrown,
~~Where the rude Rock more charm'd my sight~~
Than Phrygian Marble, or the Parian Stone.
I find the Shades that did our Joys conceal,
Not Him who made me love those Shades so well.
Here the prest Herbs with bending Tops betray
Where oft entwin'd in amorous Folds we lay;
I kiss that Earth which once was prest by you,
And all with Tears the with'ring Herbs bedew.
For thee the fading Trees appear to mourn,
(10.) And Birds defer their Songs till thy Return:
Night shades the Groves, and all in silence lye;
All, but the mournful Philomel and I;
With mournful Philomel I join my Strain;
~~With her I wake, with her I joyn my Strain;~~
Of Tereus she, of Phaon I complain!

A Spring there is, whose silver Waters show
Clear as a Glass, the shining Sands below;
A flowry Lotos spreads its Arms above,
Shades all the Banks, and seems itself a Grove;
Eternal Greens the mossy Margin grace,
Watch'd by the Sylvan Genius of the Place.
Here as I lay, and swell'd with Tears the Flood,
Before my sight a Watry Virgin stood;
She stood and cry'd; "O you that love in vain,
"Fly hence, and seek the far Leucadian Main:
"There stands a Rock from whose impending Steep
"Apollo's Fane surveys the rolling Deep;
"There injur'd Lovers, leaping from above,
(11.) "Their Flames extinguish, and forget to love.
"Deucalion once with hopeless Fury burn'd,
"In vain he lov'd, relentless Pyrrha scorn'd;
"But when from hence he plung'd into the Main,
"Deucalion scorn'd, and Pyrrha lov'd in vain.
"Haste Sapho, haste, from high Leucadia throw
"Thy wretched Weight, nor dread the Deeps below!
She spoke, and vanish'd with the Voice — I rise,
And silent Tears fall trickling from my Eyes.
I go, ye Nymphs! those Rocks and Seas to prove;
How much I fear! but ah, how much I love?
I go, ye Nymphs! where furious Love inspires;
Let Female Fears submit to Female Fires!

To

Melius quam Scroop.

minus placent.

minus placent — fere Melius Scroop

Pulchre

Pulchre — et Scroop

minus placet — nec Scroop

Pulcherrime

Bene.

Bene.

Bene.

Stent. 19 lines.

Paraphrasis

Rocks — priori loco sint.

Bene

Paraphrasis

44

I view the Grotto, once the Scene of Love;
Rocks around,
The ~~Moss below,~~^ the hanging Roofs above;
Which charm'd me more, with native Moss oergrown,
~~Where^ the rude Rock more^ charm'd my sight^ alone~~
Than *Phrygian* Marble, or the *Parian* Stone.
Shades that did our joys conceal
I find the ~~Grove, beneath whose gloomy Shade~~
Not Him who made me love those Shades so well.
~~Our panting Limbs on springing Flow'rs were laid;~~
~~But Thee I find not; Thee I seek alone!~~
<For> ~~Not Flow'rs nor Shades delight, now thou art gone!~~
Here the prest Herbs with bending Tops betray
~~mem--alter~~ Stet: oft entwin'd ~~in Am'rous Folds~~ we lay
Where ~~to^ our^ Weight the willing^ Earth gave^ way;~~
~~amrous folds~~
I kiss that Earth which once was prest by you,
~~in folds~~
~~<(10.)>~~And all with Tears the with'ring Herbs bedew.
For thee the fading Trees appear to mourn,
(10.) And Birds defer their Songs till thy Return:
Night shades the Groves, and all in silence lye,
~~wakefull~~ *Philomel*
All, but the mournful ~~Nightingale~~ and I;
mournful *Philomel* I join my Strain,
With ~~her^ I wake, with her I joyn my Strain;~~
Of *Tereus* she, +of *Phaon* I complain!
A Spring there is, whose silver Waters show
Clear as a Glass, the shining Sands below;
⟷
A flow'ry Lotos spreads its Arms above,
Shades all ye Banks
~~The Shaded Streams~~, and seems itself a Grove.
Eternal Greens the mossy Margin grace,
11. Watch'd by the Sylvan *Genius* of the Place.
Here as I lay, and swell'd with Tears the Flood,
~~<(11.)>~~Before my sight a Watry Virgin stood;
She stood and cry'd; "O you that love in vain,
"Fly hence, and seek the far *Leucadian* Main:
"There stands a Rock from whose impending Steep
< > "*Apollo*'s Fane surveys the rolling Deep;
Stent "There injur'd Lovers, leaping from above,
⟷
19 lines. (11.) "Their Flames extinguish, and forget to love.
"*Deucalion* once with hopeless Fury burn'd,
"In vain he lov'd, relentless *Pyrrha* scorn'd;
"But when from hence he plung'd into the Main,
"*Deucalion* scorn'd, and *Pyrrha* lov'd in vain.
"Haste Sapho, haste, from high *Leucadia* throw
"Thy wretched Weight, nor dread the Deeps below!
She spoke, and vanish'd with the Voice -- I rise,
And silent Tears fall
~~The big round Drops run~~ trickling from my Eyes.
+
Rocks Seas
I go, ye Nymphs! those ~~Seas~~ and ~~Rocks~~ to prove;
ah ~~more~~
How much I fear! but ~~oh,~~ how much I love?
I go, ye Nymphs! where furious love inspires;
⟷ Let Female Fears submit to Female Fires!

melius ~~<ferè>~~
quam Scroop.

~~The Rocks around~~

~~wch charmd me more with~~

~~hoary moss o'ergrown~~

~~native~~

~~<than>~~
~~<stent>~~

minùs placent
~~(Flowrs not in original~~
~~alter this 3rd line.)~~

~~minus placent~~

minùs placent
ferè melius Scroop

~~his 3rd line better than my 2d.~~

Pulchrè

Pulchrè—et Scroop

~~shades & all~~
~~Night oer ye Groves extends~~
~~her gloomy wings~~
~~all is shut in sleep yet~~
~~& all is hushd but Philomela~~
~~mournful I sings~~
~~With Philomela Sapho joins her~~

minus placent--nec Scroop

Pulcher-
—rime

Benè

Benè

Benè

Paraphrasis ~~Quere si~~
~~Tautologie~~ ~~delendū~~
~~+likes it~~ ← → ~~obscuri~~
tate

~~Non liquet~~

—Rocks—priori loco
sint

—Belle

Paraphrasis

To

6

Paraphras Bella — To ~~Seas and Rocks~~ Rocks and Seas I fly from Phaon's Hate,
And hope from ~~Rocks~~ Seas and ~~Seas~~ Rocks a milder Fate.
Ye gentle Gales beneath my Body blow,
Bellis-sime — And softly lay me on the Waves below!
And thou, kind Love, my sinking Limbs sustain,
Spread thy soft Wings and waft me o'er the Main,
19 lines. (12) — Nor let a Lover's Death the guiltless Flood profane!
In Phœbus Shrine my Harp I'll then bestow,
Recte et Bene — And this Inscription shall be ~~read~~ plac'd below:
"Here she who sung, to him that did inspire,
"Sapho to Phœbus consecrates her Lyre,
"What suits with Sapho, Phœbus suits with thee,
"The Gift, the Giver, and the God agree!

Bene — But why alas! relentless Phaon! why
To ~~[illegible]~~ distant Coasts must tender Sapho fly?
~~If you return, [illegible] shall stay~~ — ✕ Beauty should recommend her Mr Granville ✕ abundance of these ...
~~Not all the Gods shall force me then away.~~ — alter
~~[illegible]~~
~~For thou alone art all the Gods to me.~~
Ah! ~~canst thou doom me~~ to the Rocks & Sea;
O far more faithless, ~~and~~ and more ~~[illegible]~~ hard than they?
Ah! canst thou rather see this tender Breast
Dash'd on sharp Rocks, than to thy Bosom prest?
This Breast which once, ~~[illegible]~~ inhuman! you lik'd so well;
19 lines. (13) Pulcher-rime — Where the Loves play'd, and where the Muses dwell!
Alas! the Muses now no more inspire;
Untun'd my Lute, and silent is my Lyre;
My languid Numbers have forgot to flow,
And Fancy sinks beneath a Weight of Woe.
Ye Lesbian Virgins, and ye Lesbian Dames,
Pulchre — Themes of my Verse, and Objects of my Flames,
No more your Groves with my glad Songs shall ring,
No more — These hands ~~no more~~ shall touch the trembling String:
Phaon (my Phaon ~~I almost~~ almost had said!) Is gone, and with all those pleasures fled.
~~[illegible] fled~~ — alter
non pulchra 14 — Return fair Youth, return, and bring along
Pulchre — Joy to my Soul, and Vigour to my Song:
Absent from thee, the Poet's Flame expires,
But ah! how fiercely burn the Lover's Fires?
Epiglam: Paraphr: — pulchra — Gods! can no Prayrs, ~~[illegible]~~ tender no Numbers move
Bene — One savage Heart, ~~and~~ or teach it how to love?
~~[illegible]~~

The

41

Rocks and Seas
To ~~Seas and Rocks~~ ^ I fly from Phaon's Hate,
Paraphras
Seas Rocks
Bella-- And hope from ~~Rocks~~ ^ and ~~Seas~~ ^ a milder Fate.
Ye gentle Gales beneath my Body blow,
Bellis- And softly lay me + on the Waves below!
simè And thou, kind Love, my sinking Limbs sustain,
Spread thy soft Wings and waft me + o'er the Main,
19 lines (12.) Nor let a Lover's Death the guiltless Flood profane!
On Phoebus Shrine my Harp I'll then bestow,
plac'd
Rectè And this Inscription shall be ~~read~~ ^ below:
et "Here she who sung, to him that did inspire,
Benè "Sapho to Phoebus consecrates her Lyre,
"What suits with Sapho, Phoebus suits with thee,
"The Gift, the Giver, and the God agree!
Benè But why alas! relentless Phaon! why
⟷distant Coasts must tender + Sapho
+ To ~~those steep Cliffs, that Ocean, must I~~ fly?
~~+Beauties shoud recorded be, Mr Granville & a hundred of others qu:~~
~~no God invokd shall be~~
Leucadia salubrior + ~~If You return, thy Sapho~~ ^ ~~too shall stay,~~
unda, left out.
dele ye 2^d 2 lines. ~~+13 Not all the Gods shall force me then away:~~
~~No Gods I will invoke~~ + ~~Nor Love, nor Phoebus~~ ^ ~~then invok'd shall be,~~ alter
~~possessd of thee~~
+ ~~For You alone are all the Gods to me.~~
Stet sic. & adde<nda?> Stet ~~Canst thou committ~~
Formae meritis Phebus Bene ~~Ah! canst thou doom me~~ to the Rocks and Sea,
duobus aliis versib: Ah canst thou doom me
~~wouldst~~
~~If thou return, oh more than Phebus~~ and ~~fierce unmov'd~~
~~fair~~ O far more faithless ~~and~~ more ~~hard~~ than they?
hard
~~coud~~
~~No God like thee woud ease thy Saphos~~ ~~O far more hard & far more fierce~~
Benè Ah! canst thou rather see this tender Breast
melius quã
Scroop Dash'd on sharp Rocks, than to thy Bosom prest?
~~my~~ in vain!
19 lines. (13) This Breast which once, ~~ah once! you~~ ^ lik'd so well;
Where the Loves play'd, and where the Muses dwell:
Pulcher-
rimè Alas! the Muses now no more inspire;
Untun'd my Lute and silent is my Lyre;
My languid Numbers have forgot to flow,
And Fancy sinks beneath a Weight of Woe.
Ye Lesbian Virgins, and ye Lesbian Dames,
Pulchrè Themes of my Verse, and Objects of my Flames,
No more your Groves with my glad Songs shall ring,
No more
^These hands ~~no more~~ shall touch the trembling String:
quae vobis ante placebat almost ~~almost~~ ~~him~~ ~~those Delights are~~
<i.e.> cithara mea Phaon (My Phaon I^+ ~~almost~~ ^ had ^ said!) ~~Is gone, and wth all y^se Pleasures fled~~
~~all those^ Pleasures~~
Rectè ~~gone, and all thatb pleasing with him~~
Non pulchre 14. ~~Is+fled,^with Phaon: your Delights are fled.~~ + alter
Return, fair Youth, return, and bring along
Pulchrè Joy to my Soul, and Vigour to my Song:
Absent from thee, the Poet's Flame expires,
Exclam: Paraphr:-- But ah! how fiercely burn the Lover's Fires?
Pulchra
\+ tender
Gods! can no Prayrs, ~~no Sighs~~, no ^ Numbers move
or
Benè One savage Heart, ~~and~~ ^ teach it how it love?
41 ~~or raise a dying Fire~~ The

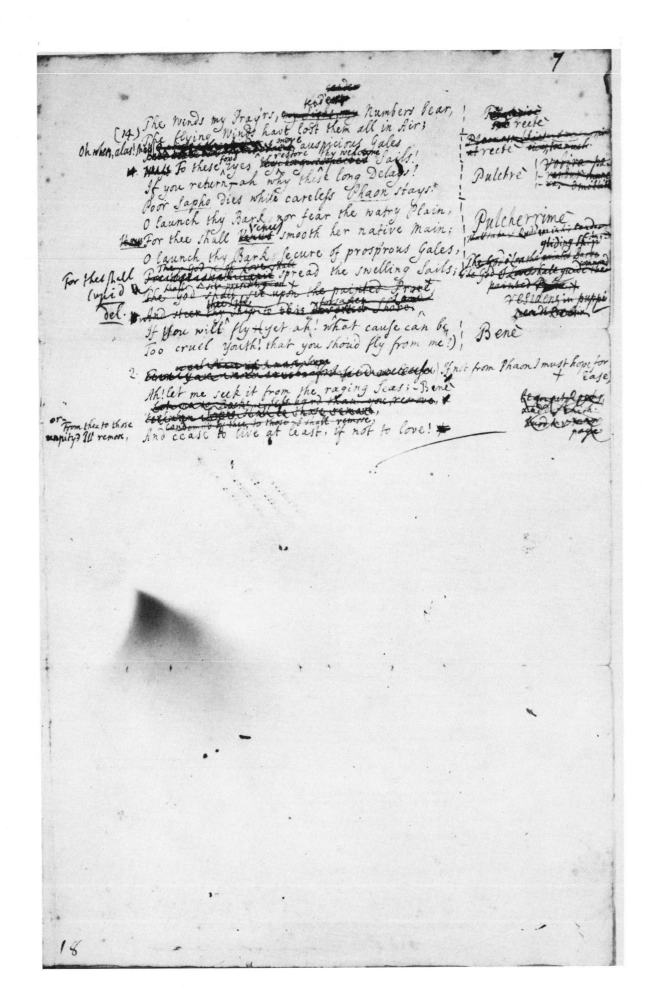

~~tender~~
tender
The Winds my Pray'rs, ~~my Sighs, my~~ Numbers bear, ⟷
(14) ⟷ rectè
The flying Winds have lost them all in Air;

~~O might those kinder~~ more
Oh when, alas! shall ~~And, shall at last more kind~~ auspicious Gales ^ — Pleonasm (~~kinder & more auspi-cious, too much~~
fond restore thy welcome
~~14.~~ ~~Waft~~ To these Eyes ~~thy long expected~~ Sails! ^ ^ ^ — at rectè

If you return -- ah why these long Delays?

Poor _Sapho_ dies while careless _Phaon_ stays. — Pulchrè — votiva pa-rantur mune-ra, omittitur

O launch thy Bark nor fear the watry Plain,

Venus
~~Venus~~ For thee shall ~~Venus~~ smooth her native Main; — Pulcherrimè
~~Shall take the rudder in his tender hand~~

O launch thy Bark secure of pros'prous Gales,

~~gliding ship~~
<2> ~~The God of Love shall~~ — ~~The God o' Love the painted Barge command~~
For thee shall _Cupid_ ~~For thee shall Cupid~~ spread the swelling Sails; ^

~~shall sit presiding on~~ +
~~The God shall sit upon the painted Prore,~~ + — ~~The God of Love shall guide the painted Prore~~ + ~~residens in puppi~~ ⟷

~~thee safe~~ ~~forsaken Land~~
del. ⟷ ~~And steer thy Ship to this deserted Shore~~. ^ ^ ^

If You will fly -- (yet ah! what cause can be

Too cruel Youth! that you shou'd fly from me?) — Benè

~~cruel Phaon if I must hope~~
2. ~~From you more cruel if I find no ease~~ — If not from Phaon I must hope for + + Ease,

Ah! let me seek it from the raging Seas; — --Benè

~~Let me to Rocks, less hard than you, remove~~ +
~~Forsaken Sapho shall to these remove~~
Or-- ~~Condemn'd by thee, to those I shall remove~~,
From thee to those unpityd I'll remove — And cease to live at least, if not to love! + — ~~begin at Rocks & add ye Epist~~. ~~<third> in ye former page~~.

Sapho to Phaon

NOTES TO THE TRANSCRIPTS

Page:Line	
1:1	Heart *overwrites* Soul.
1:4	*The words I have placed in pointed brackets are puzzling. I take the final letters in the line to be* 11 *(for* lines); *but this may be quite wrong;* the. is *may be judged an alteration of* the *to* this, *yet the period and the failure to cancel* e *is unlike Pope.*
1:11–12	*For* Lyricis *and* Barbitos, *see Ovid, 11. 6, 8.*
1:11, 13	*A cross before 1. 11 and a cross within 1. 10 are canceled.*
1:15	Involve *seems to overwrite and replace an unfinished word, perhaps beginning with the letters* com.
1:21	*The* W *of* Winds *overwrites* w.
1:28	The . . . more *overwrites* No more the Lesbian Dames.
1:32	*In the transcript,* can st *is an error for* canst.
1:34	*I now think that* Love *overwrites* Cares *and* lost *overwrites* cast *(instead of vice-versa).* Therefore Love *and* lost *should appear in the transcript line.*
1:36	the *appears to overwrite* and.
1:44	*For* improbe, *see Ovid, 1. 20.*
2:1–2	*For* si mihi difficilis, *see Ovid, 1. 31.*
2:22	*The indecipherable word may be* ye.
2:22a	sure *seems to overwrite a word, possibly* once.
2:33	A *of* All *overwrites* a.
2:43	*For* nova praeda, *see Ovid, 1. 51.*
2:47	*For* remittite, *see Ovid, 1. 53.*
2:53	yr. *seems to overwrite* the.
2:66	*For* haut *in TS, read* haud.

Page:Line	
3:3	*The apparent underscoring of* Cares *seems to indicate not emphasis but a space left blank and later filled in.*
3:28	while *overwrites something illegible.*
3a:76	B *of* Be *overwrites* be.
4:7	*The obscure mark immediately above and to right of* pale *may be a small cross, as elsewhere in this manuscript.*
4:10–11	*For* astrictum . . . frigore, *see Ovid, 1. 112. An illegible word precedes* Damp *in l. 11.*
4:26	*In the transcript,* Ofspring *is erroneously transcribed with two f's.*
4:54	Then . . . as *overwrites an erasure.*
4:56	quaere si delend *should be struck through in TS.*
4:73	*The illegible word at far right is perhaps* dele!
5:39	*Before* watch'd, *what appears to be the numeral* 11 *is erased.*
6:7, 9	*The + mark after* me *in each line is canceled.*
6:23–24	*For* Leucadia . . . salubrior, *see Ovid, 1. 187.*
6:25–26	*Between these lines in the transcript a revision of 1. 26 has been inadvertently omitted:* Gods I will invoke possest of thee *(intended to follow from* No, *altered from* Not, *in 1. 26. The revision is repeated in the left margin, 11. 26–27).*
6:29–30	*For* forma . . . Phoebus, *see Ovid, 1. 188.*
6:41	in vain *overwrites an illegible word or words.*
6:51	my . . . Songs *overwrites an erasure.*
7:2	tender *appears to be altered from* tend'rest.
7:11	*The dash overwrites a comma.*
7:12–13	*For* votiva . . . munera, *see Ovid, 11. 211–12.*
7:25	*For* residens in puppi <puppe>, *see Ovid, 1. 215.*

Epistle to Jervas

INTRODUCTION

THIS EARLY DRAFT of Pope's *To Mr. Jervas, with Fresnoy's Art of Painting, Translated by Mr. Dryden* is tucked away on the back of one leaf of the *Iliad* manuscript[1] like some happy green valley remembered by a traveler among "th' Eternall Alpine Snow" (TS, 84); of which it speaks. Very possibly it served just such a distractive and recreative function for Pope in the course of a task of translation so vast and forbidding that it gave him nightmares.[2] Certainly, at any rate, the lines look back with considerable nostalgia to what seems to have been for Pope a golden year—the twelvemonth from roughly the spring of 1713 to the late winter of 1714, when he lived in the house and haunted the studio of the fashionable London portrait painter Charles Jervas, in an atmosphere that obviously combined a good deal of joyous camaraderie with apprenticeship to the painter's art, and, possibly with more profit for Pope, to the painter's "eye."[3] By the autumn of 1715, when he jotted this version on the back of the beginnings of *Iliad IX*, he was two years and two volumes into the project, but still had four volumes and five years to go. Small wonder that his mind should suddenly be flooded with memories of an interlude in his life when "Long summer suns rolld unperceivd away"—when two kindred spirits had met at night to share the excitement of their day-time achievements—and when each dreamed aloud, in his own art's terms, of taking together that great eighteenth-century journey across the Alps to Rome, which Jervas had already once taken and Pope, because of his crazy constitution, must have known he would never take.

When Pope published this epistle in his *Works* of 1717, the joy of the comradeship, the enthusiasm for the new craft, and the dream of Italy have been reoriented, deepened, but at the same time in some degree depersonalized by their submergence in a more elegiac emotion lamenting the frailty and mutability of all things human, including the painter's and the poet's arts. The manuscript draft, though it lacks this kind of sobriety and density, conveys a tousled breathlessness that is ingratiating in its own right. The four-way proportion that seems intended by the first couplet to assume some such form as "Dryden is to Fresnoy as my effort is (failing to be) to Jervas" fades out almost at once into a simple contrast between the faintness of his own imagery and Jervas's "unexhausted Mine" and "endless Stream of fair Ideas." Yet the very exaggeration of this tribute witnesses to the excited sense of discovery—of a whole new world opening in front of one's eyes—that Mr. Ault reminds us every beginning art student feels as he learns to see and that the rest of the draft maintains. In the printed poem this glowing passage is reshaped into a considerably more generalized pronouncement on the inferiority of artistic precept to artistic vision (*TE*, ll. 39–46).

The second paragraph of the draft vanishes from the printed poem altogether. This was unquestionably a gain, for the hyperbole of placing Jervas, even in his own time, on a double pinnacle for both painting performance and painting criticism—

> of Jervas only future Times shall tell
> None practis'd better, none explain'd so well
> (TS, 27–29)

—would clearly have exceeded even a poet's license. Yet, again, there is something attractive about the ardor of the tribute, which is not quite recovered in the printed poem's more orthodox compliment to the effect that Lady Bridgewater's beauty will last on Jervas's canvas "a thousand years" (*TE*, l. 18).

Particularly interesting as evidence of the hustle-bustle of this draft is the name Leandro (TS, 22, 24), with which Pope replaces Vasari's to denominate a writer on painting who did not paint—or if he did: "The Artist lost, ye Critic yet remains" (TS, 23). After much vain pursuit of this shadowy figure (who has often reminded me of the bogus poet in *Dunciad*, Book II), I conclude, hesitantly, that he is partly a ghost, but, so far as he is real, is Leonardo da Vinci.[4] Leonardo, in the Augustan age, proves to be an exceedingly elusive figure. Everybody knows, admires, and collects Raphael: in the index to George Vertue's *Notebooks*, our best guide to what degree of information a genuinely sophisticated art connoisseur had at his disposal in Pope's time, Raphael fills a whole page.[5] By contrast, Leonardo has only the briefest entry, listing—significantly, I think—his *Trattato della Pittura* and a few paintings in the Arundel and Charles I collections.

What I suspect happened is that Pope, the novice painter, fumbling for a name in the midst of his Trojan wars, puts down one, almost the right one, that he associates honorifically with a *Trattato*, but otherwise with an artist whose paintings are little known: he "painted but in vain" (TS, 22). Discovering later (perhaps at the same time that he refreshed his memory of the other Italian painters whose names occur in the 1717 poem but not in the draft) that he has got the name wrong, and reflecting perhaps further on the egregiousness of making Jervas match Raphael in his painting and top Vasari in his art criticism (without ever having written, so far as we know, a line!), he decides to cancel this particular compliment altogether.

NOTES

1. British Library, Add. MS. 4807, f. 128 v.

2. "Though I conquered the thoughts of it in the day, they would frighten me in the night. I dreamed often of being engaged in a long journey and that I should never get to the end of it. This made so strong an impression on me that I sometimes dream of it still. . . ." (Spence, No. 197). It is not impossible that the dream journey relates in some subconscious way to the poem's journey through desolate mountain snows to longed-for Rome.

3. For a full and sensitive discussion of this apprenticeship and its possible effects, see Norman Ault, *New Light on Pope* (London: Methuen, 1949), ch. 5. Ault, however, prints a transcript of the manuscript epistle to Jervas without blottings (pp. 72–73) that quite disguises its tentative and exploratory character.

4. Since art critics and historians are known universally by their last names, Leandro/Leander ought to be a last name; but no appropriate person with such a surname can be identified in Thieme-Becker, the McGraw-Hill *Encyclopedia of World Art* (15 vols. 1959–68), the *Encyclopedia Italiana,* or Julius Schlosser, *Die Kunstliteratur: Ein Handbuch zur Quellenkunde der neueren Kunstgeschichte* (Vienna; A. Schroll, 1924). Nor is there any one with Leander for his Christian name who quite fits the bill. Thieme-Becker has a Leandro—"Bentnam des Reder, Christ"—but he seems otherwise a shadowy personage and is, in any case, not likely to have been known to Pope.

5. *The Notebooks of George Vertue* (Publications of the Walpole Society, Oxford: The Unversity Press, 1947), 29:216–17.

1

This small well-polish'd gem, the work of years
In Dryden's diction still more bright appears
Yet here how faint each Image seems to shine
Match'd with thy Soul's rich unexhausted mine
Whence endless Streams of fair Ideas flow
Strike on the Sketch, or on the Canvas glow
Where Beauty, waking all her forms, supplies
An Angel's sweetness, or a Berkley's Eyes.
Nature her [illegible] to thee [illegible] Graces [illegible]
And only gave to make those Beauties known
For this of Jervas [illegible] self shall tell
None practis'd better, none explain'd so well
[illegible]
[illegible]
2 Leandro's [illegible] Fresnoy [illegible]
The Artist lost, the Critic yet remains
Of Raphael writ as if [illegible] wrought
1 [illegible]
Of Jervas only [illegible] shall tell
None practis'd better, none explain'd so well
[illegible]
[illegible]
She only saw what others could not know;
Or if they saw it, only thou canst show.

2

Like friendly Colors [illegible] kind arts unite
Each from the other [illegible] & light
[illegible]
They [illegible]
Their Birth, their Features [illegible]
[illegible]
Of forms they differ and as Sisters are like
2 [illegible]
1 [illegible]
[illegible] wear the day
[illegible] roll unperceiv'd away
[illegible] each finding like a friend
Something to blame [illegible] to commend
1 Smit with the love of Sister Arts we came
& met congenial, mingling flame with flame
How oft [illegible] in pleasing tasks we wear the day
Long summer suns roll unperceiv'd away
[illegible]
& form the distant Journeys in our thought
Together [illegible]
Together trod th' Eternal [illegible]
We [illegible] in some vast Ruin's shade
Or [illegible] beneath some [illegible] laid
2 [illegible]
[illegible] Ideas [illegible]
[illegible] Art to Art [illegible]
1 [illegible] Rome's decays [illegible] supplies
[illegible] Imaginary Rome arise
Beneath an [illegible]
[illegible]
[illegible] Fresco [illegible]
[illegible] Urn
Here arts rich Relicks from [illegible] call
A mouldring [illegible] a faded Wall
There
well studyd [illegible] the Eye

In kindred studies labors might we [illegible] the day
& Summer suns roll unperceiv'd away

This small well-polishd Gem (ye work of years)

In Drydens diction still more bright appears

Yet here how faint each Image seems to shine

Matchd wth thy Souls rich unexhausted Mine

Whence endless Streams of fair Ideas flow

Rise on
Strike on ye Sketch, or on ye Canvass glow

her
Where Beauty, waking all Forms, ~~& thence~~ supplies

An Angels Sweetness or a Berkleys Eyes.

to thee has all her Graces shown
Nature her ~~Beauties shows to thee alone~~

thee words Graces
And ~~only~~ gives to make those ~~Beauties~~ known

~~For this of Jervas Envys self shall tell~~

~~None practised better, none explaind so well~~.

~~In some we value those have written or w^t these have~~
~~We value What they writ, not w^t they~~ wrought

~~The Writer lives, ye Painter Artist is forgot~~
~~still is <known>~~

Evn ~~might~~ painted wth unfruitful pains
~~Leandro~~ Fresnoy ~~painted but in vain~~
2
The Artist lost, ye Critic yet remains

Leandro Verse is
If Raphael writ or if ~~Vasari~~ wrought The ~~Poems~~ perishd
1
~~The Writer still or Painter is forgot~~ or ye Piece forgot.

future Times
Of Jervas only ~~Envys self~~ shall tell

None practisd better, none explaind so well

~~taught~~
~~Of all fair Natur~~ ⟶ ~~Thou alone~~

when
~~Hast seen her Secrets, or if seen hast shewn~~

ee ~~canst~~
~~If others saw y^n only thou hast show~~

⟷
~~Or thou hast known w^t others coud not know~~

~~Or if others knew twas only thou coudst show~~
~~<You only knew~~ ⟶ ~~others coud not know~~
~~Thou only knowst w^t others have not known~~
~~canst show~~
~~Or If they knew <tis> only thou hast shown~~
~~others saw <y^m> You only knew w^t others coud not know~~
~~Or w^t if others knew it you only show~~.

sawst
Thou only ~~knowst~~ w^t others coud not know;

Or if they saw
If others ~~knew~~ it, only thou coudst show.

Like friendly Colors our kind arts write

Each ing
~~&~~ from ye mixture gather sweets & light

~~Both like as~~ ~~yet not <both y^e>~~
~~<As> Sisters <next> alike be not ye same~~

They ~~Each~~ meets each other mingling flame wth flame

~~Tho not ye same <ye Sisters>~~ ~~<are>~~ alike

Their ~~<Air>~~ their features wth resemblance strike

~~As~~ ~~as~~
~~Like sisters different, & like sisters like~~
~~Thus So Twins may differ <& be> Twins alike~~
thus are
thus
~~Thus So Sisters vary, so are Sisters like~~
vary
As Twins they ~~differ~~ and as Twins are like

2 ~~They meet like Lovers, mingling flame wth flame~~

1 ~~Both like as Sisters, yet not look ye same~~

~~In equal studies have past worn y^e~~
~~Together thus we oft had past ye sumers day~~
worn ye day

Long ~~summer suns~~
2 While & ~~Suns on Suns~~ rolld unperceivd away
Suns on Suns

Then meet ~~<at night>~~, each finding like a friend

Something to blame & something to comend

Smit wth ye Love of Sister Arts we came
1
~~<elated>~~
& met congenial, mingling flame with flame

How oft ~~Lost~~ in ye pleasing Labors of ye day — While Suns on Suns

Long Summer Suns rolld unperceivd away — How oft in fancy

At night we met each — long amusement
& form the distant Journeys in our Thought — sought

Smit wth ye Love of Arts methinks
~~Together~~ we go
Together tread th' Eternall Alpine Snow
we ~~<snow>~~

Now catch y^e ~~<breeze>~~ in some vast Ruins Shade
~~<Now in some>~~
Or talk ~~Now shun ye Heats~~ beneath some Ruin laid

~~Converse~~ delighted in ye pompous Shade

Notions awake & vive — Now sleep where
2 ~~Awake Ideas~~ Images renew — Tullys worthy head was layd

From Art to Art ye pleasing Track pursue

Each Ruin w^{th} < >
~~While~~ Fancy joind wth Art Times decays supplies

1 ~~<sees>~~
&~~<here>~~ Imaginary Romes arise — each step we take
New Scenes rise round new notions wake
~~Beneath an Amphitheatres vast Shade~~
Thou oer thy Raphaels monument should ~~We~~
Now ~~<Here oer a>~~ mourn
~~Great Raphaels art in~~ fading Fresco

to dream
I ~~There Now~~ wait inspiring dreams at Maros Urn

Here Arts rich Reliques for our sorrows call

marble
A moulderd ~~Homer~~ or a faded Wall

There

well studyd busts attract ye Eye

In kindred studies labors might we wear ye day

& suns on suns roll unperceivd away

Epistle to Jervas

NOTES TO THE TRANSCRIPTS

Line

9 waking *is altered from* wakes her.
12 shows *is altered from* showd.
14 gives *is altered from* gave.
17 those *overwrites an illegible word.*
18 W *of* What *overwrites* w.
21 unfruitful *overwrites an illegible word.*
31 fair *overwrites an illegible word; the illegible word following* Natur *is possibly* teaches *or* taught.
35 *Pope's* yn (then) *was perhaps intended to be* ym (them).
42 they *overwrites an illegible word, probably* any.
48 coudst *seems to be altered from* canst.
53 *The illegible word before* Sisters *may be* As.
54 each *seems to overwrite* oth *of* other *and probably a preceding* ye.

Line

56 Air *overwrites an illegible word, possibly* Face *or* Mien *or both.*
59 differ *overwrites an illegible word, probably* vary.
65 like *seems to overwrite* as.
68 thus we oft had *overwrites illegible words, probably* In equal studies.
73 Meet *overwrites an illegible word, possibly* judgd; at night *overwrites* each Work.
86 breeze *may overwrite another word, conceivably* wind.
99 We: *Pope evidently intended* Weep *but changed his mind.*
109 *For* wear, *Pope seems first to have written* p (*for* pass?).

The Dunciad

INTRODUCTION

1

AS INDICATED IN the general introduction above, all *Dunciad* manuscripts have disappeared. There is, however, a record of the manuscripts that lie behind the 1728 and 1729 texts of the poem in the register of manuscript variants set down by Jonathan Richardson, Jr., in copies of the 1728 and 1736 editions.[1] Of the manuscripts that lie behind the *New Dunciad* of 1742 and the revised *Dunciad* in four books of 1743, nothing whatever is known. Very probably Pope destroyed them in the conflagration of which Spence writes, shortly before his death. If he did not, doubtless Bolingbroke did.[2]

A note in Pope's hand along the upper margin of the title page of the copy of the 1728 edition used by Richardson informs us that "This book is corrected by the First Broglio MS. as the / Ed. of 1736 is from the Second. / A. Pope." A similar note appears on the title of the copy of the 1736 edition that Richardson used: "N. This Book is alter'd from the Second MS; as ye / 1st Ed. 1728 is from the First MS. A. Pope."[3] Both title pages bear the signature: "Jonat. Richardson jun. / Queen's Sq."

Richardson's practice is to insert the variant manuscript readings above or below or in the margin near the printed lines concerned. When the variants are numerous and complicated, as often happens, he branches out to the tops and bottoms of his pages as well as the bottoms and tops of facing pages, and, if required, even to the titles, half titles, and fly leaves in the front matter. Usually, though not always, he calls attention to the parts of the printed text that have replaced the inserted manuscript material by underscoring them with dashes. Where he neglects to do this, meaning, together with the exigencies of the pentameter line, normally suffices to clarify the situation. The reader, I think, will have no serious difficulty in reconstructing from the following pages the content and general appearance of Richardson's insertions.

The procedures used here to represent these insertions are as follows.

1. In the heading of each page, the first figure (a Roman numeral) designates the book of the *Dunciad* that is in question. The third figure is the number of the relevant page in the edition of 1728 (or 1736). The second figure gives the inclusive line numbers of the lines on that page. This, I believe, will assist readers who do not have access to the 1728 and 1736 editions to visualize their verse texts page by page. In the 1736 edition, which contains the commentary derived from the 1729 Variorum, often no more than two lines of verse appear per page; in the 1728 edition, which lacks commentary, the lines of verse on a page average about twenty.

2. Next are given in order the verses for which Richardson has indicated manuscript variations. *Only* these verses are reproduced, numbered (in the left margin) as in the Twickenham edition, with the 1728 (or 1736) line number (if different) in parentheses. The verses not reproduced may be found by consulting a 1728 or 1736 text, or (what is generally available) the *TE Dunciad A* text, which is the text of the 1729 Variorum edition equipped with textual notes that permit the recapture of the 1728 text.

3. In the plan of representation used here, the manuscript variants noted by JR above or beside a given line are inserted in the line and placed between asterisks. These are the earlier readings. The parts of the line that in the printed text have replaced them, indicated by JR with an underscoring line of dashes, are signalized instead by underscorings. Thus, at page 1, line 1, of 1728—"Book and the Man I sing, the first who brings"—Richardson underscores with dashes the fifth through ninth words and in the right-hand margin writes beside them: "who first from Grubstreet." In the scheme used here, this appears as: "Book and the Man I sing, the first who *who first from Grubstreet* brings.[4]

4. Not infrequently, Richardson indicates that a given word or phrase in the printed text had two manuscript predecessors, one of which he places immediately above the material that has succeeded it in the printed line, the other in the margin. In I 69 of 1728 (*TE*, 79), for instance—"She, tinsel'd o'er in robes of varying hues"—he underscores "She, tinsel'd o'er" with dashes, inserting "Refulgent She" above the line and "She high enthron'd" in the margin. Since it is impossible to know for certain which of the two manuscript readings is prior, I regularly give the insertion above the line first:

I 79(69) She, tinsel'd o'er *Refulgent She* *She high enthron'd* in robes of varying hues.[5]

5. Sometimes in a larger manuscript variant of several words, one or more of those words will have been further revised, as in I 64 of the 1728 text. Here Richardson's collations indicate that the manuscript first read "And two-shap'd Tropes" where we now

have "Figures ill-pair'd," and was subsequently revised to "Figures ill-joynd." In such situations I have used double underscoring within the single underscoring to designate the word or words that in the published text replace the intermediate manuscript reading—for example, in the line cited: "*Figures ill-pair'd* *joynd* *And two-shap'd Tropes* and *Similes* unlike."

6. On the rather rare occasions when Richardson gives a manuscript variant that has a further variant contained *within* it, the interior variant is set off by double asterisks within the single asterisks that denote the encompassing larger variant.

7. Following the 1728 or 1736 verses with their manuscript variants duly inserted between asterisks comes my own description of whatever scribal marks Richardson has affixed to them, such as brackets, cue-words, underscorings (i.e., full underscorings, not his succession of dashes), cross-references to other parts of the poem, and so forth. Here, editorial intrusions appear in italic letter, Richardson's markings in roman. Page numbers in these descriptions refer to the original editions, 1728 and 1736; as do JR's line numbers. My own line numbers, in italics, are those of the Twickenham edition.

8. Last to appear in the present scheme of representation are the variants, usually one or more couplets in length, which Richardson has entered on the appropriate page as readings entirely omitted from or superseded by the printed text, and for which, as noted earlier, he sometimes uses all available free space. For the reader's convenience, the readings he has inserted at the top of a page always come first, with any scribal directions that concern them; then those at the foot of the page; and then those (often written transversely to the type block) at the sides. To facilitate reference to these verses, which of course lie outside the numbering scheme of the printed texts, I have lettered them consecutively with the letters of the alphabet.

9. As with manuscript variants in the printed lines, single asterisks are used to enclose an insertion and double asterisks to enclose an insertion within an insertion.

2

Readers will find, I think, many sources of interest in this record of the *Dunciad* manuscripts. The most dramatic, to my mind, is the skeleton plan of most of *Dunciad* IV, which was apparently already present in "the Second MS." (there proposed as a plan for "Canto 2d") before publication of the 1729 edition, but replaced, perhaps because it was politically explosive, by the opening of Book II that we are now all familiar with.[6]

Richardson's record yields other interesting discoveries, too. One is that, even in the earlier of the two manuscripts, the poem was already formed substantially as we know it, though the proposed plan for Canto 2d just mentioned points to an earlier less settled stage to which it is now our sole clue. The comparatively finished structure of the poem's events already in the earlier manuscript bears out the temporal implications of Pope's statement (doubtless referring to Swift's first visit to Twickenham in 1726) that "the first sketch of the poem was snatched from the fire by Dr. *Swift*," and of George Sherburn's shrewd guess that the poem thus saved was probably a piece of some years' standing, entered upon originally to satirize the choice of Elkanah Settle as City Poet (in December 1718)—or possibly his debut in that role in the succeeding lord mayor's pageant in 1719, when the incumbent was Sir George Thorold.[7] Abandoned but then reconsidered on Swift's initiative, the poem on this theory would have been gestating for seven or eight years by the date of the "First Broglio MS." and hence would have already passed through those provisional stages of which we will find so much clearer a record in some of the manuscripts presented later in this volume.[8]

Striking too are the names found only in Richardson's record. The first manuscript refers in the text to nineteen contemporaries and partial contemporaries whose names either do not appear or would not otherwise be certainly known to have appeared[9] by name in the 1728–29 printed texts: Anthony Alsop, John Baber(?), Joshua Barnes, Richard Bentley, Colonel Martin Bladen, Henry Bland, the Honorable Robert Bruce (?), Edward Bysshe, Henry Cromwell, "Catalogus" Fraser, Henry Kelsall, John Lawton (?), Michael Maittaire, ———N——n, Mary Pix, Sir Richard Steele, Dr. John Tanner (?), Joseph Trapp, ———Travers, Edward Wicksteed, and John Wootton. To these, the second manuscript adds Samuel Bradford, Bubb Dodington, Walter Carey, Thomas Gordon, Benjamin Hoadly, William Pattison, Thomas Purney, Thomas Tickell (?), and ——— W——m.[10]

A surprising name in the above list, at first glance, is Steele's. Introducing the heroic contest in Book II to see who can stay awake while being read to from dull authors, Dulness in the manuscript offers consolation prizes to those who lose but keep at least partly awake:

> To Him who nodding steals a transcient Nap,
> We give Tate's Ovid, & thy Virgil, Trap.
> Unable Heads that Sleep and Wake by fits,
> Win Steel, well-sifted from all Alien Wits.[11]

Here, evidently, Pope recalls an ancient grievance. The implication that Steele is among those who "Sleep and Wake by fits" very well suits the circumstances surrounding the genesis and publication of *Guardian,* No. 40. Steele's journal, *The Guardian,* in which Pope was assisting him at this time, had carried essays on pastoral in the spring of 1713, highly praising those of Ambrose Philips, omitting even to mention Pope's (Nos. 22, 23, 28, 30, 32). Irritated at what must have seemed either an intended slight or a remarkable oversight on his associate's part, Pope wrote and sent to Steele anonymously an essay ironically praising Philips's poems for their "simplicity" and condemning his own for being something else and better. Steele printed the paper as *Guardian,* No. 40, without detecting the irony—a solid confirmation, it may be permissible to think, of the inattention with which Pope credits him here.[12] By 1728 when their acquaintance had for many years lapsed and their sympathies had led them in totally different paths (Steele was a strong Hanoverian Whig, Pope essentially a Tory), Pope had no particular reason to spare Steele, yet in the end did so from motives or feelings at which today we can only guess. Possibly from 1729 on it was because Steele was dead.

3

Apart from Steele's, the names supplied by the manuscripts appear to have slid into verse for about the same reasons as those we have long been acquainted with in the printed editions. A few, always, are the names of friends. Among the persons just listed, William Kent and John Wootton belong to this category. They are evoked as close friends of Gay who testify to the extreme likeness between the real Gay and the bogus effigy poet that the booksellers try to seize:

> With laughg. Eyes yt twinkled in his head,
> Well-lookd, well-turnd, well-naturd, & well-fed.
> So wondrous like that Wootton's self mt. say,
> And Kent wd. swear, by- G——d it must be Gay.[13]

Another few names—fewer in the *Dunciad* as a whole than one tends to believe till one looks into the matter—spring from personal pique or resentment or a wish to retaliate for injuries received. In the lists above, so far as I can discover, only Bentley, Steele, and Tickell qualify as having offended Pope personally. Far the larger number of names in the lists as in the published poem itself appear there either because they were well-known public examples of this or that frailty or foible (the garrulous Fraser, the long-winded Bruce, Travers the coffeehouse politician, the quack Dr. Tanner); or because they were offensive on ideological grounds (as bad writers—Pattison, Pix, and Purney; as verbal critics—Bentley and Barnes; as flatterers—Webster and Tickell; as silly patrons—Bubb Dodington: as pick-thanks of the Walpole establishment—Gordon, Hoadly, Trapp); or because they had been offensive not to Pope himself but to his friends or to persons he admired.

In the manuscript, for example, one of the poet's signs of the approaching collapse of civilization at the end of *Dunciad* III is that England has made "Her boasted Newton, C____ys Deputy."[14] The statement is not literally true. Carey was Warden of the Mint during 1725–27, when Newton was Master. But Carey seems to have been a cocky aggressive sort—"a sad dog," said the Prince of Wales; "among the most obnoxious men of inferior degree," wrote the second earl of Egmont—a bureaucrat who subsequently, as secretary of the lord lieutenant of Ireland, made himself unpopular by talking of "*his* administration" and generally putting on "airs."[15] If one supposes that Carey conducted himself under Newton at the Mint as he conducted himself later, it is easy to catch the figurative truth of Pope's description and its status in his mind as one more testimony to the current disarray of values. The reference probably dates to 1726–27, when the poem was being actively worked on and Carey was still employed in the Mint. Once he had moved on to become one of the lords of trade (by 1728), his example ceased to be useful, and the verse naming him was cut.

A similar quite impersonal distaste seems to lie behind the naming of Samuel Bradford among those who "preach in vain" (*TE,* 3:200). There was a "Br——" in the text of the 1728 published edition and a "B**" in the text of 1729; but since the abbreviation was mistaken in Curll's *Key* for a reference to James Bramston,[16] it is only through the further clue given in the Richardson collations ("Br——d"),[17] that one can certainly identify him. Bradford's offense in Pope's mind was apparently a lack of taste—combined, perhaps, with some disparagement, real or imagined, of Atterbury and Bolingbroke, both of whom the poet greatly admired. A staunch Whig, appointed one of the royal chaplains by William III, Bradford became Bishop of Carlisle in 1719 and in 1723, on Atterbury's trial and exile, his immediate successor in the see of Rochester and deanery of Westminster. Such obvious ingratiation with the government of Walpole and George I might have sufficed to make him suspect in Pope's eyes, but there was a further ground of annoyance, set forth in the poet's note to "naked mourns the Dormitory wall" (again, in Pope's view, one of the ubiquitous signs of cultural neglect, like the decay of Inigo Jones's Banqueting House at Whitehall, the ruinous condition of Savoy House, the appointment of men like Colley Cibber and Ambrose Philips to positions of influence) toward the close of *Dunciad* III:

> The Dormitory in Westminster was a building intended for the lodging of the King's Scholars; toward which a sum was left by Dr. *Edw. Hannes,* the rest was raised by contributions procured from several eminent persons by the interest of Francis [Atterbury] late Bishop of Rochester, and Dean of *Westminster.* He requested the Earl of *Burlington* to be the *Architect,* who carried on the work till the Bill against that learned Prelate was brought in, which ended in his banishment. The shell being finished according to his Lordship's design, the succeeding Dean and Chapter employ'd a common builder to do the inside, which is perform'd *accordingly.*[18]

Perhaps then, it was a simple prejudice on Pope's part in favor of the architectural work of his friends Atterbury and Burlington that qualified Bradford for the *Dunciad,* though clearly the inferior quality of the Dormitory interior had to be recognizable by many if the satire were to take effect. Bradford's categorization among uninspiring preachers, on the other hand, he won for cause. Those who turn to his eight Boyle Lecture Sermons on "The Credibility of the Christian Revelation, from its Intrinsick Evidence," or indeed any of nearly two dozen others, will see little reason to quarrel with Pope's view that Dulness had early sealed him for her own.

Names, of course, can be dangerous, particularly the names of those approved by a governmental establishment. One notices with interest, therefore, that Pope never went further than "Br——" and "B**" in his editions, or further than "Br——d" in his manuscript. Though there is no hard evidence one way or other, it is tempting to believe that the several gaps in the manuscripts—which include much of Book I and the famous diving game in Book II, among others—are owing to the presence of names that Pope did not want even young Richardson to see. We shall encounter this question again in the manuscript of the *Epistle to Burlington.*

A further interesting aspect of the manuscripts—to which there is space here only to call attention—is the exuberance and freedom of the writing when Pope is not yet revising for his ultimate audiences. At the Latinate end of the scale, fascinating words crop out that are never allowed to see print: "ennucleate" (1728, t.p. verso, line g), "incrassate" (1736, p. 179; III 17), "disploding" (half title recto, line f), and several more.[19] Likewise at the Anglo-Saxon end are encountered such happy inspirations as "Here slidder'd Curl"[20] (instead of "There fortun'd Curll to slide")—sacrificed, we may suppose, as an archaism or dialectical form that would not be widely understood and would almost certainly be ridiculed.

A particularly instructive instance of this sort of purification is the word *Toupie* (for *toupée*) in the lines describing the rallying of Dulness's minions near the beginning of Book II:

> A motley mixture! in long wigs, in bags,
> In silks, in crapes, in garters, and in rags.[21]

In the second manuscript, which forms the basis of the 1729 text and therefore dates at least as early as 1728, the first line of this couplet evidently read (unmetrically): "A motley mixture—in Toupies, Bobs, and bags." Here, it appears, the difficulty was not that the word was too old but that it was too new. The first English use of "toupie" recorded by the *OED* occurs in Fielding's *Grubstreet Opera* in 1731. Obviously still a neologism in 1728, it was excluded from Pope's line when printed, at the expense of a rather pleasing tonsorial heterogeneity that had placed alongside the bag wig and the bob wig the toupie, a type of wig "in which the front hair was combed up over a pad, into . . . a top knot" *(OED).* Fifteen years later it would seem that the word had acclimated itself, for Pope prints it apparently without a qualm in *Dunciad* IV, line 88:

> What e'er of dunce in College or in Town
> Sneers at another, in toupee or gown.

True to his own maxim in the *Essay on Criticism,* Pope usually succeeds, in his published texts, in not being the first by whom the new is tried nor yet the last to lay the old aside.

NOTES

1. I wish to thank the trustees of the New York Public Library for permission to print the Richardson collations, and, most particularly, Lola Szladits, curator of its Berg Collection, for her kind assistance. On the role played by Richardson in the preservation of Pope's manuscripts, see *Collected in Himself: Essays Critical, Biographical, and Bibliographical on Pope and Some of His Contemporaries* (Newark, Del.: University of Delaware Press, 1982), p. 325, companion to this volume.

2. Spence, Nos. 139–40. Pope's will left to Bolingbroke executive power over all his unpublished papers. See *Collected in Himself,* p. 325.

3. Among the 1728 issues, JR uses a copy of Griffith, No. 199. His 1736 edition is Griffith, No. 405.

4. Below, p. 101.

5. Below, p. 102.

6. Below, pp. 127–28. See also *Collected in Himself,* pp.339–43.

7. See *TE,* 5:xiv and 201 n.

8. See especially the epistles to Burlington and Fortescue, and the Morgan Library manuscript of the *Essay on Man.*

9. See below on Bradford, Trapp, Travers, Tickell, pp. 152, 117.

10. Identifications of several of the lesser-known names in these lists may be had by consulting the index and biographical appendix of *TE,* 5, which draws on information that Elwin and Courthope supplied in their edition about the names in the JR collations. Names not found in *TE,* 5, are briefly identified below at the point of next appearance. N——n *may be Mrs. Nelson ("Sappho") of Binfield, but see below, 113n.*

11. Below, p. 116.

12. It is now generally believed that Tickell was the author of these essays, but the traditional attribution (and obviously Pope's) is to Steele. *Guardian,* No. 40, is collected in the volume of Pope's *Prose Works,* edited by Norman Ault (Oxford: Basil Blackwell, 1936).

13. The manuscript lines are Pope's picture of the real Gay; the equivalent lines in the published text describe the effigy.

14. Below, p. 155.

15. See Romney Sedgwick, *The House of Commons,* 1715–1754 (London: HMSO, 1970), 1 (*sub* Carey, Walter [1685–1757]).

16. *TE,* 3:200 n.

17. Below, p. 152.

18. *TE,* 5:189 n.

19. Below, pp. 111, 147, 112.

20. Below, p. 139.

21. Below, p. 137.

Dunciad 1728

Title page recto

At top of the page: N. This Book corrected from the First Broglio MS. as the / Ed. 1736 is from the Second. / A. Pope. *To the right of this:* Jonat. Richardson jun. / Queen's Sq.

I, 1-8. P. 1.

I 1 Book and the man I sing, the first who *who first from Grubstreet* brings

I 2 The *Smithfield* muses to the ears *Courts* of kings.

I 5 Say from what cause, in vain *tho so* decry'd and curst,

At top, to right of scroll border: The Title was torn / off on purpose. *Beside the title THE DUNCIAD:* An Heroic Poem. *Ll. 3-4 are bracketed with comment:* inf. <=*infra: referring to lower part of the page*>.

In blank space below text:

(a) v. 3 I sing; say Great ones (You these works inspire)

(b) Since thus *If so* Joves will, & *or* Brittains Fate require)

(c) X Say what the Cause that still this Taste remains,

(d) And when a Settle falls a Tibbalds reigns?

At foot of the page:

(e) X Why, from what cause, th' Im̃ortal Race remains,

In ll. 3-4, Pope (or Richardson?) shows some uncertainty about completing the parenthesis.

I, 9-28. P. 2.

I 15 Still her old *lost* empire to confirm *restore* she tries,

I 28(18) A yawning ruin hangs and nods *seems to nod* in air;

I 29(19) Keen, hollow *Eternal* winds howl thro' the bleak recess,

I 35(25) Here stood her Opium, here she nurs'd *kept* her Owls,

Ll. 29-30 (19-20) *are bracketed with comment:* insertd. *In l. 32*(22) cave of Poverty *is underscored. In l. 38*(28), *the blanks are filled in.*

At foot of the page:

*(a)*v. 17<*TE, 27*> There yawns a Ruin pervious to ye Air,

(b) Some say in *Kentstreet,* others in *Rag-Fair.*

I 39(29) Hence hymning *weeping* Tyburn's elegiac lay,

I 40(30) Hence the soft sing-song *Nothings* on Cecilia's day,

Ll. 43-56(33-46) are bracketed, with comment: ins[d]. <=inserted>. Line 57(47) is marked inf.<=infra>.

At foot of the page:

(a) v. 47<TE,57> Here she beholds how Hints in Embrio lye

I 63(53) There *Now* motley Images her fancy strike,

I 64(54) Figures ill-pair'd, *joynd* *And two-shap'd Tropes* and Similes unlike.

I 65(55) She sees a mob of *Now sees contending* Metaphors advance,

I 66(56) Pleas'd with the madness of the mazy *th' unmeasur'd* dance;

I 67(57) How *Now* Tragedy and Comedy embrace;

I 68(58) How *Now* Farce and Epic get a jumbled race;

I 71(61) Here gay Description AEgypt glads *Her<e?> unconfind Descr. paints* with showers,

I 74(64) Fast by, fair *There smiling* vallies of eternal green,

I 75(65) On cold December fragrant *flow'ry* chaplets blow,

Ll. 63-64(53-54) are bracketed with a 2 and ll. 65-66(55-56) with a 1, indicating Pope's intention to reverse their order. To left of the figure 2, a canceled indecipherable word, possibly mob; below 2 and the canceled word, a word or phrase not readily legible, possibly & sim. It may therefore be that Pope's original version of l. 64(54) was And two-shap'd Tropes & similes unlike; for in this case JR does not indicate what part of the printed line the phrase And two-shap'd Tropes is to replace. Ll. 63-64(53-54) have a marginal caret just above them; ll. 69-72(59-62) are bracketed, with comment: inf. <=infra>

At foot of the page:

(a) aft. v. 52 <TE,62> Here Atom Swarms of thin conceits unwraught,

(b) There Hints like Spawn flow quick'ning *slow quickned* into Thought.

(c) aft. v. 58 <TE,68> On Sum̃er's Neck his Arms here Autumn flings,

(d) And Naked Winters marry blooming Springs.

I 79(69) She, tinsel'd o'er *Refulgent She* *She high enthron'd* in robes of varying hues,

To right of l. 82(72): Twas <cf. l. 83(73)> -- But here a leaf torn out -- to v. 225 <TE, 235>. Below l. 82(72): Here ye whole process -- v. 217 <TE, 227>. The words below l. 82(72) are bracketed and marked with a delta for deletion.

I, 87-202. Pp. 6-11.

On these pages there are no insertions, but the missing letters in ll. 102-3(92-93) *on p. 6 and l. 116*(106) *on p. 7 are filled in.*

I, 203-20. P. 12.

I 227(217) Here to her Chosen all her works *the whole Process of her Art* she shows;
I 228(218) Prose swell'd *swells* to verse, Verse loitring *loitres* into prose:

At left of 227(217)*:* See aft v. 72 *<TE, 82>*. *Vertically, beside ll. 227-30*(217-20)*, five dots.*

At foot of the page:

(a) How Unideal Thoughts now Meaning find,
(b) Now leave -- to Ozell *<TE, 240>*.

I, 221-40. P. 13.

I 236(226) Less human genius *Science* than God gives an ape,
I 237(227) Small thanks *With thanks* to *France*, and none to *& thanks to* *Rome* or *Greece*,
I 240(230) Can make a *C--r, Jo--n,* *Bladen* or *O--ll.*
I 244(234) Something betwixt *between* a H-- and Owl)
I 245(235) Perch'd on his crown. All hail! and hail again *behold, she crys, ye Day*
I 246(236) My son! the promis'd land expects thy reign. *The prom^{sd} Nat^{n} now exp^{cts} thy Sway*
I 247(237) Know *Since* *Settle*, cloy'd with custard and with praise,
I 248(238) Is gather'd to *Now sleeps among* the Dull of antient days,
I 249(239) Safe, where no *Where neither* criticks damn, no duns molest,
I 250(240) Where G--n, B--, and high-born H--d rest!

At l. 237(227) *JR's indications of revisions remain equivocal. He underscores* Small . . . none to *as words not found in the MS. line, but his insertion in the right margin is* With France & / thanks to. *My rendering above is therefore conjectural. A* no *at far right of l. 237*(227) *perhaps indicates that* no thanks to *was a possible MS. alternative to* and none to, *or that* no *was an alternative to* Small. *In l. 240*(230), C--r *and* O--ll *are filled out, and* Bladen *is written above* Jo--n; *below* C--r, Jo--n *is inserted* Shadwell, Welstead. Bladen *is Martin Bladen, minor playwright and translator of Caesar's "Commentaries." The MS. variants of l. 250*(240) *are also imprecisely indicated. The margin contains:* Touchin *<John Tutchin>*, Banks. *Below* G--n . . . high-born *are inserted* Dunton Baber Gildon, *with slash marks between, apparently as alternative contestants for the* G--n *slot. The missing letters in* Howard *have been filled in.* Baber, *as the TE editor notes (p. 93), is presumably J. Baber.*

At foot of the page:

(a) X v. 231 *<TE,241>* And now, my Son, the Goddess Mother cry's,
(b) Maternal Dullness breathing on his Eyes,
(c) Be thou my Son. Behold the destind Day,

(d) The promisd Nation now expects thy Sway.

(e) *Below the above passage:* ^{X}Now Night involves the Scene. The Goddess crys,

I, 241-50. P. 14.

I 251(241) I see a King! who leads *Take thou ye sceptre, rule* my chosen sons

I 252(242) To lands *realms* that flow with clenches and with puns:

I 253(243) Till each fam'd theatre *Rule till both theatres* my empire own,

I 254(244) Till *Albion*, as *Hibernia*, bless my *And near our Monarchs Dullness fix her* throne.

I 255(245) I see! I see! -- Then rapt, she spoke *said* no more.

I 259(249) Hoarse thunder to its bottom shook *shook ye bottom of* the bog,

The insertion in l. 251(241) *seems to call for an alteration of* To *to* In *in 252*(242) *that JR neglected to make. Above the insertion, he records an alternative to its first four words:* G-- save King T--. *Ll. 253-56*(243-46) *are bracketed, with a caret above that perhaps indicates they are added. The period in l. 255*(245) *is revised to a dash.*

At foot of the page:

(a) aft v. 242 <*TE*,*252*> God save King T --- Grubstreet own our choice,

(b) And Hawker Heralds roar with rusty Voice.

II, 1-8. P. 15.

II 15(1) The sons of *Dulness* meet: *She summons all her Sons;* an endless band

II 16(2) Pours forth, and leaves unpeopled *dispeopled* half the land,

II 17(3) A motley mixture! in *of* long wigs, in *&* bags,

A marginal 2 *beside ll. 17-20*(3-6) *and a* 1 *beside 21-22*(7-8) *indicate Pope's intention to reverse their order.*

II, 9-28. P. 16.

II 13(9) Now herald hawker's rusty voice *To these ye Queen by Trumpets sound* *The Goddess now by Hawkers Voice* proclaims

II 23(11) In that wide space the Goddess *Amid that Area wide she* took her stand

II 26(14) A Church collects *invites* the saints of *Drury-lane*.

II 27(15) With authors, stationers *Booksellers* obey'd the call;

II 33(21) No meagre, muse-rid mope, adust and *Not such as Garrets lodge of Visage* thin,

II 34(22) In a dun night-gown of his own loose *Who like a N^{t}. G^{n}. round him wraps his* skin;

II 36(24) Twelve starving *starv'ling* bards of these degen'rate days.

II 37(25) All as a partridge plump, full-fed *Plump as a P^{ge} ruddy, round,* and fair,

II 39(27) With pert flat eyes she window'd well its *Laugh^{g}. Eyes y^{t} twinkled in his* head,

II 40(28) A brain of feathers, and a heart of lead *Well-lookd, well-turnd, well naturd, & well fed;*

In the MS. variants of l. 13(9), *a further marginal alternative to* by Hawkers Voice *is* to grace the day. *A notation to*

right of l. 14(10)--With Authors v. 15 *<TE, 27>--and a bracket and caret beside ll. 23-26*(11-14) *seem to indicate that these lines are added. In the space between ll. 26 and 27*(14 *and* 15)*:*

(a) With Authors, Stationers--the feild of G-- all;

(b) Ev'n Booksellers obey y^{e} Hawker's call.

Following l. 28(16)*:* Who sit inf *<=infra>. Ll. 29-32*(17-20) *are bracketed.*
Inserted after l. 40(28)*:*

(c) So wondrous like that Wootton's self m^{t}. say,

(d) And Kent w^{d}. swear, *by G-- it must be Gay*

(e) All gaze v. 35 *<TE, 47>*

Wootton *is John Wootton, animal and landscape painter;* Kent *is William Kent, painter, designer, architect, landscape gardener; both were friends of Pope.*
At foot of the page, the lines called for by the cue following l. 28(16)*:*

(f) Who sit at Counters or at Rails who stand,

(g) From Pauls, Moorfeilds, Pye corner, or ye Strand;

(h) And last in infamous *impudent* Disorder came,

(i) Pyrates, & Publishers, unknown to Fame.

(j) In Fleetstreet fair the Goddess chose ye place,

(k) And *There* mark'd the Barriers, & Prescrib'd the Race.

(l) And first (for Dullness, gentle Queen! delights

(m) In Jokes, & feeds her Subjects with strange *Friends with wondrous* Sights)

(n) To Nimble Stationers proposd the Prize,

(o) And sets a Phantome Poet *raisd a Poets Phantome* in their Eyes.

The first four of the above lines are marked with a bracket and a delta for deletion.

Beside ll. 27-38(17-26) *at right angles to the text:* To these in Sport she first proposd ye Prize / And raisd a Poets Ph--- / Not such as -- v. 21. *<Above, TE, 2:33*(21)*>. In the margin beside l. 36*(24)*:* Qualia hũc / hom.*<inem>* produ- / cit corp.*<ora>* tellus, *which Pope quotes from Aeneid 12 in his 1729 note on l. 35. In the margin beside l. 38*(26)*:* Tum dea nu- / be cava -- Aen. 10, *which he quotes in his 1729 note on l. 31. At foot of the page, cued to the inserted MS. line* Pyrates . . . fame: Multi praeterea quos fama obscura, *which Pope quotes from Aeneid 5. 302.*

II, 29-48. P. 17.

II 47(35) All gaze with ardour: some, a Poet's name, *the Author's fame,*

II 48(36) Others, a sword-knot and lac'd *his Lace & Birthday* suit inflame:

II 49(37) But lofty *L--t* *awfull Tryphon* in the circle rose;

II 52(40) He spoke, and who with *L--t* *Tonson* *Tryphon* shall contend?

II 54(42) Stood dauntless *C--l*. "Behold that *your* rival here!

II 57(45) Swift as a bard the *his* bailiff leaves behind,

II 58(46) He left huge *L--t*, *fat Tonson | Tryphon* and out-stript the wind.

Ll. 41-46(29-34) *are bracketed, possibly to signal them as lines not in the MS. or as replacing some part of the MS. passage quoted at foot of p. 16. Here, in l. 58*(46) *and elsewhere, a vertical slash mark between words indicates that they are alternatives of which the better is still to be decided.*

II, 49-66. P. 18.

II 61(49) So lab'ring on, with shoulders, hands, *arms* and head,

II 63(51) With steps unequal *L--t* *Tonson* urg'd the race, *Tryphon w. Arms expanded **With arms expanded Tryphon** rows his State*

II 64(52) And seem'd to emulate great *Jacob's* *his Uncle's* pace. *And left-legd Jacob seems to emulate.*

II 66(54) Which *C--l's* *Corinna* chanc'd *.... Harlot happ'd* that morn to make.

II 69(57) Here fortun'd *C--l* to slide: loud shout the *Here slidderd Curl: loud shout the Laugh^{g}.* band,

II 70(58) And *L--t, L--t, **Jacob, Jacob** rings thro' all *Tryphon moves **flies** ye Glory of* the *Strand.*

II 77(65) And him and his, if more devotion warms *In him and his if greater **And if in Him and His more** Grace abound*

II 78(66) Down with the *Bible*, up with the *Pope's Arms*. *Then let mine Host of Sksp^{rs} H^{d} be crownd*

At right of ll. 63-64(51-52)*, the cue:* So first. *A note to l. 64*(52) *quotes Virgil's description of Ascanius following his father:* Sequiturq<*ue*> patrem non passibus equis <*Aeneid*, 2.74>. *A note to the earlier reading of l. 66*(54) *identifies the harlot as:* One M^{rs}. Thomas who calld her self &c. *This is the same person as Curll's Corinna, but the different rhythm established in the MS. reading (*Harlot happ'd *for* Corinna chanc'd*) suggests that* C--l *may stand, alternatively, for Cromwell, the name of Pope's early friend whose mistress Mrs. Thomas is said to have been. For reasons unclear, JR has underscored* my bards *and* I *in l. 75*(63). *A note to the MS. version of l. 78*(66) *reads:* Host of Shakespears head -- Tonsons sign.

In the margin at foot of the text, marked with a delta for deletion:

(a) (b) If He and His more Pious trim ye Scale, / Then let mine Host of S^{s}. h^{d}. prevail.

Also below the text, but separated from the above:

(c) v. 65 In Him and His unless more Grace appear,

(d) This Days bright Garland *wreath of conquest* let not Tryphon wear.

Below this couplet, related by a marginal line and check mark to the MS. insertion at foot of p. 19, and clearly intended as a transition to ll. 79(67) *ff:*

(e) Brown Cloacina heard her Servant call,

(f) From her black Grottos near ye Temple Wall.

(g) A place --

II, 67-86. P. 19.

II 79(67) A place there is, betwixt *between* earth, air, and seas,

II 81(69) There in his seat *Throne* two spacious Vents appear,

II 82(70) On this he sits, to that *this* he leans his ear,

II 85(73) All vain petitions, sent by winds on high, *Petitions vain yt daily vex ye Sky,*

II 87(75) Amus'd he reads, and then returns the *Jove reads them oer & wth these usefull* bills

II 88(76) Sign'd with that *Wipes that rich* *Ichor* which from Gods distills.

II 89(77) In office here fair *black* *Cloacina* stands,

II 92(80) And plac'd it next him *foremost* a distinction rare!

II 94(82) The *This* Goddess favour'd him, and favours yet.

At right of l. 80(68)*:* Lull'd -- inf.

At foot of the page, bracketed, and marked with a check mark:

(a) v. 67<*TE,79*> A Place there is between Earth, Air, & Seas,
(b) Calld by the Gods the Thund'rer's House of Ease.
(c) Where in her Throne two spacious vents appear,
(d) On One she sits, to One applys her Ear:
(e) There lists delighted to ye Jest unclean
(f) Of Link-boys vile, & Watermen obscene.
(g) Then with Mist's Journals, & with Tanner's Bills
(h) Wipes that rich Ichor which a God *Goddesses* distills.
(i) Oft as she fish'd these nether -- v. 81

Below these lines at foot of the page: Cloacina Gay's Trivia 157 quote. Tanner's Bills *are probably advertisements for the quack remedy called "The Anodyne Necklace," said to have been invented by Dr. John Tanner. A tract about the necklace may be seen in Plate 5 of Hogarth's "A Harlot's Progress." It was still advertised in the early nineteenth century.*

II, 87-106. P. 20.

In l. 108(96) *the missing letters are filled in.*

At foot of the page:

(a) aft. v. 88<*TE,100*> How
(b) How
(c) See 2^{d}. MS. As
(d) And
(e) Th impassive Form from his Embraces flies *His empty arms th impassive air confess*
(f) The Phantome Spectre vanishd, Shouts ascend *And melts to air; Loud Laughter Shakes* ye Skies
(g) All of ye Idol vanish'd but the Dress.
(h) Th' unhappy Stationer, his Author gone,
(i) Now grasps an empty *Joseph* for a *John*. v. 108
(j) But She good
(k) Pleas'd
(l) A Riding coat
(m) So call'd

II, 107-24. P. 21.

At foot of the page:

(a) Pleasd at her Wit, & of Applauses vain,

(b) Dullness, good Queen, repeats the Jest again.

(c) Another Poet, & another rise,

(d) Curl, not Discourag'd, at each Quarry flies.

(e) Forthwith she drest, like Addison & Prior,

(f) Two Wicked Imps of her own Grubstreet Quire.

(g) A *Two* wicked Spright *Imps* she drest in Pope's attire *like Pope & Prior*

(h) The same the *their* voice the *their* mein, and the *their* Attire.

The first couplet is bracketed; the second and fourth are bracketed and marked with deltas for deletion; then the whole passage is bracketed and marked with a delta.

A note below the passage reads: [N. a Leaf torn out -- to v. 172 <*TE, 183*>.]

II, 125-64. Pp. 22-23.

In l. 141(128) *on p. 22, and in l. 159*(148) *on p. 23, the missing letters are filled in. No collations from the MSS. are made on these pages. On p. 22, the printer gives the number 130 to line 131, a misnumeration by one line that continues through Book II. To avoid unnecessary complications for those who wish to follow these notes with the text of 1728 before them, I have let this error stand in my own marginal numbering through the remainder of this book.*

II, 164-81. P. 24.

II 183(172) But now for Authors nobler palms *Tasks* remain:

II 184(173) Room for my Lord! three Jockeys *six Huntsmen* in his train;

II 186(175) He grins, and looks *Who silent looks* broad nonsense with a stare.

II 187(176) His honour'd *Lordship's | secret* meaning, Dulness thus exprest.

II 189(178) He chinks *chinkd* his purse, and takes *took* his seat of state,

II 190(179) With ready quills the Dedicators *Listning Authors* wait,

II 191(180) Now at his head the dex'trous task *Tindal & Gordon at his head* commence,

Ll. 185 and 192(174 and 181) *are marked:* inf.

At foot of the page:

(a) v.174<*TE, 185*> In ye blew String a Jocky Leads ye Bear,

(b) v.181<*TE, 192*> The quickning Numskull fancies *feels ye* fancied Sense. *Possibly JR's error?*

II, 182-201. P. 25.

II 196(185) Then his *the* nice taste directs our *all* *He turns Subscriber to all* *Operas*:

II 197(186) ** *B--y* his mouth with *Classic* flatt'ry opes,

II 198(187) And the puft *Orator* bursts *breaks* out in tropes.

II 199(188) But *O--* *While Oldmixon* the *Poet*'s healing balm

II 201(190) Unlucky *Unhappy* *O--*! thy lordly *Lord &* master

II 209(198) As *So* taught by *Venus*, *So, great Achilles!* *Paris* learnt the art

II 210(199) To touch *Achilles'* only tender *thy only penetrable* part,

II 211(200) Secure, thro her, *Secure from all* *By Venus taught* the noble prize to carry,

Ll. 194-95(183-84) *are bracketed with a* 3, *ll. 196-97*(185-86) *with a* 2, *and ll. 198-99*(187-88) *with a* 1, *indicating Pope's intention to rearrange them.* B--y *in l. 197*(186) *is of course Richard Bentley.*

At foot of the page:

(a) aft. v. 183<*TE,194*> Now to his Heart y[e] Titillation comes,

(b) He pants with Courage, & *His beating bosom pants* with Love of Drums:

(c) *Bentley* His mouth now *w.[th]* Bentley's kind Instruction *Classic Flatt'ry* opes,

(d) He grows *bawls | roars* an Orator, & out fly Tropes.

*In line (c) above, the alternative indicated by the insertion of *Bentley* seems to be:* Bentley his mouth with Classic Flatt'ry opes. *An insertion above* Bentley's *looks like* Bl-- with, *possibly suggesting an alternative reading in which the name has one syllable: e.g.,* His Mouth now Bl-- with kind instruction opes. *If so, the intended name may be that of Henry Bland, whose writings in support of the regime had just brought him (in 1728) the deanship of Durham.*

(e) v. 188<*TE, 199*> *Concanen,* from his Soft, & Giving *Palm,*

(f) Strives to extract y[e] Poets healing Balm.

(g) Unhappy *Concanen*! --- faster.

(h) A Nicer part sly W--r chose to probe,

(i) Latent beneath y[e] Cinctures *Tassels* of his Robe.

(j)(k) Where y[e] broad azure Cincture joynd to hold The Starry Gem distinct wth varied Gold.

(l) This well observd, unheeded by the rest,

(m) He brought his Sister, & she tickled best.

(n) So great Achilles

Cued to Latent . . . Robe *is a quotation:* Ilia subter / caecū vuln[s] <=*vulnus*> habes /<*sed*> lato qd <=*quod*> balte:/us auro Prae-/tegit. Pers. Sat. iv <*43-45*>. *Pope quotes from memory, omitting* sed, *adding* q[d]. W--r *in line (h) is Edward Webster, on whom see TE, V 458.*

II, 202-20. P. 26.

II 213(201) Now turn to diff'rent *other* sports (the Goddess cries)

II 218(206) With *By* *Thunder* rumbling *Thunders rattling* from the mustard-bowl.

II 219(207) With *horns* and *trumpets* now to madness *fury* swell,

II 221(209) Such *These* happy arts attention can command,

II 222(210) When *Tho* fancy flags, and sense is at a stand:

II 225(213) And *But* his this *Drum*, whose hoarse heroic base

II 228(216) The Monkey-mimicks rush discordant *The monkey-mimicks critics all rush* in;

II 230(218) And *R--*, and railing, Brangling, and *Welsted at Wicksted, Budgel at* *B--*,

II 231(219) *D--s* and *And loud tongu'd* Dissonance; And captious art, *& each sustains his part*

II 232(220) And *With* snip-snap short, and interruption smart.

In l. 224(212), *JR underscores* chatt'ring *--why is unclear. I am unable to identify Wicksted in line 230*(218). *In line 231*(219), *it remains unclear what words have replaced* & each sustains its part *--JR's dashes underscore only D--s* and.

At top of the page:

_(a)_ aft. v. 202<_TE,214_> The Head who wins not may ye Ear confound,

_(b)_ And force attention, not by Sense, but Sound.

Under this, also at top of the page:

_(c)_ The Last, not wholly to Lament his fate,

_(d)_ A Groat to Drink, or --'s Works compleat.

Written in left margin at right angles to the entire printed text:

_(e)_ These happy Arts Attention shall command,

_(f)_ When Fancy flags, & Sense is at a stand.

_(g)_ Now try we first *Then try we next* who Catlike growl & *best can* whine,

_(h)_ The next who *Or who in* chatt'ring match the Monkey Line:

_(i)_ Who emulates an _Owl_ shall then surpass,

_(j)_ But He the Cheif whose Braying shames an _Ass_.

_(k)_ Two Slip-shod Muses . . . p. 27 a<_t_> top

In line (g) of the above passage, Then try we next _was inserted, then canceled, then reinserted as indicated._

At foot of the page:

_(l)_ For Noise & Nonsense next behold ye Prize!

_(m)_ Whose Voice Stentorian loudest shakes ye Skies.

_(n)_ Who fails to ravish, or com̃and ye Heart,

_(o)_ With Skspears Nature, or with Johnson's Art,

_(p)_ Shall wake ye Sense, & terrifie ye Soul,

_(q)_ With rolling Thunders from ye Mustard-Bowl,

_(r)_ Move dullest minds, *The dullest move* from Passion quite at ease,

_(s)_ With Show'rs of Paper, or by Hail of Pease.

_(t)_ With Horns, & Trumpets teach the <_blank_> to *now to Vengeance* swell

_(u)_ Or *Now* sink to *in* sorrows with a Tolling Bell.

_(v)_ From Pathos, and from Ethos quite at ease,

_(w)_ Alarm an Audience with a Storm of Pease.

These marg.

Lines (r)-(s) above are bracketed and marked with a delta, probably because lines (v)-(w) make a similar point.

Title page verso

At l. 227 JR notes: See Reverse of ye Title Page. _The title page verso to which this direction points, along with the end of p. viii and the recto of the half title immediately following p. viii (all front matter) is crammed with MS. versions of passages corresponding roughly to Book II 213-56 but including a passage that in the printed editions makes part of Book III._

On the verso of the title page:

In Margin ye Corrections, ye other as first writ. _Since I follow JR's example here to preserve for readers the appearance of his page, underscored words now indicate earlier readings--_"as first writ." _With_ "P. 27" _(see the headings), the former scheme_ *returns.*

Vociferation

(a) (215)*<TE, 227>* Now thousand Tongues are heard in one loud Din,

(b) Welsted & Wicksted at each other grin; *Sudden ye Monkey critics all rush in*

(c) Twas mouthing, chatt'ring, answring, Snip-snap *chattr^{g}. grin^{g}. mouth^{g}. jabbring* all,

(d) Kelsal at Cibber *Welsted at Wicksted* Cibber at Breval.

(e) Now, shrugging, all was wrong, now, nodding, right,

(f) Now Freinds they hug, now Enemies they bite. *now they writhe & bite*

(g) Scramble o'er *Enucleate* empty Authors, and dispute

(h) For Shells *Those Nuts* of which a Maggot is the Fruit.

(i) Dire was the din. Not mine the Goddess cries *Not mine (the Goddess cries But cry's unheard)*

(j) But scarce was heard, Not mine to judge this Prize But scarce was h^{d}.

(k) Inf. Such equal-- *<cf. line (z)>*

(l) Scarce was the goddess heard! while thus *Not mine* she cries,

(m) Tis not in me to judge this *<blank>* *Not mine to judge ye well-contested* Prize

(n) In louder Music be this Jargon *Babel* drown'd,

(o) Now bray my Asses, *Sound forth my Brayers* & these Tongues confound.

(p) Forthwith each Windpipe trumpets forth an Ass, *Owl hoots to owl, & Ass intones to Ass.*

(q) Dry sound! that twangs *Harmonic Twangs* of Leather, Horn & Brass.

(r) As when -- *<cf. line (dd)>*

(s) Forthwith he sounds the Trumpet of an Ass,

(t) A *Dry* Sound compos'd of *y^{t} twangs of* Leather, Horn & Brass!

(u) She lists delighted while her *Far oer ye rest sonorous* Blackmore brays,

(v) And crowns him more than Ass *And more than Ass is crown'd* with Deathless Praise.

(w) No Voice like His, so bold, so clear, so strong,

(x) None sung so Loudly & none sung so Long.

In line (j) above, the N *of* Not *is altered from* n; *in line (f), JR seems to have omitted* and *or some other syllable before* now . . . bite.

Below this, on the same page:

(y) this Prize.

(z) Such equal Noise, such equal Merit strike,

(aa) Ye all have won, or all have lost alike.

(bb) Lest ye Well-argued Strife should never end, *But lest ye strike for ev. s^{d}. extend,*

(cc) Sound forth my Brayers, & ye Welkin rend. *So.nd my whole Chorus, & ye Contest end.* *Strait in one *<blank>* ye Voice extend **ye Welkin rend** *

(dd) As when the grave She Doctors wait before

(ee) Some gouty Miser's triple-bolted Door

(ff) In early morning on their Foals they call,

(gg) And break his vision of ye Dev'l & all.

(hh) So rose the Bray -- shook -- Long -- And

(ii) Each Windpipe Labours, Ass intones to Ass,

(jj) Dry Sound --

(kk) Far o'er --

Marginally, beside lines (dd)-(gg) in the passage above:

(ll) ʢ conspire

(mm) Wits, Critics, all in Unharmonious Quire

(nn) Now Burnet grumbles like a snarl^{g}. Dog,

(oo) Lewd <*blank*> now rymes, & rubs a grunt^{g}. Hog.

(pp) By Gods an Owl <*These two words are a cue for line (p) above?*>

P. viii

On p. viii at top upper margin, but cued to the note at top of title page verso: + Vociferation. *At foot of page cued to the MS. insertion ending* Young & Fair <*line (aa)*> *on half title recto:* ++ young & fair

(a) With scornful Smile at this the Hag reveald

(b) The brindled Monster in her Robe conceal'd.

(c) When thus ye Hag: now blush ye Prepossest;

(d) Lo! here ye Cat I suckled at my Breast:

(e) Well have ye Judg'd -- Then scornfull she reveal'd

(f) The brindled Monster in her Robe conceal'd -- own. As MS. 2 in Ed^{n}. 1736. p. 157.

(g) Now thousand Tongues -- as ll. 215 <*TE, 227*>. Corrected.

Half title recto

On recto of the half title following p. viii, preceded by JR's note:

Not<*e*>. This, ye page but one after what is MS. in ye Leaf p. 26. That on ye Reverse of ye title-page is between.

(a) ll.201 Now turn to diffrent Sports (ye Goddess crys)

(b) And learn my Sons ye wondrous Power of *Noise*.

(c) Who fail to ravish or to steal the *To move, to raise, to ravish ev'ry* Heart

(d) With Shakespear's Nature, or with Johnson's Art

(e) Can wake ye Sense & terrify *Hard task! yet fail we not to shake* ye Soul

(f) With grumbling *Discharg^{g}.* | *Displod^{g}.* Thunders from ye Mustardbowl.

(g) With Horns & Trumpets to wild Fury *With Horns & Drums the mind to Fury* *The Mind to madness wth French Horns we* swell,

(h) Or *And | Now* sink in Sorrows by *with* a Tolling Bell:

(i) These *Such* happy Arts Attention can command,

(j) When *Tho'* Fancy flags & Sense is at a stand.

(k) Try then new Arts *These <*carrols*> hers | This D--ky hers* whose feebly plaining **Elegiac** Lines *Try new ones then, these Cat-calls be ye bribe*

(l) Match the thin Music of ye Cat that whines. *Of him whose *Chatter*^{g}. shames ye Monkey tribe.*

(m) And who can form his *But his this Drum whose* hoarse Heroic Base

(n) To *Draws* the loud Trumpet *Clarion* of the Braying Ass.

(o) Now thousand tongues

The couplet Try then . . . that whines *<lines (k)-(l)> is marked with a delta for deletion.*

Below the above lines, a passage found only in part in the printed text (TE, III 141-44):

(p) Two slipshod Muses traips'd before ye Throng,
(q) With Heads unpind but meditating Song.
(r) Locks discomposd *Disorderd Hairs* as started *starting* from a Dream
(s) And never wash'd but in Castalia's Stream.
(t) First in thin *In feeble* treble Infantine & low,
(u) Pix plaintive pules, like tender Kitten's Woe;
(v) Now strains ye Tenor to a Sharper Squall,
(w) New mewing melts in many a dying Fall.
(x) More *But | Then* tragic N--n swells with deeper Rage,
(y) Like the base Murmur of Grimalkin sage.
(z) But who, alass! for fifty five declare? *In vain! small fav^{r}. Nymphs of 50 share,*
(aa) Each strait gave sentence for *All gave y^{r} Suffrage to* the Young & Fair.
(bb) Then swells
(cc) Harmonic

*The entire passage above--*Two slipshod . . . Harmonic *<lines (p)-(cc)>--is bracketed and marked with deltas for deletion.* N--n *in line (x) is possibly Lady Frances Norton (1640-1731), but I cannot discover that she had any special connection with "the tragic" or with drama. For* Pix *see TE, V 452.*

Next follows on this same half title recto:

(dd) As when the Long eard Mother milkd before *eer day ye Milky Mothers wait **stand** *
(ee) The gouty *At some sick* Miser's triple-bolted Door *Gait*
(ff) For her *their* defrauded absent *<blank>* makes *children **Foals they** make*
(gg) A cry *moan* so loud that all the *Guild* awakes.
(hh) Sore sighs S^{r}. Gilbert, starting at ye Bray,
(ii) From dreams of Millions, & a *Groat to pay*!
(jj) Such Chatter rises; *So swells each Windpipe;* Ass intones to Ass,
(kk) Harmonic Twang of Leather Horn & Brass. Such as from labr. 1. | 11. 233. High sounds *<TE, II 245-46>*
(ll) But high *far* o'er all Sonorous Blackmore's Strain
(mm) Street, Walls, & Skies bray back to Him again
(nn) In Tuthill Feilds the Asses in amaze
(oo) Prick all their Ears, & wondring cease to graze.
(pp) From George's Feilds *Thames wafts it then to Rufus -- *
(qq) Heavn takes his Praises *And Hungerford reechos--*
(rr) Confessd supreme in both ye Powers of Song *With Blackmore Blackmore shouts th' applauding Throng*
(ss) None sung so loudly & none sung *Who sings so *loudly*, & who sings* so *long*. Diving. N*<ote>*. Y^{e} Leaf torn out to v. 319 *<in 1728's misnumbering, 317; TE, 331>*. Slow mov'd

In lines (pp) and (qq) the phrases indicated by JR to be replaced (underscored) are not metrically equivalent to those replacing them.

II 235(223) But that this well-disputed game *strife* may end,

In l. 246, JR corrects the third t *of* attempted *to* r.

At top of p. 27:

from p. 20 marg.]

aft. v. 214 <*TE, 226*>

(a) III 141(149) Two shrill-voicd Dames *appeard* *Two slip-shod Muses stepd **traipst** before ye throng,

(b) III 142(150) Muse<*s*> <*blank*> for ever *With heads unpin'd, but* meditating Song;

(c) III 143(151) With Locks uncomb'd *L^{s} discompos'd* as newly wak'd from Dreams,

(d) III 144(152) And never wash'd but in Castalia's Streams.

(e) With smallest *First in thin* Treble, feeble, thin *Infantine &* low,

(f) Pules plaintive Pix *Pix plaintive pules* like tender Kitten's Woe.

With Base inf

At foot of p. 27:

(g) With Base more Tragic, that all Hearts appalls, *N--n in Tragic Base, grown deep wth Age,*

(h) In hoarser growles Grimalkin N--n squalls. *Like ~~gray~~|~~old~~ **hoarse** Grimalkin growls wth deeper rage.*

(i) But *~~the~~* Charms of Fifty little favour share,

(j) All damnd the Hag who durst oppose ye Fair.

(k) Scornful she smil'd, & learn from hence said She

(l) Gainst Justice, Truth, & Nature to decree.

(m) Lo here the Cat I nourishd at my Breast,

(n) Behold *& blush* for ever all ye prepossest.

(o) With that her Robe the grizly Beast reveald;

(p) But Sentence past can never be repeald.

(q) Yet, Daughter, thou, she said, this Prize *the Goddess cryd* resign,

(r) Content the Nobler qualities are *This ill-judgd Prize, a Nobler shall be* thine:

(s) Tho' Hers the Voice of Love, & whining Moan,

(t) Arms, & the venom'd Scratch are all thy own.

(u) Now thousd. Tongues v. 215 <*TE, 227*>

(v) The goddess said

In (j) of the above passage, who *overwrites* that. *The entire passage is bracketed and marked with a delta for deletion.*

Also at foot of p. 27, two distinct couplets written at right angles to the above passage, the first cued with a + to lines (q)-(r) of that passage, to which it is an alternative, the second marked delta for deletion:

(w) All stand abash'd, but Dullness thus: Resign

(x) Daught^{r} this Prize, ye nobler part is Thine.

(y) With Smiles ye Goddess loud exulting crys,

(z) Tis not in us to judge this noble Prize.

Above these couplets, in the right-hand margin, written at right angles to the entire printed text:

(aa) Now strains ye Tennor to a Sharper Squall,

(bb) Now Mewing melts in many a dying Fall:

(cc) More tragic N--n, *N--n, now more than* half a Cat with Age

(dd) Like hoarse *grey* Grimalkin growls with deeper Rage.

(ee) But who alass for Fifty five declare?

(ff) Each gave ye conquest to ye Young & Fair.

(gg) To whom ye Hag: Now blush ye prepossest,

(hh) Behold ye Cat I suckled at my Breast.

(ii) Hers was ye Voice,

In the left-hand margin, again written at right angles to the printed text:

(jj) Hers was the Voice of Love, & Whining Moan,

(kk) The Fire, the Rage, the Scratch are all thy own.

II, 241-60. P. 28.

To left of ll. 257(245)*ff, JR's note:* This Game is wholly / torn out, / from the pre:/ceed^{g}. verse -- so long <*TE, 256*>/ to v. 317, Slow movd <*TE, 331*>.

He inserts weekly *beside the asterisks in l. 268*(258) *and writes out the abbreviated names at ll. 254, 271*(242, 259).

II, 261-316. Pp. 29-31.

These pages have no insertions, but JR writes out the abbreviated names in ll. 279, 293, 302, 324, 325 (267, 281, 288, 310, 311).

II, 317-34. P. 32.

II 335(321) Hear you! in whose grave *My Critics in whose* heads, as equal scales,

II 337(323) Which most conduce to sooth the soul in *Indolence &* *bless Mank^{d}. wth* slumbers,

II 338(324) My *H*--'s *Henley's* *Hoadley's* periods, or my Bl--'s *Blackmore's* numbers?

II 339(325) Attend the *See now the* *This mighty* trial we propose to make:

II 343(329) To him we grant our *Him we invest with* amplest pow'rs to sit

II 345(331) To cavil *critic* censure, dictate, right or wrong,

II 346(332) Full, and *And his th'* eternal privilege of tongue.

To left of l. 331(317), *referring back to his notation at l. 257*(245) *that the page containing the Diving Game is torn out, JR writes:* [See ad v. 245 <*TE, 257*>.]

At foot of the page, four lines:

(a) v. 317<*TE, 331*> This done, the Goddess, from the Sable Flood,

(b) Moves to her quarters in the Walls *Gates* of Lud;

(c) The Tribes persue; and now to close the Games,

(d) A gentler Exercise the Queen proclaims.

These lines are followed by an alternative for the second couplet, with <ad?>*(for addendum?) over the first word:*

(e) Her Priest attends: In honor of whose <*blank*>

(f) She calls her Critics now to close ye Games Hear you

Next follows an alternative version of ll. 343-46(329-32)*:*

(g) aft. v. 328<*TE,342*> His be the *our* Licence, which shall ever last,

(h) On all my Authors, present, future, past,

(i) To critic -- And his th' eternal

Then follow eight lines not printed in any form:

(j) Yet not to plunge Well Willers in Dispair,

(k) Who haply slumber shall some Guerdon *some Reward shall* share.

(l) To Him who nodding steals a transient Nap,

(m) We give Tate's Ovid, & thy Virgil, Trap;

(n) Unable Heads that Sleep and Wake by fits,

(o) Win Steel, well:sifted from all Alien Wits.

(p) Nay who successless quite but <*blank*> *only gape* & wish

(q) Shall gain the whole Poetic Art of Bysshe.

(r) Three Cambr.

Lines (n)-(o) are bracketed and marked with a delta for deletion. Trap in line (m) is the Rev. Joseph Trapp; Steel in line (o) is Sir Richard Steele; Bysshe in line (q) is Edward Bysshe, whose "Art of English Poetry" appeared in 1702.

To left of lines (j)-(m) above, a Latin quotation: nemo / nemo in hoc nu:/mero nihi non / donatus alibit. <*Aeneid, 5. 305. Pope probably quotes from memory, reading* in *for* ex.>

II, 335-56. P. 33.

II 349(335) Each *All* prompt to *The same at* query, answer, and debate,

II 350(336) And smit with *The same their* love of poesie and prate.

II 355(341) Then mount the Clerks; and in one lazy *in one low equal* tone,

II 356(342) Thro' the long, heavy, painful page *lines* drawl on,

II 357(343) Soft creeping words on words the *each restless* sense compose,

II 358(344) At ev'ry line *page* they stretch, they yawn, they doze.

II 361(347) Thus oft they rear, and oft the head *their heads* decline,

II 362(348) As breathe, or pause, by fits *As less or more are breath'd* the airs divine.

II 365(351) Thrice *B--l* *Budgel* aim'd to speak, but thrice suppress

II 367(353) *C--s* *Collins* and *T--d*, prompt at Priests *ever prompt alike* *Ev'n thou, O Toland, ever prompt **tho prepard** * to jeer,

II 368(354) Yet silent *In silence* bow'd to *Christ's no-kingdom* here.

II 369(355) Who sate the nearest, by the words *nearest sate by <*blank*> full w.^{ds}* o'ercome

II 370(316) Slept first, the distant nodded *Dropt first, ye Distant only* to the hum.

To right of l. 349(335)*, part of the quotation from Virgil's Eclogues, 7. 4-5, that Pope quotes at TE, 348:* Arcades ambo Et Cantare pa/:res, & respondere parati. *To right of l. 352*(338)*, the line Pope quotes from Ovid's Metamorphoses, 13.1,* *at TE, 352:* Consedere duces, & vulgi stante corona. *Ll. 353-54*(339-40) *are marked with a caret. Ll. 359-62*(345-48) *are marked on the left with a* 1 *and ll. 363-68*(349-54) *with a* 2 *to indicate Pope's intention to reverse their order.*

At foot of the page, the first couplet cued by a + to a marginal note reading Hom. Linus. <*Il. 18. 569-71*>*:*

(a) aft. 338<*TE,352*> And first preludes a Laureat youth, with *And first a Laureat Youth in gentle* Lays

(b) Of gentlest *Preludes a | Intones a* Lullaby to Brunswick's Praise:

(c) aft. 352<*TE,366*> Next Philips dropt, & Thule left half sung,

(d) Next, Collins! ceas'd thy Turbulence of Tongue.

(e) aft. 348<*TE,362*> Now Philips yawns, & Thule left half sung,

(f) Loud Boyer, gifted with his Mothers Tongue:

(g) Then first Centlivre found her Voice to fail,

(h) Then Br. himself unfinishd left his Tale:

(i) And Travers fam'd for Coffee house debate,

(j) And Norton faild, tho born at Billingsgate.

(k) All slept, then first Centlivre's Voice did fail,

(l) And Br. himself unfinishd left his Tale:

(m) Evn He sate mute. The Clerks no longer read,

(n) And all lay *was* hushd as Folly's self lay Dead.

The entire passage is bracketed and marked with deltas for deletion. In line (h), Br. *is evidently Bruce (below, p. 34: TE II, 380), but I can discover nothing about him. Beside line (h) is written* Last, *though it is not clear whether this refers only to the passage or to the line as well, in which it might be a possible alternative for* Then. *A "Master Travers"--line (i)--appears as a coffee-house gossip in Swift's "The Quidnunckis."* Norton *in line (j) is Benjamin Norton Defoe. In line (k),* V *of* Voice *overwrites a word, possibly* thy.

In the right margin, written at right angles to the above lines:

(o) And now to this side -- As Verse or P<*rose*>

(p) And -- who Lectures c^d. ten Hours prolong,

(q) Loud Boyer gifted w.th his Mother's Tongue.

(r) Norton hims. untir'd in foul Debate,

(s) Wits lay on Wits, on Cr.-- And all was 372 <*TE, 386*>.

(t) Then down are rolld ye Books, fall'n oer em lies

(u) Each gentle Clerk, & muttr^g. seals his Eyes.

II, 357-76. P. 34.

II 371(357) Then down are roll'd the books; stretch'd *fall'n* o'er em lies

II 373(359) As what a Dutchman plumps into the lakes, *a lake*

II 374(360) One circle first, and then a second makes, *Will first One Circle, then a hund^d. make,*

II 375(361) What Dulness dropt among *amid* her sons imprest

II 377(363) So *Felt* from the midmost the nutation *Catchd by the midmost first, the nodding* spreads

II 379(365) At last *length* *C--re* *Centlivre* felt her voice to fail,

II 380(366) And *** *Bruce* himself unfinish'd left his Tale.

II 381(367) *T--s* and *T--* *Travers and Trap* the church and state gave o'er, *forgot*

II 382(368) Nor *** *Kelsal* talk'd *harangu'd,* nor S--- *Selkirk* *Laughton* whisper'd more.

II 383(369) Ev'n N--n, gifted with his mother's tongue *tho fam'd for foul debate*

II 384(370) Tho' born at Wapping, and from Daniel sprung *Sprung from Defoe & born at Bil^{gate}*

II 385(371) Ceas'd his loud bawling breath, and dropt the head; *Ev'n He sate mute on Critics Critics spread*

II 388(374) And stretch'd on bulks, as usual, Poets *And Bards around on Bulks, as usual* lay.

II 389(375) Why should I sing what bards *Except whom in her Walks* the Nightly Muse

Beside ll. 371-72(357-58) a bracket, with comment: add. Beside l. 390(376), the notation: [Here MS. torn off.] In l. 382(368), harangu'd calls for a monosyllabic name nowhere provided by the collations. Bruce in l. 380(366) is unidentified. Laughton may be John Lawton, who had a post in the excise under Walpole and so may have been associated in Pope's mind with the unfriendly gossip about "Timon" emanating (as he thought) from the Treasury.

At foot of the page:

(a) aft. v.364 <TE, 378> Not more when Winds succeed some heavy Rain,
(b) Unumberd nod the Poppies of the Plain.
(c) The Clerks themselves dropt down on either side
(d) Down roll the Volumes, oer each Volume lies,
(e) The gentle Clerk, & muttring shuts his Eyes
(f) Then first Centlivre

Line (c) above is marked with a delta for deletion; lines (a)-(e) are bracketed and marked with a delta for deletion. Below the above passage, and also marked with a bracket and delta for deletion:

(g) v. 367<TE, 381> Travers & Trap, untird in long debate,
(h) One for the Church, the other for the State,
(i) Fraser, who talk'd ten Volumes o'er by heart,
(j) And Boyer gifted with his Mother's Art,
(k) All slept *Lay mute* ev'n Norton calm in Silence slept,
(l) Sprung from Defoe, & born at Bilingsgate:
(m) Wits rolld on Wits, on Critics Critics spread,
(n) And all was hush'd -- v. 372 <TE, 386>

Below these lines: 362 <JR's error for 364; TE, 378> x Blackmore's Job. A waving Sea of Heads. Fraser in line (i) was called "Catalogue" Fraser for the range of his reading (Egmont, "Diary," 19 April 1730, 1:95).

II, 377-82. P. 35.

At l. 393(379), JR fills out the missing letters in the name.

III, 1-10. P. 36.

III 1 But in her Temple's last recess enclos'd *ye T^{s} holiest holy spread,*

III 2 On Dulness' lap th' Anointed head repos'd. *was laid **reposd** th' anointed Head.*

III 4 And soft besprinkled with Cimmerian dew.

III 6 Which only heads refin'd *well purgd* from reason know:

III 7 Hence from *on* the straw where *as* _Bedlam's_ prophet nods,

III 8 He hears loud *high* Oracles, and talks with Gods;

In l. 4, JR underscores Cimmerian, _but gives no MS. variant for it unless possibly one that has been erased. See, however, his first line at foot of the page._

At top of the page:

_(a)_ First T--d sits in all his Glory crown'd,

_(b)_ With ev'ry Emblem of his Empire round

_(c)_ Fast by the Throne, there Bridewell Lictors *Here Bridewell Lictors in dread order* stand

_(d)_ The Bedlam Prophets in <_blank_> Band

In the upper right margin, written at right angles to the printed page, but seemingly cued to the above verses:

_(e)_ In yon thick Mist see Durfey not alone,

_(f)_ Each Modern Science bows before his Throne.

In the upper left margin, written at right angles to the printed page:

_(g)_ Each Modern Science by its proper *modern* *Each may be well distinguishd by its* Type

_(h)_ Stand round: *Lo! there* _Divinity_ with Box *_Pot_* & _Pipe_

_(i)_ There *next* Broad Philosophy with _Breeches tore_

_(j)_ Music with Crotchets, & a tedious *Poor English Music there with dismal* _Score_

_(k)_ More *There* happy History with Pots of *There Hist'ry with her better Comrade* Ale

_(l)_ Consoles *To cheat* *Relieves* by fits her long desastrous *Melancholly* Tale.

At foot of the page:

_(m)_ v. 4,5.<_TE,III 4-5_> And sprinkled oer his Lids Lethean Dew;

_(n)_ O'er all his Brain extatic Raptures flow,

_(o)_ Which only H^{ds}. well-purg'd from Reason know.

_(p)_ Hence fro ye Straw -- He hears -- Hence the Fools -- The Acr. --

_(q)_ A thousand <_blank_> watchd the Holy Place,

_(r)_ And glorious Visions of the mighty race.

_(s)_ In the soft Arms of Sleep & Death convey'd,

_(t)_ He seems descended to th' Elysian Shade:

_(u)_ There in a dusky -- Old Bavius sits v. 15 <_TE, 15_>

_(v)_ Instant away they Veerd, just shake their Ears

_(w)_ Knock at ye Gate of Life (which Curl & Mears

_(x)_ Set wide to all) assume a Calf-Skin dress,

_(y)_ Demanding Birth, Impatient for the Press.

_(z)_ Millions -- v.23 <_TE, 23_>

In the left margin beside the four lines (v)-(y): postp. <= _postponenda_>. _In line (v),_ they . . . shake _overwrites an erasure._

III, 11-28. P. 37.

III 11 The Maids romantic wish, *Maiden's reverie* the Chymists flame,

III 13 And now *Now swift* *Hence swift* on Fancy's easy wing convey'd,

III 14 The King descended to *The Monarch wanders in* th' *Elyzian* shade.

III 19 Instant when dipt, away they wing *take* their flight,

III 21 Demand *Assume* new bodies, and in Calf's array *Calf-skin Dress*

III 22 Rush to the World, impatient for the day. *from ye Press.*

III 24 Thick as the Stars of night, or *As thick as Stars, as thick as* morning dews,

III 26 As thick as eggs at *round* *W--d* in pillory.

III 27 Wond'ring he gaz'd: When lo! a Sage *priest* *form* appears,

Ll. 17-18 are bracketed. In the space above l. 27 is inserted but then marked with a delta for deletion: Wond'ring He gaz'd, when Bavius thus begun. *L. 27 is bracketed and marked at opening with an interrogation point.*

At top of the page:

(a) v. 19<*TE, 19*> These soon as dipt all instant take their flight

(b) Where Brown & Mears --

(c) Demanding *There take new* Bodies, & a calf-skin Dress,

At foot of the page:

(d) v. 17<*TE, 17*> And proof to *Proof to all* *Proof against* Sense, impenetrably dull,

(e) With Achillaean Thickness arms the *each* Scull

(f) v. 27<*TE, 27*> When lo! grave Settle's rev'rend Form appears,

(g) By his broad Sh--

(h) Known by his Band, & by the Suit he wore,

III, 29-48. P. 38.

III 29 Known by the band *The spreading Band* and suit which *Settle* wore,

III 30 (His only suit) for twice three *Six* *Ten* years before.

III 35 Oh! born *giv'n* to see what none can see awake!

III 38 The hand of *The sacred* *Bavius* drench'd thee o'er and o'er.

III 40 What mortal knows his *Thou know'st not, Son, thy* pre-existent state?

III 41 Who knows how long, *Thou know'st not how* thy transmigrating soul

III 42 Did from *Boeotian* to *Boeotian* *Did down from $Dutchm^{n}$ into Dut^{an}* *Did long frō D^{n} down to D^{n}* roll

Ll. 31-32 are marked postpone, *but the directive may include 29-34. Below l. 42, the cue* Then turn'd, *on which see below. Ll. 43-48 are bracketed.*

At top of the page, marked with a delta for deletion:

(a) Amaz'd he stood, when Bavius thus begun

(b) With Speech Familiar, as from Sire to Son.

(c) O giv'n to see ------- v. 35 <*TE, 35*>

At foot of the page:

(d) aft. v.42<*TE,42*> Then turnd Ap-rice, Vandunck, & Numbers more,

(e) Who Cambrian Leek or <*blank*> Laurel wore.

(This couplet repeats one written at right angles to the text that is cued by a guideline to the words Then turnd, *as noted above.) After this couplet follows the cue:* For this. 53; *and below that:*

(f) v.38 <*TE,38*> These Arms my T--d, *The Sacred Bavius* drench'd thee oer & oer
(g) I made Thee proof to all the points of Sense,
(h) Impenetrable Dullness thy Defence.
(i) Know, unrememb'ring of thy former fate

<*JR writes in error* inrem'bring *and* state.>

(j) What Dullness grac'd thy prae-existent State:
(k) Thou wert Ap-rice, Vandunck, & numbers more,
(l) Who Cambrian Leek, or High *Low* Dutch Lawrel wore.
(m) What tho no Bees around thy Cradle flew
(n) Nor on thy Lips distill'd their golden Dew?
(o) Yet have I oft <*blank*> in their Stead,
(p) A swarm *What swarms* of Drones have buzz'd about thy Head.
(q) When you *If thou* like Orpheus, strike ye vocal *warbling* Lyre,
(r) Attentive *How listning* Blocks stand round thee & admire.
(s) Come then

The couplet (g)-(h) is bracketed and marked with a delta for deletion. Vocal *in the next to last line overwrites or is overwritten by* warbl^{g}. *The final two words are a cue to lines inserted at foot of the following page.*

III, 49-68. P. 39.

III 53 For this our Queen unfolds *has purg'd* to vision true
III 55 Old scenes of glory, times long cast behind, *Scenes of old Glories, all her ancient reign*
III 56 Shall first *thus | now* recall'd rush forward to thy mind; *brain;*
III 57 Then stretch thy sight o'er all her rising reign, *to Triumphs yet behind,*
III 58 And let the past and future fire thy brain. *Mind.*
III 60 Her boundless Empire over *stretch'd o'er* *spread o'er* seas and lands.
III 61 See round the Poles *Pole* where keener spangles *freezing Planets* shine,
III 63 (Earths wide extreams) her sable flag display'd; *sabled ensign spread;*
III 64 And all the nations cover'd in *safe beneath* her shade!
III 68 He, whose long *Wall* the wand'ring *Tartar* bounds. *That early dawn wth sudden Night surrounds*

Ll. 49-52 are bracketed. Goddess *is inserted above* our Queen *in l. 53, but JR gives no indication what it is to replace--possibly* For this. *Parentheses are inserted before* for *and after* view *in l. 54. Beside ll. 65-68 the comment:* add *(for* addenda*?) To right of l. 67:* Lo! He--. *In l. 68 it is not clear how the marginal insertion (here asterisked) is to function, since JR gives no underscoring dashes.*

At top of the page:

(a) Let scenes of Glory past enflame thy mind;

(b) How wide our Empire once, & unconfin'd.

At foot of the page, all but the last couplet bracketed and marked for deletion:

(c) Come then, (for Dullness sure accords this grace,)

(d) Come & Survey the Wonders of the Place.

(e) Survey thy Progeny, th' illustrious Throng, *Sight* *Behold em as they pass, Illustrious Sight!*

(f) In Nature's Order as they move along. *rise to Light.*

(g) Ascend this Mount, from whence thine Eye comands

(h) Her Spacious Empire, spread oer Seas & Lands.

III, 69-84. P. 40.

III 71 Thence to the South as far extend thy *thine* eyes;

III 74 And lick up *swallow* all their *Physick* of the *Soul*.

III 75 How little, see! *now* that portion of the ball,

III 76 Where faint at best *short & faint* the beams of science fall!

III 80 The freezing *streams of* *frozen* Tanais thro' a waste of snows,

III 81 The North by myriads *millions* pours her mighty sons,

III 82 Great *Stern* nurse of *Goths*, of *Alans*, and of *Huns*.

III 83 See *Alaric*'s stern port, the martial *godlike* frame

Ll. 69-74 are bracketed with a bracket possibly meant to be continuous from that on p. 39 noting add<*enda*>. *Ll. 79-82 are bracketed with a* 1, *ll. 77-78 with a* 2, *and ll. 83-84 with a* 3, *indicating proposed rearrangements.*

At foot of the page:

(a) v. 77,78 Rebellious Europe parted from her reign,

(b) How soon she gather'd to her Wings again?

The above lines, marked with a delta for deletion, are followed by two couplets, of which the first is also marked for deletion:

(c) Southward as fast from Libya's torrid <*blank*>

(d) Swift *Lo!* to her aid the Glorious Vandals fly.

(e) As swift <*JR erroneously writes* stift> behold! from yet remoter Skies.

(f) In Dullness great the Glorious Vandal<*s*> rise.

III, 85-102. P. 41.

III 85 See! the bold *Millions of* *Ostrogoths* on *Latium* fall;

III 86 See! the fierce *Millions of* *Visigoths* on *Spain* and *Gaul*.

III 90 And saving Ignorance enthrones *restores* by Laws.

III 91 See *Christians*, *Jews*, one *a* heavy sabbath keep;

III 93 Lo *See* *Rome* herself, proud *the* mistress now no more

III 98 Oh glorious ruin! and *** *a Varius | Vigilius* burn'd.

III 105 See'st thou an *Isle*, by Palmers, Pilgrims *Beh^{d} yon neighbr^{g} Isle, all over* trod,

III 106(100) Men bearded, bald, cowl'd, uncowl'd, shod, *In tracks of Pilgrim[ge] by feet* unshod,

III 107(101) Pee'ld, patch'd, and *Oer-run with* pieball'd, linsey-woolsey brothers,

Ll. 85-86 are bracketed with a 3, *ll. 93-98 with a* 2, *and ll. 105-8 with a* 1, *indicating proposed rearrangements. In l. 98, parentheses are inserted before* Oh *and after* ruin.

At top of the page:

(a) Then from a Mountains Cloudy Top the Guide

(b) Shows all the Kingdoms of the Goddess wide

(c) From where the North first pourd her mighty Sons,

(d) Stern Nurse of Alans, Visigoths, & Huns:

(e) Where dull Maeotis sleeps, & hardly flows,

(f) The frozen Tanais thro' a waste of Snows.

In the space between ll. 92 and 94, two lines marked for deletion:

(g) How lies *Behold* Iërne once in Science proud,

(h) Fat as Boeotia in one foggy Cloud?

At foot of the page, nine lines, in passages of four, three, and two, the first couplet marked for deletion:

(i) Who <*blank*> & bath'd in Childrens Blood,

(j) Yet fought for Easter, or a <*blank*> of wood.

(k) Could weep devoutly when an Image spoke,

(l) And groan in concert with a Saint of Oak.

(m) Allmighty Dullness! what a Sea of Blood

(n) For early Easter, or a Stick of Wood.

(o) Thus visit not --- Oh spread -- v. 108

(p) All this, persued the Sire, was once our own,

(q) Now Shorter Limits bound her <*blank*> Throne.

The blank space in (j) above contains an opening mark that could be s *for* Stick, *as below in line (n).*

III, 103-20. P. 42.

III 113(107) Thus visit not thy *Nor visit thus thine* own! on this blest age

III 115(109) And see my son, the hour is on *The hour my son already wings* its way

III 116(110) That lifts *bears* our Goddess to imperial sway:

III 117(111) This fav'rite Isle, long sever'd *parted* from her reign,

III 120(114) What aids, what armies, to assert her *their|our|the* cause!

III 121(115) See *Lo!* all her progeny, illustrious sight!

III 122(116) Behold, and count them *In Nature's order* as they rise to light

III 123(117) As *Berecynthia*, *pleasd Cybele* while her offspring vye

Ll. 111-12(105-6) *are bracketed, with a* 1 *to left of 111*(105), *and a* 2 *to left of 112*(106), *indicating Pope's intention to reverse them.*

At foot of the page:

(a) v. 109<*TE,115*> Here once more, Son, but in a milder Way,

(b) The Goddess meditates Imperial Sway

(c) The Time revolving, rip'ning Fates Decree,

(d) Much from her Sons she hopes, & most from Thee.

(e) Then look thro' Fate -- v. 113 <*TE,119*>

III, 121-38. P. 43.

III 127(121) Not with less glory *triumph* mighty *Dulness* crown'd,

Presumably following Pope's MS., JR notes the proximity of take *in l. 128*(122) *and* takes *in l. 131*(125) *by underscoring them. He fills out the names at ll. 134, 175, 176*(128, 137, 138). *In the space between ll. 134 and 135*(128 *and* 129) *he inserts:*

Famish'd to Modesty as Ed. 1736. p. 190 -- to -- Sighs return. <*l. 140*> Behold yon pair <*l. 141*>

Ll. 135-40(129-34) *are bracketed.*

III, 139-53. P. 44.

III 167(143) Ah *D*--, *G*-- ah! what ill-starr'd *frantic* rage

III 168(144) Divides a friendship long confirm'd by *on the verge of* age?

III 169(145) Blockheads with reason wicked wits *Men of Wit* abhor,

III 171(147) Embrace, embrace *again* my Sons! be foes no more!

III 142(150) In lofty madness *With heads <unpinn'd &>* meditating song,

III 145(153) *H*-- and *T*-- *H--d & W--y* glories of their race!

III 146(154) Lo *H--ck*'s fierce, and *M*--'s *Concanen next **meek** & Michel's* rueful face!

The names are filled out at l. 167(143). *At ll. 143 and 144*(151 *and* 152) *JR's collations simply repeat the first two words of each printed line:* With tresses; And never. W--y *in l. 145*(153) *is doubtless Lady Mary Wortley Montagu, and* T-- *is Elizabeth Thomas.* M *and* Michel *in l. 146*(154) *both refer to Michael Maittaire, classical scholar.*

At foot of the page:

(a) aft. v.154<*TE,146*> One *Cook* great of Stomach, one of greater *Horneck fierce of* Mind,

(b) And thousand thousand nameless names behind.

(c) See Pix & slip-shod W-- traipse along,

(d) With heads unpinn'd, & meditating Song &c -- streams.

III, 159-76. P. 45.

(159) How proud! how pale! how earnest all appear! *studious all **is** y^r <=*their*> chear*

III 195(161) Pass these to nobler sights: Lo *But lo! amidst yon crowd where* *H*-- stands,

III 196(162) Tuning *And tunes* his voice, and balancing *balances* his hands,

(171) While *But* happier *Hist'ry* with her *lov'd* comrade *Ale*,

Ll. 199-200 are bracketed, with comment: add *(for* addenda?*). The name in 199 is filled out; the names in 200 are not filled out but a final letter is added to each, giving:* K--t, B--d, W--n. *In 1728: 168-70 <TE(textual note, ll. 192-94)>,* box and pipe, breeches tore, *and* score *are underscored. In 1728, after l. 172 <TE(textual note, ll. 191-94, last verse)>:*

(a) Dull Woolston Scourge of Scripture mark with awe,

(b) And duller Jacob, blunderbuss of Law.

At foot of the page:

(c) v.161 Pass these for nobler Scenes, Lo! yonder spread

(d) The fog where *<blank>* *Lo yonder Mist there A--s* musefull head.

(e) Mark *But* where the thickest *th' obscurest* Darkness veils ye place,

(f) There *Great* Barnes, there *Great* Bentley, & their num'rous *the poring* race.

(g) A lumber house --

(h) With twice ten thousand Volumes in their Head.

(i) Are ever read.* ---- v. 176 *<TE, 190>*

(j) On yonder part what Fogs of gather'd *pregnant clouds of thickend* Air

(k) Invest the Scene, there musefull sitts Mattaire.

What *in line (j) above seems to be a slip of JR's pen for* where. *In line (d),* Mist *puns on the name of Nathaniel Mist, and* A--s *is presumably Alsop's.* Barnes *in line (f) is Joshua Barnes, the editor of Homer. The form of line (j) called for by the MS. reading might be:* Yonder what <*or* where>. . . Air.

III, 177-94. P. 46.

III 183(179) Right well mine eyes arede *eye aredes* that myster wight,

(183) But oh! what scenes, what miracles *wonders rise* behind?

(184) Now stretch thy view *Eye* *Extend thy Eyes,* and open all thy Mind.

III 237(193) Then *Thence* a new world to nature's laws unknown,

The name H-- *in l. 184*(180) *is filled out to* Herne. *After l. 186*(182) *is inserted (but also marked for deletion):* Now, Sire, to Nobler Scenes extend thine Eyes.

At top of the page: inf cornfeilds / on fire. *Then follows:*

(a) Up start the Furies! sooty Feinds advance,

(b) And lilly-handed Ladies joyn the dance.

(c) Now walk the Trees, now Rivers upward rise,

(d) Whales sport in Groves, & Dolphins in the Skies.

(e) [Here, torn off to v. 207 *<TE, 253>*. Angel, &c

Below this passage is repeated Cornfields, / on fire, *cued by a + to its appearance at top of page.*

At foot of the page:

(f) aft.184.*<TE, textual note, ll. 201-28, l. 2> Then wondrous* -- as Ed. *<17>*36 -- to War.

(g) And Pegasean Horse come flying in

(h) And justling Knights in Panoply of Tin.

(i) Speard in *Robd in* *Then from* a radiant Cloud *behind her veil* of Sarcenet White

(j) The rising *Forth-beaming | The peeping* Cynthia sheds her Silver Light

(k) Then swiftly fleet the Shades of Night *Swift the brown Shadows breaking melt* away

(l) And lo! three Suns illuminate the Day

(m) <*Blank*> three Tapers raisd at pleasure higher

(n) Illuminate their Light, & set their Flames on fire.

(o) Thick Darkness blots out those, then downward pour,

(p) Wide oer the darkned Landscape, Snow or Shower.

(q) Up start supra Earthquakes. M. Aetna --

In the final six lines above, three insertions are apparently cues rather than variant readings: Whose *below* And lo; Earthquakes *above* Thick; *and* M. Aetna *above* Wide oer. *The blank in line (m) is probably intended to contain* And lo! *as in line (l).*

III, 195-214. P. 47.

III 241(198) The *Here* forests dance *walk* the *Now walk the trees, now* rivers upward rise,

III 254(208) Her magic charms on *Her charms & darken* *Her charms & brood oer* all unclassic ground:

III 255(209) Yon stars, yon suns *Yon suns proud heighth* he rears at pleasure higher,

At foot of the page, but marked for deletion:

(a) aft. 210<*TE*, *236*>. His Light'ning's Flash, his mimic Thunders roll,

(b) Like Jove's own Delegate, from Bowl to Bowl.

III, 215-32. P. 48.

(217) B--th in his *her* cloudy tabernacle shrin'd,

III 266(220) Here shouts all *Drury*, there all *Here *Drury* shouts, there bellows* *Lincoln's-Inn*;

III 267(221) Contending Theatres our *Her* empire raise,

The names in ll. 262-64(216-18) *are filled out.*

At foot of the page:

(a) v. 215<*TE*, *261*> See opposite, with Cibber at his sides,

(b) Booth in his Cloudy Tabernacle rides.

(c) In flying Dragons, & in the Clouds *Fields* of Air,

(d) Seer wars with Seer, here Rich, & Cibber there.

(e) With flying Dragons Cibber; see beside *by his Side*

Below this passage JR's notation: No more MS.

III, 233-86. Pp. 49-51.

There are no insertions in pp. 49-51, but the names in ll. 319-22(271-74) *are filled out.*

Dunciad 1736

Front Flyleaf Recto

Canto 2^{d}

(a) The Sons of Dullness meet

(b) Pours

(c) A

(d) In

(e) On

(f) In

(g) All

(h) And all

(i) High on a Bed of State, that far outshone,

(j) Fleckno's proud Seat, or Querno's nobler Throne

(k) ---- exalted sate. Around him bows

(l) The Laureate Ba *Laurelld Train* & breathes Poetic Vows.

(m) With Kingly Joy he hears their Loyal Lies *With Kingly Pride ye genl. Joy he spies*

(n) And sees his Subjects *marks each Subjects* Transport in their Eyes *while he Lyes*

(o) His Strut, his Grin, and his dead Stare *His strut, his stare, his stupid Eye* they praise,

(p) And gaping *grinning* Crowds grow foolish as they gaze.

(q) With Kingly Pride ye gen'ral Joy he spies,

(r) And marks *sees* his Subject's Love in all their Lyes.

(s) Addresses & Homages p^{d}. to ye New King: Tibbalds. Satire on 3)

(t) Universities, ^{2}Inns of Court, ^{1}Governors to Travelling Noblemen

(u) Academy of Musick, Virtuosos (ye Corruptions of Each)

(v) 1 B--y with ye Cantabrigians 2 <*blank*> wth ye Oxonians

(w) 3 A French Refugee Governor with his Pupils.

(x) Addresses spoke by these 3)

(y) 4 Inns of Court Students 5 Travelling Physicians, to make

(z) fine Gentlemen at Paris, not collect Simples at Alexandria

(aa) 6 Virtuosos useless. Editions, Statues, Paintings, silly Affecta-

(bb) tion of Taste. Then introduce ye Directors of Musick with all

(cc) their Set of fine Gentlemen of Taste. All telling Dullness

(dd) & their King Tibbalds what they will perform with <y^{r}>

(ee) Lives and Fortunes for her, & what they have done in

(ff) bringing up ye Youth to such Ends for ye Next Age. Virtue.

Front Flyleaf Verso

(a) First came a Band, not better taught than fed,

(b) For Books their Hands, & Trenchers gracd their Head,

(c) From where thro Works Pontific murmuring fall,

(d) To lull ye Sons of Jesus & Clare Hall,

(e) Cam's slothful Streams; where B--ly holds his C^{t}

(f) And Alma Mater lies dissolv'd in Port.

(g) With Forehead plough'd by many a deep Remark,

(h) Before them frown'd that awfull Aristarch.

(i) His Hat, that never stird to Mortal Pride,

(j) W--r with rev'rence raisd *seazd*, & laid aside.

(k) Low bow'd the rest, but B--ly just did Nod *did but Nod*,

(l) So Sober Quakers please both Man & God.

(m) Since Fate, Great King, has plac'd thee on ye Throne

(n) (To all Great Kings my Zeal was ever known),

(o) Behold ye Youth educated by my Precepts are presented to thee

(p) Good Men & True we untill *Sworn even* <*JR's markings indicate that this phrase replaces* Good Men & True we un> Death ye ways of sense to fly

(q) And Wicked Wit wth all her Works defy.

(r) & for ever quit Putid, Vernacular & English Wit

(s) I make them Loyal, learn'd I suffer none,

(t) Be that ye pride of Our great Self alone.

(u) Satire on Neglect of Politeness in B--ly's address. & Time-

(v) serving

(w) Oxf^{d}. Description of a Head of a House.

(x) Tutors Leading up their Pupils

(y) His Address, a Satyr on ye Bad Education, Mad Principles.

Title Page

At top of the page: N. This Book is alter'd from the Second MS: as y^{e} / 1st Ed. 1728 is from the First MS. A. Pope. *Immediately below this:* Jonat. Richardson jun / Queen's Sq. *At foot of the page between the double rule before* London: Tota illa poetarum manus in me venenatos sales suos effudit. Scrib. Bent. 27]

On the blank verso of p. 64, following the prose prolegomena that occupy pp. 1-62:

Edm. Curll.

Impudence

Whipt at Westminster

During his being tost in ye Blanket, they recited this Latin / Verse, *Ibis ab excusso missus ad astra sago*, wch as soon as / he was taken out of it, he askd ye Young Gentlemen his / Tossers to know ye English of, that (says he) I may print / an account of it.

Supposititious Works of ye D. of Buckingham. brought to / ye Bar of ye H of L.^{ds} while he was receiv.^{g} ye Reprimand of y^{e} / House on his Knees, ye Chancellor using accidentally ye Ex- / -pression R.^{t} Hon. Duke of B. he rose up & corrected him: By y^{r} Ldsps leave, not R^{t} Hon. but Most Noble.

I, 1-2. P. 66.

In l. 2, Smithfield *is underscored. To left of the single footnote, which begins* This Poem *and ends* March, 1728-9:

Arma virumq cano / Trojae qui primus -- / Inferretq Deus La: / tio -- / Virg. <*Aeneid, 1. 1-6.*>

I, 3-4. P. 67.

I 3 Say great Patricians! (since your selves inspire *You these Works inspire!

I 4 These wondrous works; so Jove and Fate require). *So Jove's high Will & Britain's Fate require*

In l. 3, Patricians *is underscored.*

I, 5-6. P. 68.

I 5 *At foot of the page immediately below the word* Imitations*:* v. 5. Musa, mihi causas Memora -- <*Aeneid*, 1. 8.>

I, 7-8. P. 69.

In l. 8, Pallas *is underscored.*

I, 9-22. P. 70.

I 16 *To right of l. 16, the cue:* There. v. 27. *Ll. 17-26 are bracketed, with carets presumably indicating that the passage was inserted later. In ll. 9-16,* Dulness *(both occurrences),* Chaos, *and* Night *are underscored.*

I, 23-28. P. 71.

I 28 A yawning ruin hangs and nods *seems to nod* in air;

At foot of the page:

v. 27 There yawns a Ruin pervious to the Air
(Some sing in Kent-street, others in Rag-Fair).

I, 20-32. P. 72.

I 29 Keen hollow *Eternal* winds howl thro' the bleak recess,

To right of l. 32: Tibbald had wrote a Poem / calld The Cave of Poverty. See Note 106. *In l. 33,* Poverty *and* Poetry *are underscored.*

I, 33-38. P. 73.

I 33 *In ll. 34-38,* Quidnunc's, Guild-hall, Opium, Owls, *and* Curls *are underscored. To right of note on l. 33:* a Denomination gi: / ven to certain gentle: / men of a Political Club / constantly inquiring / What news now? Qd nunc?

I, 39-44. p. 74.

I 41 Sepulchral Lyes our holy *hallow'd* walls to grace,

I 44 Four guardian Virtues, round, support *With evry *Virtue* that upheld **upholds** * her throne.

Ll. 43-44 are bracketed. To left of l. 43: see 223-26. *In ll. 39-42,* Tyburn's, Cecilia's, New-year Odes, *and* Grubstreet *are underscored.*

I, 45-48. P. 75.

I 45 Fierce *First* champion Fortitude that knows no *nothing* fears

I 46 Of *Nor* hisses, blows, or *nor* want, or *nor* loss of ears:

I 47 Calm Temperance, whose blessings those partake *Next Vestal Temperance, that blest can make*

In ll. 45-48, Fortitude *and* Temperance *are underscored.*

I, 49-54. P. 76.

I 49 Prudence, whose glass presents th' approaching jayl: *Here P.... with a Patron for her Bail,*

I 50 Poetic Justice, with her lifted *And there Poetic Justice holds her* scale;

I 51 Where in nice balance, truth with gold she *Gainst Twenty Reasons ten Guineas* weighs <*A monosyllabic adjective is called for between* ten *and* Guineas, *but evidently not decided on.*>

To right of l. 52: Here all y[e] Process. 227. *In ll. 49-54,* Prudence, Poetic Justice, Chaos, *and* Somethings *are underscored.*

I, 55-62. P. 77.

In ll. 55-59, Jacob, Third-day, poem, play, hints, nonsense, *and* Maggots *are underscored.*

I, 63-72. P. 78.

I 64 Figures ill-pair'd, *-joynd* *o'erwrought* and Similies unlike.

In ll. 63-72, Images, Figures, Similies, Metaphors, Tragedy, Comedy, Farce, Epic, Description, AEgypt, Zembla *and* Barca *are underscored. Ll. 69-70 are bracketed, with comment:* add.

I, 73-84. P. 79.

I 74 There painted *smiling* vallies of eternal green,

I 75 On cold December fragrant *rosie* chaplets blow,

I 79 She, tinsel'd o'er *high-enthron'd* *Refulgent she* in robes of varying hues,

I 83 'Twas on the *that great* day, when Thorold, rich and grave,

Ll. 77-78 are bracketed, with comment: add. *Ll. 83-88 are bracketed. In ll. 75 and 84,* December *and* Cimon *are underscored.*

At foot of the page:

(a) v. 83. 'Twas on the day when thro' the broad *Cheapside*

(b) Gigantic Forms in Cars triumphal ride:

(c) Those pompous Glories with the Night were *'Twas night & all those pompous Glories* o'er,

(d) And yet in *Settle*'s song live one day more.

In line (b), triumphant *is altered to* triumphal.

I, 85-88. P. 80.

I 86 Glad chains, warm furs, broad banners, *streamers* and broad faces)

I 87 Now Night descending, the proud *all the* scene was o'er,

I 88 But *yet* liv'd, in Settle's numbers, one day more.

I, 89-94. p. 81.

I 89 Now May'rs and Shrieves all hush'd and satiate *in pleasing slumbers* lay,

I 90 Yet *and* eat, in dreams, the custard of the day;

I 91 While *But* pensive Poets painful vigils keep.

I 93 Much to the mindful Queen the feast *Much to her mind the solemn feast* recalls,

I, 95-102. P. 82.

I 95 Much she revolves their arts, their ancient *former* praise,

I 101 She saw old Pryn in restless Daniel *good Withers yet in W--y* *Still in Defoe she saw bold Withers* shine,

In l. 99, Bruin *is underscored.*

I, 103-4. P. 83.

I 104 And all the mighty mad in Dennis *And Dunton foaming still in **Whatleys** **Welsted's** * rage.

Above all the *in l. 104, JR inserts* venom'd, *apparently indicating that a MS. variant was either* And, venom'd, all the mad, *or, more probably,* And all the venom'd mad.

I, 105-6. P. 84.

Ll. 105-8 are bracketed. In mid-page, beside the note on Nahum Tate: Nahum Tate, a Poet / who had no sort of / Harm in him; where: / fore it seems none to a:/ ny person who is said to follow him.

At foot of the page:

(a) v. 105. But cheif her darling Tibbald fills her thought,

(b) With rising Worlds, & Monsters yet unwrought;

(c) Feinds, Monsters, Gods amazing Leagues prepare,

(d) And in her Cause, engage Hell, Earth, & Air!

Leagues *in line (c) possibly overwrites a word now illegible.*

I, 109-10. P. 86.

I 110 And pin'd, unconscious of his rising *the Birth of* fate;

I, 115-16. P. 89.

I 116 Where yet unpawn'd, much learned lumber *the Spoils of Sturbridge* **Philemon*'s Labours* lay:

I, 117-20. P. 90.

I 117 Volumes, whose size *bulk* the space exactly fill'd,

Ll. 119-20 are bracketed. In ll. 117-18, exactly fill'd *and* gild *are underscored.*

At foot of the page (as alternative to ll. 119-20):

v. 119. add. Or where the Pictures for ye Peice attone,

Sav'd by the Graver's Work, & not their own.

I, 121-22. P. 91.

I 121 Here swells the *bends a* shelf with Ogilby the great:

In l. 121 Ogilby *is underscored.*

I, 123-24. P. 92.

I 124 Here all *Hither* his suff'ring brotherhood *brethren all* retire,

Above all, may *is inserted and then canceled. To left of 121 n., with caret indicating its position after* large Volumes, *the insertion:* as well in Verse as Prose.

At foot of the page:

(a) aft. v. 124. Here Christian Quarles, thy picturd Works are thrown,

(b) And all who Benlowes as Maecenas own.

(c) or. Polemics huge, of Strength to fortifie

(d) The feeble Bandbox, or ensure *uphold* the Pye.

The two couplets above are bracketed and marked with deltas for deletion. Below them: Benlowes. A gent. of Oxfordshire in ye time of Ch. ye 1 who spent his / whole fortune upon ye Poets of those days, Quarles, Phineus Fletcher, &c. / His Anagram wch cost him ye foresaid Estate.

I, 125-30. P. 93.

I 127 But high *far* above, more solid Learning *in Time's old Varnish* shone

I 130 One *some* clasp'd in wood, and one *some* *or bound* in strong cow-hide,

Ll. 127-30 are bracketed and marked: add. *Beneath l. 130, marked with a delta for deletion:* Twelve Volumes, twelve, of massy weight, & size v. 135. *In ll. 125-28,* Vatican *and* Classics *are underscored.*

I, 131-34. P. 94.

I 134 And here *there* the groaning shelves *Philemon* bends.

Ll. 131-34 are bracketed and marked: add.

I, 135-46. P. 95.

I 135 Of these twelve volumes, twelve of amplest *of enormous* size,

I 136 Redeem'd from tapers *spices* and defrauded pyes,

I 140 Founds the whole pyle, of all his *those* works the base;

I 143 Then he. *thus.* Great Tamer of all human *O *Dullness*! victor of all* art!

I 145 Dulness! whose good old cause I yet *Whose good old cause unprosprous|unhappy I* defend.

In ll. 141-45, Quarto's, octavo's, *and* good old cause *are underscored.*

I, 147-62. P. 96.

I 147 O *Oh* thou of business the directing soul,

I 148 To human heads like *as* byass to the bowl,

I 153 And, lest we err by Wit's wild dancing *Reason's wandring* light,

I 155 Ah! still o'er *Britain* stretch that peaceful *Oh mayst thou yet o'er Britain stretch that* wand,

I 157 Where rebel to thy throne if *Where 'gainst thy throne if rebel* Science rise,

Ll. 147-50 are bracketed, with comment: add, *as are ll. 161-62. In l. 159,* Scholiasts *is underscored.*

At foot of the page:

(a) aft. v. 160. Like them, worn pale, with Nightly Sweats of Brain

(b) My righteous Labours long advancd thy reign.

(c) Blind with vile Types, wth N^{t}ly Sw. of Br--

(d) Worn pale, my Lab....

Both couplets are bracketed and marked with deltas for deletion.

I, 163-66. P. 97.

I 163 Old puns restore, lost blunders nicely seek, *Lost Puns or Blunders to each Line restore,*

I 164 And crucify poor *Shakespear* once a week. *o'er & o'er*

I 165 For thee I dim *dim^{d}* these eyes, and stuff *stuff^{d}* this head,

I 166 With all such reading as was never *no man e'er* read;

Ll. 163-66 are bracketed and marked: add. *To right of l. 166:* From those sup<*plying*>--167. *Below l. 166:*

(a) And had ye grace to read what none e'er read,

(b) And thought that Learn^{g} which none e'er w^{d} read;

(c) And took for Learning all that none e'er read;

I, 167-80. P. 98.

Ll. 169-82 are bracketed, with a caret beside 181-81 as if to signify added. *To left of ll. 173-74, JR calls attention to the distinction between 1736* Critiques *and MS. (and 1728)* Critics: NB Not that my Quill / to Critics was confin'd. (confin'd *overwrites an illegible word, possibly* designed.)

I, 181-94. P. 99.

I 183 Had Heav'n decreed such *these|our* works a longer date,

I 185 But see great *thy* Settle to the dust *grave* descend,

I 186 And all thy *her* cause and empire at an end!

I 189 But what can I? my Flaccus cast aside, *Thus, thus at least I show*

I 190 Take up th' Attorney's (once my better) guide? *My Zeal <,> thy long try'd Confessor below*

I 193 Yes, to my Country I my pen consign, *Let *Prin* <*Prynne*> & *Withers* now their Wreaths resign*

I 194 Yes, *I* from this moment, mighty Mist! am thine,

Ll. 191-94 are bracketed and marked with a caret.

I, 195-98. P. 100.

Ll. 195-96 are bracketed and marked with a caret.

I, 199-206. P. 101.

I 199 Fair *Pure* without spot; then greas'd by grocer's hands,

I 200 Or shipp'd with *Ward* to ape and monkey *barbrous Indian* lands,

I 203 With that, he lifted thrice the sparkling *fatal* brand,

I, 207-8. P. 102.

I 207 The opening *Th' unfolding* clouds disclose each work by turns,

To left of l. 208 n: T--ds & a watch:/maker, See his Pre:/face to it. <*TE, V 88.*>

I, 209-12. P. 103.

I 209 In one quick *Quick in one* flash see *Proserpine* expire,

I 211 Then gush'd *burst* the tears, as from the *Trojan*'s eyes

I, 213-18. P. 104.

I 216 Down sunk the flames, and with *in* a hiss expire.

In l. 213, Dulness *is underscored.*

I, 219-26. P. 105.

Ll. 223-26 are bracketed. At l. 221 JR has corrected the printer's error by placing a 2 *above* her *and a* 1 *above* him.
At foot of the page, bracketed:

(a) v 223-226. (For, long-time shelterd in that kind retreat,
(b) His gratefull Muse has eterniz'd ye Seat.)
(c) v 43-52 'Twas here in clouded Majesty she shone,
(d) With ev'ry Virtue that upholds her Throne.
(e) First, Champion *Fortitude* that nothing fears,
(f) Nor Hisses, Blows, nor Want, nor Loss of Ears.
(g) Next Vestal *Temperance* that blest can make
(h) Who Hunger and who Thirst for scribling sake.

In right margin, at right angles to the text, bracketed, and cued to the preceding passage by a +*:*

(i) Here *Prudence* with a Patron for her Bayl,
(j) And there Poetic Justice holds her Scale.
(k) 'Gainst Twenty Reasons Ten <*blank*> Guineas weighs,
(l) And Solid Pudding against Empty Praise.
(m) Here all ye Process. v. 227.

I, 227-40. P. 106.

I 227 Here to her Chosen all *Here all the process of* her works she shews;

I 234 Yet *And* holds the eel of science by the tail.

I 236 Less human genius *Learning* than God gives an ape,

In ll. 231-32, prologues, prefaces, *and* notes *are underscored. In l. 9 of 240 n, JR indicates that the MS. variant of* remark *is* observe.

At foot of the page:

(a) v. 233-4 were: How shuffled *Scenes* now Thebes now Athens turn,
(b) And Kings dye raving e'er they yet were born.

(c) How Time hims.<*elf*> stands still at her com̄and, *(d)* Realms shift y^r place, & Ocean turns <*to land*>.

Below this insertion, cued to MS. 233-34 by a +: Et modo me Thebis modo ponit Athenis. Hor. <*Epistles*, II.i.213>.

I, 241-42. P. 107.

In l. 242, Opium *is underscored. In l. 9 of 240 n, JR indicates that the MS. reading of* valuable translations *was* many valuable translations.

I, 243-48. P. 108.

I 245 Perch'd on his crown. All hail! and hail again, *Behold, she crys, the day*

I 246 My son! the promis'd land expects thy reign. *That gives the promis'd nation to our sway.*

I 247 Know, *Since* *Settle* cloy'd with custard, and with praise,

Between our *and* sway *in his insertion in l. 213, JR has canceled a word that may be* prey. *In l. 248, he capitalizes the* d *of* dull.

I, 249-56. P. 109.

Ll. 250-60 are bracketed.

At foot of the page, bracketed and marked with carets:

(a) v 250-260. Where *Gildon*, *Banks*, & high-born *Howard* rest.

(b) Take thou the Sceptre, rule *Then hail King Tibbald. Rule* my chosen sons,

(c) First Ed. In lands that flow with Clenches, & with Puns.

(d) Rule till each Theater my Empire own,

(e) And near our Monarchs, *Dullness* place *fix* her Throne.

(f) I see, I see --- Then Rapt she spoke no more --

(g) God save King *Tibbald*! Grubstreet alleys roar.

I, 263-64. P. 111.

I 263 Loud *Hoarse* thunder to its bottom shook the bog,

I 264 And the hoarse *loud* nation croak'd, God save King Log!

JR underscores the last four words of l. 264.

II, 1-2. P. 114.

Ll. 1-12 are bracketed and marked with carets. To left of the last four lines of the prose argument of Book II: See spare Leaf / bef. ye Title Page. *This is the material eventually used in Book IV.*

II, 13-26. P. 117.

II 15 She summons all her sons: *The sons of Dullness meet* An endless band

II 17 A motley mixture! in long wigs, in *Toupies, Bobs &* bags,

II 23 Amid that area wide she *In that wide space the Goddess* took *chose* her stand,

Ll. 13-14 are bracketed and marked inf. <=*infra*>. *In l. 25, JR inserts parentheses around* so . . . ordain. *In ll. 25-27,* May-pole, piety, *and* church *are underscored.*

At foot of the page:

The Second Canto. [begins]

(a) The Sons of Dullness meet: an endless Band

(b) + Quiq pii vates --

(c) Quiq sui memores alios facere merendo. Aen. 6 <*663, 665*>.

Then follows:

(d) v. 22. Rank'd side by side ye Patron & the Scrub *There hand in h^{d} wth each Poetic Scrub*

(e) Each Quarles his Benlowes, & each Tibbalds *Stood ev'ry Benlowes & stood ev'ry* B--

Below this, a couplet written as one line:

(f) The herald Hawker's rusty Voice proclaims *(g)* Heroic Prizes & adventrous Games.

In right margin, written at right angles to the text and cued to the final line above:

(h) The Goddess now by Hawkers Voice proclaims *(i)* Heroic --- Games. Amid that area -- v. 23.

In line (e) above, B-- *is Bubb Dodington.*

II, 27-38. P. 118.

II 31 A poet's form she plac'd *sets* before their eyes,

II 32 And bad *bids* the nimblest racer seize the prize;

II 34 Twelve *The* starveling bards of these degen'rate days.

II 35 All as *Plump as* a partridge plump, full-fed, *ruddy, round* and fair,

Ll. 31-46 are bracketed. In l. 30, Dulness *is underscored. To left of l. 32:* Shakespear. <*1 H 4: 3.3.3.*>

At foot of the page:

(a) v-46. To these in sport she first proposd ye Prize,

(b) And raisd a Poet's Phantom in their Eyes:

(c) Not such as Garrets lodge with Visage thin,

(d) Who like a Night gown round him wraps his Skin,

(e) But such a Bulk as no twelve Bards c^{d} raise,

(f) The starv'ling Bards ---

(g) Plump as a Partridge, ruddy, round, & fair,

(h) She formd this Image ---

II, 39-46. P. 119.

II 39 With pert flat *laughing* eyes she window'd well its head,

At foot of the page, the passage inserted at foot of p. 118 continues:

(a) With Laughing Eyes that twinkled in his head,
(b) Well look'd, well turn'd, well natur'd, & well fed:
(c) So wondrous like that Wootton's self might say,
(d) And Kent would swear, By G-- it must be Gay.
(e) All gaze---

Below this, a note on Wootton and Kent: Two Eminent Painters, intimate friends of ye true Mr. Gay. *See 1728: p. 16, lines (c) and (d).*

II, 47-48. P. 120.

II 47 All gaze with ardour: some a poet's name *ye authors fame*
II 48 Others, a sword-knot and lac'd suit *his lace, & birthday suit* inflame.

II, 49-54. P. 121.

II 49 But lofty Lintot *awfull Tonson* in the circle rose;
II 52 He spoke, and who with Lintot *Tonson* shall contend!

At foot of the page, a note on Curll: 54. Edmund Curl, Bookseller, y^e most Impudent Fellow of his Age. / He stood in y^e Pillory at Charing Cross, Feb. 24. $172\frac{7}{8}$.

II, 57-64. P. 123.

II 58 He left huge Lintot *fat Tonson* and outstrip'd the wind.
II 60 On feet *legs* and wings, and flies, and wades, and hops,
II 63 With legs expanded Bernard *steps unequal Lintot* urg'd the race,
II 64 And seem'd *seems* to emulate great Jacob's *his Uncle's* pace.

The second MS. variant for l. 64 suggests that the variant JR meant to record for l. 63 was steps unequal Tonson.

At foot of the page:

(a) v. 63,4. With Arms expanded Tonson rows his State,
(b) And left-leg'd Jacob seems to emulate.

Below this, the note: Alluding to Dryden's Verse on Old Jacob: / "With Two Left legs &c., *and also the further note:* 63. Sequiturq. patrem non passibus equis. Virg. <*Aeneid,* II 724.>

II, 65-66. P. 124.

II 66 Which *Curl*'s *Corinna* chanc'd *happ'd* that morn to make:

In l. 2 of 66 n, the name is filled out.

II, 67-72. P. 125.

II 69 Here fortun'd _Curl_ to slide; *Here slidder'd _Curl_* loud shout the *laughing* band,

II 70 And _Bernard_! _Bernard_! *_Jacob_! _Jacob_!* rings thro' all the _Strand_.

II 71 Obscene with filth the miscreant *Varlet* lies bewray'd,

Above Bernard! Bernard! _JR inserts_ Lintot Lintot, _then overwrites with_ Jacob Jacob, _then cancels the whole._

II, 73-78. P. 126.

Ll. 77-78 are bracketed.

At foot of the page, a couplet marked with a delta for deletion:

_(a)_ v. 77,8. And if in Him and His more grace abound,

_(b)_ Then let mine Host of Shakespear's Head be c^{d}.

Below this: v. 73. Si quid habent veri vatum praesagia -- Ov.<_id, Metamorphoses, 15. 879._>

II, 77-90. P. 127.

Ll. 79-92 are bracketed and marked with a caret.

II, 91-104. P. 128.

II 93 Oft, as he fish'd her *these* nether realms for wit,

II 99 Re-passes Lintot, *Tonson* vindicates the race,

II 103 A shapeless shade, it melted from his *When lo! the shapeless shadow melts from* sight,

JR revises l. 95 to read: Renew'd by ordure (sympathetic force!). _Ll. 101-12 are bracketed._

At foot of the page, also bracketed:

_(a)_ v. 101-- How Jove, still just, defeats Man's erring Aim!

_(b)_ How Hope deludes, how Fortune shifts ye Game!

_(c)_ As Curl rapacious spreads his Eager Hand,

_(d)_ And ye plump Phantom stands, or seems to stand,

_(e)_ See 1st. MS. His frustrate Arms th' impassive Air confess,

_(f)_ All of the Idol vanish'd but the Dress. Un-

II, 105-10. P. 129.

II 108 And whisk 'em back to _Evans_, _Young_, and *to Gay, to Young, to* _Swift_.

At top of the page:

_(a)_ 105. Baffled yet present still amidst Dispair,

_(b)_ To seize his Papers, _Curl_, was next thy Care.

(c) His Papers all ye Sportive Winds uplift,

At foot of the page, the passage inserted at foot of p. 128 continues:

(d) Unhappy Stationer! his Author gone,

(e) Now grasps an empty *Joseph* for a *John*. v. 120

Below this, the note: Joseph Gay, a fictitious Name put by Curl before several papers / of Verses, Rape of a Smock, Confederates, Hoop-Peticote, & others / printed by him.

II, 111-20. P. 130.

Ll. 113-32 are bracketed and marked with carets.

II, 133-34. P. 133.

II 134 With that she gave him *But royal Tibbald,|But ye kind Monarch,* (piteous of his case,

At foot of the page:

(a) 133. But Royal Tibbald to console his Slave,

(b) A figurd Rug, (Indulgent Monarch) gave.

(c) There *Dulness* trac'd in wry-mouth'd Portraiture,

(d) The Fates her Martyrs militant endure. v. 137.

II, 135-36. P. 134.

II 135 A shaggy tap'stry *Gives him a Rug well* worthy to be spread

II 136 On *Codrus*' old, or *Dunton*'s *Durfey's* modern bed;

Below l. 136:

There *Dullness* trac'd &c p. 133. bot.<*tom*>.

II, 139-40. P. 136.

II 139 Ear-less *Dauntless* on high, stood un-abash'd *Defoe*,

II 140 And *Tutchin* flagrant from the scourge *Lash* below:

At foot of the page:

139. Daniel Defoe stood in y^e Pillory for certain Papers, call'd the / Reviews. He thereupon no whit abashed, publish'd an *Hymn to / the Pillory*, a Pindaric Ode. It appears from hence that this Poem was writ before Mr *Curl* hims.<*elf*> stood in the / Pillory, which happen'd not till Feb. $172\frac{8}{9}$.

II, 141-42. P. 137.

II 141 There *Ridpath*, *Roper*, cudgell'd *There Kick'd & Cudgeld Ridpath* might ye view,

JR puts parentheses around l. 142.

II, 145-50. P. 139.

II 149 See in the circle *at the barrier* next _Eliza_ plac'd,

II 150 Two babes of love close clinging to *round* her waste;

In ll. 2-3 of 140 n, beside upon which . . . hang'd, _the correction:_ but upon petition/ing to be hanged, / was pardon'd. _In the Imitations for l. 148,_ Hal.<_ifax_> _is added after_ in the looms.

II, 151-56. P. 140.

II 152 In flow'rs and pearls *In rich brocade* by bounteous _Kirkall_ dress'd.

At 149 n, opposite For the two Babes, _the addition:_ She had 2 Bas:/tards, others say / three.

At foot of the page, bracketed and marked with a delta for deletion:

_(a)_ aft. 152. Pearls on her Neck, & Diamonds in her Hair.

_(b)_ See 1st. Ed. And her fore Buttocks to the Navel bare.

II, 159-70. P. 142.

II 162 That on his vigour and superior *gigantic* size.

II 164 It rose, and labour'd to a curve *an arch* at most:

II 168 The wild _Maeander_ wash'd the Artist's *For straining more it flys in his own* face:

II, 179-82. P. 145.

II 179 Thou triumph'st, Victor of the high-wrought *well-p-st* day,

II 180 And the pleas'd dame, soft smiling, leads *moves* away.

II, 183-98. P. 146.

II 187 His honour'd *secret* meaning Dulness thus exprest;

II 189 He chinks his purse, and takes his seat of *in* state:

II 191 Now at his head the dex'trous task *T--l & Go--n at his head* commence,

II 196 Then his nice taste directs our *all* Opera's:

II 197 _Bentley_ his mouth with *His mouth now Bentley's* classic flatt'ry opes,

In ll. 187 and 198, Dulness _and_ tropes _are underscored. In l. 191,_ Go--n _is Thomas Gordon, who appears in the 1743 "Dunciad" as Silenus._ T--l _may be Matthew Tindal but may also be Thomas Tickell, whose name would make his participation in a tickling contest appropriate._

II, 199-200. P. 147.

II 199 But *Welsted* most *Oldmixon* the poet's healing balm

At foot of the page: Oldmixon. He prefacd the Court Poems, publishd by Curl, & / imputed them to M[r] Pope in 1706. 8[o].
JR's date is clearly a slip of the pen for 1716.

II, 203-12. P. 149.

II 204 And quick sensations skip from vein to *thro' ev'ry* vein,

II 209 As *So* taught by Venus, Paris learnt the art

II 211 Secure, *So sure* thro' her, the noble prize to carry,

In ll. 207 and 212, Queen of Love *and* Secretary *are underscored.*

At foot of the page, marked with a delta for deletion:

(a) aft. 208. Bids her un-mark'd a nicer part to probe,

(b) Latent, beneath the Cincture of his Robe. See 1st. MS.

II, 213-20. P. 150.

II 218 With Thunder rumbling *ratling* from the mustard-bowl,

II 219 With horns and trumpets now to madness *Fury* swell,

In l. 214, Noise *is underscored.*

II, 221-32. P. 151.

II 230 And Noise, and *Norton*, Brangling, and *W-st-d at W-ck-d, B-dg-l at* *Breval*,

II 231 *Dennis*, and *And loud-tongu'd* Dissonance; and captious art,

At top of the page, some indicators as to where the following passages in the MS. relate to the printed poem:
[See III 141 & aft. 172]/ [See p. 196 & 197] *To left of these:*

(a) v. 226. Two slipshod Muses traips'd before y[e] throng,

(b) With Heads unpin'd, but meditating song,

(c) Disorder'd locks as starting wild from *from their* Dreams,

(d) And never wash'd but in Castalia's streams.

(e) In feeblest Treble, Infantine & low,

(f) Pules plaintive Pix, like tender Kitten's Woe;

At foot of the page, continuing the above:

(g) Now strains y[e] Tenor to a sharper Squall,

(h) Now mewing melts in many a dying fall.

(i) But Tragic N--n growls with deeper Rage,

(j) Like y[e] base Murmur of Grimalkin's Age:

(k) Q. if obscure In vain! small favour Nymphs of Fifty share

(l) All gave their Suffrage to ye Young & Fair.

(m) Phaedrus Fab. Lib. <5.No.5> When thus the Hag: now blush ye Prepossest!

(n) Behold ye Cat I suckled at my Breast! Well -- marg.

In right margin, at right angles to the text, continuing the above:

(o) Well have ye judgd -- Then scornfull she reveal'd

(p) The brindled Monster in her Robe conceald.

(q) The King Pacific rose; He cry'd, Resign,

(r) Sister, this Prize; a Nobler shall be thine:

(s) Tho' Hers the Voice of Love, & tender moan,

(t) The Scratch, ye Rage, the Fire, are all thy own.

In same margin, to right of the above lines, an alternative passage:

(u) Then, lift^{g}. high ye Beast her Robe conceals,

(v) To Thee, O King, an injur'd Muse appeals!

(w) ---breast. Hers was ye Voice --- then held ye Beast to view,

(x) The Beast beg'd Justice wth a dolefull Mew.

(y) The King

(z) Now thousand t. v. 227.

II, 233-48. P. 152.

II 233 Hold (cry'd the Queen) A Cat-call each *ye all alike* shall win,

II 235 But that this well-disputed game *strife* may end,

II 238 At some sick miser's triple- *trebly* bolted gate,

II 245 Such, as from lab'ring *groaning* lungs th' Enthusiast blows,

In l. 240, Guild *is underscored. Ll. 245-46 are bracketed and marked:* add.

II, 249-56. P. 153.

In ll. 252 and 256, courts *(both occurrences),* loudly, *and* long *are underscored.*

II, 257-60. P. 154.

II 258 (As morning *Ev'ning* prayer and flagellation end)

II 259 To where *Where fam'd* *Fleet-ditch* with disemboguing streams

II, 265-68. P. 157.

II 267 Who flings most filth *Mud* and wide pollutes around

II 268 The stream, be his the Weekly *London* *all H-d-y-s* Journals bound;

At foot of the page:

(a) 266. And whose th' Alacrity of sinking well.

II, 269-72. P. 158.

II 271 In naked majesty *Oldmixon* *great Dennis* stands,

At foot of the page:

272. at magnos membrorum artus &c. Aen. 5. <*422.*>

272. *Milo*, who was kill'd by undertaking to pull an oak to peices / which was too strong for him.

II, 273-74. P. 159.

At close of 271 n: See p. 147.

II, 275-82. P. 160.

II 279 Next *Smedley* **Eusden** div'd; slow circles dimpled o'er

II 280 The quaking mud *Just where he sunk* that clos'd, and op'd *closing op'd* no more.

II 281 All look, all sigh, and call on *Smedley* *Eusden* lost;

II 282 *Smedley* *Eusden* in vain resounds thro' all the coast.

In the Imitations for l. 281, below the Roscommon quotation: ut litus Hyla Hyla <*Virgil, Eclogues, 6. 44*.>

II, 283-90. P. 161.

II 287 True to the bottom, see *Concanen* creep *as Concanen creeps* *Room & Wheetly* <*Whatley?*> creep,

II 288 A cold, long-winded native of the deep! *deeps*

II 289 If perseverance gain the Diver's *He pleads this only Merit for the* prize,

Ll. 283-84 are bracketed, with comment in left margin: These 2 lines / torn off. *To right of l. 283:* See 1 Ed. *To right of l. 287:* See 1 Ed.

At foot of the page:

(a) See 1st. Ed. Far worse unhappy Diaper succeeds,

(b) He search'd for Coral, but he gather'd Weeds.

(c) True to ye bottom Room & Whatly creep,

(d) Long-winded these, as Natives of the Deep.

(e) This only Merit pleading for the Prize

The more nearly correct spelling of Stephen Whatley's name in the above lines suggests that the spelling inserted in the printed text represents a slip of the pen.

II, 291-94. P. 162.

Ll. 291-92 are bracketed and marked with a caret. Ll. 293-96 are bracketed.

At foot of the page:

(a) v. 293. But nimbler *Welsted* labours at ye Ground

(b) See 1st. Ed. Circles in Mud, & darkens all around.

(c) No Crab ---

II, 295-302. P. 163.

II 298 Downward to climb, and *or* backward to advance.

II 300 And loudly claims the Journals *H-d-y* and the Lead.

II 301 Lo *Smedley* *Dennis|Eusden* rose in majesty of mud!

II, 303-14. P. 164.

II 303 Shaking the horrors of his ample *beetle|sable* brows,

II, 315-22. P. 165.

II 317 As under seas *Alphaeus'* *As Alphaeus under seas by* secret sluice

II, 323-28. P. 166.

II 324 And *Shadwell* nods the poppy *poppies* on his brows;

II 327 And "Take (he said) these robes *the gown* which once were <*Pope or JR neglects to singularize the verb*> mine,

II, 329-42. P. 167.

II 331 Slow moves *Then march'd* the Goddess from the sable flood,

II 333 Her Critics there *last* she summons, and proclaims

II 337 Which most conduce to sooth *bless* the soul in *with* slumbers,

II 338 My *Henley*'s *H-dl-y-s* periods, or my *Blackmore*'s numbers?

II 341 Sleep's all-subduing charms *Pow'r* who dares defy,

In l. 341, Sleep *is underscored.*

At foot of the page:

338. H-dl-y the reverend Author of the London Journals subscrib'd / Brittannicus, in ye year <*blank*> in accusation & Invective agst. / Bishop Atterbury after his Sentence was executed in yt yr. / In this Paper, then under his Direction, were publish'd 2 false &c. *In the first sentence,* in ye year *is struck through.*

II, 343-56. P. 168.

To left of ll. 347 and 352, carets. To left of l. 352, the notation sup. *In ll. 347 and 351,* Sophs, Templars, *and* gentle readers *are underscored.*

At top of the page:

(a) aft. 352. And first a Laureate Youth, in gentle Lays,

(b) Preludes a Lullaby in Brunswick's praise.

At foot of the page:

(c) aft. v. 346. Yet not to drive Well-wishers to despair,

(d) Who haply slumber shall some Guerdon share:

(e) To him who Nodding steals a transient Nap,

(f) We give Tate's Ovid, or thy Virgil Tr--.

(g) Unable Heads that Sleep & Wake by fits

(h) Win *Steel* well sifted from all Alien Wits.

(i) Nay who successless only gape & wish

(j) Shall win ye whole *Poetic Art* of *Bysshe*.

All four couplets are bracketed and marked with carets; the last but one is marked with a delta for deletion. In the right margin, beside the third and fourth couplets: nemo ex hoc/num. mihi non / donat abibit. / Aen. 5. <*305:* donat *should read* donatus>

II, 357-68. P. 169.

II 367 *Toland* and *Tindal*, prompt at priests *ever prompt* to jeer,

In l. 368, Christ's No Kingdom *is underscored. Beside l. 365 n, marked for insertion before the final sentence:* He was no less fa:/mous for mak^{g} / Speeches ab^{t} ye S. Sea, / & for presenting a / Glass of Wine to his pres^{t} Majesty in his / Journey to Newmar:/ket, 1728.

II, 369-78. P. 170.

II 371 Then down are roll'd the books; stretch'd *and* o'er 'em lies

II 375 What Dulness dropt among *amid* her sons impress

II, 379-82. P. 171.

II 380 *Motteux* *And B--* himself unfinish'd left his tale,

II 381 *Boyer* the State, and *Law* the Stage *Tr--s and Tr-- the Church & State* gave o'er,

II 382 Nor Kelsey talk'd, nor Naso *S--k--k* whisper'd more;

At 379 n, JR inserts version of *before* Homer.

II, 383-86. P. 172.

Ll. 383-86 are bracketed.

At top of the page:

(a) v. 383. Evn *Norton*, gifted with his Mothers Tongue,

(b) Tho' born at Wapping, & from Daniel sprung,

(c) Ceas'd his loud bawling Breath, & dropt the head;

II, 387-94. P. 173.

II 390 Did slumbering visit, and convey *convey'd* to stews:

II 391 Who *Or* prouder march'd, with magistrates in state,

II 393 How *Laurus* *Dennis|Eusden* lay inspir'd beside a sink,

In l. 389, nightly Muse *is underscored.*

II, 395-96. P. 174.

II 395 While *All* others, timely, to the neighboring Fleet

In l. 395, Fleet *is underscored.*

III, 1-8. P. 177.

In l. 2, Dulness *is underscored. Opposite* Virg. AEn. 7 *in the Imitations:* simulacra videt volitantia <*l. 89*>.

At foot of the page:

(a) But in her Temple's Holyest Holy spread,

(b) In Dullness lap was lay'd *reposd* th' anointed Head.

III, 17-20. P. 179.

III 17 And blunt the sense, and fit it for a scull

JR's collations show that the MS. line omits And blunt *and inserts* incrassates & encrusts; *but how these alterations are to eventuate in a pentameter line remains obscure, unless he meant to retain* And *with the addition of some following word such as* then.

III 18 Of *to* solid proof, impenetrably dull

III 19 Instant when dipt, away they wing *take* their flight,

III, 21-26. P. 186.

III 21 Demand *Assume* new bodies, and in Calf's array,

III 24 Thick as the stars of night, or *As thick as stars, as thick as* morning dews,

III 26 As thick as eggs at *round* *Ward* in Pillory.

III, 39-54. P. 183.

III 42 Might *Did* from *Boeotian* to *Boeotian* roll!

III 45 And all who since, in mild benighted *Albion's clouded* days,

III 53 For this, our Queen unfolds *has purg'd* to vision true

Ll. 39-46 are bracketed, as are ll. 47-52. Ll. 41-42 are marked with a 2 *and ll. 43-44 with a* 1 *to indicate intention to rearrange.*

At foot of the page, the first two lines are bracketed and marked for deletion:

(a) Then turn'd *Ap-rice*, *Vandunk*, & numbers more,

(b) Who *Cambrian* Leeks, or *Low-Dutch* Lawrel wore

(c) But blind

III, 55-70. P. 184.

III 60 Her boundless empire over *spread o'er* seas and lands.

III 65 Far eastward cast thine *thy* eye, from whence the sun

III 66 And orient Science, at a *one* birth begun.

Ll. 67-68 are bracketed.

At foot of the page, bracketed:

(a) v.67 Lo! He whose Wall *He whose long Wall* the erring Tartar bounds

(b) (One Man Immortal!) all *her* Works confounds.

(c) That early *hopefull* dawn with sudden Night surrounds

Marginally, beside the final line to signal it as an alternative to the preceding one: or. *Beside the preceding line, possibly as an alternative to* (One man Immortal!)*:* Obscure for Dullness, *canceled.*

III, 71-88. P. 185.

III 71 Thence to the south extend thy gladden'd *as far extend thine <*overwritten by* thy>* eyes;

III 74 And lick up *swallow* all their Physic of the soul.

III 75 How little, mark! *now|see!* that portion of the ball,

III 76 Where, faint at best *Where short or faint* *Where uneclypst* the beams of Science fall:

III 77 Soon as they dawn, *Scarce had they dawn'd,* from *Hyperborean* skies,

III 79 Lo *See* where *Maeotis* sleeps, and hardly flows

III 81 The North by myriads *millions* pours her mighty sons,

III 83 See *Lo!* Alaric's stern port, the martial *godlike* frame

III 85 See *Lo!* the bold *Ostrogoths* on *Latium* fall;

III 86 See *Lo!* the fierce *Visigoths* on *Spain* and *Gaul.*

Ll. 77-78 are bracketed. At 73-74 n, l. 4, cued for insertion before Medicine: Ψυχῆς 'Ιατρειον, / _Medela Animae._

At foot of the page, the first couplet marked for deletion:

_(a)_ v. 77,8 Southward, behold! from Libya's torrid skies,

_(b)_ Against her throne ye glorious Vandals rise.

_(c)_ aft. 82 As swift, behold! from yet remoter skies,

_(d)_ In Dullness great, ye glorious Vandals rise.

III, 89-94. P. 186.

III 90 And saving Ignorance <u>enthrones</u> *restores* by Laws.

In l. 91, an exclamation point is inserted after See; Christians _and_ Jews _are underscored._

III, 95-106. P. 187.

III 105 <u>Behold yon</u> *See'st thou an* Isle by Palmers, Pilgrims trod,

Ll. 97-102 are bracketed and marked with a caret. Ll. 103-4 are bracketed.

At foot of the page:

_(a)_ v.103 Lo Statues, Temples, Theatres oerturn'd

_(b)_ (Oh glorious Ruin!) and <u>a _Varius_</u> *_Vigilius_* burn'd

_(c)_ A Phidias &c

The cue A Phidias _is preceded by a marginal_ or.

III, 107-20. P. 188.

III 117 This fav'rite Isle, long <u>sever'd</u> *parted* from her reign,

III 120 What aids, what armies, to <u>assert</u> *assist* her cause?

_In l. 112,_ Dulness _is underscored._

III, 121-34. P. 189.

III 121 <u>See</u> *Lo!* all her progeny, illustrious sight!

III 122 <u>Behold and count them,</u> *In Nature's order* as they rise to light.

III 123 As Berecynthia, *As pleas'd Cybele* while her offspring vye

III 127 Not with less <u>glory</u> *triumph* mighty Dulness crown'd.

III 129 And <u>her</u> *all* _Parnassus_, glancing o'er at once,

JR notes the repetition in ll. 128 and 131 by underscoring take _and_ takes. _In l. 130 he capitalizes_ dunce.

III, 135-46. P. 190.

III 139 Thee shall *For Him* each Ale-house, thee *him* each Gill-house mourn,

Ll. 135-38 are bracketed. In margin below l. 140: Behold yon fair - 173. *In margin, beside l. 141:* See p. 151 & 197.

At foot of the page, the second couplet marked for deletion:

(a) v. 135,138 Famish'd to Modesty that other see,

(b) O Live! & P--n shall live in thee

(c) Alas no longer on this Earth *globe* he shone

(d) Than *But* just to show *prove* that *Curl* & he were one.

Below these lines:

(e) Fate gives not here the short-lived youth to shine,

(f) But just to shew his Friendship, Curl, was thine.

(g) For him

A partly erased line between the two passages (evidently JR's error) reads: Alass no longer on this Earth he shone

P--n *in line (c) is William Pattison, one of Curll's minions who is said to have died in Curll's house. Pope jestingly assumes that he is an invention of Curll's.*

III, 147-48. P. 191.

At top of the page, evidently continuing the passage at foot of p. 190:

(a) For Him the Beauties of the Bar deplore;

(b) All Drury wept but graceless Harry *Edmund* swore

(c) For Him each Alehouse, Him each Gill-house mourn'd

(d) And answ'ring Gin-shops sow'rer Sighs return'd

Graceless Harry *in line (b) is possibly Curll's son Henry.*

III, 149-50. P. 192.

To left of l. 150: p. 204.

III, 167-72. P. 196.

III 167 Ah *Dennis*! *Gildon* ah! what ill-starred *frantic* rage

III 169 Blockheads with reason wicked wits *Men of Wit* abhor,

III 171 Embrace, embrace *again* my sons! be foes no more!

Ll. 169-70 are bracketed, with the comment: inf.

At top of the page:

(a) 172. Lo Dunton, *Purney* Horneck, Glories of their Race,

(b) Concanen, Cook and Mitchel's ruefull Face

(c) Cook, great of Stomach, Dunton great *feirce* of Mind,

(d) With thousand thousand nameless Names behind!

(e) How proud, how pale, how pensive is *all* their chear!

(f) How Rhymes eternal gingle in their Ear!

(g) Pass these v. 195

At top of this passage, a note: Quote Jacob p. 304. *At left of its first line:* v.172 -gone. *Beside it, vertically:* See 1 Ed. v. 153.

Between verse text and Notes:

(h) See next two slipshod Muses -- with Heads -- vid. inf. * p. 151.

(i) With Tresses sta-- and never wash'd

(j) H--d & W--y glories of their race, vid. sup.

At foot of the page:

(k) See Pix & slipshod W-- traipse along [vid. sup & p. 151]

(l) With Heads unpin'd but meditating Song.

(m) With Tresses staring from Poetic Dreams,

(n) And never wash'd but in Castalian Streams. v. sup. & 1 Ed. v. 149

[v. 169 These 2 verses were originally in ye *Essay on Criticism* aft. v. 33

(o) Tho' such, with reason, Men of Sense abhor,

(p) Fool against Fool, is barb'rous Civil War]

III, 173-78. P. 197.

III 173 Behold yon Pair, in strict *close* embraces join'd;

III 174 How like in *their* manners, and how like in *their* mind!

In the notes at v. 175-76, l. 10, following 1715, *the insertion:* by W. Wilkins.

At top of the page:

(a) See next two Slipshod Muses traipse along See v. 141

(b) In lofty Madness meditating Song

(c) With tresses staring from Poetic Dreams,

(d) And never washd but in Castalia's Streams.

(e) Heywood & W--, glories of their Race!

(f) Lo! Horneck's stern, Concanen's *& Mitchels* rueful face!

(g) Cook great of / Stomach p. 196

III, 179-80. P. 198.

Below l. 180: Ah Dennis -- 167. *At foot of the page, a note on Thomas Burnet and George Duckett:* 180. One of them was made *Consul* at Lisbon, ye other / *Commissioner* of Trade in ye Reign of K. George 1.st

III, 181-82. P. 199.

III 182 Of sober face, with learned *With visage from his shelves wth* dust besprent?

III 183 Right well mine eyes *eye* arede *aredes* the myster wight,

III 184 On parchment scraps y-fed, and *Wormius* hight, *He wonnes in Haulkes & Hernes, & Herne he hight.*

In the margin opposite this insertion: vid. Ed. prima.

At foot of the page:

He is a person unambitious, & of great Moderation, as appears by / his Wish in these lines / One hundred pound a year, I think would do / For me, if single, & if Married, Two.

III, 185-86. P. 201.

Below l. 186: But oh what scenes - See aft. v.222.

III, 187-90. P. 202.

At left of l. 189: p. 204

III, 197-200. P. 204.

III 197 How fluent *hony'd* nonsense trickles from his tongue!

III 200 While Kennet, Hare, *Br--d* and Gibson *W--y* preach in vain.

Below l. 200: Round him each Science -- as 1st Ed. III. 167-172. / On yonder inf.

At top of the page:

(a) inf. *Woolston*, ye *Dull Woolston* scourge of Scripture mark with awe, v. 147

(b) And duller *Jacob*, Blunderbuss of Law.

At foot of the page:

1st Ed. v. 172 Woolston &c. sup.

(c) *-Tale* On yonder part what Fogs of gather'd Air

(d) Involve ye Scene! There musefull sits *Mattaire*.

(e) But where ye thickest Darkness veils ye place

(f) W--m, B--y, all the poring Race,

(g) v. 189 A lumber house of Books in ev'ry head,

(h) Are ever reading, & are never read.

(i) But who is he v. 181

Between lines (c) and (d) of this passage, the insertion: And Jacob. W--m *in line (f) is unidentified.*

III, 201-16. P. 205.

Ll. 201-8 are bracketed and marked with a caret.

III, 217-30. P. 206.

III 229(227) He look'd, and saw a Sable Socr'rer rise, *Seer arise*

III 232(230) And ten-horn'd fiends and Giants rush to *threaten* war.

*Ll. 225-30(*223-28*) are bracketed, with caret. Between ll. 228 and 229:*

(a) Strange Knights on Pegasean Horse advance. *(b)* And Lilly-handed Ladies joyn in dance.

At 229 n, ll. 6-7(1. 5) actually represented *is inserted to replace* introduced.

At top of the page:

(c) inf. But oh! What scenes, what Miracles behind?

(d) Now stretch thy Views, & open all thy Mind.

(e) He look'd, & saw a sable Seer arise

(f) Swift to whose hand --- 228.

(g) Strange Knights, & Pegasean Steeds advance,

(h) And Lilly-handed Virgins joyn in dance.

(i) All sudden --

The last couplet above is marked with a delta for deletion.

At foot of the page:

(j) sup. But oh! What Scenes, what Miracles behind? 1 Ed. v. 183.

(k) Now stretch thy Eye *View* & open all thy Mind!

(l) Then wondrous Sounds, unknown to nature, rise,

(m) Then wondrous Sights, unseen by Mortal Eyes.

(n) All sudden, Lyons roar, *Gyants roar* *Gorgons hiss* & Dragons glare

(o) Feirce Gyants, Feinds, & Furies threaten War!

III, 231-44. P. 207.

III 233(231) Hell rises, Heav' descends, and dance *meet* on Earth,

III 234(232) Gods, imps, and monsters, *Gods, Mortals, Fairies* music, rage, and mirth

III 236(234) Till one wide *full* conflagration swallows all.

III 237(235) Thence *Then* a new world to Nature's laws unknown,

III 239(237) Another *Cynthia* her new journey *progress* runs,

Ll. 245-52(243-50) *are bracketed. In l. 244*(242), Egg *is underscored.*

At foot of the page:

(a) 1 Ed. v.243<*TE,245*> No word the King could speak; yet ask'd in thought,

(b) What God or Daemon all these Marvels wrought?

(c) To whom

III, 245-52. P. 208.

Ll. 253-54(251-52) *are bracketed with a* 2, *and, on p. 209, ll. 255-56*(253-54) *with a* 1 *to indicate intention to rearrange.*

At foot of the page, continuing passage at foot of p. 207:

(a) To whom the Sire: in yonder Cloud behold,
(b) Whose fluid *sarcenet* skirts are edgd with flamy *tinsel* Gold,
(c) A Godlike Youth: See *Jove*'s own Bolts he flings,
(d) Rolls ye loud Thunder, & ye Tempest wings.

Beside this passage, the notation: See 1 Ed.

III, 255-72. P. 209.

Ll. 271-72 are bracketed and marked with a caret.

At foot of the page:

255-6 Alluding to two sublime Verses of Dr. Young.
260 Alluding to a Noble Verse of Mr. Addison.

III, 277-78. P. 212.

III 278 To me committing their eternal *immortal* praise,

III, 279-82. P. 213.

III 281 Tho' long *all* my Party built on me their hopes,
III 282 For writing pamphlets, and for roasting *burning* Popes;

In l. 282, Popes *is underscored.*

III, 283-90. P. 214.

III 286 To Dulness, *Ridpath* *Boyer* is as dear as *Mist*.
III 287 Yet lo! in me what authors *Poets* have to brag on!
III 290 Should wag two serpent-tails in *at* *Smithfield* fair.

Immediately below l. 290: Far better Fates - p.215 *At 281 n,* and dyd City Poet / in 1722 *is inserted in place of* and there dyed.

III, 291-306. P. 215.

Ll. 291-94 are bracketed, with comment: sup; *ll. 301-2 with comment:* inf. *and ll. 303-4 with a caret.*

At top of the page, the first four lines bracketed.

(a) in vain Still in rotation, like a Rolling Stone,

(b) Thy giddy Heaviness shall lumber on,

(c) marg. From one low Patron to another stray,

(d) And lick up ev'ry Blockh^{d} in its way.

(e) Thy Dragons U-- & L-- shall taste,

(f) And from each Show rise Sillier than ye Last.

At foot of the page:

(g) Far better Fates, my Son, attend thy reign,

(h) Wits shall oppose, & Criticks write in vain;

(i) Thy Dragons, Peers & Potentates shall taste,

(j) And from each show rise duller than ye last.

(k) From humble Booths, to Theatres, & Courts,

(l) Her Seat imperial *Dullness* now transports.

(m) To aid her cause -- 305

To right of the third line above: Still in rot.<*ation: III 295*> Sup.<*ra*>. *In the fourth line* duller *overwrites a word now illegible.*

In line (e), U-- & L-- *presumably mean* Universities & Lords.

III, 313-20. P. 217.

III 317 This, this is he, foretold by ancient rhymes *Lays* *by ancient Bards foretold*

III 318 Th' *Augustus*, born to bring Saturnian times *days!* *an Age of Gold!*

Ll. 319-20 are bracketed. Below l. 320: (a) B-- sit oer Poems, *Cibber* over Plays.

At top of the page, bracketed with a marginal notation that reads 318. /Age of gold / marg., *these verses:*

(b) I see th' unfinish'd Dormitory wall, [See 1. Ed. v.275]

(c) I see ye Savoy totters to her Fall,

(d) The Sons of *Isis* reel ye Townsmen's sport,

(e) And Alma Mater Lies dissolv'd in Port. Swift.

At foot of the page:

(f) Beneath whose reign shall wondring Britain see

(g) Her boasted *Newton*, C--ys Deputy

(h) Knight each Sr Richard for his wretched *Sr Richard knighted for adopted* writ,

(i) And thee, my *Ambrose*, thee, prefer'd for *Wit*.

(j) *Benson*, sole Judge of Architecture sit,

The third line above is marked for deletion; the fourth is marked with a 2 *and the last with a* 1, *indicating intention to rearrange.*

In line (a), B-- is presumably Bubb Dodington. In line (g), C--y *is Walter Carey, Warden of the Mint when Newton was Master of the Mint.* Swift *in (e) seems not to be a cue but perhaps evidence that this line was Swift's contribution.*

III, 321-22. P. 218.

After l. 322: [No more MS.]

III, 323-24. P. 219.

To right of l. 323: p. 217 at top

Epistle to Burlington

INTRODUCTION

1

THE ONLY SURVIVING AUTOGRAPH of the *Epistle to Burlington* is a single folio leaf, measuring 11⅞ by 7¼ inches, preserved in the Pierpont Morgan Library. It contains on its two sides sixty-four lines of the poem, plus a few marginal and interlinear additions (some later incorporated, some not) amounting to twelve lines more. This body of verse, when augmented by subsequent revisions and insertions (and in one instance contracted by the postponement of eight lines to a later point), eventually constituted the entire epistle up to the description of Timon and his villa (ninety-eight lines).

The cue for one of these later insertions—on Sabinus and his son: ll. 89–98 of the *TE* text—is already present in the autograph beneath Pope's l. 46 (TS, 2:27). Though it is of course impossible to be certain, the available evidence suggests that this passage was already in existence when Pope began to copy out the present manuscript—perhaps as one of several sketches gathering toward "ye Gardening Poem" of which he spoke to Spence in May of 1730;[1] for the occurrence of the same cue twice below Pope's l. 76 (TS, 2:59, 60) presumably indicates that these lines were to be the first on the autograph's next leaf, now destroyed or lost.[2] Line numbering seem also to confirm the prior existence of this insertion. To his fortieth line Pope correctly assigns the marginal figure "40," but to his fiftieth the figure "60," on no discernible ground unless to accommodate the ten verses devoted to Sabinus and his heir.

The autograph reveals also some characteristic hesitations about the ordering of verse paragraphs. If second thoughts prompt Pope to interpolate Sabinus before Vitellio/Villario, third thoughts apparently prompt him to reconsider. Accordingly, he cancels the Sabinus cue beneath his l. 46, firmly numbers the Vitellio/Villario lines both "First." and "(1)"—probably at the same time entering their cue to the right of the canceled Sabinus cue—and at this point either drops a "2." beside a "Thro'" already present beneath l. 76 (TS, 2:59) or drops both number and cue to the left of other catchwords that he now strikes out. Sabinus, we may guess, is slated on reflection to follow Vitellio/Villario because it illustrates the impermanence of undertakings not responsive to "Sense" or "the Genius of the Place" through two generations and so has broader implications than the example of Vitellio/Villario, who tires of the fussy artifices of his manufactured landscape within a decade.[3]

Meantime, the poet has rethought the placing of ll. 47–54/64 (TS, 2:28–38). This is the paragraph acknowledging the economic trickle-down of rich men's extravagances to benefit the poor, while at the same time proposing an alternative based on productive use. As it stands in the autograph, the passage arises from and comments on the general scene of conspicuous consumption sketched in the preceding forty-six lines:

> Yet hence the Poor are cloathd, ye Hungry fed
> Health to himself, and to his Infants Bread
> The Lab'rer bears: What the hard Heart denies
> The Charitable Vanity supplies.
> ~~Wouldst thou do better? Let~~
> ~~What better can be? till~~ the Golden Ear
> Another Age shall see
> Imbrown the Slope and nod on the Parterre,
> Deep Harvests bury all his Pride has plann'd
> And laughing Ceres re-assume the Land.

On reflection, Pope has numbered this passage "3).", thus reassigning it to follow rather than precede the sketches of Vitellio/Villario and Sabinus and son. His thought is perhaps that "hence" of l. 47 and "better" of l. 51/61, as well as "the hard Heart" of l. 49, take on additional cogency if the passage is seen to address not merely a generalized scene of consumption but the activities of specific individuals, and (more important) the age's ordinary oversights rather than its egregious follies. Placed after the somewhat sympathetic (even touching?) portraits of Vitellio/Villario and Sabinus, with the earlier generic "hard Heart" and "charitable Vanity" now relocated more personally in these recognizable contemporary types and at the same time extended to the reader by the shift from "the" to "thy" (ll. 49, 50; TS, 2:30, 32),[4] the passage picks up new voltage.

Just possibly, the notion of successive generations brought to mind by Sabinus and his son also inspired what I take to be the happiest single alteration in the autograph. This is the alteration from the seeming resignation of "What better can be?" and the dependence on human resolve of "Wouldst thou do better?" to a serene affirmation of nature's indwelling power over the long term to make good her losses—a confidence always latent in the figure of laughing

Ceres if taken seriously, but now for the first time clearly precipitated out: "Another Age *shall* see. . . ." (italics mine). Once put forward as nature's judgment on the misguided efforts of Vitellio/Villario and the two Sabinuses, no great step was required to transfer her doom to the works of the poem's exemplary offender: Timon. Thus, the passage could be postponed to become the coda of that portrait.

No great step was required, but, as in some other poems we shall be looking at, it was not taken at once. The eight lines on the "better" way remained attached to Vitellio/Villario and Sabinus and son through three printed editions and were removed to the conclusion of the Timon protrait only with the *Works, Volume II,* of 1735.

2

A contemporary transcript of the entire *Epistle to Burlington* survives today at Chatsworth among the Devonshire archives. It is said to be in the hand of John Ferret, Burlington's estate agent, and must have been copied by him from the manuscript that Pope sent to Burlington on 4 April 1731, eight months before he printed. An accompanying letter shows that Burlington had seen the poem in a still earlier state when the two men last met. On that occasion there had been talk of using it to preface Burlington's second publication of Palladio drawings (a book never actually issued), and apparently with this possibility in mind Pope now tells him he has added some "lines . . . toward the End of the Common Enemy, the bad Imitators and Pretenders, which perhaps are properer there than in your own mouth."[5]

The passage referred to must be a version of ll. 23–38 of the TE text, which in the Chatsworth transcript and the first three printed editions *succeed* the Timon portrait and are introduced by a couplet—

In you, my Lord, Taste sanctifies Expence,
And Splendor borrows all her Rays from Sense

—whose first line follows an altogether narrower trajectory than the line replacing it in the editions of 1735 and after:

'Tis Use alone that sanctifies Expence.

What possibly happened here is that when Pope moved the eight lines ending in the Ceres image, with its strict reminder in the quasi-legal senses of "reassume" that man is steward not owner, and made them the turning point of his poem (abuses ended, restoration begun), he saw more plainly than before that from the first mention of "Miser" and "Prodigal" his underlying theme had been "use"—something, in fact, on the order of an Augustan parable of the talents. "Use," moreover, had clear logical connections with his declared theme of "Taste," being the fruition in which informed taste eventuated but which false taste betrayed by amassing possessions it was unable to enjoy: "Not for himself he sees, or hears, or eats."

At any rate, whatever the background of associations impelling him, Pope was at pains to improvise for the 1735 editions a substantial passage that further exemplified this theme, matching now his introductory couplet on Burlington and architecture with another on Bathurst and farming:[6]

Who then shall grace, or who improve the Soil?
Who plants like BATHURST, or who builds like BOYLE.
'Tis Use alone that sanctifies Expence,
And Splendor borrows all her rays from Sense.
  His Father's Acres who enjoys in peace,
Or makes his Neighbours glad, if he encrease;
Whose careful Tenants bless their yearly toil,
Yet to their Lord owe more than to the soil;
Whose ample Lawns are not asham'd to feed
The milky heifer and deserving steed;
Whose rising Forests, not for pride or show,
But future Buildings, future Navies grow:
Let his Plantations stretch from down to down,
First shade a Country, and then raise a Town.
(*TE*, ll. 177–90)

A Tory or Country-Party point of view, no doubt; and deeply indebted, some would say, to the facilitating myths of an aggressive agrarian capitalism. Let that be as it may. Whatever their partisan resonances, there is present in these lines, as in those that follow on the falling arts it is Burlington's province to renew, what has been rightly called an ideal of civilization: a Britain Redivivus in which "Art and Nature, Beauty and Use, Industry and Decorum, should be reconciled, and humane culture, even in its most refined forms, be kept appropriately aware of its derivation from and dependence on the culture of the soil."[7] If the vision is more paternalistic than we can now approve, it nevertheless invokes principles of sound stewardship of natural resources and a consciousness of responsibilities attending on privilege that our own Utopian fancies would do well to imitate.

In April of 1731, when he sent the poem to Burlington, Pope had thought it appropriate to attach the new lines on the "bad Imitators and Pretenders" to the address with which the poem ends—saying to Burlington, in effect, "Though your rules will inevitably be abused by all who follow new models slavishly, proceed nevertheless with your Palladian ambitions:

make falling Arts your care,
Erect new wonders, and the old repair. . . ."

Once the Ceres passage had been transferred, however, to become the judgment of nature on pride (in some sense an English version of *Ozymandias*) and once the lines on responsible estate management had been conceived, the whole set of the poem was necessarily affected. The "golden Ear," seen now as the assured final transmutation of the gold of miser and prodigal, provided a natural bridge to the lines on cheerful tenants and deserving steeds, and both passages together swept grandly toward the Vergilian dream of the poem's close. Dwelling in this context on the mistakes of those who

> Reverse your Ornaments, and hang them all
> On some patch'd dog-hole ek'd with ends of wall

would have been unbearably anti-climactic, and the lines were accordingly removed to the forepart of the poem with the other instances of misguided "Expence."

3

The Chatsworth transcript clearly represents a somewhat later stage of the poem than the autograph fragment, even though the latter, in appearance, gives every sign of having set out to be fair copy, possibly even printer's copy. Postponement of the Ceres passage to follow Vitellio/Villario and Sabinus and his heir has already taken place in the transcript, which in some instances (e.g., "proud Versailles thy Glory falls"—l. 41; TS, 2 : 19) also incorporates revisions made in the autograph. On the other hand, the transcript is by no means a simple copy of the autograph with its indicated revisions and rearrangements consummated. Even within the portion of the poem that the autograph fragment contains, the transcript twice differs in ways for which the autograph offers no precedents. Before Pope's l. 29, for instance (TS, 1 : 69), a couplet inserted interlinearly elaborates the nature of "Sense":

> 'Tis in yourself you must this Light perceive,
> Jones & Le Notre have it not to give.

In the transcript, with no authority whatever from the autograph, this couplet appears several lines further on, immediately following the compliment to Stow. Equally significant is the allusion found in the transcript's variant of this couplet. Where the autograph names Jones and Le Notre, and then as a canceled replacement Gibbs and Bridgman, the transcript introduces an entirely new name: Mansart—i.e., J. H. Mansart, who was responsible for much of the finest French building, including parts of Versailles, during the two decades from 1684 to 1706. Both variants make it plain that the text from which John Ferret copied the Chatsworth transcript, though evidently later than the autograph, was in some degree independent of it.[8]

A knottier problem is posed by revisions in the autograph that appear in the published texts but not in the transcript. A typical cluster is found in ll. 37–40 of the autograph (TS, 2 : 10–17), ll. 35–38 of the Chatsworth transcript. In the autograph these read:

> Begin with Sense *this*, of ev'ry Art the Soul,
> Parts answ'ring Parts shall slide into a whole,
> Nature shall *join* you; Time shall make it *and yr Work shall* grow
> A work *Something* to wonder at—perhaps a Stow

The transcript incorporates the revised reading of l. 37, but not those of ll. 39 and 40. The printed texts incorporate all three.

Two explanations seem possible. Either the copy from which the printer set type for the early editions afforded an oddly eclectic text, close in general form to the Chatsworth transcript, yet incorporating some revisions from the autograph while eschewing others; or, alternatively, revisions in the autograph that appear in the printed editions but not in the transcript found their way into the autograph during the eight months between the date when the manuscript from which Ferret copied was sent to Burlington and the date of publication. At that time (we may suppose), via the autograph, these improvements reached the copy prepared for the printer. The latter supposition seems considerably more plausible.[9]

4

A modest light possibly is thrown on the formation of some passages in the epistle by five scraps of paper preserved with other Pope memorabilia at Mapledurham House. These contain portions of the poem, primarily from the description of Timon's villa, beginning with the final four lines on Sabinus's heir (ll. 95–98 of the TE text) and ending with a fragment of the passage on imitators and pretenders—which, as we have seen, were in the manuscript sent to Burlington (therefore also in the Chatsworth transcript) and in the early editions immediately succeeded *TE*, l. 180.

Scrap 1, a torn half sheet, has *TE*, ll. 95–98, followed (again as in the transcript, the early editions, and the cues of the autograph) by *TE*, ll. 169–76.[10] Scrap 2, verso of scrap 1, has *TE*, ll. 99–112, lacking ll. 103–4, which are, however, found in the transcript and early editions. Scrap 3 continues with *TE*, ll. 115–34, lacking ll. 123–26 and 129–32, which are likewise found in the transcript and the early editions. Line 115 is introduced by the gloss: "His Garden." Scrap 4 is the verso of Scrap 3 and contains *TE*, ll. 147–48 and 151–62—again present in the transcript and early editions. Line 163 is introduced by the gloss: "att Dinner." Scrap 5 contains *TE*, ll. 179–80 in the pre-1735 form and *TE*, ll. 23–36, lacking ll. 29–34—which also exist in the transcript and the early editions. (In the Chatsworth transcript, the equivalents are ll. 145–52, 159–60).

Neither the authority nor the chronological status of these fragments is easy to determine. They are very crudely copied in an unsophisticated hand (not Martha or Teresa Blount's) on scraps of paper seemingly torn off for the occasion. They reflect an arrangement of the poem similar to that of the autograph cues, the Chatsworth transcript, and the early editions: i.e., Sabinus and his heir are directly followed, as in these other texts, by the lines on trickle-down-extravagance and nature's judgment on pride; and the passage on blunderers and imitators comes after the description of Timon's villa. The absence from the fragments of many lines found in the transcript suggests that they represent an early phase of the poem when its parts were still expanding. The last half-dozen lines on Scrap 5, for instance—

just as they are, yett shall yr Noble rules
fill half ye land with imitating fools
who random drawings from yr sheets shall take
& of one beauty many plunders[11] make
shall call ye Winds thro long Arcades to roar
proud to catch cold att a venetian door

—have a rough and ready completeness as they stand, even though not yet smoothed out grammatically or satirically enlivened by the brilliant inventions of ll. 29–34.

Yet if the Mapledurham fragments *are* early, it is difficult to explain why they remain closer to the printed texts than the Chatsworth transcript and why they sometimes incorporate readings that are found only among revisions to the autograph and in the early editions—revisions that presumably, therefore, date later than April of 1731, when Pope sent a completed manuscript to Burlington that did not include them. Thus (to cite only two examples) where the transcript has in l. 63 (*TE,* l. 95) "Instead of these one flourishd. Carpet views," Scrap 1 and the early editions have "One boundless Green, or," etc. Likewise, where the transcript has in l. 71 (*TE,* l. 173) "Wouldest thou Do better: Let the Golden Ear"—a reading derived from the autograph's first revision at this place but apparently oblivious of its second—Scrap 1 and the early editions have "Another age shall see," etc.

All things considered, it seems probable that the Mapledurham fragments do represent an early stage of the poem's composition—it is very difficult, in fact, to account for them in any other way. Yet anomalies remain that without benefit of the missing leaves of the autograph (or perhaps even with them) put certainty beyond reach.

NOTES

1. *TE,* 3. 2:xxi; Spence, No. 310.

2. Jonathan Richardson, Jr., son of Pope's close friend the painter, entered collations from this autograph on unbound sheets of the quarto *Works, Volume II,* of 1735, now in the Huntington Library. His entries, which stop with l. 76 of the autograph, and his notation at that point ("No more MS") make it abundantly clear that even circa 1735–36 there was no access to the rest of the poem in manuscript. That Pope withheld or had destroyed the rest because of names or jottings in the portrait of Timon that he did not wish seen seems to me a reasonable hypothesis.

3. The *TE* editor silently omits many of the notes and glosses that the poet inserted in his editions from 1735 on, in particular one that sheds light on Vitellio/Villario: "For want of this *Sense,* and thro' neglect of this Rule"—i.e. to consult the genius of the place—"men are disappointed in the most expensive undertakings. Nothing without this will ever please *long,* if it pleases *at all.*"

4. This may of course be read as if addressed to a composite Vitellio/Villario/Sabinus/and son rather than to the reader.

5. *Correspondence,* 3:188.

6. Pope may refer to the introduction of Bathurst and farming when he says in the letter of 4 April: "the few Words I've added in this Paper may . . . ease you too in another respect," meaning that he has eased Burlington by making the good health of Britain less directly independent on one man and one art.

7. F. R. Leavis, "Pope," in his *Revaluation* (London: Chatto & Windus, 1935), p. 80. One should not overlook here in Pope's emphasis on arboriculture the conscious or unconscious influence of an economic and ecological need strongly felt in England since John Evelyn's time: the need for intensive reforestation of a country that had become almost entirely denuded of its trees by centuries of iron-smelting and, most especially, by the shipbuilding required for the great wars with France, 1689–1713. The effect of this and other mundane considerations on the evolution of the new English landscape has yet to be studied.

8. Pope's habit of continuous revision makes nonce changes of this sort less surprising than they might be in another writer. See the revisions inserted in a copy of his octavo *Works, Vol. II,* of 1736 (Griffith, No. 430), apparently intended for a later edition but never used: see *Collected in Himself* (Newark, Del.: University of Delaware Press), p. 322, 344–45.

9. That any inference from this autograph is possibly suspect may, however, be the lesson of the revision in l. 10 (TS, 1:37). Here Pope first wrote, and in all texts till 1744 retained, the reading "Rarities for Sloan." In 1732 the word "Rarities" drew fire for being insufficiently explicit from Thomas Cooke, one of Pope's dunces, who wrote:

> What knowledge, what Meaning, is conveyed in the word *Raritys!* Are not some Drawings, some Statues, some Coins, all Monkish Manuscripts, and some Books, *Raritys?* . . . Fy, fy; correct and write,
>
> Rare Monkish Manuscripts for Hearne alone,
> And Books for Mead, and Butterflys for Sloane.
>
> *Sir Hans Sloane* is known to have the finest collection of Butterflys in *England,* and perhaps in the World.

During several editions Pope paid no attention to this stricture—perhaps rightly, since Sloane's rarities were not merely butterflies but of many sorts, and the satirical point, after all, was directed toward those who collected rarities simply because they were rare, despite the fact that the knowledge required to appreciate them belonged only to serious students like Sloane. In the so-called deathbed edition of his epistles, however, Pope revised to "Butterflies for Sloane," a reading that is clearly visible in the autograph as an alternative to "Rarities."

Was this, then, an alternative that occurred independently to Pope during the poem's composition, as the *TE* editor supposes, but was rejected at the time, "perhaps because Pope had not been able to discover for certain whether Sloane was a serious lepidopterist"? or was it inserted in the autograph in response to Cooke's criticism (an example of Pope's usual readiness to learn from enemy as well as friend) at some point between 1732 and the period (c. 1735–36) when the young Richardson made his collations, this reading among them? The second view seems to me far more credible. If it is sound, then in at least one instance (another, I believe, involves the word "dirty" in l. 9, which like "Butterflies" appears to be written in a different ink) the autograph of the epistle has become a record not merely of compositional alterations, but of alterations made after publication and so casts a degree of question over any compositional conclusions drawn from it.

10. Scrap 1 also omits *TE,* ll. 171–72; but as this leaves a predicate without subject, I assume it to be a copyist's slip.

11. Without much doubt this is another copyist's slip, despite its curious relevance.

OF TASTE:

AN

EPISTLE

To The

EARL of BURLINGTON.

TIS strange, my Lord, the Miser should employ
His cares to gain the Wealth he cant enjoy:
Is it less strange, the Prodigal should waste
His Wealth on that for which he has no Taste?
Not for himself but Fountain, Gems he buys;
Pictures, to raise the noble shout of Praise;
For Topham, Drawings & far-fetchd Designs;
For Pembroke, Statues, brazen Gods, and Coins;
Rare Monkish Manuscripts for Herne alone;
And Books for Mead, & Rarities for Sloan.
Think we all these are for Himself? No more
Than his fine Wife, alas or finer Whore.
For what has Virro builded, painted, planted?
Only to show how many Tastes he wanted.
What brought vile Carnio's ill-got wealth to waste?
Some Dæmon whisperd, "Carnio have a Taste".
Heav'n visits with a Taste the wealthy Fool,
And needs no Rod, but [illegible] with a Rule.
The merry Fates to punish aukward Pride,
Bids Babo build, and [illegible] Guide;
A [illegible] Sermon! at each Years Expence,
That never Coxcomb reachd Magnificence.
Oft' have You hinted to your Brother Peer,
A certain truth, which many buy too dear:
Something there is, that should precede Expence,
Something to govern Taste itself—'Tis Sense;
Good Sense, which only is the Gift of Heav'n,
And tho' no Science, yet is worth the Seven:
To build, to plant, whatever you intend,
To rear the Column, or the Arch to bend,
To swell the Terras, or to sink the Grot;
In all, let Nature never be forgot:
Con-

OF T A S T E :
AN
E P I S T L E
To The
EARL of BURLINGTON.

, we think ~~the Miser still imploys~~

still
stet ~~All own it strange~~, that Misers ~~should~~ imploy
~~his cares~~ ~~What he ne'r enjoys~~

~~all own~~, that Misers still employ
'Tis strange, ~~my Lord, the Miser should employ~~

Their Cares to gain ye Wealth they ne'r ~~they ne'r~~ | ~~never can enjoy~~
~~His Cares To gain the Wealth he cant~~ enjoy:

~~will~~
Is it less strange, the Prodigal should waste

~~That~~ His to purchace what he ne'r can~~not~~ taste?
~~His~~ Wealth ~~in that for which he has no Taste~~?

~~Not for himself, but Fountain, Come he buys~~;

of price for Howard, or for
Pictures, ~~to raise the noble shout of~~ Guise;

sought
For Topham, Drawings & far-~~fetchd~~ Designs;

Curio dirty
For ~~Pembroke~~, Statues, brazen Gods, and Coins;

Rare Monkish Manuscripts for Herne alone;

Butterflies
And Books for Mead, & Rarities for Sloan.

Think we all these are for Himself? No more

~~(My Lord)~~ (My Lord)
Than his fine Wife, ~~alas~~ or finer Whore.

built and
For what has Virro ~~builded~~, painted, planted?

Only to show how many Tastes he wanted.

~~proud~~ Sir Shylock's
What brought ~~vile Carrio's~~ ill-got Wealth to waste? ~~vile Arthur's~~

Knights shou'd ~~Arthur have~~
Some Daemon whisper'd, "~~Carrio~~ have a Taste."

Heav'n visits with a Taste the wealthy Fool,

Mo--s
And needs no Rod, but ~~Sh--~~ ++ with a Rule.
~~B--n~~

See sportive
~~The merry~~ Fate~~s~~, to punish aukward Pride,

Dado sends ~~gives~~ him such a
Bid~~s~~ Babo build and ~~sent him (as a)~~ Guide;

~~T' inforce this truth by~~ ~~evry~~
standing
A ~~Living~~ Sermon! at each Years Expence,

That never Coxcomb reachd Magnificence.

Oft' have You hinted to your Brother Peer,

A certain truth, which many buy too dear:

Something there is, that should precede Expence,

Something to govern Taste itself -- 'tis Sense;

Good Sense, which only is the Gift of Heav'n,

fairly
And tho' no Science, yet is worth the Seven:

~~'Tis in yourself you must this Light perceive~~,

To build, to plant, whatever you intend,

To rear the Column, or the Arch to bend,

To swell the Terras, or to sink the Grot;

In all, let Nature never be forgot:

Con-

---

we think
'Tis strange, ~~all own~~, that Misers
still employ

Their gain ye enjoy~~s~~
~~His~~ cares to ~~gain the~~ Wealth they ner

or or eats,
Not for himself he sees, ~~he~~ hears,
~~Ne'r can~~
Artists must chuse his Pictures
Music, Meats

He buys Designs
~~To buy~~ for Topham Drawings &

For Pembroke Statues, & for Curio
Coins

Rare Monkish --

And Books

Must have ye skill
~~Shall~~ Bishops, Lawyers, Statesmen

To build, to plant, judge Paintings, w^t y^y will

And
Then ~~Then~~ why not honest Kent our Treaties
draw

Bridgman explain ye Gospel, Gibs ye Law?

A Light, wch in yourself y^u must perceive

~~Jones & Le Nôtre have it not to give~~
~~For Gibs & Bridgman~~ have it not to
give

Jones & LeNôtre

Consult the Genius of the Place in all;
That tells your Waters or to rise, or fall,
Here bids ascend the future Mount, & here
Invites to scoop the circling Theatre.
Begin with Sense, of ev'ry Art the Soul,
Parts answ'ring Parts, will slide into a whole,
Nature shall join you; Time shall make it grow
A Work to wonder at—perhaps a Stow.[x]
Without it, proud Versailles! thy Glory falls,
And Nero's Terraces desert their Walls.
The vast Parterres a thous[an]d hands shall make,
Lo! Cobham comes, and floats them with a Lake;
Or cut wide Views thro' mountains to the Plain,
You'll wish your Hill & sheltred Seat again.
(3.) Yet hence the Poor are cloath'd, the Hungry fed;
Health to himself, and to his Infants Bread
The Lab'rer bears: What thy hard Heart denies
Thy charitable Vanity supplies.
Another Age shall see the golden Ear
Imbrown thy Slope, & nod on thy Parterre,
Deep Harvests bury all thy Pride has plann'd
And laughing Ceres re-assume the Land.
First. (1) Behold Villario's ten years toil compleat!
His Arbours darken, his Espaliers meet;
The Wood supports the Plain; the Parts unite,
And strength of Shade contends with strength of Light;
His blooming Beds a waving Glow display,
Blushing in bright Diversities of Day,
With silver-quiv'ring Rills mæander'd o'er:
—Enjoy them You! the Master can no more:
Tir'd with the Scene Parterres & fountains yield,
He finds at last he better likes a Field.

2. Thro'

So Thames's Store who adds a creeping Rill,
This year may dip it, but the next shall fill;
Ev'n in an Ornament, its Place remark,
Nor in an Hermitage set Dr Clark.

[x] The Seat & Gardens of the Lord Viscount Cobham in Buckinghamshire.

Consult the Genius of the Place in all;

That
~~Twill~~ tells your Waters or to rise, or fall,

bids ascend
Here ~~shall it point~~ the future Mount, & here

Invites to scoop the circling Theatre.

sense
Begin with ~~this,~~ of ev'ry Art the Soul,

Parts answ'ring Parts, will slide into a Whole,

Time shall make it
Nature shall join you; ~~and y^r Work shall~~ grow

A Work
~~Something~~ to wonder at -- perhaps a +Stow.

proud Versailles! thy Glory
Without it, ~~Babylons proud Garden~~ falls,

And Nero's Terraces desert their Walls.

The vast Parterres a thous.d hands shall make,

Cobham
stet Lo! ~~Bridgman~~ comes, and floats y.m wth a Lake

Or cut wide Views thro' Mountains to ye Plain,

You'l wish your Hill & sheltred Seat again.

~~Thro' his young Woods &c~~ Behold Vi

| 3.) Yet hence the Poor are cloathd, ye Hungry fed

Health to himself, and to his Infants Bread

The Lab'rer bears: What Thy hard Heart denies

Thy charitable Vanity supplies.

~~Wouldst thou do better?~~ Let
~~What better can be! till~~ the golden Ear
Another Age shall see

Imbrown thy Slope, & nod on thy Parterre,

Deep Harvests bury all thy Pride has plann'd

And laughing Ceres re-assume the Land.

At
~~Nor waits one Curse alone on the Profuse, Ev'n when they gain the Taste, yy lose the Use.~~

First. (1) ^ ^ Behold ~~Vitellio~~'s ten years toil compleat!
Villario's

Espaliers
His Arbours darken, ~~and~~ his ~~Arches~~ meet;

The Wood supports the Plain, the Parts unite,

And strength of Shade contends with strength of Light

y waving Glow
His bloom~~ing~~ Beds a ~~dazling Scene~~ display,

in
Blushing ~~with~~ bright Diversities of Day,

With Silver-quiv'ring Rills maeander'd o'er:

Master
--Enjoy them You! the ~~Owner~~ can no more:

Tir'd with the Scene Parterres & fountains
~~The gouty Owner on his Couch is thrown~~ yield

He finds at last he better likes a Field.
~~And humbly begs you that you walk alone.~~

2. Thro' ~~Vatia's~~
~~At~~ ~~Thro'~~ &c
~~Timon's~~

To Thames s store who adds a creeping Rill,

may but
This year ~~he~~ dig~~e~~ it, ~~&~~ ye next shall fill.

Evn in an Ornament, its Place remark,

Nor in an Hermitage set Dr Clark.
D ++ +

+The Seat & Gardens of the
Lord Viscount Cobham in
Buckinghamshire.

Epistle to Burlington

NOTES TO THE TRANSCRIPTS

Page:Line

1:9 gain *overwrites* gather.

1:10 they *is altered from* he.

1:14 that *is altered from* the, *and* Misers *from* Miser.

1:16 gain *is altered from* gather, *and* Wealth *from* what.

1:17 T *of* To *overwrites* t.

1:21 *The first* he *is altered from* they.

1:25 Howard *overwrites* Methuen; *in the margin* n'er can *is very nearly overwritten by* Artists must chuse *(l. 23). Howard is probably Hugh Howard (1675–1737), a painter and noted collector. Methuen is Sir Paul Methuen (1672–1757), whose collection of Italian paintings is still intact and may be viewed today. (Names identified in the TE notes, 3. 2:134–39, are not enlarged upon here.)*

1:26 Guise *is possibly John Guise (B.A. Oxford 1701, d. 1765), regimental commander and eventually general, who bequeathed a valuable collection of paintings to Christ Church. His shout might be "noble" because of his courage in soldiering. An alternative is Sir John Guise (c. 1677–1732), brother-in-law of Pope's friend Edward Blount. But I can find no evidence that he had collecting or artistic interests.*

1:31, 36 dirty *appears to be a later insertion, as does* Butterflies.

1:33 Monkish *overwrites* Books.

1:45 Carrio *is unidentified.* Arthur *is Arthur Moore (1666?–1730), mentioned in the "Epistle to Dr. Arbuthnot," (ll. 23–24).*

1:46 Knights *may be Robert Knight of Barrels in Warwickshire (son of the fugitive cashier of the South Sea Company), who in 1727 had married Bolingbroke's half-sister. To the extent that his wealth came from his absconding father, Pope may have thought it "ill-got." But I find no evidence of lavish building.*

Page:Line

1:49 Mo——s *is probably the builder Roger Morris (1695–1749), and the reference is perhaps a hit at Dodington, at whose seat at Eastbury Morris was working at least by late 1732, when possibly the name was first inserted in the autograph.*

1:50 Sh—— *seems to have been altered at some point to* R——, *i.e. Thomas Ripley.*

1:51 B——n *is probably William Benson (1682–1754), whom Pope also ridicules in the* Dunciad *(1729: III, 325; 1743: IV, 110).*

1:54 The . . . Fates *overwrites an erasure.*

1:57 sent . . . a *overwrites an erasure.* Bridgman *is of course Charles Bridgman (d. 1738), one of the earliest of the "liberating" landscape gardeners;* Gibs *is James Gibbs (1682–1754), the architect.*

1:58 *The last word in the line is* evry, *canceled.*

1:60 Living Sermon *overwrites an erasure, possibly of* Truth inforc'd; at *overwrites* by; each *overwrites an erasure, possibly of* evry.

1:62 hinted *overwrites an erasure, possibly of* whispred.

1:69 *In the manuscript,* perceive *appears to be struck through, but it is impossible to be sure.*

2:22 a . . . hands *overwrites an erasure, and* shall make *two illegible words, possibly* now rise.

2:27 *The canceled letter or number before* Thro' *is probably* 2, *relating to* 1 *at l. 42 and* 3 *at l. 28.*

2:30 Thy *seems to have been altered originally from* the.

2:32 Thy *is altered from* The. *In this and the preceding alteration Pope may also have tried out* His *and* His *before settling for* Thy *and* Thy.

2:36 *The first* thy *overwrites* the.

2:42 *Pope has struck out both carets.*

2:49 His blooming *and the* B *of* Birds *overwrite an erasure.*

2:52 With silver-quiv'ring *and the* R *of* Rills *overwrite an erasure.*

The Chatsworth Text

A LETTER TO THE EARL OF BURLINGTON

Tis Strange, my Lord the miser Should Imploy
his Cares to Gain the Wealth he Can't enjoy
Is it Less Strange, the Prodigal Should Waste
his Wealth to Purchase What he Cannot Taste
not for himself but Fountain, Geems he Buys
Pictures of Price, for Howard, or for Guise
For Topham Drawings and far sought Designs
For Curio Statues, brazen Gods and Coins
Rare monkish manuscripts for Hearne alone
And Books for Mead: and Rarities for Sloan
Think Wee, all these are for himself; no more
Than his fine Wife, alas! or finer Whore.
For What has Virro builded, Painted, Planted
only to Shew how many Tastes he Wanted
Heaven visits With a Taste the Wealthy Fool
And needs no Rod but Shxx With a Rule
See! Sportive Fate, to Punish aukward Pride
Bids Bubo build, and gives him Such a guide
A Standing Sermon: at Each Years expence
That never Coxcomb reachd. Magnificence
Oft have You hinted to Your Brother Peer
A Certain Truth, Which many buy Too Dear
Something there is, that Should precede Expence
Something to Govern Taste it Self—tis Sense
Good Sense Which only is the Gift of Heavn
And tho no Science, Yet is Worth the Seven
To Build, to plant, Whatever You intend
To Rear the Column, or the Arch to bend
To Swell the Terras, or to Sink the Grot
In all, Let Nature never be forgote
Consult the Genius of the Place in all
That Tells the Waters or to rise or fall—
Here bids ascend the future mount, and here
Invites to Scoop the Circling Theatre.
Begin With Sense of every Art the Soul
Parts answ'ring Parts Shall Slide into a Whole
Nature Shall joyn You: and Your Work Shall Grow
Something to Wonder at—Perhaps a Stow
Tis in Your Self You must this Light Perceive.
Mans art <= Mansard?> <,> LeNotre have it not to give:
Without it, Proud Versailles: thy Glory falls,
And Nero's Terrasses desert their Walls
The vast Parterres a thousand hands Shall make
Lo! Bridgman Comes and Floats them With a Lake
Or Cut Wide Views thro' mountains to the Plain
You'l Wish Your Hill and Shelterd. Seat again
Behold Vitellio's ten Years Toil Compleat
His Arbors Darken, his Espaliers meet
The Wood Supports the Plain, the Parts Unite
And Strength of Shade Contends With Strength of Light
His Bloomy beds a Waving Glowe Display:
Blushing in bright Diversities of Day:
With Silver quiv'ring Rills Maeand'r'd o'er
—Enjoy them, You, the Master can no more
Tir'd of the Scene Parterres and Fountains Yield
He finds at Last True Joy is in the Field
Thro' his Young Woods, how Pleas:d Sabinus Strayd:
Or Sate Delighted in the thick'ning Shade
With Annual Joy the red'ning Shoots to greet,
And See the Stretching Branches Long to meet
His Sons Fine Tast an op'ner vista Loves
Foe to the Dryads of his Fathers Groves
Instead of these one flourishd. Carpet views
With all the mournfull Family of Yews
the thriving Plants ignoble Broomsticks made
Now Sweep those allies they Were Born to Shade
Yet hence the Poor are Clothd. the hungry Fed
Health to himself: And to his Infants Bread
The Lab'rer bears: What thy hard heart Denies
Thy Charitable Vanity Supplies - - - - -
Wouldest thou Do better: Let the Golden Ear
Inbrown thy Slope: and nod on thy Parterre
Deep Harvests bury all thy Pride has Plann'd
And Laughing Ceres, Re asume the Land—
At Timons Villa let us Pass a day:
Where all Cry out: What Sums are thrown away
So proud So grand, of that Stupendous air
Soft and agreeable Come never there
Greatness With Timon, dwells in Such a draught
as Brings all Brobdignag before Your thought
To compass this, his Building is a Town
His Pond An ocean his Parterre a Down
Who but must Laugh When he the Master Sees

A Puny Insect Shiv'ring at a Breeze
Lo! What huge heaps of Littleness around
The Whole a Labour:d Quarry above ground.
Two Cupids squirt before a Lake behind
Improves the keenness of the northern Wind
His gardains next Your admiration Call
On ev'ry side you look behold the Wall
No Pleasing Intricacies intervene
No Artful Wildeness to Perplex the Scene
Grove nods at Grove, Each Ally has a Brother
And half the Platform just reflects the other
The Suffering Eye inverted Nature Sees
Trees Cut to Statues, Statues thick as Trees
With here a Fountain never to be play:d
And here a Summerhouse, that knows no Shade—
Here Amphitrite Sails thro' myrtle bow'rs
There gladiators fight and dye in flow'rs
unwater:d See the Drooping Sea horse Mourn
And Swallows roost in Nilus Dusty Urn.
Behold my Lord advances o'er the green
Smit With the mighty Pleasure to be Seen
But soft—by regular approach—not Yet
First thro the length of Yon hot Terras Sweat.
And When up ten Steep Slopes You've draggd. your thighs
Just at his Study Door he'l bless Your Eyes
His Study! With What authors is it Stord.
In Books not authors, Curious is my Lord
To all their Dated Backs he turns You round
These Aldus printed, those De Suëul has bound
Lo some are vellom and the Rest as good
For all his Lordship knows: but they are Wood
For Lock or Milton tis in vain to Look
These Shelves admit not any modern book
And now the Chappels Silver bell you hear
That Summons You to all the Pride of Prayr
Light Quirks of Musick: broken and uneven
Make the Soul Dance upon a jig to heaven
on painted Cielings you Devoutly Stare
Where Sprawl the Saints of Verrio or Laguerre
on gilded Clouds in fair expansion lye
And bring all Paradise before Your eye
To Rest, the Cushion and Soft Dean invite
Who never mentions Hell To Ears polite
But hark the Chiming Clocks to Dinner Call
A hundred footsteps scrape the marble Hall
The rich Buffet well Color'd Serpents grace
And gaping Tritons Spew to Waish Your face
Call not this Dinning, that an Eating Room
No thats a Temple, this a Hecatomb
A Solemn sacrifice, perform'd in State
You Drink by measure, and to minutes eat
So quick retires each flying Course Youd. Swear
Sancho's Dread Doctor and his Wand Were there
Between each act the trembling Salvers Ring
From Soupe to Sweet wine and God bless the king
In Plenty Starving, tantalizd. in State
And Complisantly helpd. to all I hate
Treated Carest, and tird. I Take my leave
Sick of his Courtly Pride from Morn to Eve
I Curse Such lavish Cost, and Little Skill
And Swear no Day Was Ever Past So Ill
In You my Lord Taste Sanctifies Expence
For Splendor borrows all her rays from Sense
You Show us Rome was Glorious not profuse
And Pompous Buildings once Were things of use
Just as they are: Yet Shall Your noble Rules
Fill half the Land With Imitating Fools
Who randome drawings from Your Sheets shall take
And of one Beauty many blunders make
Load some vain Church With old Theatric State
Turn Arcs of Triumph to a Gardain Gate
Reverse Your ornaments, and hang them all
on Some Patcht Doghole ek'd With Ends of Wall
That With four Slices of Pilaster on't
And lac'd With bits of Rustic, is a front
Shall Call the Winds thro Long Arcades to Roar
Proud to Catch Cold at a Venetian Door
Conscious they act a True Palladian Part
And If they Starve they Starve by Rules of Art
Yet thou Proceed: be fallen arts thy Care
Erect new Wonders and the old Repair
Jones and Palladio to themselves Restore
And be what'ere Vitruvius Was before
While Kings Call forth th'Ideas of thy mind
Proud to Accomplish What Such hands Designd.
Bid harbors open; Public Ways Extend
And Temples: Worthier of the God: ascend
Bid the Broad arch the Dangerous flood Contain
Far chearing Beacons light their Subject main
Back to its bounds th' incroaching Surge Command
And Roll obedient Rivers thro the Land.
Till Tyber Stoop to Thames and his White hall
Rise With the fortune of Romes Capitol
These Honors: Peace to happy Britain Brings
These are Imperial Works and Worthy Kings

The Mapledurham Fragments

Scrap 1

one boundless green or florished carpett views
with all ye mournfull Family of Yews—
the thriving plants ignoble broomsticks made
now sweep those allies they were born to shade
yett hence the poor are clothed the hungry fed
health to himself & to his infants bread
another age shall see ye golden Ear
imbrown thy slope & nod on thy parterre
deep harvests bury all thy pride has planned
& laughing Ceres re'assume the land

Scrap 2

att Timons Villa lett us pass a day
where all cry out, what Sums are thrown away
so proud so great of yt <that> stupendious Air
soft and agreeable come never there
to compass ys <this> his building is a town
his pond an ocean his parterre a down
who but must laugh, the Master when he sees
a puny insect shivering att a Breeze
lo! what huge heaps of littleness around
the whole a laboured Quarry above ground
two cupids squirt before: a lake behind
improves ye keeness of ye northern Wind

Scrap 3

His Garden: no pleasing intricacies intervene
no artfull Wildness to perplex ye Scene
grove nods att grove each ally has a Brother
and half ye platform just reflects ye other
the suffering Eye inverted nature sees
trees cutt to statues, statues thick as trees
with here a fountain never to be played—
and there a summer house that knows no shade
behold my Lord advances o'er the green
smit with ye mighty pleasure to be seen
his study wth what authors is it stored
in books! not authors curious is my Lord

Scrap 4

& now ye Chapels Silver Bell you hear
yt [that] summons you to all the pride of prayer
light quirks of musick, broken & uneven
make ye Soul dance upon a jigg to heaven
on painted Ceilings you devoutly Stare
where sprawl the Saints of Verio or Laguerre
to rest ye Cushion & soft Dean invite
who never mentions Hell to Ears polite
att dinner in plenty starving tantalized in state
& complaisantly helped to all I Hate
treated caressed & tired I take my leave
sick of His civill pride from morn to Eve

Scrap 5

<In> you my Lord taste sanctifies expence
for splendor borrows all her rays from Sence
you show us Rome was glorious not profuse
& pompous buildings once were things of Use
just as they are, yett shall yr Noble rules
fill half ye land with imitating fools
who random drawings from yr sheets shall take
& of one beauty many plunders make
shall call ye Winds thro long Arcades to soar
proud to catch cold att a venetian door

The First Satire of the Second Book of Horace or The Epistle to Fortescue

INTRODUCTION

1

AMONG THE MANUSCRIPTS of Pope's maturity, that of his first Horatian imitation,[1] now in the Berg Collection of the New York Public Library, is comparatively simple and straightforward. This is perhaps because (in a sense) the poet's first or "Ur-manuscript" was Horace's Latin poem, which determined some aspects of the larger structure for him. Once this structure had been reconceived in terms contemporary to the poet's Augustan audience, it was certain to attract whatever elements were most germane to it from the inventory of satiric intentions, themes, verse fragments, images, and intonations that were jostling in his mind at the time. This was the period of the early 1730s, when Pope was working on the epistles to Burlington (14 December 1731) and Bathurst (15 January 1733), and on the *Essay on Man* (to appear in four epistles: 20 February, 29 March, 8 May, 1733; 24 January 1734), while at the same time putting together the "Bill of Complaint"—composed by snatches and laminated of many layers—which became the *Epistle to Dr. Arbuthnot* (2 January 1735), not to mention the poem we are concerned with here (15 February 1733).[2] These circumstances together—i.e. a structure ready to hand and a swirl of poetic "ideas" eager to find a local habitation—probably account for much of the ease and speed with which, we are told, the poem was produced—in "about two days," says Bolingbroke, who is credited by Pope with having suggested that he imitate this satire in the first place.[3]

Some hint of the creative chaos from which, as Swift noted, Pope could eventually cause a poem to "rise" may be implicit in a fragment of paper preserved at Mapledurham House, though the document is as difficult to interpret as it is to account for. One side of the fragment, in an unidentified hand belonging neither to Martha nor Teresa Blount, bears five couplets, the first two of which constitute ll. 223–24 and 239–40 of the *Epistle to Bathurst,* as we now know it; the last three, ll. 77–78 and 29–32 of this first Horatian imitation:

to balance fortune by a just expence
joine with Oeconomy, magnificence

is there a Lord yt <that> knows a cheerfull Noon
without a fidler flatterer or buffoon

His 2d poem

Who'ere offends att some unlucky time
~~Slides~~[4] slides into verse & hitches in a rhyme

lett all yr Muse's softer art display
lett ‸smooth ye tunefull Lay‸ ~~Carolina~~[5]
Lull with Amelia's liquid Name ye Nine
& sweetly flow thro all ye Royal Line

On the opposite side of the fragment, in the same hand, are again five couplets, this time all from the imitation of Horace (35–36, 75–84):

for justly Caesar scorns ye poets Lays
it is to History he trusts for praise
Peace is my dear Delight—not fleury's more
but touch me, & no minister so sore
Who'eer offends att some unlucky time
Slides into verse & Hitches in a Rhyme

Slander & poison dread from Delia's Rage
Hard words or Hãging if yr judge be—
from furious Sappho yett a sadder fate
poxed by her Love, or libelled by her Hate

The inscription of couplets from the Horatian poem on the same scrap of paper with couplets from the *Epistle to Bathurst* and under the vague rubric "His 2d poem" inclines one to suppose that we have here some early stage in the growth of the imitation or in the growth of both poems. Yet the readings of these verses are far closer to the final printed edition than to the known manuscripts—are, in fact, all but identical. A notable instance is the couplet on Sappho, here matching to a tittle what appears in the first printed text; whereas the closest we come to this in the manuscript is a couplet somewhat differently phrased, quite differently positioned (Sappho's lethal fury, in the manuscript, is listed among other threats to the poet's life; it has not yet been moved to become Sappho's version of the natural power to hurt that all creatures share, each in its way) and given to the poet's interlocutor:

> Alas my Friend! yr days can n'er be long.
> In flow'r of youth you perish for a Song.
> How oft from Sapho have I feard yr fate
> P—xd by her love or poisond by her hate
> (TS, 8:3–4; see also 6:4–5)

Since I see no plausible way to reconcile this couplet in its later form with an early phase of the poem, the only safe conclusion to be drawn from the Mapledurham fragment—if, indeed, it is not simply an arbitrary selection of verses culled for reasons unknown from a late stage in the poem's development—is that possibly some sort of apology for satire and for himself as satirist had become linked in Pope's mind with some sort of mock panegyric of the royal family, and that this association of ideas *may* have been arrived at even before Bolingbroke planted the suggestion of imitating Horace's satire in his mind. If so, this too might help account for the remarkable expedition with which the work was completed. All this, however, is the purest speculation.

2

Reporting to Swift on the day after publication that he had sent him both the imitation—"a Parody from Horace"—and the *Epistle to Bathurst,* published a month earlier, Pope adds:

> I never took more care in my life of any poem than of the former of these, nor less than of the latter: yet every friend has forc'd me to print it, tho' in truth my own single motive was about a score of lines towards the latter end, which you will find out.[6]

Without much doubt, the passage referred to is all or part of ll. 105–32 of the printed poem, which in the first edition lacked ll. 119–20 and so amounted to twenty-six lines. It was here that Pope had taken the crucial step of reconceptualizing Horace's poem by (1) expanding its image of the support the satirist Lucilius had from men of influence and affairs like the great Scipio and Laelius Sapiens, even though Lucilius spared no one in his satire but Virtue and her friends, and (2) applying it to his own situation at Twickenham.

What the manuscript allows us to follow in some detail is the careful shaping of this theme (TS, 6) as the poet brushes away all that might contaminate it with the wrong colorations—impressions of private self-indulgence or domestic trifling (the ranking of teacups, for instance, or dressing food for dinner); allusions that could be misinterpreted as politically dissident or malcontent (the evocation of so many great French patrons of the arts under Louis XIV, always subject to contemptuous dismissal as Jacobite nostalgia, paticularly when cited by a Roman Catholic); and comparisons too scholastic or backward-looking ("another Scipio," TS, 6:51; "Here Cyrus-like," TS, 6:55). What remains at last is a sturdy English and Popian disdain for bought poets in the phrase "pension'd Boileau" (which does not fail, however, to glance tacitly at Walpole's kind of "Pensioner," noticed in the *Epistle to Bathurst,* ll. 339–402, especially 394); an appraisal of the Sun King's rule along official eighteenth-century British lines as *of course* unbearably oppressive ("ev'n in Louis' reign"); and a rather disarming portrait of a poet doing in his country retreat what a long tradition of moral philosophy urged that any man should do.

If, as the Mapledurham fragment *may* indicate, the notion of defending his role as satirist had associated itself early on in Pope's mind with some mischievous cadences inspired by the royal family, his gradually clarifying sketch of a private world where the satirist is valued and supported by great men for his contribution to the common welfare might easily call forth, as its antithesis and justification, a teasing representation of a public world in which a poet is seen to be blocked from both epic and lyric outlets by the inappropriateness of the available subjects, who are at the same time his unappreciative audience—all this managed, however, as a compliment to their nicer taste in art and their strenuous concern for deeds not words in life.

The shaping of this passage on royalty in the manuscript (TS, 1–3) is fully as instructive as that of the passage on Virtue and her friends. From what appears to have been at first largely an intended romp through the incongruity of writing poetry at all about such a prosaic family as the Hanoverians, it refines soon into a demonstration of the ease and grace with which a certain contemporary poet can make one "Sacred to Ridicule" simply by sliding one's name into verse. And not only into verse, but into such verse as can fix forever in the grotesque museum of comedy both a king's passion for warlike postures (and, perhaps, in the big sounds added in the second edition, his well-known tendency to temper tantrums and outright bluster):

> What? like Sir Richard, rumbling, rough and fierce,
> With ARMS and GEORGE and BRUNSWICK crowd the Verse?
> Rend with tremendous Sound your ears asunder
> With Gun, Drum, Trumpet, Blunderbuss & Thunder?
> (Ll. 23–26)

and a queen's and princess's susceptibility to insipid flatteries such as put even the Nine Muses to sleep and only a Cibber could bear to write:

> Then all your Muse's softer Art display,
> Let Carolina smooth the tuneful Lay,
> Lull with Amelia's liquid Name the Nine,

And sweetly flow through all the Royal Line.
(Ll. 29–32)

The last verse, with its hovering pun on "Line" and its delicate intimations of the havoc to be expected if this poet's ink actually did flow through the entire family, seems a particularly exquisite invention; and since it appears unaltered in printed text, manuscript, and Mapledurham fragment, may belong among those genial seeds, or "nameless somethings," as the *Dunciad* calls them, from which this poem ultimately sprang.

3

What is very clear, at any rate, both from printed text and manuscript, is that three themes very much occupy Pope's mind as he sets about reinterpreting Horace's Latin. One is the low estate of literature as symbolized in a royal family indifferent to it, a situation that has not always and everywhere existed, as the names of Charles, James, Louis, Dryden, and Boileau are calculated to remind us. Another is his own future as a satirist in view of the scandal lately raised about him (aided and abetted, he seems to have felt, perhaps even generated, by court and administration busybodies) when his ridicule of Timon's villa in the *Epistle to Burlington* was misread as ridicule of the Duke of Chandos and his estate "Cannons."[7] The third—a theme that impinges heavily on the other two—is Robert Walpole.

Thanks to Fortescue, the poem's interlocutor, who at one time was Walpole's private secretary as chancellor of the exchequer, Pope had stayed on good terms with the minister through the 1720s, even occasionally attending his "Sunday-Tables."[8] By 1733, however, for reasons that are obscure but probably have much to do with the temperaments of the two men as well as with the administration's treatment of Gay,[9] Pope's undisguised admiration of Bolingbroke,[10] and latterly (perhaps) some real or imagined action or inaction on Walpole's part in connection with the Chandos affair that Pope felt to be unfriendly,[11] all this had changed. How much changed, the imitation bears vivid witness. Somewhat crudely evoked in the manuscript through the usual battery of Opposition referents,[12] Walpole's power and its implications become in the printed text the unidentified but pervasive presence to which all other topics relate, from the unnamed persons at the opening "to whom my Satire seems too bold" to the frankly acknowledged supreme authority at the close (higher, it is hinted, than either church or throne) at whose nod "The Case is alter'd" and "the Judges laugh."

Though this is not the place to offer a reading of the finished poem,[13] those who examine the manuscript with care will have little difficulty in seeing that a question of power and its right uses—power of the king, the minister, the law, and the satirist—lies at its heart.

4

Physically, the manuscript consists of four leaves, the first measuring in inches, 12 9/16 by 8 1/16, the second and third, 12 9/16 by 8, and the fourth 6 1/2 by 7 7/8. To the second leaf is affixed a scrap of paper measuring 5 7/16 by 3 5/8, whose verso contains a physician's prescription and whose recto Pope has used as a sort of scratch pad for the material on the first leaf, no doubt while still in bed.[14]

As a whole, the manuscript is less appealing to the eye than many of Pope's, largely because it shares with the manuscript of the *Epistle to Dr. Arbuthnot* the unusual characteristic of not being entirely an autograph. As readers will quickly notice, only pages 3, 7, and 8 are wholly in Pope's hand. The intrusion of an amanuensis is probably owing to the circumstance that Pope at the time was ill at Lord Oxford's in Dover Street and therefore, having mentally formulated parts of the poem, as was often his habit, had them taken down by one of Oxford's secretaries in a first draft to be worked on anew.

NOTES

1. Though we know from Spence (Nos. 321a, 322) that Pope imitated "above a third" of Horace's satires and epistles, several of these remained unpublished and have not survived. Of the imitations known, this is the earliest.

2. The dates in parentheses are publication dates.

3. Spence, No. 321.

4. The copyist's first effort yielded something like "slitts."

5. Again a scribal slip.

6. 16 February 1733 (*Correspondence,* 3:438).

7. George Sherburn, "'Timon's Villa' and Cannons," in *Huntington Library Bulletin* 8 (1935): 131–52; John Butt, "A Master Key to Popery," in *Pope and His Contemporaries,* ed. J. L. Clifford and L. A. Landa (Oxford: Clarendon Press, 1949), especially pp. 46–47; and *TE,* 3. 2:172–74.

8. E.g. Pope to Fortescue, 5 August [1727] and 7 June 1730 (*Correspondence,* 2:441; 3:112).

9. From the point of view of his friends, Gay's failure to receive government patronage or a sinecure such as many far lesser men enjoyed was proof positive of the Walpole administration's cultural indifference.

10. During the 1730s, as the partisan spirit on both government and Opposition sides grew, this friendship was much harped upon by Walpole's writers.

11. Some unease on the point seems to lurk in Pope's rather cryptic remarks to Fortescue on 18 March 1733 (*Correspondence,* 3:357); and perhaps also in Butt, "A Master Key to Popery," where most of the "misinterpreters" of Timon's villa are seen to be court and administration creatures.

12. In the Opposition arsenal of innuendo, reference to "a Great Man" (TS, 3:28; 6:8; 8:7), "Macheath" (TS, 5:6, 7:30), "base Attorneys" who pervert the laws (TS, 9:2), and political "screening" of malefactors (TS, 7:16: see also 6:43; 8:19) were capable of being, and usually were intended to be, understood as hits at Walpole.

13. For a variety of interpretations, see "The Muse of Satire", *Collected in Himself: Essays Critical, Biographical, and Bibliographical on Pope and Some of His Contemporaries* (Newark, Del.: University of Delaware Press, 1982); Thomas Maresca, *Pope's Horatian Poems* (Columbus, Ohio: Ohio State University Press, 1966), pp. 37–67; and, *The Garden and the City: Retirement and Politics in the Later Poetry of Pope* (Toronto: University of Toronto Press, 1969), pp. 174–87.

14. The verso of the pasted-down fragment, which so far as can be ascertained reads, "Please to take one of / the Draughts going to Bed / and the other in the Morning. / For Mr. Pope." has been eliminated from the sequence of photographs and transcripts of this manuscript.

The first ~~thoughts~~ of a great Genius are precious—

The
FIRST SATIRE
of the Second Book of
HORACE.

Imitated in a Dialogue between W. F. Esq. H..... on ye one pt. and A. P. of T.... Esq. on ye other.

Fortescue—

P.
F×× I scarce can think it, but am told,
There are to whome my Satire seems too bold:
Scarce to wise Peter Complaisant enough,
And something said of Chartres much too rough.
Timorous by nature, of the rich in awe,
I come to Council learned in the Law.
You'll tell me like a freind, whate'r it be
My case; & (as you use) without a Fee.
F. "I'd write no more." P. Not write? but then I think;
And for my soul I cannot sleep a wink.
I nod in Company, I wake all night;
Fools rush into my head, & so I write.
F. "You could not do a wiser thing for your life
"Why if the nights seem tedious—take a Wife.
"Or talk with Hollins; Hollins ~~shall~~ will advice.
"Hartshorn, or something that shall close your eyes.
"[But ~~If you~~ must you write; ~~then sing~~ compile ~~the~~ your Sovereign's ~~why write~~ praise;
"You'll gain at least a Knighthood, or the Bays."
P. [What? like a torrent, rumbling, rough, & fierce,
With Arms, & George; & Fredrick, ~~charge~~ crowd ye verse?

<1>

The first thoughts of a great Genius are precious--

The

FIRST SATIRE

of the Second Book of

HORACE.

Imitated in a Dialogue between W.F. Fortescue

Esq. A on ye one p^{t}

and A.P. of T.... Esq. on y^{e}

other.

P.

F + + I scarce can think it, but am told
There are to whome my Satire seems too bold:
Scarce to wise Peter Complaisant enough,
And something said of Charters much too rough.
Tim ~~e~~ rous by nature, of the rich in awe,
I come to Council learned in the Law.
You'll tell me like a freind, whate'er it be
My case; & (as you use) without a Fee.

F. P.

"I'd write no more." Not write? but then I think;
And for my soul I cannot sleep a wink.
I nod in Company, I wake all night,
Fools rush into my head, & so I write.

F.

"You could not do a worse thing for your life
"Why, if the nights seem tedious — take a Wife.
will
"Or talk with Hollins; Hollins ~~shall~~ advise
"Hartshorn, or something that shall close your eyes.
our
But you ? ~~then sing~~ compile ~~the~~ Sovereign's
"~~If you~~ must write, ~~why write Augustus~~ praise;
"You'll gain at least a Knighthood, or the Bays."

P. [What? like a torrent, rumbling, rough, & fierce,
crowd
With Arms, & George, & Fred'rick, ~~charge~~ ye verse?

Then, all at once, my Genius
~~[illegible]~~ to display,
Let Carolina smooth the tuneful lay
With soft Amelia's name delight the nine.
And smoothly flow thro' all the Royal line —
Alas! our Monarch scorns Poetick lays,
'Tis to History he trusts for praise
Thrown in his face, 'tis what he'll scarcely support;
~~[illegible]~~
his own Laureates, who
~~[illegible]~~ From ~~[illegible]~~, or ~~[illegible]~~ preach at court.

F. Better be Cibber, ~~[illegible]~~ who you will —
" Than thus blaspheme all money & Quadrille,
weightiest
" Abuse the City's ~~[illegible]~~ men in metre
ridicule the Rich yet
" Or ~~[illegible]~~ ~~[illegible]~~ hurt in Peter
Even Those ~~[illegible]~~ you name not, hate you
" ~~[illegible]~~
all Priors P. — What should ail 'em!
~~And shakes at every Balaam every Timon.~~
F. " ~~[illegible]~~ trembles for themselves in Balaam.
Each good man
~~[illegible]~~

P. Yet all men none deny
~~[illegible]~~ have their pleasures, ~~[illegible]~~
~~To~~ Scarsdale his ~~[illegible]~~, Dashy his ~~[illegible]~~ Ham-pye,
~~[illegible]~~
sips & dances
Fidotta ~~[illegible]~~ till she see
The doubling Lustres dance as well as she.
Ball
A Boy Lords Fanny loves, a Wench his Brother
Like in all else as one egg to another
my Joy it is ~~[illegible]~~ in Rhime to speak
~~[illegible]~~ as plain
downright
As ~~[illegible]~~ Shippen or as old Montaigne
Whose ~~their~~ Soul
~~[illegible]~~, as certain to be lov'd as seen,
Stands ~~[illegible]~~ boldly
~~[illegible]~~ forth, nor keeps a thought within
In mine, what spots (for spots there are) appear
Will
~~Shall~~ prove at least the Medium must be clear
whatever is in my head, is in my quill
~~[illegible]~~
think will
Verseman or Proseman, ~~call~~ me which you like.
Papist or Protestant, or both between,
Like Good Erasmus in an honest mean,
In Moderation placing all my glory,
While Tories call me Whig, & Whigs a Tory.

Then at once my
~~Or~~ all ~~my Tuneful~~ Genius
~~Then the whole art of Numbers~~ to display

tuneful
Let Carolina smooth the ~~tunefull~~ lay

With soft Amelia's name delight the nine

And sweetly flow thro' all the Royal Line—

Alas, our Monarch scorns Poetick lays,

It is to History he trusts for praise

~~<he cant>~~
~~nicer Ear can scarce~~ support,
~~Praise~~
Thrown in his face tis what he ~~cant~~ 'll scarce

~~such~~
~~He bears no Panegyricks of that sort~~,

his own Laureates, who
~~Except~~ From ~~Laureats~~, or ~~that~~ preach at Court

[Better
F. "~~Yet I'd~~ be Cibber, Harris, who you will—

thus blaspheme all mony
"~~Rather~~ Than ~~rail at Riches~~ & Quadrille,

weightiest
"Abuse the City's ~~best good~~ men in metre

ridicule the Rich y[t]
"Or ~~laugh at~~ ^ ~~that put their~~ trust in Peter

Even Those ~~whom~~ you name not, hate you—
~~"Who scapes you now, expects you still to rhyme on~~
P.--What shd ail em?

~~And shakes at evry Balaam, evry Timon.~~
F. ~~"Alas! y[y]~~ trembles ~~for~~ himself in Balaam.
Each good man

~~Why faith tis hard~~

~~who'l deny~~
~~this is~~
P. Yet all men none deny ~~I have mine~~
~~All Mortals~~ have their pleasures, ^ ~~<Wine>~~

Bottle,
To Scarsdale his ~~<Hare>~~. Darty his Ham pye.
Scribling
~~Ham pyes are Dartye's joy, & <C ts> mine~~

sips & dances
Ridotta ~~plyes the sideboard~~ 'till she see

The doubling Lustres dance as well as She.

Ball
A Boy Lord Fanny loves, a Wench his Brother

Like in all else as one egg to another

My Joy it is ~~to~~ ~~Tis all my Joy~~ in Rhime to speak
~~write~~
~~I love in verse to speak my mind~~ as plain
downright
As ~~Master~~ Shippen or as old Monteigne

Whose ~~Their~~ Soul
~~In them~~, as certain to be lov'd as seen,

Stands ~~nobly~~ boldly keeps
~~The Soul stood~~ ^ forth, nor ~~kept~~ a thought within.

In mine, what spots (for spots there are) appear

Will
~~Shall~~ prove at least the Medium must be clear.

WWhatere is in my head, is in my quill
~~Virtue I love, at Vice alone I strike~~

think will
Verseman or Proseman, ~~call~~ me which you like,

Papist or Protestant, or both between,

Like Good Erasmus in an honest mean,

In Moderation placing all my Glory,

While Tories call me Whig, & Whigs a Tory.

× The lines are weak, another's pleas'd to say

Then all at once the ...

Yet good & just, are themes you sing

not over good & just a generous King

Some Heros ... or Statesmen ... may find

Such to your Name have been wondrous kind

The bold Maeonian ...

Paints & immortalizes ...

Heros & Statesmen read: but our Epistles

So good a Jest & fit, a great man whistles

... can detect, & scarce support

... on Laureate or ...

The lines are weak <another's> pleasd to say

& Boden writes a hundred such a day
Ld Fanny

with
Or ~~like~~ bold Budgel starting
frõ ye course

line

~~<Start full>~~

~~Paint ye bold chief~~

~~The fiery Ode with Budgels fire & force~~

Paint the
~~Paint~~ angels trembling at ~~his~~ falling Horse

Few panegricks touch their nicer ear

And

scarce
They can bear their Laureats twice a Year

my
& justly Caesar scorns Then all at once &c to—
~~ye Line~~
Poets lays

—Flattry his ears detest
& scarce support
Frõ his own —
Court

It is to

Genrous
Yet Good & Just <are> themes y^{u} ~~chuse~~ sing

'Why not our good & just & genrous King?

I'll take ye first Occasion, I declare

then
'~~Or~~ some <Stat> Hero ~~yet~~, or Statesman y^{u} may find,

'Such to y^{r} <Homer> have been wondrous kind

The bold Maeonian y^{t} in lofty s^{ds}

Paints & immortalises blood & w^{ds}

Heros & Statesmen read: but oer Epistles

Of Good & Just & Fit, a Great Man whistles

~~Our Prince, my friend, disdains Poetick Lays. It is to History---~~

~~thing~~ his
~~Flattry<s> a thing his ears detest & scarce support~~

his
~~Frõ their own Laureates or who~~

But done abruptly how ye K. w^{d} stare?

Evn this were Better, I

all maintain it still

F* [There are, I forget, you only lashed the dead
The heirs of such ... [illegible]
I'd never use my Satyr, or my Sword,
To draw, when no man gives me a cross word
When neither Cutthroats, Cheats or Theives appear;
Nor Lonsdale, Bl—n or Macheath are near.

P. Save but our Army; & let Love incrust
Swords, Pikes & Guns with everlasting Rust!
Peace is my Hearts delight - not Fleury's more;
But touch me & no Minister so sore:
Who ere offends, at some unlucky time,
Slides into verse, & hitches in a ryme,
the wight's ... no more nor less, his whole life long,
Than the sad Burthen of some merry song.

[Slander & lyes expect from W—'s rage
Hard words or Hanging if your Judge be P—
[Its proper Power to hurt, each creature feels,
Bulls aim their horns, & Asses lift their heels:
But no man wonders he's not stung by Pug.
and a Bears ... not to kick, but Hugg.
mistaken Monsieur
... Lamend fled to save his throat,
When nothing was in danger but his Note.

1 (Slander & lies expect from W—'s rage.
Hard words or hanging if your Judge be Page.
But go drink with Walpole or with Charters eat,
They'll never poison you, they'll only cheat.
... my Weapon is to write, & to be ... short
Whether I lie in country or at Court, ...
If mild old age, with faint but chearful ray
Attend to gild the Evening of my day
Or Death's black wing already be displayd
To wrap me in the universal Shade;
Whether the darkend room to muse invite,
... [illegible]
With Pen and ink, or Mattrices & a clout
Like Lee ... or Budgell I will write &
... me Paper, Mattrices & a clout.
... abroad at home in Bedlam or ... in mint

or sick or well, or in my wits or out
or in my wits or out
With pen and ink, or mattrices & a clout
In Exile, Durance, Bedlam or ye Mint.
Like Lee I'll versify, like Budgel print

F. "['Twere safer yet you only lashed the dead
"The heirs of such would hardly break your head
I'd never use my Satyr, or my Sword,
To draw, when no man gives me a cross word,
When neither Cutthroats, Cheats, or Theives appear,
Nor Henly, Bl--n, or Macheath, are near.

our / let
P. Save but ~~the~~ Army! & ~~may~~ Jove incrust
Swords, Pikes, & Guns with everlasting Rust!
Hearts
Peace is my ~~dear~~ delight--not Fleury's more,--
But touch me, & no Minister so sore:
Whoere ~~Th~~ offends ~~wight~~
~~That wretched name,~~ at some unlucky time,
Slides into verse, & hitches in a ryme;
The ~~He'll be That Man's~~
Wight's ~~And is~~ no more ~~n~~or less, his whole Life long,
Than the sad Burthen of some merry Song.

[Slander & Lyes expect from W---ys rage
Hard words or Hanging if your Judge be P---

Its proper Powr to hurt
~~Its strength by nature evry~~ creature feells,
~~Where lies its strength~~ to hurt each
Bulls aim their horns, & Asses lift their heells:
But no man wonders he's not stung by Pug,
~~A Wolf will bite you, but a Bear will hug~~
And a Bears Talents not to kick, but hugg.
~~What wonder that you are not stung by Pug.~~
Mistaken Monsieur
~~Yet silly~~ Remond fled to save his throat,
When nothing was in danger but his Note.
1 | Slander & lies expect f[m] W---'s rage,
Hard words or hanging if your Judge be Page
~~Go~~
But drink with Waters, or with Charters eat,
They'll never poison you, they'll only cheat.

Weapon / my pen
[~~Now~~ My ~~Talent~~ is to ~~write~~, & to be
~~But to apply & cut the matter~~ short--
Country
~~Exile~~
Whether I live in ~~Country~~ or at Court,
~~Abroad, at home, in Bedlam or ye Mint Like Lee Ill versify like Budgel print.~~
If mild Old age, with faint but chearful ray
Attend to gild ye Evening of my day,
Or Deaths black wing already be displayd
To wrap me in the universal Shade;
the
Whether ~~some~~ darkend room to muse invite,
whitend / ~~Walls~~ / ~~I'l~~
Or ~~some plain bare~~ Wall provoke ye Skewr to write
~~whitend~~
~~Whether at home, in Bedlam or the Mint~~
With Pen and ink, or Mulbries & a clout
~~Like Lee I'll versify, like Budgell print~~
or Budgell I will write &
~~Deny~~ me Paper, Mulb'ries & a clout,
~~For sick or well, or in my wits or out~~
Abroad at ~~large~~ home, in Bedlam or ye Mint
Like Lee I'll ~~versify~~, ~~like~~ Budgel ~~print~~

~~or without~~
~~Or rich or poor, with paper~~
~~By G-- Ill write with mulbries~~
~~and a clout~~
~~Or sick or well, or in my Wits or out~~

~~Confind or sick, with paper or without~~
Or sick or well, in Bedlam or ye Mint
rich poor, with paper or with out
~~By G-d~~ Ill write
~~do't with Mulbries & a~~
Or or ~~clout~~
~~Or Rich or poor~~, sick, well,
Or in my wits or out
With pen and ink, or mulbries & a clout
In Exile, Durance, Bedlam, or ye Mint,
Like Lee I'll versify, like Budgel print

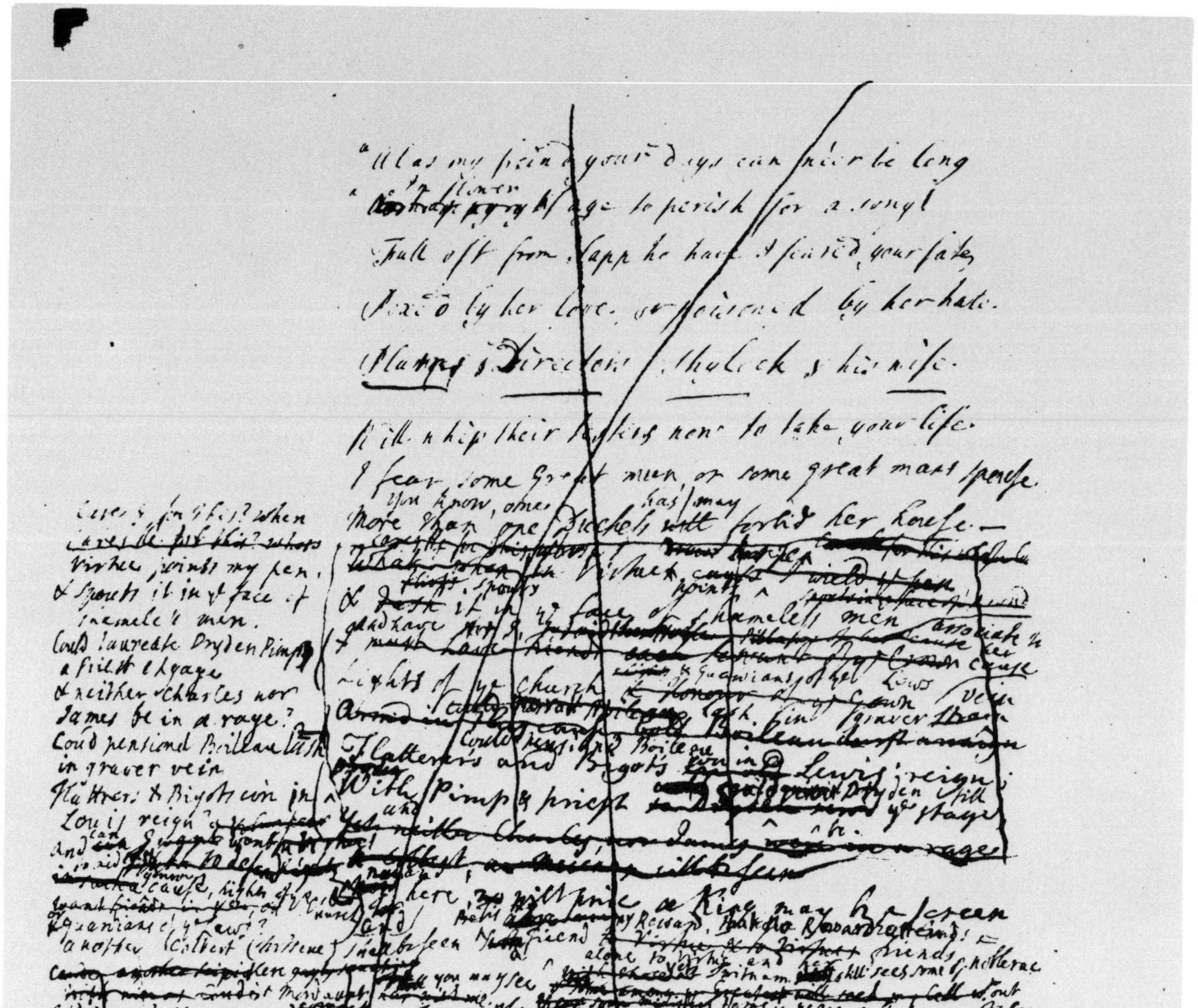

"Alas my friend, your days can ne'er be long
"In flower of age to perish for a song!
Full oft from Sapph he have I feared your fate,
Pox'd by her love, or poison'd by her hate.
Flattery's Directions / Shylock & his wife.
Will whip their [illegible] to take your life.
I fear some Great men, or some great man's spouse
More than one Duchess will forbid her house.

[illegible struck-through and interlined revisions]

Lights of ye Church [illegible]
Flatterers and Bigots ev'n in Lewis' reign.
With Pimp & priest [illegible] Dryden still ye stage

[illegible struck-through and interlined revisions]

No pimp of pleasure, & no Spy of State.
An eye that prys not, tongue that ne'er repeats,
Fond to spread friendships, pleas'd to cover heats,
Unplac'd, unpension'd, meaning all men well,
This all, who know me, know; who love me, tell.
And who, unknowing, slander, let 'em be
Scribblers or peers, alike are Mob to me.
This is my plea, and this my precedent,
Unless my learned Council shall dissent.

Cures? for this? when [illegible]
Virtue, points my pen,
& Spoots it in ye face of
shameless men.
Could laureate Dryden Pimp
& friar engage
& neither Charles nor
James be in a rage?
Could pensioned Boileau lash
in graver vein
Flatterers & Bigots ev'n in
Louis' reign
[illegible]
Mordaunt ye may see
to dress a dinner or to
[illegible]
the feast of [illegible] flow of soul

Care I for this? when
~~Cares he for this? whose~~
virtue points my pen,
& spouts it in ye face of
shameless men

Could laureate Dryden Pimp
& Priest engage
& neither Charles nor
James be in a rage
Could pensiond Boileau lash
in graver vein
Flattrers & Bigots evn in
Louis reign

can a Volunteer
And ~~can~~ I ~~want~~ want ~~in Virtue~~'s
⟵⟶
to aid ~~Truth to defend~~ ~~lights~~

genrous
~~in such a~~ ^ cause, Lights of y^e
~~want friends in you, oh~~ Church

or
~~&~~ guardians of ye Laws?

Another Colbert (Fortscue) shall be seen,
~~Condé another Scipio~~ Here ~~gayly shuntring~~

~~will~~
~~With him as Condé~~ & Mordaunt <has> with me

~~correct~~
Wd dress a Dinner or ~~wd~~ prune a tree

~~The <grave> Lamoignon softend at a Joke~~
To form
~~Design~~
~~Draw up~~ a Quincunx ~~dispose or dispose~~ ^
The Teacups range & discipline

~~<Here>~~ ~~<will>~~
Mordant ~~&~~ Cobham ~~oft here design~~
form the verdant Lines
To form ye Quincunx or to range
ye Vines
the orderd
~~embatteld~~ vines
To
~~Or spread ye Quincunx or to form~~
~~ye Lines~~

~~unconquerd~~)
en
Here (Spain forgott~~en brave~~
Mordant y^u may see

To dress ~~the Brocoli or~~ prune
a dinner or to
a ye tree

Or St John mingle wth ye friendly
bowl

Reason & y^e
The feast of ~~Eloquence &~~ flow of
Soul

"Alas my freind your days can ne'er be long
In flower
"~~<Unhappy>~~ of age to perish for a song!
Full oft from Sappho have I feared your fate,
Poxed by her love, or poisoned by her hate.
Plums and Directors, Shylock & his wife
Will whip their testers now to take your life
I fear some Great Man, or some great mans spouse
You know, one has|may
More than one Duchess ~~will~~ forbid her house—
~~Cares~~ he for this ~~whose~~ < >
~~Cares He for this when~~ ~~draws~~ <his> pen
~~What? When in~~ Virtue~~s cause~~ ^ ~~I wield ye pen~~
points

~~flirts~~ spouts ~~spouts in ye face of proud~~
& ~~dash~~ it in ye face of shameless men

associate to
And have not I ~~<to> did~~ <this → ~~Pillars of her~~ cause her cause
~~I must have Friends, each Servant of ye Crown~~
~~& Lights~~ ~~& Guardians of ye Laws~~
~~Lights of ye Church & Honour of ye Gown~~

3

Vein
~~could < moral > Boileau~~ lash in graver ~~Strain~~
~~Armd in this cause, bold Boileau durst arraign~~
could pensiond Boileau

2

evn in
Flatterers and Bigots ~~in old~~ Lewis' reign;
~~Dryden~~ ~~could~~ could ~~<great>~~ Dryden fill
With Pimp & priest ~~has~~ ^ ~~Dryden servd~~ ye stage,

1

and be
~~Yet neither Charles nor James were in a rage~~

~~A Colbert, or Mecenas will be seen~~

~~<Nay>~~ and
~~<Now>~~ here, ~~<no>~~ with pride, a King may be a Screen
For
And
Be Tis my
⟵⟶ my Reward, that no Reward attends
~~Sworn~~ Friend ~~to Virtue & to Virtues~~ friends
A alone to Virtue and her

Yet
~~With those at~~ Twitnam ~~<still>~~ still sees some of noble race
~~Evn~~
~~St John among the Greatest will seek my Cell w^{th}~~ out

~~& evn some ministers~~ Heros in peace & Statesmen ^ of place
~~Another Laelius~~
& St. John mingle~~s~~ with ye flowing bowl
The feast of Reason & ye Flow of Soul

Here Cyruslike brave
Mordant yu may see
To form a Quincunx or

Me
~~Envy shall~~ own s ~~tho' loath shall own I please y^e~~ Great
domestic with the
No pimp of pleasure, & no spy of State
An eye that prys not, tongue that ne'er repeats,
Fond to spread friendships, pleas'd to cover heats.

Unplac'd, unpension'd, meaning all men well,
This all, who know me, know; who love me, tell.
n
And who, unkowing slander, let 'em be
Scribblers or peers, alike are Mob to me.

This is my plea, and this my precedent,
Unless my learned Council shall dissent.

What? arm'd for Virtue when I point the pen
& spoil it in yr face
Can there be wanting, to defend her Cause,
Lights
~~Lights~~ Patrons champions or
2 World Laureat Dryden — for her
& neither Charles
1 Could pension'd Boileau lash in
Flatterers
and I, nor strip the gilding off a Knave ~~unplac'd, unpens~~ unpay'd ~~no Mortals Slave~~
Unplac'd, unpension'd, no mans Heir, or Slave?
~~Friends, Patrons champions (doubt not) will be seen,~~
nor
~~& here a Statesman black to be screen~~.
I will, or perish in ye glorious Cause:
Hear this & tremble, you who scape ye Laws!
To Virtue only & her friends a friend
~~& leave ye rest to~~ murmur or commend
The World beside may or
In Twitnam grottoes
Life. distant
There, my retreat
x [~~Neither~~ Fixing, I nor wear my Sabres or my Sword
To draw wth no
Of ~~[illegible]~~, Thieves & Cutthroats when ye Coast is clear,
& ~~not a~~ nor the Captain nor Macheath appear.
Save but one army &c.

Fills up a Verse
~~Breaking~~
no more ~~[illegible]~~ nameless, alas!

What? armd for Virtue when I point ye pen
& spout it in ye face
Can there be wanting, to defend her Cause
Lights or
Friends, Patrons, Champions—— Nor here
2 Could Laureat Dryden
& neither Charles
1 Could pensiond Boileau lash in
Flatt'rers
not strip the Gilding off a Knave
~~<unpla>~~
And I, ~~unplac'd unpens unpayd no mortals slave~~
Unplacd, unpensiond, no man's Heir, or Slave?
~~Friends, Patrons, Champions (doubt not) will be seen~~,
Nor
~~& here here a Statesman blush to be a Screen~~.
I will, or perish in ye Glorious Cause:
Hear this, & tremble, you who scape ye Laws!
To Virtue only & her friends a friend
~~I leave ye rest~~ to murmur or commend
The world beside may or
In Twitnam Grottoes
Like distant
There, my retreat
Know, I nor
~~I neither~~ wear my Satires or my Sword
To draw wn no
Of ~~Cheats~~ Thieves & Cuthroats when ye Coast is clear,
nor the
& ~~not a~~ Captain nor Macheath appear.
our
Save but ~~ye~~ army &c.
Fills up a Verse
~~Bears up~~
~~out~~
No more nor less, alas!

Alas my Friend! yt days can ne'r be long.
In flow'r of youth you perish for a Song!
How oft from Sapho have I fear'd yt fate
P-x'd by her Love or poison'd by her hate
Plumms & Directors, Shylock & his Wife
Will whip their Jesters now to take yr life.
I dread some Great man, or some great man's Spouse
You know, one Duchess has forbid her house—
Is this my Care when Virtue arms my pen
& points it in ye face of shameless Men
Could Laureate Dryden Pimp & ~~Poet~~ Fry'r engage
& neither Charles nor James be in a rage
Could pension'd Boileau lash in graver vein
Flatt'rers & Bigots ev'n in Louis Reign?
And can I want, to aid this bribeless Cause
Lights of ye Church, or Guardians of ye Laws!
Another Colbert (F x x) shall be seen
& here, with pride, a King may be a Screen
I leave ye World to murmur or commend
To Virtue only & her friends a friend
In Twitnams Grottoes, all yt noise yy keep
Like distant thunders but promotes my sleep
There's my Retreat
The Best Companions my Retreat shall grace,
Chiefs, out of War, & Statesmen, out of place:
That Eye, whose lightning thrill'd th' Iberian Lines
Has form'd my Quincunx & has rank'd my Vines
& St John mingles with my friendly bowl
The ~~Heir~~ Feast of Reason & ye Flow of Soul.
Envy ~~shall~~ must own, I live among ye Great
No Pimp of Pleasure & no Spy of State,
~~No Flincher, out of pow'r, & in, no Slave,~~
~~(For her nor Friend nor Servant, but a Knave)~~
With eyes yt pry not, Tongue yt ne'r repeats,
~~Fond~~ to spread friendships, but to cover Heats
Not medling, nor reserv'd: ~~but meaning~~ intending well,
This all who know me, know; who love me, tell:
& who, unknown, defame me, let em be
Scriblers or Peers, alike are mob to me

Alas my Friend! y^r days can n'er be long.
In flow'r of youth you perish for a Song!
How oft from Sapho have I feard y^r fate
P-xd by her love or poisond by her hate
Plumms & Directors, Shylock & his Wife
Will whip their Testers now to take y^r life.
I dread some Great man, or some great man's spouse
You know, one Duchess has forbid her house—
Is this my Care when Virtue arms my pen
Or spouts it in ye face of shameless Men
~~Fy~~ Fry'r
Could Laureate Dryden Pimp & ~~Priest~~ ^ engage
& neither Charles nor James be in a rage
Could pensiond Boileau lash in graver vein
Flattrers & Bigots even in Louis Reign?
And can I want, to aid this bribeless Cause
Lights of ye Church, or Guardians of ye Laws?
Another Colbert (F ++) shall be seen
& here, with pride, a King may be a Screen
I leave ye World to murmur or commend
To Virtue only & her friends a friend
In Twitnams Grottoes, all ye noise y^y keep
Like distant Thunders but promotes my sleep
There, my Retreat
The Best Companions my Retreat shall grace
Chiefs, out of War, & Statesmen, out of place:
That Eye whose Lightning thrilld th' Iberian Lines
Has formd my Quincunx and has rankd my Vines
& St John mingles with my friendly bowl
The ~~His~~ Feast of Reason & ye Flow of Soul.
must
Envy ~~shall~~ own, I live among ye Great
No Pimp of Pleasure & no Spy of State
~~Forsaken~~
(No Flincher, out of pow'r, & in, no Slave,
For he's nor Friend nor Servant, but a Knave)
With Eyes y^t pry not, tongue y^t ne'r repeats,
but
Fond to spread friendships, ~~&~~ to cover Heats
intending
Not medling, nor reservd: ~~but meaning~~ well
This all who know me, know; who love me, tell:
& who, unknown, defame me, let em be
Scriblers or Peers, alike are Mob to me

"The Courts are open to whoe'er shew cause,
"And base Attorneys will pervert the Laws;
"Consult the Statute, prim: I think it is
"Ricardi Sexti; or anno ~~non~~ Eliz:
"See Libels, Satyrs — there you have it — read
Libels & Satyrs? lawless things indeed!
But grave Epistles, bringing vice to light
Such as a King might read, a Bishop write,
Such as Sr Robert has approv'd — "Indeed—
"The case is alter'd, By all means proceed.
"In such a cause the plaintiff will be hiss'd
"My Lords the Judges laugh, & you're dismiss'd

This is my Plea, on this
I rest my Cause.
What says my Councel
learned in ye Laws?
"Agreed, agreed — But still
"I say, beware!
"Laws are explain'd by
" men; so have a care
" I well remember ye severe
book: in ancient times
"A man was hang'd for very
honest rymes

Mr. Pope says of this Parody from Horace (in a Letter to Dr. Swift) that it was writ in two mornings, & that he never took less care of any thing in his life. see vol. IX. p. 231.

"The Courts are open to whoe'er show cause,
"And base Attorneys will pervert the laws;
"Consult the Statute, prim: I think it is
"Ricardi tert: or anno non. Eliz:

" See Satyrs--- There you have it--read
~~Of~~ Libels, ~~Ballads, Be It Enacted -- Read~~

lawless things
Satyrs? ~~Those are vile~~ indeed!
Libels, & ~~Ballads? oh that point's agreed,~~

<ye> grave Epistles,
But ~~moral Satire~~ bringing vice to light

a might
~~the~~ King ~~would~~ read a Bishop
Such as ~~the King would read, or Gibson~~ write

has approvd--
Such as Sr Robert ~~would present~~ --"Indeed --

By all means
"The case is alter'd; ~~you may then~~ proceed.

will
"In such a cause, the plaintiff ~~would~~ be hissed
"My Lords the Judges laugh, & youre dismissed

This is my Plea, on this
I rest my cause.

What says my Council
learned in ye Laws?

"Agreed, agreed--But still
"I say, beware!

"Laws are explaind by
"Men, so have a care severe

I will remember yt
"~~There want not Prece-
dents :~~ in ancient times

"A man was hangd for
very honest rymes

Mr. Pope says of this Parody from Horace (in a Letter to Dr. Swift) that it was writ in two mornings, & that he never took less care of any thing in his life. See vol. ix. p. 231.

The First Satire of the Second Book of Horace or Epistle to Fortescue

NOTES TO THE TRANSCRIPTS

Page:Line	
1:1	*The hand is unidentified.*
1:7	*Pope's* A . . . *presumably stands for* Advocate.
1:14	*In the manuscript Pope seems to have struck out an obscure mark to left of* And, *conceivably quotation marks wrongly placed.*
1:16	lea *of* learned overwrites some illegible letters.
1:19	*The initial here (and throughout) appears to be a later insertion.*
1:20	*The first pair of quotation marks was evidently at one stage canceled;* N *of* Not *overwrites* n.
1:22	*The second* I *overwrites* &.
1:26	*The* W *of* Wife *overwrites* w.
1:28	Hollins: *John Hollings (1683?–1739), Fortescue's physician. See Pope to Fortescue, November 1735 ("Correspondence," 3:508).*
1:29	Shorn *of* Hartshorn *overwrites some illegible letters, perhaps only a freer spelling of* Hartshorn.
1:32	*In the transcript, the interrogation point is raised to l. 31 to clarify the situation.*
1:36	A *of* Arms *overwrites* a. Frederick: *Frederick Louis, Prince of Wales (1707–51).*
2:7	the *is altered from* th'.
2:17	F *of* From *overwrites* f.
2:19	Harris *overwrites* Harvey? Harris: *This is evidently John Harris (1680–1738), from 1729 Bishop of Llandaffe, of which Pope records his opinion in "One Thousand Seven Hundred and Thirty Eight": Dial I, 134 n: "A poor Bishoprick in Wales, as poorly supplied." (See TE, 4:364). The relation of Cibber/Harris to l. 17 perhaps suggests that Harris had been on occasion a flattering preacher at Court.*
2:21	T *of* Thou *overwrites* t.

Page:Line	
2:23	City's *overwrites* cities.
2:27	*Pope first writes (and then overwrites) the beginning of l. 36:* All Mor[tals].
2:30	s *is added to* tremble, *then apparently struck out;* himself *is altered from* themselves.
2:33	who'l deny *is altered from* who denies.
2:38	Hare *is possibly* whore, *or possibly used in the sense of* whore. *If so, Pope may have had in mind Scarsdale's earlier well-publicized pursuit of the actress Anne Bracegirdle or perhaps a more current liaison. On his feats with the bottle, see TE, 4:370.*
2:40	*The bracketed word ends with* ts *but seems not to be* Couplets, *though this would be the best counterpart to Horace's pedibus . . . laudere verba. Possibly the word begins with* l, *not* C. *In that case, in view of Pope's fondness for them, the word should be* lampreys.
3:1	another *overwrites* Ld Fanny.
3:3	Boden: *Unidentified.*
3:6	*What I have placed in brackets may equally well be* tastfull.
3:19	are *overwrites an illegible word.*
5:6	*For John Henley (1692–1756), see TE, 4:365 and TE, 5:444. For Thomas Bladen, ibid., 5:430. Macheath is of course the name of the hero of Gay's recently produced "Beggar's Opera" and also a nickname sometimes thereafter bestowed on Walpole.*
5:8	*The exclamation point overwrites a comma.*
5:13	offends *is altered from* offending.
5:28	then *overwrites* that.
5:30–31	*Considerably revised, these two lines became ll. 53–54 of "Sober Advice." For the story, see TE, 4:79 n.*
5:31	N *of* Note *overwrites* n.
5:32	*The identifying* W *looks like a later insertion.*

Page:Line	
5:32–33	*The figure* 1 *seems to have been altered from* 2.
5:33	your Judge be *is altered from* you're judg'd by.
5:45	O *of* Old *overwrites* o.
5:48	*In the transcript, this line is inadvertently indented.*
5:51–56	*To the left of Pope's bracket, an indecipherable number or symbol.*
5:56	*Following l. 56 the transcript should read as follows:* 56a. Free ~~Rich, and with Paper, < ——— > and without~~ 56b. ~~Abroad~~ 57. ~~Whether at home, in Bedlam or the Mint~~
6:3	of *overwrites* yr.
6:10	*If there is a specific reference in* one Duchess *it is probably to Katherine, Duchess of Buckinghamshire, who at this time was much at outs with Pope.*
6:12	*The first* for *is altered from* of; *the second* when *overwrites* whose; <his> *overwrites an illegible word.*
6:19	not *overwrites an illegible word, possibly* nor; <this> *seems to overwrite* her, *and the following word may be* Cause.
6:32	great *overwrites an illegible word, possibly* civil.
6:34	*In the manuscript, the figure* 1 *is overwritten by the* i *of* in *in l. 32.*
6:39	*The illegible word is probably* my, *modifying* genrous *in l. 42. Colbert is John Baptiste Colbert (1619–83), chief finance minister under Louis XIV, patron of artists, supporter of the French Academy, and founder of the Academy of Sciences.*
6:45	that . . . attends *overwrites* shall; *the final* s *of* sees *is added.*
6:51	H *of* here *overwrites* h. Condè: *Louis II de Bourbon, Prince of Condè (1621–86), one of Louis XIV's great generals who was also a patron of the arts.*
6:52	*A possible alternative reading of* St. John *is* & some.
6:54	Mordaunt: *Pope's good friend Charles Mordaunt, Earl of Peterborow, to whom ll. 129–32 of the printed poem are devoted.*
6:60	Lamoignon: *Guillaume de Lamoignon, eminent French justice, whom Boileau makes the deus ex machina of his "Le Lutrin."*
6:67	Cobham: *Sir Richard Temple, to whom Pope later addressed his epistle "Of the Knowledge and Characters of Men." (See TE, 3, pt. 2.)*
6:68	*The first* of *is altered from* to.
8:11	Fy *is perhaps a false start for* Fry'r.
8:32	e *of* live *overwrites* d.
8:33	*Pope seems to have struck out a terminal comma or semicolon, though why is not clear.*
9:28	*The reference is to Warburton's edition (9 vols., 1751).*

*An Essay on Man**

INTRODUCTION

AS A RECORD of Pope at work, the most revealing documents we have are probably the two manuscripts of the *Essay on Man,* one now in the Pierpont Morgan Library, the other in the Houghton Library at Harvard. Taken together, they open up a considerable view over that terrain of the imagination that stretches between what Dryden called "wit writing" and "wit written"—wit writing being "no other than the faculty of imagination in the writer, which, like a nimble Spaniel, beats over and ranges through the field of Memory till it springs the Quarry it hunted after"; wit written being "that which is well defin'd, the happy result of thought, or product of that imagination." In the following pages, I attempt to trace some of the maneuverings of "wit writing," in so far as these may be guessed at from the marginalia and revisions in the manuscripts of the *Essay on Man.*[1]

1

The marginalia take many forms. Some (as is noticed in the companion volume *Collected in Himself*) supply a running précis of the poem's thought such as was used to compose the "Argument" prefixed to each epistle in the later printed editions: "Of Man, as an Individual," "His Middle Nature," "His Powers and Imperfections," etc. Some point connections or make references. In the Morgan manuscript, for example, line 6 of Epistle I—"A mighty Maze! of Walks without a Plan"—carries the annotation: "Inconsistencys of Character, ye Subject of Ep. 5." This is presumably a reference to the contents of what we now call *Moral Essay* I and, possibly, *Moral Essay* II. At line 8, on the other hand—"Or *Orchard,* tempting with forbidden Fruit"—we are referred to "The Use of Pleasure, in Lib. 2," a topic on which the poet never got around to writing at all.[2]

Other marginalia throw light on the evolution of the *Essay* to its four-epistle form. We know from Spence that at a very early stage (May 1730) the poem was to have been complete in one epistle, and while the manuscripts offer no clues to this first phase, the "Finis" following Epistle II in the Morgan manuscript (together with the insertion at the head of this epistle of some of the lines to Bolingbroke that ultimately came to rest in the peroration to Epistle IV) suggests the possibility of a second phase when the *Essay* was thought complete in two epistles. A similar "Finis," closing Epistle III in both manuscripts, makes it reasonably certain that there was a third or three-epistle phase, especially if this evidence is taken in conjunction with the fact that the Harvard manuscript was plainly meant to be complete in three epistles, and that Epistle III concludes in both manuscripts with lines which were later postponed to the latter part of Epistle IV. A glance at the marginal queries on the last two pages of Epistle III in the Harvard manuscript will show, in fact, that at one time or other the poet debated postponing most of their contents to Epistle IV. Thus the disposition of the poem into its present parts was arrived at slowly, and, by the time Pope set down the queries here referred to, had shifted from the plan of which he spoke to Spence in May of 1730 to that which Bolingbroke described to Swift in a letter of 2 August 1731: "Three Epistles I say are finished. The fourth he is now intent upon."[3]

A considerable group of Pope's marginalia have the character of editorial annotations: they name an authority or supply an analogue for what is being attempted in the verse. So in the Morgan manuscript, opposite lines 75–76 of Epistle I—

> The blest today is as completely so
> As who began a thousand years ago—

occurs the comment: "Lucretius of death reverst. lib. 3. finè"; and the argument of lines 117–22 in the same epistle—

> Love, Hope and Joy, fair pleasure's smiling train,
> Hate, Fear, and Grief, the family of pain;
> These mix'd with art, and to due bounds confin'd,
> Make and maintain the balance of the mind:
> The lights and shades, whose well accorded strife
> Gives all the strength and colour of our life—

receives a similar glossing from a prosier source: "Arist[otle] Eth[ica] l. 7. c. 11. ~~of ye mean~~ reduces all

*This introduction first appeared in *Alexander Pope: An Essay on Man. Reproductions of the Manuscripts in the Pierpont Morgan Library and the Houghton Library. With the Printed Text of the Original Edition* (Oxford: Printed for Presentation to the Members of the Roxburghe Club, 1962). I have somewhat revised and shortened it for publication here. As noticed in the General Introduction, I reproduce the manuscripts of the *Essay* in this collection, partly because the earlier volume is hard to come by, but primarily because it lacks transcripts, without which large parts of the more heavily worked pages remain obscure.

ye Passions under Pleasure & Pain as their universal Principles. The Mean between opposit Passions makes Virtue, ye Extremes Vice."[4]

Marginalia of this expressive kind are rare in the Harvard manuscript; but it contains two which bring into play some interesting associations with Pope's friends. The first has to do with a couplet in Epistle I describing degrees of sensitivity in the sense of smell. This first ran in the Morgan manuscript as follows:

> Degrees of *Smell,* the stupid Ass between,
> And Hound, sagacious on the tainted green![5]

Subsequently, "the stupid Ass" was corrected to "each vulgar Brute" (perhaps on the ground that "ass" was an explosive word, as it still is in contexts like this), and then, rather oddly, to "the headlong Lioness," with a consequent revamping of the line: "Of *Smell,* the headlong Lioness between." To this verse Pope appended in all the printed editions beginning with 1734 a note descanting on the defect of scent in lions: "The manner of the Lions hunting their Prey in the Deserts of Africa is this; at their first going out in the night-time they set up a loud Roar, and then listen to the Noise made by the Beasts in their Flight, pursuing them by the Ear, and not by the Nostril. It is probable, the story of the Jackall's hunting for the lion was occasioned by observation of the Defect of Scent in that terrible Animal." This note, with its remarkable misinformation, does not appear in either of the manuscripts, but beside the couplet in the Harvard manuscript Pope has written "Cheseld."[6] The name is that of his friend, the physician and anatomist William Cheselden, from whom presumably he had the story; and its presence in the manuscript is a tonic reminder that the so-called Age of Reason was still an age when old lore was not yet disentangled from new learning.[7]

The other note in the Harvard manuscript that invokes the authority of a friend occurs in Epistle III. Here—between the couplet celebrating the instinctive equipment of the animals:

> Say, where full Instinct is th' unerring guide,
> What Pope or Council can they need beside?—
> (83–84)

and that which disparages the rational equipment of mankind:

> Reason, however able, cool at best,
> Cares not for service, or but serves when prest—
> (85–86)

a passage is inserted in a hand that is certainly not Pope's:

> While Man with opening Views of various ways
> Confounded by ye aid of Knowledge strays.
> Too weak to chuse, yet chusing still in haste
> One moment gives ye Pleasure & Distaste.[8]

Pope has marked the lines at beginning and end "DrA"—as the work in other words, of his friend Arbuthnot, in whose poem ΓΝΩΘΙ ΣΕΑΥΤΟΝ: *Know Your Self* of 1734 (lines 63–66) they will be found. Arbuthnot's poem did not appear in print till after the *Essay* had been published. According to its preface, however, it was "wrote several years ago," and so can have been known to Pope, or can even have been in process of composition during the period 1730–31, when the Harvard manuscript was made. It would be interesting to know, in view of the close ties between the two men and the general similarities of the two poems, whether Arbuthnot's second couplet above, which occurs in a far less effective form in the only known manuscript of *Know Your Self,* does not perhaps owe something to Pope, whose distinctive rhythm it has; and whether, in turn, Pope's lines on Newton (2. 31–34) and those which immediately precede and follow them—

> Go, wond'rous creature! mount where Science guides,
> Go, measure earth, weigh air, and state the tides;
> Instruct the planets in what orbs to run,
> Correct old Time, and regulate the Sun. . . .
> Go, teach Eternal Wisdom how to rule—
> Then drop into thyself, and be a fool!
> (19–22, 29–30)
> Could he, whose rules the rapid Comet bind,
> Describe or fix one movement of his Mind?
> Who saw its fires here rise, and there descend,
> Explain his own beginning, or his end?
> Alas what wonder! Man's superior part
> Uncheck'd may rise, and climb from art to art:
> But when his own great work is but begun,
> What Reason weaves, by Passion is undone—
> (35–42)

do not owe something, in general conception at least, to Arbuthnot's poem as well as to Pascal:

> With Look erect, I dart my longing eye,
> Seem wingd to part, & climb my native Skye.
> I strive to mount; But strive alas in vain,
> Tyd to this massy Globe by magick chain.
> Now on swift thought I flye from pole to pole,
> View worlds around their Flaming Centers Roll. . . .
> I weigh the ponderous planets in a scale,
> & trace the Blazing Comets Fiery Trail.
> These godlike thoughts, while eager I pursue,
> Some glittering trifle, offerd to my view,
> A Gnat or insect of the meanest kind
> Can Rase the new Born image from my Mind.
> Some Beastly want, urging, importunate,
> Vile as the grinning mastifs at my gate,
> Calls off from heav'nly truth this reasoning me
> & tells me I'me a Brute as much as he. . . .
> Lur'd by some vain conceit, or shamefull Lust,
> I flag, I drop, & Flutter, in the dust.[9]
> (27–32, 35–44, 47–48)

2

One group of marginalia in the Morgan manuscript takes us about as close to the actual processes of composition as with Pope we are likely to get. These are the poet's prose formulations of his thought as he gropes his way into and through his paragraphs of verse. Marginalia of this type are found at their best only in the pages of Epistle IV, the roughest of all Pope's surviving working papers. If we wish to follow "wit writing" in some of its earliest fumblings, we must look at a few of these with care.

Pope's first annotation in Epistle IV is an impromptu sketch of arguments evidently intended for its close, under the title "Elenchus in fine":

1. Happiness ye End of Man. God implants ye desire in all man kind, and he shows not ye End wthout ye Means, wch is *Virtue.*
2. He implants further a desire of Immortality wch at least proves he wd have us think of & expect it, & he gives no desire in vain to any Creature.
   ~~appetite Nature assigned to all~~ this
   As God plainly gave [yt?] Hope [or?] instinct, it is plain Man should entertain it. Hence flows his greatest Hope & greatest Incentive to Virtue.
   Hobs
3. Hope his sum̃ũ bonum, not Possession-----always something to come. So on to Im̃ortality.[10]

In the pages of the epistle that have survived, Pope never reaches this part of his argument. Instead, his mind begins to play with a series of defining propositions on the character of happiness, which he jots down in a tangled knot a little farther along the page:

1. That Happiness is ~~Social~~
   Equal
2. Therefor dwells in no Excess
3. Is social
4. Not external
   but mental
   That to be equal it must be ^
5. Necessity that External Goods shd be unequal for Order & Com̃on Good.

By the time he reaches "Page 2d,"[11] Pope has begun to distribute these headings along the margin, cueing them to passages of verse that are growing and reforming almost as fast as set down. Proposition No. 4, as a sample, is cued to this passage:

~~If ye great aim were Genral Bliss 'tis clear Nature & God cd never place it here~~
~~The of all if Heavn's indulgent aim, It could not place in Riches, Powr, or Fame~~
[1.] ~~If Bliss in these were plac'd, One greatly blest~~
~~In Fortune's Goods were one supremely blest~~
~~Sensual Joys~~
~~With Powr Wealth Pleasure *One* profusely blest,~~

paind
[2.] ~~Others were hurt~~, impoverishd, or opprest:

On all alike suppose them to
[3.] ~~Or did [this? that? the?] [these?] Goods on all *alike*~~ descend,

[4.] If all were equal, must not all contend?

[5.] In what (Heavns hand impartial to confess)

men
[6.] Need ~~all~~ be equal but in Happiness?

~~If Heaven to all meant~~ For all were Happiness designed,
tis
~~Which to secure,~~ ~~And genral if that Happiness, tis~~ clear

[7.] ~~This to bestow, if its indulgent aim,~~
Nature and God cd never place it *here*

~~could~~
[8.] ~~It must not place in Riches, Powr, or Fame,~~

~~then only~~
[9.] See therefore, Peace of Mind is at a stay!

~~Others~~
[10.] The rest, mad Fortune gives & takes away.

where
~~on~~ All but that ~~can~~
[11.] ~~Tis this sole~~ Point ~~where~~ Happiness stand~~s~~ still,

s
[12.] And taste~~s~~ ye Good, without the Fall to Ill.
~~How widely then at happiness we aim~~
On outward goods we build our Bliss in vain &c.

Of these twelve lines and their several emendations, all were ultimately discarded except 3–6 and 11–12, which in the printed text became the basis of line 63–64, 53–54, and 311–12.

"Page 3d"[12] of the manuscript brings forth two additional prose propositions, with verse to match—

particular
6. All^Happiness relates to General so cannot cen-
   s
   ter in ~~it~~self.

8. That ye Good Man is not unhappy, & ye Bad happy, ev'n in ye Gifts of fortune but has ye advantage—

followed by a third:

7. The chief Happiness of Man, Benevolẽce.[13]

Beyond this point numbered propositions disappear, and we begin to encounter jottings that are much more tangled, more tentative, more intimately expressive of the mind's effort to blaze a path through the thicket of its own conceptions:

Leaf 2, verso. In ye gifts of Fortune there is always that wish for more. So also there is in ye gifts of ye mind, Knowledge, Prudence, Temperance, Fortitude Only in Benevolence none.

Ibid. In ye gifts of ye mind a man wishes himself more knowledge, more Virtue, temperance, fortitude. No man wishes himself more Benevolence. Therefore it is ye only Compleat Happiness, having no *wish,* wch implies a want.

Upon ye whole account & in ye general course of things
Leaf 3, recto.^The good man has always ye advantage of ye bad, for he is not excluded frõ any of those Pleasures or Goods wch a bad man can possess, & he has Pleasures besides wch ye bad can have no feeling of, in his Virtue &c.

Ibid., verso. But you say Good men want necessaries, Bread, &c. he may not deserve these? Bread is ye Rewd of toil, & he may be Indolent or *weak* yet Good. His Goodness is rewded by consciousness Quiet Content &c. It is better he shd starve yn yt ye Naturall & General order of things shd be perverted. Must a Miracle be wrought contrary to yt Course, in his favor? more yn in Natural Philosophy.

3

Among the marginalia of this kind, we occasionally catch a fleeting glimpse of the whole range of the process of composition. At the hither end, the preliminary prose, passing into verse so fast that a phrase or sentence set down as prose is actually sucked into and made part of the verse line. On the thither end, the wide field of memory (to recur to Dryden's terms), over which the spaniel imagination seems to be ranging among the shadows of old books and remembered reading.

For a fine example of verse sucking prose into its own vortex, we may turn to leaf 2, verso. Here, as we have already noticed, Pope meditates on the nature of benevolence, trying out, in a note not yet quoted, this description:

> Benevolence a Pleasure one is never weary of, always occasions of exercising it. If disappointed, one is comforted in ye thing itself, & ye will, wch can be sd of no other pleasure even of ye mind.

Having got this far, and having tentatively roughed out the idea in an interlineary couplet—

> The joy unequald if our End we gain
> And
> Evn frustrate unattended wth a pain
>   if we miss attended wth no Pain—

the poet goes on to a new sentence:

> There is one thing still wanting in the happiness of a bad man, yt he wd be thought a good one.

This too he roughs out in an interlineary couplet, but in his haste to get the couplet down he actually incorporates into it the final five words of the prose, canceling "a" and "one," and placing the period after "good":

> Give Bad men all ye happiness they would
> They   want
> Still one ~~he wants~~ wch is to be thought ~~a~~ good. ~~one~~.

The opposite end of the composing process glances out upon our attention toward the foot of leaf 3, verso, where a note says, just above the prose passage about good men lacking bread: "See Woolaston 71.110.182." The reference is to three passages in William Wollaston's *the Religion of Nature Delineated,* a book that we know from Pope's correspondence he had read soon after its publication in 1724.[14] Space is wanting to consider all three passages, but one of them, beginning on page 110, will give some notion of the relevance of Wollaston to this part of Pope's argument. To sharpen the relevance as much as possible, I interpolate in square brackets certain verses from Epistle IV.

> Against all this it has been . . . *objected* of old, that things do not seem to be dealt according to *reason,* virtuous and good men very oft laboring under adversity pains, persecutions; whilst vitious, wicked, cruel men prevail and flourish. But to this an *answer* . . . is ready. . . . 1. We are not always certain, who are *good,* who *wicked.*
>
> [The good must merit God's peculiar care;
> But who, but God, can tell us who they are?]
> (135–36)
>
> . . . Opposite parties make a merit of blackening their adversaries, and brightening their friends, *undeservedly* and *unmeasurably.* . . . . . . and people of differing religions judge and condemn each other by their own tenents; when *both* of them cannot be in the right, and it is well if *either* of them are.
>
> [One thinks on Calvin Heav'n's own spirit fell;
> Another deems him instrument of hell;
> If Calvin feel Heav'n's blessing, or its rod,
> This cries there is, and that, there is no God.]
> (137–40)
>
> .2 It rarely happens that we are competent judges of the *good* or *bad fortune* of other people. . . . We do not see the *inward* stings and secret pains, which many of those men carry about with them, whose *external* splendor and flourishing estate is so much admired by beholders:
>
> [The good or bad the gifts of Fortune gain,
> But these less taste them, as they worse obtain.]
> (83–84)
>
> nor perhaps sufficiently consider the *silent* pleasures of a lower fortune, arising from temperance, moderate desires, easy reflexions, a consciousness of knowledge and truth. . . .
>
> [O fool! to think God hates the worthy mind,
> The lover and the love of human-kind,
> Whose life is healthful, and whose conscience clear;
> Because he wants a thousand pounds a year.]
> (189–92)
>
> . . . But suppose the pleasures of some, and the sufferings of some others, to be just as they appear: still we know not the *consequences* of them. The pleasures of those men may lead to miseries greater than those of the latter, and be in reality the greater misfortune: and, again, the sufferings of these may be preludes to succeeding advantages.
>
> [Fortune her gifts may variously dispose,
> And these be happy call'd, unhappy those;
> But Heav'n's just balance equal will appear,
> While those are plac'd in Hope, and these in Fear;
> Not present good or ill, the joy or curse,
> But future view of better, or of worse.]
> (67–72)
>
> . . . 3. Men ought to be considered as *members* of familes, nations, mankind, the universe, from which they cannot be separated: and then from the very *condition of their being* it will appear, that there must be great inequalities; that the innocent cannot but be sometimes involved in general calamities or punishments,

[But Fools the Good alone unhappy call,
For ills or accidents that chance to all.
(97–98)
Think we, like some weak Prince, th' Eternal Cause
Prone for his fav'rites to reverse his laws?]
(121–22)

nor the guilty but share in public prosperities; and that the good of the *whole* society or kind is to be regarded preferably to the present pleasure of any *individual,* if they happen to clash.[15]

["Remember, Man, "the Universal Cause
Acts not by partial, but by gen'ral laws;"
And makes what Happiness we justly call
Subsist not in the good of one, but all.]
(35–38)

A final specimen of Pope's marginalia brings us into contact with both ends of the composing spectrum at the same time. At the head of leaf 3, verso, Pope sets down in the scholastic manner the question he is about to argue and the position he is about to take: "Cur bona Malis, mala Bonis accidunt? Principio negatur." A sketch of two phases of the argument follows immediately:

[1.] Tis one part of ye Goodness of Providence yt
To bear his adverse & his prosprous fate
felicity & Misfortune succeed alternately, yt men
may bear ye one with moderation, & ye other
this, with moderation that. Yet still aspiring to a better State.
W *That State wch Virtue gives*
with *Patience,* & raise their minds to ye Search
of wt is better & more durable, in Virtue itself
&c. *& Wisdom finds*[16]

[2.] Difference of Fortune, Powr, &c right in Providence
sure knew
That Powr who made ye Difference ~~knows ye~~
best; See Peace. Pasc. 291,311. Were all men equal, all men wd contest.

Here, Pope's interlineations show us prose drawn into the orbit of verse, while the reference at lower right leads once more through the field of memory to Pascal's *Thoughts on Religion and Other Subjects,* in the English translation by Basil Kennett of 1704.[17]

4

In an interesting essay, George Sherburn points out that the growth of one of Pope's poems usually involved "four stages of mental and manual labour . . . : (1) making notes for the poem, sometimes detailed, in prose; (2) the composition of verse paragraphs; (3) the arrangement of the fragments in an effective structure; and (4) the polishing and perfecting of lines."[18]

Evidence from the Morgan and Harvard manuscripts of the *Essay on Man* suggests that it may be possible to refine somewhat on this sketch. The earliest stage, without question, was a cluster of prose notes—probably a kind of commonplace book. For the *Essay on Man,* we know from Spence that Pope had "very large (prose) collections on ye Happiness of Contentment," and "a long letter" from Bolingbroke, to say nothing of Bolingbroke's mysterious "dissertation," which, according to Lord Bathurst, Pope "turned into that fine poem."[19] All this belonged to the precompositional phase of the *Essay,* and none of it has survived except, just possibly, one trace. For the sake of completeness this "trace" deserves to be noticed here, before we go on to consider the remaining steps in the growth of the poem.

As with so many other poems of Pope's, Jonathan Richardson the younger was given the manuscripts of the *Essay on Man* to collate.[20] Richardson's ordinary practice, as we have seen, was to record the variant manuscript readings in the margins of a printed text; but in the case of the Morgan manuscript of the *Essay,* he made a condensed transcript of the manuscript itself, apparently finding it impossible otherwise to register so many variants. This transcript, now in the Berg Collection of the New York Public Library,[21] is prefaced by two leaves of prose, also in Richardson's hand, which read as follows. On the first leaf, recto, appear simply the words: "Maxim order belonging to Essay on Man N 1." On the verso of this leaf and the recto of the next, Richardson has listed seven "maxims":

Maxim. 1. That ORDER requires all Degrees of
Partial
~~Single~~ *Imperfection* [supposing all ways
predominating
ORDER preponderating Good] to compose a
1.163.iv.47. *Perfect Whole.*[22]
2. That then, "There must be *somewhere such a Rank as Man*". 1.48.
3. That to compose that Rank the Individuals must be as they are.
4. That then a *Borgia* or a *Cataline* are not Obnoxious to Punishment because it was their Lot to be such, & not a *Cato* or a *Socrates.*
5. That then the Imputation on Providence of an Unjust Distribution of Goods & Ills, to Ill & Good Men ceases.
6. That God's Justice being accountable for a Future State is Error.
Providence
7. That ~~God~~ is not Subject to ye Contingency of what We may Act; but that God is *All in All,* & all his Attributes Intire & Clear.

The verso of the second leaf contains these additional notations:

1. That Man, & all other Creatures, & Things, in general & in particular are alike Usefull, ~~to~~ in their Place, to ye Coñon Cause; in the same mañer as the Stones, Bricks, Mortar, Timber, Lead, Glass, Nails &c are to a House, where if some are more *Considerable,*
You'll answer:
all are alike *Necessary.* ~~But then you'll say~~, This is True, but then ye Materials must be good in their kind. & so they were Originally as they came from God. ORDER

in Nature or ye Universe consists in a continual Opposition of Extreams kept in due Bounds.

"ORDER is Heav'n's first Law—
iv.47.
from whence our Happiness.
"But Mutual Wants this Happiness encrease,
"All Natures Diff'rence keeps all Nature's Peace.
iv.53.cont.1:161.
The same is in Man: Two Principles in Human Nature reign,
"*Self Love* to urge, & *Reason* to restrain.
ii.45&c.
"The rising Tempest puts in acy ye Soul,
"Parts it may ravage, but preserves ye whole.
ii.95&c.

Corolary 1. As this *ORDER* ~~is~~ makes the *Happiness* of the whole, (which *Happiness* is its Essense, & Sole End!), so, the nearer Every Individual approaches, in Himself, to ORDER, that is to TEMPERANCE, +note whose other Name is VIRTUE; by just so much the Nearer He approaches to *Happiness*.

+ which is suffering some Ill for ye Good of the Whole, as Infinite Wisdom hath done in ye Universe.

Though it is obviously impossible at this late date to assess the significance of these notations with any assurance, one may perhaps be permitted to draw a few tentative inferences from them:

1. Their survival among Richardson's collations of the Morgan manuscript, and the careful preservation of variant readings that they seem to show (Single: Partial; preponderating: predominating; God: Providence; to: in; But then you'll say: You'll answer; is: makes) strongly suggest that they are not Richardson's own work, but, like the transcript they accompany, his copy of Pope's.

2. The references to lines in the first, second, and fourth epistles as they are numbered in the printed editions show that these notes were not written down, in this document, till after the poem had been published. They cannot therefore, as they stand, be an exact copy of the prose materials the poet used in composing; but this need not exclude the possibility that they in some way relate to those materials.

3. The argument presented by the seven maxims, and by the two added notes, both of which appear to be amplifications of Maxim 1, bears hardly more than a laughable resemblance to the *Essay* as a poem, and only a very limited resemblance to the *Essay* as a "system of Ethics"—the poet's own phrase in the "Design" prefixed to all editions of the poem beginning with 1734.

4. Apart from the quotations from Epistles II and IV with their corresponding line numbers, there is nothing in these notes and maxims that cannot, at a pinch, be referred to the argument of the first epistle of the *Essay,* and therefore, but more plausibly, to a projected version of the poem at a time when it was still being conceived of as complete in one epistle and as primarily a theodicy, justifying Providence for having made a universe that does not exclude moral evil any more than it excludes natural evil.

5. Given these hypotheses and facts, the notes and maxims may best be accounted for, I suspect, by supposing that they are a late redaction of materials that, in their earliest form, preceded composition of the poem. Just possibly, they take us in the general direction of that "dissertation," or "long letter," or "series of propositions,"[23] that Bolingbroke is said by various eighteenth-century sources to have contributed for the poet's guidance. The apparent drift of Maxims 3–6, for instance, fits rather better with what we know of Bolingbroke's thought than with anything Pope was finally willing to set down in either the manuscripts or the published poem. Moreover, in the *Essay* as we know it, the argument that guilty men—"a Borgia or a Catiline" (I.156)—cannot be eliminated from a universe in which all possible degrees of "goodness" have been realized, including that degree which can fail and fall into evil, is qualified by the acknowledgement that no particular man is compelled to be a villain: even "Nero reigns a Titus, if he will" (II.198).

6. An alternative explanation of these materials is, of course, that they are precisely what they appear: an abstract of "points" drawn up by Pope, or possibly by Richardson, for some unspecified purpose after the poem was in print. This explanation seems less satisfactory than the other, if one reflects how improbable it is that a man who knew the completed poem, whether the author or another, would draw up such a misleading summary of its argument—a summary that ignores Epistle III entirely and barely implies a portion of the contents of Epistles II and IV.

7. All things considered, it seems somewhat easier to believe that we have here a late adaptation of a very early prose scheme. If so, it is the best evidence we possess at present about the role played by prose in the pre-compositional stage of the *Essay,* and it does not give us much ground for thinking that the prose of this stage (if it could be found) would have an especially illuminating relationship to the finished poem.

5

We come now to the later steps in the poem's composition. Working from his collections of prose notes, Pope would appear to have hammered out, probably as brouillons on scraps of paper that have not come down to us, clusters of couplets on various themes.[24] When enough of these were in a tentatively finished form, he began the making of a first rough draft of the poem as a whole. Epistles II, III, and IV of the Morgan manuscript seem to belong to such a draft, though from the middle of leaf 2, verso, in Epistle IV, through part of leaf 3, verso, we are plainly very close to, or even in, the brouillon phase. The sometimes still uncertain direction of the argument at this stage; the use of all sorts of marginalia to question, expand, analogize, explain; and the incentive function served by the main column of verse, around which new couplets accumulate like the proverbial pearl around the irritating grain of sand: these are matters which have been sufficiently illustrated in the foregoing paragraphs and in the earlier introductions in this volume. Their ultimate effect was to transform a preliminary rough draft into a preliminary final draft.

Once this process was complete, it seems to have been Pope's habit to prepare a fair copy for the inspectión and criticism of his friends. In the case of the *Essay on Man)* and probably in many other cases, Pope's passion for revision being what it was), this became a working paper too. To instance only from Epistle II of the *Essay,* lines 25–28, 91–92, 215–16, 261–72 of the printed poem have no originals in the Morgan manuscript, but first occur (with one exception, as interlineations or marginal additions) in the Harvard manuscript. Conversely, the following lines of Epistle II in the Morgan manuscript have no successors in the Harvard manuscript. After line 18 (within a passage dropped from both manuscripts before printing):

> If Gods we *must be,* 'cause we *would be,* then
> Pray hard, ye Monkies! & ye may be Men.[25]

After line 34:

> Ah turn the Glass! it shows thee all along
> As weak in Conduct, as in Science strong.[26]

After line 104:

> Virtue dispassioned naked meets *to* the fight,
> & void of *Arms* can * Comes without *Arms,* & *
> conquers but by *Flight.*[27]

After line 148:

> Its *own best forces* lead the mind astray,
> Just as with *Teague* his *own Legs* ran away.[28]

After line 184:

> *See* Thus So dulcet Pippins from the Crabtree
> come
> *As* The Sloe's rough juices *melts* so thus into a
> Plum[29]

After line 214 (but following a passage dropped from both manuscripts before printing):

> To strangle in its birth each rising Crime
> Requires but little, just to think in time.
> In evry Vice, at first, in some degree
> *Still in ye Thing deceived or ye Degree,*
> We see some Virtue, or we think we see.
> And spite of all ye Frenchman's witty lies
> *Wicked but by degree or by surprise*
> Most *Our* Vices are but *still are* Vir-
> tues in disguise[30]

And after line 240:

> What urges *One* thro just and thro unjust, Lust
> To present *private* Lucre, or to present *private*
> Op'rates in *All,* & is itself the Cause
> Of what restrains them, Government & Laws.[31]

This last omission casts a further interesting side-light on the evolution of the poem from a two-epistle to a three-epistle form; for by the time the Harvard manuscript was copied out, these lines had migrated and been revised to become lines 269–72 of Epistle III.

6

In the meantime, as the poem moved from the Morgan state to the Harvard state and on toward print, two developments of the first importance occurred. First, the poem gradually found its decorum. In the *Essay on Man,* this is a decorum of abstractions, universals, types. We are taking a survey. Our view is wide, circumspective; our tone, despite some lively sallies, grave. Names in the *Essay on Man,* as was pointed out earlier in these volumes, take on a notably generalizing and exemplary cast.[32] Even geographical sites are snatched by their contexts from our actual terraqueous globe to that other *Theatrum orbis terrarum* where the topographers have always been poets, and Tweed and Zembla, York and Orcades lie down peaceably side by side. In Epistle IV this state of affairs alters somewhat because the character of the poem alters. Argument is now as far as possible submerged; the successive cosmic, psychological, and historical perspectives of Epistles I–III narrow to focus on man in his mundane contemporaneity; and the pervasive theme of the vanity of human wishes invites, even demands, illustration from all quarters: Caesar and Eugene (244), Lucrece and the Howards (208, 216), Alexander and Charles XII (220), Aurelius and Pope's mother (235, 110). Yet even in this most contemporary and allusive of the epistles, the names have as much the status of symbolic types as persons, and sometimes, almost, the status of figures in a myth.

The *Essay*'s decorum, then, was to be grave, so far as this allowed excursions to the gay, and abstract, so far as this was compatible with rhetorical force. But the right combination was not easily found. The lines quoted below, for example, may have been jettisoned for a variety of reasons, but surely in part because they were too "familiar," and, in the final couplet, too "low":

> Boast we of Arts? A Bee can better hit
> The Squares than Gibs, ye Bearings than Sr
> Kit
> To poise his Dome a Martin has ye knack
> While bold Bernini lets St Peters crack. . . .
> Sweet as Berselli's ye wild Woodlarks note
> Yet never lost his Stones to mend his throat.[33]

A passage like the following must have been excluded at least partly because it was frivolous:

For more Perfection than this State can bear
In vain we sigh: Heav'n made us what we are.
More *As* wisely, sure, a modest Ape might aim
To be like Man, whose faculties and frame
He sees, he feels; than *as* you or I to be
An Angel Thing we neither know nor see:
Observe his Love of tricks, his laughing face
How near he edges elbows on our race
What human tricks! how risible of face!
(An elder Brother too, to human Race)
"It must be so—why else have I a Sense
"Of more-than-monkey Charms and Excellence?
2 T 1 3
"Why else ~~to~~ walk on two have I essay'd?[34]
"And why this ardent Longing for a Maid?
So Pug might plead, & call his Gods unkind,
Till set on-end, and marry'd to his mind.[35]

And the revision of such a couplet as this—

Envy, in Criticks and old Maids the Devil,
Is Emulation in the Learn'd and Civil—

to this—

Envy, to which th'ignoble mind's a Slave
Is Emulation in the Learn'd or Brave—[36]

must have been motivated to some extent by the feeling that the tone was becoming too chatty.

One notices even in Epistle IV that the poet is at some pains not to adopt too immediate a perspective, not to give up classic marble for contemporary brick. The couplet that finally became:

And more true joy Marcellus exil'd feels
Than Caesar with a senate at his heels—
(257–58)

held in the manuscript, among other possibilities, "honest Sh[ippen]" for Marcellus, and "W[alpole]" for Caesar.[37]

7

The other important change that took place in the poem as it evolved from the Morgan to the Harvard to the published text lay in the arrangement of verse paragraphs. One example must suffice—a short passage of six lines in Epistle III whose final arrangement appears to have cost Pope more effort than any passage of similar brevity in the *Essay* and is surely one of the minor triumphs of "wit writing":

Man, like the gen'rous vine, supported lives,
The strength he gains is from th' embrace he gives.
On their own Axis, as the Planets run,
Yet make at once their circle round the Sun:
So two consistent motions act the Soul;
And one regards Itself, and one the Whole.
(311–16)

The felicity of these lines at this point needs little emphasis. They not only sum up much that the epistle, and much that the poem, has so far said; they also affirm the peculiar blend of terrestrial and cosmic, homely and grand, scientific and legendary, immediate and remote, which is the characteristic mode of the poem's outlook on the human situation—and, while affirming it, manage to say something about human nature that is psychologically acute. The center of their poetic energy lies obviously in the juxtaposition of the two similes, one drawn from Newton's principle of gravitation, one, ultimately, from the legendary marriage of the vine and elm. But this juxtaposition was long in coming.

The couplet on man-as-vine appears first in the Morgan manuscript in this context:

Prefer we then the greater to the less
For Charity is All men's Happiness.
Man like ye genrous Vine supported lives,
The Strength he gains is from th' Embrace he gives.
Th' extended World is but one Sphere of bliss
To him, who makes anothers blessing his.
Parent or Friend first touch the virtuous mind,
His Country next, & next all humankind [etc.][38]

By the following page,[39] it is being tried out in this context:

Let us, my [St. John] this great Truth profess,
One is our Duty, and our Happiness:
Each like ye genrous Vine supported lives,
The Strength he gains is frō
And Faith and Morals end as they began,
All, in the Love of God, and Love of Man.

Toward the beginning of Epistle IV, it reappears in a third context:

Hear first this Oracle What Happiness we call
Consists not in ye Good of one, but all.
Man like ye genrous
The Strength
And ev'ry Bliss that Individuals find
Still some way leans & harkens to the Kind.[40]

A page later, it has rejoined one of the couplets with which it began, but in a new order and a somewhat new milieu:

Of human nature Wit its worst may write,
We all revere it in our own despite:
No Bandit fierce, no Tyrant mad with pride,
No cavern'd Hermit, rests Self-satisfyd
Who most to scorn it, or renounce pretend
Seek an Approver, or wd find a friend.
Man like the gen'rous Vine supported lives,
The Strength he gains is from th' Embrace he gives.
Hear then this Oracle, nor think it less:
True CHARITY is *mans chief Happiness*.[41]

Two pages after this, the simile on gravitation is struck out, almost at a blow, as a marginal insertion beside a passage on the joys of benevolence:

Round their own Center as *~~Self movd, self centerd as~~* the Planets run
Yet take an ampler compass round ye Sun

Thus 2 consistent motions act urge *two
different motions thus impell* ye Soul
& one regards itself & one ye Whole.[42]

On the same page, in the opposite margin, man-as-vine returns. The two similes are at last within striking distance of each other, though man-as-vine still keeps to its original environment of meaning:

True happiness, tis sacred truth I tell
Lies but in thinking right and meaning well.
The only Bliss Heavn can on all bestow
Wch who but *feels* must taste, but *thinks* must know.
Man like ye genrous Vine
The Strength he gains
Greater as kinder, to wtere [whate'er] degree
& Height of *Highest* Bliss but *is* height of Charity.

This is as close to joining as the two similes ever come in the surviving pages of the Morgan manuscript. The crucial step was taken in the Harvard manuscript. There, the couplet on man-as-vine was transcribed as part of the passage of Epistle III in which we first met with it in the Morgan manuscript—naturally enough, since no Epistle IV had yet been thought of—and the whole passage was set down as the last paragraph but one of the epistle. But then came the decision to add a fourth epistle; this paragraph of Epistle III was canceled for removal there; Epistle III remained without a proper conclusion—what was to be done? It was then, if one may playfully recur to Dryden again, that the spaniel imagination was dispatched on a vital errand. Its first quarry seems to have been the simile on gravitation. It retrieved this from the margin of Epistle IV in the Morgan manuscript (which was by this time in existence) and plunked it down, in a slightly amended version, immediately beneath the canceled paragraphs of Epistle III.[43] Its second quarry was the simile of man-as-vine. Possibly it fetched this from the canceled paragraphs of Epistle III, possibly from one of its appearances in Epistle IV. In any case, the couplet was nosed out among all the possibilities that were available, inserted in the Harvard manuscript just above the gravitation simile, and the potential of the two comparisons became fulfilled in their dynamic relation to each other. Good writing, Pope had said in his *Essay on Criticism,* implies "a *Happiness* as well as *Care.*" This is true. But as our present example shows, the happiness is seldom distinguishable from the care.

8

For most poems, the story of composition would now be closed. The *Essay* had grown from jottings—through brouillons of verse—through a first and then a second transcript—through a hundred visions and revisions posterior to the transcripts—and finally to a published poem. But Pope went on puttering, as he did with most of his major work, until he died. In the various editions intervening between the first and last of his lifetime, he omitted 18 lines, added 62, rearranged dozens, and revised upwards of 150.

The most significant of his additions, as Professor R. W. Rogers has reminded us, were made in 1743–44: "to temper statements on which constructions antithetical to orthodox dogma could be placed."[44] What is especially interesting for our record of Pope at work is that several of these additions were not newly composed for the occasion. Instead, Pope returned to his manuscripts, especially the Morgan manuscript, and simply reaffirmed what had been present in them from the start. The following couplet, for instance, in the edition on which Pope and Warburton collaborated, was amended to read "knowledge" for "Being"—

His Being measur'd to his state and place,
His time a moment, and a point his space—
(I. 71–72)

possibly because, in Professor Rogers's words, "the assertion that man's 'being' is measured to his state and place seemed to some to deny the possibility of a future life."[45] In the Morgan manuscript, however, Pope had written "Knowledge" in the first place, and the line was so transcribed in the Harvard manuscript, from which it was later canceled in favor of "Being."[46]

Likewise in Epistle III of the Pope–Warburton edition the poet added after this couplet—

For Modes of Faith let graceless zealots fight;
His can't be wrong whose life is in the right—
(305–6)

this one:

In Faith and Hope the world will disagree,
But all Mankind's concern is Charity.

"To some of Pope's readers," says Professor Rogers, "the first couplet standing alone was objectionable because it seemed to declare that all religions were indifferent as to their forms and object. The additional couplet buttressed Warburton's argument that Christianity and the natural religion of Pope were not in effect antithetical because the ethical ideals of the two were the same."[47] Again, however, Pope had written the buttressing couplet in the Morgan manuscript as far back as 1730–31.[48]

9

The most interesting of all Pope's later additions to the *Essay* was not published in his lifetime and never became part of the poem. This is a series of revisions inserted on a surviving leaf of the first quarto edition of the *Essay* (1734), which was at one time Warburton's, later the property of John Murray the publisher, and is now in the possession of the Yale Library. The revisions were made with the evident intent of turning the generalized sketch of "Misery in

Grandeur," which occupies lines 287–308[49] of Epistle IV, into a portrait that without ceasing to suggest a type could be counted on to evoke a particular person: John Churchill, the great Duke of Marlborough.

Pope was never among the Duke's admirers. Few Tories were after 1708, when the controversies about prolongation of the wars in France became acute. Pope, moreover, counted among his close friends several men whose dislike of Marlborough for private or public reasons was intense: Robert Harley, first Earl of Oxford, to whose prosecution for high crimes and misdemeanors after the death of Queen Anne Marlborough lent his warmest support; Bolingbroke, who told Pope the unlikely story that a Junto of Whigs, including Marlborough, had studied to assassinate him and the Earl of Oxford during their tenure as Secretary of State and Lord Treasurer;[50] Swift, whose attacks on Marlborough's policies and character in the *Examiner* had been among the most telling ever made; and there were others.

Living in such a milieu, Pope not surprisingly reflects in his poems and letters most of the charges that circulated against the Duke in the enemy camp, some true, some partly true, some scandalously false. That—for example—in his youthful days at the court of Charles II, Marlborough had become the gallant of the Duchess of Cleveland and been paid some thousands of pounds for his attentions, though he refused on a later occasion to lend the Duchess twenty guineas at a card game.[51] That he had betrayed James II in the affair of '88, assuring the king of his support with one hand while welcoming in the Prince of Orange with the other.[52] That he was grasping, rewarded his soldiers poorly, made a private fortune from the army supply accounts and military plunder.[53] That his last years were senile and miserable, dominated by the furious humors of his wife Sarah and her unending squabbles with sons-in-law and daughters.[54] That his funeral, though the most ostentatious in living memory, was unaccompanied by any genuine national sorrow.[55] That his unremitting efforts for perpetuation of his line and fortune, extending even to obtaining an act of parliament that permitted his honors and estates to descend through the distaff side, were destined to be circumvented by a just Providence, who between 1703 and 1733 snatched away his one surviving son, three of his four daughters, his eldest daughter's only son, two of three sons belonging to his second daughter, all three sons of his fourth daughter, etc.

To these charges Pope returns with vehemence in the revisions on the quarto leaf. Alteration of the first ten lines was easy, for the reason that in all probability they had been intended for the Duke from the start:

> There, in the rich, the honour'd, fam'd, and great,
> See the false Scale of Happiness compleat!
> In hearts of Kings or arms of Queens who lay,[56]
> (How happy!) those to ruin, these betray.
> Mark by what wretched steps Great + + *their
>   Glory* grows,
> From dirt and sea-weed as proud Venice rose;
> One equal course, how Guilt and Greatness ran,
> *In each, how Guilt and Greatness equal ran,*[57]
> And all that rais'd the Hero sunk the Man.
> Now Europe's Lawrels on his *their* brows behold
> But stain'd with Blood, or ill exchang'd for Gold.
> (287–96)

Marlborough's addiction to "Gold," Pope knew, was the one charge from which not even his best friends could exonerate him. So in the revision the poet strikes out lines 297–302[58] of the printed sketch in favor of a more extensive disquisition on avarice:

> O Wealth ill-fated! which no act of Fame
> E'er taught to shine or sanctified from shame.
> What wonder tryumphs never turn'd his brain
> Fill'd with mean fear to lose mean joy to gain
> Hence see him modest free from pride or shew
> Some Vices were too high but none too low
> Go then indulge thy age in Wealth & Ease
> Stretch'd on the spoils of plunder'd palaces
> Alas what Ease those furies of thy life
> Ambition Av'rice & th' imperious Wife [etc.]

But looking over the last two couplets, the poet evidently decided to improve the force of "Wealth & Ease". He therefore canceled the two lines on wealth that introduce the passage, revised them slightly, and paired them with the two on ease, the whole insertion flowing smoothly back into the printed sketch at line 303:

> Alas what *wealth,* which no one act of fame
> E'er taugh[t] to shine, or sanctified from shame
> Alas what *Ease* those furies of thy life
> Ambition Av'rice & th' imperious Wife
> The trophy'd Arches, story'd Halls invade (303)
> And haunt their[59] slumbers in the pompous
> Shade.

After line 300 Pope inserted a much longer manuscript passage, this one expatiating on the emptiness of the Duke's later career as hostile gossip had presented it:

> No joy no pleasure from successes past
> Timid & therefore treacherous to the last
> Hear him in accents of a pining Ghost
> Sigh, with his Captive for his ofspring lost[60]
> Behold him loaded with unreverend years
> Bath'd in unmeaning unrepentant tears
> Dead, by regardless Vet'rans born on high
> Dry pomps & Obsequies without a sigh
> Who now his fame or fortune shall prolong
> In vain his consort bribes for venal song
> No son nor Grandson shall the line sustain
> The husband toils th' Adulter ‸er‸ sweats in vain:
> In vain a nations zeal a senate's cares
> "Madness & lust (said God) be you his heirs"
> "O'er his vast Heaps in drunkenness of pride"
> "Go wallow Harpyes and your prey divide".

Pope cannot have entered these revisions on the quarto leaf much before April 1734,[61] when the quarto was published; and since from about 1734 the Duchess of Marlborough joined Pope's circle of political acquaintances in opposition to Walpole and became gradually one of his own friends, they can hardly have been proposed for a position in the poem later than that year. It seems probable on all counts that they were written down in the quarto during the months of 1734 when Pope was revising his poems of the early thirties for his collected *Works, Volume II*, of 1735. And there is a good deal of evidence to suggest that, like the passages discussed in the preceding section, they represent a return to the manuscript rather than a new *ad hoc* creation. For one thing, Pope wrote to Bethel, 8 September 1731, stating that he was "busy in the Moral Book I told you of"—i.e., the *Essay on Man* and *Moral Essays*, and that "many exemplary Facts & Characters fall into it daily, but which render it less fit for the Present Age. The Fate of the Marlborough family is a Great one, which the death of the Marquess of Blandford has renewd my Reflections on. *Solus sapiens dives* is very true."[62] This allusion points plainly to some sort of character of Marlborough, with which Pope is concerned at approximately the period when he was "intent upon"[63] the fourth epistle; and since Pope says "renewd," it is not impossible that his current "Reflections" were by way of addition to some existing already.[64]

Whatever the truth may be on this last point, there is strong evidence in the Morgan manuscript for believing that most or all of the lines Pope set down on the quarto leaf in 1734 date from the time when the poem as a whole was composed. The latter pages of Epistle IV are lacking in the manuscript, as noticed earlier; but at the foot of leaf 3, recto, Pope has huddled down in haste a few scrawled lines and cues for lines that belong to the Marlborough portrait. First, a complete couplet:

> Let gatherd Nations next their chief behold
> How blest wth Conquest yet unblest wth Gold.

Next, a cue indicating that four of the verses in the first manuscript insertion were already extant elsewhere in some form:

> Wt wonder—low.

Next, a group of cues, probably indicating that the remainder of the first insertion and lines 303–4 of the printed sketch were also extant elsewhere in some form:

> [rest?] [?]
> Go then & steep thy age in Wealth & Ease
> Stretched on ye spoils
> Alas
> The trophyd arch, ye storied hall
> pompous shade.

Then two verses and several cues, indicating that lines 286–8 and 305–8 of the printed sketch are either taking shape fast, or, more plausibly, have already taken shape in another place—including, apparently, lines no longer known:

> In one mans fortune mark & scorn ym all
> him the famd & most
> In one, most vain, most honord, famd & great
>
> See ye false Scale
> But oh! not dazled wth his
> Compute
> [address led?][65] his youth.

Finally, at the very end, a jotting that points to one line in the second manuscript insertion and to the idea governing its last eight lines:

> thy name & fortune shall.

The conclusion appears inescapable that Pope composed the portrait of Marlborough, or a version of it, in 1730–31; for a time contemplated recapturing it for the 1735 editions; and then suppressed it, partly in deference to the new political alignment of Marlborough's duchess. But *only* partly, I think. Though Pope told Spence that he had omitted from his "Moral Poem" one of the best characters he had ever written and presumably meant this one,[66] he must have been secretly, or on other occasions, wiser than this. The sketch he had finally evolved for the *Essay* as we have it is superbly balanced. There is an elegiac sigh in the movement of the lines, and if there is also a sting, it is the sting that comes from facing the necessary imperfection of human things, the oft-told tragic story of great gifts ruined by some mole of nature, some dram of e'il. The covert references to the modern instance are muted, and at the same time reasserted, by the generalized pattern to which they are subsumed. Or, to put it another way, the "ancient story" has materialized again, has become modern once more, and therefore "ancient" in a richer sense.

Not much of this survived the revisions Pope put down on the quarto leaf. There the universal was eliminated in favor of the unique. The marble was covered over with brick. The tragic tone became strident, not to say shrill. And the modern particulars were not only no longer seen *sub specie aeternitatis*, some of them were not even applicable. Marlborough *did* have—for instance—a grandson living, who assumed the dukedom in January 1734.

Pope was a warm-hearted man and far from the monster of perfidy that the nineteenth century loved to paint. But I suspect no one who has lived long with him would care to guarantee that, if he had really thought the character of Marlborough one of the best he ever wrote, or even appreciably better than the sketch he first printed, he would not have found ways and means to make it eventually appear in the poem, despite the affiliation of the Duchess with his party and eventually with himself.[67]

NOTES

1. The Morgan Library manuscript of the *Essay on Man* is written on leaves of varying sizes, and each epistle is contained in a gray-blue paper wrapper. Epistle I consists of seven leaves measuring 8⅞ in. by 7³⁄₁₆ in. Leaf 1 is a cover leaf, the text beginning on leaf 2, recto, and ending on leaf 7, recto (verso, blank). Epistle II consists of five leaves. In this case, leaves 1 and 5 are both cover leaves, and the text runs from leaf 2, recto, through leaf 4, verso. Leaf 1 measures 11⁷⁄₁₆ in. by 8 in., the other leaves 12½ in. by 8 in. Epistle III is extremely irregular. Leaf 1, a cover leaf, measures 11⅞ in. by 8 in. Leaves 2 and 3 are ruled ledger paper measuring 11⅞ in. by 7⅞. Leaf 4 is also ruled ledger paper, but has been cut down at the top so that it is only 11½ in. long. Leaf 5 is mutilated, its top half crudely torn away—evidently by Pope himself, since Richardson imitates this feature of the manuscript in his transcript. (Richardson's note on the torn leaf shows that it was originally "wafered over" the bottom of leaf 3 so that "God in the Nature of each Being founds" [TS, 33:4 ff.] would follow directly on "Yet never lost his Stones to mend his Throat" [TS, 30:57]. With the cancellation of ll. 44–47 on leaf 3v [TS, 30], the passage just quoted from the recto of the torn leaf would adjoin the passage on instinct [leaf 3v, TS, 30:1–43], as in the final published text. Since in the present manuscript the torn leaf is mounted *after* leaf 4v [TS, 32], to which the material on its verso pertains, I have respected that arrangement.) Leaf 6 is exceptionally long—12½ in. Leaf 7, roughly of small quarto size, 8⅞ in. by 7³⁄₁₆ in., has been folded to make four pages, which Pope has numbered 7–10. Leaf 8, exactly half the size, 7³⁄₁₆ in. by 4⁷⁄₁₆ in., became at some early time displaced to the end of Epistle IV. Its recto is paged 11; its verso, blank except for some later irrelevant notations, is pasted to the inside of the gray-blue wrapper at the end of Epistle IV, is therefore not available for photography, and therefore is not reproduced below. The text of Epistle III begins on the recto of leaf 2 and ends on the recto of leaf 8. Epistle IV consists of five leaves. Leaf 1 (a cover leaf) and leaves 2, 3, and 5 are ruled ledger paper measuring 11⅞ in. by 7⅞ in. Leaf 4, which is not ledger paper, measures 11⅞ in. by 7½ in. The text of the epistle begins on leaf 2, recto, and ends on the verso of leaf 5.

The Houghton Library manuscript of the *Essay* occupies 39 pages of a quarto notebook, in a gray-blue paper wrapper. Epistle I begins on page 1 of the notebook and ends on page 12; Epistle II begins on page 15 and ends on page 28; Epistle III begins on page 31 and ends on page 43. Pages 13–14, 29–30, 44–50 are blank. Page 50 is followed by an inserted leaf, the recto of which contains eight lines of verse under the title: "Incipit Liber Secundus. / Epist. I. Of Ye Limits of Reason." (The verses have been published by Professor Sherburn in "Pope at Work," *Essays on the Eighteenth Century Presented to David Nichol Smith* [Oxford, 1945], pp. 59–60). The pages of the notebook measure 11¹¹⁄₁₆ in. by 9½ in.

2. The lines quoted are given as in the manuscript: Epistle I, leaf 1, recto. References to the Morgan manuscript (MLM) in this introduction will be made to epistle, leaf, and recto or verso, counting as leaf 1 of each epistle the first leaf to contain text. References to the Harvard manuscript (HLM) will be made to the pages, which Pope has numbered consecutively from Epistle I through Epistle III.

Quotations from the *Essay* that are not explicitly cited from one or other of the two manuscripts under consideration follow the Twickenham text and line numberings.

For a full account of the "system of Ethics in the Horatian way" of which these and several unwritten poems were once planned to be part, see Miriam Leranbaum, *Alexander Pope's "Opus Magnum," 1729–1744* (Oxford: Clarendon Press, 1977).

3. *Correspondence,* 3:214.

4. MLM, Epistle II, leaf 2, recto. For other examples, see the companion volume, *Collected in Himself* (Newark, Del.: University of Delaware Press, 1982), pp. 331–32.

5. MLM, Epistle I, leaf 4, verso.

6. HLM, p. 9.

7. The notion that lions have defective scent was current in the eighteenth century: see the notes on this passage in the Twickenham Edition. But I have found nowhere else the idea that lions hunt by ear.

8. HLM, p. 34.

9. I quote from the manuscript text of the poem, as reproduced in G. A. Aitken's *The Life and Works of John Arbuthnot* (1892), pp. 439–42.

10. Epistle IV, leaf 1, recto. Pope's reference is apparently to Hobbes's *Leviathan* (1651), pp. 25 and 47, or to his *Humane Nature* (1650), pp. 74–75.

11. Leaf 2, recto.

12. Leaf 2, verso.

13. The propositions appear in this order in the manuscript. Though it is impossible to be sure, proposition 8 seems originally to have been numbered 7 and then renumbered when proposition 7 was conceived.

14. Wollaston's book, privately printed in 1722, was not published till 1724. Pope refers to it in a letter to Bethel dated 12 July 1723, but the date, as Professor Sherburn notes (*Correspondence,* 2:179 n.), is questionable.

15. For other passages influenced by Wollaston's book, see the Index in the Twickenham Edition of the *Essay.*

16. I have distinguished the verse lines by italics to show the absorption of *with Patience* from the prose line into the verse.

17. The relevant passage from Pascal is quoted in the companion volume to this, *Collected in Himself,* p. 331.

18. "Pope at Work," in *Essays on the Eighteenth Century presented to David Nichol Smith* (1945), p. 52.

19. Spence, Nos. 310–11, and also Spence, Volume 2, pp. 632–33. On Bathurst's testimony, see Sherburn's "Two Notes on the Essay on Man," in *Philological Quarterly* 12 (1933):402, and R. W. Rogers, *The Major Satires of Alexander Pope* (Urbana, Ill.: University of Illinois Press, 1955), p. 46.

20. *Richardsoniana* (1772), p. 264.

21. I am again grateful for permission to publish.

22. The brackets occur in the original.

23. The latter phrase is Joseph Warton's: see his *Essay on the Genius and Writings of Pope,* vol. 2 (1782), p. 62.

24. Conceivably some of the Mapledurham fragments (above, pp. 167, 168) represent such brouillons.

25. Leaf 1, recto.

26. Ibid.

27. Leaf 2, recto.

28. Leaf 2, verso. Teague is the comic Irishman in Robert Howard's play *The Committee,* who explains (V, i) that his legs are not under his own control but the devil's.

29. Ibid. (None of Pope's variants in these passages is canceled).

30. Leaf 3, recto.

31. Leaf 3, verso. (None of Pope's variants is canceled).

32. See *Collected in Himself,* pp. 119–20.

33. MLM, Epistle III, leaf 2, verso. Matteo Berselli (whose dates are not known) was an Italian operatic tenor performing in London during the 1720s.

34. The numberings indicate Pope's projected rearrangement.

35. HLM, pp. 16–17. (None of Pope's variants for "observe . . . face" is canceled).

36. HLM, p. 22.

37. MLM, leaf 3, verso. Though a preference for Marcellus and Caesar was no doubt dictated by political discretion, the point still holds. The English names do not have the same symbolic resonance.

38. MLM, Epistle III, final page (numbered 10) of the folded leaf which follows leaf 5.

39. Epistle III, final half-leaf, recto (p. 11).

40. MLM, Epistle IV, leaf 1, recto. Pope at first reversed the order of the man-as-vine couplet and that following it, but then shifted it to the position indicated here.

41. MLM, Epistle IV, leaf 1, verso. In transcribing this passage and the earlier passages incorporating the man-as-vine couplet, I have not attempted to register variant readings.

42. MLM, Epistle IV, leaf 2, verso.

43. HLM, p. 43.

44. R. W. Rogers, *Major Satires of Alexander Pope* (Urbana, Ill.: University of Illinois Press, 1955), p. 103.

45. Ibid.

46. MLM, Epistle I, leaf 2, recto; HLM, p. 4.

47. Rogers, *Major Satires,* p. 105.

48. MLM, Epistle III, final page (numbered 10) of the folded leaf which follows leaf 5.

Pope also added IV. 173–80 in the edition prepared with Warburton—according to Professor Rogers (p. 105), in order to subsume "the idea of a future life" and thus "allay criticism of Pope's intention in Epistle I, lines 9 ff." For the third couplet in this passage—

> Go, like the Indian, in another life
> Expect thy dog, thy bottle, and thy wife—

Pope turned to lines in MLM, Epistle IV, leaf 1, verso:

> By outward Goods who thinks this Bliss is given,
> Hopes, Indian-like, his Wife & Dog in Heavn;

and for the fourth couplet—

> As well as dream such trifles are assign'd,
> As toys and empires, for a god-like mind—

to lines in MLM, Epistle IV, leaf 3, verso:

> Far other & more worthier far has Heav'n assignd[:]
> Toys, Gowns, & Empires for a God-like mind!

A further addition from the manuscripts, possibly on similar moral and theological grounds, was the famous passage on man as child, II, 275–82. See *Collected in Himself*, p. 337–38.

49. The line numbers are again those of the Twickenham text. On the quarto leaf, they are 283–304. A facsimile of the passage was published by Elwin and Courthope as frontispiece to volume 3 of Pope's *Works*. I am in debt to the Yale Library for permission to publish here from the autograph.

50. See Pope's letter of 21 May [1731] to Edward Harley, the first Lord Oxford's son (*Correspondence*, 3:199).

51. Pope alludes to this in his *Imitations of Horace: Satires* I. 2.9–10.

52. See *Essay*, IV. 289 ("hearts of Kings") and the second manuscript insertion transcribed below.

53. Pope's poems contain many allusions to Marlborough's tightfistedness: see his *Epistle to Dr. Arbuthnot*, 392; *Imitations of Horace: Epistles* II. ii. 33–51 and I. i. 126–27.

54. See *Essay*, IV. 312–14 and the second manuscript insertion below.

55. See the second manuscript insertion below.

56. The "arms of Queens" (*Essay*, IV. 289) may be a loose way of referring to Marlborough's supposed affair with the Duchess of Cleveland, mistress to Charles II.

57. In this line Pope cancels only *In each* and *equal.*

58. There was also a point at which Pope momentarily restored lines 297–98, striking out the part of his earlier cancellation that concerned these two lines.

59. Pope forgot to revise "their" in this case.

60. Marlborough's "Captive" is evidently Tallard, the French general who became his prisoner at the battle of Blenheim in 1704 and who had lost his son in the battle: see Addison's poem *The Campaign*, 335–50. The idea seems to be that Marlborough now laments, like Tallard, the loss of an heir (his son having died of small pox the year before Blenheim).

61. The quarto of course may have been in print somewhat before its publication date.

62. *Correspondence*, 3:327. The Marquess of Blandford, son to Henrietta, Marlborough's eldest daughter, had died on the 24th of August.

63. Above, p. 190.

64. Writing to Atterbury on 27 July [1722] (*Correspondence*, 2:127), Pope makes the suggestive comment that "at the time of the Duke of Marlborough's funeral [9 August 1722], I intend to lye at the Deanery, and moralize one evening with you on the vanity of human Glory." Perhaps some of his moralizings soon took the form of verse.

65. These words, if correctly transcribed (as I believe they are), perhaps glance at his supposed advancement through the favor of the Duchess of Cleveland: see above, n. 57.

66. Spence, No. 366: "I have omitted a character (though I thought it one of the best I had ever written) of a very great man who had every thing from without to make him happy, and yet was very miserable; from the want of virtue in his own heart—P. [Though he did not say who this was, it seemed to have been that of the Duke of Marlborough. . . S.]"

67. Pope made a further insertion on the quarto leaf. It has nothing to do with Marlborough, but for the record should be mentioned here. Marked to enter the poem after Epistle IV. 315, it reads as follows:

> Ev'n while it seems unequal to dispose,
> And checquers all the good man's joys with woes
> Tis but to teach him to support each state
> With Patience this, with moderation that
> And raise his base on that one solid joy
> Which conscience gives & nothing can destroy.

Like the manuscript lines on Marlborough, these seem to me to accomplish nothing that the poet had not already accomplished better. I suspect he came across them when returning to the Morgan manuscript for the Marlborough insertions. As the reader will recall, he had interlineated an early version of them in Epistle IV at the top of leaf 3, verso. A more finished version will be found on the same page in the right margin. What is again significant, I think, is that the lines were never allowed to be printed.

Epist. I. Of Man, in ye Abstract, with respect to the Universal System.

<1,2>

in y^e Abstract,

Epist. 1. Of Man with respect to the

Universal System.

1

Awake my Memmius, leave all meaner things
To working Statesmen & Ambitious Kings. ×
~~Let us~~ Let us, Since Life ~~my Friend~~ can little more supply
Than just to look about us, and to die;
Let us Expatiate, ~~free~~, o'er all the Scene of Man;
×+ A mighty Maze! of Walks without a Plan;
+ Or Wilde, where Weeds and Flowrs promiscuous shoot; ×
Or Orchard, tempting with forbidden Fruit. +
Together let us beat this ample Field,
Try what all the open, what all the covert yield, ×
Of all who blindly creep, the tracks explore, ×
And all the dazled race who sightless soar;
Eye Nature's walks, shoot Folly as it flies, ×
And catch the Manners living as they rise;
Laugh where we must; be candid where we can;
~~And~~ But vindicate the Ways of God to Man.

But

× Laelius

× Inconsistency of Character, ye Subject of Ep. 5

× passions, Virtues &c. ye Subject of Ep. 2.

× ~~wild~~ Pleasure, in Lib. 2.

+ the use of ~~Books, and~~ Dress

× Of the Knowledge of mankind ~~the Character, &c.~~ Epistle 1st of Book 2.

× Learning & Ignorance, Subject of Epist. 3 of Book 2.

× The rest In general.

Awake my Memmius, leave all meaner things

groveling low-thoughted
To working Statesmen & ambitious Kings.

Let us, ~~my Friend~~
~~Let us~~ Since Life can little more supply
^ ^

Than just to look about us, and to die)

~~Let us~~ ~~we~~
Expatiate, ~~free~~, o'er all the Scene of Man;
^

\+ + A mighty Maze! of Walks without a Plan;

\+ Or Wilde, where Weeds and Flowrs promiscuous shoot;

Or Orchard, tempting with forbidden Fruit.

Together let us beat this ample field,

all all
Try what the open, what the covert yield,

Of all who blindly creep, the tracks explore,

And all the dazled race who sightless soar;

Eye Nature's walks, shoot Folly as it flies,

And catch the Manners living as they rise;

Laugh where we must; be candid where we can;

But
And vindicate the ways of God to Man.

But

\+ Inconsistencys of Character, y[e] Subject of Ep. 5.

\+

\+ Passions, Virtues &c. y[e] Subject of Ep. 2.

~~wild~~
\+ The use of Pleasure, in Lib. 2.
~~deckd, and~~
~~drest~~

Of the Knowledge of mankind
\+ ~~The Characters see~~ Epistle 1st of Book 2.
^ ^

\+ Learning and Ignorance, Subject of Epist. 3 of Book 2.

The rest
\+ ^ In general.

~~But~~ Say first, of God above, or Man below,
What can we reason but from what we know?
not used { ~~Thro endless worlds His endless works are known;~~
~~But ours to trace him only in our own.~~
Of Man, what see we but his Station here,
From which to ~~argue~~ reason, or to which refer?
~~Thro worlds unbounded~~ Tho' if God be known, 'tis ours to trace him only in our own.
3d page. Of this vast Frame, the Bearings, & the Ties;
The close Connections, nice Dependencies,
x qu. ~~the confining~~ And Centres just, has Thy pervading Soul
Look'd thro', or can a Part contain the Whole?
Is the strong Chain that draws all to agree,
And drawn supports, upheld by ~~God~~ Him, or thee?
He who can all the flaming limits pierce
Of Worlds on worlds, that form one Universe,
Observe how System into System runs,
What other Planets, & what other Suns?
What ~~other Man dwells in~~ vary'd Being peoples ev'ry Star?
May tell, why Heav'n has made us as we are.

When the proud Steed shall know, why Man now reins
His stubborn neck, now drives him o'er the plains;
Pag. 4th. When the dull Oxe, why now he breaks the clod,
Now wears a Garland an Ægyptian God;
Then shall Man's pride & dulness comprehend
His Action's, Passion's, Being's Use and End;
Why doing, suff'ring, check'd, impell'd, and why
This hour a Slave, the next a Deity?

Pre-

Say
~~But~~ first, of God above, or Man below,

What can we reason but from what we know?

δ ~~Thro endless worlds His endless works are known;~~

~~But ours to trace him, only in our own.~~

Of Man, what see we but his station here,

reason
From which to ~~argue,~~ or to which refer?

Thro worlds unbounded tho y[e] God be known, Tis ours to trace him only in our own.

3[d] page. Of this vast Frame, the Bearings, & the Ties,
His
The close Connections, nice Dependencies,

~~All centring just~~
+ qu. And Centres just, has Thy pervading Soul

Lookd thro', or can a Part contain the Whole?

Is the strong Chain that draws all to agree

~~Him~~
And drawn supports, upheld by God, or thee?

He who can all the flaming limits pierce

Of Worlds on worlds, that form one Universe,

Observe how System into System runs,

What other Planets, & what other Suns?

vary'd Being peoples
What ~~other Habitants in~~ ev'ry Star?

May tell, why Heav'n has made us as we are.

When the proud Steed shall know, why Man now reins

His stubborn neck, now drives him o'er the plains,

Pag. 4.th When the dull Oxe, why now he breaks the clod,

Now wears a Garland an AEgyptian God;

Then shall Man's pride & dulness comprehend

His Action's, Passion's, Being's Use and End;

Why doing, suff'ring, check'd, impell'd, and why

This hour a Slave, the next a Deity?

Pre-

9

Presumptuous Man! the reason wouldst thou find
Why made so weak, so little, and so blind?
First if thou can'st, the harder reason guess,
Why fram'd no weaker, blinder, and no less?
Ask of thy Mother Earth, why Oaks are made
Taller or stronger than the Plants they shade?
Or ask of yonder argent Fields above,
Why Jove's Satellites are less than Jove?

\+ 8 lines wanting here
15. Pag.

Respecting Man whatever wrong we call,
May, must be right, as relative to All.
In human works, tho' labor'd on with pain,
A Thousand movements scarce one purpose gain;
In God's, one single can its end produce,
Yet serves to second too some other Use.
So Man, who here seems Principal alone,
Perhaps acts second to some Sphere unknown,
Touches some wheel, or verges to some Gole;
'Tis but a part We see, ~~not here a Part~~, & not a Whole.

Then say not Man's Imperfect, Heav'n in fault:
Say rather, Man's as perfect as he ought:
p. 6. If to be perfect in a certain Sphere;
What matter, soon or late, or ~~[illegible]~~ here or there?
The Blest to Day is as completely so, As, who began ten thous.^d years ago.
In the same hand, the same all-plastic Pow'r,
Or at the Natal, or in the Mortal hour.
[Heav'n from all Creatures hides the Book of Fate,
All but the Page prescrib'd, their present State;

His Knowledge measur'd to his State & Place
~~[illegible]~~
His Time a Moment, and a point his Space

\+ Lucretius of death reversst. Lib. 3. fine.

omitted

From

Presumptuous Man! the reason wouldst thou find
Why made so weak, so little, and so blind?
First if thou can'st, the harder reason guess,
Why fram'd no weaker, blinder, and no less?
Ask of thy Mother Earth, why oaks are made
Taller or Stronger than the Plants they shade?
Or ask of yonder argent Fields above,
Why Jove's Satellites are less than Jove?

Respecting Man whatever wrong we call, (5.pag.
May, must be right, as relative to All.
In human Works, tho', labor'd on with pain,
A Thousand movements scarce one purpose gain;
In God's, one single can its end produce,
Yet serves to second too some other Use.
So Man, who here seems Principal alone,
Perhaps acts second to some Sphere unknown,
Touches some wheel, or verges to some Gole;
Tis but a part
We see, ~~but here a Part~~ &, not a Whole.

Then say not Man's Imperfect, Heav'n in fault:
Say rather, Man's as perfect as he ought:

His Knowledge measur'd to his State & Place
\+ ~~Lord of a Span & Hero of a Day;~~
~~In one short Scene, to strut, & pass away.~~

Point
His Time a Moment, and a ~~Span~~ his Space

p. 6. If to be perfect in a certain Sphere,
matter, soon or late, or
What ~~then imports it whether~~ here or there?
The Blest today is as completely so, As who began ten thous.[d] years ago.

† Lucretius of death
reverst. lib. 3.fini<s.>

In the same hand, the same all-plastic Pow'r,
~~As~~ ~~in~~
Or in the natal, or the Mortal hour.
[Heav'n from all Creatures hides the Book of Fate,
All but the Page prescrib'd, their present State;

From

From Brutes what men, from men what Spirits know;
Or who could suffer Being here below?
The Lamb thy Riot dooms to bleed to day,
- Had he thy Reason, would he skip & play?
Pleas'd to the last, he crops the flowry food,
And licks the hand just rais'd to shed his blood.

7th Oh blindness to the future! kindly given,
That each may fill the Circle mark'd by Heav'n,
Who sees with equal eye, as God of All,
A Hero perish, and a Sparrow fall:
No Great, no Little! ~~'Tis~~ as much decreed
That Virgils Gnat should die, as Cæsar bleed.

† Vid Epist 3. of animals † for Verse

Hope humbly then, with trembling pinions soar!
Wait the great Teacher, Death, & God adore!
What Bliss above, he gives not thee to know,
But gives that Hope to be thy bliss below.
Hope springs eternal in the human breast;
Man never is, but always to be blest;
The Soul uneasy, & confin'd at home,
Rests, and expatiates in a Life to come.

6 lines omitted here →

8. ~~See~~ [Lo!] the poor Indian, whose untutor'd mind
~~Seeks~~ [Sees] God in Clouds, or ~~on the wings of~~ [hears him in the] Wind;
His Soul, [thought] proud Science never taught to stray,
Far, as the Solar Year, or †milky Way;
Yet Nature's flattery this Hope has given;
Behind his cloud-topt Hills he ~~frames~~ [builds] a Heaven,
~~Some happier World, wth woods or wonders infold,~~
~~Where never Christian pierced for thirst of Gold.~~

Some

† the ancient Opinion yt ye Souls of ye Just went thither
See Tully Somn. Scipion. Manil. l.

From Brutes what Men, from Men what Spirits know;
Or who could suffer Being here below?
The Lamb thy Riot dooms to bleed to day,
Had he thy Reason, would he skip & play?
Pleasd to the last, he crops the flowry food,
And licks the hand just rais'd to shed his blood.
7th. Oh blindness to the future! kindly given,
That each may fill the Circle mark'd by Heav'n,
Who sees with equal eye, as God of All,
\+ A Hero perish, and a Sparrow fall:
No Great, no Little! and as much decreed
That Virgils Gnat should die, as Caesar bleed.

\+ Vid Epist 3. of Animals
<frõ> Verse

Hope humbly then, with trembling pinions soar!
Wait the great Teacher, Death, & God adore!
What Bliss above, he gives not thee to know,
But gives that Hope to be thy bliss below.
Hope springs eternal in the human breast;
Man never <u>is</u>, but always <u>to</u> <u>be</u> blest;
The Soul uneasy, &, confin'd at home,
Rests, and expatiates in a Life to come.

8. ~~See~~ Lo! the poor Indian, whose untutor'd mind
~~Seeks~~ Sees God in Clouds, or ~~on the Wings of~~ hears him in the Wind;
His soul, proud Science never ~~learnt~~ taught to stray, thought
Far, as the Solar Year, or+ milky Way:
Yet Nature's flattery this Hope has given;
Behind his cloud-topt Hills he ~~frames~~ builds a Heaven,
Some Happier World, wth Woods on Woods infold,
Where never Christian piercd for thirst of Gold.

\+ The ancient opinion y^t y^e
Souls of y^e Just went thither
See Tully Somn. Scipion. Manil. 1.

Some

~~Some safer World, in depth of woods embrac'd,~~
~~Some happier Island, in the watry Waste,~~
~~Where Gold nere grows, & never Spaniards come,~~
~~Where Trees bear maize, & rivers flow w.th Reeds~~
~~Exil'd, or chain'd, he lets you understand~~
~~Death but returns him to his native Land;~~
~~Or firm as Martyrs, smiling yields the ghost,~~
~~Rich of a Life, that is not to be lost.~~

Where ~~Captives~~ Slaves once more
their native Land behold,
No Fiends torment, × nor Christians thirst for Gold.

But does He say, the Maker is not good,
Till he's exalted to the State he would? "Himself alone high heavens peculiar Care?
~~[illegible]~~
~~He wants for Bliss in a remoter Sphere,~~ [illegible] ~~his only care?~~
~~Himself~~ alone made happy,
~~Not proudly claims it~~ when he will, and where: (~~9~~)
Go, wiser Thou! and in thy Scale of Sense   4 lines omitted here
Weigh ~~here~~ thy Opinion against Providence; (9)
Call Imperfection what you fancy such;
Pronounce ~~His acts~~ too little or too much;
Destroy all Creatures for thy Sport or Gust;
Yet, if unhappy, think tis He's unjust;
Snatch from his hand the Balance & the Rod,
Re-judge his Justice; be the God of God!

In Pride (my Friend) in Pride, our Error lies,
Our Sphere we quit, and rush into the Skies.
Pride still is aiming at the blest Abodes;
Men would be Angels, Angels would be Gods;
Aspiring to be Gods if Angels fell,
Aspiring to be Angels, Men rebell:
And who but wishes to invert the Laws 10
Of Order, sins against th' Eternal Cause.

Ask

Some safer World, in depth of Woods embrac'd,
Some happier Island, in the watry Waste,

Slaves
Where ~~Captives~~ once more
their native land behold,

torment
Nor ~~r~~ Fiends nor Christians thirst for
Gold.

~~Where Gold n'er grows, & never Spaniards come,~~
~~Where Trees bear maize, & Rivers flow wth. Rum~~
~~Exil'd or chain'd, he lets you understand~~
~~Death but returns him to his native Land;~~
~~Or firm as Martyrs, smiling yields the ghost,~~
~~Rich of a Life, that is not to be lost.~~

But does He say, the Maker is not good,
Till he's exalted to the State he wou'd?

Himself alone high heavns peculiar
~~Not just, unless himself alone his~~ Care?

~~<or>~~ ← → ~~himself~~
~~Arraign Not Justice the blessings not <un>determind <pres~~cribd>~~< > his only Care?~~
~~He waits for Bliss in a remoter Sphere,~~
Himself alone made happy
~~Nor proudly claims it~~ when he will, and where; ~~(9)~~
Go, wiser Thou! and in thy Scale of sense (9)
Weigh ~~here~~ thy Opinion against Providence;
Call Imperfection what you fancy such;
Pronounce He Acts too little or too much;
Destroy all Creatures for thy Sport or Gust;
Yet, if unhappy, think tis He's unjust;
Snatch from his hand the Balance & the Rod;
Re-judge his Justice; be the God of God!

In Pride (my Friend) in Pride, our Error lies,
Our Sphere we quit, and rush into the Skies.
Pride still is aiming at the blest abodes;
Men would be Angels, Angels would be Gods;
Aspiring to be Gods if Angels fell,
Aspiring to be Angels, Men rebell:
And who but wishes to invert the Laws (10
Of Order, sins against th' Eternal Cause.

Ask

II.

Ask for what End the Heav'nly Bodies shine?
Earth for whose use? Pride answers, 'Tis for mine:
For me young Nature paints her vernal bower,
Suckles each herb, and pencils ev'ry flow'r;
Annual for me, the Grape, the Rose renew
The juice nectareous, and the balmy dew;
For me, the Mine a thousand treasures brings;
For me, Health gushes from a thousand Springs;
Seas roll to waft me, Suns to light me rise;
My footstool Earth, my Canopy the Skies!

But errs not Nature from this gracious End,
From burning Suns when livid Deaths descend?
When Earth quakes ~~quick~~ swallows, or ~~[illegible] when~~ Tempests ~~or when Oceans~~ sweep
Towns to one grave, ~~and~~ Nations to the Deep?
Blame we for this the dread Almighty Cause?
"No ('tis reply'd) he acts by Gen'ral Laws;
"Th'exceptions few; some Change since all began;
"And what created, perfect?"— Why then Man?
If the great End be human happiness,
And Nature deviates, how can Man do less?
Nature as much a constant course requires
Of Show'rs & Sunshine, as of Man's Desires;
As much eternal Springs and cloudless Skies
As Man for ever temp'rate, calm, & wise.
If Plagues or Earthquakes break not Heav'n's design
Why then a Borgia or a Catiline?

From

II.

Ask for what End the Heav'nly Bodies shine?
Earth for whose use? Pride answers, Tis for mine:
For me young Nature paints her vernal bower,
Suckles each herb, and pencils ev'ry flow'r;
Annual for me, the Grape, the Rose renew
The juice nectareous, and the balmy dew;
For me, the Mine a thousand treasures brings;
For me, Health gushes from a thousand Springs;
Seas roll to waft me, Suns to light me rise;
My footstool Earth, my Canopy the Skies!

But errs not Nature from this gracious End,
From burning Suns when livid Deaths descend?
quakes or ~~Inundations~~ when Tempests
11th) When Earth ~~quick~~ swallow~~s,~~ ~~or when Oceans~~ sweep
a
Towns to one grave, ~~and~~ Nation~~s~~ to the Deep?
Blame we for this the dread Almighty Cause?
"No (tis reply'd) he acts by Gen'ral Laws;
"Th' exceptions few; some Change since all began;
"And what Created, perfect?" - Why then Man?
If the great End be human happiness;
And Nature deviates, how can Man do less?
Nature as much a constant course requires
Of Showrs & Sunshine, as of Man's Desires;
As much eternal Springs and cloudless Skies
As Man for ever temp'rate, calm, & wise.
If Plagues or Earthquakes break not Heav'n's design
Why then a Borgia or a Catiline?

From

From whence all Physical or moral Ill?
'Tis Nature, wandring from th' Eternal Will. } ×
Why charge we here our Maker, there acquit? (12
In both, to reason right is to submit.

Better for Us perhaps it might appear,
Were there all Harmony, all Virtue here;
That never Air or Ocean felt the Wind,
That never Passion discompos'd the mind:
But All subsists by Elemental Strife,
And + Passions are the Elements of Life: + See Epist. 2. Vers
The genral Order, since the Whole began,
Is kept in Nature, and is kept in Man.

III. What would this Man? now upward will he soar,
And little less than Angel, would be more;
Now looking downward, just as griev'd appears
To want the Brawn of Bulls, the Fur of Bears. {18
Made for his use all Creatures if he call, — 13.
Say what their use, had he the Pow'rs of all?
Nature to each, without profusion kind,
The proper Organs, proper pow'rs assign'd,
Each seeming want compensated of course,
Here, due degrees of Swiftness, there of Force;
With quickest
With eyes dele
Each Beast, each Insect happy as it can,
Is Heav'n unkind to nothing but to Man?
So justly all proportion'd to each State,
Nothing to add, and nothing to abate:
Shall man, shall reasonable Man, alone,
Be, or endow'd with all, or pleas'd with none?

From whence all Physical or Moral Ill?
'Tis Nature, wandring from th' Eternal Will.
Why charge we here our Maker, there acquit? (12
In both, to reason right is to submit.

Better for Us perhaps it might appear,
Were there all Harmony, all Virtue, here;
That never Air or Ocean felt the Wind,
That never Passion discomposd the mind:
But All subsists by Elemental Strife,
And + Passions are the Elements of Life: +See Epist. ~~3~~ 2. Vers.
The gen'ral Order, since the Whole began,
Is kept in Nature, and is kept in Man.

III What would this Man? now upward will he soar,
And little less than Angel, would be more;
Now looking downward, just as griev'd appears
To want the Brawn of Bulls, the Fur of Bears. ~~13~~
Made for his use all Creatures if he call, 13
Say what their use, had he the Pow'rs of all?
Nature to each, without profusion kind,
The proper organs, proper pow'rs assign'd,
Each seeming want compensated of course,
Here, due degrees of Swiftness, there of Force;
δ With quickest ~~dele~~
With eyes
Each Beast, each Insect happy as it can,
Is Heavn unkind to nothing but to Man?
So justly all proportion'd to each State,
Nothing to add, and nothing to abate:
Shall man, shall reasonable Man, alone,
Be, or endow'd with all, or pleas'd with none?

see, thro whole Life
× ~~Behold~~, thro all a gradual Scale arise,
Of Sensual, and of mental Faculties!
vast / Mans Imperial
14- ~~How wide the~~ Range of Sense, from ~~human~~ race
To the green Myriads in the peopled Grass!
What / be ~~between~~ / wide
~~How many~~ Modes of Sight twixt each extreme,
The Mole's dim Curtain & the Lynx's Beam!
the [illegible] headlong [illegible] / Lioness
vel delend ~~Degrees~~ Of Smell, ~~the~~ [illegible] between,
And Hound, sagacious on the tainted green!
Of Hearing, from the Life that fills the Flood,
To that which warbles thro the vernal Wood!
In the nice Bee, what sence so subtly true
From poisnous herbs extracts the healing dew!
The Spiders touch, how exquisitely fine,
Feels at each thread, and lives along the line!
How Instinct varies! what a Hog may want
Compard with thine, half-reasining Elephant!
Instinct
× Twixt that, and Reason, what a nice Barrier,
For ever sep'rate, yet for ever near!
15- Remembrance and Reflexion, how allied!
What thin partitions Sense from Thought divide!
And middle natures, how they long to join,
Yet never pass th' insuperable Line!
Without this just Gradation, could they be
Subjected these to those or all to thee?
The Pow'rs of all subdu'd by thee alone,
Is not thy Reason all those pow'rs in one?

The

See, thro whole Life
Behold, thro all a gradual Scale arise,
Of Sensual, and of mental Faculties!
Vast Mans imperial
14- ~~How wide the~~ Range of <u>Sense</u>, from ~~human~~ ^ race
To the green Myriads in the peopled Grass!
What be ~~between~~ wide
~~How many~~ Modes of <u>Sight</u> twixt each ^ extreme,
~~to~~
The Mole's dim Curtain & the Lynx's Beam!
headlong
the ~~each vulgar brute~~ lioness
vel ~~Degrees~~ Of <u>Smell</u>, ~~the stupid Ass~~ ^ between,
delend
And Hound, sagacious on the tainted green!
Of <u>Hearing</u>, from the Life that fills the Flood,
To that which warbles thro the vernal Wood!
In the nice Bee, what sence so subtly true,
From pois'nous herbs extracts the healing dew!
The Spiders <u>touch</u>, how exquisitely fine,
Feels at each thread, and lives along the line!
How <u>Instinct</u> varies! what a Hog may want
Compar'd with thine, half-reas'ning Elephant!
~~Instinct~~
Twixt that, and <u>Reason</u>, what a nice Barrier,
For ever sep'rate, yet for ever near!
15- <u>Remembrance</u> and <u>Reflexion</u>, how allied!
What thin partitions <u>Sense</u> from <u>Thought</u> divide!
And <u>middle</u> <u>Natures</u>, how they long to join,
Yet never pass th' Insuperable Line!
Without this just <u>Gradation</u>, could they be
Subjected these to those, or all to thee?
The Pow'rs of all subdu'd by thee alone,
Is not thy Reason all those pow'rs in one?
The

The bliss of Man (could Pride that blessing find)
Is, not to know nor think beyond Mankind;
No self-confounding Faculties to share;
No Senses stronger than his brain can bear.
Why has not man a microscopic Eye?
For this plain reason, Man is not a Fly:
What the advantage, if his finer eyes -16
Study a Mite, not comprehend the Skies?
His Touch, if tremblingly alive all o'er,
To smart, and agonize at ev'ry pore?
Or quick Effluvia darting thro his brain,
Dye of a Rose, in aromatic pain?
If Nature Thunder'd in his opening Ears,
And stunn'd him with the Music of the Spheres,
How wd he wish that Heav'n had left him still
The whisp'ring Zephyr and the purling Rill?
Who finds not Providence all-good, & ~~all~~-wise,
Alike in what it gives, & what denies?

See, thro' this Air, this Ocean & this Earth,
All Matter quick, and bursting into Birth.
Above, how high progressive Life ~~must~~ may go? (17
Around, how wide? how deep extend below?
Vast Chain of Being! which from God began,
Ethereal Essence, Spirit, Substance, Man,
Beast, Bird, Fish, Insect: What no Eye can see,
No Glass can reach! From Infinite to Thee!
From Thee to Nothing! — On superior Pow'rs
Were we to press, inferior ~~must~~ might on ours:

Or

The bliss of Man (could Pride that blessing find)
Is, not to know ~~n~~or think beyond Mankind;
No self-confounding Faculties to share;
No Senses stronger than his brain can bear.
Why has not Man a microscopic Eye?
For this plain reason, Man is not a Fly:
What the advantage, if his finer eyes -16
Study a Mite, not comprehend the Skies?
His Touch, if tremblingly alive all o'er,
To smart, and agonize at ev'ry pore?
Or quick Effluvia darting thro his brain,
Dye of a Rose, in aromatic pain?
If Nature Thunder'd in his opening Ears,
And stunnd him with the Music of the Spheres,
How w^{d} he wish that Heav'n had left him still
The whisp'ring Zephyr and the purling Rill?
Who finds not Providence all-good, ~~all~~ & -wise,
Alike in what it *gives*, & what *denies*?

See, thro' this Air, this Ocean & this Earth,
All Matter quick, and bursting into Birth.
Above, how high progressive Life ~~must~~ may go? (17
Around, how wide? how deep extend below?
Vast chain of Being! which from God began,
Ethereal Essence, Spirit, Substance, Man,
Beast, Bird, Fish, Insect: What no Eye can see,
No Glass can reach! From Infinite to Thee!
From Thee to nothing!--On superior Pow'rs
Were we to press, inferior ~~must~~ might on ours:

Or

~~Or leave in Nature wch it hates, a void,~~

Or in wch Creation leave ~~a Gap~~, a Void,

~~Or leave a Gap in the Creation void,~~

~~The [illegible] broken if a Step destroyd.~~

Where, ~~one~~ Step broken, the ~~great~~ Scale's destroy'd.

From Nature's Chain whatever Link you strike,

Tenth, or ten thousandth, breaks the Chain alike.

~~yet more, ever~~ and if each Systems in Gradation roll,

Alike essential to th' amazing Whole.

181 The least confusion but in one, not all

That System only, but the Whole must fall.

All this dread Order, shall it break? For thee?

Vile Worm! O madness! Pride! Impiety!

This after (All are but Parts of one stupendous Whole:

Nature the Body is, and God the Soul;

Varied thro all, & yet in all the same,

~~Strong in the~~ Powerful in Earth, as in th' ætherial Frame,

Warms in the Sun, refreshes in the Breeze,

Glows in the Stars, and blossoms in the Trees,

2 Breathes in our Soul, informs our mortal ~~Lives~~ part,

× As ~~full~~, as perfect in a ~~Hair~~, as Heart

As full, as perfect, in vile man y^t^ mourns, As the rapt Seraphim y^t^ sings & burns,

19 Lives thro all Life, extends thro all Extent,

1. Spreads un-divided, operates un-spent,

To this no high, no low, no great, no small,

It fills, it bounds, connects, and equals all.

Put first (Just as absurd, for any Part to claim

To be another, in this gen'ral Frame;

As

~~Or leave in Nature w^{t} it hates, a void,~~
Or in [ye full] Creation leave ~~a Chasm,~~ a void,
~~Or leave a Gap in the Creation void,~~
~~The Scale is broken if a step destroy'd.~~
Where, a~~ne~~ step broken, the great Scale's destroy'd.
From Nature's chain whatever Link you strike,
Tenth, or ten thousandth, breaks the Chain alike.
~~Yet more: ev'n~~ [and if each] System~~s~~ in Gradation roll,
Alike essential to th' amazing Whole.
18) The least confusion but in one, not all
That System only, but the Whole must fall.
All this dread Order, shall it break? For thee?
Vile Worm! O Madness! Pride! Impiety!

This after (
All are but Parts of one stupendous Whole:
Nature the Body is, and God the Soul;
Varied thro all, & yet in all the same,
~~Strong in the~~ [Pow'rful in] Earth, as in th' aethereal Frame,
Warms in the Sun, refreshes in the Breeze,
Glows in the Stars, and blossoms in the Trees,
Lives--
2 (Breathes in our Soul, informs our mortal part,
As full, as perfect, in a Hair, as Heart,
As full, as perfect, ~~In~~ → in vile man y^{t} ~~ungrateful~~ mourns, As the rapt Seraphim y^{t} sings & burns.
19 (Lives thro' all Life, extends thro' all Extent,
1. Spreads un-divided, operates un-spent,
To this no high, no low, no great, no small,
It fills, it bounds, connects, and equals all.

Put first (
Just as absurd, for any Part to claim
To be ~~stand~~ another, in this gen'ral Frame;
As

6

As if the Foot, ordain'd the Dust to tread,
Or Hand to toil, aspir'd to be the Head;
As if that Head, the eye or ear repin'd
To serve mere Engines to the ruling Mind;
Just as absurd, to mourn the Tasks or Pains
The great, directing Mind of All ordains.

all are but parts &c

Cease then, nor Order Imperfection ~~call~~ name,
~~On which depends the Happiness of all~~ Our proper Bliss depends on what we blame.
~~On what thou can'st~~ Safe and content Know thy own point: This just, this kind Degree
Of Blindness, Weakness, Heav'n bestows on thee.
Submit! in this, or any other Sphere,
Secure to be as blest as thou canst bear.
All Nature is but Art, unknown to thee;
All Chance, Direction which thou canst not see; ← 2 lines omitted here
And spite of Pride, and in thy Reason's spight,
One truth is clear; "Whatever Is, is Right."

274. Thy will be done, in Earth as it is in Heaven

As if the Foot, ordain'd the dust to tread,
Or Hand to toil, aspir'd to be the Head;
As if that Head, the eye or ear repin'd
To serve mere Engines to the ruling Mind;
Just as absurd, to mourn the Tasks or Pains
The great, directing <u>Mind</u> <u>of</u> <u>All</u> ordains.

all are but parts &c.

name
Cease then, nor Order Imperfection ~~call~~,

Our proper Bliss depends on what we blame
~~On which depends the Happiness of All:~~

~~See and confess~~
~~On that thy own~~: This just, this kind degree (20
Know thy own point.

Of Blindness, Weakness, Heav'n bestows on thee.
Submit! in this, or any other Sphere,
Secure to be as blest as thou canst bear.
All Nature is but Art, unknown by thee;
All Chance, Direction which thou canst not see;
And spite of Pride, and in thy Reason's spight,
One truth is clear: "Whatever <u>Is</u>, is <u>Right</u>."

274. Thy will be done, in Earth as it is in Heaven

No 2

Learn me ourselves &c

n° 2

Learn we ourselves &c

1×

his Powers & Imperfections.

Epistle II.

2 His middle nature; [illegible]
1 Of man consider'd in respect to himself as an Individual.
[illegible] Passions. the Predominant Passion.
[illegible] Virtue & Vice.
5 The Ends of Providence answered in all this.

1. Learn we ourselves, not God presume to scan,
And know, the Study of Mankind is Man.
Plac'd on this Isthmus of a middle State,
A Being darkly wise, & rudely great.
With too much knowledge for the Sceptic side,
And too much Weakness for a Stoic's Pride,
He hangs between, uncertain where to rest;
Whether to deem himself a God or Beast;
Whether [illegible] Mind or Body to prefer,
Born but to die, & reas'ning but to err;
Alike in Ignorance, (his Reason such)
Whether he thinks too little, or too much.
Chaos of Thought & Passion, all confus'd,
Still by himself abus'd & dis-abus'd:
Created half to rise, & half to fall;
Great Lord of all things, yet a prey to all;
Sole Judge of Truth, in endless Error hurl'd;
The Glory, Jest, and Riddle of the World.

Go reas'ning Man! assume the Doctors chair,
As Plato high, as Seneca severe;
Fix moral Fitness, give all others rule;
Then drop into thyself and be a Fool.

2 Go, [illegible] go mount where Science guides,
Go measure Earth, weigh Air, & state the Tydes,
Instruct erratic Planets where to run,
Correct old Time, & regulate the Sun.

Angels themselves, I grant it, when they saw
One mighty Man unfold All Nature's Law
Admir'd an Angel in a human shape!
And show'd a Newton, as we show an Ape.

[illegible]
Can He
Who tells each Planet where to roll,
Describe or fix one movement of his Soul?
Who marks their points, to rise and to descend, knows he his [illegible] beginning or end?
Or more of God or more of Man can find,
Than this, that One is good, & one is blind?

[illegible] Man's superior Part
[illegible] mounts, unchecked, & soars from Art to Art,
But, when his own great Work is but begun,
What Reason weaves, by Passion is undone.

× This stanza omitted in printed version

× Come then my Friend, my Genius come along,
Oh Master of the Poet, and the Song!
And while the Muse, transported, unconfin'd,
Soars to the Sky, or stoops among mankind,
Teach her like thee (in various nature wise)
To fall with Dignity, with Temper rise;
Form'd by thy Converse, happily to steer
From Grave, to Gay, from lively, to severe:
Powerful with Art, or Eloquent with Ease;
Intent to reason, or polite to please!
Me× whose Love excus'd my labors past,
Matures my present, & shall bound my last!

1. Of man in yt abstract
His middle nature, his Powers & Imperfection.

2. His Capacity how limited.

For more perfection than this State can bear
In vain we sigh: Heav'n made us as we are.
[illegible]
As justly sure a modest Ape might aim
To be like man, whose faculties & frame
He sees, he feels; as you or I to be
An Angel-thing we neither know nor see.
2 Observe how [illegible] face?
[illegible]
It must be so! else why so warm a Sense
Of more-than-monky Charms & Excellence
[illegible] to walk on two essay'd
And why this ardent Longing for a Maid?
So Pug might plead, & call his Gods unkind,
Till set on-end, & marry'd to his mind.

1 Go, wing'd with Reason, mount where Science guides
2 2. Then [illegible] Glass — blind.
[illegible] themselves — Ape
4 [illegible] next, assume the [illegible] chair
As Plato — Fool

3 His Powrs & Imperfections.

EPISTLE II.

2 His middle nature ~~mixd of Greatness & Imperfections.~~
1 Of Man considerd wth respect to Himself as an Individual

capacity of Selflove, & Reason. ~~<That>~~ Why ye former ye stronger. The
4 Of his ~~Faculties~~; ~~Reason~~, Passion s, The Predominant Passion.
His two Principles
Of
5 The Use of y^{t} ~~Pass~~ and ye other Passions. Virtue & Vice.

& Human Happiness
The Ends of Providence answerd in all this.

we ourselves
1. Learn ~~then Thyself~~, not God presume to scan,

But
~~And~~ know, the Study of Mankind is Man.

Plac'd on this Isthmus of a middle State,

A Being darkly wise, & rudely great.

With too much knowledge for the Sceptic side,

And too much weakness for a Stoic's Pride,

He hangs between, uncertain where to rest;

Whether to deem himself a God or Beast;

Whether his Mind or Body to prefer,

Born but to die, & reas'ning but to err;

his
Alike in Ignorance (~~that~~ Reason such)

~~Who~~ ~~who thinks~~
Whether he thinks too little or too much:

Chaos of Thought & Passion, all confus'd,

Still by himself abus'd & dis-abus'd:

Created half to rise, & half to fall;

Great Lord of all things, yet a prey to all;

Sole Judge of Truth, in endless Error hurl'd,

The Glory, Jest, & Riddle of the World.

~~--mind~~ ~~Thing~~
(↔) Go reas'ning Man! assume the Doctors chair,

high
As Plato ~~deep~~, as Seneca severe;

Fix Moral Fitness, give all others rule;

Then drop into thyself, & be a Fool.

2. Go reas'ning Man! guides,
(↔) ~~Wouldst thou be more~~? go mount where Science

Go measure Earth, weigh Air, & state the Tydes,

Instruct ~~erratic~~ Planets ~~where~~ to run,

Correct old Time, & regulate the Sun.

(↔) Angels themselves, I grant it, when they saw

One mighty Man unfold All Nature's Law,

Admir'd an Angel in a human shape!

\+ And show'd a Newton, as we show an Ape.

+Job man is as a wild ass & y^{e} son of man
~~<Then> turn the glass! it shows thee all along~~

as the Fole of a wild ass.
~~As weak in Conduct, as in Science strong.~~

Can He,
Who tells each Planet ~~in what orb~~ where to roll,

Describe or fix his ~~our~~
~~Say can he fix~~ one movement of ~~his~~ Soul?

own
Who mark s their Points, to rise and to descend, knows he his Beginning or his End?

Or more of God or more of Man can find,

Than this, that One is good, & one is blind?

Alas what wonder? Man's superior Part

There ~~soars~~ mounts uncheckd & soars
~~Joins truth to truth, or mounts~~ frõ Art to Art:

But
~~But~~ when his own great Work is but begun,

What Reason weaves, by Passion is undone!

Come then my Friend, my Genius come along,

Oh Master of the Poet, and the Song!

And while the Muse, transported, unconfin'd,

Soars to the Sky, or Stoops among Mankind,

thro'
Teach her like thee (~~by~~ various Fortune wise)

To fall with Dignity, with Temper rise;

steer her ~~an~~ easy flight
Formd by thy Converse happily to steer

From Wit to Sense Reason Profit to Delight
From Grave to Gay, from lively to severe:

artful to persuade, polite to please!
Oh Powrful with Art, or Eloquent with Ease;

in Busness, elegant in ease!
Intent to reason, or polite to please!

Love
M + whose ~~Smile~~ excusd my labors past,

s shall bound
Mature my present, & direct my last!

1. Of man in ye abstract
His middle nature, his Powers & Imperfections

how limited
2. His Capacity & ~~Faculties~~

this
[For more perfection than ~~our~~ state can bear

as
In vain we sigh: Heav'n made us ~~w^{t}~~ we are.

~~If Gods we must be 'cause we would be, then~~

~~Pray hard, ye Monkies! & ye may be Men.~~

wisely
As ~~justly~~ sure a modest Ape might aim

~~break forth~~
To be like Man, whose faculties & frame

He sees, he feels; as you or I to be

An Angel-thing we neither know nor see.

Else why this Love of Tricks, this laughing
2 Observe ~~how close he edges on our~~ face?

~~What human Action, what a laughing face?~~
(An Elder Brother too, to Human race.)

else
1 'It must be so: ~~else~~ why so warm a Sense

'Of more-than-Monky Charms, & Excellence

~~have I else~~ why else have I
'~~Else Why so oft~~ To walk on two essay'd

'And why this ardent Longing for a Maid?

So Pug might plead, & call his Gods unkind,

Till set on-end, & marryd to his mind.

Go, reasning Man—
1. [~~Go, winged with Reason, mount where Sciẽce~~
guides

2. Then turn ye Glass — blind.

[~~Angels~~ themselves — ape

4. [Go next, assume the ~~sober Ethic Chair,~~

As Plato — Fool

2 x

3. His two Principles

X Selflove & Reason.

3 ~~Two different Principles our Nature move;~~ Two Principles in human nature reign,
Selflove, to urge, & Reason, to restrain;
~~One spurs, one reins; that Reason, that Self Love.~~
Nor this a good, nor that a bad we call,
Each works its end, to move or govern all.

omitted

Of good and evil Gods, what frighted Fools,
Of good and evil Reason, puzled Schools,
Deceiv'd, deceiving, taught, to these refer:
Know, both must operate, or both must err.
And to their proper Operation still
Ascribe all Good, to their improper, Ill.

X Most necessary.

Selflove, the Spring of Motion, acts ye Soul
Reason's comparing Balance, rules ye whole.
The primal Impulse, & the controlling weight,
To give the Motion, & to regulate.
Man, but for that, no action cd attend,
And but for this, were active to no End.
Fixt, like a Plant, on his peculiar spot
To draw nutrition, propagate, & rot:
Or Meteor-like, flame lawless thro' the Void,
Destroying others, by himself destroy'd.

X Selflove ye stronger & why?

Most strength, the moving Principle requires,
Active its task, it prompts, impells, inspires:
Sedate & quiet the comparing lies,
Form'd but to check, delibrate and advise.
Selflove still stronger as its Objects nigh,
Reason's at distance & in prospect lye;

qu. X

This sees immediate Good, by present Sense,
Reason the future, & the Consequence:
Thicker than Arguments, Temptations throng,
~~Still grows~~ At best more watchful this, but that more strong.
~~Modes of Selflove the Passions we call,~~
~~Reason itself more nicely shares for all:~~
Both fly from Pain, to Pleasure both aspire,
With one aversion, & with one Desire;
But greedy this its Object will Devour,
That sips the hony, yet not wounds the Flower.
Love, Hope, & Joy, fair Pleasure's smiling Train;
Hate, Sadness, Fear, the Family of Pain.
The soft, reward the Virtuous, or invite;
The fierce, the wicked punish, or affright.
This Light and Darkness in our Chaos join'd,
Tis Reason's task to sep'rate in the mind;
To blend them well, & harmonize their Strife,
~~Makes all the Strength & Colour of our Life.~~
X The Passions. & their use.

Those yt imparted court a nobler aim,
Exalt their kind & take some Virtues Name
~~Let subtle Schoolmen~~ ... in Pleasures &c

— Strong (2) Let subtle Schoolmen teach these friends to fight
More studious to divide than to unite;
~~Let Wit & ... reason split~~
Wt all ye ... dexterity of Wit;
Wits, just like fools, at war abt a name
Have full as oft no meaning, or ye same:

X Their End the same.

~~Grace & Nature, Vice & Virtue ... ... will be found~~
~~Know Pleasure, Good, ...~~
Neither Selflove & Reason both aspire,
To join their pleasure ... desire;
But greedy that its Object wd devour,
This taste ye Hony & not wound ye flower.
~~The Action of ye Stronger to suspend~~
Reason still use, to Reason still attend
Attention Habit & Experience gains
This strengthens Reason, yt Selflove restrains.
Modes of Selflove ye Passions we may call,
Tis real Good, or seeming moves em all:
But since not every Good we can divide,
& Reason bids us for our own provide;
Passions selfcentred, if their means be fair,
List under Reason & deserve her care;

X 3. His Two Principles
Self Love & Reason.

~~sep'rate~~ Two Principles in human nature reign,
~~Two diffrent Principles our Nature move;~~

Selflove, to urge, & Reason, to restrain.
~~One spurs, one reins ; this Reason, that Self Love~~.

Nor this a good, nor that a bad we call,

Each ~~has~~ works its end, to ~~urge, and~~ move or govern all.

Of good and evil Gods, what frighted Fools,

Of good and evil Reason, puzled Schools,

Deceivd, deceiving, taught, to These refer:

Know, both must operate, or both must err:

And to their proper Operation still

Ascribe all Good, to their improper, Ill.

X Both necessary

Selflove, The Spring of ~~Action lends the force;~~ Motion acts ye Soul

~~alter~~
Reason's comparing Balance ~~states ye Course~~: ~~the~~ ~~rectifies regulates ye Whole~~ rules ye whole. X

δ 3
The primal Impulse, & ~~the poising~~ controuling Weight,

To give the Motion, & to regulate.

Man, but for that, no Action c^d attend,

And but for this, were active to no End.

Fixt, like a Plant, on his peculiar spot

~~To~~ Just draw nutrition, propagate, & rot:

Or meteor-like, flame lawless thro' the Void,

Destroying others, by himself destroy'd.

X Self Love ye stronger, & why

Most strength, the moving Principle require<s;>

Active its task, it prompts, impells, inspires:

Sedate & quiet the comparing lies,

Formd but to check, ~~to balance, to~~ delibrate and advise.

Selflove ~~the~~ yet stronger as its Objects ~~near~~ nigh,

qu. X
~~diminishd as remote appear~~
Reason's at distance & in prospect lye;

This sees immediate Good, by present Sence,

Reason the future, & the Consequence:

Thicker than Arguments, Temptations throng

~~That grows~~ <is> At best more watchful, this, but that more stro<ng>
Let subtile—

~~Virtues name~~

strong (↔) Let subtile Schoolmen teach these friends to fight

More studious to divide than to unite;

& Grace &
Nature, ~~&~~ Sence ~~& Grace~~ & reason
~~Let Metaphysick comon~~ reason split

mad
W^{th} all y^e ~~dull~~ mad dexterity of wit;

Wits, just like fools, at war ab^t a name

X Have full as oft no meaning, or ye same:

~~Modes of Self-Love the Passions the we call,~~

~~Reason itself more nicely shares in all:~~

Both fly from Pain, to Pleasure both aspire,

With one Aversion, & with one Desire;

But greedy this its Object will devour,

That sips the hony, yet not wounds the Flowr.

Love, Hope, & Joy, fair Pleasure's smiling Train;

Hate, Sadness, Fear, the Family of Pain.

Their End y^e same.
~~Know too nice distinctions $hones^t$ Sence will shun;~~
~~Know Pleasure Good & Happiness are one.~~

The soft, reward the Virtuous, or invite;

The fierce, the Wicked punish, or affright.

~~To this End~~
~~Hither~~ To ~~this~~ to this end to ~~y^e~~ one Good
To Selflove & Reason ~~both~~ aspire,

~~W^{th} one~~ Pain their aversion ~~& wth one~~ pleasure ~~its~~ their desire;

This Light and Darkness in ~~thy~~ our Chaos join'd,

Tis Reason's task to sep'rate in the mind:

To blend them well, & harmonize their strife,

~~Makes all the Strength & Colour of our Life~~.

But greedy that its object w^d devour,

This taste ye Hony & not wound ye flowr.

~~Pleasures are ever~~ &c

[The Passions. & their use.

~~The Action of ye stronger to suspend~~

Stet ~~<Still>~~ Reason ~~imploy~~ still use, to Reason still attend

Attention Habit & Experience gains

This strengthens Reason, y^t Selflove restrains

Those y^t imparted court ~~a~~ ~~boast some~~ nobler aim,

Exalt their Kind, & take ~~a~~ some Virtues Name
~~rise in~~

~~Let subtil Schoolmen~~ Pleasures &c

~~<(3)>~~ Modes of Selflove ye Passions ~~the~~ ~~if~~ may we call,

Tis ~~Still~~ ~~But~~ real Good, or seeming moves em all.

But ~~And~~ since not evry Good we can divide,

~~&~~ Reason bids us for own provide,

Passions selfcentred, if their means be fair,

List under Reason & deserve her care;

Go on

Here [illegible]

In [illegible] Apathy (the Stoic's boast)
If Virtue fix, tis fixt as in a Frost,
Contracted all, retiring to the breast;
But strength of mind is Exercise, not Rest.
[illegible]
[illegible] puts in act ye Soul;
Parts it may ravage, but preserves the Whole:
On life's vast ocean diversely we sail,
Reason the Card, but Passion is the Gale
[illegible]
The Compass, if no powrful Gust arise?

Not God alone in the still Calm we find;
He mounts the Storm, & walks upon the Wind.

Passions, like Elements, tho' born to fight,
Yet mix'd & soften'd, in His work unite:
These, tis enough to temper and imploy;
But what composes man, can man destroy?
Suffice, that Reason follow Nature's road,
Compound, [illegible] & imitate the God.
[illegible]
And treat with Passion more as friend [illegible]
[illegible] not every Good we can divide,
(And Reason bids us for our own provide)
Passions, whose Ends are honest, means are fair,
List under Reason, & demand her care:
Such as, imparted, boast a farther aim,
[illegible] Virtue's name.

Pleasures are ever in our hands, or eyes,
And when in act they cease, in Prospect rise:
Present to grasp, & future, still to find,
The whole Employ of Body & of Mind.
All spread their charms; but charm not all alike;
[illegible]
[illegible]
One Master Passion hence, in the breast,
Like Aaron's Serpent, swallows up the rest.
[illegible] Glory please,
Or (more strong than all) the Love of Ease
That Byass, Nature to each temper lends,
And several men directs to several ends.
[illegible]
[illegible] Reason [illegible]
[illegible] the Judge, [illegible] to persuade
[illegible] change [illegible] made
To serve the present Sovereign all along,
But remove a weaker for a strong.
As Man, perhaps, the moment of his breath
Receives the lurking Principle of Death,

torpid

3 x Postpone

Postpone

Hent hic:

x used in printed version

Deleted 2 only

omitted

The soft reward [illegible] virtuous [illegible] invite
The [illegible] wicked punish, or affright
Love, Hope, & Joy, fair Pleasures smiling train
Hate, Sadness, Fear, ye [illegible] of Pain:
These mixed with art, & to due bounds confin'd,
Make & maintain the Balance of the mind.
[illegible]

reduces all ye Passions under Pleasure & Pain as their universal Principle [illegible]

[illegible]

[illegible] internal faculties controll
[illegible] and hence one Master Passion in the breast

[illegible]

[illegible] Life is [illegible], even at Life's expence
The Merchant's [illegible] Sages Indolence,
The Monk's Humility, the Hero's pride,
All, all alike find Reason on their side.
[illegible] persuade
[illegible] choice we make, or justify it, made;
Proud of her Easy Conquest all along,
While she [illegible] for ye strong.

So when small Humors gather to a Gout,
The Doctor fancies he has driv'n 'em out.

X The Predominant Passion, and its strength over Reason

Go on | ~~after- makes a Knave~~
here | ~~-body acts wth mind~~

Rest fro Passion
In ~~passive~~ Apathy (the Stoic's boast)   torpid   ~~Postpone~~
torpid

by
If Virtue fix, tis fixt as in a Frost,

in
Contracted all, retiring to the breast;   ~~Postpone~~

is
But strength of mind ~~asks~~ Exercise, not Rest.

~~meets~~ ~~& void of~~ ~~can~~
~~Virtue dispassiond naked to the fight Comes without Arms, & conquers but by flight~~

~~Passions like Tumults but~~ put s in act ye Soul;
The rising Tempest

Parts it may ravage, but preserves the Whole:

wide
On Life's ~~blind~~ Ocean diversly we sail,

Reason the Card, but Passion is the Gale,   Stent hic

all   δ
~~A tedious Voyage! where how useless lies~~
dele these 2
~~The Compass, if no pow'rful Gust arise?~~   only

Nor God alone in the still Calm we find;

He mounts the Storm, & walks upon the Wind.

Passions, like Elements, tho' born to fight,

Yet mix'd & soften'd, in His work unite: X ~~Use of ye Passions.~~

These, tis enough to temper and imploy,

But what composes Man, can Man destroy?

Suffice, that Reason follow Nature's Road,

Subject
Compound, ~~them well,~~ & imitate the God.   δ [The soft reward ye Virtuous or invite

~~Tis here to rectify, not overthrow,~~   Love Hope   The fierce the Wicked punish, or affright

And treat with Passion more as friend ~~than foe~~.   Love, Hope, & Joy, fair Pleasures smiling train

Hate, Sadness, Fear, ye Family of Pain:

The most pursue ~~& <chuse> ye things y^y choud~~

~~For~~ since
^ ~~It is~~ not evry Good we can divide,   Or if they deviate, 'tis in ~~search of Good~~

And since not   These mixd with art, & to due bounds confin'd

(And Reason bids us for our own provide)   Make, & maintain, ye Balance of the mind.

Those
~~That~~ Lights & Shades, to harmonize whose strife

Passions, whose Ends are honest, means are fair,   Makes all ye Strength & Color of thy Life

List under Reason, & demand her care:
~~Then~~
~~Extremes in Nature &c~~
Such as, imparted, boast a farther aim,   Arist Eth. l. 7.c.ll. ~~overleaf~~
~~of ye mean~~
rise, & take a   ~~Virtues name~~   reduces all ye Passions under Pleasur<e>
~~Rise up Exalted in some Virtue's name~~.   & Pain in their universal Principles
The mean between opposit Passions
X makes Virtue, ye Extremes Vice.

Pleasures are ever in our hands, or eyes,

And when in Act they cease, in Prospect rise:

grasp &
Present to ~~seize, or~~ future ~~to obtain~~ still to find;

The whole Employ of Body & of ~~Brain~~ Mind.

objects
All spread their charms; but charm not all alike,   ~~on~~ diff~~rent~~ ~~Senses~~ diffrent~~ly~~ ^ strike,

~~stronger~~ ~~stronger Passions~~   Hence Passions rise, and
~~On diffrent Senses diffrently they strike~~;   ~~Stronger or Weaker~~, more or less, inflame,

< > Responsive ⟷ to each Organ of the frame   As strong or weak the s
~~Stronger or weaker, more or less inflame,~~   ~~Proportiond to each~~ Organ of ye frame.

~~Or more or~~ less our Natures take ye flame,   δ Nor here internal Faculties controll
~~As Organs vary, or the Body's frame.~~

the
[~~One Master Passion hence, in evry breast~~   Nor Soul on body acts but that on Soul,

And hence one master Passion in the breast
Aaron's
Like ~~Moses~~ Serpent, swallows up the rest; | Aaron's | each
As man perhaps &c

Let Powr, or Knowledge
& ~~Whether Wine& Woman~~, Gold, or Glory please,   Reason our judge, here sits but to persuade

oft
Or ~~(yet~~ ^ more strong than all) the Love of Ease ^   Thro Life tis followd, ev'n at Life's expence:

The Merchants Toil, ye Sages Indolence,

The Monks Humility, ye Hero's pride,

All, all alike find Reason on their side.

That Byass, Nature to each temper lends,

And sev'ral men directs to sev'ral ends; on Lifes

Tis Nature's Road, & must be followd still,   <here acts>
~~This ruling Passion, be whatere it will,~~   ~~Reason, our Judge, sits only to persuade~~
^   ^
The
~~Each~~ choice we make, or justify it, made;

yet
no Guide, ~~is~~ but a Guard from ill.
~~It conquers~~ Reason, ~~or can charm it still~~:   ~~<an>~~
Proud of her Easy Conquest all along,
No more   but Pleader
~~At best~~, the Judge, ~~sits only~~ to persuade   re ~~<a>~~ Passions
While she ~~but~~ moves ~~y^e~~ weake~~r~~ for ye strong;
Each   we make ~~&~~ or justify it made,
~~The~~ change ~~is right that higher Pow'r has made~~
^   ^   ^   ^

To serve the present Sovreign all along,
Or
~~And~~ but remove a weaker for a strong.

Man ~~must~~   ~~he receives~~   ~~change into~~
<up>ye rest. As ~~Man~~, perhaps, the moment of his breath   So when small Humours gather to a Gout,
^   ^

Receives the lurking Principle of Death,   The Doctor fancies he has driv'n 'em out.

As—

+ The Predominant Passion,

~~over reason~~
The   and its Strength, ~~over Reason~~

Th

4

The young disease that must subdue at length
Grows with his growth, & strengthens wth his strength,
So cast and mingled with our very [From the very nature of our] frame,
The mind's disease, its ruling Passion came.
Each vital humors wch shd feed the whole,
Soon flows to this, in body & in soul.
Whatever warms the heart, or fills the head,
As the mind opens, & its functions spread,
Imagination plies her dang'rous art,
And pours it all upon the peccant part.
Nature its Mother, Habit is its Nurse;
Wit, Spirit, Faculties, but make it worse;
Reason itself but gives it edge & pow'r,
As Heav'ns blest beam turns Vinegar more sour!
Ah! if she lend not Arms as well as Rules,
Can Reason more, than tell us we are fools?
Teach us to mourn our nature, not to mend,
A sharp Accuser, but a helpless Friend! yes—
. . . Good wth ill,
On this Passion . . . our Principle.
By this, the Mercury of Man is fix'd;
Strong grows the Virtue, with his Nature mix'd:
The Dross cements what else were too refin'd,
And in one Int'rest Body acts with Mind.
The surest Virtues thus from Passions shoot,
Wild Natures Vigor working at the root.
What Crops of Wit and Honesty appear
From Anger, Obstinacy, Spleen, or Fear?
Lust, thro some certain Strainers well refin'd
Is gentle Love, and charms all Womankind.
Envy, in Criticks and old Maids the Devil,
Is Emulation in the Learn'd & Civil:
Nor Virtue, male or female can we name,
But what or grows on Pride or grows on Shame.
And Nero reigns a Titus, if he will;
The fiery Soul abhorr'd in Catiline,
In Decius charms, in Curtius is divine!
The same Ambition can destroy or save,
. . . Extreams

We, wretched Subjects tho' to rightful sway,
In this weak Queen, some Fav'rite still obey.

Yes: Nature's Road must ever be prefer'd:
Reason is here no Guide, but still a Guard:
'Tis hers to rectify, not overthrow,
And treat this Passion more as friend than foe.
. . . Life 'tis follow'd, ev'n at Life's expence;
The Merchant's Toil, ye Sage's Indolence,
The Monk's Humility, the Hero's Pride,
All, all alike find Reason on their side.

4 The young disease that must subdue at length
Grows with his growth, & strengthens wth his strength,
cast and mingled with our very
So ~~from the very nature of our~~ frame,

The mind's disease, its Ruling Passion, came.
Each
~~Those~~ vital humor~~s~~ wch sh^{d} feed the whole,
or
Soon flows to this, in body & in soul.
Whatever ~~or~~ warms the heart, or fills the head
its
As the Mind opens, & ~~her~~ functions spread
Imagination plies her dang'rous art,
And pours it all upon the peccant part.
Nature its Mother, Habit is its Nurse;
Wit, Spirit, Faculties, but make it worse;

wretched
We, ~~sad~~ Subjects, tho to rightful sway,
or ~~And we who vainly boast her rightful sway~~
gives
Reason itself but ~~lends~~ it edge & pow'r,
this
In ~~our~~ weak Queen, some Fav'rite still obey.
As Heav'ns blest beam turns Vinegar more sour:
or ~~Its own best forces lead the mind astray,~~
X Or frō turn
-- Friend! ~~No more~~ a Judge, ~~but~~ Pleader to persuade
~~Just as with Teague his own Legs ran away.~~
The choice we make--Proud of an easy Conquest all along
[Ah if she lend not Arms as well as Rules,
~~Its Use~~,
~~and~~
While she ~~but~~ removes weak Passions for ye strong So w^{n} small humors-the Dr-
Can Reason more, than tell us we are fools?
Its ~~must~~
must
Teach us to mourn our Nature, not to mend,
Necessity in Yes! Nature's Road ~~sh~~^{d} ever be preferrd:
A sharp Accuser, but a helpless Friend! Yes—
directing Reason is here no Guide, but still a Guard. --side
Th' Eternal ~~that~~
~~Yes, Heavns kind~~ Art, ~~still~~ mingles Good wth ill,
Tis hers to rectify, not overthrow,
~~Ev'n Ev'n Evn~~ best
men to
~~Oft~~ on this Passion, ~~grafts~~ our Principle.
different & treat this Passion more as friend y^{n} foe.
purposes
~~Tis thus~~
By this, the Mercury of Man is fix'd;
~~powrful~~ ~~mightier Nature~~
~~That Byass Nature to each temper lends~~
~~A mightier Powr the strong direction lends,~~
his Nature
Strong grows the Virtue, with ~~the Passion~~ mix'd:
~~& sevral men impells to sevral Ends~~:
~~& sevral men impels to sevral ends.~~
The Dross cements what else were too refind,
~~<sea> to~~
~~On Life's blind Ocean diverse points we sail~~,
And in one Int'rest Body acts with Mind.
A mightier powr the strong direction sends, & sevral men impells to sevral Ends.

~~Passions~~
~~Reason ye Card, but Passion all ye Gale.~~
~~In passive apathy &c~~
~~How oft with Passion, — to none~~
~~The fairest fruits our expectation mock,~~
Like varying Winds by other ~~<various>~~ Passions tost,
to Balance of
ye Mind
~~A tedious Voyage, where all useless lies~~
Th' Eternal Art &c
As fruits ungrateful to ye Planters care
On savage stocks
~~This drives~~ ~~<them all ways>~~ to a certain Coast
~~But thrive~~ inserted learn to bear ~~Savage Stock~~:
~~The compass, if no~~ <blank> ~~gust arise~~
~~The sloe's rough juices melt into a plum, See dulcet Pippins from~~ ~~thy crabtree come~~
~~<them>~~
This drives them us constant
our
~~Th' Eternal Art, that mingles Good wth Ill~~
The surest Virtues ~~thus~~ from Passions shoot
2 Wild Nature's Vigor working at the root.
Let Powr or Knowledge, Gold or Glory please
& ~~Thus~~ So
~~Ev'n on this Passion grafts our Principle~~
~~So dulcet Pippins from the Crabtree come,~~
The so ~~thus~~
1 ~~As sloe's rough juices melts into a Plum~~;
Or (oft more strong than all) ye Love of Ease,
Tis thus &c
~~Let~~ Thro Life tis followd, evn at Life's expence,
What crops of Wit and Honesty ~~we bear~~,
appear
The Merchant's Toil, ye Sages Indolence,
The Monks Humility, the Heros Pride;
or
From Anger, Obstinacy, Spleen, ~~& Fear~~?
And
~~All <&>~~ all alike find Reason on their side.
Ambition, Courage, Justice can supply, Ev'n Avarice Prudence, Sloth Philosophy.
~~This powrful Byas A mightier Powr this strong Direction sends~~
Lust, thro some certain Strainers well refin'd,
~~Th' Eternal Art y^{t} mingles Good wth Ill~~
Is gentle Love, and charms all Womankind.
~~And sevral men impells to sevral Ends~~ ~~(before)~~
Envy, in Criticks and old Maids the devil,
~~Evn on this Passion~~ — &c
Is Emulation in the Learn'd & Civil.
~~<still>~~educing
~~Yet~~ Th' Eternal Art, ~~that mingles~~ Good
from Ill
~~Ambition, Courage, Justice can supply,~~
6 ~~Ev'n Av'rice Prudence, Sloth Philosophy~~
Grafts
~~Evn~~ on this Passion our best Principle
Nor Virtue, male or female can we name,
But what or grows on Pride or grows on Shame.
~~&~~ Tis thus ye Mercury &c
art
~~By y^{t} <same> Bent, to Virtue, Vice, inclin'd,~~
Its ~~use~~ Providential use, to
X ~~The predominant~~ Passion Fixe~~s~~ our Principle & secure~~s it~~ our Virtue.
Know, ~~evry ruling~~ ~~Thus evry ruling Passion of the mind~~
~~evry ruling Passion of ye mind~~.
--Shame dele
+ How oft with Passion Virtue points her charms!
~~Thus stands~~
~~Stands to some Virtue, and some Vice inclind~~. Thus
~~as to~~ Nature
then
Then shines The Hero, ~~dazzles, or~~ ye Beauty warms:
or
~~Who Hector's valor Brutus~~
son or Brutus who had
~~Peleus~~ great
~~What made Achilles or Augustus~~ known,
~~worth had known~~
Check but its Force, ~~&~~ compass, short of Ill
~~Turn but the Byas from the side of ill~~
Had ~~Fulvia~~ been a Whore, or Helen none?
Lucrece
And Nero reigns a Titus, if he will;
abhorrd
The fiery Soul ~~we curse~~ in Catiline,
Each
~~<The>~~ Passion thus, the our
~~By ye same art each~~ Byass of ~~ye~~ Mind Extreams in Nature
&c to Black & White
In Decius charms, in Curtius is divine!
The same Ambition can destroy or save,
Is turnd to Virtue, or to Vice inclind
And
Thus Nature gives us (let it check our pride) ~~It~~ makes a Patriot, as it makes a Knave
~~& either makes a Patriot, or a Knave.~~
~~Ev'n Nature~~ Extremes
The Virtue nearest to our Vice allyd
This Light & Darkness--Tis Reasons
~~& evry~~ Alike y^{e} ruling Byass of our mind
or
Is turnd to Virtue ~~and <is>~~ to Vice inclind Check but
~~And <is> not more turnd to Ill y^{n} to Good~~
~~not of itself~~
θ ~~In passive apathy &c~~ ~~Behind~~

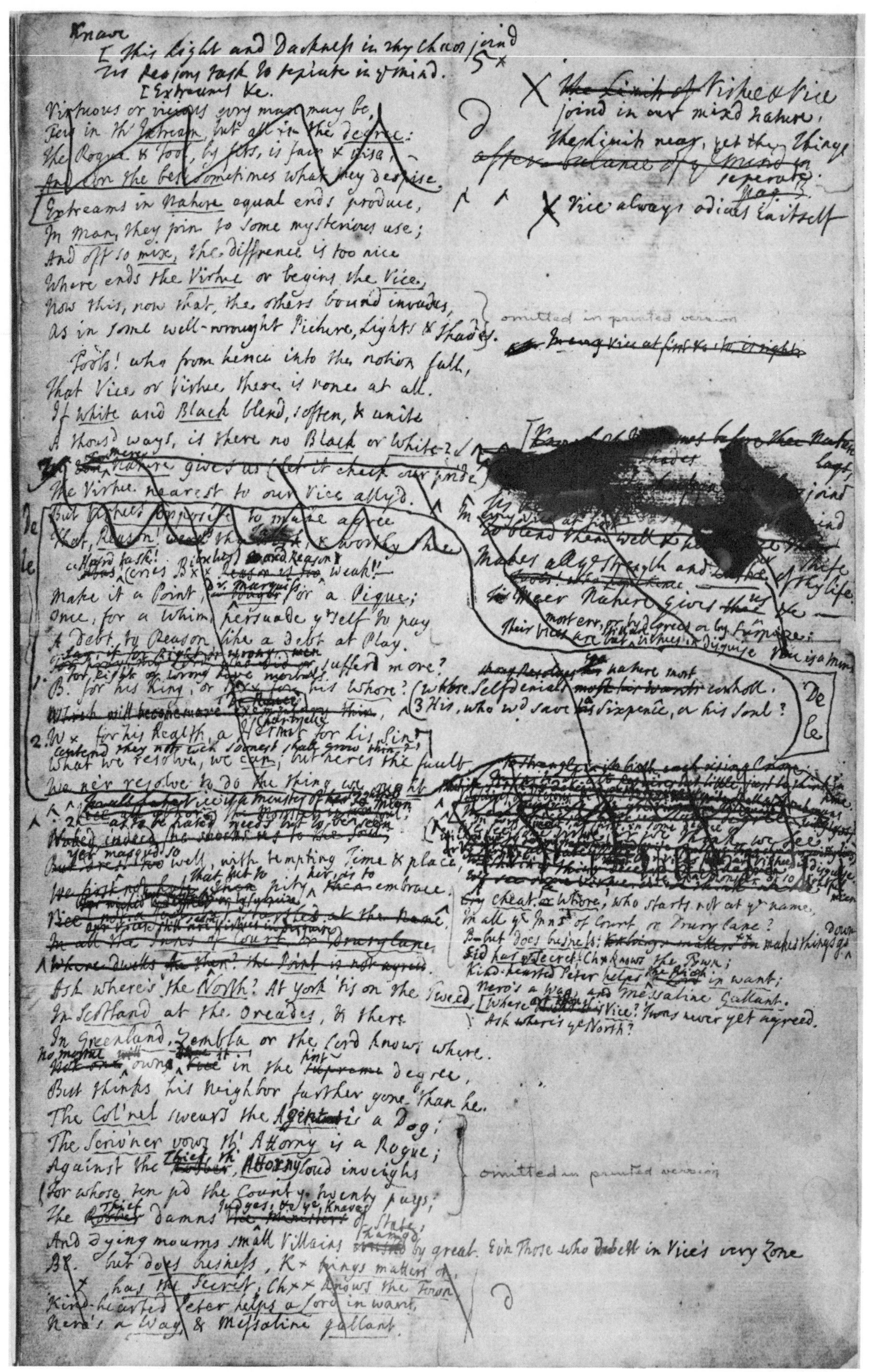
Knave
[This Light and Darkness in thy Chaos joind
Let Reasons task to seperate in y^e mind.
[Extreams &c.
Virtuous or vicious every man may be,
Few in th' Extream, but all in the degree;
The Rogue & Fool, by fits, is fair & wise,
And even the best sometimes what they despise.
Extreams in Nature equal ends produce,
In Man, they join to some mysterious use;
And oft so mix, the difference is too nice
Where ends the Virtue or begins the Vice.
Now this, now that, the others bound invades,
As in some well-wrought Picture, Lights & Shades. } omitted in printed version
Fools! who from hence into the notion fall,
That Vice or Virtue there is none at all.
If White and Black blend, soften, & unite
A thousd ways, is there no Black or White?
...
The Virtue nearest to our Vice allyd.
...
Make it a Point, ... for a Pique;
Once, for a Whim, persuade y^rself to pay
A Debt, by Reason like a debt at Play.
...
Ask where's the North? At York 'tis on the Tweed,
In Scotland at the Orcades, & there
In Greenland, Zembla or the Lord knows where.
No mortal owns ... in the ... degree,
But thinks his neighbor further gone than he.
The Col'nel swears the Agent is a Dog,
The Scriv'ner vows th' Attorny is a Rogue;
Against the Thief, th' Attorny loud inveighs
For whose ten pd the County twenty pays; } omitted in printed version
The Thief damns Judges, & ye Knaves of State;
And dying mourns small Villains hang'd by great.
... but does business, K×× brings matters ...
... has the Secret, Ch×× knows the Town
Kind-hearted Peter helps a Lord in want,
Nero's a Wag, & Messaline gallant.

X ~~the limit of~~ Virtue & Vice
joind in our mixd nature;
the limit near, yet the Things
... seperate way.
X Vice always odious in itself
...
Cheat & Whore; who starts not at ye name,
In all ye Inns of Court, or Drury lane?
B— but does business; ... on makes things go down
Sid has ye Secret; Ch× knows the Town;
Kind-hearted Peter helps the Brib in want;
Nero's a Wag, and Messaline Gallant.
[Where ... is Vice? Twas never yet agreed.
Ask where's ye North?
Ev'n Those who dwell in Vice's very Zone

Knave
[This Light and Darkness in thy Chaos joind
Tis Reasons task to sep'rate in ye mind.
[Extreams &c
Virtuous or vicious evry man may be,
Few in the Extream, but all in the degree: δ
The Rogue & Fool, by fits, is fair & wise,
And evn the best sometimes what they despise.
[Extreams in Nature equal ends produce,
In Man, they join to some mysterious use;
And oft so mix, the diffrence is too nice
Where ends the Virtue or begins the Vice.
Now this, now that, the others bound invades,
As in some well-wrought Picture, Lights & Shades.
Fools! who from hence into the notion fall,
That Vice or Virtue there is none at all.
If White & Black blend, soften, & unite
A thous^{d} ways, is there no Black or White?
~~For~~ Mere
~~<Tis> Evn Nature gives us (let it check our pride)~~
The Virtue nearest to our Vice ally'd.
But Virtues opposite to make agree
is Task
That, Reason! ~~were~~ thy ~~Work~~, & worthy thee
de
Hard task! ibulus) ‹—› and ~~Reasons~~
"~~Alas~~ (cries B + + ~~Reason is too~~ weak!"—
le
d^{r} Marquiss
Make it a Point, ~~a Wager~~, or a Pique;
Once, for a Whim, persuade y^{r}self to pay
A Debt to Reason, like a Debt at Play.
~~Say, if for Right or Wrong men~~
~~For pray, my Lord, who did or~~ suffer~~d~~ more?
For Right or Wrong have mortals
1, B. for his King, or B + + for his Whore?
~~Which will become more exemplary thin~~,
De Rance
Chartreux
2. W + for his health, a Hermit for his Sin?
Contend they not wch soonest shall grow thin?
What we resolve, we can; but heres the fault
We ne'r resolve to do the thing we ought
frightful
For all ~~<hate>~~ Vice is a Monster of ~~her so~~ mien
~~Vice all abhor~~, ~~The Monster is <too> foul~~;
2 As to be hated needs but to be seen
~~Naked, indeed, she checks us to the Soul~~,
Yet masqud so
~~But drest too~~ well, with tempting Time & place,
That but to her, is to
~~We first not hate, then~~ pity, ~~then~~ embrace.
~~but mistake~~
~~For Wicked by degrees or by surprise~~
~~Vice! not a Soul but startles at the Name~~,
seem
~~Our Vices still are Virtues in disguise~~
~~In all the Inns of Court, or Drury lane~~.
art thou
~~Where dwells she then? the Point is not agreed.~~ [Where ~~dwells this~~ Vice? 'Twas never yet agreed
Ask where's the North? At York 'tis on the Tweed, Ask where's ye North?
In Scotland at the Orcades, & there
In Greenland, Zembla, or the Lord knows where.
No mortal ~~will~~ < > it first
~~Not one~~ owns ~~Vice~~ in the ~~supreme~~ degree,
But thinks his Neighbor further gone than he.
The Col'nel swears the Agent is a Dog;
The Scriv'ner vows th' Attorny is a Rogue;
Thief, th'
Against the ~~Robber~~, Attorny loud inveighs
(For whose ten pd the County twenty pays;
Thief Judges, & ye Knaves
The ~~Robber~~ damns ~~the Ministers~~ of State,
hangd
And dying mourns small Villains ~~crushd~~ by great.
Bl. but does bus'ness, K + brings matters on,
+ has the Secret, Ch ++ knows the Town,
Kind-hearted Peter helps a Lord in want, δ
Nero's a Wag, & Messaline gallant.

5

X ~~The Limits of~~ Virtue & Vice
Joind in our mixd Nature,
The Limits near, yet the things
~~after balance of ye mind in pag. 3~~
seperate.
X Vice always odious in itself

~~In every Vice at first &c to is right~~

[~~Know <that> Extremes before thee Nature lays~~
<The Lights and> ~~Shades~~
<The light &> darkness in thy chaos joind
Tis Reasons task to seprate in the mind
~~To blend them well & harmonize their~~ strife
In evry Vice at first
Colour
Makes all ye Strength & ~~Lustre~~ of thy life.
~~Fools! who from hence~~ —
us
Tis Meer Nature gives ~~thee~~ &c —
Most err, by degrees or by surprise;
still are
Their Vices are but Virtues in disguise
Vice is a Mons<ter>
~~can~~
~~strong Resolves his~~ Nature most
Whose Selfdenials ~~more his Wants~~ controll,
a
3 His, who w^{d} save ~~his~~ Sixpence, or his Soul? De le

~~To strangle in its birth each rising Crime~~
~~In spite of all Requires but little, just to think in time~~.
~~But in ye thing deceivd or the degree~~
~~Virtuous, or Vicious &c to despise In spite of all the Frenchmans witty lyes~~
[~~In evry Vice, at first, in some degree~~
~~In evry Vice, at first, in some degree~~
We see some Virtue, or we think we see
~~Wicked but by degrees or by surprise~~ ~~And(spite of all the Frenchmans witty lies)~~
but
~~<For all save vice>~~ Our Vices ~~<still>~~ are Virtues in disguise.
~~Still in ye Thing deceivd, or ye Degree~~
Vice is a monster of so frightful mien
~~We see some Virtue, or we think we see~~
A a
~~Cry~~ Cheat! ~~or~~ Whore! who starts not at ye name,
In all ye Inns of Court or Drury lane?
down
+ + makes things go
B — but does bus'ness; K + brings matters on
Sid has ye Secret; Ch + knows the Town;
the Rich
Kind-hearted Peter helps a Lord in want;
Nero's a Wag, and Messaline Gallant

Ev'n Those who dwell in Vice's very Zone

6x

X The Ends of Providence
& Human happiness,
our Passions, answered in [illegible]
particular instances
X How usefull to different
orders of men. That proper frailties &c
X To Society. That forming each
X To ye Individuals [In every state
see some change
Comfort
&c.

X and in Passions [illegible] every
part of Life
[with every stage
of Man, new Passions rise
Hope travels thro, nor
quits him when he dies

Ev'n they who dwell in Vice's very Zone
Or never feel the rage, or never own;
What happier Natures shrink at, with affright,
The hard Inhabitant contends is right.

[illegible]

Vice or Virtue, Self directs it still;
Each Individual seeks a several Goal;
But Heav'ns great View is One, and that the Whole.
That counterworks each Folly & Caprice,

[illegible]

To private Lucre or to private Lust,

[illegible]

A fellow-Creature master, or a Servt or a Friend;
For like assistance mutually call,
Till each man's Weakness grows ye Strength of all.
Wants, Frailties, Passions, closer still ally
The common Int'rest, & endear the Tye.
To these we owe true Friendship, Love sincere,
Each home-felt joy that Life inherits here;
Yet from the same we learn, in its Decline,
Those joys, those friends, those int'rests to resign;
Taught half by Reason, half by slow decay,
To welcom Death, & calmly pass away.
With Man's each Age, some new Passions rise,
Hope travels thro nor quits him when he dies.
Behold the Child, by Nature's kindly law,
Pleas'd with a Rattle, tickled with a Straw;
Some livelier Plaything gives his youth delight,
A little louder, but as empty quite;
Scarfs, Garters, Gold, amuse his riper stage,
& Beads & Prayrbooks are the Toys of age:
Pleas'd with this Bauble still, as that before,
Till tir'd he sleeps, and all the Care is o'er!
Observant then, how from Defects of mind
Springs half the Bliss, or Rest of humankind;
How Pride repairing what Wisdom [illegible] destroy;
In Folly's cup how laughs the Bubble Joy;
How Fancy & [illegible] gilds w ever-changing rays
Those painted Clouds yt beautify our days;

Thro Life's long Dream what glowing Visions reign
How Nature gives no Vanity in vain?
[illegible] Confess, one Comfort [illegible] still will rise,
'Tis this; tho Man's a Fool, yet God is Wise.

Finis

~~beneath her~~
6x Evn they who dwell in Vices very Zone
Or never feel the rage, or never own;
What happier Natures shrink at, with affright,
The hard Inhabitant contends is right.
In
Thus spite of all the Frenchmans witty lies
are
Most Vices ~~seem~~ but Virtues in disguise.
Virtuous & vicious every man must ~~will~~ be,
~~In evry Vice at first in some degree~~
Few in th' Extreme, but all in ye degree;
~~We see some Virtue, or we think we see~~.
Best
The Rogue & Fool by fits is fair & wise & evn ye ~~Best~~, by fits,
wt they despise
Tis but by parts Man follows Good or ill,
For
~~And~~ Vice or Virtue, Self directs it still;
Each Individual seeks a sev'ral Goal;
X But Heav'ns great View is One, & that the Whole.

X The Ends of Providence
& Human Happiness,
answerd in ~~all <this>~~
our Passions & ~~very~~ our very
~~our~~ imperfections
~~<the Passions> Frailties & Vices~~
frailties
Frõ wants, ~~frõ follies~~
~~observe it well~~:
~~<&>~~ frõ defects of mind
~~See~~ Springs half ye Joys
or Rest of human kind
Particular instances
X How useful to different
orders of men. That proper frailties &c
Shame — &c

<Till evry>
That thy ~~our~~ and
~~This~~ counterworks ~~his~~ folly & caprice ~~<makes>~~ evry
That draws some Virtue out of evry Vice becomes by force <divine>
~~And public Good extracts from private Vice~~ The Scale
~~Of certainty by F<aith>~~,
~~Defects of Happiness by Hope supplyd~~,
<Sense>
Of ~~<Wit by Pride>~~
~~What urges One thro just & thro' unjust~~,
present present With e<vry age>
δ To private Lucre or to private Lust, bid som<e new passion rise>
Hope tr<avels thro nor>
Op'rates in all, & is itself the cause quits h<im when he dies>
Of what restrains them, Government & Laws. Behold <the child, etc.>
δ ~~See now Self Love a Principle divine~~,
~~A Scale to measure others good by thine~~.

X To Society That forming each
X To ye Individuals [In evry state.
~~<And whom>~~ See some strange
Comfort
&c
Stent
post-pone-to ye third

That forming each on other
~~Created each on our fellow creatures~~ to depend
A ~~fellow creature~~ Master, or a Servt or a Friend.
bids them
For like assistance mutually ~~we~~ call,
Till each man's Weakness grows ye Strength of all.
Wants, Frailties, Passions, closer still ally
The common Int'rest, & endear the Tye.
δ To these we owe true Friendship, Love sincere,
Each home-felt joy that Life inherits here:
Yet from the same we learn, in its decline,
Those joys, those friends, those int'rests to resign,
Taught half by Reason, half by mere decay
To welcome Death, & calmly pass away.

and ~~to~~ in
X ~~To Passions ye happiness of~~ evry
part of Life
[With evry ⟷ age
of Man new Passions rise
Hope travels thro, nor
quits him when he dies.

see
~~makes~~ some still a-
Vice | With Mans each Age, ~~see some~~ new Passions rise,
Hope travels thro nor quits him when he dies

[Behold the Child, by Nature's lucky law!
Pleasd with a Rattle, tickled with a Straw;
Some livelier Plaything gives his Youth delight,
A little louder, but as empty quite;
Scarfs, Garters, Gold, amuse his riper stage,
& Beads & Prayrbooks are the Toys of Age:
this that
Blest with ~~each~~ Bauble still, as ~~all~~ before;
At last he sleeps, and all the Care is o'er!
~~mark~~ ~~Passions or~~
Observant then how from Defects of Mind
or
Springs half the Bliss ~~and~~ Rest of humãkind?
repairs ~~<as fast as>~~ Wisdom wd
How Pride ~~rebuilds~~ what ~~Reason can~~ destroy,
In Folly's cup how laughs the Bubble, Joy?
wth ever dchanging rays
How Fancy's ~~Sunshine~~ gilds ~~a thous ways~~
Those painted Clouds yt beautify our days?

Visions
glowing ~~prospects~~
Thro what ~~gay delusions~~ reign
~~How~~ Life's long Dream ~~new Prospects entertain~~,
How no
~~And~~ Nature gives ~~not~~ Vanity in vain?
And evn Selflove becomes by force divine The scale to measure others Good by thine;
Mark & Confess, one Comfort ~~ever will arise~~
See, & still in all will rise—
'Tis this; tho Man's a Fool, yet God is Wise.

Finis

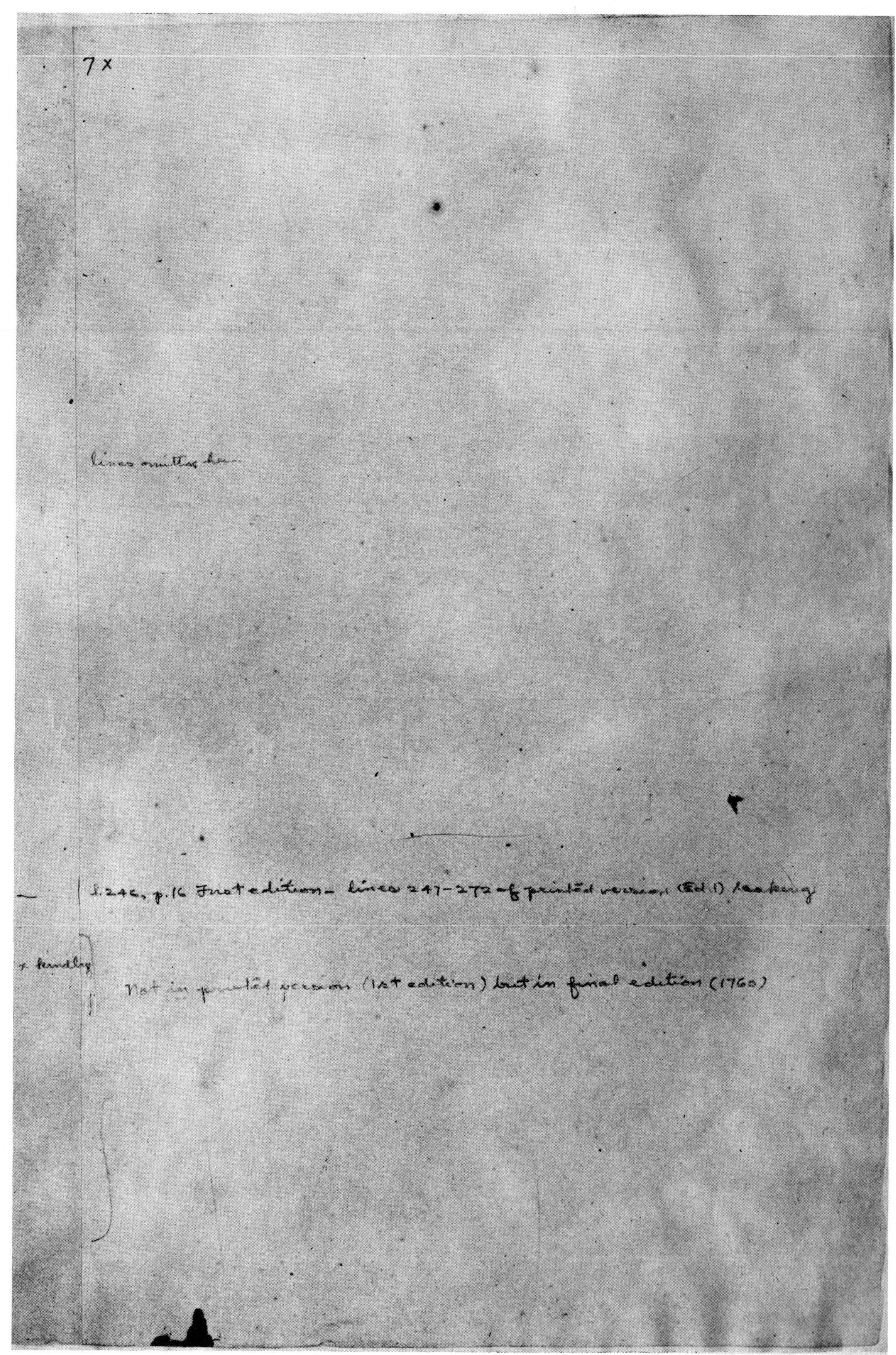
7x
lines omitted here
l.246, p.16 First edition— lines 247–272 of printed version (Ed.1) lacking
x kindly
Not in printed version (1st edition) but in final edition (1760)

1

M. S. B.

Learn Dulness learn'd. &c

Learn Dulness learn! &c

1.

~~Epistle III.~~

~~Put this after~~

Learn, Dulness, learn! an Universal Cause
~~Must act by General, not~~ by ~~partial~~ Laws.
[works to ones End, but works various]
In all thy Madness of Superfluous Health,
Thy Trim of Pride and Impudence of Wealth,
Let that great Truth be present Night & Day,
But most be present, if thou preach or pray.

~~Begin here.~~ Incipit

While man exclaims, see all things for my use!
See man for mine, replies a pamperd Goose.
What care to tend, to ~~house~~ lodge, to cram, to treat him,
All this he knew, but not that twas to eat him.
As far as Goose cd judge, he reasond right,
But as to Man, mistook the matter quite:
And just as short of Reason ~~shall he~~ he Man will fall
Who Thinks all made for one, not one for all.

Look Nature thro' & see the Chain of Love
~~That~~ Combining all below and all above.

Look nature here

omitted in printed version

Learn Dulness
works to one End
In all thy madness
Thy
Let
But

See

1.

~~Epistle III.~~

~~Put this after~~

~~2.~~ Learn Dulness, learn! an Universal Cause
Works to one End but works various
~~Must act by genral, not~~ by ~~partial~~ Laws.
In all thy Madness of Superfluous Health,
Thy Trim of Pride and Impudence of Wealth,
Let that great Truth be present Night & Day,
But most be present, if thou preach or pray.

Incipit — Look Nature

~~Begin~~ While Man exclaims, See all things for my use!
1.
~~here.~~ See Man for mine, replies a pamperd Goose.
lodge
What care to tend, to ~~house~~, to cram, to treat him,
~~1.~~ All this he knew, but not that twas to eat him.
As far as Goose c^d^ judge, he reasond right,
But as to Man, mistook the matter quite:
Man will
~~he~~ ~~Thou~~
And just as short of Reason ~~shall we~~ fall Learn Dulness
Works to one End
In all thy Madness
~~To~~
\+ Who think'~~st~~ all made for one, not one for all. Thy
Let
~~3~~ [Look Nature thro', & see the Chain of Love But —
<~~Next~~> Combining all below and all above.

See

2.

See lifeless Matter moving to one End;
× Each single Particle to other tend,
Attract, attracted to, the next in place,
By Nature form'd its Neighbor to embrace.
Behold it next, with various life endu'd,
~~Still to their~~ Centre ~~tends~~, the ~~common~~ general Good.
See dying Vegetables Life sustain,
See Life dissolving vegetate again.
Nothing is foreign; Parts relate to Whole:
One all-preserving, all-connecting Soul
Unites ~~all~~ each Being; greatest with ye least.
~~Nor more~~ Made Beast ~~for~~ in aid of Man ~~than~~ and Man of Beast.
~~More ample views, more general ends[?]~~
~~Each for his own & Neighbors Happiness:~~
~~Or while Man exclaims All~~
Each serving & serving, nothing stands alone
~~The chain holds on, and where it ends, unknown.~~
~~Has God thou Fool! work'd solely~~ for thy Good,
~~Thinkst not all Creatures design'd for thy Good,~~
Thy Joy, thy pastime, thy attire, thy Food?
Know, ~~all~~ nature's children ~~with one~~ claim her equal care, ~~are most~~;
The Fur What warms ~~a Monarch~~ Sir Gilbert warm'd ~~an~~ a Bear first
× If for thy Table feeds the wanton Fawn,
× Nature as kindly spreads for him the Lawn.
× Tis not for thee the Sky-lark mounts & sings,
Joy lifts his voice & elevates his wings.
Tis not for thee the Linnet pours her Throat,
Loves of his own & Raptures swell the note.
The bounding Steed you gracefully bestride
Shares with his Lord ye pleasure and the Pride.
× Think not thy own the Seed yt strows ye Plain:
The Birds of Heaven shall vindicate their ye Grain.
Think not thy own the Harvest of ye year
Part pays, and justly, the deserving Steer.
The Hog yt plows not, nor obeys thy Call,

Lives on the Labors of this Lord of all.
Know Nature's children claim alike her care. The Fur yt warms ye warm'd a Bear.
While Man exclaims &c. W one for all. Tis true

all forms yt perish other forms supply
By turns they catch ye vital breath & die
Like bubbles on ye Sea of Matter born
They rise, they break & to yt Sea return.
Nothing is foreign—

All served & serving, nothing stands alone
nor general ends
More ample views
Each for his own & Neighbors happiness
All served & serving, Nothing stands alone
The Chain holds on, & where it ends unknown
More ample views & general
Each for his own & Neighbors
all Nature's— happiness

line 457 (p. 7) Ed. 1

7 lines omitted here

2.

See lifeless matter moving to one End,
Each single Particle to other tend,
Attract, attracted to, the next in place,
By Nature form'd its Neighbor to embrace.
Behold it next, with various Life indu'd,
~~Press to one~~
same press ~~of commutual~~
~~Still~~ To the ^ Centre ~~tend~~, the ~~common~~ Good.
general
See dying Vegetables Life sustain,
See Life dissolving vegetate again.
^^ Nothing is foreign; Parts relate to Whole:
One all-preserving, all-connecting Soul
each
Unites ~~all~~ ^ Being, greatest with ye least
in aid of and of
~~Nor more~~ Made Beast ~~for~~ Man ~~than~~ Man ~~for~~ Beast.
seu ~~delend.~~ ~~More ample Views, more genral ends confess~~
~~Stet~~ ~~Each for its own, & neighbors Happiness~~
Stet ~~or~~ ~~While Man exclaims &c~~ — — —
to- Each servd & serving, Nothing stands alone
~~Who thinks all made for one not one for all~~
The Chain holds on, and where it ends, unknown!
[~~Has God, thou Fool! work'd solely~~ for Thy Good
Solely ~~Think not all Creatures destin'd for thy Good,~~ ^
Thy Joy, thy pastime, thy attire, thy Food?
claim her equal
δ Know ~~All~~ Nature's children ~~with one~~ care, ~~are nurst~~;
Sir Gilbert a Bear
The Fur that warms ~~a Monarch~~ warm'd ~~an Ermine first~~
If for thy Table feeds the wanton Fawn,
s him
Nature as kindly spread~~e~~ for his the Lawn.
Tis not for thee the Sky-lark mounts & sings,
Joy lifts his voice & elevates his wings.
Tis not for thee the Linnet pours her throat,
Loves of his own & Raptures swell the note.
The bounding Steed you gracefully bestride
Shares with his Lord ye pleasure and the Pride.
Think not thy own the Seed y^t strows ye Plain,
their
The Birds of Heavn shall vindicate ye grain.
Think not thy own the Harvest~~s~~ of ye year,
Part pays, and justly, the deserving Steer.
The Hog y^t plows not, nor obeys thy Call,
Lives on the Labors of this Lord of all.
Know Natures children claim alike her care The Fur y^t warms Sr G. warmd a Bear.
While Man exclaims &c. to--one for all. Tis true

supply
All forms y^t perish other forms
^ By turns they catch ye vital breath
& die
^ Like bubbles on ye Sea of Matter borne
They rise they break &
to y^t Sea return.
Nothing is foreign—

All servd & serving
nothing stands alone
more genral ends confess
More ample views
Each for its own & neighbors happiness
~~More powrful each as needful to ye rest~~
~~& Each in Proportion as it blesses blest~~
Each servd & serving, Nothing stands alone
The Chain holds on, & where it ends unknown.
Ends confess
More ample views & genral
Each for his own & neighbors happiness.
all Natures—

3

×'Tis true the ~~Strong the weaker still~~ Powrful still ye Weak controll, (line 53, p. 8, Ed. 1)
And ~~powrful Man is Master~~ Man's, the Wit and Tyrant of ye Whole
~~Him therefore~~ But Man alone great Nature checks: He ~~only knows~~ knows,
He ~~only~~ feels ~~another~~ alone, all others Wants & Woes:
For some his Int'rest prompts him to provide, for more his Pleasure, & for more his Pride.
Say will the Falcon, stooping from above,
Smit with his varying plumage, spare the Dove?
× Turns He his Ear while Philomela sings?
Admires her Eye ye Insect's gilded wings? – line 60 omitted
Man cares for all: to Birds he gives his woods, = line 61 – p. 8 – Ed. 1
To Beasts his Pastures & to fish his floods.
2 ~~For~~ some all feed on one
~~For~~ more th'extensive
All feed on one proud Patron & enjoy Th'Extensive Blessing of his Luxury
That very Life his learned Hunger craves
He saves from ~~Torment~~ Famine ~~or~~ fro' ye Savage ~~Famine~~ saves:
Nay feasts the animal he dooms his Feast,
And till he ends the Being, makes it blest.
The favour'd Man, by Touch ethereal slain,
Not less foresees ye Stroke, or feels ye pain.
The Creature had his Feast of Life before;
The ~~Man~~ Thou too must perish when ~~this~~ thy Feast is o'er.

To each unthinking Being Heav'n a friend = line 75
Gave not ye useless knowledge of its end
To Man he gives it, but with such a view
As while he fears it, makes him hope it too.
The Hour conceal'd, tis so remote a fear,
That Death tho nearer still, seems never near.
~~Perpetual Wonder~~ Great standing Miracle! that Heav'n assign'd
Its only thinking thing this Turn of mind. = line 82, p. 8 (Ed. 1)

~~All, all enjoy the Power Bliss that suits them best,~~
Or by Reason or with Instinct blest,
~~To equal Bliss by one direction tend~~
And find the means proportion'd to their End.
~~Reason prefer to Instinct if you can~~
~~In this his God directs, in that but Man.~~
N.B. ~~And~~ say where full Instinct is th'unerring guide,
What Pope or Council can they need beside? = line 88
~~This serves them always, that nor serves us long:~~
~~One must go right, ye other may go wrong.~~

[Right margin:] Whether with Reason or with Instinct blest
Know all enjoy ye Power that suits em best
To equal Bliss by that direction tend

Reason

3

Powrful still y^e Weak
Tis true the ~~Strong the weaker still~~ controll,

Man's the Wit and Tyrant
And ~~powrful Man is Master~~ of ye Whole

But Man alone great knows
~~Him therfore~~ Nature checks: He ~~only knows,~~

alone, all others
He ~~only~~ feels^ ~~anothers~~ Wants & Woes:

For some his Intrest prompts him to provide, For more his Pleasure, & for more his Pride.

Say will the Falcon, stooping from above,

Smit with his varying plumage, spare the Dove?

\+ Turns He his Ear while Philomela sings?

Admires her Eye y^e Insects gild~~ed~~ wings?

Man cares for all: To Birds he gives his woods,

To Beasts his Pastures & to fish his floods.

For some all feed on one

δ For more Th' extensive

All feed on one proud Patron, & enjoy Th' Extensive Blessing of his Luxury

That very Life his learned Hunger craves

Famine ye Savage
He saves from ~~Torment~~ — & frõ ~~Famine~~ saves:

Nay feasts the animal he dooms his Feast,

And till he ends the Being, makes it blest:

The favour'd Man, by Touch aetherial slain,

Not less foresees ye Stroke, or feels ye pain.

The Creature had his Feast of Life before;

Thou too thy
The Man must perish when his Feast is o'er:

To each unthinking Being Heavn a friend

Gave not ye useless knowledge of its end

To Man he gives it, but with such a view

As while he fears it, makes him hope it too.

The Hour conceald, tis so remote a fear,

That Death tho nearer still, seems never near

~~Perpetual Eternal~~
Great standing Miracle! that Heavn assignd

Its only Thinking Thing this Turn of Mind. ^

Bliss
~~All, all enjoy the Powrs that suits them best,~~

Or by Reason, or with Instinct blest,

Good
~~To equal Bliss by one direction tend,~~

And find the means proportiond to their End.

~~Reason prefer to Instinct if you can,~~

~~In this tis God directs, in that but Man:~~

say
\+ δ And^ where full Instinct is th' unerring guide,

What Pope or Council can they need beside?

~~This serves them always, that ner serves us long;~~

~~One must go right, y^e other may go wrong.~~

with
[Whether ~~by~~ Reason or with
Instinct blest

Know, all enjoy y^e Powr
that suits em best

that
To equal Bliss by ~~one~~
direction tend^

Reason

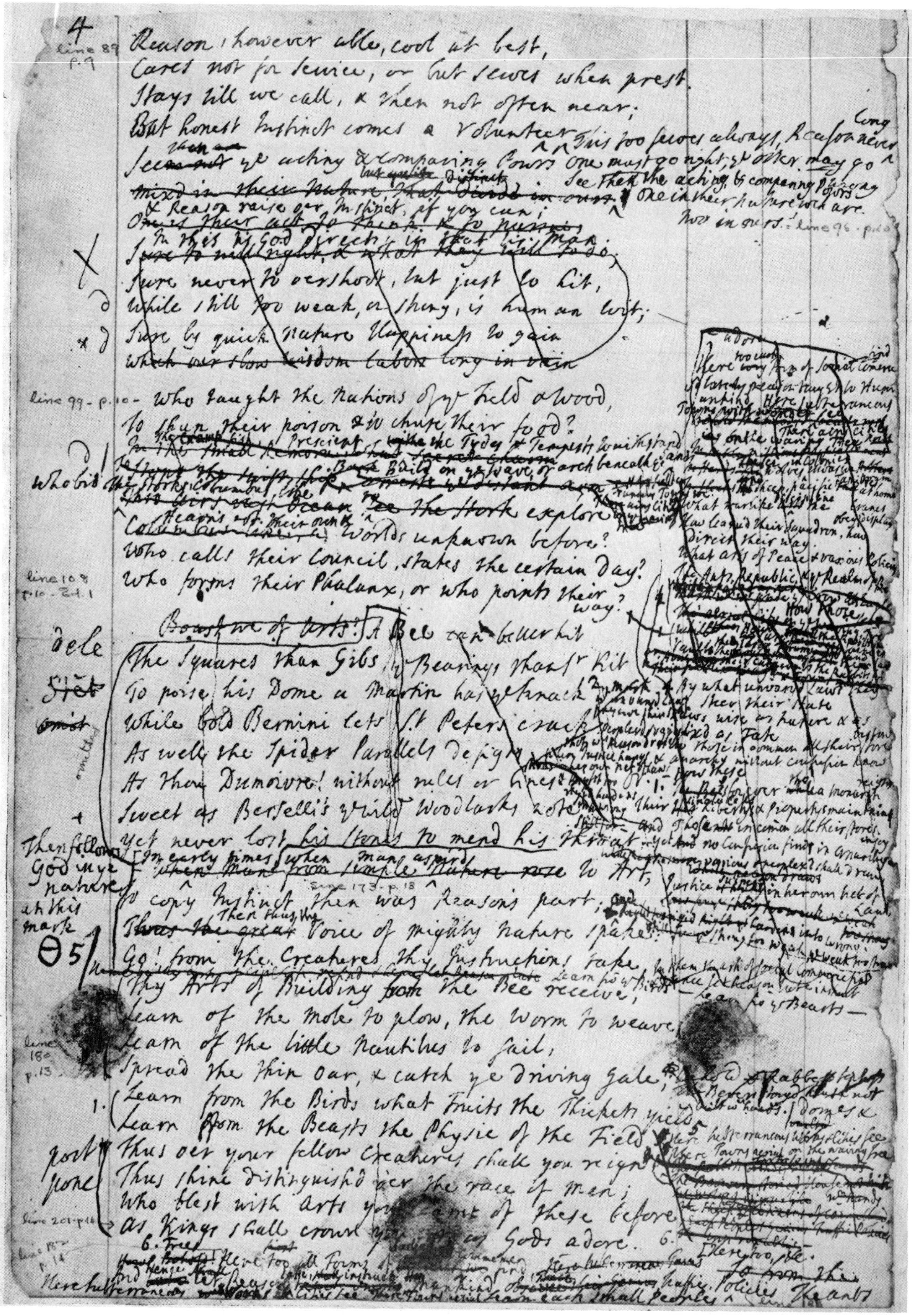

4 line 89 p. 9

Reason, however able, cool at best,
Cares not for service, or but serves when prest,
Stays till we call, & then not often near;
But honest Instinct comes a Volunteer;
Sees then ye acting & comparing Powers
[illegible]
& Reason raise o'er Instinct, if you can;
[illegible]
In this 'tis God directs, in that 'tis Man.
[illegible]
Sure never to o'ershoot, but just to hit,
While still too weak, or strong, is human wit;
Sure by quick Nature Happiness to gain
Which wiser slow Wisdom labors long in vain

line 99 - p. 10 - Who taught the Nations of ye Field & Wood,
To shun their poison & to chuse their food?
[illegible]
Who bid the Stork, Columbus like, explore
Worlds unknown before?
Who calls their Council, states the certain day?
Who forms their Phalanx, or who points their way?

line 108 p. 10 - Ed. 1

dele

Boast we of Arts! A Bee can better hit
The Squares than Gibs, & Bearings than Sr Kit
To poise his Dome a Martin has ye knack
While bold Bernini lets St Peters crack
As well the Spider Parallels designs
As thou Dumoivre! without rules or lines
Sweet as Berselli's wild Woodlarks note
Yet never lost his Stones to mend his Throat

Then follows God in ye nature at this mark

In early times when Man aspir'd to Art,
To copy Instinct then was Reason's part;
Thus then to Man the Voice of mighty Nature spake:
Go! from the Creatures thy Instructions take,
Thy Arts of Building from the Bee receive;
Learn of the Mole to plow, the Worm to weave;
Learn of the little Nautilus to sail,
Spread the thin Oar, & catch ye driving gale;
Learn from the Birds what Foods the Thickets yield
Learn from the Beasts the Physic of the Field
Thus o'er your fellow Creatures shall you reign
Thus shine distinguish'd o'er the race of men;
Who blest with Arts you learnt of these before
As Kings shall crown you, or as Gods adore.

line 180 p. 13

line 201 p. 14

line 182 p. 14

Reason, however able, cool at best,
Cares not for service, or but serves when prest.
Stays till we call, & then not often near;
But honest Instinct comes a volunteer.

Then ~~are~~
Seem ~~not~~ ye acting & comparing Powrs
~~but quite distinct~~
~~Mixd in their Nature, that divide in ours.~~

& Reason raise oer Instinct, if you can;
~~One is their act, to think & to pursue~~ ;

In this tis God directs, in that tis Man.
~~Sure to will right, & what they will to do.~~
Sure never to oershoot, but just to hit,
δ While still too weak, or strong, is human Wit;
Sure by quick Nature Happiness to gain
\+ δ ~~Which our slow Wisdom labors long in vain~~

Who taught the Nations of y^e Field & Wood,
To shun their Poison, & to chuse their food?

The ~~Cramp fish~~ Prescient ~~with~~ the Tydes & Tempests to withstand
~~In the small Remora, what secret charm~~
δ ~~To~~ ~~Bark~~ Build on y^e Wave or arch beneath ye Sand
~~Stops the swift ship, arrests ye distant arm~~

Who bid the Storks, Columbus like ~~to~~
~~Thro Airs vast Ocean, see the Stork~~ explore
Heavn's not their own &
~~Columbus like, a~~ Worlds unknown before?
Who calls their Council, states the certain day?
Who forms their Phalanx, or who points their way?

~~Boast we of Arts?~~ A Bee can better hit
dele The Squares than Gibs, y^e Bearings than Sr Kit
~~Stet~~ To poise his Dome a Martin has y^e knack
~~omit~~ While bold Bernini lets St Peters crack
As well the Spider Parallels designs
As thou, Dumoivre! without rules or lines
\+ Sweet as Berselli's y^e wild Woodlarks note
Yet never lost his Stones to mend his throat

Then follows God in y^e nature at this mark θ5
In early times, when Man aspir'd
~~When Man from simple Nature rose~~ to Art,
To copy Instinct then was Reason's part;
Then thus the
~~Thus the great~~ Voice of mighty Nature spake:
Go! from the Creatures thy Instructions take,
~~Hence be thy Arts of Civil Life refind & hence let Reason late~~

Learn frō y^e Birds -- Learn frō y^e Beasts --

2\. Thy Arts of Building from the Bee receive,
Learn of the Mole to plow, the Worm to weave;
3\. Learn of the little Nautilus to sail,
Spread the thin oar, & catch y^e driving Gale;
1\. Learn from the Birds what Fruits the Thickets yield,
Learn from the Beasts the Physic of the Field.
Thus oer your fellow Creatures shall you reign

post pone
Thus shine distinguishd o'er the race of Men;
Who blest with Arts you learnt of these before,
As Kings shall crown you, or as Gods adore.

6\. Tree
~~first~~ <social> Commerce
~~<How>Behold!~~ Here too all Forms of ~~<G. ment> we~~ find ~~Here subterraneous Towns~~
Hence ~~shall~~ late ~~shall~~ instruct ~~Trace~~
And ~~late~~ Let Reason ~~teach <y> to~~ Mankind ~~Observe their Genius~~, Traffic, Policies The Ants
Learn each small People's

Here subterraneous ⟷ Works & Cities see There Towns aerial

~~Here sub terraneous Towns we see~~
~~There airy Cities on ye waving tree~~

1

2 Mark
w^t unvaryd Laws
preserve their State
Perplexd & <various>
those wch Reason draws
When Justice hangs
in her own Net of Laws
& Right too rigid hardens into Wrong
still for

This too serves always, Reason never long
One must go right, ye other may go wrong

See then the acting & comparing Powrs
One in their Nature, wch are two in ours.

~~adore~~

Here ~~evry~~ too each Form of Social Comerce find
So late by Reason taught to Humankind

Here subterraneous Towns with wonder see

~~Behold th embodyd Locusts rush ing forth~~

There airy cities on the waving Tree

~~In sable millions frō ye inclement north~~

~~<The>~~ ee in Colonies
~~In Herds the~~ Wolves invasive ~~Robbers~~ roam

And Families
~~In Flocks the~~ Sheep, pacific ~~race~~ at home

Discipline
What warlike ~~arts~~ the <blank> Cranes obey display

How leagu'd their Squadron, how direct their Way

What Arts of Peace & various Policies
The Ants Republic & ye Realm of Bees

<While as sure>
2 ~~Mark wth w^t pride ye Crow or Eagle <see>~~
~~How those~~

~~Th aerial City on ye waving Tree~~

1 ~~<While> their House ⟷ the Rabbits~~
~~the large Forum ⟷ sand~~
~~Vault the large Dome ⟷ their~~
~~How large their Catacombs the Rabbits fo<und>~~
~~Their public Ways & Forums underground~~

4 By what unvaryd Laws they steer their State
Laws wise as Nature & as fixd as Fate

How those in common all their Store bestow
& anarchy without confusion know

—How these
Or 1. <e> tho reign ~~e~~
~~The Bee s~~ forever ~~while~~ a monarch

Their single Cells
~~His~~ Liberty s & Property s maintain ~~e~~

And Those in comon all their stores enjoy

Yet ~~And~~ no confusion find in Anarchy

~~While Reason more~~ various & perplexd shall draw
~~While Reason draws~~

suspend
Justice ~~is hung~~ in her own Net of Laws

~~Laws for ye Strong too weak, ye Weak too strong~~

And
~~& Right too rigid Right y^t~~ hardens ~~e~~ into Wrong
Still for ye Strong too weak, ye Weak too strong

In them the Arts of Social Commerce find
& hence let Reason late instruct

<4.> Behold ye Rabbits fortress

The Beavers storyd house not built with hands domes & ~~vaults~~

5
~~<5>~~ Here Subterraneous Works & Cities see
~~<5>~~ There Towns aerial on the Waving Tree

~~Behold~~ ~~Fortress in y^e~~
~~The Rabbits <Fortress ⟶ Sands~~

~~The Beavers storied House not built wth hands~~

~~<See>Wolves <invade> like~~
~~The Sheep ye Citizens of comon stand~~

~~Each Peoples Genius, Traffic, Policies~~

~~The ants republic~~--

6 [Here too &c

~~Go from the~~

5

line 113. p. 10 So from the first th' Eternal Order ran
Creature to Creature linkd, & Man to Man!
Heavn that but made a world the whole to bless
Plac'd in Society that happiness
From private sparkles rais'd ye public flame
And bad Self-love & Social be the same
Quicken'd with this spirit new-born Nature mov'd,
Each first admir'd its Being, then it lov'd
Each, seeks a pleasure not possess'd
Seeks, to be taught, not seeks, to be alone,
Each Sex desires alike, and Two are one.

Origin of Society / Foundation of Society.

line 119. p. 11 Not only Man, but all that range the wood
That wing the wide air, or roll along the flood
This, ardor, minute, animates, one nature feeds
The vital Lamp, & swells the genial seeds.
All spread their Image with one ardour stung
All love themselves, reflected in their Young.
The Beast, the Bird, their common charge attend,
The Mothers nurse it, and the Sires defend;
But taught to range the wood, or wing the air,
There Instinct ends, & Passion & the Care

There stops the Instinct & there ends the Care

line 130. p. 11 The Link dissolv'd, each seeks a fresh Embrace,
Another Love succeeds, another Race.
A longer care Man's wanting Kind demands,
That longer care contracts more lasting bands;
Reflection, Reason, still the tyes improve,
At once extend the Interest, & the Love.
With Choice we fix, with Sympathy we burn,
And ev'ry tender Passion takes its Turn.
And still new needs, new Helps, new Habits rise,

Origin of Family Societies

line 139. p. 11 That graft Benevolence on Charities:
And now one Brood, and now another grows;
line 148. These nat'ral Love maintain'd, habitual those;
Scarce had the last the Parents' care outgrown
Before they saw those Parents want their own.
Mem'ry & Forecast just returns engage;
That pointed back to Youth, this on to Age
While Pleasure, Gratitude, Hope, combine,
line 149. p. 12 Stretch the long Interest, & support the Line

When man from simple nature &c

Serving & send, for nothing no Being stands alone
The chain holds on, & where it ends unknown
one life, one light, one Earth, one Air

The last scarce ripen'd into perfect Man
Sees helpless Him from whom ye Race began
Led by whose art they learnd to pierce ye wood
Learnd to command the Fire, controll the flood
Draw forth ye monsters of the abyss profound
Or fetch th' aerial Eagle to the ground.
Mem'ry &c.

5

So from the first th' Eternal Order ran

Creature to Creature linkd, & Man to Man.

Each serves to each, of mutual Use & Care, Heirs of one life, one light, one Earth, one Air.

Heavn that but made a World the Whole to bless

Placd in Society that happiness

From private Sparkles raisd ye public flame

And bad Selflove & Social be the same.

~~Quick Strong~~ with spirit mov'd,
~~This ye first~~ this ~~Impulse~~ new-born Nature ~~mov'd~~,

Each its it loved;
~~Origine of~~ ~~Man first admird his Being, then he lov'd~~

Each ~~sought~~ a Pleasure not possest
~~Society~~ ~~Society he sought, nor sought~~ alone,
seeks

es are
Foundation Each sex desires alike, and two ~~were~~ one.

of Society Not only Man, but all that range the wood

wide
~~That~~ Wing the air, or roll along the flood

This ~~ardor~~ Impulse
~~One Spirit~~ animates, one nature feeds

The vital lamp, & swells the genial seeds:

one ~~ardor impulse~~ ardor stung
All spread their Image w^{th} ~~this Impulse stung~~

All love themselves, reflected in their Young.

~~offspring tend~~
The Beast, the Bird, their common charge attend,

~~them~~ it, and
The Mothers Nurse~~s~~ ~~&~~ the Sires defend~~s~~ ;

But
~~Till~~ taught to range the wood, or wing the air, There stops y^e Instinct & there ends y^e Care

~~stops There ends ends the Love &~~
\+ ~~There Instinct ends its Passion & its Care~~
~~Nature ends y^e~~

The Link dissolvd, each seeks a fresh Embrace,

Another Love succeeds, another Race.

~~<But>~~
A longer Care Man's wanting Kind demands,

~~Those~~ ~~s~~
That longer Care contract~~s~~ more lasting bands;

~~Origine of~~ Reflection, Reason, still the tyes improve,

Family extend
At once ~~prolong~~ the Intrest, & the Love.
Societies

we ~~they~~
With Choice ~~they~~ fix, wth Sympathy we burn,

And ev'ry tender Passion takes its Turn.

And still new Needs, new Helps, new Habits rise,

That graft Benevolence on Charities:

And now and now grows,
\+ ~~And now~~ one Brood, ~~& now~~ another ~~rose~~,

These nat'ral Love maintain s ~~d~~, habitual those;

have
~~Scarce had the last the Parents Care outgrown,~~
~~see~~
~~Before they saw those Parents want their own.~~

Mem'ry & Forecast just returns engage,

them
That points back to Youth, this on to Age,

Pleasure and ~~&~~ ~~all~~ combine,
While Gratitude, Hope, ~~Pleasure, Intrest join,~~

Stretch the long Int'rest, & support the Line.

When Man from simple Nature &c

for Nothing
Serving & servd, no Being stands alone

The Chain holds on, & where it ends
unknown

ripen'd
The last scarce ~~strength~~
~~end~~ into perfect Man

Sees helpless Him from
whom ye Race began

~~Led by~~
~~<Learnd> from whose~~
Led ~~Taught~~ by whose art they
learnd to pierce ye Wood,

Learnd to command the Fire, controll
ye flood

Draw forth ye Monsters of th' abyss
profound

or fetch ~~d~~ th' aerial
Eagle to the ground.

Mem'ry &c.

6 Origine of Political Societies.

Line 204. p. 15 — Thus rose one little State: another near

Grew by like means & join'd thro Love or Fear.

For Love & Nature's Dictate, Murder not.

For Want alone each Animal contends,

Tygers with Tygers, ... friends.

... the common mother crown'd

She pour'd her Acorns, Herbs & Streams around.

... Neighbours to invade ...

... to fight, for Sunshine or for Shade

ORIGIN of MONARCHY

... when crown'd by Nature first Patriarch sate

King, Priest, & Parent of his growing State: line 217 - p. 15

... taught to command the fire, Control the flood;

Draw forth the monsters of the abyss profound

And fetch the soaring Eagle to the ground. line 223, p. 15

On him their second Providence, they hung line 218

Their Law, his Eye; their Oracle his Tongue. line 219 - p. 15

Till weak, & old, & dying, they began (line 224)

Whom they rever'd as God, to mourn as man:

Then looking up from Sire to Sire, explor'd,

line 227 - p. 16 → One great first Father, & that First ador'd.

Or plain Tradition that this All begun

Convey'd unbroken Faith fro Sire to Son,

The mighty Workman from the Work was known, (line 230 - p. 16)

And simple Reason never sought but one.

Ere Wit oblique broke that steddy Light

Man like his Maker saw that all was right

To Virtue in the paths of Pleasure trod,

line 235 - p. 16 → And own'd a Father when he own'd a God.

Twas simple Worship in the native Grove,

Religion, Morals, had no name but Love;

Love all the Faith & all th' Allegiance then;

line 237 - p. 16 - For Nature knew no Right Divine in Men,

[Origine of true Religion & Government, from ye Principle of Love.

6 Origine of Political Societies. <32>

Thus rose one little State; another near
Grew by like means, & joind thro Love or Fear;
~~Fear <Each> wd forbid wd forbid to quarrel engagem^t^~~
~~More like they lovd than quarreld on the spot,~~
& The neighbors leagud to guard their common Spot,
~~For~~ Love is Nature's dictate, Murder not.

For Want alone each animal contends,
Tygers with Tygers, that removd, are
~~Remove but that, & Tygers will be~~ friends.
Their untaught wants
~~Their unlearnd Wants~~ the common Mother crownd,
Plain Natures
~~Mere All Natures~~ wants ye comon
~~all their~~

She pourd her Acorns, Herbs, & Streams around.
~~<This> all their Wealth no~~ for ~~Rapine~~ to ~~wd~~
What Treasures then
~~No Treasures then for Neighbors to~~ invade;
& What need to
~~What Cause to~~ fight, for Sunshine or for Shade
Did here
~~These States had But each obeyd each ruld his own~~ & few ye Fears ~~to awe W^n^ Love was Liberty & Nature Law~~
~~Each had a Lords, tis true, but each its own,~~

~~or controlled by one~~?
~~Why all one Kingdom, why must all be~~
~~Not all Subjected to the rule of One,~~

Each State was ~~not~~ seprate still ~~seprate States subject~~ tho not alone ~~Till comon~~
~~Unless where from one Lineage all began,~~
[Thus States were formd, but yet no sole Monarch known ORIGIN OF MONARCHY
Till common Intrest placd ye sway in One.
~~And swelld into a Nation from a Man~~
Then godlike Virtue or in Arts or Arms Diffusing Blessings or averting Harms, ~~Where ye same Virt~~
~~There crownd by Nature~~
The same the Sons first lovd & then obeyd One man ye Father of a People made
[When crown'd by Nature ~~the first~~ hoary Patriarch sate
Till then by Nature
King, Priest, & Parent of his growing State
He taught ye wondring Youth to pierce ye wood
~~He taught the Arts of Life, the Means of Food~~
~~They saw him pierce~~ Taught to command ye Fire, controul ye flood,
~~To pierce the Forest & to stem the flood~~ Draw forth ye Monsters of ye abyss ~~deep~~ profound
~~Draw~~ ~~below~~
To ~~Draw from ye secret Deeps the finny Drove~~
~~from above~~
And fetch d the soaring Eagle to the ground.
On him their second Providence, they hung
Their Law, his Eye, their Oracle his Tongue.
Till weak, & old, & dying, they began
Whom they rever'd as God, to mourn as Man:
Then looking up from Sire to Sire, explor'd,
One great first Father, & that First ador'd.
Or
~~One~~ plain Tradition that this All begun
Conveyd unbroken Faith frō Sire to Son,
The mighty Workman from the Work was known,
And simple Reason never sought but One.
had ~~n~~ that
Ere Wit oblique broke ~~Natures~~ steddy Light
<had>
Man like his Maker saw that all was right
~~In paths of pleasure~~ | To Virtue in ye Paths of Pleasure trod,
~~Chearful pursud her straight & equal road~~
~~found~~ ~~found~~
And ownd a Father when he ownd a God.
Twas simple Worship in the native Grove,
Religion, Morals had no name but Love,
Love all the Faith, &
~~Plain Gratitude was~~ all th' Allegiance then,
knew
For Nature ~~found~~ no Right Divine in Men,

Left margin:

Fear wd forbid ye unpractisd to engage
& Natures dictate ~~wd be~~ Love, not ~~Rage~~.
Blood & ~~Death &~~ rage
Much cause to join & little <Commerce & Love were> ~~powerful~~ Fear to awe
W^n^ Love was Liberty & Nature Law.

Superfluities & wants on each side-- one State had Water another Fruit. What each wanted might cause Quarrels, but it was imediatly stopd by one giving what it did not want ye other to ~~one~~ y^t^ did.

Did here ye Trees wth ruddier x Foe.
~~happier~~ burthens bend?
& there ye Springs in purer
~~clearer~~ rills descend?
~~all~~ —made
W^t^ War w^d^ ravish Commerce coud bestow,
~~sent him back~~
& he returnd a Friend, who came a Foe.
~~<what other> tempted to~~
~~No Treasure invade~~
~~and~~ ←→ who w^d^
~~No cause to fight for~~
←→
~~& half ye cause~~ Commerce
~~W^n^ Beauty~~ Conveni
~~<Commerce>~~ ence Change
~~Beauty <& Love>~~
must strongly ~~draw~~
W^n^ Love was Liberty
~~& Nature Law~~
Still evry State its nature Lord w^d^ own
Unless ye Common
~~Good was placd in~~
~~One~~

Unpractisd Man yet knew no murdering Skill
& Nature's dictate was to love not kill
~~might prompt to love but not to kill~~
For say what makes ye Liberty of Man ←→ ~~were each no <slender>~~
~~Commerce & Love~~ Not doing what
< ~~When Love~~ he will but w^t^ > he can
& ~~Love was Liberty~~
If w^t^ he likes, another
What serves one Will when
How shall he keep
A weaker might
His Safety did his
All joind to guard
Did here &c. — Foe. [Thus States
Or there
~~<Then>~~ ~~removd~~
~~And~~ half ye Cause of Contest was
When Beauty might be kind to all y^t^ lovd
Did here the Trees a ruddier— foe

~~<one>~~
~~Much cause to joyn & little Fear to awe~~
~~When Love was Liberty & Nature~~
Unless ye common ~~Good was~~ Intrest joind in one When
~~charmd~~ ←→ ~~whose Virtues~~ ~~whose~~ Dy<ing>
~~placd in one~~ Stand ←→ ~~whence~~ ←→
~~&common Intrest many joind in one~~
~~Defence. <There Gratitude or ye same~~ ~~The~~
~~ye same Love~~
~~The Father of a people made~~
For
~~For ye same Virtues wch his~~ ←→
~~his sons had swayd~~ ~~A King~~,
~~a Sire obeyd~~

←→[Origine of true Religion & Government, from y^e^ ~~same~~ Principle of Love.

Wood
Ere yet the guilty altar blushd with blood;
Love all ye Faith & all the Allegiãce then,

~~And~~ No

(7

[God, in the Nature of each Being founds — line 109 - p. 10 (Ed. 1)
Its proper Bliss, and marks (sets) its proper Bounds
But as he formd a Whole, the whole to bless
Plac'd in Society that happiness;
2 So from the first th' eternal Order ran
And Creature linkd to Creature, Man to Man — line 114 - p. 10
From private sparkles rais'd yͤ general flame — line 140, p. 12
1 And bid Self Love & Social be yͤ same.
Quick, with this Spirit, newborn Nature moved, } omitted
Itself, each Creature in its species loved, }
Each sought (sought) a pleasure not possest alone, — line 121 - p. 11
Each Sex desired alike, (till) two were one. 122.
Not only Man, but all
wing the wide } omitted
One Ardor (This Impulse) animates: One Nature feels }
The vital Lamp,

~~<For evry Creature>~~ ⟷
~~to mend his Throat~~
⟷

[God in the Nature of each Being founds

sets
Its proper Bliss, & marks its proper Bounds
But as he formd a Whole, the whole to bless
Plac'd in Society that happiness
So from the first th Eternal Order ran
2 And Creature link'd to Creature, Man to Man
From private Sparkles raisd ye genral flame
1, And bid Selflove & Social be ye same.
Quick, with this Spirit, newborn Nature moved;
Itself, each Creature in its species loved,
~~seeks~~
Each ~~sought~~ a pleasure not possesst alone,
till were
Each sex desired alike, ~~&~~ two ~~are~~ one.
Not only Man but all
Wing the wide
This Impulse animates: one Nature feeds
~~One Ardor~~
The vital Lamp,

King Priest

7th

Who taught their wondring youth

Taught to comand

Draw forth ye monsters of th'abyss profound

& fetch ye aerial Eagle

~~[illegible]~~

~~What they revere~~

To — God's adore[illegible] at Nature spoke, Obsequent Man

at this mark — Cities were built, Societies were made — obey'd

Here rose one little State — fear

Did here ye Trees

And then ye thousand

Wt War cd ravish, Commerce cd

& he return'd

Thus States were form'd, ye name of K. unknown

Till Common Intrest

line 202 - p. 14

line 214

line 219 p. 15

Sees

Mem'ry &

That pointing back

While

Stretch the long

[When man fro simple nature rose to art [illegible]

Thus rose one little State, another near

Grew by like means, & joind thro Love or Fear

~~Form'd Larger States~~: One ~~Ruler yet un-~~

Till common Intrest plac'd ye Sway in One:

then Virtue only, or

[illegible]

same the Sons first in a Sire obey'd

One Man the Father

Till then, by Nature crown'd, each

King Priest & Parent of his growing

On him their second Providence, they hung

Their Law his Eye, their Oracle

Till

&c. to Love of man.

[False faith, false Policy at once begun Stet

↔

King Priest

their
Who taught ~~ye~~ ^ wondring Youth

Taught to command

Draw forth ye Monsters of th' abyss profd

& fetch ye aerial Eagle

~~Now withring~~

~~Whom they reverd~~

To-Gods adore [Great Nature spoke, observant Man obeyd

at this mark
Cities were built, Societies were made

⧖ Here rose one little state -- fear

Did here ye Trees

And there ye Streams in

Wt War cd ravish, Commerce cd

& he returnd

Thus States were formd, ye Name of K. unknown

Till Common Intrest

^ ^ Sees

Mem'ry &

That pointing back

While

Stretch the long

When Man frō simple Nature rose to art To <copy> Instinct t<hen>

^ ~~Thus~~ rose one little State; Another ne<ar>

Grew by like means, & joind thro Love or Fear

~~The name of Monarch King~~
~~Form'd larger States: One Ruler yet un-~~
^ ~~known,~~

Till common In'trest plac'd ye Sway in One:

~~Twas~~ Then
~~Then~~ ^ Virtue only, or

Diffusing

first
The same the Sons ~~had~~ in a Sire obey'd

~~(&c) blest~~

One Man the Father

Till then, by nature crown'd, each

King Priest & Parent of his growing

On him their second Providence yy hung

~~He~~

Their Law his Eye, their Oracle

Till &c to Love of Man.

false Policy at once
[False Faith, ~~& broken Governmt~~ ^ begun stet

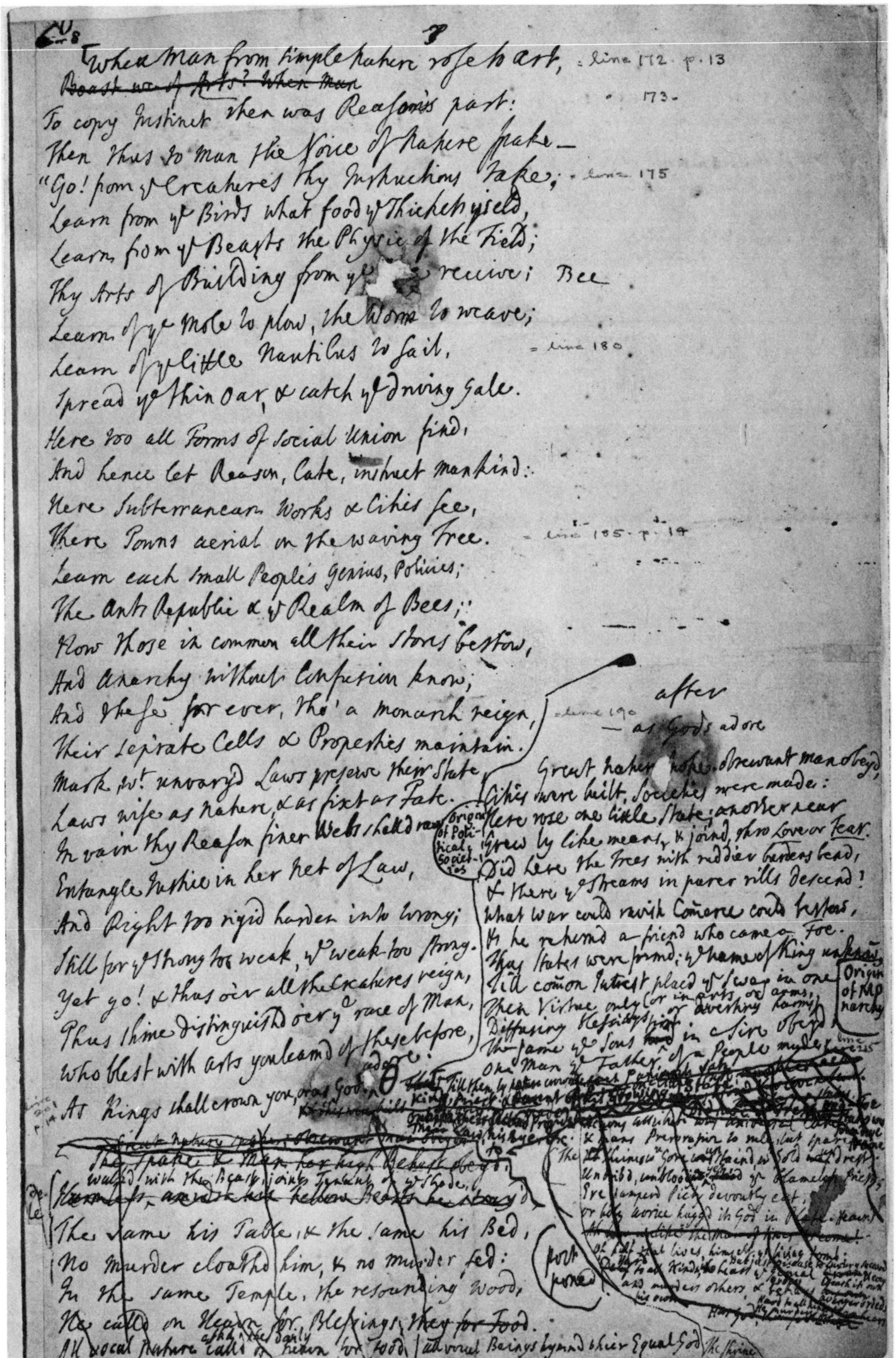

When Man from simple Nature rose to Art,

~~Beast was of Arts? When Man~~

To copy Instinct then was Reason's part:
Then thus to Man the Voice of Nature spake—
"Go! from ye Creatures thy Instructions take;
Learn from ye Birds what food ye Thickets yield,
Learn from ye Beasts the Physic of the Field;
Thy Arts of Building from ye Bee receive;
Learn of ye Mole to plow, the Worm to weave;
Learn of ye little Nautilus to sail,
Spread ye thin Oar, & catch ye driving gale.
Here too all Forms of social Union find,
And hence let Reason, late, instruct mankind:
Here Subterranean Works & Cities see,
There Towns aerial on the waving Tree.
Learn each small People's Genius, Policies;
The Ants Republic & ye Realm of Bees;
How those in common all their Stores bestow,
And Anarchy without Confusion know;
And these for ever, tho' a monarch reign,
Their separate Cells & Properties maintain.
Mark wt. unvary'd Laws preserve their State,
Laws wise as Nature, & as fixt as Fate.
In vain thy Reason finer Webs shall draw,
Entangle Justice in her Net of Law,
And Right too rigid harden into wrong;
Still for ye strong too weak, ye weak too strong.
Yet go! & thus o'er all the Creatures reign,
Thus thine distinguish'd o'ery race of Man,
Who blest with Arts you learn'd of these before, adore
As Kings shall crown you, as Gods [illegible]

after — as Gods adore

Great Nature spoke, obsequious man obey'd,
Cities were built, Societies were made:
Here rose one little State, another near
Grew by like means, & join'd, thro Love or Fear.
Did here the Trees with ruddier burdens bend,
& there ye Streams in purer rills descend?
What War could ravish Comerce could bestow,
& he return'd a friend who came a Foe.
Thus States were form'd; ye name of King unknown
Till comon Interest plac'd ye sway in one.
Then Virtue only (or in arts, or arms,
Diffusing blessings or averting harms)
The same wch. in a Sire ye Sons obey'd
One Man ye Father of a People made.
[illegible]

Origin of Political Societies

Origin of Monarchy

~~Great Nature spoke, obsequious Man obey'd~~
~~The Snake & Man for high Behest obey'd,~~
walk'd with the Beast, joint Tenant of ye Shade.
~~[illegible]~~
The same his Table, & the same his Bed,
No Murder cloath'd him, & no murder fed:
In the same Temple, the resounding Wood,
~~We call'd on Heav'n for Blessings, they for Food.~~
All vocal Nature calls to Heav'n for food | All vocal Beings hymn'd their Equal God | the shrine

Unbrib'd, unbloody, [illegible]
Pre[illegible] devoutly [illegible]
[illegible]

post poned

↔
6 or 8 ~~3~~

[When Man from simple Nature rose to Art,
~~Boast we of Arts? When Man~~
To copy Instinct then was Reason's part:
Then thus to Man the Voice of Nature spake--
"Go! from ye Creatures thy Instructions take;
Learn from ye Birds what food ye Thickets yield,
Learn from ye Beasts the Physic of the Field;
Thy Arts of Building from ye e receive; Bee
Learn of ye Mole to plow, ye Worm to weave;
Learn of ye little Nautilus to sail,
Spread ye thin Oar, & catch ye driving Gale.
Here too all Forms of Social Union find,
And hence let Reason, late, instruct Mankind:
Here Subterranean Works & Cities see,
There Towns aerial on the waving Tree.
Learn each small People's Genius, Policies;
The Ants Republic & ye Realm of Bees;
How those in common all their Stores bestow,
And Anarchy without Confusion know;
And these for ever, tho' a Monarch reign,
Their sep'rate Cells & Properties maintain.
Mark, w^t unvary'd Laws preserve their State,
Laws wise as Nature, & as fixt as Fate.
In vain thy Reason finer Webs shall draw,
Entangle Justice in her Net of Law,
And Right too rigid harden into Wrong;
Still for ye Strong too weak, ye Weak too strong.
Yet go! & thus o'er all the Creatures reign,
Thus shine distinguishd o'er ye race of Man,
Who blest with Arts you learnd of these before,
adore. θ
As Kings shall crown you, or as God. ^
~~Great Nature spoke; observant Man obeyd~~
~~She spoke & Man her high Behest obeyd~~,
Walkd with the Beasts, joint Tenant of ye Shade,
de ~~Harmless, amidst his Fellow Beasts he stray'd,~~
le ^
The same his Table, & the same his Bed,
No Murder cloathd him, & no Murder fed:
In the same Temple, the resounding Wood,
He calld on Heavn for Blessings, ~~they for Food.~~
asked the daily
All vocal Nature calld on heavn for food. | All vocal Beings hymned their Equal God

after
—as Gods adore
Great Nature spoke, observant Man obeyd,
Cities were built, Societies were made:
Here rose one little State; another near
Grew by like means, & joind, thro Love or Fear.
Did here the Trees with ruddier burdens bend,
& there ye Streams in purer rills descend?
What War could ravish Comerce could bestow,
& he returnd a friend who came a Foe.
Thus States were formd, ye name of King unknow,
Till comon Intrest placd ye Sway in one
Then Virtue only (or in arts or arms,
Diffusing blessings, or averting harms)
first
The same ye Sons ~~had~~ in a Sire obeyd,
One Man ye Father of a People made.

(Origin of Political Societies)

(Origin of Monarchy)

~~The~~ Till then by Nature crownd each Patriarch sate
King Priest & Parent of his growing State
On him their second Providence
Their Law his Eye &c

~~So rose one little State, another near~~
~~Grew by like means & joind thro love or fear~~
~~Formd larger States~~
~~Did here ye Trees ↔ Foe~~
~~Thus States were formd ↔ (for One)~~

Heavns attribute was Universal Care
& Man's Prerogative to rule, but spare.
The Shrine
un un
The ~~No~~ Shrine~~s~~ wth Gore ~~was~~ staind, wth Gold ~~was~~ drest;
yet
Unbribd, unbloodied ~~stood~~ ye blameless Priest;
Ere pamperd Piety devoutly eat,
Or holy Avrice huggd its God in Plate. Heavn's
~~Ah how unlike the Man of times to come!~~
post Of half that lives, himself ye living tomb:
But just Disease to Luxury succeeds
Hard
~~Deaf~~ to all Kinds, who hears y^e genral ~~Groan~~ & evry
groan
pone δ Death its own
& murders others, & betrays ~~his own.~~ avenger breeds
his own
Hard to all kinds, Man hears
He murders others
~~Has God thou fool~~ —

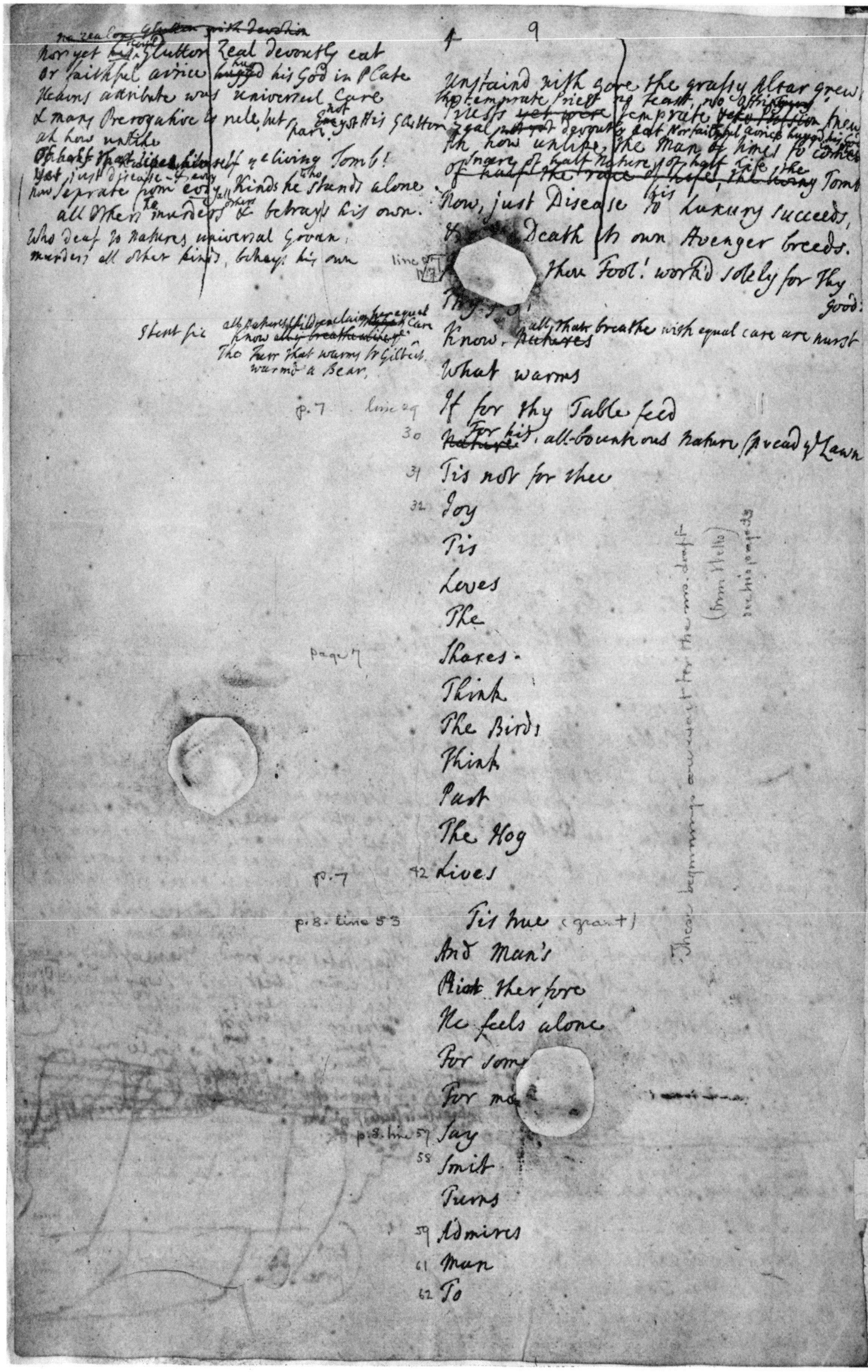

4 9

Nor yet a Glutton Zeal devoutly eat
Or faithful avice hug his God in Plate
Heavens attribute was universal Care
& man's Prerogative to rule, but spare. not yet His Glutton
ah how unlike
Of half that live, himself ye living Tomb!
Yet, just disease —
now seprate from each Kind, he stands alone
all others murders & betrays his own.
Who deaf to Natures universal Groan,
murders all other kinds, betrays his own

Unstaind with gore the grassy Altar grew,
The temprate Priest no feast, no Offring knew,
Priests temprate
Zeal devoutly eat Nor faithful avice hugg'd his God
Ah how unlike, the Man of times to come!
of half the race of Life, the living Tomb
Now, just Disease to Luxury succeeds,
& Death its own Avenger breeds.

line 27 Thee Fool! work'd solely for thy good:

Know. all that breathe with equal care are nurst

Stent fie — Know all that breathe — The Furr that warms St Gilbert warm'd a Bear.

What warms

p.7 line 29 If for thy Table feed
30 For his all-bounteous Nature spread ye Lawn
31 Tis not for thee
32 Joy
Tis
Loves
The
page 7 Shares.
Think
The Birds
Think
Past
The Hog
p.7 42 Lives

p.8. line 53 Tis true (grant)
And Man's
Riot therfore
He feels alone
For some
For more
p.8. line 57 Say
58 Smit
Turns
59 Admires
61 Man
62 To

(Those beginning ... for the ms. draft (from Hello) see this page 33)

~~No zealous Glutton with devotion~~
could
Nor yet ~~his~~ Glutton Zeal devoutly eat
hug
Or faithful av'rice ~~huggd~~ his God in Plate

Heavns attribute was Universal Care

& Man's Prerogative to rule, but spare.

Ah how unlike

Of half that live d himself ye living Tomb!

Yet just disease— & evry
who
Now Seprate from evry Kinds he stands alone
all
To others
All others murders & betrays his own.

Who deaf to Natures universal Groan

Murders all other kinds, betrays his own

All Natures Children claim her equal
Stent hic ~~nurst~~ Care

Know ~~all yt breathe alike ye~~ ^

The Furr that warms Sr Gilbert
warmd a Bear,

4 9

Unstaind with gore, the grassy Altar grew,

The temprate Priest no Feast, no Offring ~~Fury~~
Priests ~~yet were~~ temprate, ~~yet no Passion~~ knew
not
~~Ere~~ yet His Glutton Zeal ~~not yet~~ devoutly eat Nor faithful avrice huggd his God
in Plate

Ah how unlike the Man of times to come

Snare of half Nature, of half Life the
~~Of half the race of Life, the living~~ Tomb
his
Now, just Disease to Luxury succeeds,

& ev'ry Death its own Avenger breeds.

H thou Fool! work'd solely for Thy
good:

Thy Joy,

all that breathe with equal care are nurst
Know, ~~Natures~~

What warms

If for thy Table feed

For his, all-bounteous Nature spread ye Lawn
~~Nature~~

Tis not for thee

Joy

Tis

Loves

The

Shares

Think

The Birds

Think

Part

The Hog

Lives

Tis true

And Man's

Him therfore

He feels alone

For some

For mo

Say

Smit

Turns

Admires

Man

To

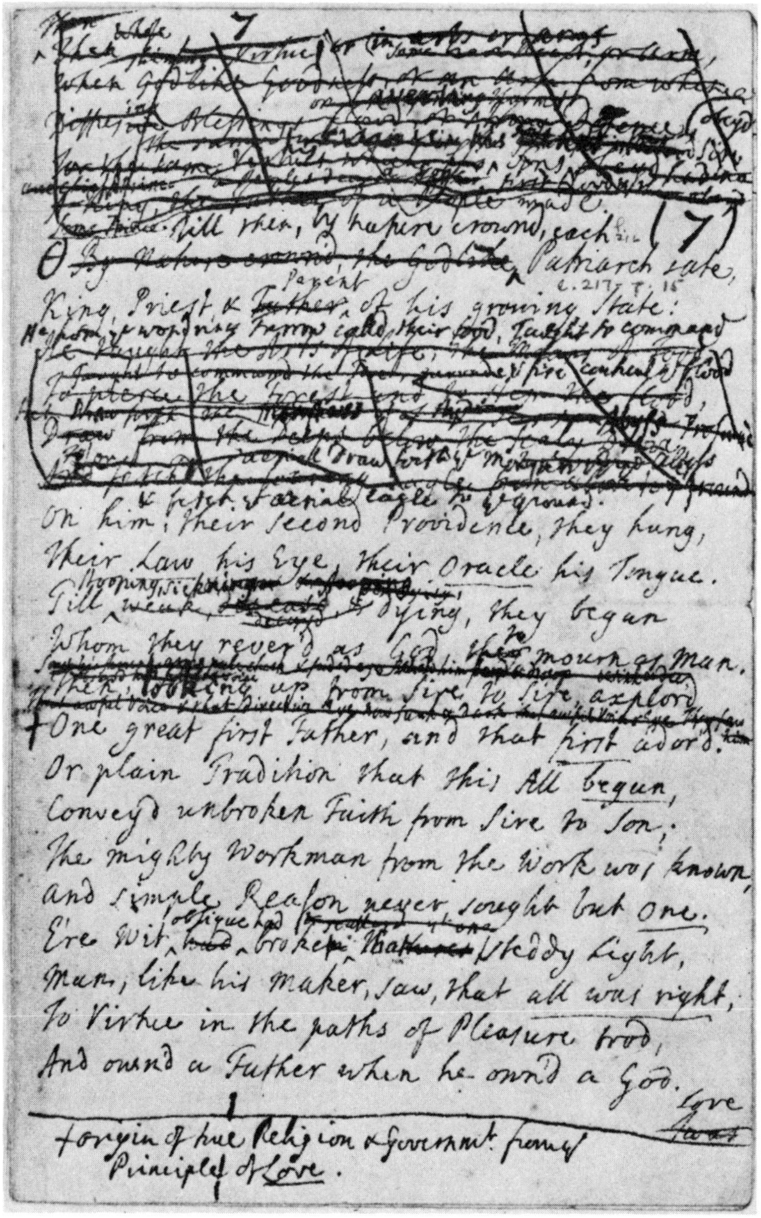

7

Till then, by Nature crownd, each Patriarch sate,
King, Priest, & Parent of his growing State:

& fetch th' aerial Eagle to y^e ground.

On him, their second Providence, they hung,
Their Law his Eye, their Oracle his Tongue.
Till drooping, sickning, dying, they began
Whom they reverd as God, to mourn as Man.
Then, looking up from Sire to Sire explord
One great first Father, and that first adord.
Or plain Tradition that this All begun,
Conveyd unbroken Faith from Sire to Son;
The mighty Workman from the Work was known,
And simple Reason never sought but One.
Ere Wit oblique had broke that steddy Light,
Man, like his Maker, saw, that all was right,
To Virtue in the paths of Pleasure trod,
And ownd a Father when he ownd a God.

Love

Origin of true Religion & Government from
Principle of Love.

~~Then Whose~~ ~~or in Arts or Arms~~
^ ~~Then shining Virtue~~ ~~some brave Heart, or Arm,~~

~~When Godlike Goodness, or an Arm from whence~~

~~ing~~ ~~or averting Harms~~
~~Diffusive Blessings flowd, or strong Defence~~

~~sons~~
~~The same <which in a sire his> < > obeyd~~ ~~obeyd~~
~~sire~~
~~For the same Virtues which his Sons obeyd~~ ~~had in a~~

~~a~~ ~~<son>~~
~~One Chief~~ | ~~A Prince a Peoples <dearer> Father~~ ~~first lovd & then obeyd~~
~~A King, the Father of a People made~~.
~~Some Prince~~

(7)

Till then, by Nature crownd, each
~~By Nature crown'd, the Godlike~~ ^ Patriarch sate,

Parent
King, Priest, & ~~Father~~ ^ of his growing State:

He from ye wondring Furrow calld their food, Taught to command
~~He taught the Arts of Life, the Means of Food~~
ye fire, controul ye flood

Taught to command the Fire, pervade
~~To pierce the Forest and to stem the flood,~~

~~<deeps>~~
~~stet~~ ~~Draw forth the Monsters of the <Seas>< >Abyss Profound~~
~~Draw from the Deeps below the scaly Drove~~
Draw forth ye Monsters of ye Abyss

~~To~~ | ~~or~~ ~~aerial~~
~~And fetch d the soaring Eagle from above to ye ground~~
& fetch ye aerial Eagle to ye ground.

On him, their second Providence, they hung,

Their Law his Eye, their Oracle his Tongue.

stooping, sickning ~~<&> stooping dying,~~
Till ^ ~~weak, diseasd, &~~ dying they began
~~decayd~~

to
Whom they rever'd as God, ~~they~~ mourn as Man.

~~Saw his shrunk arm, pale cheek, & faded eye Beheld him <stand> & droop & wish to die,~~
~~Observd his <feeble>~~ voice

Then, looking up from Sire to Sire explor'd

~~That awful Voice & that directive Eye Now sunk & dark that awful Voice & Eye They saw~~
~~him~~

\+ Onegreat first Father, and that first ador'd.

Or plain Tradition that this All begun,

Conveyd unbroken Faith from Sire to Son;

The mighty Workman from the Work was known,

And simple Reason never sought but One.

oblique had ~~& scatterd y^t one~~
E're Wit ^ ~~had~~ ^ broke~~n~~ ^ that | steddy Light,

Man, like his Maker, saw, that all was right,

To Virtue in the paths of Pleasure trod,

And own'd a Father when he own'd a God.
Love
1 ~~Twas~~

+Origin of true Religion & governm^t from y^e
Principle of Love.

8 ~~Heavn's vaulted Temple, or~~
~~He knew no Temple but~~
~~Feasts~~ ~~Worship in the native Wood;~~
line 236 p.16 ~~Ere yet the Grassie Altar blushed with Blood~~
Love all the Faith, & ~~all~~ th' Allegiance then;
For Nature knew no Right Divine in Men,
No Ill could fear in God; nor understood
A Sov'reign Being but a Sov'reign Good.
True Faith, true Policy, united ran,
That was but Love of God, & this of Man.

False Faith, ~~& wicked Government~~ false Policy, at once begun
Th' enormous Thought of many made for One.
Force first made Conquest, & that Conquest Law;
Then Superstition gave the Tyrant awe;
~~[illegible]~~ next stood the Tyranny, ~~[illegible]~~ indulgent it aid,
And Gods of Conqu'rors, Slaves of Subjects made.
She, ~~midst the Lightning's Blaze~~ ~~[illegible]~~ thunder [illegible]
~~[illegible]~~ when mountains ~~[illegible]~~ or Earthquakes rent ye ~~[illegible]~~ ground
~~The~~ When Weak to bend, ~~the~~ & Fierce to fear began,
At Pow'r unseen, & mightier far than Man:
From opening Earth ~~thought~~ [illegible] Fiends infernal nigh,
And Gods supernal, from the bursting Sky;
Here Hell ~~was~~ she fixd, & there ~~the bright~~ divine abodes;
Fear made ~~their~~ her Devils, & weak Hope ~~their~~ her Gods;
Gods partial, changeful, passionate, unjust,
Whose Attributes were Rage, Revenge, or Lust;
Such as the Souls of Cowards ~~[illegible]~~ might conceive,
And form'd like Tyrants, Tyrants w'd believe.
~~[illegible]~~ Zeal

8

~~Heavns Vault ye Temple, or~~
~~The He knew no Temple but~~
~~Twas~~ ~~Worship in the native Wood,~~
~~E're yet the Grassie Altar blush'd with Blood.~~
Love all the <u>Faith</u>, & all th' <u>Allegiance</u> then;
For Nature knew no Right Divine in Men,
No Ill could fear in God; nor understood
A Sov'reign Being but a Sov'reign Good.
True Faith, true Policy, united ran,
That was but Love of God, & this of Man.

false Policy, at once
False Faith, ~~& wicked Government~~ begun
Th' enormous Thought of Many made for One.

~~calld~~
~~then was Virtue then & Conquest Law~~
Force first made <u>Conquest</u>, & that Conquest <u>Law</u>;
Then <u>Superstition</u> gave the Tyrant awe;
Next ~~shard~~ shard ~~&~~ ←→ and lent it
~~Then learnd~~ the Tyranny, ~~it shar'd, to~~ aid,
And Gods of Conqu'rors, Slaves of Subjects made

sound
She, midst the Lightnings Blaze ←—— &> Thunders ←——→
~~When all the bellowing Air~~ ~~groaning ground~~ <~~shattering s~~^d>
<~~Rav'd~~> When Mountains ~~cleavd~~ or Earthquakes rent y^e
~~Split the huge Oak, &~~ rockd ~~the rending~~ Ground

~~&~~ when &
\+ ~~The~~ Weak to bend, ~~the~~ Fierce to fear began,
At Powr unseen, & mightier far than Man;

showd ~~taught~~
From opening Earth ~~thought~~ Fiends infernal nigh,
And Gods supernal, from the bursting Sky;

she divine
Here Hell ~~they~~ fixd, & there ~~the bright~~ abodes;

her her
Fear made ~~their~~ Devils, & weak Hope ~~their~~ Gods:
Gods partial, changeful, passionate, unjust,
Whose Attributes were Rage, Revenge, or Lust;

~~Priests~~
Such as the Souls of Cowards might conceive'~~d~~
And form'd like Tyrants, Tyrants w^d believe.
'~~d~~

~~soon~~ Zeal

(9) l. 262. p. 17

Zeal now, not Charity, became the Guide;
And Hell was built on Spite, & Heaven on Pride.
The Glutton Priest, first tasted living Food
[illegible] his grim Idol smear'd with human blood;
Heaven's dread thunder [illegible] on all below,
And plays the God an Engine on his Foe.

So drives Selflove, thro just & thro unjust, l. 270
To one mans Power, ambition, Lucre, Lust:
The same Selflove, in all, becomes the cause
Of what restrains him, Government & Laws.
~~Selflove forsakes the Path it first pursued~~
~~And finds the private in the publick Good.~~
For say, wt makes the Liberty of Man?
Not doing what he will, but what he can:
If what he likes, another likes as well,
What serves one Will when many Wills rebell? l. 275
How shall he keep, what, sleeping or awake,
A weaker may surprize, a Stronger take?
His Safety must his liberty restrain;
All join to guard what each desires to gain.
2 Selflove forsook ye path it first pursu'd & found ye private in ye public good.
Forc'd into Virtue thus by Self-Defence
1 Ev'n Kings learn'd Justice and Benevolence.
Then Poets, Legislators, then
~~Then Legislators, Poets then~~, restore
The Faith & Morall, Nature gave before; line 287 p. 18
Relum'd her ancient Light, not kindled new;
If not Gods Image, yet his Shadow drew;

Taught

seemd
<1> Now sacred ^ Th'aetherial
vault ~~was~~
sacred now
no more

Zeal now, not charity, became the Guide,

<2> ~~Now~~
And Hell was built on Spite, & Heav'n on Pride ^

~~The native wood seemd sacred now no more~~ ~~charg'd with~~
~~& Altars <grew> marble <y^t^ were stone before>~~

altars grew marble now
and reekd
wth Gore

The Glutton Priest, first tasted living Food

s Then smear'd
~~Smear'd~~ ^ his grim Idol ~~next~~ ^ with human blood,

Hurld dread Thunderbolts ~~dealt~~
Heavn's ~~Bolts~~ ^ ~~or Blessings hurld~~ on all below,

And playd the God an Engine on his Foe.

So drives Selflove, thro just & thro unjust,

one mans Powr, Ambition, Lucre,
To ~~present Passion, Lucre, Powr, or~~ Lust:

same Selflove
The~~n op'rating~~ ^ in All, becomes the cause

him,
Of what restrains ~~them~~, ^ Government & Laws

~~Selflove forsakes the Path it first pursud~~

~~And finds the private in the publick Good.~~

w.^t^ makes
For say, ~~where lies~~ the Liberty of Man?

Not doing what he will, but what he can:

If what he likes, another like as well,

one many
What serves ~~his~~ Will when ^ Wills rebell?

How shall he keep, what, sleeping or awake,

A weaker may surprize, a stronger take?

His Safety must his Liberty restrain;

All join ~~d~~ to guard what each desires to gain.

2 --Selflove forsook ye path it first pursud & found ye private in
^ ye public
good.

1 (Forcd into Virtue thus by Self-Defence
Ev'n Kings learn'd Justice and Benevolence.

~~First~~ Legislators ~~Philosophers~~
Then ~~First~~ Poets, ~~first~~ then ~~Lawgivers~~
~~Then Legislators, Poets then~~, restore

The Faith & Morall, Nature gave before,

Relum'd her ancient Light, not kindled new;

If not Gods Image, yet his Shadow drew;

Taught

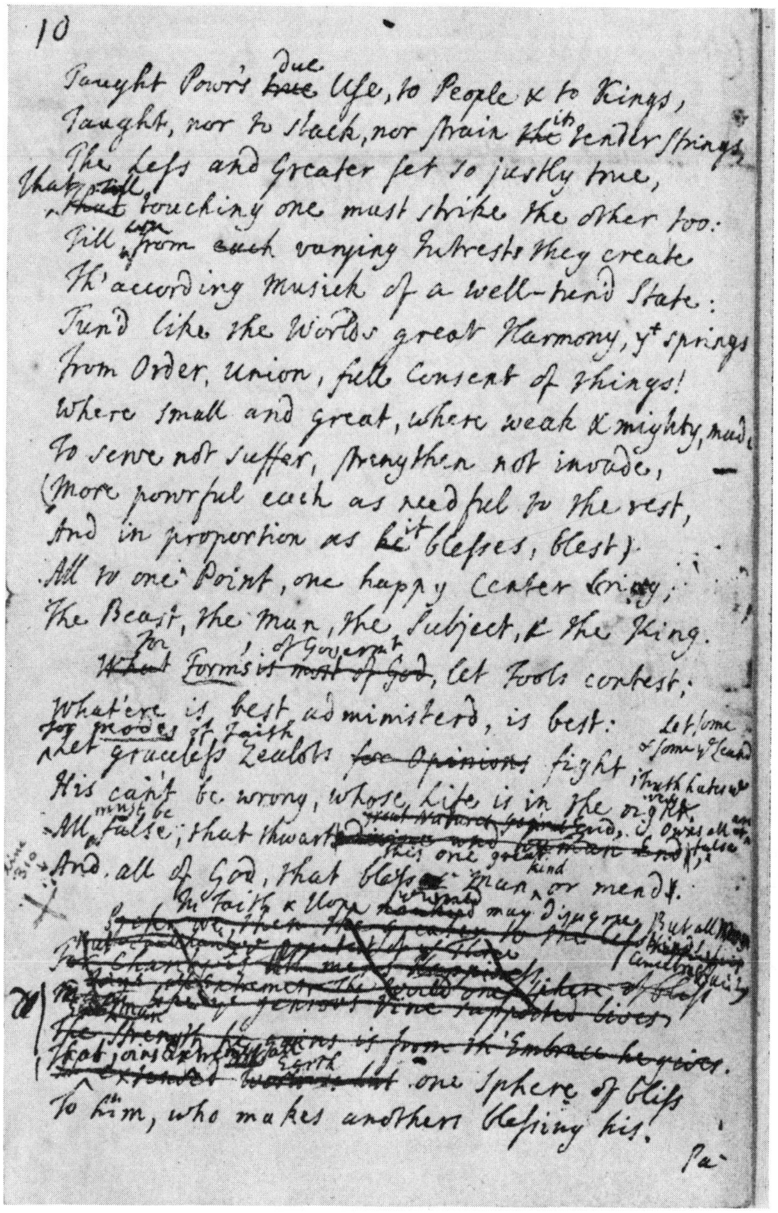

10

Taught Pow'r's due Use, to People & to Kings,
Taught, nor to slack, nor strain its tender Strings;
The Less and Greater set so justly true,
That still touching one must strike the other too:
Till jarring from varying Intrests they create
Th'according Musick of a well-tun'd State:
Tun'd like the World's great Harmony, y^t springs
From Order, Union, full Consent of things!
Where small and great, where weak & mighty, made
To serve not suffer, strengthen not invade,
(More powrful each as needful to the rest,
And in proportion as it blesses, blest)
All to one Point, one happy Center bring;
The Beast, the Man, the Subject, & the King.
For Forms of Governt let Fools contest;
Whate'er is best administerd, is best:
For modes of Faith let graceless Zealots fight
His can't be wrong, whose Life is in the right.
All must be false, that thwart this one great End;
And all of God, that bless mankind, or mend.
In Faith & Hope mankind may disagree,
[illegible]
[illegible]
[illegible]
[illegible]
[illegible]
[illegible]
Extended Earth ... one Sphere of bliss
To him, who makes another's blessing his.

Pa

due
Taught Powr's ~~true~~ Use, to People & to Kings,

its
Taught, nor to slack, nor strain ~~the~~ tender strings,

The Less and Greater set so justly true,

That Till
^ ~~That~~ touching one must strike the other too:

evn
Till ^ from ~~each~~ varying Intrests they create

Th'according Musick of a well-tun'd State:

Tun'd like the Worlds great Harmony, y^t springs

From Order, Union, full Consent of things!

Where small and great, where weak & mighty, made

To serve not suffer, strengthen not invade,

(More powrful each as needful to the rest,

it
And in proportion as ~~he~~ blesses, blest)

All to one Point, one happy Center bring;

The Beast, the Man, the Subject, & the King.

For s of Goverm[t],
~~What~~ Form s ~~is most of God~~, let Fools contest;

What'ere is best administerd, is best:

For modes of Faith
Let graceless Zealots ~~for Opinions~~ fight;
^
His can't be wrong, whose Life is in the right.

Let some
& some ye Learnd
Truth hates y^e
very

must be ~~great Natures gen'ral~~ End,
All ^ false, that thwart ~~divine and human Ends~~,
this one great

are
Owns all ~~is~~ ^
false

kind
And all of God, that bless~~es~~ Man ^ or mend~~s.~~

ye world
In Faith & Hope ~~mankind~~ may disagree
~~Prefer we then the greater to the less~~

But all Man
kinds ~~is~~
concern Charity

~~But < > Charity ye greatest of ye Three~~
~~For Charity is All mens Happiness~~.
~~Joins all Extremes, the World one sphere of bliss~~

~~Man like ye genrous Vine supported lives~~,
δ <Each> | Man

~~The Strength he gains is from th' Embrace he gives.~~

That joins Extreams, all
~~orb~~ Earth
~~Th extended World is but~~ one Sphere of bliss
^
To him, who makes anothers blessing his.

Pa-

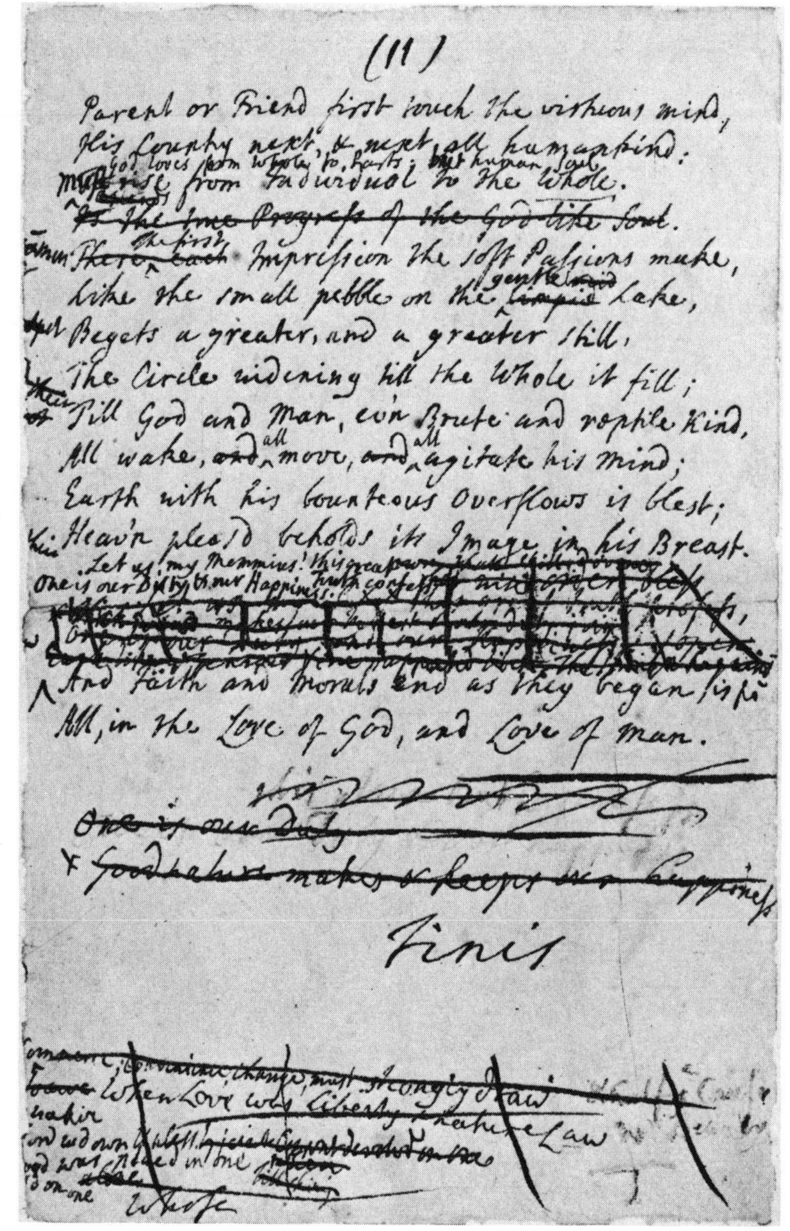
(11)

Parent or Friend first touch the virtuous mind,
His Country next, & next all human kind:
God loves from Whole to Parts; but human soul
Must rise from Individual to the Whole.
There, the first Impression the soft Passions make,
Like the small pebble on the gentle Lake,
Begets a greater, and a greater still,
The Circle widening till the Whole it fill;
Till God and Man, ev'n Brute and reptile Kind,
All wake, all move, all agitate his mind;
Earth with his bounteous Overflows is blest;
Heav'n pleas'd beholds its Image in his Breast.
And Faith and Morals end as they began,
All, in the Love of God, and Love of Man.

Finis

(11)

Parent or Friend first touch the virtuous mind,
His Country next, & next all humankind:
God loves from Whole to Parts; but human Soul
Must rise from Individual to the Whole.
^ ~~Ascends~~
~~Is the true Progress of the God-like Soul~~.
The first
~~<coṁon>There each~~ ^ Impression the soft Passions make,
gentle ~~lucid~~
Like the small pebble in the ^ ~~limpid~~ Lake,
~~<Spot>~~ Begets a greater, and a greater still,
~~<Mur>thur~~ The Circle widening till the Whole it fill;
<not> Till God and Man, ev'n Brute and reptile Kind,
all all
All ~~wake~~, ~~and~~ ^ move, ~~and~~ ^ agitate his Mind,
Earth with his bounteous Overflows is blest;
<their> Heav'n pleasd beholds its Image in his Breast.
Let us, my Memmius! this great ~~own that skill divine~~
Truth confess
One is our Duty & our Happiness ~~with Order bless~~
~~Let us, my + + this great Truth profess~~,
~~Which joins makes our Intrest & our duty join~~
~~One is our Duty and our Happiness~~ ~~open~~
~~Each like ye genrous Vine supported lives, The Strength he gains~~
And Faith and Morals end as they began is frõ
^
All, in the Love of God and Love of Man.
~~One is our Duty~~
+ ~~Good nature makes & keeps our happiness~~

Finis

~~Commerce, Convenience, Change, must strongly draw~~
~~to awe~~ ~~When Love was Liberty & Nature Law~~
~~<native>~~
Lord w^d own Unless ~~by joint Consent devolvd on One~~
<G>ood was placd in one ~~When~~
~~alone~~
<'d> on one ~~Till~~ ~~<sikning>~~
Whose

N° 1

Popes Hymne to God &c & Epistle 4th.

n° 1

Popes Hymne to God &c & Epistle 4th.

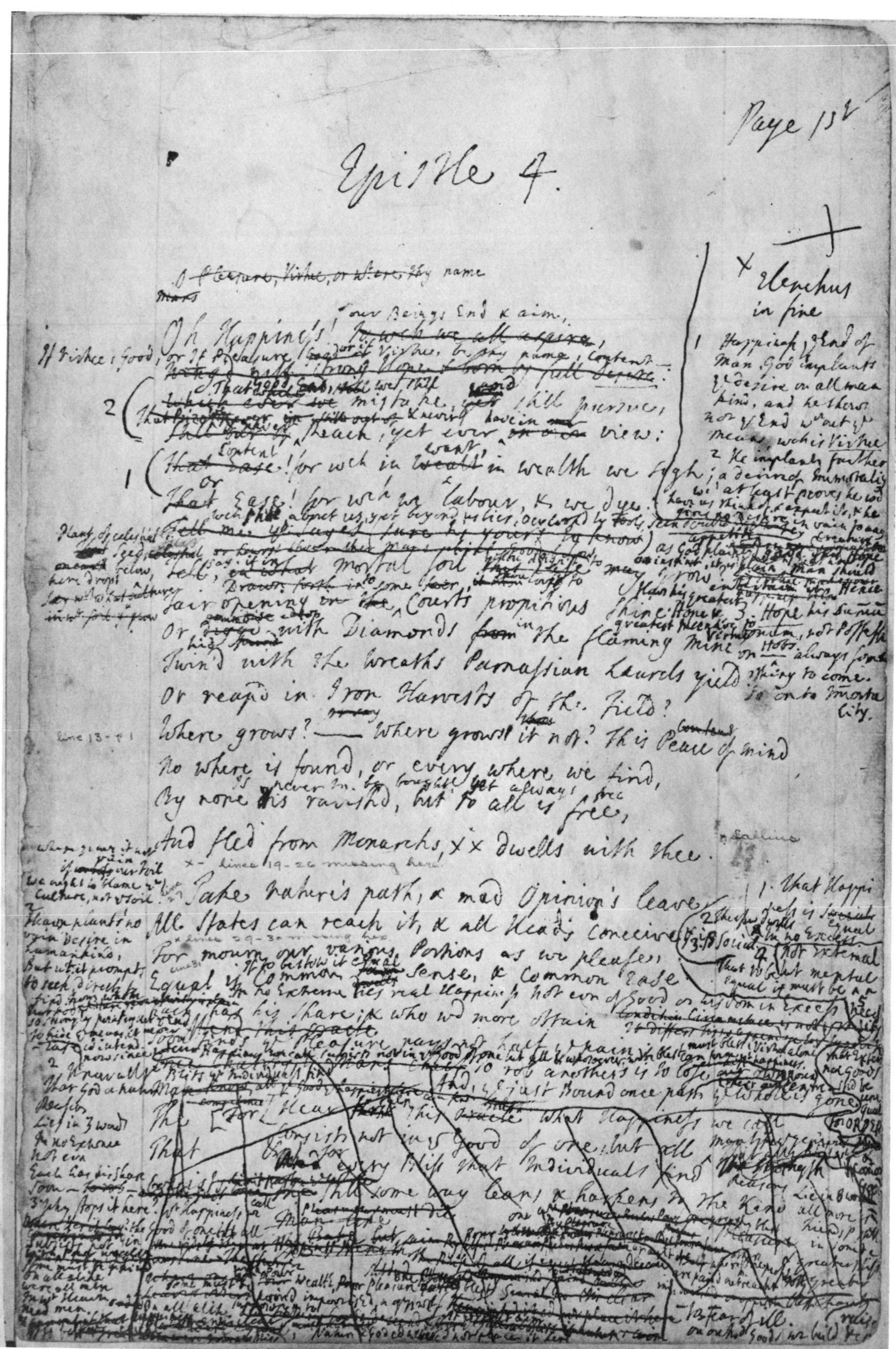

Page 13

Epistle 4.

Oh Happiness! our Being's End & aim,

That Ease! for wch in want, in wealth we sigh;

That Ease! for wch we labour, & we dye.

Fair opening to some Court's propitious shine,

Or dug with Diamonds in the flaming mine?

Twin'd with the wreaths Parnassian Laurels yield

Or reap'd in Iron Harvests of the Field?

Where grows? — Where growst it not? This Peace of mind

No where is found, or every where, we find,

By none 'tis ravish'd, but to all is free,

And fled from Monarchs, x x dwells with thee.

Take Nature's path, & mad Opinion's leave,

All States can reach it, & all Heads conceive

For mourn our various Portions as we please,

Equal is Common Sense, & Common Ease

Elenchus in fine

Epistle 4.

O Pleasure, Virtue, or wt ere thy name

Mans

our wch Beings End & aim,

Oh Happiness! to wch we all aspire,

or if

If Virtue, Good, or If Pleasure, Good, or Virtue be thy name, Content--

Wingd with strong Hope & born by full Desire :

Good End, still we still and

That while <who>

2 Which ever we mistake, yet still pursue,

we

That Prize never in Still out of & never have in <our>

& never

Still out of Reach, yet ever in our view:

Content Want

That Ease! for wch in Wealt in Wealth we sigh;

1

Or

That Ease! for wch we labour, & we dye:

Wch still about us, yet beyond us lies, oerlookd by Fools, seen double by ye Wise.

Tell me, ye Sages (sure tis yours to know)

or < hearst thou rather >Mans chief Good below

Say, if in thou deignst to

Tell, in what mortal Soil this Ease may grow?

thou

if thou lovst to

to

Drawn forth in some fair

Fair opening in the Court's propitious Shine;

<——> deep in

Or diggd with Diamonds from the flaming mine?

hid found

Twin'd with the Wreaths Parnassian Laurels yield?

Or reap'd in Iron Harvests of the Field?

Or say thou Content

Where grows? ----Where grows t it not? This Peace of Mind

No where is found, or every where we find,

Is never to be bought yet always free

By none Tis ravishd, but to all is free,

And fled from Monarchs, + + dwells with thee.

Take Nature's path, & mad Opinion's leave,

All States can reach it, & all Heads conceive.

For mourn our various Portions as we please,

If to bestow it equal

Equal is Common <——> Sense, & Common Ease.

dwells

In no Extreme lies real Happiness Not evn of Good or Wisdom in excess

Each has his Share; & who wd more obtain

Soon finds ye Pleasure pays not half ye pain

Now since wtever Happiness we call Consists not in ye Good of one but all & whosoever wd must bless, Virtue alone be blest can form yt happiness. Round their own Centre

TRUE Charity is Mans chief

To rob anothers is to lose our own

And, ye just Bound once past, ye Whole is gone

MAN like

Know all ye Good ye happiest here can find

THE

Truth

then

THAT [For Hear first this Oracle What Happiness we call

Man like ye gen'rous Vine

That all alike

Consists not in ye Good of one, but all

^ The Strength

limit past ye Whole

, and the just <——>

CONSISTS Reasons

& For

And every Bliss that Individuals find

Still some way leans & harkens to the Kind

3. Why stops it here? Wt happiness we call

Where lies it say? the Good of one but all

<Consists not in>

subsists not in

How widely then at Happiness we

With Powr wealth

Man like ye genrous Vine The strength

Some must be paind

with Powr

On all alike When one <wth> Powr wealth Powr Pleasure <——> blest

Some must be

Were all men Leaves others paind impoverishd or oppress

suppose ym to

In <wt> Heavn <——> On all alike <did outward>Goods descend

Mad men

& genral if that Happiness tis clear>

<If all were equal>

<——> genral Bliss

Pleasure must die

Man like

Bate but

The strength aim

The bliss of all if equal Heavn decree

wth Pleasure, Riches, Powr one greatly blest

By Pleasure <Riches> Pleasure

Powr<——>pleasure<——>others

By selfish Pleasures <——> <or aught> of Self where One

profusely

are paind outreacht

subdud<——>impoverishd paind<——>impoverishd or oppress blest

one <proves>

Genral<——> tis clear

Heavn<——> cd not place it here

great aim

<If yt> general bliss <ye whole to win>

Nature & God cd never cd not place it here

Lie in 3 words

All more is

Friendsp still <is >

& greater Bliss

<wth> greater

Charity

-to-Fear of ill. raise

on outwd Goods we build &c

Plant of celestial

That Seed, celestial

on earth below,

here dropt ^

Say wth what culture

in wt soil yu grow

Where grows it not

vain

if we lose our toil

We ought to blame ye culture not ye soil.

<2>

Heavn plants no vain Desire in humankind,

But what it prompts to seek directs to find. <From whom>

That God & Nature gave it<plainly>is plain

so strongly pointing at ye End ATTEND this Oracle

To hide ye means, it never

—Ease cd intend.

2 Know all ye Bliss yt Individuals find

That God or Nature

Reasons to -- Competence

Lies in 3 words

In no Extreme

Not evn

Each has his share

soon-To rob-

\+ +

Elenchus

in fine

1 Happiness ye End of Man. God implants ye desire in all man kind, & he shows not ye End wthout ye Means, wch is Virtue

2 He implants further a desire of Immortality wch at least proves he wd have us think of & expect it, & he gives no desire in vain to any appetite Creature

As God plainly gave this Hope or instinct, it is plain Man should entertain it. Hence flows his greatest Hope &

Tis Virtue makes your Happiness below

3. Hope his summ greatest Incentive to Virtue Bonum, not Possessi

Hobs on --- always some thing to come.

So on to Imorta lity.

1.That Happi ness is social equal

2 Therfore dwells in no Excess

& is

3. Social

4. Not External but mental

That to be equal it must be ^ ^

5 neces sity that Exter nal Goods shd be une qual for ORDER & comon Good

Man like the generous Vine
The strength he gains
Pleasure must die, the Blaze of Glory sink,
Bate but what others feel, nay wt they think.
Of human nature wit its worst may write,
We all revere it in our own despite:
line 39 No Bandit fierce, no Tyrant mad with pride,
No cavern'd Hermit, rests self-satisfy'd.
Who most to hate or quit mankind [illegible] pretend
line 42 p.3 Seek an approver, or wd find a friend.
Man like the generous Vine supported lives,
The strength he gains is from th' Embrace he gives.

Hear then this Oracle, nor think it less:
True CHARITY is mans chief Happiness.
~~The utmost Bliss the Happiest here can find~~
~~Or God or Nature [illegible] to more Mankind~~
Reason's whole Bliss what God to mortal singly can dispense
Lyes in three words, Health, Peace, & Competence.
All more is Friendship, shar'd in some degree:
And highest Bliss but is highest Charity.

Thro' selfish Pleasures, Riches, Power or Fame,
[illegible] Outward Good internal Bliss sustain,
Wrong ye materials, & ye labor [illegible]
By Outward Goods who thinks that Bliss is given,
Indian-like, [illegible] Life & Dogs [illegible] Heaven.
~~Increase of these is but Increase of Pain~~
Wrong ye materials, & he builds in vain.
[illegible] Sons of Earth! that still attempt to rise
By Mountains pil'd on Mountains, to the Skies:
The Gods with laughter on such madmen gaze,
[illegible]

[illegible] Equal, must not all contest?
[illegible] Heaven [illegible] impartial to confess,
[illegible] be equal, but [illegible] Happiness?
See, Peace of mind [illegible] is [illegible] a Stay:
The rest, mad Fortune gives, & takes away.
The single Point where Happiness
stands still,
& tastes ye Good, without ye fear of Ill.

3. That ORDER requires some outward Goods to be unequal

Yet blinder they wh Heaven's great scheme

Man like the genrous Vine
The Strength he gains
Pleasure must die, the Blaze of Glory sink,
what ^{t} others
Bate but what others feel, nay ~~w they~~ think.
Of human nature Wit its worst may write,
We all revere it in our own despite:
<2> No Bandit fierce, no Tyrant mad with pride,
No cavern'd Hermit, rests Self-satisfyd.
hate or quit mankind
<1> Who most to ~~scorn it, or renounce~~ pretend
Seek an Approver, or w^{d} find a Friend.
Man like the gen'rous Vine supported lives,
The Strength he gains is from th' embrace he gives.

Hear then this Oracle, nor think it less:
True CHARITY is mans chief Happiness.
~~The utmost Bliss the Happiest here can find boast~~
~~singly~~
~~Or God or Nature grant to mere Mankind~~
What
~~Reasons whole~~ ~~All~~ God to Mortal singly can dispense
Lyes in three Words, Health, Peace, & Competence.
shar'd
All more is Friendship, ~~still~~ in some degree:
r but r
And highe~~st~~ Bliss, ~~is~~ highe~~st~~ Charity.

1. On outw^{d} Goods we build this bliss in vain
<2.> The Wrong ~~y^{e}~~ Materials ~~but increase our Pain~~ frustrate all our pain

then
How widely ~~alas~~ at Happiness we aim
By selfish <> Pleasures, Riches
~~By Powr~~ by ~~Wealth by Knowledge~~ Powr or Fame!
no Encrease of outw^{d} Good no
1. ~~With~~ outward Goods internal Bliss sustain,
Wrong ye Materials, & ye Labor vain. Contentment
By outward Goods who thinks this Bliss is ~~given~~,
~~Takes~~ ~~Hopes~~ take to
Would ~~Bears~~ Indian-like ~~his~~ Wife & Dog ~~in~~ Heavn
Stent. ~~Encrease of these is but Encrease of Pain~~
<2 >Wrong ye Materials, & he builds in vain.
+ ~~Still when y^{e}~~ still attempt
~~Blind~~ Sons of Earth! that ~~once more hope~~ to rise
Blind
By Mountains pil'd on Mountains, to the Skies;
such Madmen
The Gods with Laughter on ~~y^{r} Labour~~ gaze
Sure to be buryd ~~in th' enormous Heap they raise~~
~~And bury such in the mad Heap they raise~~
~~Sure to be buried in the Heap y^{y} raise~~
~~Tis Peace of Mind alone is at a Stay~~ ⟷
[~~Wit Riches Strength if givn to an excess Others oerreach impovrish & oppress~~
~~The rest mad Fortune~~ < > ~~gives or takes away~~
With Powr Wit Wealth
And ~~If <with these> mankind~~ alike suppose them
~~Some must be greater Suppose them all wth equal fortune~~ blest
If all were ~~all men~~ ~~all men~~ w^{d}
~~If all were~~ Equal, must not all contest?

In what then ⟷ ~~Just to all~~
~~In what~~ Heavns ~~hand~~ impartial to confess
~~heavns image~~
~~men all~~ need all in
What Need ~~all~~ be equal but ~~their~~ Happiness?
therfore ~~therfore~~
See Peace of Mind ~~alone~~ is at a stay!
or
The rest, mad Fortune gives, ~~&~~ takes away.
~~<Tis>~~ The single
~~In this sole~~ Point where Happiness
stands still
& tastes ye Good, without ye fear of ill.

Pleasures Indiv.
~~blessings~~
+ + The strongest ~~noblest Plea~~
duals find | ~~sures of ye Mind~~
All hold of mutual Con-
~~verse with y^{e}~~ Kind
Can sensual Lust or selfish
Rapine know
Such, as frō Bounty, Love
or Mercy flow +
All all lasting of mortal
~~The~~ strongest ~~Joy~~ Joys ~~is of y^{e}~~ Mind
Whatever stronger Joys ~~of hum<an>~~
~~mind~~
ye happiest
find
Still ⟷ ~~All~~ some way leans
& harkens to ye Kind.
Tis shard, tis Friendship, Love, in some degree

<Still w^{n}> ye Sons of Earth
⟷ —raise
That it must be Mental to be Equal
greatly blest If all were
one <made> Equal
In these suppose it placd ⟵ ~~equal~~ must not
Others were hurt, impoverishd or opprest all contest
⟵ ~~blest~~
Or did they equally on all descend
Blind
~~Mad~~ Sons of Earth y^{t} still
~~Still w^{n} ye Sons of Earth~~
~~aspire~~ attempt to rise
to ye Skies
By Mountains pil'd on Mountains
The Gods wth laughter on such Madmen gaze
Sure to be buried in ye Heap y^{y} raise ⟷
Order is Heavns g. Law: ⟷
hence
Tis confess
Some are & must be greater y^{n} ye rest
More strong, more wise; but infrence hence
That such are Happier, is a gross mistake
Say not Heavns here profuse—& for—
You find w^{n}<Laws>& their Ends are known
Twas for ye thous^{d} He Happiness we ~~aim~~—
~~How wide alas at~~
~~By Wit, by Wealth, by Knowledge, or by Fame~~
~~Nature's~~
3. That Order requires ~~some~~ outw^{d} Goods to be unequal
That
~~The~~ mutual wants to —
~~helps to~~ comon Blessing
~~Each <man> Each <strength> to other~~
tend~~s~~
those their
& these his Strength, & ~~y^{r} his~~ Wisdom lend
~~In what then~~ While
Benevolence a double pay receives
<Tis > blest in w^{t} it takes, & w^{t} it gives
Wch if its
~~If~~ to bestow impartial ~~its~~ aim
~~It~~ It can not ⟷ place in Riches Powr or fame,
~~<It must not rest>~~
Order is Heavns great Law Yet blind
blest
In these if Bliss were placd, one greatly
Others were hurt impoverishd or oppress
~~By outward Goods~~
[~~Order is Heavns great Law &c~~
Yet blinder they to Heavns g^{t}
Scheme

Page 2d.

1. That Happiness in men [Comon] is equal

Common Ease

Know all ye Bliss yt Individuals find
That God or Nature grant to mere mankind,
Reasons whole pleasure, all ye Joys of Sense
Lies in three words, Health, Peace & Competence.

2 dwells in no Extremes

In no Extreme dwells real Happiness
Not ev'n of Good, or ~~Wisdom~~ Knowledge in Excess.
Each has his Share, & who wd more obtain
Soon find, ye Pleasure pays not half ye pain.

3 and is Social

Why stop it here? — what Happiness we [illegible]
~~And higher Bliss but higher change~~
Subsists not in ye Good of one but all
~~[illegible]~~

Fear of Ill

On outward Goods we build our Bliss in vain?

2 [mental]

The wrong materials frustrate all the pain.
Still when the Sons of Earth attempt to rise
By mountains pil'd on mountains, to the Skies?
The Gods with laughter on the madmen gaze,
Sure to be buried in the Heaps they raise! ORDER

~~[illegible]~~

4. That Happiness to be equal must not be External but mental.

Others were impoverish'd, or opprest: One properly blest,
Or all alike superior them to descend,
If all were equal, must not all contend?
In what (Heav'ns hand impartial to confess)
Need men be equal, but in Happiness?
~~[illegible]~~ For all were Happiness [illegible] clear [illegible],
It could not place in Riches, Power, or Fame. [illegible] & God cd never place it here

x Health & Competence

See therefore, Peace of Mind is at a stay!
The rest mad Fortune gives & takes away.
All but that Point where Happiness stands still,
And tastes ye Good without the Fall to Ill.

—Heap ye raise

3

5. Necessity of External Goods shd be unequal for ye sake of Order & comon Good of Society

ORDER is Heav'n's great Law: Tis hence confest
Some are, & must be, Greater than ye rest,
More strong, more wise: But [illegible] to make
That such are Happier, 'tis a gross mistake.
Her Gifts tho Fortune
& these we call unhappy
Equal almost ye balance

all this to bottom of page omitted

Happiness this world can know all ye [illegible] Wealth Ease Pow'r Pleasure, One properly Blest Another's pain'd, impoverish'd or opprest. On all alike

On outward Goods we build our Bliss in vain &c.

Page 2^{d}.

comon
1. That ^ Happiness in Man
is equal

-- Common Ease

Know all ye Bliss y^{t} Individuals find
That God or Nature grant to mere mankind,
Reasons whole pleasure, all ye Joys of Sense
2 dwells in | Lies in three Words, Health, Peace & Competence.
no Extremes | In no Extreme dwells real Happiness
Not evn of Good, or ~~Wisdom~~ Knowledge in Excess.
Each has his share, & who w^{d} more obtain
Soon find^{s}, ye Pleasure pays not half ye pain.
3 and is | Why stops it here? -- What Happiness we call
Social | ~~And higher Bliss but higher Charity~~
Subsists not in ye Good of One but all.
For evry ~~Good y^{t} Individuals find Still some way~~

how
why we ~~were~~ in
Fear of Ill [On outward Goods ~~we~~ build ~~that~~ Bliss in vain?
2 The wrong materials frustrate all the pain.
When will
5 But mental | Still ~~when~~ the Sons of Earth attempt to rise
By mountains pil'd on mountains to the Skies?
Just Heavn with laughter ye vain toil surveys
Such folly still surveys
The Gods with laughter on the Madmen gaze,
Still ~~Oerwhelms~~ & <&> buries Madmen in those
Sure to be buried in the Heaps they raise!

~~here~~
~~If ye great aim were Genral Bliss 'tis clear Nature & God c^{d} never place it~~

~~or Fame~~
~~of All if Heavns indulgent Aim, He could not place in Riches Powr~~
[~~The Bliss in these were plac'd, One greatly blest~~ with Powr Wealth
4. That Happi- ~~In Sensual Joys were one supremely blest~~ ~~Pleasure Or ought of Self; where~~
^ One profusely blest,
paind
ness, to be Equal, ~~Others were hurt~~, impov'rishd, or oppress:
must not be
On all alike, suppose them to
External but ~~Or did These Goods on all alike~~ descend,
Mental 1. If all were equal, must not all contend?
In what (Heavns hand impartial to confess)
men
Need ~~all~~ be equal, but in Happiness?

~~Heavn to all meant~~ tis For all were Happiness
~~Which to secure <and> gen'ral~~ ~~If that Happiness, tis~~ clear designd,
~~This to bestow if its indulgent aim~~ Nature & God c^{d} never place it
here
could
It ~~must not place in Riches, Powr, or Fame:~~

~~then only~~
See therfore, Peace of Mind is at a stay!
Health
x &
Competẽce | + ~~others~~
The rest mad Fortune gives & takes away.

where
~~On~~ All but that ~~can~~
~~Tis this sole~~ Point ~~where~~ Happiness stand~~s~~ ~~still~~,
And taste~~s~~ ye Good, without the Fall to Ill.

~~How widely then~~
~~vain~~
~~at Happiness we~~ aim
On outward Goods we build
--Heap y^{y} raise | ORDER is Heavns great Law. Tis hence confest — our Bliss in vain &c.
5. Necessity 3 Some are, & must be, greater than ye rest,
~~The~~ But if ~~you will~~ you
y^{t} External More strong, more wise: ~~but~~ Inf'rence~~s~~ to make
Goods sh^{d} be un- That such are Happier? tis a gross mistake.
equal for ye Her Gifts tho Fortune
sake of & these we call unhappy

Order & Comon
Equal almost ye balance
Good of Society

Count all y^{t} in this world can ^ bless or please
~~Wealth<with>Powr~~ Wealth Fame
Ease
Knowledge
Powr ^ Pleasure One
To rob another's ~~—~~
profusely blest
Another's pain'd,
impoverishd, or
opprest.
On all alike

ORDER)

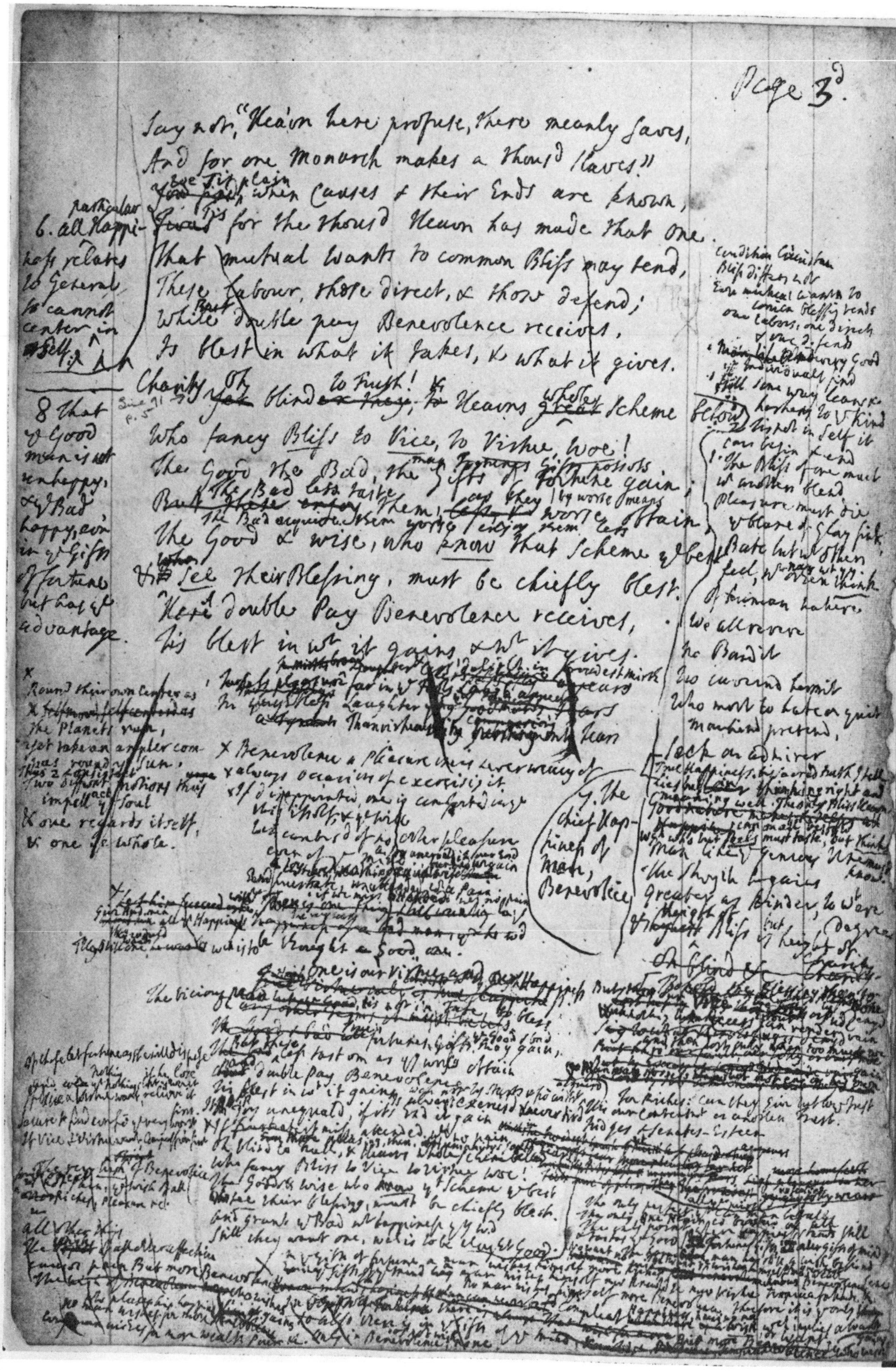

Page 3d.

Say not, "Heav'n here profuse, there meanly saves,
And for one Monarch makes a thous^d slaves!"
Yet 'tis plain when Causes & their Ends are known,
'Tis for the thous^d Heav'n has made that One.

6. all Happiness relates to General & cannot center in Self.

That mutual wants to common Bliss may tend,
These labour, those direct, & those defend;
While But double pay Benevolence receives,
Is blest in what it takes, & what it gives.

Charity Oh blind to Truth! & to Heavns whole great Scheme
Who fancy Bliss to Vice, to Virtue, Woe!
The Good the Bad, the many Fortune's Gifts possess
But the Bad lets raise them, by worse means obtain,
The Good & wise, who know that Scheme the best
Who See their Blessing, must be chiefly blest.
Here double Pay Benevolence receives,
'Tis blest in wt it gains & wt it gives.

8 that ye Good man is not unhappy, & ye Bad happy, even in ye Gifts of fortune but has ye advantage.

Round their own Centres as the Planets run, yet take an ampler compass round ye Sun; thus 2 consistent, two different motions thus impell ye Soul & one regards itself, & one ye whole.

Benevolence a pleasure every way of always occasion of exercising it

9. The chief Happiness of Man, Benevolence

The vicious man ...

'Tis blest in wt it gains ...

Who fancy Bliss to Vice, to Virtue woe!
The Good & wise who know ye Scheme ye best
Must see their Blessing, must be chiefly blest.

Say not, "Heavn here profuse, there meanly saves,

And for one Monarch makes a Thousd Slaves."

We Tis plain
~~You find~~ when Causes & their Ends are known,

Tis
~~Twas~~ for the Thousd Heavn has made that One.

That mutual Wants to common Bliss may tend,

These labour, those direct, & those defend;

~~But~~
While double pay Benevolence receives,

Is blest in what it takes, & what it gives.

Charity Oh to Truth! & whole
~~Yet~~ blinder ~~they, to~~ Heavns ~~great~~ Scheme below

Who fancy Bliss to Vice, to Virtue Woe!

may Fortunes Gifts possess
The Good, the Bad, the Gifts of Fortune gain;

The Bad less taste as they | by worse means
~~But these enjoy~~ them ~~less, &~~ worse obtain
The Bad acquire them worse enjoy them less

The Good & Wise, who know that Scheme ye best

~~Who~~
& ~~&~~ see their Blessing, must be chiefly blest.

A
~~Here~~ double Pay Benevolence receives,

Tis blest in wt it gains & wt it gives.

~~broad~~ & less delight in broadest Mirth
~~In Mirths Laughter less Pleasure appears~~
~~<less joy>~~
Far Less Pleasure far in ye Fool's Laugh appears
~~<maidens>~~
In thoughtless Laughter yn ye ~~Good Mans Tears~~
~~Compassions~~
A ~~Tyrants~~ Than virtuous Pity bursting into Tears

+Benevolence a Pleasure men never weary of
+Always occasions of exercising it
+If disappointed one is comforted in ye
thing itself & ye Will
Wch can be sd of no other pleasure
evn of ye mind. The Joy unequald if our End
our End we gain
<A Joy wch nothing ⟷ wise obtain>
Evn frustrate unattended wth a Pain
& if we miss attended wth no Pain
~~There is one thing still wanting to ye~~

The very least

~~happiness of a bad man, yt he wd~~
be thought ~~a~~ good one.

One is our Virtue and our Happiness
~~High~~ ~~<consists to>~~
~~True Virtue only is true Happiness~~

The Vicious Man <hates ye Good> tis not in Fate to bless
~~On any other terms it must be less~~

True, ye Good & bad
~~The Good & bad all~~ Fortunes Gifts may gain,
Of those let fortune as she will dispose
But these
~~The bad~~ less taste em as yy worse obtain
n nothing if he lose
And even ~~yt~~ nothing but ye worst And
~~But~~ double pay Benevolence
acquird
Wch not by starts & frō without
Tis blest in wt it gains
If Vice & Virtue want, relieve it
Is always exercisd & never tird
first. < >
Its joy unequald, if its End it gain
Secure to find evn frō ye very worst
& If ~~frustrate~~ it miss attended wth no pain
If Vice & Virtue want Compassion first
~~Evn~~ More pleasing, then, Humanity's soft tears

Oh blind to Truth, & Heavns whole Scheme below

Who fancy Bliss to vice to Virtue Woe!

The Good & Wise who know yt Scheme ye best

Who see their blessing, must be chiefly blest.

And grant ye Bad wt happiness yy wd

Still they want one, wch is to be thought good.

In ye Gifts of fortune a man wishes himself more Riches
a
In ye Gifts of ye mind evry man wishes himself more knowledge, more Virtue, tempräce, fortitude, &c
The No man wishes himself more Benevolence. Therefore it is ye only ~~thing~~
<Heavn intends hapiness of Man can never be> Happiness having no
Compleat ~~when there is a~~ wish, wch implies a want
gains
In ye Gifts of Fortune, ~~there is always that wish for more~~
But more Benevolence who wishes
So also there is in ye Gifts of ye Mind, ~~Knowledge, Prudence, Temprance, Fortitude~~

<does> not wish
Only in Benevolence none

Particular
6. All Happiness relates to General so cannot center in Self;

8. That ye Good Man is not unhappy, & ye Bad happy, ev'n in ye Gifts of fortune but has ye advantage.

\+
Round their own Center as
\+ ~~Selfmovd, selfcenterd as~~
the Planets run,
Yet take an ampler compas round ye Sun.

Thus 2 consistent ~~urge~~
Two diffrent motions thus
act
Impell ye Soul
& one regards itself,
& one ye Whole.

(ye)
will
X ~~Let him succeed <as he>~~
Give Bad Men
~~<Grant him>~~ all ye Happiness
they would
want
They Still one ~~he wants~~ wch is to

~~object~~
The very wish of Benevolēce
⟷
is not <Pain>, ye wish of all

~~<Honor>~~ Riches Pleasure &c.

All other things
wish
The ~~object~~ of all other affections
causes pain But more Benevolence
who wishes
The wish of Benevolence
gains
Who places his happiness <in it>

No man wishes for more Benevolence
Evry man wishes for more Wealth, Powr, &c.

Condition, Circumstance
Bliss differs not
Ease mutual Wants ~~e~~ to
Comon blessing tends
One labors, one directs
& one defends

~~Man like~~ And every Good
yt Individuals find
still some way leans &
harkens to ye Kind
2 Tis not in self it
can begin & end
1 The Bliss of one must
wth another blend
Pleasure must die
ye blaze of Glory sink,
Bate but wt others
nay wt yy
feel, wt others think

Of human nature
We all revere
No Bandit
No cavernd Hermit
Who most to hate or quit
mankind pretend,
Seek an admirer

7. The chief Happiness of Man, Benevolēce

[True Happiness, tis sacred truth to tell
in
Lies but ~~our~~ thinking right and
meaning well. The only Bliss Heavn
~~Good Nature makes & keeps all~~
~~Happiness~~ can on all bestow
wch who but feels must taste, but thinks must know.
Man like ye genrous Vine
The Strength he gains
Greater as kinder, to wtere
Height of but degree
& ~~Highest~~ Bliss is height of
Charity

~~Oh blind &c~~ — ~~Charity~~ —

[Behold the Blessing then to
⟷ none
But thro our Folly
~~Lost but by~~ Vice⟷ or Pride denyd
Errour

Wch nothing but Excess can render vain
~~Say to what this blessing is denyd~~

and then lost only when too much we
~~But thro our fault, our folly, or our pride~~
gain
~~But by Excess of~~⟵ ~~Good made vain~~

Man may possess⟵ but>not enjoy his own
⟷
For Riches: can they give but to ye Just
His own Contentmt or anothers Trust.
Judges & Senates-- Esteem
<yt> ~~appears~~
in
~~Mirth The broadest laugh of Mirth less pleasd~~ ⟵
⟵~~soft Tear More pleasing far her~~ ~~more home felt~~
~~Evn fruitless Pitys soft & mourning Tears sigh~~ ~~pleasure in her~~
than unfeeling
~~Feels more of pleasure The broadest Joy gay folly wears~~
all ye mirth

The only perfect yt can Man befall
The only one Heavn cd bestow on all
The only point where happiness stands still
& tastes ye Good | In Fortunes Gifts, <in> also Gifts of Mind
No want nor The happiest man has still a wish / behind
greater
The want <yt> wishes himself< more >Wealth <Sense>
⟷ wishes ~~(But) Benevolence~~ knows Benevolence

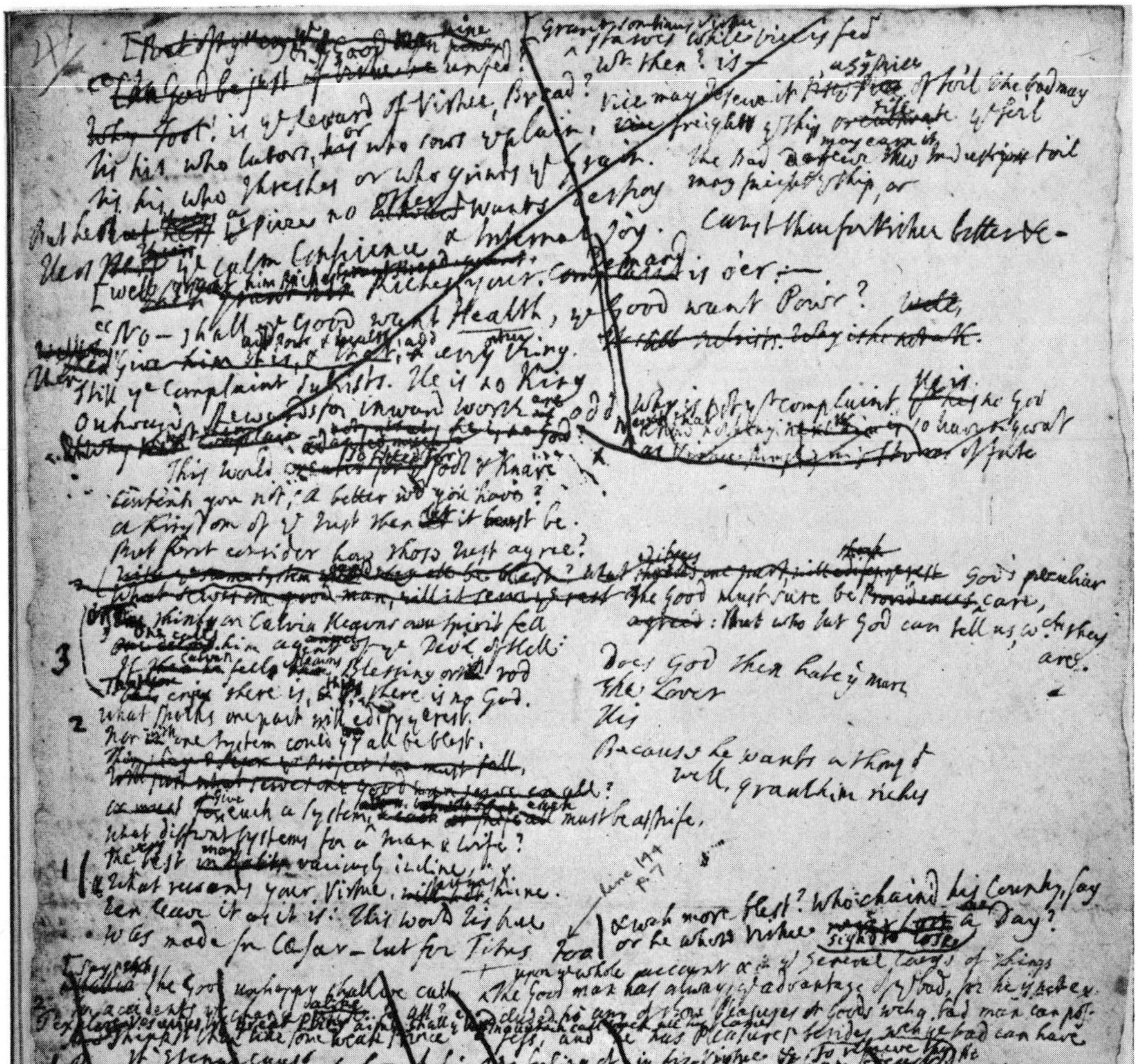

[~~But oft yu say ye~~ ~~pine~~
& ye Good Man ~~pines~~
"~~Can God be just if Virtue be~~ unfed?

Why Fool! is ye Reward of Virtue, Bread?

or
Tis his who labors, ~~his~~ who sows ye plain,

Tis his who threshes or who grinds ye Grain.

~~theirs~~ a other
But hers ~~But hers ye~~ Prize no ~~outward~~ Wants destroy

~~Theirs~~
Hers ~~Next~~ ye calm Conscience & Internal Joy,

[Well, grant him Riches, ~~grant Bread, grant~~ Demand
~~Then grant her~~ Riches, your ~~Complaint~~ is o'er:—

"No--shall ye Good want Health, ye Good want Pow'r? Well,

~~Well~~|~~Why~~ Add Powr & Wealth, add other
~~Then Give him this, & that~~ & evry thing
Then

Still ye Complaint subsists. He is no King

are
Outward Rewards for inward Worth ~~is~~ odd

~~not then~~
~~Oh Why then complain not that he is no God?~~

~~adapted much to~~
so fitted for
This World ~~created for~~ ye Fool & Knave

Contents you not: a better wd you have?

let
A Kingdom of ye Just then ~~let~~ it ←——→ be

But first consider how those Just agree?

could
2 ~~With ye same System <will> they all be blest~~?

~~What serves one good man, will it serve ye rest~~?

One <Some> think~~s~~ on Calvin Heavns own spirit fell

One calls ~~angel~~
~~One deems~~ him agent of ye Dev'l of Hell:

3
Calvin Heavns its
If ~~then he~~ feels ~~the~~ Blessing or ~~the~~ rod

That ~~<Those>~~ this
~~This~~ cries there is, & ~~yt~~, there is no God.

What shocks one part will edify ye rest,

2
wth ~~we~~
Nor ~~in~~ one System could yy all be blest;

~~Then say <O Peer> yr Project too must fall~~,

~~Will just what serves one Good man serve em all~~?

Give ~~<alters,~~ ~~that>~~ each
~~Or must For~~ each a System, ~~each at Strife all~~ must be at Strife,

What diffrent Systems for a Man & Wife?

very may
The best ~~in Habit~~, variously incline,

1
punish
& What rewards your Virtue, ~~will not~~ mine.

<Een> leave it as it is: This World tis true

Was made for Caesar—but for Titus too

[Say next
~~Shall we~~ the Good unhappy shall we call,

alike
2 For accidents yt chance ~~alike~~ to all?

T'explore Vesuvius if great Pliny aims Shall ye kind mountain call back all his flames?

~~And~~ Thinkst thou like some weak Prince
th' Eternal Cause

1 Prone for his Favorites to break his Laws

3 Shall on ye air new Motions be imprest ~~To ease the~~

trembles
~~And when ye threatning~~ Timber ~~nods~~ fro high

If ye loose

Honor & Shame fro no condition rise,

Act well your part, there all ye merit lies.

we have
Oft of 2 Brothers, one shall be surveyd

Fluttring in rags, one flaunting in Brocade,

A Cobler apron'd, or a Parson gownd,

A Friar hooded, or a Monarch crownd.

"What differs more (you cry) than Crown & ~~Hood~~? Cowl?

~~wise~~ and ~~wise Fool & Bad a~~
~~A good man & a bad man wise & good~~.

You'l find, if once yt Monarch acts ye Monk,

Or ~~If~~ Cobler-like that Parson will be drunk,

want of it
Worth makes ye Man, & ~~Folly makes~~ ye Fellow,

The rest, is all but Leather or Prunella.

Stuck oer wth Titles or hung round wth Strings

That thou mayst be, by Kings, or Whores of Kings, &c.

The noblest blood
~~Let the pure blood of an illustrious race In quiet flow frō Lucrece to Lucrece Swell~~ ←——→
&c ~~rich~~
But to make Wits of Fools & Chiefs of Cowards
wise weak brave

What can?--Not all ye Pride of all the H——
blood
as X Church
(once) all Colleges
beside.

Europe
Let gatherd Nations next their Chief behold

<New> blest wth Conquest, yet more blest wth Gold

< >
Wt wonder—Lord. Go then & <steep> thy Age in Wealth & Ease

Stretcht on ye Spoils. Alas, The trophyd
arch ye storied hall
pompous shade

[Grant sometimes Virtue
starves while Vice is fed

Wt then? is —

as ye Price
Vice may deserve it ~~tis ye Price~~ of Toil The bad may

till
Vice freights ~~e~~ ye ship or ~~cultivate~~ ye Soil

may earn it
The Bad deserve thro Industrious Toil
may freight ye ship, or

Canst thou for Virtue better &c—

It still subsists. Why is he not a K.

He is
Why is not yr complaint ~~yt hes~~ no God

<Next> that ←→
Know, nothing ~~next him~~ is so brave and great

As Virtue perishd in ye Storms of fate

~~edifyes~~ ~~shock~~
~~What shocks one part, will edify ye rest~~

God's peculiar
The Good must sure be ~~Providence's~~ care,

~~Agreed~~: But who but God can tell us, wch they
are.

Does God then hate ye man

The Lover

This

Because he wants a thousd

Well, grant him riches

& wch more blest? Who chain'd his Country, say

~~one~~
or he whose Virtue ~~never lost~~ a Day?
sighd to lose

Upon ye whole account & in ye General Course of things The Good Man has always ye advantage of ye bad, for he is not excluded frō any of those Pleasures & Goods wch a bad man can possess, and he has Pleasures besides wch ye bad can have no feeling of in his Virtue &c

Oh Blameless Bethel's ~~suffring~~ To relieve thy
breast. He

Tis Peace of Mind alone is at a stay

The rest mad Fortune gives or takes away

Shall Gravitation cease till you pass by?

~~threatning~~ nods
~~The < loose>~~ Ruin wh it ~~hasts~~ to fa<ll>
Or shall some

For Chartres head reserve ye hanging
wall

No — in a Scene for higher Heavn
imparts

Rewds for ~~spotless hands~~ & honest
~~searching heads~~ hearts

The Good & bad, ye wiseman & ye fool.

may
~~thy Heart &~~ Gallop in thy
brest—&c —beside
~~But gain Esteem~~
~~or Love | fame~~
~~praise | to fools or Cow <ards>~~

~~Wt can?~~

Grasp all ~~vast~~
X ~~Include~~ ye Worlds--
In one close

In one mans fortune mark & scorn ym all

~~him~~|the famd & most
In ~~one~~, most ←——→ most honord, ~~famd&~~ great

Youth
See ye false Scale--But oh not dazled wth his--Compute--address led his
this name & subject shall

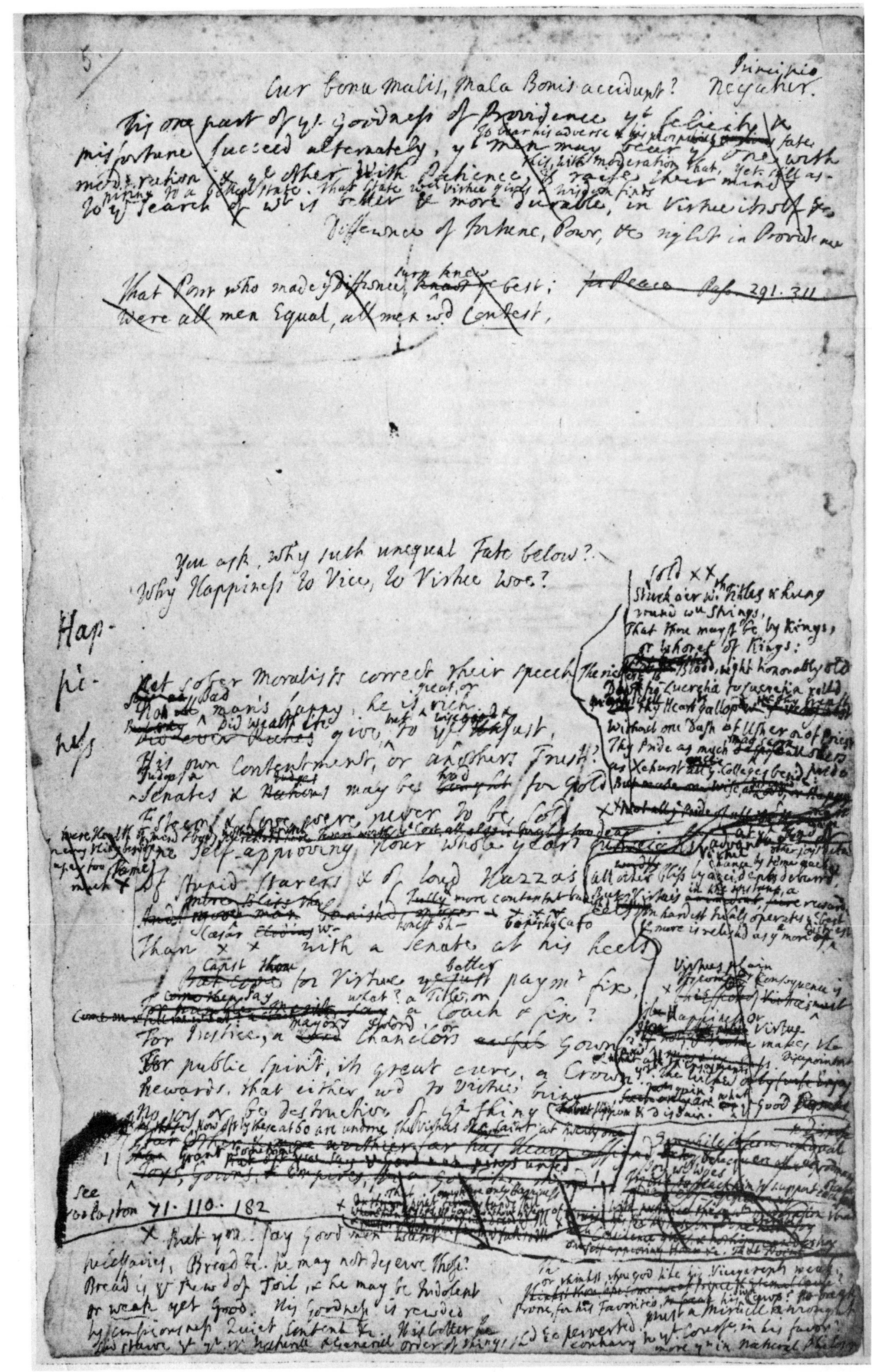

5

Cur bona malis, mala Bonis accidunt? Principio Negatur.

Tis one part of ye goodness of Providence yt felicity & misfortune succeed alternately, yt men may bear ye one with moderation & ye other with Patience, & raise their minds to ye search of wt is better & more durable, in Virtue itself &c

Difference of Fortune, Pow'r, &c right in Providence

That Pow'r who made ye difference, knows best: Were all men Equal, all men wd Contest,

You ask, why such unequal Fate below?
Why Happiness to Vice, to Virtue Woe?

Hap-
pi-
ness

Let sober Moralists correct their speech
No man's happy, he is rich.
Did wealth ere give, to ye Just,
His own Contentment, or another's Trust?
Senates & Nations may be bought for Gold
Esteem & Love were never to be sold
The self-approving hour whole years outweighs
Of stupid starers & of loud Huzzas
Than Caesar with a Senate at his heels
for Virtue ye just paym.t fix,
what? a Title, or a Coach & six?
For Justice, a Mayor's or Chancelor's Gown
For public spirit, its great cure, a Crown.
Rewards, that either wd to Virtue bring
No joy, or be destruction of ye thing

See Woolaston 71. 110. 182

Principio <50>

Cur bona malis, Mala Bonis accidvnt? Negatur.

Tis one part of ye Goodness of Providence y^t felicity &
To bear his adverse & his prosprous←→fate
misfortune succeed alternately, y^t men may bear ye one with
this, With moderation that, yet still as—
moderation & ye other With Patience, & raise their minds
piring to a better State, That State wch Virtue gives & Wisdom finds
to ye Search of w^t is better & more durable, in Virtue itself &c

Difference of Fortune, Powr, &c right in Providence

sure knew
That Powr who made ye Diffrence ~~knows y^e~~ best;

Were all men Equal, all men w^d Contest. ~~See Peace. —Pasc. 291. 311.~~

You ask, why such unequal Fate below?

Hap- Why Happiness to Vice, to Virtue Woe?

Let Sober Moralists correct their speech

pi- ~~Say a~~ Bad great, or
Not ~~ill~~ mans happy, he is rich.

~~But say~~ Did Wealth ere but wise ~~good~~ &
ness ~~Did ever Riches~~ give to y^e ~~Un~~Just,

His own Contentment, or anothers Trust?

Judges & ~~Judges~~ had
Senates & ~~Nations~~ may be ~~bought~~ for Gold

Esteem & Love were never to be sold

nothing grutch
Were Health of Mind & Body ~~purchasd here Twere worth ye Cost, all else is bought too dear~~
For evry thing besides
y^u pay too One self-approving Hour whole years outweighs
much Fame
X Of stupid Starers, & of loud Huzza's

~~More Bliss the~~ ~~Tully~~ more contentm^t banishd ~~Tully~~
And A good man banishd more + + + + feels
honest Sh— banishd Cato

Caesar ~~Clodius W—~~
Than W + + with a Senate at his heels

Canst thou better
~~But come~~, for Virtue y^e ~~just~~ paym^t fix,

~~Come then~~ Say what? a Title, or
~~For humble Merit, say~~ a Coach & Six?
~~<Come Merit tell us what?>~~ a Coach & Six?
Mayors sword, or
For Justice, a ~~Lord~~ Chanc'lors ~~awful~~ Gown?

For public Spirit, its great Cure, a Crown.

Rewards, that either w^d to Virtue bring

No Joy, or be destructive of ye thing.

2 ~~<How oft by these>~~ How oft by these at 60 are undone The Virtues of a Saint at Twenty one
~~<those>~~
~~Far other & more worthier far has Heavn assignd~~
1 Grant sometimes ~~But oft youl say ye Good man pines~~ unfed
~~Than~~
~~Toys, Gowns, & Empires for a god-like Mind!~~

See That our where only happiness
Woolaston 71. 110.182 ~~In this one~~ point happiness stands still

X And tastes ye Good without ye fear of
~~Where men~~ < > ye Good nor dread ye Ill
~~& grasps ye Good nor fears ye fall to Ill~~

+ But youl say Good men want

Necessaries, Bread, &c. he may not deserve These?

Breed is ye Rew^d of Toil, & he may be Indolent

or weak yet Good. His Goodness is rew^{d}ed

by Consciousness, Quiet, Content &c. It is better he

sh^d starve y^n y^t ye Naturall & General Order of Things sh^d be perverted
contrary to y^t Course in his favor?
more y^n in Natural Philosop<hy>

sold + +

Stuck oer wth Titles & hung
round wth Strings,
That thou mayst be by Kings,
or Whores of Kings:

~~Thy boasted~~
~~<Patrician>~~ Blood right honorably old
The richest
Down frõ Lucretia to Lucretia rolld

May swell & in thy breast
~~Let~~ thy Heart Gallop ~~wth ye very best~~

Without one Dash of Usher or of Priest

may scorn
Thy Pride as much ~~despise~~ all others
pride
once
As X Church all ye Colleges beside:

~~<esteemd>~~
~~But make one Wise, or Lovd, or Happy~~
~~Man~~
X X ~~Not all ye Pride of all ye H—~~ can

At ye End
Advantage of
Virtue other joys debar<rd>
chance by time each

~~worldl~~y
All other bliss by accidents debarrd,

in the Instant, a
But Virtue's ~~an imediat, sure~~ reward.

In hardest trials operates ye best

distrest
& more is relishd as ye more ~~op~~

Virtues plain
Its < >Consequence is
~~Or~~
~~The Effect of Virtue~~'s ~~must~~
is ~~be~~ Happiness Or
←———→ Virtue
~~If not, ye Virtue~~ makes the
~~misery less~~ disappointm^t
What are th' Enjoyments
y^t The Wicked ~~only sense Enjoy~~
~~<fools>~~ gain?
what
~~Such only~~ are ~~<as>~~ ye Good <forsake>
←→ but fly from & disdain
to ~~dispose~~
~~Evn while it seems unequal~~
~~<Or to> & chequers all ye goodmans~~
Joy with Woes State
~~Tis but to teach him~~ to support each ←—
~~With patience this with moderation that~~

eternal
~~To~~ raise his fix his Passion ~~<at one →Joy~~
W^{ch} ~~Conscience gives, & nothing can destroy~~
One self-approving Hour &c That ~~Point~~

Th
or thinkst thou God like his Vicegerents weak,
~~Thinkst thou, like some weak Prince th Eternal Cause~~?

~~a~~ own
Prone for his Favorites, ~~to break~~ his Laws? No break
Must a Miracle be wrought

Say next, the good unhappy shall we call
For accidents which chance alike to all?
Pliny who inspires Vesuvius favring Plinys aim
forget to thunder & call back the Flame
Yet hemm'd wth Plagues & breathing deathful air
Marseilles good Bishop still maintains ye Chair.
Brave Sydney falls, amid ye martial strife!
Not that he's virtuous, but careless of Life.
Disease, not Virtue, wither'd Digby's bloom
Or untimely sunk to ye Tomb.
Yet hemm'd with Plagues & breathing deathful air
Marseilles good Bishop holds the Chair! How long in green old age
And kinder Heaven's had Heavens Decree
Preserv'd a Parent to ye Poor, & me?

But, shall Vesuvius, favring Plinys aim,
Forget to thunder, & call back the flame?
Think we like some weak Prince, th' Eternal Cause,
Prone for his Favorites to break his Laws?
Or shall on air new motions be imprest
Oh blameless Bethel! to relieve thy Breast? shall

Say next, the <u>Good</u> unhappy shall we call
For accidents which chance alike to <u>all</u>?

Did fierce Vesuvius
~~Pliny who studious~~ favring Pliny's aim

Forget to thunder &
~~T'explore Vesuvius perish~~ call back the Flame?

Yet hem̃d wth Plagues & breathing deathful air

yet maintains
Marseilles good Bishop still ~~possesst~~ ye Chair.

~~That~~
Brave Sidney falls, amid ye martial Strife!

~~Twas not for his virtues~~ ~~Contempt~~
Not that he's virtuous, but profuse of Life.

Disease, not ~~snatchd Arbuthnots hopeful~~
~~Disease~~, Not Virtue, witherd ~~Digbys~~ bloom
Digbys

~~<thee>~~
Disease not ~~sunk Digby to~~
~~& buried Worth untimely in~~ ye Tomb.
& sent thee Crags, untimely to y^e^

Yet hemm'd with Plagues & breathing deathful air

How long held holds
^ Marseilles good Bishop ~~still maintains~~ the Chair? How long in green old age

~~How~~ ~~kinder~~ has Heavns
~~And~~ long kind chance, ~~or~~ Heavn'~~s more kind~~ Decree

~~Has lent a~~
~~Lends an old~~ Parent to ye Poor, & me?
~~Spares~~ Preservd a

But ~~fierce~~
~~Say,~~ shall Vesuvius, fav'ring Plinys aim

the
Forget to thunder, & call back ~~his~~ Flame

δ Think we like some weak Prince, th' Eternal Cause,
Prone for his Favorites to break his <u>Laws</u>?

Or air
~~Say~~ shall on ~~the Air~~ new motions be imprest
Oh blameless Bethel! to relieve thy Breast?

~~Shall~~

2 ~~<Say> not tis Virtue but too soft a~~
~~<Tis Virtue>~~
~~tis the Virtuous mind but fragile frame~~

~~soft a~~
2 ~~Not for their Virtue but too <fine> a frame~~

2 ~~<That>~~ , ~~ends~~
<1> ~~Walsh ends his race a Scudamore her~~
name

~~their~~
~~(&)~~ ~~Think not Virtue more tho Heavn ner~~
~~Unites so many Digbys in one~~

~~<Fame>~~ ~~<was his> doom~~
~~<Fierce glory>~~
Fierce Virtue was thy
1 ~~Thy~~ Love, not ~~Virtue~~, Falkland, ~~was thy~~
doom

←——→
~~Soft←——→of Virtue~~ nipt Louisas bloom

Disease
←——→not Virtue (more tho Heavn
ner gave)
Lamented Digby sunk thee to ye Grave
~~Unites so many Digbys in ye Grave~~
~~That joind so many Digbys in a Grave~~

When the loose ~~Timber~~ Ruin trembles from on high,
Shall Gravitation cease, till you pass by;
~~Or when~~ and ~~or~~ nodding, as ~~when~~ it totters to its fall
~~For~~ For Chartres' ~~head~~ brains reserve the hanging wall?
Think we like some weak Prince th' Eternal Cause Prone for his favorites to break his Laws? Must the good
~~Shall not his justice~~ [illegible] persue [illegible] ears
~~Who~~ Who ye lewd father gave ye dire disease?
Were just as wise of Nature to complain
That righteous Abel was destroy'd by Cain.
Of evry evil since ye world began
The real source is not in God but Man.

Say wt rewards ~~[illegible]~~ this idle World ~~[illegible]~~ ~~high Heaven~~ imparts
~~Rewards~~ fit for knowing to searching heads, or honest hearts?

Ruin
~~When the loose Timber trembles from on high~~,

Shall Gravitation cease, till you pass by;

and as ~~when~~ it
~~Or when it~~ nodding, totters to its fall

brains
For Chartres' head reserve the hanging Wall?

Think we like some weak Prince th'Eternal Cause Prone for his favorites to break his Laws?

Say w[t] ←→ ~~alas~~ World ~~reward~~
~~the fit~~ rewards ~~Think not~~ this idle ~~Scene~~ ~~high Heaven~~ imparts
^ ^

or fit for knowing
~~Rewards~~ or
~~Rewards~~ to searching heads, & honest hearts?
^

Must y[e] good
~~Shall not y[e] virtuous~~ Son enjoy
perpetual
~~ill at~~ ease
Tho
~~When~~ y[e] lewd Father gave
y[e] dire disease?

Twere just as wise of na-
ture to complain

That righteous Abel was
destroyd by Cain.

Of evry Evil since y[e] world
began

The real source is not in
God but Man.

Essay on Man: Morgan Library Manuscript

NOTES TO THE TRANSCRIPTS
EPISTLE I

MS/TS Page:Line	
MLM 2r/TS 3:1*	Laelius. *Words and other markings inserted in the manuscript in a much later hand, not Pope's or Richardson's, have been omitted in the transcript.* Memmius: *Gaius Memmius, to whom Lucretius dedicated his "De Rerum Natura," and whose career had many parallels with Bolingbroke's, including exile. (Proper names are identified in these notes if they do not appear in the published editions.)*
MLM 2r/TS 3:5	S *of* Since *overwrites* s *and the initial bracket of a parenthesis (closed after l. 6).*
MLM 2r/TS 3:9	*Exclamation point overwrites comma.*
MLM 2v/TS 4:27	other *appears to overwrite an illegible word or illegible letters.*
MLM 3r/TS 5:11	tho' *is altered from an illegible word.*
MLM 3r/T.S 5:12	purpose *overwrites an erasure.*
MLM 3r/TS 5:25	*Pope at first underscored* Time *and* Space, *then blotted the underscorings.*
MLM 3r/TS 5:29	is *is altered from* as; as completely *overwrites an illegible word.*
MLM 3v/TS 6:12	and *overwrites* tis.
MLM 3v/TS 6:13	Virgils Gnat: *the insect forming the subject of the first-century* A.D. *poem "Culex," formerly attributed to Virgil;* should *is altered from* shall.
MLM 3v/TS 6:30	H *of* Hope *overwrites* h.
MLM 4r/TS 7:20	r *of* Nor *is altered from* t.
MLM 4r/TS 7:24	He acts *overwrites* His Care.
MLM 4v/TS 8:13	when *overwrites an illegible word, probably* where.
MLM 4v/TS 8:20	C *of* Created *overwrites* c.
MLM 5r/TS 9:15	looking downward *overwrites an erasure.*
MLM 5r/TS 9:16	brawn *overwrites the erasure of an illegible word, possibly* Horns.
MLM 5r/TS 9:17	all Cr *appears to overwrite an erasure.*
MLM 5r/TS 9:19	Nature *overwrites an erasure.*
MLM 5v/TS 10:13	O *of* Of *overwrites* o.
MLM 5v/TS 10:18, 19	sence so subtly true *and* extracts *seem to overwrite erasures.*
MLM 5v/TS 10:25	*To left of* Twixt *Pope has canceled a* 2, *indicating his intention at one time to reverse ll. 25–26 and 27–28. See below at l. 27.*
MLM 5v/TS 10:27	*The* 1 *of* 15 *overwrites a figure* 1, *indicating reversal of couplets;* allied *is altered from an illegible word ending in* y'd.
MLM 5v/TS 10:34	thy *is altered from* the.
MLM 6r/TS 11:1	that *is probably altered from* the.
MLM 6r/TS 11:2	Is, not *overwrites an erasure, possibly of* His Bliss.
MLM 6r/TS 11:13	Nature *is altered from* Nature's; Thunder'd *is probably altered from* Thunder; in his opening *overwrites an erasure.*
MLM 6r/TS 11:18	-good, all- *appears to overwrite an erasure.*
MLM 6v/TS 12:5	broken *overwrites* altered.
MLM 6v/TS 12:6	a *is altered from* o *of* one; great *overwrites* whole.
MLM 6v/TS 12:5–6	*In the transcript these lines are too widely spaced.*
MLM 6v/TS 12:14	F *of* For *is altered from* f *and the question mark then inserted.*
MLM 6v/TS 12:20	Pow'r *of* Powerful *overwrites an illegible word, apparently Great.*
MLM 7r/TS 13:14	*Above* own *Pope has inserted* fix'd, *unintentionally omitted from the transcript.*

*MLM refers to the Morgan Library manuscript and TS represents "transcript."

Epistle II

MS/TS Page:Line	
MLM 2r/TS 17:31	M *(for Memmius) overwrites the first of two* xx *and is altered from* St. *(for* St. John).
MLM 2r/TS 17:34	*To the right of this line, in pencil,* Sense & Intellect *is written in a hand that may be Pope's; it is omitted from the transcript.*
MLM 2r/TS 17:45, 54, 61, 68	*To left of each of these couplets Pope has obliterated a number, indicating an intent at one time to rearrange.*
MLM 2r/TS 17:53–54	Go reasning Man *and* Wouldst thou be *appear to overwrite erasures.*
MLM 2r/TS 17:58	*Above* erratic *a hand that may be Pope's has written in pencil* the *and above* where, *again in pencil,* in what orbs; f *of* face *is altered from* r.
MLM 2r/TS 17:60	An *is altered from* And, *the* d *being overwritten by* E *of* Elder.
MLM 2r/TS 17:61	*Above* Angels themselves, *a hand that may be Pope's has inserted in pencil* But he who tells.
MLM 2r/TS 17:66	W *of* Why *is altered from* w; T *of* To *is altered from* t.
MLM 2r/TS 17:67–69	*These lines (in left column) seem to overwrite large erasures.*
MLM 2r/TS 17:68	*For* <Then> *in the transcript, read* Ah.
MLM 2r/TS 17:72	H *of* He *overwrites* w.
MLM 2r/TS 17:73	tells *is altered from* tell.
MLM 2r/TS 17:76	Marks *is altered from* mark; Points *appears to be altered from an illegible word;* and *overwrites* or; knows *is altered from* know; he *is altered from* we *and both the first and second* his *from* our.
MLM 2r/TS 17:79	Alas what wonder *overwrites illegible words.*
MLM 2r/TS 17:86	Ethic *seems to overwrite an erasure.*
MLM 2v/TS 18:27–28	that *is altered from* this *and* this *from* that.
MLM 2v/TS 18:42	nigh *is altered from* near.
MLM 2v/TS 18:49	A *of* At *is altered from* a *and* that *from* this.
MLM 2v/TS 18:52	*The cue word* strong *should be preceded in the transcript by a dash.*
MLM 2v/TS 18:71	*The second* this *is altered from* one *and* Good *from* End.
MLM 2v/TS 18:81	*In the manuscript,* a *is overwritten by a caret.*
MLM 3r/TS 19:16	it *is altered from* they.
MLM 3r/TS 19:24	r *of* Nor *is altered from* t.
MLM 3r/TS 19:47	Lights *and* Shades *are altered from* Light *and* Shade.

MS/TS Page:Line	
MLM 3r/TS 19:54	E *of* Exalted *is altered from* e.
MLM 3r/TS 19:67	Responsive *is altered from and overwrites illegible words.*
MLM 3r/TS 19:79	*The parentheses overwrite commas.*
MLM 3r/TS 19:84	That *is altered from an illegible word, perhaps* This.
MLM 3r/TS 19:92	but *appears to overwrite* yet.
MLM 3r/TS 19:93	It *is altered from* Or; conquers *appears to be altered from* answers.
MLM 3r/TS 19:96	Passions *is altered from* one.
MLM 3r/TS 19:97	*The first* ye *possibly overwrites* yt, *the second overwrites* a.
MLM 3v/TS 20:3	mingled *overwrites an illegible word, just possibly* mixd.
MLM 3v/TS 20:5	The *is altered from* Each.
MLM 3v/TS 20:10	Whatever *is altered from* What-e're.
MLM 3v/TS 20:21	still *is altered from* all.
MLM 3v/TS 20:24	Just *is altered from* Tis. Teague: *see Introduction, n. 28.*
MLM 3v/TS 20:34	mingles *overwrites* mixing.
MLM 3v/TS 20:43	his *overwrites* our.
MLM 3v/TS 20:57	learn to bear *overwrites* on to.
MLM 3v/TS 20:62	that mingles *is altered from* still mixing.
MLM 3v/TS 20:66	juice *was altered from* juices *and* melts *from* melt *before the line was canceled.*
MLM 3v/TS 20:74	A *is altered from* a; powr *overwrites an illegible word;* this *seems to be altered from* the.
MLM 3v/TS 20:76	impells *overwrites an illegible word.*
MLM 3v/TS 20:80	from *overwrites* wth.
MLM 4r/TS 21:35	and *overwrites* our.
MLM 4r/TS 21:36	B **: *unidentified. The unrevised line calls for a name of two syllables, which, until l. 39 was revised, might be that of either lord or commoner.*
MLM 4r/TS 21:48	B.: *this might refer to any of several Blounts notable for their loyalty to the throne, including Pope's friend Edward Blount; but perhaps especially to Mountjoy Blunt (1597?–1666), staunch supporter of Charles I;* more *overwrites* most, *or vice-versa.* B **: *unidentified. Suitable candidates abound.*
MLM 4r/TS 21:50	Which . . . become *overwrites erasures.*
MLM 4r/TS 21:52	De Rancé: *Armand Jean le Bouthillier de Rancé (1626–1700), abbot of La Trappe, whence came the Trappist order officially called Cistercians of the Stricter Observance.*
MLM 4r/TS 21:54	W+: *unidentified—possibly Pope's former schoolmate, "Mr.*

MS/TS Page:Line	
	Webb," who married the widow of the Blount sisters' uncle in 1732.
MLM 4r/TS 21:66	Frenchman: *La Rochefoucauld.*
MLM 4r/TS 21:72	Startles *is altered from* startled.
MLM 4r/TS 21:76	*The second exclamation point is altered from a comma.*
MLM 4r/TS 21:83	+ +: *Any two-syllabled name will serve.*
MLM 4r/TS 21:84	B——; K+: *see below, l. 97.*
MLM 4r/TS 21:86	Sid; Ch+ +: *below, l. 98.*
MLM 4r/TS 21:88	Agent is *overwrites an illegible word, possibly Adjutant's.*
MLM 4r/TS 21:91	Attorney *overwrites* he has.
MLM 4r/TS 21:97	B1.: *probably Sir John Blount, one of the most unscrupulous directors of the South Sea Company, on whom Pope added a long note to the Epistle to Bathurst (TE, 3. 2:104).* K+: *probably Robert Knight, fugitive cashier of the South Sea Company, who was said by his son to have fled to save the reputation of the ministry.*
MLM 4r/TS 21:97–98	*Pope compressed parts of these lines into l. 14 of the "Epilogue to the Satires." Dialogue 1 (TE, 4:298).*
MLM 4r/TS 21:98	+: *this nameless reference seems intended to cover any government official who uses his office for private gain; but in l. 5 Pope's allusion is to "Sid"—apparently either Sidney Godolphin, one of Walpole's predecessors in the Treasury who was also thought to have feathered his own nest, or Sidrophel, the quack in Hudibras to whom Walpole was sometimes compared by the Opposition. Pope perhaps intended the reference (which he never printed) to be read in whatever sense the individual reader preferred.* Ch+ +: *Francis Chartres. See TE, 3. 2:85–86.*
MLM 4r/TS 21:99	Peter: *Peter Walter. See TE, 4:392.*
MLM 4v/TS 22:16	Man *overwrites* we; follows *is altered from* follow.
MLM 4v/TS 22:27	Springs *is altered from* springing *and subsequently from* Spring (*when* Joy *was altered from* Joys); draws *overwrites an illegible word.*
MLM 4v/TS 22:31	Defects *partly overwrites* Each Want.
MLM 4v/TS 22:49	them *overwrites* us.
MLM 4v/TS 22:60	*The canceled word is probably* of (*Pope having thought he had already written* Age).
MLM 4v/TS 22:81	And *appears to overwrite* How.
MLM 4v/TS 22:84	in all *overwrites an illegible word;* can *overwrites* wd.

Epistle III

MS/TS Page:Line	
MLM 2r/TS 27:5	g *of* genral *is altered from* G.
MLM 2r/TS 27:20	*Final* l *of* shall *is altered to* t *and then back to* l.
MLM 2r/TS 27:24	*As indicated in the transcript,* thinks *is altered from* think'st.
MLM 2r/TS 27:27	*The canceled word* may *equally well be* Vast.
MLM 2v/TS 28:8	T *of* To *overwrites* t; *the first* the *is altered from* that.
MLM 2v/TS 28:20	M *of* Made *overwrites* m.
MLM 2v/TS 28:24	its *is altered from* his.
MLM 2v/TS 28:28	*This line partly overwrites l. 27;* servd & serving *appear to be altered from* serves *or* servd, *or* serves, is served.
MLM 2v/TS 28:29	work'd solely *overwrites illegible words, perhaps* thought only.
MLM 2v/TS 28:35	Sir Gilbert: *Sir Gilbert Heathcote (1651?–1733), a founding director of the Bank of England, whose wealth and parsimony Pope often ridicules.*
MLM 2v/TS 28:36	t *of* that *overwrites* W.
MLM 2v/TS 28:43	his *is altered from* her, *but Pope has neglected to make this alteration in l. 42.*
MLM 3r/TS 29:21	*Ampersand appears to overwrite* or.
MLM 3r/TS 29:37	Whether *seems to overwrite an illegible word.*
MLM 3v/TS 30:5	Bu *of* But *overwrites* Wh (*for* When).
MLM 3v/TS 30:7	Then *is altered from* Thus.
MLM 3v/TS 30:11	*Pope has inserted and then canceled a question mark after* ours.
MLM 3v/TS 30:22	*In the manuscript,* forth *of l. 22 is overwritten by* on the *of l. 24.*
MLM 3v/TS 30:30	*In the manuscript,* roam *of l. 30 is partly overwritten by* Families *of l. 31.*
MLM 3v/TS 30:34,8	Storks *is altered from* stork *and* Worlds *from* World.
MLM 3v/TS 30:45	Gibs: *James Gibbs (1682–1754), friend of Pope and architect of many renowned buildings including St. Martin-in-the-Fields.* Sir Kit: *Sir Christopher Wren.*
MLM 3v/TS 30:49	Bernini: *architect and sculptor (1598–1680) whose work on the interior of St. Peters and the elliptical piazza before it did not, in fact, include the dome, which had shown signs of cracking.*
MLM 3v/TS 30:53	Vault *appears to be altered from* Vaults.
MLM 3v/TS 30:55	Berselli: *see Introduction, n. 33.*
MLM 3v/TS 30:60	*In the manuscript* <various> *is partly overwritten by* fixd, *which*

MS/TS Page:Line	
	appears in the transcript as the antepenultimate word of this line.
MLM 3v/TS 30:65	Thus *is altered from* Twas.
MLM 3v/TS 30:72	from *appears to overwrite* to.
MLM 3v/TS 30:73	Those *overwrites* The Ants.
MLM 3v/TS 30:76	find *is altered from* finds.
MLM 3v/TS 30:99	*The first* Works *overwrites* Towns; *the figure* 5 *in left margin overwrites* 4 *or vice-versa; the figure* 5 *above this line appears to overwrite* 6.
MLM 4r/TS 31:9	mov'd *is altered from* moves.
MLM 4r/TS 31:11	loved *is altered from* loves.
MLM 4r/TS 31:17	desires *is altered from* desird.
MLM 4r/TS 31:20	W *of* Wing *overwrites* w.
MLM 4r/TS 31:28	attend *appears to overwrite* tend *and a final* s *added at one point to* charge.
MLM 4r/TS 31:30	Mothers . . . defend: *altered from* Mother nurses & the Sire defends, *as indicated in the transcript.*
MLM 4r/TS 31:34	*The first* ends *overwrites an illegible word.*
MLM 4r/TS 31:48	they *is altered from* we.
MLM 4r/TS 31:52	And now *overwrites* Still as; and *is altered from* as.
MLM 4r/TS 31:66	points *is altered from* pointed.
MLM 4r/TS 31:68	and *overwrites ampersand.*
MLM 4r/TS 31:69	Draw *is altered from* Drew; *its first two letters overwrite* To.
MLM 4r/TS 31:72	fetch *is altered from* fetchd, *as shown in the transcript.*
MLM 4v/TS 32:12	Fear *and* awe *overwrite illegible words, probably* aids *and* draw.
MLM 4v/TS 32:13	serves *is altered from* served.
MLM 4v/TS 32:15*	shall *is altered from* should.
MLM 4v/TS 32:30	What need to *is altered from* Who woud.
MLM 4v/TS 32:51	averting *overwrites* Father of a people.
MLM 4v/TS 32:55	obeyd *overwrites* godlike.
MLM 4v/TS 32:57	When . . . first *is altered from* By Nature crown'd the hoary.
MLM 4v/TS 32:60	Parent *overwrites* Father.
MLM 5r/TS 33:13–14	moved *is altered from* moves *and* loved *from* loves.
MLM 5r/TS 33:15	seeks *possibly overwrites an illegible word.*
MLM 6r/TS 35:51	On him their second *overwrites illegible words.*
MLM 6r/TS 35:63	unbloodied *is altered from* unbloody.
MLM 6r/TS 35:70	who *is altered from* he.
MLM 6v/TS 36:6	*The second* yet *overwrites an ampersand and the* n *of* no.
MLM 6v/TS 36:11	Of . . . himself *overwrites* Snare of half Nature.
MLM 6v/TS 36:12	*In the transcript* Tomb *should not be canceled.*

MS/TS Page:Line	
MLM 6v/TS 36:13	Yet *overwrites* Now.
MLM 6v/TS 36:18	To *is altered from* he.
MLM 6v/TS 36:45	Him *overwrites* But.
MLM leaf folded quarto; Q 1r/TS 37:4	averting *overwrites an illegible word, possibly* reforming.
Ibid./TS 37:7	his *overwrites* the.
Ibid./TS 37:24	Monsters *may overwrite an obliterated word.*
Ibid./TS 37:32	ning *of* Sickning *appears to overwrite an illegible word.*
Ibid./TS 37:42	*In the transcript* One *and* great *should be more widely spaced.*
Ibid./TS 37:48	broke *is altered from* broken; that *is altered from* Natures.
MLM leaf folded quarto; Q 1v/TS 38:16	made *is altered from* gave.
Ibid./TS 38:22	*Much of this line overwrites obliterated words, including* When *of l. 23.*
Ibid./TS 38:28	*Semicolon is altered from exclamation point.*
Ibid./TS 38:41	*In the manuscript,* 'd *appears confusingly after* Zeal *of l. 42.*
MLM leaf folded quarto; Q 2r/TS 39:3	was *overwrites an illegible word.*
Ibid./TS 39:16	playd *seems to be altered from* plays.
Ibid./TS 39:35	desires *is altered from* desir'd.
Ibid./TS 39:36	*In the transcript* Selflove *should read* Self Love; found *overwrites* finds.
MLM leaf folded quarto; Q 2v/TS 40:9	Intrests *is altered from* Intrest.
Ibid./TS 40:33–34	Man *of* Man/kinds *overwrites* Mans *or* Mens; kinds *of* Man/kinds *overwrites* Happiness.
Ibid./TS 40:39	Man *overwrites an illegible word, probably* Each.
MLM 8r/TS 41:3	but *overwrites* thy.
MLM 8r/TS 41:4	Must *overwrites* To.
MLM 8r/TS 41:22	Which *overwrites* This; joins *appears to be altered from* joind.
MLM 8r/TS 41:35	*The final word in this line looks more like* shining *than like* sikning *or* skning *(Pope's abbreviations for* sickening?*), but only the latter two have relevance to what Pope is writing about at this point.*
MLM 8r/TS 41:29–36	*In pencil, partly overwritten by these lines, but I believe in Pope's hand:* this plain truth profess/ One is our Duty & our Happiness.

*MLM 4v/TS 32:19, 21, 23 *Notice is not taken in the transcripts of the mutilated words at extreme right, possibly:* &; fr[iend], Pr[iest].

EPISTLE IV

MS/TS Page:Line	
MLM 2r/TS 45:12	*In the transcript,* <who> *should possibly read* <We>.
MLM 2r/TS 45:23	still *appears to overwrite an illegible word, possibly* all.
MLM 2r/TS 45:24	*In the transcript* appetite *should fall immediately below* desire *in l. 23.*
MLM 2r/TS 45:26–30	*In the extreme right margin these lines overwrite seven illegible words, of which the last five are:* Virtue makes our Happiness below.
MLM 2r/TS 45:30	*For* ~~thou~~ *in the transcript, read* thou.
MLM 2r/TS 45:47	Yet *is altered from* but.
MLM 2r/TS 45:48	T *of* Tis *is altered from* t.
MLM 2r/TS 45: 65, 72, 74, 76, 78	*I have capitalized here the first word of each of Pope's cues in order to distinguish the main column of verse from the scribblings that engulf it.*
MLM 2r/TS 45:82	*The canceled words may be* bound once.
MLM 2r/TS 45:83	*In the manuscript,* CONSISTS *appears just to the left of* limit . . . Whole *in l. 81. I have rearranged it to make its relation to the other cues clear.*
MLM 2r/TS 45:93	*In the manuscript, Pope's cue phrase* The Strength *(designed to match* Man like *in l. 74) is overwritten by the two words that in the transcript have been placed to precede it:* Happiness we. *The word* aim *immediately following the cue in the transcript should ideally appear in the line next above.*
MLM 2r/TS 45:106	never *overwrites an illegible word.*
MLM 2v/TS 46:9	S *of* Self *overwrites* s.
MLM 2v/TS 46:31	in some degree *overwrites an illegible word or words.*
MLM 2v/TS 46:39	widely *is altered from* wide *and its* ly *overwrites* alas.
MLM 2v/TS 46:40	Others *overwrites an illegible word or words.*
MLM 2v/TS 46:44	With *overwrites* By.
MLM 2v/TS 46:61	yr *overwrites* yt.
MLM 2v/TS 46:64	mad *overwrites an illegible word, possibly* vast.
MLM 2v/TS 46:67	is at *is overwritten by a canceled illegible word or words.*
MLM 2v/TS 46:73	suppose them *overwrites illegible words.*
MLM 2v/TS 46:78	these *overwrites* this.
MLM 2v/TS 46:81	*As indicated in the transcript, Pope has left his choice of* receive *or* receives *unsettled.*
MLM 2v/TS 46:82	Tis *overwrites* Be *or vice-versa;* it *in both occurrences overwrites* we *or vice-versa;* give/s *shows Pope's indecision, as in l. 2.*
MLM 2v/TS 46:84	their *overwrites* in; impartial *overwrites an illegible word or words.*
MLM 3r/TS 47:17	t *of* Wealth *overwrites* W *of* With.
MLM 3r/TS 47:20	why *overwrites an illegible word, possibly* to *or* we.
MLM 3r/TS 47:32	Oerwhelms *is altered from* oerwhelm; oer *of* oerwhelms *overwrites an ampersand.*
MLM 3r/TS 47:38	The *overwrites* if.
MLM 3r/TS 47:39	Sensual Joys *overwrites* Fortunes Goods.
MLM 3r/TS 47:74	*Interrogation point overwrites semicolon or vice-versa;* tis *is altered from* is.
MLM 3v/TS 48:15, 17	*The obscure marks to left of* Man *and* still *may be the figures* 2 *and* 1.
MLM 3v/TS 48:15	And *overwrites* etc.
MLM 3v/TS 48:33	their *is altered from* the.
MLM 3v/TS 48:47	bursting *overwrites an illegible word, possibly* grieving.
MLM 3v/TS 48:57	Joy . . . ←——→ *overwrites illegible words, of which the first is* Heav'n.
MLM 3v/TS 48:58	Evn *overwrites* And.
MLM 3v/TS 48:63, 65	they *overwrites* he; They *is altered from* He.
MLM 3v/TS 48:68	and our *overwrites illegible words;* then *overwrites an illegible word, possibly* Bliss.
MLM 3v/TS 48:72	Man *overwrites an illegible word.*
MLM 3v/TS 48:83	bl *of* blest *appears to overwrite letters that I take to be* pl *(for* pleased).
MLM 3v/TS 48:86	s *of* Its *overwrites an illegible word, possibly* The *first, and then* A; *the letters above and to right of* Its *remain indecipherable, though conceivably they represent* eir *of* their.
MLM 3v/TS 48:96	know *overwrites an illegible word, possibly* see.
MLM 3v/TS 48:100	In *and* <in> *each overwrite an illegible word, probably* all; *in the transcript* also *should read* other.
MLM 4r/TS 48:99	ye . . . Fortune *overwrites illegible words.*
MLM 4r/TS 49:5	ess *of* Happiness *is overwritten by an illegible word.*
MLM 4r/TS 49:12	*In the manuscript, the* rs *of the first* hers *overwrites* B *of the* But *that in the transcript follows it.*
MLM 4r/TS 49:26	*The meaning of the obscure mark to left of* Oh *is unclear.*
MLM 4r/TS 49:37	ne *of* One *seems to overwrite* S *of* Some, *but the reading remains*

MS/TS Page:Line	
	dubious, as Pope seems also to have tried This *and* They.
MLM 4r/TS 49:45	cries *is altered to* cry *and then back to* cries.
MLM 4r/TS 49:62	next *overwrites an illegible word.*
MLM 4r/TS 49:77	If *overwrites something illegible, probably* Wn; till *overwrites* if; you *overwrites an illegible word, probably* he.
MLM 4r/TS 49:89	*The first* wise *overwrites an illegible word.*
MLM 4r/TS 49:91	yt *is altered from* ye.
MLM 4r/TS 49:92	that *is altered from* the.
MLM 4r/TS 49:96	or *may overwrite an ampersand.*
MLM 4r/TS 49:106	all *overwrites* ye.
MLM 4r/TS 49:114	steep thy Age *may overwrite illegible words.*
MLM 4v/TS 50:21	No *is altered to* Not *and back to* No.
MLM 4v/TS 50:24	j *of* Unjust *is altered to* J.
MLM 4v/TS 50:32	X Church: *Christ Church, one of the wealthiest of the Oxford colleges.*
MLM 4v/TS 50:33	nothing grutch: *in no way wanting, stinted, begrudged.*
MLM 4v/TS 50:41	Sh——: *William Shippen (1673–1743), acknowledged Jacobite M.P., one of the most respected members of the Opposition.* Cato: *Marcus Porcius Cato "Uticensis" (presumably a Roman equivalent for Bolingbroke), who had favored Pompey, resisted Caesar.*

MS/TS Page:Line	
MLM 4v/TS 50:43	Clodius; *Publius Clodius, who exiled Cicero, removed Cato to Sicily, and was notorious for various forms of bribery.* W——: *Walpole, who is of course also identifiable as Caesar and Clodius.*
MLM 4v/Ts 50:45	thou *appears to overwrite* them.
MLM 4v/TS 50:47	S *of* Say *is altered from* s.
MLM 4v/TS 50:53	For *overwrites* To.
MLM 4v/TS 50:54	O *of* Or *appears to overwrite* or.
MLM 4v/TS 50:71	this *is altered from* these; *on the transcript* with *should read* wth.
MLM 5r/TS 51:7, 9	*The number* 2 *appears to overwrite* 1 *in both instances.*
MLM 5r/TS 51:18	Virtue *overwrites an illegible word.*
MLM 5v/TS 51:21	Disease *overwrites either* Deep Grief *or* Thy Grief.
MLM 5v/TS 51:22	N *of* Not *overwrites* n; Digby; *Robert Digby, warm friend of Pope's, who had died relatively young in 1726.*
MLM 5v/TS 51:27	Crags: *James Craggs the younger, secretary of state, who died of smallpox in 1721 at the age of 35.*
MLM 5v/TS 51:37	fierce *overwrites an illegible word.*
MLM 5v/TS 51:38	Pliny: *Pliny the Elder, who was asphyxiated while seeking a closer view of the eruption of Vesuvius in 79 A.D.*

ETHIC EPISTLES.

THE

FIRST BOOK,

TO

Henry St. John Lord B.

AWAKE my St. John! quit all meaner things
To puzzling Statesmen, and to blustring Kings.
Let Us, since Life can little more supply
Than just to look about us, and to dye,
†† Expatiate free o'er all the Scene of Man:
6 A mighty Maze! ~~of Walks~~ but not without a Plan;
7 ~~Or~~ A Wilde, where Weeds and Flow'rs promiscuous shoot;
8 Or ~~Orchard~~ Garden, tempting with forbidden Fruit.

This Exordium relates to ye Whole work, [illegible] in general, then in particular. the 6th, 7th & 8th verse allude to ye Design of Providence in ye whole, [illegible] ye Constitution of ye Human mind, whose Passions [illegible] the Temptations of mis-applyed Selflove, [illegible] wrong pursuits of Power, false Happiness & false Pleasures. — The 10 [illegible]

Proposition. 6th verse, alludes to ye Subject of this first Epistle, ye State of M[an] [illegible] & hereafter, disposed by Providence, tho to him unknown.
7th verse, to ye Subject of ye second, ye Passions, their good or evil.
8th verse, to ye Subject of ye 4th, of mans various pursuits of Happiness or Pleasure.
10th verse, to ye subjects of ye second ~~book~~ Epistle of ye second, the Characters of Men & Manners.
13. 14.
11. & 12th verse, to ye Subject ~~of~~ of ye first Epistle of ye second book, the Limits of Reason, Learning & Ignorance.
16. Verse, to ye Subject wch runs thro ye Whole Design, the justification of ye Methods of Providence.

† [illegible] Exordium relates to [illegible] work. The 6th, 7th & 8th Lines allude to ye Subjects of This Book; the General Order & Design of Providence; the Constitution of the human Mind, whose Passions cultivated, are Virtues, neglected, Vices; the Temptations misapplyed Self love, & wrong pursuits of Power, Pleasure, and false Happiness. 10, 11, & 12, &c. allude to ye Subjects of ye following Books; the [illegible] Learning & Ignorance [illegible] Manners [illegible] The Last Line [illegible] moral Drift of ye Whole [illegible] Justification of ye Ways of Pro[vidence] [illegible] manners of men.

ETHIC EPISTLES.

The

First Book,

To

Henry St. John Lord B.

Awake my St. John! quit all meaner things
~~zled~~ ~~flatter'd~~
To puzling Statesmen, and to blustring Kings.

Let Us, since Life can little more supply

Than just to look about us, and to dye,

+ + Expatiate free o'er all the Scene of Man:

but not
6 A mighty Maze! ~~of Walks~~ without a Plan;

A
7 ~~Or~~ Wilde, where Weeds and Flow'rs promiscuous shoot;

Garden
8 Or ~~Orchard~~, tempting with forbidden Fruit

<This> Exordium relates to
ye Whole Work. The 6th. 7th. & 8th. Lines
to
~~only~~ allude ye Subjects of This
Book; the General Order and Design
of Providence; the Constitution
of the human Mind, whose Passi-
<ons>, cultivated, are Virtues, neg
<lec>ted, Vices; the Temptations
<of> misapplyd Selflove, & wrong pur
Pleasure, and
suits of Power false Happiness.

vers^{s}
<The> 10th, 11th, & 12th, &c. allude to y^{e}
subjects of ye following books; the
<y^{e}> Characters <and> capacities of Men;
<Limits> of ~~Mans~~ Learning and Ignorãce,
knowledge of Mankind and the
~~ye Use of Reason, the various~~
~~Characters of Men, &~~ Manners
<of ye Age> ~~and~~ The last Line

sums up Moral &
~~expresses~~ ye main Drift of
~~<y^{e}> design, wch runs thro~~ ye Whole
~~Viz~~ <y^{e}> Justification of ye Ways of Provi<dence>
Viz < >

first in general, then
This Exordium relates to ye Whole Work, ~~not only that part~~ in particular. The 6. th7.th & 8th verses allude <to y^{e}>

2. ~~7th to the~~
Design of Providence in ye Whole, ~~treated in this Epistle~~, ye Constitution of ye Human Mind, whose Passions <cultivated>
~~in ye this second Epistle the 8th to 3 ye Temptations to~~ false Happiness & falss Pleasures.--The 10th

the Temptations of mis-applyd Selflove, & ~~pursuits of~~ wrong pursuits of Power.
Proposition. 6th Verse, alludes to ye Subject of this first Epistle, ye State of Man <here>
& hereafter, disposed by Providence, tho to him unknown.
7th verse, to ye Subject of ye Second, ye Passions, their good or evil.
8th verse, to ye Subject of ye 4th. Of mans various pursuits of Happiness or Pleasure. < ye manners of Men. >

Epistle of ye second, the
10th verse. to ye Subjects of ye second book Characters of Men & Manners.
13. 14.

of ye first Epistle of
11. & 12th verse. to ye Subject ~~of~~ ye second book, the Limits of Reason, Learning & Ignorance.

the
16. verse, to ye Subject wch runs thro ye whole Design, ~~to~~ justification of ye Methods of Providence.

Together let us beat this ample Field,
Try what the Open, what the Covert yield,
Of all that blindly creep the Tracts explore,
And all the dazzled Race that sightless soar:
Eye Nature's Walks; shoot Folly as it flies;
And catch the Manners living as they rise;
Laugh where we must; be candid where we can;
But Vindicate the Ways of GOD to Man.

Say first, of God above or Man below,
What can we reason but from what we know?
Of Man what see we but his Station here,
From which to reason, or to which refer?
Thro' Worlds unbounded tho' the God be known
'Tis ours to trace him only in our own.
Of this vast Frame, the Bearings and the Tyes,
The close Connections, nice Dependencies,
The Centres just, has Thy pervading Soul
Look'd thro'; or can a Part contain the Whole?
[Is the strong Chain that draws all to agree
And drawn supports, up-held by God or Thee?
[He who ~~can all the flaming Limits~~ thro vast Immensity can pierce
See ~~Of~~ Worlds on Worlds, ~~that form~~ compose one Universe,
Observe how System into System runs,
What other Planets ~~and~~ wait on what other Suns,

What

Together let us beat this ample Field,
10. Try what the Open, what the Covert yield,
11 Of all that blindly creep the Tracts explore,
12 And all the dazzled Race that sightless soar:
Eye Nature's Walks; shoot Folly as it flies;
And catch the Manners living as they rise;
Laugh where we must; be candid where we can;
16 But Vindicate the Ways of GOD to Man.

Say first, of God above or Man below,
What can we reason but from what we <u>know</u>?
Of Man what see we but his Station here,
From which to reason, or to which refer?
Thro' Worlds unbounded tho' the God be known
'Tis ours to trace him only in <u>our</u> <u>own</u>.
Of this vast Frame, the Bearings and the Tyes,
The close Connections, nice Dependencies,
The Centres just, has Thy pervading Soul
Look'd thro', or can a Part contain the Whole?
[Is the strong Chain that draws all to agree
And drawn supports, up-held by God or Thee?

thro vast Immensity can
[He who ~~can all the flaming Limits~~ pierce

See compose
~~Of~~ Worlds on Worlds, ~~that form~~ one Universe,
Observe how System into System runs,

wait on
What other Planets and what other Suns,

What

He who thro' vast Im
See Worlds on Worlds
Observe how System
What other 3
What vary'd Being peoples ev'ry Star;
May tell, why Heav'n has made us as we are.

When the proud ~~Steed shall~~ [courser] know; why Man [restrains] ~~now reins~~
His [fiery course,] ~~stubborn neck~~, ~~now~~ [or urges] drives him o'er the Plains;
When the dull Oxe, why now he breaks the Clod,
Now wears a Garland, an Ægyptian God;
Then shall Man's Pride and Dulness comprehend
His Action's, Passion's, Being's, Use and End;
Why doing, suffering, check'd, impell'd; and why
This hour a Slave, the next a Deity.

Presumptuous Man! the reason would'st thou find
Why made so weak, so little, and so blind?
First, if thou can'st, the harder reason guess,
Why form'd no weaker, blinder, and no less!
Ask of thy Mother Earth, why Oaks are made
Taller or stronger than the Plants they shade?
Or ask, of yonder argent Fields above,
Why Jove's Satellites are less than Jove?

Of Systems possible, if 'tis confest
That Wisdom infinite must form the best,
Where all must full, or not coherent be,
And all that rises, rise in due degree;
Then, in the Scale of Life & Sense, 'tis plain
There must be, somewhere, such a Race as Man
And all the question (argue e'er so long)
Is only this, If God has plac'd him wrong?
Is but if God has plac'd his creature wrong?

Respecting Man, whatever Wrong we call,
May, must be, right, as relative to All.
In human works, tho' labour'd on with pain
A thousand Movements ~~scarce~~ one purpose gain;
In God's, one single can its end produce,
Yet serves to second too some other use:

So

<3>

He who thro' vast Im
See Worlds on Worlds
Observe how System
What other 3
What vary'd Being peoples ev'ry Star;
May tell, why Heav'n has made us as we are.

~~Courser~~ restrains
When the proud Steed shall know, why Man ~~now reins~~
fiery course or urges
His ~~stubborn neck~~, ~~now~~ drives him o'er the Plains;
When the dull Oxe, why now he breaks the clod,
Now wears a Garland, an AEgyptian God;
Then shall Man's Pride and Dulness comprehend
His Action's, Passion's, Being's, Use and End;
Why doing, suffering, check'd, impelld; and why
This hour a Slave, the next a Deity.

Presumptuous Man! the reason wouldst thou find
Why made so weak, so little, and so blind?
First, if thou can'st, the harder reason guess,
Why form'd no weaker, blinder, and no less?
Ask of thy Mother Earth, why Oaks are made
Taller or stronger than the Plants they shade?
Or ask, of yonder argent Fields above,
Why Jove's Satellites are less than Jove?
Respecting Man, whatever Wrong we call,
May, must be, right, as relative to All.
In human works, tho' labour'd on with pain
A thousand Movements scarce one purpose gain;
In God's, one single can its end produce,
Yet serves to second too some other use:

Of Systems possible, if 'tis confes<t>
That Wisdom infinite must form y^{e} b<est>
Where all must full, or not coherent be,
And all that rises, rise in due degre<e>
Then, in the Scale of Life & Sense, 'tis pl<ain>
There must be, somewhere, such a Race <as>
M<an>
e'
And all the question (argue ~~ne~~'r so long)
\+ Is only this, If God has plac'd him wr<ong>
+Is but if God has plac'd his
creature wrong?

So

4

So Man, who here seems Principal alone,
Perhaps acts second to some Sphere unknown,
Touches some Wheel, or verges to some Gole;
'Tis but a Part we see, and not a Whole.

Then say not Man's Imperfect, Heav'n in fault:
Say rather Man's as perfect as he ought:
His [Being] Knowledge measur'd to this State and Place,
His Time a Moment, and a Point his Space.
post pone
If to be perfect in a certain Sphere,
What matter, soon or late, or here or there?
The Blest to day, is as compleatly so,
As who began ten thousand years ago:
[Safe in the hand of one disposing]
In the same hand, the same all-plastic Pow'r,
Or in the mortal, or the natal Hour.

Heav'n from all Creatures hides the Book of Fate,
All but the Page prescrib'd, their present State;
From Brutes what Men, from Men what Spirits know,
Or who could suffer Being here below?
The Lamb thy Riot dooms to bleed to day,
Had he thy Reason, would he skip and play?
Pleas'd to the last, he crops the flow'ry food,
And licks the hand just rais'd to shed his blood.
Oh Blindness to the future! kindly giv'n,
That each may fill the Circle mark'd by Heav'n;

Who

So Man, who here seems Principal alone,
Perhaps acts second to some Sphere unknown,
Touches some Wheel, or verges to some Gole;
'Tis but a Part we see, and not a Whole.

Then say not Man's Imperfect, Heav'n in fault:
Say rather Man's as perfect as he ought:
Being
His ~~Knowledge~~ measur'd to this State and Place,
His Time a Moment, and a Point his Space.
post | If to be perfect in a certain Sphere,
pone | What matter, soon or late, or here or there?
The Blest to day, is as compleatly so,
As who began ten thousand years ago:
Safe in the hand of one disposing
In the same hand, the same all-plastic Pow'r,
Or in the mortal, or the natal Hour.

Heav'n from all Creatures hides the Book of Fate,
All but the Page prescrib'd, their present State;
From Brutes what Men, from Men what Spirits know,
Or who could suffer Being here below?
The Lamb thy Riot dooms to bleed to day,
Had he thy Reason, would he skip and play?
Pleas'd to the last, he crops the flow'ry food,
And licks the hand just rais'd to shed his blood.
Oh Blindness to the future! kindly giv'n,
That each may fill the Circle mark'd by Heav'n;

Who

5

Who sees with equal eye, as God of All,
A Hero perish, or ~~and~~ a Sparrow fall:
No Great, no Little! 'Tis as much decreed
~~That Virgil's Gnatt~~ should dye, as Cæsar bleed.

Atoms or Systems ~~into the ... in~~
~~Systems like Atoms~~ in one ruin hurl'd
And now a Bubble burst ~~break~~ & now a World

Hope humbly then; with trembling pinions soar;
Wait the great Teacher, Death, and God adore.
What bliss above, he gives not thee to know,
But gives that Hope to be thy bliss below.
Hope springs eternal in the human breast;
Man never is, but always to be blest:
The Soul, uneasy and confin'd at home,
Rests, and expatiates in a Life to come.

If to be perfect in a certain State,
What matter, here or there, or soon or late,
Safe in ye hands of one disposing Pow'r
Or in the natal, or the mortal Hour.
And He thats blest to day, as fully so,
As who began three thousand years
ago?

Lo! the poor Indian, whose untutor'd mind
Sees God in Clouds, or hears him in the Wind;
His Whose Soul proud Science never taught to stray,
Far as the Solar Walk ~~Year~~ or Milky way:
~~This Hope kind~~ Yet simple Nature ~~Nature~~ to his hope has giv'n,
Behind his the cloud-topt Hills ~~he builds a~~ an humbler Heav'n,
Some safer World in depth of woods embrac'd,
Some happier Island in the watry waste,
Where Slaves once more their native land behold,
No Fiends torment, nor Christians thirst for Gold.

But does He say, the Maker is not good,
Till he's exalted to that ~~the~~ State he wou'd,
Himself alone high. Heavns peculiar care,
Alone made happy, when he will, and where?
To be, contents his natural desires,
He asks no Angel's Wings, or Seraph's fires, ~~Go~~
But ~~And~~ thinks, admitted to that equal Sky,
His faithful Dog shall keep him company. Go

Who sees with equal eye, as God of All,
 or
A Hero perish, ~~and~~ a Sparrow fall:
 ^ ^
No Great, no Little! \\'Tis as much decreed
~~That Virgil's Gnatt~~ should dye, as Caesar bleed.

Hope humbly then; with trembling pinions soar;
Wait the great Teacher, Death, and God adore.
What bliss above, he gives not thee to know,
But gives that Hope to be thy bliss below.
Hope springs eternal in the human breast;
Man never is, but always to be blest:
The Soul, uneasy and confin'd at home,
Rests, and expatiates in a Life to come. ^

Lo! the poor Indian, whose untutor'd mind
Sees God in Clouds, or hears him in the Wind;
His
~~Whose~~ Soul proud Science never taught to stray,
 Walk
Far as the Solar ~~Year~~ or Milky Way:
 Yet simple to his hope
~~This Hope, kind~~ Natures ~~Flattery~~ has giv'n,
 the an humbler
Behind ~~his~~ cloud-topt Hills ~~he builds a~~ Heav'n,
Some safer World in depth of woods embrac'd,
Some happier Island in the watry Waste,
Where Slaves once more their native land behold,
No Fiends torment, nor Christians thirst for Gold.

But does He say, the Maker is not <u>good</u>,
 what
Till he's exalted to ~~the~~ State he wou'd,
Himself <u>alone</u> high Heav'ns peculiar care,
<u>Alone</u> made happy, <u>when</u> he will, and <u>where</u>?
To <u>be</u>, contents his natural desire s, ~~Go~~
He asks no Angel's Wings, or Seraph's fires,
But equal
~~And~~ thinks, admitted to that Sky,
His faithful Dog shall keep him company. Go

Atoms or Systems ~~thro th' <Emanation>~~
 ruin
~~Systems like Atoms~~ in one ~~nothing~~ hurld
 burst,
And now a Bubble ~~break~~ & now a World.
 ^

If to be perfect in a certain State,
What matter, here, or there, or soon or late
Safe in y[e] hands of one disposing Pow'r
Or in the natal or the mortal Hour;
And He thats blest today, as fully so,
As who began three thousand years
 ago?

6

Go wiser Thou, and in thy Scale of Sense
Weigh thy Opinion against Providence;
Call Imperfection what we fancy such;
Pronounce He acts too little or too much;
Destroy all Creatures for thy Sport or Gust,
Yet, if unhappy, think 'tis he's unjust;
Snatch from his hand the Balance and the Rod;
Re-judge his Justice; be the God of God!

In Pride, my Friend, in Pride our error lies;
All quit their Sphere, and rush into the Skies.
Pride still is aiming at the blest Abodes,
Men would be Angels, Angels would be Gods.
Aspiring to be Gods if Angels fell,
Aspiring to be Angels, Men rebell;
And who but wishes to invert the Laws
Of ORDER, sins against th' Eternal Cause.

Ask for what end the Heav'nly Bodies shine?
Earth for whose use? Pride answers, 'Tis for mine.
For me ~~young~~ kind Nature ~~does~~ wakes her ~~vernal~~ genial Pow'r,
Suckles each Herb, and ~~pencils~~ spreads out ev'ry Flow'r:
Annual for me, the Grape, the Rose renew
The juice nectareous and the balmy dew:
For me, the Mine a thousand treasures brings;
For me, Health gushes from a thousand Springs:

Go wiser Thou, and in thy Scale of Sense
Weigh thy Opinion against Providence;
Call Imperfection what we fancy such;
Pronounce He acts too little or too much;
Destroy all Creatures for thy Sport or Gust,
Yet, if unhappy, think 'tis he's unjust;
Snatch from his hand the Balance and the Rod;
Re-judge his Justice; be the God of God!

In <u>Pride</u>, my Friend, in <u>Pride</u> our error lies;
All quit their Sphere, and rush into the Skies.
Pride still is aiming at the blest Abodes,
Men would be Angels, Angels would be Gods.
Aspiring to be Gods if Angels fell,
Aspiring to be Angels, Men rebell;
And who but wishes to invert the Laws
Of ORDER, sins against th' Eternal Cause.

Ask for what end the Heav'nly Bodies shine?
Earth for whose use? Pride answers, 'Tis for me.
For me ~~young~~ kind Nature ~~decks~~ wakes her ~~vernal~~ genial Pow'r,
Suckles each Herb, and ~~pencils~~ spreads out ev'ry Flow'r:
Annual for me, the Grape, the Rose renew
The juice nectareous and the balmy dew:
For me, the Mine a thousand treasures brings;
For me, Health gushes from a thousand Springs:

Seas roll to waft me, Suns to light me rise,
My Footstool Earth, my Canopy the Skies.

But errs not Nature from this gracious end,
From burning Suns when livid Deaths descend,
When Earth-quakes swallow, or wn Tempests sweep,
Towns to one Grave, and Nations to the Deep?
Blame we for this the ~~dread~~ wise Almighty Cause?
No ('tis reply'd) he acts by Gen'ral Laws,
Th' Exceptions few, some Change since all began,
And what created, perfect? — Why then Man?
If the great End be Human Happiness,
And Nature Deviates, how can Man do less?
Nature as much a constant course requires
Of Show'rs and Sunshine, as of Man's Desires;
As much eternal Spring and cloudless Skies,
As Man for ever temp'rate, calm, and wise.
If Plagues and Tempests break not Heav'ns design,
Why then a Borgia, or a Catiline?
Pride from Pride our very reas'ning springs,
~~From whence all Physical or Moral Ill?~~
Account for moral as for nat'ral ~~things~~:
~~Yet Nature wandring from th' Eternal Will.~~
Why charge we ~~here our Maker, there~~ Heav'n in those, in these acquit?
In both, to reason right is to submit.

Better

Seas roll to waft me, Suns to light me rise,
My Footstool Earth, my Canopy the Skies.
    But errs not Nature from this gracious end,
From burning Suns when livid Deaths descend,
When Earth-quakes swallow, or w^{n} Tempests sweep,
Towns to one Grave, and Nations to the Deep?
wise
Blame we for this the ~~dread~~ Almighty Cause?
No ('tis reply'd) he acts by Gen'ral Laws,
Th' Exceptions few, some Change since all began,
And what created, perfect? -- Why then Man?
If the great End be Human Happiness,
And Nature deviates, how can Man do less?
Nature as much a constant course requires
Of Show'rs and Sunshine, as of Man's Desires;
As much eternal Spring and cloudless Skies,
As Man for ever temp'rate, calm, and wise.
If Plagues and Tempests break not Heav'ns design,
Why then a Borgia, or a Catiline?
    Pride, from Pride, our very reas'ning springs,
From ^ ~~whence all Physical or Moral Ill?~~
    Account for moral as for nat'ral things
'~~Tis Nature wand'ring from th' Eternal Will~~.
Heav'n in those, in these
Why charge we ~~here our Maker, there~~ acquit?
^
In both, to reason right is to submit.

Better

8

[Better for Us, perhaps, it might appear,
Were there all Harmony, all Virtue here;
That never Air or Ocean felt the Wind;
That never Passion discompos'd the Mind:
But All subsists by Elemental Strife,
And Passions are the Elements of Life.
The Gen'ral ORDER, since the Whole began,
Is kept in Nature, and is kept in Man.

What would this Man? now upward will he soar,
And little less than Angel, would be more:
Now looking downward, just as griev'd appears
To want the ~~Brawn~~ strength of Bulls, the Fur of Bears.
Made for his use all Creatures if he call,
Say what their use, had he the Pow'rs of all?
Nature to each, without profusion kind,
The proper Organs, proper Pow'rs assign'd;
Each seeming Want compensated of course,
Here due degrees of Swiftness, there of Force:
Each Beast, each Insect, happy as it can,
Is Heav'n unkind to nothing but to Man?
So justly all proportion'd to each State;
Nothing to add, and nothing to abate;
Shall Man, shall reasonable Man alone,
Be, or endow'd with all, or pleas'd with none?

Be-

[Better for Us, perhaps, it might appear,
Were there all Harmony, all Virtue here;
That never Air or Ocean felt the Wind;
That never Passion discompos'd the Mind:
But All subsists by Elemental Strife,
And Passions are the Elements of Life.
The Gen'ral ORDER, since the Whole began,
Is kept in Nature, and is kept in Man.

What would this Man? now upward will he soar,
And little less than Angel, would be more:
Now looking downward, just as griev'd appears
To want the ~~Brawn~~ Strength of Bulls, the Fur of Bears.
Made for his use all Creatures if he call,
Say what their use, had he the Pow'rs of all?
Nature to each, without profusion kind,
The proper Organs, proper Pow'rs assign'd;
Each seeming Want compensated of course,
Here due degrees of Swiftness, there of Force:
Each Beast, each Insect, happy as it can,
Is Heav'n unkind to nothing but to Man?
So justly all proportion'd to each State;
Nothing to add, and nothing to abate;
Shall Man, shall reasonable Man alone,
Be, or endow'd with all, or pleas'd with none?

Be-

Thro gen'ral Life, behold the

9

[Behold ~~thro' all a gradual~~ Scale arise,
Of sensual, and of mental Faculties!
what vary'd
Vast Range of Sence! from Man's imperial Race,
To the green Myriads in the peopled Grass.
What Modes of Sight, betwixt ~~ye Lynxes Ray~~ each wide Extream,
The Mole's dim Curtain and the Lynx's Beam; ~~ye Day~~
Of Scent, the headlong Lioness
~~Degrees of Scent, the vulgar Brute~~ between, + Chesseld.
And Hound sagacious on the tainted Green;
Of Hearing, from the Life that fills the Flood,
To that which warbles ~~thro'~~ in the vernal Wood.
In the nice Bee, what Sense so subtly true
From pois'nous herbs extracts the healing dew:
The Spider's Touch, how exquisitely fine,
Feels at each thread, and lives along the line.
How Instinct varies; what the Hog may want
Compar'd with thine, half-reas'ning Elephant:
Twixt that, and Reason, what a nice Barrier,
For ever sep'rate, yet for ever near:
Remembrance and Reflection, how ally'd,
What thin partitions Sense from Thought divide;
And middle Natures, how they long to joyn,
Yet never pass th' insuperable Line!
Without this just Gradation, could they be
Subjected these to those, or all to thee?
The Pow'rs of all subdu'd by thee alone,
Is not thy Reason all those pow'rs in one?

The

Thro gen'ral Life behold the
~~Behold thro' all a gradual~~ Scale arise,
Of sensual, and of mental Faculties!

What varyd
Vast Range of <u>Sence</u>! from Man's imperial Race,
To the green Myriads in the peopled Grass,

~~ye Lynxes Ray~~
What Modes of sight, betwixt each wide Extream,

& ~~<yr> Day~~
The Mole's dim Curtain and the Lynx's Beam;

Of scent, the headlong Lioness
~~Degrees of Scent, the vulgar Brute~~ between,

~~certain~~ ~~o'er~~
And Hound sagacious on the tainted Green;
Of Hearing, from the Life that fills the Flood,

in
To that which warbles ~~thro'~~ the vernal Wood.
In the nice Bee, what Sense so subtly true
From pois'nous herbs extracts the healing dew:
The Spider's Touch, how exquisitely fine,
Feels at each thread, and lives along the line.
How <u>Instinct</u> varies; what the Hog may want
Compar'd with thine, half-reas'ning Elephant:
'Twixt that, and <u>Reason</u>, what a nice Barrier,
For ever sep'rate, yet for ever near:
Remembrance and Reflection, how ally'd,
What thin partitions Sense from Thought divide;
And middle Natures, how they long to joyn,
Yet never pass the insuperable Line!
Without this just Gradation, could they be
Subjected these to those, or all to thee?
The Pow'rs of all subdu'd by thee alone,
Is not thy Reason all those pow'rs in one?

The

10

The Bliss of Man (could Pride that blessing find,)
Is not to know, or think, beyond Mankind,
No self-confounding Faculties to share,
No Senses stronger than his brain can bear.
Why has not Man a microscopic Eye?
For this plain reason, Man is not a Fly:
What the advantage, if his finer eyes
Study a Mite, not comprehend the Skies?
His Touch if tremblingly alive all o'er,
To smart, and agonize at ev'ry Pore?
Or quick Effluvia darting thro' his brain,
Dye of a Rose in Aromatic pain?
If Nature thunder'd in his opening ears,
And stunn'd him with the Music of the Spheres,
How would he wish that Heav'n had left him still
The whispring Zephyr and the purling Rill?
Who finds not Providence all-good and wise,
Alike in what it gives and what denies.

See! thro' this Air, this Ocean, and this Earth,
All Matter quick, and bursting into Birth.
Above how high progressive Life may go!
Around how wide! how deep extend below!
Vast Chain of Being, which from God began,
Ethereal Essence, Spirit, Substance, Man,

Beast

<a>
The Bliss of Man (could Pride the blessing find,)
Is, not to know, or think, beyond Mankind,
No self-confounding Faculties to share,
No Senses stronger than his brain can bear.
Why has not Man a microscopic Eye?
For this plain reason, Man is not a Fly:
What the advantage, if his finer eyes
Study a Mite, not comprehend the Skies?
His Touch if tremblingly alive all o'er,
To smart, and agonize at ev'ry Pore?
Or quick Effluvia darting thro' his brain,
Dye of a Rose in Aromatic pain?
If Nature thunder'd in his opening ears,
And stunned him with the Music of the Spheres,
How would he wish that Heav'n had left him still
The whisp'ring Zephyr and the purling Rill?
Who finds not Providence all-good and wise,
Alike in what it gives and what denies.

See! thro' this Air, this Ocean, and this Earth,
All Matter quick, and bursting into Birth.
Above how high progressive Life may go!
Around how wide! how deep extend below!
Vast Chain of Being, which from God began,
Ethereal Essence, Spirit, Substance, Man,

Beast

Beast, Bird, Fish, Insect: what no Eye can see,
No Glass can reach! From Infinite to Thee!
From Thee to Nothing! — On Superior Pow'rs
Were we to press, inferior might on ours;
Or in the full Creation leave a Void,
Where one step broken, the great Scale's destroy'd:
From Nature's Chain whatever Link you strike,
Tenth, or ten thousandth, breaks the Chain alike.

And if each System in Gradation roll,
Alike essential to th' Amazing Whole;
The least Confusion but in one, not all
That System only, but the Whole must fall.
All this dread Order, shall it break? — For thee?
Vile Worm! — Oh Madness! Pride! Impiety!
3 Just as absurd, for any Part to claim.
To stand another, in this genral Frame;
1. What
As if the Foot, ordain'd the dust to tread,
Or Hand to toil, aspir'd to be the Head?
2 What
As if that Head, the eye or ear repin'd
To serve mere Engines to the ruling Mind?
4 Just as absurd, to mourn the Tasks or Pains
The great directing Mind of All ordains.

All are but Parts of one stupendous Whole,
Whose Body Nature is, and God the Soul:

Va-

Beast, Bird, Fish, Insect: what no Eye can see,
No Glass can reach! From Infinite to Thee!
From Thee to Nothing! - On Superior Pow'rs
Were we to press, inferior might on ours;
Or in the full Creation leave a Void,
Where one step broken, the great Scale's destroy'd:
From Nature's Chain whatever Link you strike,
Tenth, or ten thousandth, breaks the Chain alike.

And if each System in Gradation roll,
Alike essential to th' Amazing Whole;
The least Confusion but in one, not all
That System only, but the Whole must fall.
All this dread Order, shall it break? -- For Thee?
Vile Worm! -- Oh Madness! Pride! Impiety!
3 Just as absurd, for any Part to claim
To stand another, in this gen'ral Frame;
1. What
As if the Foot, ordain'd the dust to tread,
Or Hand to toil, aspir'd to be the Head?
2 What e
As if that Head, the eye or ear repin'd
To serve mere Engines to the ruling Mind?
4 Just as absurd, to mourn the Tasks or Pains
The great,directing Mind of All ordains.

All are but Parts of one stupendous Whole,
Whose Body Nature is, and God the Soul:

Va-

Vary'd thro' all, and yet in all the same;
Pow'rful in Earth, as in th' Æthereal Frame,
Warms in the Sun, refreshes in the Breeze,
Glows in the Stars, and blossomes in the Trees;
Lives thro' all Life, extends thro' all Extent,
Spreads un-divided, operates un-spent;
Breathes in our Soul, informs our mortal part,
As full, as perfect, in a Hair as Heart;
As full, as perfect, in vile Man that mourns,
As the rapt Seraphim that sings and burns;
To ^him^ this no high, no low, no great, no small,
It ^He^ fills, ^he^ it bounds, connects, and equals All.

Cease then, nor Order Imperfection name;
Our proper Bliss depends on what we blame.
Know thy own Point: this just, this kind degree
Of Blindness, Weakness, Heav'n bestows on thee.
Submit! in this, or any other Sphere,
Secure to be as blest as thou canst bear.
All Nature is but Art unknown to thee;
All Chance, Direction which thou canst not see;
All Discord, Harmony not understood; All partial Evill Universal Good:
And spite of Pride, and in thy Reason's spite,
One Truth is clear; Whatever Is, is Right.

Vary'd thro' all, and yet in all the same;
Pow'rful in Earth, as in th' AEthereal Frame,
Warms in the Sun, refreshes in the Breeze,
Glows in the Stars, and blossomes in the Trees;
Lives thro' all Life, extends thro' all Extent,
Spreads un-divided, operates un-spent;
Breathes in our Soul, informs our mortal part,
As full, as perfect, in a Hair as Heart;
As full, as perfect, in vile Man that mourns,
As the rapt Seraphim that sings and burns;
him
To this no high, no low, no great, no small,
He he
It fills, it bounds, connects, and equals All.

Cease, then, nor Order Imperfection name;
Our proper Bliss depends on what we blame.
Know thy own Point: this just, this kind degree
Of Blindness, Weakness, Heav'n bestows on thee.
Submit! in this, or any other Sphere,
Secure to be as blest as thou can'st bear.
All Nature is but Art unknown to thee;
All Chance, Direction which thou can'st not see;
All Discord, Harmony not understood; All partial Evill Universal Good:
And spite of Pride, and in thy Reason's spite,
One Truth is clear; Whatever Is, is Right.

15

EPISTLE II.

COME then my *Friend*, my *Genius* come along!
Oh Master of the *Poet*, and the *Song*!
~~And~~ While the Muse, ~~transported, unconfin'd,~~
~~Soars to the Sky~~, ~~or stoops among Mankind~~;
Teach her like thee, thro' various Fortune wise,
With Dignity to fall, with Temper rise,
Form'd by thy Converse, steer ~~her easy~~ flight
From grave to gay, from ~~learned~~ to ~~polite~~;
~~Artful with grace, and Natural to please, with ease~~
~~Intent in Business, elegant in Ease~~!
[**St. John!** whose Love excus'd my labors past,
Mature's my present, ~~and direct~~ my last.

Incipit I
~~Learn~~ we ourselves, not God presume to scan, — Of Man, as an Individual.
~~But know~~, the Study of Mankind is *Man*;
[Plac'd on this Isthmus of a Middle State, — His Middle Nature
A Being darkly wise, and rudely great;

With

EPISTLE II

~~Incipit III.~~

Come then my Friend, my Genius Come along!

~~Dele~~

Oh Master of the Poet, and the Song!

& ~~now~~ now stoops, or now ascends
~~And~~ While the Muse, ~~transported, unconfin'd,~~
^

To man's low Passions or his glorious Ends
~~now~~
~~Soars to the Sky~~, ~~or stoops among Mankind~~;
^

me in Men and Nature
Teach her like thee, thro' various Fortune wise,

2 1 sink
With Dignity To fall, with Temper rise,

an equal
Form'd by thy Converse, steer ~~her easy~~ flight

2 1 profit delight
From grave to gay, from ~~learned~~ to ~~polite~~:

~~W^th Grace elabrate~~ |Correct with Spirit ~~&~~ Eloquent with Ease
~~or~~
~~Artful with Grace~~, ~~and~~ ~~Natural to please~~! ~~with ease~~

Intent to reason, or polite to please
~~Intent in Buis'ness, elegant in Ease!~~

~~Incipit III.~~

[St. John! whose Love excus'd my labors past,

& shall bound
Mature's my present, ~~and direct~~ my last.
^ warm

~~Incipit I~~
~~Incipit III~~.

Know
~~Learn~~ we ourselves, not God presume to scan,

Of Man, as an Individual

The only Science Convinc'd,
~~But know~~, the Study of Mankind is Man;

[Plac'd on this Isthmus of a Middle State,

His Middle Nature

A Being darkly wise, and rudely great;

With

16

His Powers. and Imperfections.

With too much Knowledge for the Sceptic side,
~~And~~ [With] too much Weakness for a Stoic's Pride,
He hangs between, ~~uncertain where to~~ [in doubt to act or] rest,
Whether to deem himself a [part of] God or Beast;
Whether his Mind, or Body to prefer,
Born but to die, and reas'ning but to err;
Alike in Ignorance, his Reason such,
~~Who thinks~~ [whether he thinks] too little, or ~~who thinks too much~~ [or too much]:
Chaos of Thought and Passion, all confus'd,
Still by himself abus'd and dis-abus'd:
Created half to rise, and half to fall;
Great Lord of all things, yet a prey to all;
Sole Judge of Truth, in endless error hurl'd;
The Glory, Jest, and Riddle of the World!

Go—

[Come then my friend be]
For more Perfection than this State can bear
postpone In vain we sigh: Heav'n made us as we are.
~~At~~ [More] wisely, sure, a modest Ape might aim
To be like Man, whose faculties and frame
He sees, he feels; ~~as~~ [than] you or I to be
An Angel Thing we neither know nor see:
these Observe his Love of tricks, his laughing face,
(An elder Brother too, to human Race)
to "It must be so - why else have I a Sense
"Of more-than-monkey Charms and Excellence?
the "Why else to walk on two have I essay'd?
"And why this ardent Longing for a Maid?

So

His Powers and Imperfections.

With too much Knowledge for the Sceptic side,

With
~~And~~ too much Weakness for a Stoic's Pride,

in doubt to act or
He hangs between, ~~uncertain where to~~ rest,

part of
<u>Whether</u> to deem himself a ^ God or Beast;

In doubt
Whether his Mind, or Body to prefer,

~~He's born~~ ~~that~~
Born but to die, and reas'ning but to err;

Alike in Ignorance, his Reason such,

Whether he thinks or too much.
~~Who thinks~~ too little, ~~or who thinks too much~~:

Chaos of Thought and Passion, all confus'd,

Still by himself abus'd and dis-abus'd:

Created half to rise, and half to fall;

Great Lord of all things, yet a prey to all;

Sole Judge of Truth, in endless error hurl'd;

The Glory, Jest, and Riddle of the World!
Go--
Come then my friend &c.

For more Perfection than this State can bear

postpone — In vain we sigh: Heav'n made us as we are.

More
~~As~~ wisely, sure, a modest Ape might aim

To be like Man, whose faculties and frame

than
all — δ He sees, he feels; ~~as~~ you or I to be

An Angel Thing we neither know nor see:

elbows
how near he edges on our race, What human tricks! how risible of face!
Observe his Love of tricks, his laughing face,
these — ^

(An elder Brother too, to human Race)

"It must be so--why else have I a Sense
to
"Of more-than-monkey Charms and Excellence?

the — "[2]Why else [1]To walk on two [3]have I essay'd?

"And why this ardent Longing for a Maid?

So

Epis-tle on the world. His Capacity, how Limited. the Use & Extent of Learning

So Pug might plead, and call his Gods unkind,
Till set on-end, and marry'd to his mind.

(4) Go reas'ning ~~Man~~ thing! assume the Doctor's Chair,
As Plato ~~deep~~ high, ~~as Seneca~~ Pythagoras severe, in
Fix Moral Fitness, give ~~all Others~~ th' almighty rule;
Then drop into thyself, and be a Fool.

(1.) ~~Wouldst thou be more?~~ Go reas'ning Man! go mount where Science guides,
Go measure Earth, weigh Air, and state the Tydes,
Instruct the Planets in what Orbs to run,
Correct old Time, and regulate the Sun.

(3) Angels themselves, I grant it; when they saw
One mighty Man unfold all Nature's Law,
Admir'd an Angel in a human Shape,
And show'd a Newton, as we show an Ape.

(2) Then thou ~~who tellst~~ who tellst each Planet where to roll,
Describe, or fix, one movement of thy Soul?
Who mark'st their Points, to rise & to descend,
~~Knows he his~~ Explain thy own Beginning, or ~~his~~ thy End?
Or more of God, or more of Man can find,
Than this, that one is good, & one is blind?

Alas what wonder! Man's thy superior Part
There mounts uncheck'd, and soars from Art to Art:
But when his thy own great work is but begun,
What Reason weaves, by Passion is undone.

Two

Some angel thus, I grant it, when he saw
A wondring man unfold
Admir'd an Angel — & show'd a Newton

Or tread th' eternal Round their Followers trod,
Or giddy, talk of imitating God;
So Eastern madmen in a Circle run
To turn their brains to imitate the Sun.

alas! wt wonder?

Teach of Moral Fitness, fix thy maker's unerring Rule, then
Then drop into thy self
& be a Fool.

Go reas'ning thing! assume

Then thou —

Angels —

Uncheck'd, man's ... thy intellectual pt
to whim to whim ... from art to art

Epis- | So Pug might plead, and call his Gods unkind,

Till set on-end, and marry'd to his mind. [Some Angel thus, I grant it, when he saw

ape ~~<Thing>go mount where Science~~ A wondrous Man unfold

tle (4 Go reas'ning ~~Man!~~ assume the Doctor's Chair,

Admird an Angel -- & showd a Newton

high, Pythagoras

As Plato ~~deep, as Seneca~~ severe; Or tread th' Eternal Round their Follow'rs trod,

^

~~and to God give~~

on Fix Moral Fitness, give ~~all others~~ rule; proudly rave

th' almighty & giddy, talk of Imitating God;

Then drop into thyself, and be a Fool. So Eastern Madmen in a Circle run

& turn their brains to imitate the Sun.

Teach

of Moral Fitness, fix thy

Alas! w[t] wonder?

makers

unerring Rule; <then>

Then drop into Thy self

& be a fool.

[Or tread y[e] Eternal &c

--World. Go reas'ning Man!

His Capacity, (1.)~~Wouldst thou be more~~? go mount where Science guides,

how Limited. ^

Go measure Earth, weigh Air, and state the Tydes,

the Instruct the Planets in what Orbs to run,

Correct old Time, and regulate the Sun.

Then thou

(3) Angels themselves, I grant it, when they saw

Use One mighty Man unfold all Nature's Law,

Admir'd an Angel in a human Shape,

& And show'd a Newton, as we show an Ape. Thing

Go reas'ning ~~Man~~! assume

Then thou

Extent (2) ~~Can he~~ who tell'st each Planet where to roll,

Describe, or fix, one Movement of thy Soul?

of Who mark'st their Points, to rise & to descend,

Explain thy thy

~~Knows he his~~ own Beginning, or ~~his~~ End?

Angels—

Lear- δ | Or more of God, or more of Man can find,

| Than this, that one is good, and one is blind? ~~Angels~~

Uncheckd, may <mount> thy Intellectual p[t]

Frõ whim to whim <at> best frõ art to art

thy

ning. Alas what wonder? Man's superior Part

There mounts uncheckd, and soars from Art to Art:

thy

But when his own great work is but begun,

What Reason weaves, by Passion is undone.

Two

His Two Principles Self Love & Reason

Two Principles in human Nature reign;
Self-love, to urge; and Reason, to restrain;
Nor this a good, nor that a bad we call;
Each works its end, to move, or govern all: and
Of good and evil Gods, what frighted Fools,
Of good and evil Reason, puzled Schools
Deceiv'd, deceiving, taught, to These refer:
Know, both must operate, or both must err:
And to their proper Operation still
Ascribe all Good, to their improper, Ill.

Both necessary. [illegible]

Self-love, the Spring of Motion, acts the Soul;
Reason's comparing Balance rules the whole;
qu. si del. The primal Impulse, and controlling Weight,
To give the motion, and to regulate.
Man, but for that, no Action could attend,
And but for this, were active to no End:
Fix'd like a Plant, on his peculiar Spot,
To draw nutrition, propagate, and rot;
Or Meteor-like, flame lawless thro' the Void,
Destroying others, by himself destroy'd.

Why Self Love the stronger.

Most Strength, the moving Principle requires;
Active its Task, it prompts, impells, inspires.
Sedate and quiet the comparing lies,
Form'd but to check, delib'rate, and advise.
Self-love still stronger, as its Objects nigh,
Reason's at distance and in prospect lye;

This

His Two Principles Self Love & Reason

Two Principles in human Nature reign;
<u>Self-love</u>, to urge; and <u>Reason</u>, to restrain;
Nor this a good, nor that a bad we call;
Each works its end, to move, or govern all: And
Of good and evil Gods, what frighted Fools,
Of good and evil Reason, puzled Schools,
δ Deceiv'd, deceiving, taught, to These refer:
Know, both must operate, or both must err:
And to their proper Operation still
Ascribe all Good, to their improper, Ill.

Both necessary

Self-love, the Spring of Motion, acts the Soul;
Reason's comparing Balance ~~guides~~ rules the whole;
qu. si del. The primal Impulse, and controlling Weight,
To give the motion, and to regulate.
Man, but for that, no <u>Action</u> could attend,
And but for this, were active to no <u>End</u>:
Fix'd like a Plant, on his peculiar Spot,
To draw nutrition, propagate, and rot;
Or Meteor-like, flame lawless thro' the Void,
Destroying others, by himself destroy'd.

Why Self Love the Stronger

Most <u>Strength</u>, the moving Principle requires;
Active its Task, it prompts, impells, inspires.
Sedate and quiet the comparing lies,
Form'd but to check, delib'rate, and advise.
Self-love ~~yet~~ still stronger, as its Objects <u>nigh</u>,
Reason's ~~more~~ at dis~~t~~tance and in prospect lye;

This

That sees immediate Good, by present Sence,
Reason the future and the Consequence;
Thicker than Arguments, Temptations throng;
~~This grows~~ At best more watchful, this but that more strong. The action —

2 Let subtile Schoolmen teach these Friends to fight,
More studious to divide, than to unite,
And Grace & ~~Nature~~ Virtue, Sense & Reason split,
With all the ~~mad~~ wild rash Dexterity of Wit;) quære del.
Wits, just like Fools, at war about a Name,
Have full as oft no meaning, or the same.
~~Too nice distinctions honest Sense will shun;~~
~~Know, Pleasure, Good, and Happiness, are one.~~

Their End the same.

~~To this~~, Self-love and Reason ~~both~~ to one ~~Good~~ End aspire,
~~One~~ Pain their Aversion, ~~one is~~ Pleasure their Desire;
But greedy that its Object would devour,
This taste the Honey, and not wound the Flow'r. [Modes —
Pleasure, or wrong or rightly understood Our greatest Evil or our greatest Good.
The Action of the stronger to suspend,
1. Reason still use, to Reason still attend;
Attention Habit, and Experience, gains;
~~This~~ Each strengthens Reason, ~~that~~ Self-love restrains. [Let subtile —
~~Quær.~~ Quær. Each, or This & that?)

The Passions & their Use.

Modes of Self-love the Passions we may call;
'Tis real Good, or seeming, moves them all:
But since not ev'ry good we can divide,
And Reason bids us for our own provide;
Passions tho' ~~self-centred~~ selfish, if their means be fair,
List under Reason, and deserve her care;
Those that imparted, court a nobler aim,
Exalt their Kind, and take some Virtue's name.

19

That sees immediate Good, by present sence,

Reason the future and the Consequence;

Thicker than Arguments, Temptations throng;

this, but
~~This grows~~ At best more watchful,^ that more strong. The action—

2 Let subtile Schoolmen teach these Friends to fight,

More studious to divide, than to unite,

Virtue
And Grace & Nature, Sense & Reason split,

~~wild~~, rash
With all the ~~mad~~^dexterity of Wit; ~~qu. si del~~.

Wits, just like Fools, at war about a Name,

Have full as oft no meaning, or the same.

δ ~~Too nice distinctions honest Sense will shun~~;

~~Know, Pleasure, Good, and Happiness, are one~~:

End
to one ~~Good~~
Their End the same. ~~To this~~, Self-love and Reason ~~both~~^ aspire,

Pain Pleasure
~~One~~ their Aversion, ~~one is~~ their Desire;

But greedy that its Object would devour,

This taste the Honey, and not wound the Flow'r. [Modes—
Pleasure, or wrong or rightly understood Our greatest Evil or our greatest Good.

The Action of the Stronger to suspend,

1. Reason still use, to Reason still attend;

Attention Habit, and Experience, gains:

Each &
~~This~~ strengthens Reason, ~~that~~ Self-love restrains. [Let subtile--
Quaer.
Each, or This & that?)

The Passions and their Use. Modes of Self-love the Passions we may call;

'Tis real Good, or seeming, moves them all:

But since not ev'ry good, we can divide,

And Reason bids us for our own provide;

tho' selfish
Passions ~~self-centred~~, if their Means be fair,

List under Reason, and deserve her care;

Those that imparted, court a nobler aim,

Exalt their Kind, and take some Virtue's name.

Pleasures are ever in our hands or eyes,
And when in Act they cease, in Prospect rise;
Present to grasp, and future still to find,
The whole Employ of Body and of mind.
All spread their charms, but charm not all alike;
On diff'rent Senses diff'rent Objects strike,
Hence diff'rent Passions
~~Stronger or weaker,~~ more or less inflame,
As strong or weak the
~~Proportion'd to each~~ Organs of the Frame:
And hence, one master Passion in the breast
~~Nor here internal Faculties controul,~~
first
~~Nor Soul on Body acts, but that on~~ Soul.
~~& hence~~
in the breast
~~One Master Passion, hence, in ev'ry breast~~
Like Aaron's Serpent, swallows up the rest.
~~Reason, our Judge, here sits but to persuade~~
del The Choice we make, or justify it, made;
Proud of her easy Conquest all along,
While she ~~but~~ removes ~~a~~ weak ~~one for a~~ Passions for the Strong:
So when small Humours gather to a Gout,
~~The Doctor fancies he has driv'n 'em out.~~

man
As ~~each~~ perhaps, the moment of his breath
Receives the lurking Principle of Death,
The young Disease that must subdue at length
Grows with his growth, and strengthens with his strength;
his
So, cast and mingled with ~~our~~ very Frame,
The Mind's Disease, its ruling Passion came:
Each vital humor which should feed the whole,
and
Soon flows to this, in Body, ~~or~~ in Soul:

What

The Predominant Passion, and its Strength.

Pleasures are ever in our hands or eyes,

And when in Act they cease, in Prospect rise;

Present to grasp, and future still to find,

The whole Employ of Body and of Mind.

All spread their charms, but charm not all alike;

On diff'rent Senses diff'rent Objects strike,

Hence diff'rent Passions
~~Stronger or weaker~~, more or less inflame,

As strong or weak the s
~~Proportion'd to each~~ Organs of the Frame:

And hence one master Passion in the breast

qu. ~~Nor here internal Faculties controul,~~

δ

first
si del ~~Nor Soul on Body acts, but that on Soul.~~

~~& hence~~ in the breast
^ ~~One Master Passion, hence, in ev'ry breast~~

Like Aaron's Serpent, swallows up the rest:

~~Reason, our Judge, here sits but to persuade~~

The Choice we make, or justify it, made;

del Proud of her easy Conquest all along,

Passions for the
re
While she ~~but~~ moves ~~a~~ weak ~~one for a~~ ^ Strong:

So when small Humours gather to a Gout,

~~The Doctor fancies he has driv'n 'em out.~~

Man
As ~~each~~ perhaps, the moment of his breath

The Predominant Passion, and its Strength.

Receives the lurking Principle of Death,

The young Disease that must subdue at length

Grows with his growth, and strengthens with his strength;

~~in~~ his
So, cast and mingled with ~~our~~ very Frame,

The Mind's Disease, its <u>ruling</u> <u>Passion</u> came:

Each vital humour which should feed the <u>whole</u>;

and
Soon flows to <u>this</u>, in Body ~~or~~ in Soul:

What-

21

Whatever warms the heart, or fills the head;
As the Mind opens, and its functions spread,
Imagination plies her dang'rous art,
And pours it all upon the peccant part.

VIII Nature its Mother, Habit is its Nurse,
Wit, Spirit, Faculties, but make it worse;
Reason itself but gives it edge and pow'r,
As Heav'ns blest Beam turns Vinegar more sow'r;
We, wretched Subjects, tho' to lawful Sway,
In ~~that~~ this weak Queen some Fav'rite still obey.
Ah! if she lend not Arms, as well as Rules,
What can she more, than tell us we are Fools?
Teach us to mourn our Nature, not to mend,
A sharp Accuser, but a helpless Friend:
Or, from a Judge, turn Pleader, to persuade The choice we make, or justify it, made;

Its Necessity, directing Men to different purposes.

Yes: Nature's Road must ever be preferr'd; Proud of ~~her~~ an easy conquest all along, ~~While~~ She, but removes weak Passions for the strong.
Reason is here no Guide, but still a Guard;
'Tis hers to rectify, not overthrow,
And treat this Passion more as Friend than Foe.
So when small humors gather ~~the~~ to a Gout,
The Doctor fancies he has driv'n 'em out.
A mightier Pow'r the strong Direction sends,
And sev'ral Men impells to sev'ral Ends;
Like varying Winds, by other Passions tost,
This drives them constant to a certain Coast.
Let Pow'r or Knowledge, Gold or Glory, please,
Or (oft more strong than all) the Love of Ease;
Thro' Life 'tis follow'd, ev'n at Life's Expence;
The Merchant's Toil, the Sage's Indolence,

The

Whatever warms the heart, or fills the head;
As the Mind opens, and its functions spread,
Imagination plies her dang'rous art,
And pours it all upon the peccant part.
<   > Nature its Mother, Habit is its Nurse,
Wit, Spirit, Faculties, but make it worse;
Reason itself but gives it edge and pow'r,
As Heav'ns blest Beam turns Vinegar more sow'r;
We, wretched Subjects, tho' to lawful sway,
In ~~that~~ this weak Queen some Fav'rite still obey.
Ah! if she lend not Arms, as well as Rules,
What can she more, than tell us we are Fools?
Teach us to mourn our Nature, not to mend,
A sharp Accuser, but a helpless Friend:
Or, from a Judge, turn Pleader, to persuade The choice we make, or justify it, made;
Proud of ~~her~~ an easy Conque<st> all along,
While She but removes weak Passions for the strong;
So when small humours gathe[r ~~The~~ to a Gout,
The Doctor fancies he has driv'n 'em out.

Its Necessity, directing Men to different purposes.

^ [Yes: Nature's Road must ever be preferr'd;
Reason is here no Guide, but still a Guard;
'Tis hers to rectify, not overthrow,
And treat this Passion more as Friend than Foe.
A mightier Pow'r the strong Direction sends,
And sev'ral Men impells to sev'ral Ends;
Like varying Winds, by other Passions tost,
This drives them constant to a certain Coast.
Let Pow'r or Knowledge, Gold or Glory, please,
Or (oft more strong than all) the Love of Ease;
Thro' life 'tis follow'd, ev'n at Life's Expence;
The Merchant's Toil, the Sage's Indolence,

The

22

The Monk's Humility, the Hero's Pride,
and All, all alike, find Reason on their side.
Th' Eternal Art, ~~that mingles~~ still educing Good ~~with~~ from Ill,
~~Even and~~ Grafts on this Passion ~~grafts our~~ our best Principle.
'Tis thus, the Mercury of Man is fix'd;
Strong grows the Virtue with his Nature mix'd;
The Dross cements what else were too refin'd,
And in one Int'rest Body acts with Mind.
[As Fruits ungrateful to the Planter's care,
On Savage Stocks inserted learn to bear;
~~In passive Apathy (the Stoic's Boast)~~ &c. page 23
~~to the whole Balance of the Mind;~~
~~The noblest Fruits the Planters hope may mock,~~
~~Which thrive, inserted in the Savage Stock:~~
The surest Virtues thus from ~~our~~ Passions shoot,
Wild Nature's Vigor working at the root.
What crops of Wit and Honesty appear ~~we bear~~,
From Spleen, from ~~Anger~~ Obstinacy, Hate, or ~~Spleen, and~~ Fear?
See Anger, Zeal and Fortitude ~~Vain-Glory Courage, Justice can~~ supply;
Ev'n Av'rice Prudence; Sloth, Philosophy;
Lust, thro' some certain Strainers well refin'd,
Is gentle Love, and charms all Womankind;
Envy, to which th' ignoble mind's a slave, ~~in Criticks and old Maids the Devil~~,
Is Emulation in the Learn'd or Brave ~~and Civil~~;
Nor Virtue, male or female, can we name,
But what or grows on Pride, or grows on Shame.
How oft with Passion Virtue points her charms! Thus
Then shines the Hero, then the Beauty warms:
Peleus' great Son, or Brutus, who had known,
Had Lucrece been a Whore, or Helen none?

Its Providential Use, to fix our Principle,

And secure our Virtue.

Each

The Monk's Humility, the Hero's Pride,

and
All, all alike, find Reason on their side.

~~still~~ educing from
Th' Eternal Art, ~~that mingles~~ Good ~~with~~ Ill,

~~and~~ Grafts our best
~~Ev'n~~ ^ on this Passion ~~grafts~~ ^ ~~our~~ Principle.

Its Providential Use, to fix our Principle,

'Tis thus, the Mercury of Man is fix'd;

Strong grows the Virtue with his Nature mix'd;

The Dross cements what else were too refin'd,

And in one Int'rest Body acts with Mind.

[As Fruits ungrateful to the Planter's care,

And secure our Virtue.

~~In passive Apathy (the Stoic's Boast) &c. page 23~~

On Savage Stocks inserted learn to bear;

~~to the words - Balance of the Mind~~
^ ^

~~may~~
δ ~~The noblest Fruits the Planters hope mock~~,

~~Which thrive, inserted in the Savage Stock~~:

thus
The surest Virtues ^ from ~~our~~ Passions shoot,

Wild Nature's Vigor working at the root.

appear
What crops of Wit and Honesty ~~we bear~~ ^,

Spleen, from Hate, or
From ~~Anger~~, ^ Obstinacy, ~~Spleen, and~~ Fear?

See Anger Zeal and Fortitude
~~Vain-Glory Courage, Justice can~~ supply;

Ev'n Av'rice Prudence; Sloth, Philosophy;

δ Lust, thro' some certain Strainers well refin'd,

Is gentle Love, and charms all Womankind;

to which th' ignoble mind's a Slave,
Envy, ~~in Criticks and old Maids the Devil~~,

or Brave
Is Emulation in the Learn'd ~~and Civil~~;

Nor Virtue, male or female, can we name,

But what or grows on Pride, or grows on Shame.

Thus
del How oft with Passion Virtue points her charms!

Then shines the Hero, then the Beauty warms:

Peleus' great Son, or Brutus, who had known,

Had Lucrece been a Whore, or Helen none?

~~Each~~

23

~~Those that imparted, court a nobler aim,~~
~~Exalt their Kind, and take fair Virtue's name.~~

In lazy ~~passive~~ Apathy let ~~the~~ Stoick's Boast
Their ~~If~~ Virtue fix'd; 'tis fix'd as in ~~by~~ a Frost;
Contracted all, retiring to ~~on~~ the breast:
But Strength of Mind is Exercise, not Rest:
The rising Tempest puts in act the Soul,
Parts it may ravage, but preserves the Whole.
On Life's vast Ocean diversely we sail,
Reason the Card, but Passion is the Gale;
del A tedious Voyage! where how useless lies
The Compass, if no pow'rful Gust arise?

Nor God alone in the still Calm we find;
He mounts the Storm, and walks upon the Wind.

Passions, like Elements, tho' born to fight,
Yet mix'd and soften'd, in His Work unite:
These, 'tis enough to temper and employ;
But what composes Man, can Man destroy?
Suffice that Reason keep to ~~follow~~ Nature's road,
Subject, compound them, follow her, & ~~and imitate the~~ God.
del The soft, reward the Virtuous, or invite;
The fierce, the Vicious punish, or affright.
Love, Hope, and Joy, fair Pleasure's smiling Train,
Hate, ~~Sadness~~, Fear, and Grief, the Family of Pain;
These mix'd with art, and to due bounds confin'd,
Make, and maintain, the Balance of the Mind:
The Lights & Shades, whose well accorded ~~to harmonize whose~~ strife
Gives all the Strength and Colour of our Life.

~~Those that imparted, court a nobler aim,~~
~~Exalt their Kind, and take some Virtue's name.~~

lazy let
In ~~passive~~ Apathy ~~(the~~ Stoick's Boast~~)~~
Their in
~~If~~ ^ Virtue fix'd; 'tis fix'd as ~~by~~ a Frost,
to
Contracted all, retiring ~~in~~ the breast:
But Strength of Mind is Exercise, not Rest:
The rising Tempest puts in act the Soul,
Parts it may ravage, but preserves the Whole.
On Life's vast Ocean diversely we sail,
Reason the Card, but Passion is the Gale;
del | A tedious Voyage! where how useless lies
| The Compass, if no pow'rful Gust arise?
W Nor God alone in the still Calm we find;
He mounts the Storm, and walks upon the Wind.
Passions, like Elements, tho' born to fight,
Yet mix'd and soften'd, in His Work unite:
These, 'tis enough to temper and employ,
But what composes Man, can Man destroy?
keep to
Suffice that Reason ~~follow~~ Nature's road,
them ~~follow that~~ | follow her, | &
Subject, compound ^ ~~and imitate the~~ ^ God.
del | The soft, reward the Virtuous, or invite;
| The fierce, the Vicious punish, or affright:
[Love, Hope, and Joy, fair Pleasure's smiling Train,
and Grief,
Hate, ~~Sadness~~, Fear, ^ the Family of Pain;
These mix'd with art, and to due bounds confin'd,
Make, and maintain, the Balance of the Mind:
~~Those~~ whose well-accorded
The Lights & Shades, ~~to harmonize whose~~ strife
Gives all the Strength and Colour of our Life.

Thus Nature gives us (let it check our pride)
24 The Virtue nearest to our Vice allyd:

Reason the Byas turns to Good from Ill,
And Nero reigns a Titus, if he will.
The fiery Soul abhorr'd in Catiline,
In Decius charms, in Curtius is divine.
The same Ambition can destroy or save,
And makes a Patriot, as it makes a Knave.
This Light & Darkness, in our Chaos joind, Divide, before the Genius of ye mind.
Let Extremes in Nature equal Ends produce,
Extremes in man concur to General
In Man, they join to some mysterious Use;
Tho' oft so mixd, the diffrence is too nice
Where ends the Virtue, or begins the Vice;
Now this, now that, bound invades,
As in some well-wrought Picture, Lights & Shades.

Fools! who from hence into the notion fall,
That Vice or Virtue there is none at all.
If white and Black blend, soften, and unite
A thousand ways, is there no Black or White?
[Ask your own Heart, & nothing is so plain; Tis to mistake them, costs the time & pain.
This Light and Darkness in thy Chaos joind
'Tis Reason's part to sep'rate in the mind:
To blind them well, and harmonize their strife
Makes all the Strength and Colour of thy Life.

Mere Nature gives us (let it check our Pride)
The Virtue nearest to our Vice allyd:
But Virtues opposite to make agree,
That, Reason, is thy Task, and worthy thee.

Hard

Virtue & Vice joind in our Mixd Nature

The Limits near, yet the Things seperate.

The God within our Mind

Dele in the first Edit.

Del

Thus Nature gives us (let it check our pride)

24. The Virtue nearest to our Vice ally'd;

This light & darkness in ~~thy~~ our
Chaos joind,

Divide before ye Genius of ye mind

Reason, the Byas turns ~~from~~

to Good ~~or~~ ~~from~~ Ill,

qu: ~~this~~
~~Alike the ruling~~ , ~~by the will~~
~~Each Passion thus, the Byass of our Mind~~,

~~The Byas may be turn'd to Good or Ill.~~
~~Is turn'd to Virtue, or to Vice inclin'd:~~ ^ ^

~~Check but its force, or compass, short of Ill~~;

& ~~may~~
~~And~~ ^Nero reigns ~~a~~ ^a Titus, if he will.

The fiery Soul abhorr'd in Catiline,

In Decius charms, in Curtius is divine.

The same Ambition can destroy or save,

And makes a Patriot, as it makes a Knave.

[This Light and Darkness in our Chaos joind, Divide, before the Genius of ye mind.

& ~~the godlike~~
'~~Tis Reasons task to sep'rate in the Mind.~~
~~Let~~ ~~Ask thy~~

~~To serve~~
What can divide? The God within our Mind.

Virtue & Vice joind in our Mixd Nature

Extremes in Nature equal Ends produce,

Extremes in Man concur to gen'ral
In Man, they join to some mysterious Use; | dele in the first Edit.

Tho' | &
~~And~~ oft so mix'd, the diff'rence is too nice |

Where ends the Virtue, or begins the Vice; | 2 in ye

Virtue & Vice each invade
Now this, now ~~that, the others~~ bound invades, | first

As in some well-wrought Picture, Light|s & Shade|s. | 1. Edit.

The Limits near, yet the things seperate.

Fools! who from hence into the notion fall,

That Vice or Virtue there is none at all.

If White and Black blend, soften, and unite

A thousand ways, is there no Black or White?

[Ask your own Heart, & nothing is so plain; 'Tis to mistake them, costs the time & pain.

^ ~~This Light and Darkness in thy Chaos join'd~~

'Tis Reason's part to sep'rate in the mind:

To blend them well, and harmonize their Strife

del Makes all the Strength and Colour of thy Life.

Mere Nature gives us (let it check our Pride)

The Virtue nearest to our Vice ally'd:

But Virtues opposite to make agree,

That, Reason, is thy Task, and worthy thee.

Vice, &c

[~~Vice glares at first~~

detested as a Whore

~~The Light & darkness in thy~~

~~Chaos joind~~

~~Divide before ye Genius of the~~

<till>
But ~~see n~~ ~~her~~ too often ~~Mind~~
she shocks no more

Hard

25

Hard task! cries Bibulus, and Reason weak!—
Make it a Point, dear Marquis, or a Pique:
Once, for a Whim, persuade yourself to pay
A Debt to Reason like a Debt at Play.
For right or wrong have Mortals sufferd more?—
del B for his Prince, or B for his Whore?
Whose Self-denials Nature most controul,
His, who would save a Sixpence, or his Soul?
Web for his health, a Chartreux for his Sin,
Contend they not which soonest shall grow thin?
What we resolve, we can; but here's the fault,
We ne'r resolve to do the thing we ought.

~~In every Vice, at first in some degree~~
~~We see some Virtue, or we think we see.~~
Vice is a Monster of so frightful mien,
As, to be hated, ~~needs but to be~~ seen;
~~Yet masqu'd so well with tempting Time & Place,~~
~~That but to pity her, is to~~ embrace.
A Cheat! a Whore! who starts not at the Name,
In all the Inns of Court, or Drury Lane?
~~B—t~~ but does bus'ness, ~~brings matters out,~~
~~Knows the Secret Charters~~ knows the Town,
~~Kind hearted Peter helps the Rich in want,~~
Nero's a Wag; ~~and Messaline Gallant~~
Of Gallantry, and Sutton of Neglect.
Where art thou, Vice? 'twas never yet agreed:
Ask where's the North? at York 'tis on the Tweed,

In

And Vice always
Odious in itself.

But where the point of Vice was ... agreed.
first Edit.
dele.

Hard task! cries Bibulus, and Reason weak!--
Make it a Point, dear Marquis, or a Pique:
Once, for a Whim, persuade yourself to pay
A debt to Reason like a debt at Play.
Resolve, be steddy-- it requires no
For right or wrong have Mortals sufferd more?
Country, y^n to serve y^r
del B for his Prince, or B for his Whore?
Whose Self-denials Nature most controul,
His, who would save a Sixpence, or his Soul?
Web for his health, a Chartreux for his Sin,
Contend they not which soonest shall grow thin?
What we resolve, we can; but here's the fault,
We ne'r resolve to do the thing we ought.

lesser Faults
In ~~ev'ry~~ Vice, at first, in some degree
~~We see some Virtue, or we think we see,~~

Our Vices first are Virtues in disguise, Wicked but by degrees or by surprize.

[Vice is a monster of so frightful mien,

And Vice always
Odious in itself.

~~Sure~~ ~~when she first is~~ stet
As to be hated, needs but to be seen;
^
seen
But ~~grown~~ too oft familiar with her face,
~~Yet masqu'd so well with tempting Time and Place,~~

We first endure, then pity, then
~~That but to pity, her, is to~~ embrace.
^ ^

~~Knave~~ ~~at first who hears how shocks~~
A Cheat! a Whore! who starts not at the Name,

Ev'n in
In all the Inns of Court, or Drury lane?

Rogues/B— Y— Spies but serves the Crown
~~B---t~~ but doe|s bus'ness, brings matters on,
Huggins
H- r- y the Court, ~~Bladen, & Janson only know~~
~~Sid has the Secret, Chartres~~ knows the Town,
^ ^
~~Kind-hearted Peter helps the Rich in want,~~

~~you~~
Faustina some suspect
Nero's a Wag; ~~and Messaline Gallant~~.
Of Gallantry, and Sutton of Neglect.
Where art thou, Vice? 'twas never yet agreed:
Ask where's the North? at York 'tis on the Tweed,

where
But ^ The Point of Vice was
But
~~Endure~~ next a ~~knavish wh~~ ne'r ~~agreed~~
her
& next a Harlot she who damns wine ^ agreed

one
~~Vice! no creature owns it in ye first degree~~
~~But thinks his neighbor farther gone y^n he~~

~~del in y^e~~ ~~Where art thou~~

In y^e
first Edit.
dele.

In

26

In Scotland at the Orcades, and there
At Greenland, Zembla, or the Lord knows where.
No creature owns it in the first degree,
But thinks his Neighbor farther gone than he.
The Col'nel swears, the Agent is a Dog;
The Scriv'ner vows, th' Attorney is a Rogue;
Against the Thief, th' Attorney loud inveighs,
For whose ten pound the County twenty pays;
The Thief damns Judges and the Knaves of State,
And dying mourns small Villains hang'd by great.
Ev'n those who dwell beneath her very Zone,
Or never feel the Rage, or never own;
What happier Natures shrink at with affright,
The hard Inhabitant contends is right.

Virtuous and vicious ev'ry man must be,
Few in th' Extreme, but all in the Degree.
The Rogue and Fool by fits is fair and wise,
And ev'n the best by fits what they despise.
'Tis but by Parts we follow Good or Ill,
For, Vice or Virtue, Self directs it still;
Each Individual seeks a sev'ral Goal:
But Heav'ns great View is One, and that the Whole.
That counter-works each Folly and Caprice;
That disappoints th' effect of ev'ry Vice;
That Virtues ends from Vanity can raise,
Which seeks no int'rest, no reward but Praise,
And builds on Wants and on Defects of mind,
The Joy, the Peace, the Glory of mankind.

The Ends of Providence and general Good answer'd in our Passions and very Imperfections

In Scotland at the Orcades, and there
At Greenland, Zembla, or the Lord knows where.
No creature owns it in the first degree,
But thinks his Neighbor farther gone than he.

~~that agents will be Dogs~~
The Col'nel swears, the Agent is a Dog;
~~s all are~~ s
The Scriv'ner vows, th' Attorney is a Rogue;
δ Against the Thief, th' Attorney loud inveighs,
For whose ten pound the County twenty pays;
The Thief damns Judges and the Knaves of State.
And dying mourns small Villains hang'd by great.

~~fix~~ beneath her
Ev'n those who dwell ~~in Vices's~~ very Zone,
Or never feel the Rage, or never own;
What happier Natures shrink at with affright,
The hard Inhabitant contends is right.

Virtuous and vicious ev'ry man must be,
Few in th' Extreme, but all in the Degree.
The Rogue and Fool by fits is fair and wise,
And ev'n the best by fits what they despise.

The Ends of Providence and ~~Human Happiness~~, general good answerd, in our Passions and very Imperfections

or
~~Some Virtue in a Lawyer has been known, Nay in a Minister, nay on a Throne.~~
'Tis but by <u>Parts</u> we follow Good or Ill,
For, Vice or Virtue, <u>Self</u> directs it still;
Each Individual seeks a sev'ral Goal:
But Heav'ns great View, is <u>One</u>, and that the <u>Whole</u>.

each
<u>That</u> counter-works ~~our~~ Folly, and Caprice;
disappoints th' Effect
<u>That</u> ~~draws a Virtue out~~ of ev'ry Vice; ~~& can from Vanity each Virtue~~
That ~~and~~ Virtues Ends from can raise,
~~All forms of Good thro'~~ Vanity ~~conveys~~,
Which seeks no int'rest, no reward but Praise,
stet δ And builds on <u>Wants</u> and on <u>Defects</u> of mind,
The Joy, the Peace, the Glory of mankind.

~~Each~~

2
What See
~~The~~ happy
+ How useful to different Orders of Men ~~That~~ ~~proper~~
~~Each~~ Frailtys ~~wisely~~ to each Rank applyd;
Shame to the Virgin, to the Matron Pride,
~~= To Society~~ Fear to the Statesman, Rashness to the Chief,
To Kings, Presumption, and to Crowds Belief;
~~Bids~~ ~~in each~~ ~~want~~ ~~each Defect of mind~~
The Joy, the ~~Rest~~ Peace, the Glory, of Mankind,
See
~~Makes~~ some strange Comfort ev'ry State attend,
And Pride bestow'd on All, a common friend;
See
~~Bids~~ some new Passion with each Age arise,
~~Hope travell thro', nor quitt him when he dies.~~

~~Toy Indiv'd.~~
Behold
~~See first~~ the Child, by Nature's kindly Law,
Pleas'd with a Rattle, tickled with a Straw:
Some livelier Plaything gives his Youth delight,
A little louder, but as empty quite:
Scarfs, Garters, Gold, amuse his riper Stage;
And Beads and Pray'rbooks are the Toys of Age.
Blest with this Bauble still, as that before;
At last he sleeps, and all the care is o'er.

Till then, Opinion gilds with varying rays
Those painted Clouds that beautify ~~our~~ our Days;
~~+ And in every Part of Life. x~~ Void
Each want of Happiness by Hope supply'd,
~~Of Certainty by Faith~~ Vacuity of Sense by Pride;
These ~~still~~ build up ~~all that~~ ~~repair what Wisdom would~~ Knowledge can destroy;
In Folly's Cup still laughs the Bubble, Joy;
~~Life~~ One Prospect lost, another still ~~alter, every step~~ we gain,
~~And Nature gives no~~ And not a Vanity is given in vain;

Ev'n

~~How~~ 27

1
[To Society
Heav'n forming
~~Then~~ ~~Bless'd~~ ~~That~~ each on other to depend,
A Master, or a Servant, or a Friend,
~~Bids each on other for assistance call,~~
Till each ones weakness grows ye Strength of all.
Wants, Weakness, Passions, closer still allye
The common Int'rest, or endear the Tye:
To these, we owe true Friendship, Love sincere,
Each home-felt Joy that Life inherits here:
Yet from the same we learn, in its Decline,
Those Joys, those Loves, those Int'rests to resign,
Taught half by Reason, half by mere Decay,
To welcome Death, & calmly pass away.

~~[To the Individuals,~~ ~~in ev'ry State~~
~~See some strange Comfort ev'ry State attend:~~
~~And Pride bestow'd on all, a common friend;~~
[Whate'er the Passion, Knowledge, Fame, or Pelf,
Not one will change his Neighb^r with himself.
What partly pleases, totally will shock,
I question much if Toland would be Locke,
~~The~~ Nor Ross w^d be happy, nor Toland Locke
~~The Poor~~ happy, nature
The Learn'd are happy they so much explore;
The Fool is happy, that he knows no more;
The Rich are happy in the Plenty given;
The Poor contents him with the Care of heav'n.
See the blind Beggar dance, the Cripple sing,
The Sot a Hero, Lunatic a King,
See the Chymist happy in his golden views,
Paya in his madness, Welsted in his Muse.
~~Hope travels thro', nor quits them when he dies.~~
[In ev'ry State
Age of Life
See some strange Comfort ev'ry State attend,
And Pride bestow'd on all, a comon friend;
See Some strong Passion ~~each age~~ ev'ry age supply,
Hope travels thro', nor quits us w^n we die.
(omit Behold ye Child &c) Till then

[~~That~~ See
+ ~~See~~ happy
+ How useful ~~That proper~~
to different ~~Each~~ Frailties ~~wisely~~ to each Rank apply'd;
Orders of Men ^
Shame to the Virgin, to the Matron Pride,

+ ~~To Society~~ Fear to the Statesman, Rashness to the Chief,

To Kings, Presumption, and to Crowds Belief.

~~Bids <——> each on other for assistance call~~,

[~~and founded~~ ~~all on some~~
stet ~~Builds on each Want, and each Defect of Mind~~
^ ^
Peace
The Joy, the ~~Rest~~, the Glory, of Mankind.

See
Makes some strange Comfort ev'ry State attend,

δ And Pride bestow'd on All, a common friend;
^ ^
See
^ ~~Bids~~ some new Passion with each Age arise;

~~Hope travell thro', nor quitt him when he dies~~.
^ ^
^ ^ Behold
~~To ye Individ~~. ^ ~~See first~~ the Child, by Nature's lucky law,

Pleas'd with a Rattle, tickled with a Straw:

qu Some livelier Plaything gives his Youth delight.

si A little louder, but as empty quite:

del. Scarfs, Garters, Gold, amuse his riper Stage;

And Beads and Pray'rbooks are the Toys of Age.

Blest with this Bauble still, as that before;

At last he sleeps, and all the care is o'er.

Till then, Opinion gilds with varying rays

our
~~his~~
Those painted clouds that beautify ~~our~~ Days;

void
+~~And in eve-~~ Each want of Happiness by Hope supply'd,
~~ry Part of~~
~~Life~~. X— & each Vacuity
~~Of Certainty by Faith~~^ of Sense by Pride;

~~Time can e'er~~
build up all that Knowledge ~~present~~
can
These ~~still repair what Wisdom would~~ destroy,
2 ^ ^
In Folly's Cup still laughs the Bubble, Joy.

One lost, another still
~~Life's~~ Prospect~~s~~ ~~alter~~, ~~evry Step~~ we gain,
1
And not ~~one~~ a is giv'n
~~And Nature gives no~~ Vanity in vain;
^ ^
Ev'n

How
1.
[To society
<Kind> Heav'n
[~~Heav'n~~ [~~That~~, forming
+
[~~That forming~~ each on other to depend,

(A Master, or a Servant, or a Friend)

<—> Bids <Bids> each on other for assistance
~~For like Assistance mutually we~~ call

1 each ones
Till ~~each man's~~ weakness grows ye Strength of All.

2.See happy frailties the &c
but more
~~The~~ Want~~s~~, ~~Frailties~~, ~~Passions~~ closer ~~still~~ allye
Each & Weakness

~~and~~
The common Interest, ~~still~~ endear the Tye:
or

To these we owe true Friendship, Love sincere,

Each home-felt Joy that Life inherits here:

Yet from the same we learn, in its Decline,

Those Joys, those Loves, those Intrests to resign,

Taught half by Reason, half by mere Decay,

To welcome Death, & calmly pass away.

~~See founded thus~~
The [To the Individuals, ~~In ev'ry State~~)

[~~See some strange Comfort ev'ry State attend~~!

~~And Pride bestowd on all, a comon friend~~.

the Passion Pelf,
[Whatere ~~pant who will~~ for Knowledge, fame or
^
Not one will change his Neighb^r. with himself:

What partly pleases, totally will shock,
δ
I question much if Toland would be Lock.
+
~~The Rich~~ Nor Ross wd be Argyle nor Toland
Locke.

happy, Nature
~~The Poor~~ ~~blest, such wonders~~ to
The Learnd are ~~happy they so much~~ explore;

The Fool is happy, that he knows no more;

The Rich are happy in the Plenty given;

~~presuming on~~
The Poor ~~contents him with~~ the Care of Heav'n.
contents him with

See the blind Beggar dance, the Cripple sing,

The Sot a Hero, Lunatic a King,

~~blest still~~
See ~~The~~ Chymists ~~happy~~ in his golden Views

Payn in his madness, Welsted in his Muse.
Poets

~~fit~~ ~~rise~~
~~With every Age of Man new Passions~~^

~~Hope travels thro, nor quits him when he dies~~.

~~See first~~ [in ev'ry State
~~Behold the child &c~~. & Age of Life]
^ attend
See some strange comfort evry State ^

And Pride bestow'd on all a comon friend

See fitt~~ing~~
~~See~~ Some ~~<fit>~~ Passion ~~Man's each~~ age ~~supplies~~
^~~fit~~ evry supply

Hope travels thro', nor quits us w^n. we die.

Omit Behold ye child &c. [Till then
&c

28

E'vn mean Self-love becomes by force divine
The Scale to measure others Wants by thine:
See! and confess, one Comfort still must rise,
'Tis this, tho' Man's a Fool, yet God is wise.

~~Come then my friend &c. to. Last.~~
Oh when along ye Stream of Time &c. to know ~~his God~~.

Come then my Friend, my Genius come along,
Oh Master of the Poet & the Song!
And while ye Muse transported, unconfin'd,
Or Heav'nward soars, or stoops among Mankind,
Teach her, like thee, in men & manners wise,
With dignity to fall, with temper rise;
Form'd by thy converse, steer an easy flight
From grave to gay, from learned to polite.
Oh! when along the Stream of Time, thy Name
Shall fly full-spread, & gather all its fame,
Shall then my little Bark attendant sail,
Pursue the Triumph, & partake the Gale?
When Statesmen, Hero's, Kings, in dust repose,
Whose Sons shall blush their Fathers were thy Foes,
Shall then this Verse to future ~~time~~ age pretend
Thou wert my Guide, Philosopher & Friend?
That urg'd by thee, I turn'd the Tuneful Art
From Sounds to Things, from Fancy to the Heart;
For Wit's false mirror held up Nature's Light;
Show'd erring Pride, Whatever Is, is right;
That Reason, Passion, answer one great aim;
That true Self-love & Social are the same;
~~That just to find a God is all we can, & all the study of mankind is man.~~
~~The same our Duty, & our Bliss, below,~~
~~Virtue & Hope, man's only Bliss below;~~
That all our Knowledge is ourselves to know;
And blessing others, all our Bliss below.
Virtue all our Happiness

Finis. Lib. Prim.

& to love others & ourselves to know
Is all our knowledge, all our bliss, below.

To love our neighb! & ourselves to know.

Finis or

That all our knowledge is ourselves to know;
To love our neighbour all our bliss below.

Ev'n mean Self-love becomes by force divine
The Scale to measure others Wants by thine:
See! and confess, one Comfort still must rise,
Tis this, tho' Man's a Fool, yet God is wise.

Come then my friend &c. to. last.
Oh when along ye stream of Time &c. to know his God.

To end Lib. 1.

Come then my Friend, my Genius come along.
Oh Master of the Poet & the Song!
And while ye Muse transported, unconfin'd,
[Or] ~~Now~~ Heav'nward soars, [or] ~~now~~ stoops among Mankind,
Teach her, like thee, in Men and Manners wise,
With dignity to fall, with temper rise;
Form'd by thy converse, steer an easy flight
From grave to gay, from learned to polite.
Oh! when along the stream of Time, thy name
Shall fly full-spread, & gather all its fame,
Shall then my little Bark attendant sail,
Pursue the Triumph, & partake the Gale?
When Statesmen, Hero's, Kings in dust repose,
Whose Sons shall blush their Fathers were thy Foes,

Peroratio Lib. 1.

And Now, | then | transported oer [so vast a] ~~this ample~~ plain
While ye wingd Courser flies wth all her Rein,
While heavnward now her mounting Wing ~~Strength~~ she feels.
Now scatterd fools fly [trembling] ~~frighted~~ frõ her heels,
Wilt thou my St---n keep [her] ~~(now)~~ still ~~his~~ [ye] Course in sight,
Confine [her] ~~his~~ fury, and assist [her] ~~his~~ flight?
~~And~~
~~when along ye Stream~~
~~Say~~,

Shall then this Verse to future [age] ~~time~~ pretend
Thou wert my Guide, Philosopher & Friend?
That urg'd by thee, I turn'd the Tuneful Art
From Sounds to Things, from Fancy to the Heart;
For Wit's false mirror held up nature's Light,
Show'd erring Pride, Whatever Is, is right;

& [to] ~~to~~ love others & ourselves to know
Is all our knowledge, all our bliss bel
bliss, below.
& all our knowledge all our
To love our $Neighb^{r}$. & ourselves
to know.

Finis
or
That all our knowledge is our selves to know,
To love our neighbor all our bliss below.
& ~~Hope~~ & ~~Virtue all our Bliss~~

That Reason, Passion, answer one great aim;
That true Self love, & Social, are the same;
~~That just to find a God is all we can, & all the study of mankind, is man.~~
~~The same our Duty, & our Bliss, below,~~
~~Virtue, & Hope, Man's only Bliss below;~~
2 ~~And~~ [That ~~man's~~ ~~his~~] all our Knowledge, ~~Man himself~~ [is | ourselves | ~~Himself~~] to know;
And [^1 ~~is~~ ~~makes~~] blessing others, all our Bliss below.
1. ~~That~~ Virtue all our Happiness

Finis Lib. Prim.

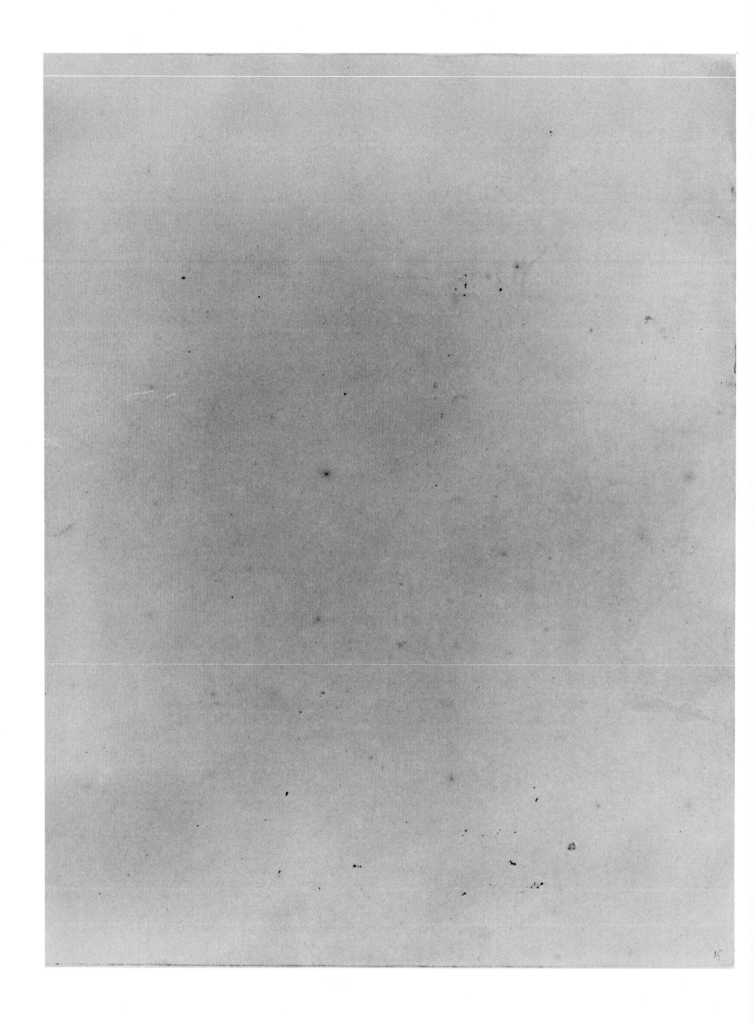

EPISTLE III.

~~Incipit II.~~

Of men with respect to Society.

WHile Man exclaims, See all things for my Use!
See Man for mine, replies a pamper'd Goose:
What care to ~~lodge~~ feed, to cram, to ~~tend~~ lodge, to treat him,
All this he saw, but not that 'twas to eat him. | Postpone.

As far as Goose could judge, he reason'd right,
But as to Man, mistook the matter quite;
And just as short of Reason Man will fall,
Who thinks all made for one, not one for all.

Incipit II. Learn, Dulness! learn, ~~an~~ the Universal Cause
~~Works to one End, but works by various Laws.~~ must act by Gen'ral, not by Partial
In all ~~thy Madness~~ ~~with~~ the Spirits of superfluous Health,
Thy^e Trim of Pride, and Impudence of Wealth,
Let that great Truth be present, night and day;
But most be present, if thou preach, or pray. | Stet

Look

EPISTLE III.

~~Incipit II~~.

Of Man with respect to Society.

While Man exclaims, See all things for my Use!
See Man for mine, replies a pamper'd Goose:
tend lodge
What care to ~~lodge,~~ to cram, to ~~tend,~~ to treat him,
All this he saw, but not that 'twas to eat him.
As Far as Goose could judge, he reason'd right,
But as to Man, mistook the matter quite;
And just as short of Reason Man will fall,
Who thinks all made for one, not one for all.

Postpone

Incipit II.

the
Learn, Dulness! learn, ~~an~~ Universal Cause
Must act by Gen'ral, not by Partial
~~Works to one End, but works by various Laws~~.

Stet

~~With~~ the Spirits
In all ~~thy Madness~~ ^ of superfluous Health,
e
Th~~y~~ Trim of Pride, and Impudence of Wealth,
Let that great Truth be present, night and day;
But most be present, if thou preach, or pray.

Look

(Insert 3. Learn then thyself)

a Lyre it with

32 Come then my Friend &c. to — bound my Last. Or wth along to brawny Sea.

View thy worth and know one

~~Loose Nature Laws, and~~ Chain of Love

The whole world one System of Society

Combining all below, and all above.

See lifeless Matter moving to One End;

~~Each~~ the single ~~Particle~~ atoms to each other tend;

Attract, attracted to the next in place;

By nature form'd its Neighbour to embrace:

Behold it next, with various Life endu'd,

~~To the same centre press, the General Good;~~

~~Press to one Centre of communal Good~~

Press to one Centre Joy:

See dying Vegetables Life sustain,

See Life dissolving vegetate again.

all forms that perish oth.r forms supply
By turns they catch the vital breath & die
Like Bubbles on the Sea of Matter born
They rise, they break, & to that Sea return

Nothing is foreign: Parts relate to Whole:

One all-preserving, all-connecting Soul

Unites each Being, greatest with the least;

made Beast in aid of Man, & man of Beast:

~~Nor more makes Beast for Man than Man for Beast:~~

Each ~~all~~ serv'd, and serving; nothing stands alone,

The Chain holds on, & where it ends, unknown.

~~Learn Dulness learn &c — pray Dulde ... &c ...~~

nothing made wholly for one. Ever or wholly for itself.

27. Has God, thou Fool! work'd solely for thy Good?

Thy Joy, thy Pastime, thy Attire, thy Food?

Think'st it thee for thee he feeds ~~the wanton Fawn~~ & for him kindly spreads for him the Lawn

Know, Nature's Children all divide her care. ~~with one care are nurs'd~~

The Furr that warms Sir Gilbert, warm'd a Bear.

~~What warms a Monarch, warm'd an Ermine first.~~

Del. superscribe the fur

~~If for thy Table feeds the wanton Fawn,~~

~~Heav'n for him all-bounteous nature spread~~

Know Nature as kindly, spreads for him the Lawn:

~~Thinks~~ thou for thee the ~~Sky~~ Lark to mounts and sings?

Joy tunes his Voice, Joy elevates his Wings;

'Tis

then thyself
Incipit 3. Learn ~~we ourselves~~,
& end it with
32 Come then my Friend &c. to-- bound my last. Oh w^{n} along to know his
God.

~~Incip. II.~~
The whole world one Systeme of Society

own
[View ~~thro'~~ thy^World; behold one
~~Look Nature thro'~~, ~~and see the~~ Chain o^ Love
Combining all below, and all above.
See lifeless Matter moving to One End;
The Atomes each
~~Each~~ single ~~Particle~~ to^other tend;
Attract, attracted to, the next in place;
By nature form'd its Neighbour to embrace:
Behold it next, with various Life endu'd,
~~To the same Centre press~~, the Gen'ral Good:
~~Press to one Centre of commutual Good~~.
Press to one Centre still, ^
See dying Vegetables Life sustain,
See Life dissolving vegetate again.
^ ^
Nothing is foreign: Parts relate to Whole:

All Forms that perish oth^{r} forms supply
By turns they catch the vital breath & die
Like Bubbles, on the Sea of Matter born,
They rise, they break, & to that Sea return.

One all-preserving, all-connecting Soul
all
Unites ~~each~~ Being, greatest with the least;
Made Beast in aid of Man, & Man of Beast:
~~Nor more makes Beast for Man than Man for Beast~~:
~~All each~~ ~~all~~
Each ~~All~~ serv'd, and serving; nothing stands alone,
The Chain holds on, & where it ends, unknown.

All Forms y^{t} perish

~~Learn Dulness, learn &c. -- pray [While man exclaims &c - all.~~

Nothing made wholly for another or wholly for itself.

~~then,~~
27. Has God, ~~thou~~ Fool! work'd solely for thy Good? Think'st thou for thee he feeds
Thy Joy, thy Pastime, thy Attire, thy Food?

ye wanton Fawn,
~~If for~~ thy Table & not as kindly
~~Know, Heav'n as kindly~~ spreads
for him ye Lawn

<&> del. Natures children
The fur --

all divide|claim her equal care,
Know, Nature's Children ~~with one care are nurst;~~
The Furr that warms Sir Gilbert, warm'd a Bear
~~What warms a Monarch, warm'd an Ermine first:~~
δ ~~If for thy Table feeds the wanton Fawn,~~
~~For his, all-bounteous Nature spread.~~
~~Heavn~~
~~Know,~~ ~~Nature~~, as kindly, spread~~s~~ for him the Lawn:
⟷ thou ~~alone~~ so s s
Know Think'st for thee the ~~Sky~~-Lark~~e~~ mount~~e~~ and sing~~e~~?
^
tunes his ~~Joy and~~ his ~~the~~
Joy ~~lifts his~~ Voice, ~~and~~ elevates ~~his~~ Wing~~s~~;
^ ^Joy

'Tis

Tis not for thee the Linnet pours his throat,
Loves of his own and Raptures swell the note.
The bounding Steed you pompously bestride,
Shares with his Lord the Pleasure & the Pride.
[illegible] the Seed that strows the Plain?
The Fowls of Heav'n shall vindicate their Grain:
[illegible] thine the full Harvest of the golden Year?
Part pays, and justly, the deserving Steer:
2 The Hog that plows not, nor obeys thy call,
Lives on the Labors of the Lord of all.
53 Grant yt the Powrful still the weak controll, 1. Know, Natures children all divide / The Fur yt warms / 3 While Man cries out / See Man for mine / to — one for all.
Be Man the Wit and Tyrant of the Whole. The Happiness of Animals mutual.
Yet Man alone great Nature checks; He knows,
He feels alone, all others Wants & Woes:
2 For some, his Int'rest prompts him to provide,
For more his Pleasure, and for more his Pride.
Say, shall the Eagle stooping from above,
Smit with her silv'ry Plumage, spare the Dove?
2 [illegible] or [illegible] the Hawk, when Philomela sings?
1 Respects the [illegible] the Insects painted wings? 2
Man cares for all: to Birds he gives his Woods,
To Beasts his Pastures, and to Fish his Floods,
All feed on one vain Patron, and enjoy
Th' extensive blessing of his Luxury.
That very Life his learned hunger craves,
He saves from Famine, from the Savage saves;

Nay

~~Say~~ his
'Tis not for thee the Linnet pours ~~his~~ throat,

his
Loves of ~~her~~ own and Raptures swell the note.
^

pompously
The bounding Steed you ~~gracefully~~ bestride,

Shares with his Lord the Pleasure & the Pride.

~~all~~ ~~only~~ Is thine, fond man:
~~Think Not~~ ~~thy own~~ the Seed that strows the Plain?
^ ^

The Fowls of Heav'n shall vindicate their Grain:

~~only~~ Thine full golden
~~Think Not~~ ^ ~~thine own~~, ^ the ^ Harvest of the Year?

Part pays, and justly, the deserving Steer:

The Hog that plows not, nor obeys thy call,
2
Lives on the Labors of the Lord of all.

Grant y^t
53 '~~Tis true~~, the Pow'rful still the weak controll,

Be
~~And~~ Man| ~~'s~~ the Wit, and Tyrant, of the Whole.

Yet
~~But~~ Man alone great Nature checks; He knows,

He feels alone, all others Wants & Woes: Say—

For some, his Int'rest prompts him to provide,
2
For more his Pleasure, and for more His Pride. All feed

shall Eagle
Say, ~~will~~ the ~~Falcon~~ stooping from above,

silv'ry
Smit with her ~~varying~~ Plumage, spare the Dove?

hears
Or turn hears|lists the Hawk
2 ~~Turns he his ear~~ when Philomela sings? 2
^

Respects the ~~Nightingale~~ <B>Jay ~~painted~~
1 ~~Admires her eye~~ the Insect's gilded wings? 1
Regards ^

Man cares for all: to Birds he gives his Woods,

To Beasts his Pastures, and to Fish his Floods, ~~For some~~ -

vain
All feed on one proud Patron, and enjoy

Th' extensive blessing of his Luxury. For some his Intrest

That very Life his learned hunger craves,

Famine the Savage
\+ He saves from ~~Torment, or~~ from ~~Famine~~ saves.
^ ^

Nay

[2 ~~All~~
Know, Natures children all divide
1.
The Fur y^t Warms

3 While Man cries out,

See Man for mine &c. as at y^e beginning,
to - one for all.

The Happiness of Animals
mutual.

Nay feasts the Animal he dooms his feast,
And till he ends the Being, makes it blest.
The favour'd Man by Touch ætheral slain
Not less forese~~en~~ces the Stroke, or ~~felt~~ feels the pain:
The Creature had his Feast of Life before;
Thou too must perish when thy Feast is o'er.

To each un-thinking Being Heav'n a friend,
Gives not the useless Knowledge of its End;
To Man ~~he gives~~ imparts it, but with such a View
As, while he ~~fears~~ dreads it, makes him hope it too:
The Hour conceal'd, 'tis so remote a fear, [so distant is the]
~~That~~ Death ~~the nearer still, seems never~~ still draws nearer, never seeming near.
Great standing Miracle! that Heav'n assign'd
Its only Thinking Thing this Turn of Mind.

Reason & Instinct operate alike to the Good of the Individual

Whether with Reason or with Instinct blest, 83
Know all enjoy that Pow'r ~~that~~ which suits them best,
~~To equal~~ alike to Bliss by that direction tend,
And find the means proportion'd to their End.
Say, where full Instinct is th' unerring Guide,
What Pope or Council can they need beside?
Reason, however able, cool at best,
Cares not for Service, or but serves when press'd,
Stays till we call, and then not often near;
But honest Instinct comes a Volunteer:
This too serves always; Reason never long;
One must go right, the other may go wrong.

Or x. While thro' the moving Views of various ways confounded, Reason and of Knowledge strays.
Qu Too weak to chuse, yet chusing still in hast, One moment gives the pleasure & distaste. Gra.

See

34

Nay feasts the Animal he dooms his feast,
And till he ends the Being, makes it blest.
The favour'd Man by Touch aethereal slain
                    ees   feels
Not less fores~~aw~~ the Stroke, or ~~felt~~ the pain:
The Creature had his Feast of Life before;
Thou too must perish when thy Feast is o'er.
    To each un-thinking Being Heav'n a friend,
Gives not the useless Knowledge of its End;
            imparts
To Man ~~he gives~~ it, but with such a View
                dreads
As, while he ~~fears~~ ^ it, makes him hope it too:
                                so distant is the
The Hour conceal'd, 'tis so remote a fear,
            still draws nearer, never seeming
~~That~~ | Death ~~the nearer still, seems never~~ near.
Great standing Miracle! that Heav'n assigned
Its only Thinking Thing this Turn of Mind.

Reason & Instinct operate alike to the good of the Individual

    Whether with Reason or with Instinct blest, 83
                        which
Know all enjoy that Pow'r ~~that~~ ^ suits them best,
alike to
~~To equal~~ Bliss by that direction tend,
And find the means proportion'd to their End.
Say, where full Instinct is th' unerring Guide,
What Pope or Council can they need beside?

| Qu
Too weak to chuse, yet chusing still in hast,
One moment gives ye Pleasure & distaste.
D^r A.

Dr A. While Man with opening Views of various ways, Confounded by ye aid of Knowledge strays.
Reason, however able, cool at best,
Cares not for Service, or but serves when pressd,
Stays till we call, and then not often near;
But honest Instinct comes a Volunteer:
    Instinct
This too serves always; Reason never long;
One _must_ go right, the other _may_ go wrong.

See

See then the Acting and Comparing Pow'rs 35
One in their Nature, which are two in ours;
And Reason prefer Instinct if you can;
In this 'tis God directs, in that 'tis Man.

Who taught the Nations of the Field and Wood,
To shun their Poyson and to chuse their Food?
Prescient, the Tydes or Tempests to withstand,
~~The Cramp-fish, Remora, the secret charm~~
Build on the Wave, or arch beneath the Sand
~~To stop the Bark, arrest the distant Train~~?
Who made the Spider Parallels design, sure as Demoivre, without rule or line?
The Storks, thro Air's wide Ocean to explore
Columbus-like, a World unknown before?
Who calls their Council, states the certain Day,
Who forms their Phalanx, or who points their Way?

Who bid the Stork, Columbus-like, explore
Heav'ns not his own, & Worlds unknown before?

~~Boast we of Arts? A Bee can better hit & insect [illegible]~~
~~Boast we of Arts? when Man aspir'd to Art,~~
When Man from simple Nature ~~rose to~~ Art,
To copy Instinct then was Reason's part. (170)
~~Then thus~~ this then the Voice of mighty Nature spake —
Go! from the Creatures thy Instructions take:
3 Learn from the Birds, what Fruits the Thickets yield;
Learn from the Beasts the Physick of the Field;
1 Thy Arts of Building from the Bee receive;
Learn of the Mole to plow, the Worm to weave;
Behold the Rabbit's Fortress in the Sands;
The Beaver's story'd House, not built with hands;
Here, Subterranean Works and Cities see,
There, ~~Domes~~ Towns aerial on the waving Tree.
† Learn of the little Nautilus to sail,
2 Spread the thin Oar, & catch the driving Gale.

Reason is taught by Instinct ~~[illegible]~~ ~~of Arts~~ the arts of Life

Then [God in the nature of each Being founds
Its proper Bliss &c. pag. 36.
to — support the line
Then, [When man from simple &c to — God's adore.
Then [Great Nature spoke &c.
— next [illegible]. Learn of the little Learn from the Birds

† Vide Oppian Halieut. Lib. 1.

Yet

qu. si δ | See then the Acting and Comparing Pow'rs
One / which are two
| ~~Mix'd~~ in their Nature, ~~but distinct~~ in ours;

prefer to
And Reason raise o'er Instinct if you can;
In this 'tis God directs, in that 'tis Man.
Who taught the Nations of the Field and Wood,
To shun their Poyson, and to chuse their Food?
or
Prescient, the Tides ~~and~~ Tempests to withstand,
| ~~The Cramp-fish, Remora, the secret charm~~
δ | Build on the Wave, or ~~and~~ arch beneath the Sand.
| ~~To stop the Bark, arrest the distant Arm~~?
Who made ye Spider Parallels design, Sure as Dumoivre, without rule or line?
The Storks, thro' Air's wide Ocean to explore
Columbus-like, a World unknown before?
Who calls the~~ir~~ Council, states the certain day,
Who forms the~~ir~~ Phalanx, or who points the~~ir~~ Way?

Who bid ye stork~~s,~~ Columbus-like, explore
his
Heav'ns not ~~their~~ own, & Worlds unknown before?

~~Boast we of Arts? A Bee can better hit &c. insert here~~) Then

X

Reason instructed by Instinct ~~Origine of Arts~~ in ye arts of Life.

~~Boast we of Arts? when Man aspir'd to Art~~,
When Man from simple Nature rose to Art,
To copy Instinct then was Reason's part. (170)
'Twas then
~~Then thus~~ the Voice of Mighty Nature spake —
^
Go! from the Creatures thy Instructions take:

[God in the Nature of each Being founds
Its proper Bliss &c. pag. 36.
to - support ye line
Then, [When Man from simple
&c, to -- Gods adore.
Then [Great Nature spoke &c.

3 Learn from the Birds, what Fruits the Thickets yield;
Learn from the Beasts the Physick of the Field; — Next too &c.
1 Thy Arts of Building from the Bee receive;
Learn of the Mole to plow, the Worm to weave; Learn of y^e little
| Behold the Rabbit's Fortress in the Sands;
δ | The Beaver's story'd House, not built with hands;
δ | Here, Subterranean Works and Cities see,
Towns
| There ~~Domes~~ aerial on the waving Tree.
\+ Learn of the little Nautilus to sail,
2 Spread the thin Oar, and catch the driving Gale. Learn frō y^e Birds

Yet

\+ Vide Oppian Halieut. Lib.1.

— and in the Forms of Society.

36 [next, ~~Here~~ too, the
~~Yet more~~, ~~each~~ Forms of ~~Law and Commerce~~ [social Union] find,
[These yet more late, let Reason teach]
And hence let Reason, late, instruct mankind:
[Here subterranean Works & Cities see; There, Towns aerial on the waving Tree.]
Learn each small People's [Genius] ~~Traffic~~, Policies,
The Ant's Republic, and the Realm of Bees;
How those in common all their Stores bestow,
And Anarchy without confusion know;
And these for ever, tho' a Monarch reign,
Their sep'rate Cells and Properties maintain.
Mark what unvary'd Laws preserve their State,
Laws wise as Nature, and as fix'd as Fate.
In vain thy Reason finer Webs shall draw,
Entangle Justice in her Net of Laws,
And Right too rigid harden into Wrong,
Still for the strong too weak, the weak too strong.
Yet go! and thus o'er all the Creatures reign,
Thus shine distinguish'd o'er the Race of Man,
Who, blest with Arts you learn'd of these before,
As Kings shall crown you, or as Gods adore.

Reason & Instinct operate to ~~[illegible]~~ ~~of~~ Society.

109 God, in the nature of each Being founds
Its proper Bliss, and marks its proper bounds;
But as he form'd a Whole, the whole to bless,
~~made~~ On mutual Wants ~~the Bond of~~ built mutual
~~Placed in Society that~~ Happiness;
~~He rais'd~~ from private Sparkles [raised] the ~~gen'ral~~ Flame,
And bade Self-love and Social be the same.
Thus, ~~So~~ from the first, Eternal Order ran,
Thus, ~~And~~ Creature link'd to Creature, Man to man.
Whate'ere of Life all-[quickning] ~~[illegible]~~ Æther keeps,
Or breathes thro' air, or shoots beneath the Deeps, [~~Quick~~]
Or pours profuse on Earth, one Nature feeds
The vital flame & swells the genial seeds. p. 8 120

[Societies] [Origine of Political,]
Great Nature spoke: Observant Man obey'd
Cities were built, Societies were made:
Here rose one little State, another near
Grew by like means, &c. p: 38

- and in the Forms of Society

36 [Next
~~Here~~ too, the Social Union
~~Yet more, each~~ Form s of ~~Law and Commerce~~ find,

yet
These more late, let Reason teach
And hence, let Reason, late, instruct Mankind:

Here Subterranean Works & Cities see; There, Towns aerial on the waving Tree.

Genius
Learn each small People's ~~Traffic~~, Policies,
The Ant's Republic, and the Realm of Bees;
How those in common all their Stores bestow,
And Anarchy without confusion know;
And these for ever, tho' a Monarch reign,
Their sep'rate Cells and Properties maintain.
Mark what unvary'd Laws preserve their State,
Laws wise as Nature, and as fix'd as Fate.
In vain thy Reason finer Webs shall draw,
Entangle Justice in her Net of Law,
And Right too rigid harden into Wrong,
Still for the strong too weak, the weak too strong.
Yet go! and thus o'er all the Creatures reign,
Thus shine distinguishd o'er the Race of Man,
Who, blest with Arts you learn'd of these before,
As Kings shall crown you, or as Gods adore.

Societies
[Origine of Political

Reason and Instinct operate to ~~ye good of~~ Society.

109.
God, in the nature of each Being founds
Its proper Bliss, and marks its proper bounds:
But as he form'd a Whole, the whole to bless,
~~Made~~ On mutual Wants ~~the Bond of~~ built mutual
~~Plac'd in Society that~~ Happiness;

Great Nature spoke: observant Man obey'd,
Cities were built; Societies were made.
Here rose one little State; another near
Grew by like means &c. p. 38.

rais'd
δ ~~He rais'd~~ From private Sparkles, the gen'ral Flame
And bade Self-love and Social be the same.

Thus, ~~So~~ from the first, Eternal Order ran,
Thus, ~~And~~ Creature link'd to Creature, Man to Man,

quick'ning
Whate're of Life all-~~fruitful~~ Aether keeps, ~~Quick~~
Or breathes thro' Air, or shoots beneath the Deeps,

Or pours profuse on Earth; one Nature feeds flood
The vital flame, & swells the genial Seeds.

Not

37

Quick, with this Spirit, new-born Nature mov'd;
[Itself each Creature in its Species]
~~Each first admir'd its being, then it~~ lov'd.
Each sought a Pleasure not possest alone;
Each Sex desir'd alike, and Two were One.
Not ~~only~~ Man [alone] but all that range the Wood,
[or beat the Sky] ~~Or Wing the Air~~, or roll along the Flood,
This Impulse animates; one Nature feeds
The vital Lamp, and swells the genial Seeds;
All spread their Image, wth like ardour ~~stung~~
[Each loves itself, the third time, in its Race]
~~All Love themselves reflected in their Young~~
The Beast, the Bird, their common charge attend,
The Mothers nurse it, and the Sires defend;
[Just] ~~Till free of earth of ocean or of air~~ taught to range the Wood, or wing the Air,
There stops the Instinct, & there ends the Care,
The Link dissolv'd, each seeks a fresh embrace,
Another Love succeeds, another Race.
A longer care Man's wanting Kind demands,
That longer care contracts more lasting bands; with choice we fix
2 Reflection, Reason, the soft Tyes improve,
3 [Wh spread at once] ~~At once extend~~ the Int'rest, and the Love,
7 And still new Needs, new Helps, new Habits rise,
That graft Benevolence on Charities; And now one brood
1 With Choice we fix, with Sympathy we burn,
And ev'ry tender Passion takes its turn. Reflection
4 And now one Brood, & now another grows,
These nat'ral Love maintains, habitual those:

~~Scarce~~

Society how far carry'd by Instinct.

Each loves itself, but not itself alone;
Each Sex desires alike, till two are one:
Nor ends the pleasure with the fierce Embrace;
Race.

Origine of Family Societies.

How far by Reason.

Quick with this Spirit, new-born Nature mov'd;

Itself each Creature in its Species
~~Each first admir'd its being, then it~~ lov'd;
δ
Each sought a Pleasure not possest alone;

Each sex desir'd alike, and Two were One.

Society how far carry'd by Instinct.

alone
Not ~~only~~ Man, ^ but all that range the Wood,

or beat the Sky
~~wide~~
~~Or Wing the Air~~, ^ or roll along the Flood,

This Impulse animates; one Nature feeds
δ The vital Lamp, and swells the genial Seeds;
All spread their Image, wth like ardour ~~stung~~;

^ Each loves itself, the third time, in its Race
~~All love themselves, reflected in their Young.~~ ^

Each loves itself, but not itself alone,
Each sex desires alike, till
two are one:
Nor ends the pleasure with the
fierce Embrace;

-Race.

The Beast, the Bird, their common charge attend,

The Mothers nurse it, and the Sires defend;

But ~~free of Earth, of Ocean, or of Air,~~
~~Till~~ ^ taught to range the Wood, or wing the Air,

There stops the Instinct, & there ends the Care,

The Link dissolv'd, each seeks a fresh embrace,

~~<1> δ~~ Another Love succeeds, another Race.

Origine of Family Socie-ties.

A longer care Man's wanting Kind demands,

That longer care contracts more lasting bands; With choice we fix

2 Reflection, Reason, the soft Tyes improve,

[How far by Reason.

<3> ~~& spread at once~~
~~At once extend~~ ^ the Int'rest, and the Love,

<2> And still new Needs, new Helps, New Habits rise,

That graft Benevolence on Charities; And now one brood

1. With Choice we fix, with Sympathy we burn,

And ev'ry tender Passion takes its turn. Reflection

~~rose~~
4. And now one Brood, & now another grows,

'd
These nat'ral Love maintains, habitual those:

~~Scarce~~

38 man

[Of ye State of Nature A]

A [Pride yet was not, nor ... ye Pride to aid;
Man walk'd wth Beast, joint Tenant of ye shade;
36 The same his Table, & ye same his bed;
No murder cloth'd him & no murder fed.
In ye same Temple, ye resounding Wood,
All vocal Nature hymn'd their equal God.
The Shrine wth Gore unstain'd, with Gold undrest,
Unbrib'd, unbloody, stood ye blameless Priest.
Heav'ns attribute was Universal care,
& man's Prerogative to rule but spare.
Ah how unlike, ye man of times to come!
Of half that live, ye Butcher & ye Tomb;
Who, Foe to Nature, hears ye gen'ral groan,
Murders their Species, & betrays his own.
But just Disease to Luxury succeeds,
And ev'ry Death its own Avenger breeds;

[not think in nature's state they trod?]
The State of Nature was ye reign of God; Self Love & Social at her birth began, Union ye bond of all things and of Man.
Pride then was not, nor arts that Pride to aid;
Man walk'd with beast joint tenant of the shade.

[or] the third ... Principle whence all began
... Bond of Nature ... of man
... arts ... ye Pride to aid;

~~The last, scarce strengthen'd~~ ripen'd into perfect Man,
Sees helpless Him from whom his Life began:
Mem'ry and Forecast just returns engage,
That pointing back to Youth, this on to Age;
Thus Pleasure, Gratitude, and Hope combin'd,
~~Still stretch the long~~ Int'rest, and ~~Support~~ present the Band.
When man from simple Nature rose to Art, To copy Instinct &c.
~~There~~ Here rose one little State; another near
Grew by like means; & join'd, thro' Love or Fear:
~~The Neighbors leagu'd to guard their common Spot~~
~~And Love was Nature's dictate, Murder not.~~
~~For Want alone each Animal contends;~~
~~Tygers with Tygers, that remov'd, are friends:~~
~~Plain Nature's Wants the common Mother crown'd,~~
~~She pour'd her Acorns, Herbs, and Streams around;~~
~~No Treasure then for Rapine to invade;~~
~~What neede to fight, for Sunshine or for Shade?~~
~~And half the Cause of Contest was remov'd,~~
~~When Beauty could be kind to all who lov'd.~~

Of Commerce

Did here the Trees with ruddier burdens bend,
And there, the Springs in purer rills descend?
What War could ravish, Commerce might bestow,
And he return'd a Friend, who came a Foe.

~~Of Monarchy~~

~~Commerce, Convenience, Change, must strongly draw~~
~~When Love was Liberty, and Nature Law.~~
~~And~~ Still every State its native Lord would own;
Till common Int'rest plac'd the Sway in One
~~Unless the Good of all repos'd on One.~~

[Right margin:]
Who taught ye ... young Youth to pierce ye Wood,
Taught to command the Fire, controul the Flood,
The Monsters of th' Abyss ...
And fetch th' Aerial Eagle to the Ground.

[Or, Instead of the Insertion A]

First was ... 'Twas then ... 35 ... to God adore.

Then Great Nature spoke.
Cities were built
Here rose—
Origine of Political Societys

Foe
Converse & Love were pow'rful charms to draw,
When Love was Liberty & Nature Law;
Thus States were form'd; the name of King unknown,
Till common Int'rest plac'd ye Sway in One.
And half the cause of Contest was remov'd,
When Beauty could be kind to all who lov'd.

Whose Then

38 Man [Of ye State of Nature

~~Line~~ Arts~~s~~
Priest
then ~~Wealth~~
A. Pride yet was not; nor ~~Gold~~ yt. Pride to aid; ^ ^
Man walk'd wth Beast, joint Tenant of ye Shade;
The same his Table, & ye same his bed;
No murder clothd him & nc murder fed.
In ye same Temple, ye resounding Wood,
Beings
All vocal ~~Nature~~ hymnd their equal God.
The Shrine wth Gore unstaind, with Gold undrest,
Unbribd, un bloody, stood ye blame-
less Priest.
Care
Heavns attribute was Universal ^
And Man's prerogative to rule but spare.
Ah how unlike ye Man of times to come!
Of half that live, ye Butcher & ye Tomb.
Who, Foe to Nature, hears ye gen'ral groan
Murders their species, & betrays his own.
just
But ~~adore~~ Disease to Luxury succeeds;
& evry Death its own Avenger breeds
~~While Great Nature <strict> observant~~
~~strict the injury to scan~~
~~Man obeyd~~
~~<Left> Man the only Beast to prey on Man.~~
~~Cities were built, Societies were~~
~~<Leaves>~~ ~~On Man let loose a fiercer~~
~~savage--man~~
Origine of
from their
The Fury-Passions ~~nursd with~~
~~Political Societys~~ Blood began
~~the great Destroyer~~
& loos'd a fiercer Savage,
~~turnd~~ ~~to~~
Man, on Man.
& Man became the Beast
to prey on Man
~~half~~ other kinds
~~The Foe to Nature <in>~~ ^ oerthrown
oer his
~~Restless he seeks dominion~~ ^ own
~~Proceeding next to <stratagem &>~~
~~To copy Instinct~~ ~~<Art>~~
Of Commerce
See him frō Nature rising slow
to art
Evn then frō Instinct Reason learnd
her part
Thus ~~thus~~ thy Voice, inspiring
~~Twas~~ then ~~ye Voice of mighty~~ ^
Nature spake
"Go, frō the Creatures thine In-
~~Of Monarchy~~

Nor think they blindly ~~<devious>~~
~~Ask not~~ in Nature's state ~~what path~~ y trod?
A
The State of Nature was ye Reign of God;
~~Her Dictates but his Will; wch Man obeyd,~~
~~For Pride was not. Joint Tenant of ye Shade~~
~~He shard wth Beasts his table & his bed~~
|or| No murder
Principle whence all began,
Union ye
Bond & ~~<Link>~~
Not more The ~~Soul~~ of Nature ~~<as> ye <soul>~~ of Man
Ye ~~Link of Nature~~ than of
~~yet~~ Arts
~~Nor Pride was not~~, nor ~~<Priest>~~ ^ yt. Pride to aid,
Man walkd
~~The last, scarce strengthen'd~~ into perfect Man,
ripen'd
~~Saw~~ his ~~birth~~ Life
Sees helpless Him from whom ~~the Race~~ ^ began: + + +
~~must~~
Mem'ry and Forecast just returns engage,
That pointing back to Youth, this on to Age;
or, Quaere of the Insertion A
~~And~~
Thus
While Pleasure, Gratitude, and Hope combine'd,
still stretch'd ye preservd Kind
~~Stretch the long~~ Int'rest, and ~~support~~ the ~~Line~~. ^ ^
^ ^ when they rising slow first was Rea
When Man from simple Nature rose to Art, To copy Instinct &c θ
Here ~~Thus~~ rose one little State; another near
Twas then ye Voice--
pag. 35.
Grew by like means; & join'd, thro' Love or Fear:
to-- as Gods adore
δ ~~The Neighbors leagu'd to guard their common Spot,~~
Then--
Great Nature spoke
~~And Love was Nature's dictate, Murder not.~~
Cities were built
~~For Want alone each Animal contends,~~
Here rose--
~~Tygers with Tygers, that remov'd, are friends:~~
~~Plain Nature's Wants the common Mother crown'd,~~ [Origine of Political Societys
~~She pour'd her Acorns, Herbs, and Streams around;~~
~~No Treasure then for Rapine to invade;~~
~~What neede to fight, for Sunshine or for Shade?~~
~~And half the Cause of Contest was remov'd,~~
~~When Beauty could be kind to all who lov'd.~~
Did here the Trees with ruddier burdens bend,
And there, the Springs in purer rills descend?
c ~~might~~
What War ~~would~~ ravish, Commerce could bestow,
And he return'd a Friend, who came a Foe.
^
~~Commerce, Convenience, Change, must strongly draw,~~
δ ~~When Love was Liberty, and Nature Law:~~ ^
Still
~~And~~ ^ ev'ry State its native Lord would own;
~~Till common Int'rest placd the Sway in One.~~
~~Unless the Good of all repos'd on One.~~
~~Whose~~ [Then

-foe
Converse & Love
were powrful charms
to draw
When Love was Liberty
& Nature Law.
Thus States were form'd;
the Name of King unknown,
Till common Intrest
placd ye sway
in One.
~~And half the cause of~~
~~Contest was remov'd,~~
~~When Beauty could be kind~~
~~to all who lov'd.~~

Selflove & Social
at her birth began
Bond
Union ye Soul of
all things and
of Man.
del
~~Pride yet--~~
~~+ + + Who taught their won-~~
~~dring Youth to pierce ye Wood,~~
~~Taught to command the Fire,~~
~~controul the Flood,~~
~~the Monsters of the Abyss~~
~~profound,~~
~~And fetch th' aerial Eagle to~~
~~the ground.~~

— of monarchy.

[~~Then, Godlike Virtue~~
~~Him~~ Virtue only,
~~Whose shining Virtue~~ (or in Arts or Arms,
Diffusing Blessings, or averting Harms)
The same ~~his~~ the Sons ~~had in a Sire~~ first ~~lov'd & then~~ in a Sire obey'd,
~~A Prince~~ One man ~~one~~, the Father of a People, made.
Till then, by ~~By~~ Nature crown'd, ~~the Godlike~~ each Patriarch sate,
King, Priest, and Parent of his growing State:
~~He taught the wondring Youth to pierce the Wood~~
~~Taught to Command the Fire, to stem the~~ controll ~~rapid~~ Flood,
~~Draw forth the Monsters of th' Abyss~~ profound,
~~And fetch th' Aerial Eagle to the ground.~~
On him, their second Providence, they hung,
Their Law his Eye, their Oracle his Tongue.
~~He crown'd the wondring Earth with golden grain,~~ He bade the wondring ~~Till stooping~~ Now drooping, sickning, dying, they began
Whom they rever'd as God, to mourn as Man!
Then looking up from Sire to Sire, explor'd
One great first Father, and that first ador'd:
Or plain Tradition that this All begun,
Convey'd unbroken Faith from Sire to Son;
The mighty Workman from the Work distinct was known,
And simple Reason never sought but One:
E're Wit oblique had broke that steddy Light,
Man like his Maker, saw, that All was right,
To Virtue in the paths of Pleasure trod,
And own'd a Father when he own'd a God.
Love all the Faith, and all th' Allegiance then;
For Nature knew no Right Divine in Men,

No

~~Ask not in Nature's State what~~ ~~The State of Nature was ye Reign of God~~ ~~[illegible] began~~ ~~[illegible] of Nature [illegible] of man~~

Origine of True Religion & Government

He bad ye wondring their food; He from the ~~fruitful~~ furrow call'd Taught to command the Fire, controll the Flood; Draw forth ye monsters of th' Abyss prof.d Or fetch th' aerial Eagle to the groud.

— From the same Principle of Love.

—of monarchy

Then, ~~Godlike Virtue~~
~~Him,~~ Virtue only,
~~Whose shining Virtue~~, (or in Arts or Arms,

Diffusing Blessings, or averting Harms),

the first ~~lovd & then~~ in a Sire
The same ~~his~~ Sons ~~had in a Sire~~ obey'd,

One man ~~and~~
~~A Prince~~, the Father of a People, made.

Till then, by each
~~By~~ Nature crown'd, ~~the Godlike~~ Patriarch sate,

King, Priest, and Parent of his growing State:

~~stent~~

~~He taught the wond'ring Youth to pierce the Wood,~~

controll rapid
δ ~~Taught to Command the Fire, to stem the Flood,~~

~~Draw forth the Monsters of th' Abyss profound,~~
~~2~~
~~And fetch th'~~ ~~Aerial~~ Eagle ~~to the ground~~.

~~1~~ On him, their second Providence, they hung,

3 Their Law his Eye, their Oracle his Tongue.

~~He crownd the wondring Earth with golden grain~~,

~~Till stooping~~, sick'ning, dying, they began
Now drooping

Whom they rever'd as God, to mourn as Man:

Then looking up from Sire to Sire, explor'd

One great first Father, and that first ador'd:

Or plain Tradition that this All begun,

Convey'd unbroken Faith from Sire to Son;

distinct
The mighty Workman from the Work was known,

And simple Reason never sought but One:

E're Wit oblique had broke that steddy Light,

Man like his Maker, saw, that All was right,

To Virtue in the paths of Pleasure trod,

And own'd a Father when he own'd a God.

Love all the Faith, and all th' Allegiance then;

For Nature knew no Right Divine in Men,

~~Nor ask~~ (~~path y^y trod~~
~~Ask not in Natures State what~~
~~The State of Nature was ye Reign of God~~
~~Selflove & Social at her birth began~~
~~Union ye Soul of Nature & of Man~~
all things

Origine of
True Religion
& Government

He bad ye wond'ring their food;
He from the ~~fruitful~~ furrow call'd

He bad ye wond'ring their food;
He from the fruitful furrow call'd

Bade them Flood;
Taught to command the Fire, controll the Main;

Draw forth ye Monsters of th' Abyss prof^d.

Or ~~&~~ fetch th' aerial Eagle to the groũd.

--From the same
Principle of Love.

No

No Ill could fear in God, nor understood
A Sovereign Being but a Sovereign Good.
True Faith, true Policy, united ran,
That was but Love of God, and this of Man.

Origin of Superstition & Tyranny, from the same Principle of Fear.

~~False Faith and wicked Government begun~~ [false Policy at once] | What first taught Souls enslav'd & Realms undone,
Th' enormous ~~Thought~~ [Faith] of many made for One; That proud exception to all Nature's Laws, T'invert the World, & counter-work its Cause.
Force first made Conquest, and that Conquest, Law;
~~Then~~ [First] Superstition gave ~~the~~ Tyrants awe,
~~Then~~ [Next] shar'd the Tyranny, ~~and~~ [then] lent it aid,
And Gods of Conqu'rors, Slaves of Subjects made.
She, 'midst the Lightning's Glare, and Thunder's sound,
When rock'd the Mountains, & when groan'd the Ground,
~~When~~ [She taught the] weak to bend, ~~and~~ [the Proud to pray] ~~to fear began,~~
~~At~~ [To] Pow'r unseen, and mightier far than ~~Man~~ [they]:
~~From opening Earth shew'd Fiends infernal nigh,~~ She, from the rending Earth & bursting Skies, Saw Gods descend, & Fiends infernal rise;
~~And Gods supernal from the bursting Sky;~~
Here ~~Hell she~~ fix'd [the dreadful,] ~~and~~ there ~~divine~~ [the blest] abodes;
Fear made her Devils, and weak Hope her Gods.
Gods partial, changeful, ~~passionate~~ [cruel, &] unjust,
Whose Attributes were ~~Wrath, Revenge,~~ [Passion, Vengeance] & Lust;
Such as the Souls of Cowards might conceive,
And form'd like Tyrants, Tyrants would believe.
Zeal ~~now~~ [then], not Charity, became the Guide,
And Hell was built on Spite, and Heav'n on Pride.
~~Now~~ [then] sacred seem'd th' Ethereal Vault no more,
Altars grew Marble ~~now~~ [then], and reek'd with Gore.

The

No Ill could fear in God, nor understood
A Sovereign Being but a Sovereign Good.
True Faith, true Policy, united ran,
That was but Love of God, and this of Man.

Origin of Superstition & Tyranny, from the same Principle of <u>Fear</u>.

~~false Policy, at once~~
~~False Faith and wicked Government begun~~ |

What first taught Souls inslav'd & Realms undone

Faith
Th' enormous ~~Thought~~ of <u>many</u> made for <u>one</u>?

That proud Exception to all Nature's Laws.
T'invert the World, & counter-work its <u>Cause</u>.

Force first made Conquest, and that Conquest, Law;
First ~~Till heavnly Terrors taug<ht> those Conqu'eror~~
~~Then~~ ~~Then~~, Superstition gave ~~the~~ Tyrant~~s~~ Awe,

& ~~First~~ shook, ~~then~~ shar'd their ye ~~Pow'r~~, & ~~lent it~~ aid

Next then
~~Then~~ shar'd the Tyranny, ~~and~~ lent it aid,
And Gods of Conqu'rors, Slaves of Subjects made.
She, 'midst the Lightning's Glare, and Thunder's sound,
When rockd the Mountains, & when groan'd the Ground,
She taught the the Proud to pray
~~When~~ weak to bend, ~~and fierce to fear began~~,
To they:
~~At~~ Pow'r unseen, and mightier far than ~~Man~~,

She, frõ the rending Earth & bursting Skies Saw Gods descend, & Fiends infernal rise.

~~taught~~
~~From opening Earth, show'd Fiends infernal nigh~~,
~~And Gods supernal from the bursting Sky~~;
the dreadful the blest
Here ~~Hell she~~ fix'd, ~~and~~ there ~~divine~~ abodes;
Fear made her Devils, and weak Hope her Gods.
cruel &
Gods partial, changeful, ~~passionate~~, unjust,
Passion, Vengeance,
Whose Attributes were ~~Wrath~~, ~~Revenge, &~~ Lust;
Such as the Souls of Cowards might conceive,
And form'd like Tyrants, Tyrants would believe.
then
Zeal ~~now~~, not Charity, became the Guide,
And Hell was built on Spite, and Heav'n on Pride.
Then
~~Now~~ sacred seem'd th' AEthereal Vault no more,
then
Altars grew Marble ~~now~~, and reek'd with Gore.

The

~~The glutton Priest first~~ [Then first the ~~pamperd~~ Flamen ~~gorge on~~ tasted] tasted living food,
~~Then~~ [next] his grim Idol smeard with human blood;
Hurl'd Heav'ns dread Thunderbolts on all below,
And play'd the God an Engine on his Foe.

So drives Self-love, thro' just and thro' unjust,
To one Man's Pow'r, Ambition, Lucre, Lust:
The same Self-love, in all, becomes the cause
Of what restrains him, Government and Laws.
For say ~~what makes~~ [where lies] the Liberty of Man?
~~Not~~ ['Tis not in] doing what he ~~will, but what he can~~ [would, but can];
If what he likes, another like as well,
What serves one Will when many Wills rebell?
How shall he keep, what, sleeping or awake,
A weaker may surprize, a Stronger take?
His Safety must his Liberty restrain,
All join to guard what each desir'd to gain.
Forc'd into Virtue thus by Self-defence,
Ev'n Kings learn'd Justice and Benevolence;
Self-love forsook the path it first pursu'd,
And found the private in the publick Good.

~~Then~~ [then] Poets, ~~Legislators then~~ [Gods & Patriots] restore
The Faith and Moral, Nature gave before;
Re-lum'd her ancient Light, not kindled new;
If not God's Image, yet his Shadow drew:

Restoration of Governmt & Religion to their first Principle.

Taught

Then first the tasted
~~pamperd~~ Flamen ~~gorg'd on~~
~~The glutton Priest first~~ tasted living food,
^

Next
~~Then~~ his grim Idol smear'd with human blood;

Hurl'd Heav'ns dread Thunderbolts on all below,

And play'd the God an Engine on his Foe.

So drives Self-love, thro' just and thro' unjust, 269

To one Man's Pow'r, Ambition, Lucre, Lust:

The same Self-love, in all, becomes the cause

Of what restrains him, Government and Laws.

where lies
For say ~~what makes~~ the Liberty of Man?

Tis not in would, but can.
~~Not~~ doing what he ~~will, but what he can~~;

If what he likes, another like as well,

What serves one Will when many Wills rebell?

How shall he keep, what, sleeping or awake,

A weaker may surprize, a stronger take?

His Safety must his Liberty restrain,

All join to guard what each desir'd to gain.

Forc'd into Virtue thus by Self-defence,

Ev'n Kings learn'd Justice and Benevolence;

Self-love forsook the path it first pursu'd,

And found the private in the publick Good.

Then rose, & Patriots, to
~~Then~~ Poets, ~~Legislators then~~, restore 285

Restoration of Governm^{t} & Religion to their first Principle.

The Faith and Moral, Nature gave before;

Re-lum'd her ancient Light, not kindled new;

If not God's Image, yet his Shadow drew:

Taught

42.

Mix'd Government.

Taught Pow'rs due Use, to People and to Kings;
Taught nor to strain, nor slack those tender Strings;
The Less, the Greater, set so justly true,
That touching one must strike the other too;
Till jarring Interests, of themselves create
Th' according Musick of a well-mix'd State.
Tun'd like the World's great Harmony, that springs
From Order, Union, full Consent of Things:
Where small and great, where weak & mighty, made
To serve, not suffer, strengthen, not invade,
More pow'rful each, as needful to the rest,
And in proportion as it blesses, blest,
Draw to one Point, & to one Centre bring,
Beast, man or Angel, Servant, Lord and King.
The Beast, the Man, the Subject, and the King.

Various Forms of each.

For Forms of Government, let Fools contest;
Whate'er is best administer'd, is best.
For Modes of Faith, let graceless zealots fight;
His can't be wrong, whose Life is in the right.

True End of All.

All must be false, that thwart this one great End;
And all of God, that bless Mankind, or mend.

~~In Faith and Hope, the World must disagree,~~
~~But all Mankinds Concern is Charity:~~
~~Man like the gen'rous Vine, supported lives,~~
~~The Strength he gains is from th' Embrace he gives.~~
~~Th' extended Earth is but one Sphere of Bliss~~
~~To him, who makes another's Blessing his.~~

Pa-

Mix'd Government.

Taught Pow'rs due Use, to People and to Kings;

those
Taught nor to strain, nor slack ~~its~~ tender Strings;

~~&~~ ~~&~~
The Less, the Greater, set so justly true,
~~&~~ ~~<For>~~
That touching one must strike the other too.

~~Made~~ And ~~soften to~~ ~~of themselves~~ ~~From jarring~~
~~and ev'n from<Till>~~jarring of themselves ~~Int'rests well oppos'd~~
~~Till, from each varying~~ Interests ~~they~~ create ~~self-~~
<&>
mix'd
The according Musick of a well-~~tun'd~~ State.

~~to~~ they move
-~~Such is~~- ~~immense~~ Government ~~to move~~
~~Till~~, Tun'd like the World's great Harmony, that springs

~~By~~ On & Love
From Order, Union, full Consent of Things: ~~& Love~~ qu.

~~the~~
~~The~~ Where small and great, where weak & mighty, made si

To serve, not suffer, strengthen, not invade, postpon

More pow'rful each, as needful to the rest,

And in proportion as it blesses, blest,

Draw and to one blest
~~All~~ to one Point, ~~one~~ ~~happy~~ Centre bring;

Beast, Man, or Angel, Servant, ~~Master, King~~ or Lord ~~and~~ King.

The Beast, the Man, the Subject, and the King.

Various Forms of each.

For Forms of Government, let Fools contest;

Whate'er is best administer'd, is best.

For Modes of Faith, let graceless Zealots
~~Let graceless Zealots for Religions~~ fight;

His can't be wrong, whose Life is in the right.

True End of All.

this One great
All must be false, that thwart ~~great Nature's~~ End;

And all of God, that bless Mankind, or mend.

[Man, like - as at ye End

Qu: si postponenda in Ep. sequ.

~~will~~
~~In Faith and Hope, the World must disagree~~,

~~Charity the greatest of the three~~
-~~Stet~~- ~~But all Mankind's Concern is Charity:~~ ~~Joins all Extremes~~: ~~All Earth one Sphere of~~ Bliss

~~Man like the gen'rous Vine, supported lives~~,

~~<qu>~~ ~~<si>~~ ~~<Standum>~~ 2 ~~The Strength he gains is from th' Embrace he gives~~.

-~~Stet~~- ~~2 The' extended Earth is but one Sphere of Bliss~~

1 ~~To him who makes another's blessing his~~.

Pa-

Parent or Friend first touch the virtuous mind,
His Country next, and next all Humankind;
God loves from Whole to Parts; but human Soul
Must rise from Individual to the Whole.
The first Impression the soft Passions make,
Like the small Pebble in the peaceful Lake,
Begets a greater, and a greater still,
The Circle widening till the whole it fill;
Till God, and Man, and Brute, and Reptile-kind,
All wake, all move, all agitate his mind;
Earth with his bounteous Overflows is blest;
Heav'n pleas'd beholds its Image in his Breast.

Let us, my S. this plain truth confess,
One is our Duty and our Happiness:
Which makes our Int'rest and our Duty joyn;
And Faith and Morals end as they began,
All, in the Love of God, and Love of Man.

On their own Axis as the Planets run,
Yet make at once their Circle round ye Sun;
So two consistent Motions act ye Soul,
And one regards Itself, & one the Whole:
Thus God & Nature link'd ye gen'ral Frame,
And bad Selflove & Social be ye same.

Finis.

Parent or Friend first touch the virtuous mind,
His Country next, and next all Humankind;
God loves from Whole to Parts; but human Soul
Must rise from Individual to the Whole.
The first Impression the soft Passions make,
Like the small Pebble in the ~~gentle~~ peaceful Lake,
Begets a greater, and a greater still,
The Circle widening till the whole it fill;
Till God, and Man, and Brute, and Reptile-kind,
All wake, all move, all agitate his Mind;
Earth with his bounteous Overflows is blest;
Heav'n pleas'd beholds its Image in his Breast.

haec om- nia in Epis. sequent.

Postpone to end ye following Epistle

Let us, my S. ~~own that Skill Divine~~, this plain truth confess,
One is our Duty and our Happiness:
δ ~~Which makes our Int'rest and our Duty joyn~~,
Thus And Faith and Morals end as they began,
316 All, in the Love of God, and Love of Man.

[Man like ye genrous Vine supported lives. The Strength he gains is by th'
Embrace he gives

On their own Axis as the Planets run,
Yet make at once their Circle round ye Sun;
So two consistent Motions act ye Soul,
& one regards Itself, & one the Whole:

[Such is great
Natures Harmony y^t
~~Form'd like ye Worlds great~~ Governm^t ~~must move~~ that springs
From Order
Where &c.
Draw to one point
& to one Centre bring
Beast Man or Angel

[Thus God ^ Thus God & Nature, link'd ye gen'ral Frame,
& bad Selflove & Social be ye same.

So ~~stands~~ moves the Worlds immense Machine on springs
Of Order Union & Consent of things

~~Good Nature makes & keeps~~
~~our Happiness~~
~~Man like ye genrous Vine~~

~~And thou whose~~ Love -- last
~~Say, when along~~--fame Shall then my feeble bark
2All in ye Love--When Statesmen--foes. Shall then
this verse

Heav'n &
Thus Go<d> Nature linkd ye genral Frame
& bid Self Love & Social be ye same
Round their
Yet make at once
So two consistent
& one regards Itself
Let us my S-- this
One is our Duty
Thus Heavn
& bade
~~And Faith~~. St J. whose Love--matures last
--last. Oh w^n along
Shall fly full spread
When Statesmen
Whose
Shall then my feeble bark
Pursue
Shall than this
Thou wert
That urg'd
From
For
Showd
That
That
Social are y^e same
That the same our Duty & our Bliss below
& Mans whole knowledge Man himself to know.

Finis

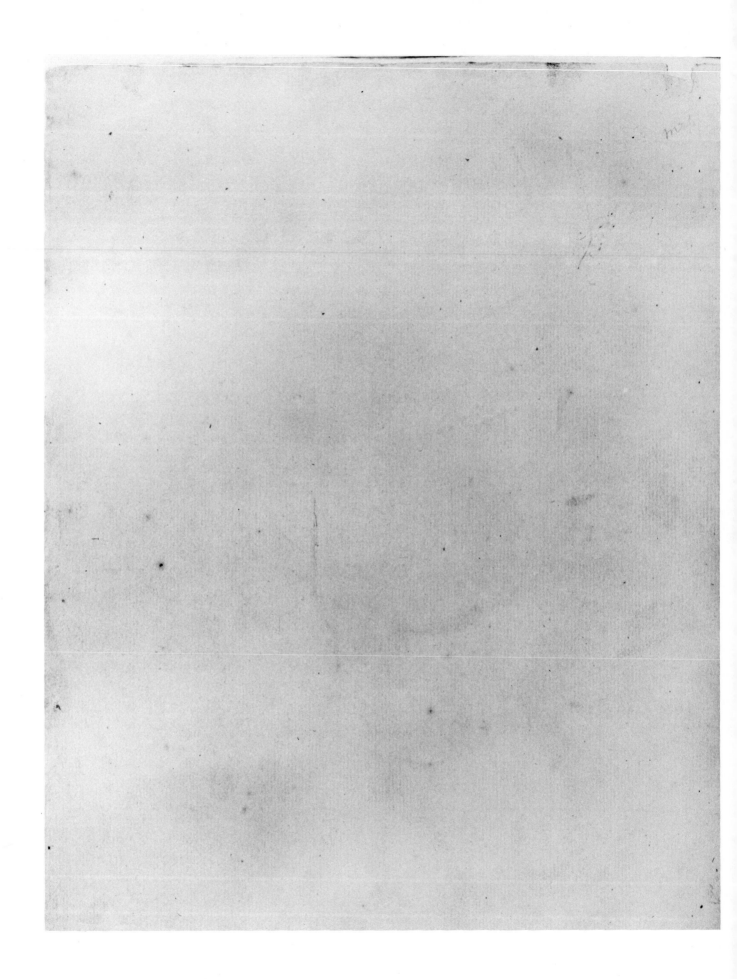

Incipit Liber Secundus.

Epist. I. Of ye Limits of Reason

And now, transported o'er so vast a Plain,
While the free Courser flies with all ~~her~~ the Rein;
While heav'nward, now, his mounting Wings she feels,
Now, ~~Scatters~~ stoops where Fools fly trembling from his heels;
Wilt thou, my Lælius! keep ye Course in sight,
~~Confine the~~ ~~thy~~ Fury, or ~~restrain my~~ assist ye Flight?
Lælius, whose Love excus'd my labours past,
Matures my present, & shall bound my last.

26

Incipit Liber Secundus.

Epist. I. of ye Limits of Reason

And now, transported o'er so vast a Plain,
the
While the free Courser flies with all ~~her~~ Rein;
While heav'nward, now, his mounting Wings ~~s~~he feels,
stoops where
Now scatterd Fools fly trembling from his heels;
Wilt thou, my Laelius, keep y^e Course in sight,
~~Or urge~~ assist
Confine the ~~my~~ Fury, or ~~restrain m~~y^e Flight?
Laelius, whose Love excus'd my labours past,
Matures my present, & shall bound my last.

Essay on Man: Houghton Library Manuscript

NOTES TO THE TRANSCRIPTS
EPISTLE I

MS/TS Page:Line	
HLM 1/TS 1:7*	*The bracketed word is probably* this, *but the canceled comma after it is then an oddity.*
HLM 1/TS 1:10	allude *partly overwrites an illegible word, probably* to.
HLM 1/TS 1:18	*Exclamation point was altered from comma when line was revised.*
HLM 1/TS 1:36	*Pope appears to have written* whoes *or* whose; ions *of* Passions *overwrites an illegible word.*
HLM 3/TS 3:1	Book *overwrites an illegible word or numerals.*
HLM 3/TS 3:9	Steed shall *is canceled, then restored;* know *is altered to* knows *and then back to* know.
HLM 3/TS 3:26	W *of* Where *overwrites an illegible word, probably* If.
HLM 5/TS 5:3	or *overwrites an ampersand.*
HLM 5/TS 5:41	*As often when stumped for the word he wants, Pope leaves a blank.*
HLM 6/TS 6:20	P *of* Pow'r *overwrites* B.
HLM 10/TS 10:2	*The first round bracket overwrites a comma.*
HLM 11/TS 11:13, 12	*The question mark in each instance overwrites a semicolon.*
HLM 12/TS 12:17	Know . . . Point *overwrites an erasure.*
HLM 12/TS 12:23	Evill *overwrites an erasure.*

Epistle II

MS/TS Page:Line	
HLM 15/TS 15:8	W *of* While *is altered from* w.
HLM 15/TS 15:12	Men *is altered from* Man.
HLM 15/TS 15:15	T *of* To *is altered from* t.
HLM 15/TS 15:20	C *of* Correct *overwrites* c; Spirit *overwrites an illegible word or words, probably* Grace *followed by an ampersand.*
HLM 15/TS 15:22	with Grace *overwrites* to know.
HLM 17/TS 17:14	thy *is altered from* the.
HLM 17/TS 17:18	T *of* Thy *is altered from* t.
HLM 17/TS 17:34, 36	tell'st *is altered from* tells, *and* mark'st *from* marks.
HLM 17/TS 17:35	thy *is altered from* the.
HLM 18/TS 18:12	*Beneath* Both necessary *Pope has erased* Why the former the stronger, *shifting this gloss to the margin of ll. 24–25.*
HLM 19/TS 19:5	A *of* At *is altered from* a; *the caret overwrites a comma.*
HLM 19/TS 19:11	d *of* dexterity *is possibly altered from* D.
HLM 20/TS 20:22–23	re *(shown in the transcript in l. 22) is inserted in the manuscript before* moves, *the* t *of* but *being altered to* r.
HLM 21/TS 21:5	*The obscure markings in left margin may read* 26 ll., *referring to the ensuing paragraph, which does have 26 lines.*
HLM 21/TS 21:22	S *of* She *is altered from* s.
HLM 22/TS 22:19	the . . . hope *overwrites an erasure, apparently of* our expectation.
HLM 22/TS 22:20	Which *overwrites an illegible word, possibly* That *or* Then.
HLM 23/TS 23:2	some *overwrites* a.
HLM 23/TS 23:4	Stoick's *is altered from* Stoicks.
HLM 23/TS 23:6	*The first* fix'd *is altered from* fix.
HLM 23/TS 23:16	*The question mark is altered from a colon.*
HLM 23/TS 23:17	*The scrawl in the left margin is evidently Pope's indication of intent not to indent this line.*
HLM 24/TS 24:7	will *is altered from an illegible word, possibly* wise.
HLM 24/TS 24:10	*In the transcript,* from *is struck through in error.*
HLM 24/TS 24:14	*As indicated in the transcript,* reigns *is altered to* reign and then back to reigns.
HLM 24/TS 24:21	The . . . Mind *is written over an erased passage or gloss.*

*HLM refers to Houghton Library Manuscript; TS is "transcript."

MS/TS Page:Line	
HLM 24/TS 24:19–21	*The meaning of the marks to left of these lines, not included in the transcript, remains obscure.*
HLM 24/TS 24:41	glares at first *overwrites* is a Monster.
HLM 25/TS 25:18	*Like other insertions in pencil in the manuscript, this line seems to have been inserted at a later time.*
HLM 25/TS 25:24	with *overwrites* to.
HLM 25/TS 25:25a	But *overwrites an illegible word.*
HLM 25/TS 25:26	ne'r *is altered from* never.
HLM 25/TS 25:31	But *overwrites an illegible word, probably* Each.
HLM 25/TS 25:34	B——: *Sir John Blunt. See MLM TS, 21:84.* Y——: *Sir William Yonge, Whig M.P., "ductile courtier and . . . parliamentary tool," as Lord Hervey describes him, whose "name was proverbially used to express everything pitiful, corrupt, and contemptible."*
HLM 25/TS 25:34–44	*See the adaptation of these lines in the "Epilogue to the Satires," Dialogue 1:13–16. Of the persons mentioned here, Yonge, Blount, Huggins, and Sutton reappear there.*
HLM 25/TS 25:35	B——t: *see above, l. 34 n.*
HLM 25/TS 25:36	Huggins: *John Huggins, notorious warden of the Fleet prison, 1713–28, was widely accused of extortion, cruelties, even murder. See TE, 4:367.*
HLM 25/TS 25:37	H–r–y: *Lord Hervey.* Bladen & Janson: *professional gamblers.*
HLM 25/TS 25:38	Sid. . . . Chartres: *see MLM TS, 21:98;* knows *overwrites an illegible word, apparently* knew.
HLM 25/TS 25:40	Peter: *see above, MLM TS, 21:99.*
HLM 25/TS 25:42	Faustina: *Faustina the Younger, cousin and wife to the philosophic Emperor Marcus Aurelius. Her reputation for gallantry, though apparently undeserved, was considerable. The English reference, if any, is not clear.*
HLM 25/TS 25:43	Nero: *possibly a glance at Walpole, who was occasionally referred to by this name among the Opposition.* Messaline: *the Emperor Claudius's profligate wife.*
HLM 25/TS 25:44	Sutton: *Sir Robert Sutton, negligent governor of the Charitable Corporation. See TE, 3. 2:100; 4:387.*
HLM 27/TS 27:11	*The second round bracket overwrites a comma.*
HLM 27/TS 27:12	Bids *overwrites* Lets.
HLM 27/TS 27:13	<Bids> *overwrites an illegible word, possibly* Lets.

MS/TS Page:Line	
HLM 27/TS 27:14	and *overwrites an illegible word;* all *is altered from* that.
HLM 27/TS 27:27	travell *is altered from* travels *and* quitt *from* quit.
HLM 27/TS 27:42	Passion *overwrites an illegible word.*
HLM 27/TS 27:43	Whatere *appears to be altered from* Let.
HLM 27/TS 27:47	What *overwrites an erasure.*
HLM 27/TS 27:49	Toland: *John Toland (1670–1722), whose "Christianity Not Mysterious" (1696) sought to reconcile Christianity with the epistemology of John Locke (l. 52).*
HLM 27/TS 27:51	Ross, Argyle: *Pope refers to the ancient hostility of these two houses (i.e. the MacDonalds and the Campbells), but perhaps more particularly to the massacre of the MacDonalds at Glencoe in 1692 under Archibald Campbell, the first duke of Argyle. For Argyle Pope first wrote* Ar——e.
HLM 27/TS 27:56, 58, 61	*Pope has unaccountably canceled terminal punctuation.*
HLM 27/TS 27:70	Payn: *unidentified.* Welsted: *Leonard Welsted. See TE, 4:393.*
HLM 27/TS 27:52	*Pope's caret overwrites a comma.*
HLM 27/TS 27:54	all that *overwrites* fast ere.
HLM 27/TS 27:81	S *of* Some *overwrites* s.

EPISTLE III

HLM 32/TS 32:10	*After* Matter *Pope has canceled a comma.*
HLM 32/TS 32:13	*Pope has canceled the second comma.*
HLM 32/TS 32:32	*In the manuscript, these four words are very lightly inserted in pencil immediately to right of l. 31.*
HLM 32/TS 32:53	Think'st *is altered from* Tis not; *immediately to left of this line, in pencil, Pope has written* Know.
HLM 32/TS 32:54	*The first* his *is altered from* the.
HLM 33/TS 33:2	his *was altered from* her *before canceling.*
HLM 33/TS 33:8	I *of* Is *overwrites* y *of* only.
HLM 33/TS 33:9	N *of* Not *is altered from* n.
HLM 33/TS 33:9, 12	*The question mark is in each case altered from a semicolon.*
HLM 33/TS 33:11	only *is altered from* all.
HLM 33/TS 33:12	N *of* Not *is altered from* n; thine *is altered from* thy; *the second* the *is altered from* thy.
HLM 34/TS 34:29–33	*This marginal passage should appear in the transcript to right of and below l. 34, being a continuation of Arbuthnot's interpolation. See Introduction, p. 191.*

MS/TS Page:Line	
HLM 34/TS 34:34	with *overwrites an illegible word, possibly* by.
HLM 35/TS 35:25	rose to *overwrites* to—Throat, *evidently a cue for the final line of the passage whose insertion is signaled by its first line in l. 22. See MLM TS, 30:44–57.*
HLM 36/TS 36:34	O *of* On *overwrites* e *of* Made.
HLM 36/TS 36:38	Sparkles *is altered from* Sparks.
HLM 36/TS 36:41	*Possibly the comma after* first *has been canceled.*
HLM 37/TS 37:11	W *of* Wing *overwrites* w.
HLM 38/TS 38:10	*To left of the line, Pope has written* 36 *(omitted inadvertently in the transcript), possibly a count of the lines calculated at some point to have been comprehended in the two marginal paragraphs here beginning* Pride yet was not *and* See him from Nature rising, *which in the final printed text amount to 38 lines.*
HLM 38/TS 38:15	<Link> *overwrites* Bond.
HLM 38/TS 38:16	their, *which is possibly altered from* the, *overwrites* 38 *(an earlier entry of the page number);* The *is altered from* That.
HLM 38/TS 38:28	*In the manuscript, the three crosses are struck through (an effect not reproducible in the transcript without confusion).*
HLM 38/TS 38:34	adore *is evidently a cue word (above, TS, 36:26) jotted down before the marginal lines were inserted.*
HLM 38/TS 38:37	stretch'd *overwrites an illegible word.*
HLM 38/TS 38:38	strict *overwrites an illegible word.*
HLM 38/TS 38:42	*In the manuscript* on Man *overwrites* made *(the final word understood in l. 44 of the transcript).*
HLM 38/TS 38:46	<Leaves> *in the manuscript was evidently intended as an alternative for* Left *in l. 42 of the transcript.*
HLM 38/TS 38:52	*In the manuscript,* B *of* Blood *overwrites* y *of* Society.
HLM 38/TS 38:60	neede *overwrites an erasure, evidently of* cause.
HLM 38/TS 38:62	Cause *overwrites an erasure.*
HLM 38/TS 38:67	And *is altered from* Or.
HLM 38/TS 38:74	Thy *overwrites an illegible word, possibly* her; inspiring *appears to overwrite a* ₰ *(for deletion).*
HLM 39/TS 39:29	rs *of* Monsters *and* of *overwrite an illegible word, possibly* draw; th' *is altered from* the, *of which the final* e *overwrites the* A *of* Abyss.
HLM 40/TS 40:9	*The question mark is possibly altered from an exclamation point.*
HLM 40/TS 40:19	midst *and* Lightning's glare *are written over erasures.*
HLM 40/TS 40:27	show'd *overwrites an erasure, perhaps of* taught.
HLM 40/TS 40:29	dreadful *overwrites an illegible word, possibly* direful.
HLM 40/TS 40:30	*In the manuscript, Pope's caret overwrites the comma after* fix'd.
HLM 40/TS 40:42, 44	*These two lines appear to overwrite an erased couplet.*
HLM 42/TS 42:11	Interests *is altered from* Interest, *the final* s *overwriting a comma.*
HLM 42/TS 42:16	Government *overwrites an erasure.*
HLM 42/TS 42:18	*Following* on *several words have been erased, of which the final three are possibly* Liberty and Love.
HLM 42/TS 42:33	*In this line, between ll. 32 and 34, four penciled words have been erased, possibly* best shall <*or* can> exercise itself.
HLM 42/TS 42:36	Religions *overwrites an erasure.*
HLM 42/TS 42:38	O *of* One *overwrites* o.
HLM 43/TS 43:19	*Several words are erased here between ll. 18 and 20, of which the first eight appear to be* If Vice turn Virtue in its own defence.
HLM 43/TS 43:22	316: *again, part of Pope's line count.*
HLM 43/TS 43:36	that *overwrites* whose.
HLM 43/TS 43:37	From *overwrites* Are.
HLM 51/TS 51:5	free *possibly overwrites an illegible word.*
HLM 51/TS 51:6	his *is altered from* her; Wings *from* Wing.
HIM 51/TS 51:8	his *is altered from* her.
HLM 51/TS 51:11	*As the transcript indicates,* ye *is altered from* my.

Epistle to Dr. Arbuthnot

INTRODUCTION

1

THE MANUSCRIPTS OF the *Epistle to Dr. Arbuthnot* have come down to us in an odd clutter of working papers, fair copies, verse fragments, and Richardson collations, written on nine folio leaves and parts of leaves.[1]

The heart of this material, as John Butt demonstrated in a brilliant lecture nearly thirty years ago, is a 260-line poem (TS, 1–7) addressed not to Arbuthnot but to Pope's friend William Cleland (1674?–1741) and probably composed entirely or mostly in 1732 in response to malicious misapplications of the Burlington epistle's "Timon" to the duke of Chandos and his elegant seat at Cannons.[2] This poem says nothing of the good doctor whom Pope credits in the published epistle with prolonging his life (*TE*, ll. 27–30); makes no reference to Gay's death, which occurred on 4 December 1732 (*TE*, ll. 255–60); contains the famous lines on Atticus but lacks those on Bufo[3] and Sporus (*TE*, ll. 231–48, 305–33); and, though it ends with a version of the well-known passage on the poet's father, shows no trace of the ensuing conclusion of the epistle as we know it, which turns to his mother and the cradle of resposing age (*TE*, ll. 406–19).

Most startling of all, perhaps, this 260-line poem reaches the published epistle's dramatic opening ("Shut, shut the door, good John, fatigu'd I said") at a point about two-thirds of the way along (Pope's numbering, ll. 167 ff; TS, 5:2–8), and places at another point thirty lines earlier (Pope's numbering, 137 ff; TS, 4:48–60), entirely distinct from that opening, the two paragraphs that in the published epistle succeed it: "What walls can guard me. . . ?" "Is there a Parson . . . ?" (*TE*, ll. 7–14, 15–26). The Cleland poem's own opening paragraph takes the form of a tribute to its dedicatee, who, after what had apparently been a distinguished military career, now held a government place as tax commissioner and, both in 1729, in connection with the *Dunciad*, and in 1731, during the brouhaha raised by the alleged attack on Chandos, had stepped forward vigorously to Pope's defense—in the latter instance, possibly with some degree of danger to his livelihood.[4] Pope's tribute to him, as we now have it (a few lines may have been cropped away at the top of the leaf, as may an early title) reads:

> And of myself too something must I say?
> Take then this Verse, the Triffle of a Day;
> And if it live, it lives but to commend
> The Man of Friendship, but no boasting Friend,
> The Man of Courage, yet not prone to fight,
> The Man of Learning, yet too wise to write.

Lame stuff, but we can see what is happening. In this earliest version of his *apologia,* the poet seeks to establish from the start images of rational and manly self-possession, intended to contrast with the narcissistic lunacies soon to be described—intended also perhaps, with one exception, to characterize the poem's author as well as the former soldier to whom it is addressed. That exception will then serve as bridge to the crucial question: "too wise to write"/ "Why did I write?"

A slightly abbreviated version of the long reflection answering this query (ll. 125–230 in the *TE* text of the published epistle) follows immediately in the Cleland poem and takes it from l. 7 to l. 94 (Pope's numbering; TS, 3:35). It is in this section that the portrait of Atticus appears, now in the expanded context that Pope had built for it before publishing it in the Pope–Swift *Miscellanies* of 1727.[5] With that context it now occupies ll. 27–94 of the Cleland poem, immediately succeeding the two paragraphs "Why did I write . . . ?" (TS, 1:13–24) and "But why then publish" (TS, 1:25–38). The clean condition of these paragraphs in the manuscript makes it reasonable to suppose that they too had been in existence, at least in Pope's mind, for some while, and that what he probably had by him when he began the Cleland poem was simply or mainly the portrait of Atticus with accumulated appurtenances: eighty-eight lines in all, which he copied down in our manuscript almost without corrections.

Lines 95–104 (Pope's numbering; TS, 3:37–80) show the first uncertainty of direction, one that will only be resolved at last in two independent papers of verses (TS, 8–9) copied out by an amanuensis but revised in Pope's hand. Line 104 (TS, 3:70) makes passing mention of a patron figure named "B——b" (Bubb Dodington). He will become Bufo in the published epistle (*TE*, ll. 34–38); but since he is already sketched marginally here as Bubo and a gap of sixteen lines in Pope's numbering occurs at this point, it seems probable that the full portrait proliferated early and was intended for inclusion in this space as part of the poem when it was still being addressed to Cleland.

Most of the remainder of the Cleland text is taken up with the familiar harassments and embarrassments of being a celebrated author. These—from which "No walls can guard me" (Pope's numbering, l. 167; TS, 4:48)—prompt at length the impatient outburst: "Shut, shut the door" (Pope's erroneous numbering, l. 160; TS, 5:2). But then follows, quite anticlimactically, an additional register of harassments and embarrassments, among them flattery of his physical deficiencies; and it is from these, confessed now to be a legacy from his parents, that he manages a transition to his father's exemplary life, with his description of which the poem ends. On the whole, an occasionally vivid 260 lines, thanks to some of the particulars, but shapeless.

2

What happened next, and when, we can only guess. In its issue of 22–25 January 1732, the London *Evening-Post* carried twelve lines of verse entitled *Horace, Satire 4. Lib. l. Paraphrased. Inscribed to the Honorable Mr.* ——.[6] In this fragment—whose subject is slander (in obvious allusion to the misinterpretations currently being put on "Timon's Villa")—early versions of several couplets used later in the published poem are imbedded: *TE,* ll. 291–92, 295–96, 289–90, 297–98, 303–4—in that order. A fuller and more accomplished rendering of this theme, roughly analogous to *TE,* ll. 283–304, appears marginally in the 260-line manuscript (TS, 3:18–42) and another briefer rendering makes part of one of the fragments (TS, 10:51–69). Neither passage can be dated, but as the latter hews close to the newspaper text, and the main purpose of the former seems to be to establish (as a further defense of the Atticus portrait, which it adjoins in the manuscript?) the poet's concern to reserve his satires for the guilty, and most particularly for such malicious gossips as those who see at Cannons "what was never there," both passages may belong to the early weeks or months of 1732, when Pope was still smarting from the reception of the *Epistle to Burlington.*

A new conclusion for the Cleland poem was probably also conceived at an early date. We know, at least, that a version of the lines on rocking the cradle of reposing age was in existence from 3 September 1731, when Pope quoted them in a letter to Aaron Hill. In this text they purport to be addressed to an unidentified "successful Youth," and the description of the poet's attendance on his mother precipitates a wish that when *he* is old and ill he may receive—from "some kind Hand, like B***'s or thine"—similarly affectionate attentions.[7] By the time these verses appear on the sheet from which they have visibly been torn in our cluster of manuscripts (TS, 14), they are appended to the praise of his father and have been made the poem's closure as in the published work. In respect of tone, however, much remains to be done. As we read them in the manuscript, the curve of Pope's feeling flows from pride in his father to concern for mother, and then, self-indulgently, to solicitude for himself. In the *Epistle to Dr. Arbuthnot,* this last concern has been displaced by a prayer for the doctor's well-being that glances only obliquely and in passing at his own.

What appears to be a first effort to meddle radically with the internal structure of the Cleland poem occupies a fresh page in the extant manuscripts (TS, 10) and incorporates the shorter passage on slanderers referred to above. In their situation on this page (ll. 1–12), the lines of the Cleland poem deploring the public's insistence on prying into authors' plans (TS, 4:8–34) no longer open anticlimactically onto a reprise of a poet's harassments and embarrassments. Instead, they introduce a third phase of his *apologia*—not only "why did I write?" and "why then publish?" but "why write Satyr?" (TS, 10:14–50). This particular defense of satire was later siphoned off, however, to contribute with other fragments to the composition of the *Epistle to Fortescue,* a process necessarily completed before 15 February 1733, when that epistle was published, but probably not begun much before late January.[8] Once this transfer had been mentally conceived, the passage on the public's prying (TS, 10:8–34) and the passage expressing the poet's resolve to protect the innocent by attacking those who slander or betray them (TS, 10:51–69) remained on the page in close conjunction. A fruitful conjunction, I am inclined to think, since after such lines on the satirist's social role and yet more especially after the fuller elaboration of this role in the margin of the 260-line poem (TS, 3), there could be no continuing with a mere bill of complaints. The materials occupying ll. 137–232 of the Cleland poem (TS, 3:47 to 6:36) had to be repositioned, and where better, Pope must have concluded (unfortunately we do not know at what date) than as prolegomena to the two questions, "why did I write?" and "why then publish?"—the third question, "why write Satyr?" being now tacitly answered in the formulations that we have seen springing up in the manuscripts from the *Evening-Post* fragment on slander. In some such moment of illumination, we may guess, Pope made the crucial leap that is registered for us in his insertion of "Incipit. (Epistle to Arbuthnot.) / (l)" at the top of the next-to-final leaf of the Cleland poem and in his general reordering of themes—reflected, still sometimes ambiguously, in large marginal numerals on pp. 1, 3, 5, 7, 8, 11, and 13.

3

The last of the extant Arbuthnot fragments to be composed was undoubtedly "Sporus." In February 1733 Pope had published the *Epistle to Fortescue,* a "rearguard," as Professor Butt aptly describes it, for the *Epistle to Bathurst,* published a month earlier, and the *Epistle to Burlington,* published in December 1731. Pope's conviction that court gossips, not least among them his former friends Lady Mary Wortley Montagu and Lord Hervey, had helped spread the lies identifying "Timon" with Chandos expressed itself in *Fortescue* in two notorious characterizations. One was of a foppish poetaster named Lord Fanny, descendant of Horace's Fannius, who seems to have been a Roman version of the wealthy scribbling dilettante of modern times who publishes his own works and circulates them as gifts to libraries:

> The Lines are weak, another's pleas'd to say,
> Lord Fanny spins a thousand such a day.
> (Ll. 5–6)

The other was of a mad poetess named Sappho by whom one was poxed if she loved, libeled if she hated—

> Slander or Poyson, dread from *Delia's* Rage,
> Hard Words or Hanging, if your Judge be *Page,*
> From furious *Sappho* scarce a milder Fate,
> P——x'd by her Love, or libell'd by her Hate
> (Ll. 81–84)

It is not easy to understand why Lady Mary and Lord Hervey should have wished to claim these characterizations (though undoubtedly intended for them) by responding publicly unless they believed their image in the public mind was such as made identification inevitable. But respond they did. In *Verses Address'd to the Imitator of the First Satire of the Second Book of Horace. By a Lady,* published scarcely more than three weeks after *Fortescue,* Lady Mary, with Hervey's assistance, gave Pope the tongue-lashing of his life. Most of the charges made were such as he had grown accustomed if not inured to: he was ignorant of Greek, misunderstood Horace, wrote "crabbed Numbers"—"Hard as thy Heart, and as thy Birth obscure" (the latter a not-very-pretty thrust at Pope's mother, who was still alive and whom in the days of their friendship Lady Mary must have known)—and in pillorying "Timon" he had *of course* been showing ingratitude to Chandos, since "even Benefits can't rein thy Hand." The deepest thrusts, however, were directed where they would hurt the most:

> If Limbs unbroken, Skin without a Stain,
> Unwhipt, unblanketed, unkick'd, unslain;
> That wretched little Carcass you retain:
> The Reason is, not that the World wants Eyes,
> But thou'rt so mean, they see, and they despise.
>
> Like the first bold Assassin's be thy Lot,
> Ne'er be thy Guilt forgiven, or forgot;
> But as thou hat'st, be hated by Mankind,
> And with the Emblem of thy Crooked Mind,
> Mark'd on thy Back, like *Cain,* by God's own Hand,
> Wander like him, accursed through the Land.

A brilliant performance, in its kind. And it may well have precipitated in its victim that rush of Hippocrene to the head to which we owe not only "Sporus," but the psychological energy that at last propelled so many and such discrete atoms as are recorded in the *Arbuthnot* manuscripts into one firm poise.

In November came a further attack. A letter in verse that Hervey had written to an old friend, Dr. William Sherwin, was published by its recipient, charging among other sillinesses that Pope's entire poetical career had been one extensive plagiarism.[9] Though this was the most ancient of canards and the whole performance feeble, Pope was understandably troubled by what looked to be a conspiracy to defame him in the highest echelons of government; for Lady Mary was a frequenter of Court and Lord Hervey was not only vice-chamberlain to the king but such a favorite with the queen that he breakfasted with her regularly and on hunting days was commissioned to ride immediately beside her chaise—"Close at the Ear of Eve is perchd the Toad" (TS, 11:10)—to entertain her.[10] It was easy to imagine what stories might there be told of a papist poet, some of whose friends were suspected Jacobites or even former servants of the Stuart pretender, and whose own private little lightnings seemed no longer to be playing about the heads of dunces but shifting dangerously toward heads of state. So concerned was Pope that he sent Arbuthnot to make inquiries. To him Hervey announced (according to his own report) that Pope

> was a rascal; had begun with me and deserved it, and that my only reason for being sorry the verses were printed, which I did not design they should be, was because I thought it below me to enter into a paper war with one that had made himself by his late works as contemptible as he was odious.[11]

This, he confided to another friend, had put Pope into a most violent fury, "and j'en suis ravi."[12]

Possibly owing to this incident; perhaps also because it would not have done to reply to a woman as he intended to reply to Hervey; perhaps, as well, because Hervey's political position made him available to the imagination both as hated individual and as symbol of the sycophancies that all courts and seats of power engender, particularly including (from Pope's Opposition view) the court of George II and the administration of Robert Walpole, Hervey bore the brunt of Pope's revenge. "Sporus"—the name of Nero's palace catamite and eunuch—said it all.

In the late spring of 1733, therefore, during the first glow of anger following the *Verses to the Imitator,* or in the early winter of 1733–34, when that first anger must have been rekindled on Arbuthnot's report that Hervey had thrown down the gauntlet, we may guess that the character of Sporus was born. One tends to stress the firstness of the anger because the portrait as we have it among the *Arbuthnot* manuscripts is not far removed from the vein of pure invective in which Pope himself had been attacked. And if the numeral "(5)" that heads it and the slant line that closes it (often with Pope a *finis* symbol) indicate an original purpose to let the portrait conclude the poem, then we clearly have here an additional instance of the happiness of Pope's second thoughts and the advantage of his settled principle of letting things "lie by" him for indefinite periods.

4

During the remainder of 1733 and the early months of 1734, Pope was probably too engrossed in other projects—the fourth epistle of the *Essay on Man,* the *Epistle to Cobham,* and the *Second Satire of the Second book of Horace* (not to mention the preparation of his poems for the *Works* of 1735, together with the editing of his letters and the first *sub rosa* negotiations that he hoped would trick Curll into publishing them) to give more than perfunctory attention to the poem in which Sporus was to be enshrined. During July, however, he was with Bathurst at Cirencester and during August with Peterborow at Southampton, both favorite haunts for his labors of composition. At one or other of these retreats he began (like Medea with the fragments of old Aeson) the formidable task of assembling the various states and pieces of his epistle—with probably other snatches we no longer have—into a reconsidered whole.

Whether at this stage the poem was still designed for Cleland, we do not know—in his own self-interest Cleland may have felt compelled to decline the honor once Sporus was in place. By late August, at any rate, if not before, the shift was made. It had been no secret for some weeks that Arbuthnot was ill with the disease from which he would not recover, and in a letter of July, in the spirit of a last request, he had urged Pope to "continue that noble *Disdain* and *Abhorrence* of Vice, which you seem naturally endu'd with," yet "with a due regard to your own Safety"[13]—advice that the Arbuthnot of the poem essentially repeats. (One wonders if, earlier in July, the real Arbuthnot had been sent the Sporus portrait.) Replying to the advice on August 2, Pope acknowledged its propriety but pointed out that "General Satire" was useless: "'tis only by hunting One or two from the Herd that Examples can be made. If a man writ all his Life against the Collective Body of the Banditti, or against Lawyers, would it do the least Good, or lessen the Body?"[14]

Following this up on August 25 he told Arbuthnot that his advice had

> worked so much upon me (considering the *Time & State* you gave it in) that I determine to address to you one of my Epistles, written by piece-meal many years, & which I have now made haste to put together; wherein the Question is stated, what were, & are, my Motives of writing, the Objections to them, & my answers. It pleases me much to take this occasion of testifying (to the public at least, if not to Posterity) my Obligations & Friendship for, & from, you, for so many years: That is all that's in it; for Compliments are fulsome & go for nothing.[15]

Nine days later he was able to add:

> we have here little News or Company, and I am glad of it because it has given me the time to finish the Poem I told you of, which I hope may be the best Memorial I can leave, both of my Friendship to you, & of my own Character being such as you need not be ashamd of that Friendship. The apology is a bold one, but True. . . .[16]

Even so, a good deal of shaking down remained. The first edition of the poem, published on 2 January 1735 with a 1734 date, still shows signs of haste, as Professor Butt has pointed out,[17] and it is not until the last of four editions dated 1735 that the text settles in details to the text we read today.

5

Close readers of the manuscripts and transcripts to follow will, I think, find much to occupy them. They will also find—what in my own experience has proved true of poetical manuscripts generally, no matter whose—that they cast little light on the questions of greatest interest. How, why, and when (for example) did Pope grasp the value of suspending his *apologia* between a command and a prayer? between a mood of partly comic exasperation and one of resignation, epitomized in the dying Arbuthnot? between images of siege, exclusion, and defense and images of domesticity, privacy, and family affection—the still center that we all struggle to protect? How certainly did he understand that the shift to Arbuthnot was a stroke of genius, enabling him not only to pay tribute to his dying friend, but to make what Arnold will call later "this strange disease of modern life" a central theme: a species of fractionating illness that within the work itself the poet's persona metaphorically shakes off in the remarkable lines following the Sporus portrait, leading at last to an identification in spirit with his father, whose "life to sickness past unknown." And was Pope ever aware—whatever old scores he might be paying off—that in Atticus, Bufo, and Sporus he had sketched out the three most dangerous giants-in-residence in his own (or any other literary lion's, or any teacher's) personal House of Pride: to begrudge and repress the talent of the young; to feed on the adulation of the second-rate; to prostitute one's services to a social, critical, political, or some other Establishment? In view of Pope's eminence in his own time over so many years, one cannot but wonder whether he was not projecting in these figures some profound temptations of his own.

On such mysteries, alas, the rest is always silence.

NOTES

1. Eight of these leaves are preserved today in the Pierpont Morgan Library in New York. With the single surviving autograph leaf of the *Epistle to Burlington* and a copy of the first edition of the epistle, they are now mounted between handsome red morocco covers in the order given below. (The numbers appearing first record the order of their succession in the Morgan Library manuscript, hereafter referred to as ML; those next appearing are the numbers of the corresponding transcripts in the arrangement given here; the final numbers are the measurements of the leaves in inches, useful in this instance for identification. These can be only approximate since some of the leaves are torn or trimmed, producing one shorter margin and one longer. Width is regularly given first.)

Leaf 1, recto and verso—the only surviving autograph fragment of the *Epistle to Burlington* (reproduced above).

Leaf 2, recto—TS, p. 7—7⅜ × 11¾

Leaf 2, verso—TS, p. 10

Leaf 3, recto—TS, p. 13—7¾ × 5¼ (right margin), or 6⅝ (left margin)

Leaf 3, verso—TS, p. 14

Leaf 4, recto—Jonathan Richardson, Jr.'s collation of ML leaf 6, recto (not transcribed)

Leaf 4, verso—ibid. of ML, leaf 6, verso (not transcribed)

Leaf 5, recto—ibid. of ML, leaf 7, recto (not transcribed)

Leaf 5, verso—ibid. of ML, leaf 7, verso (not transcribed)

Leaves 4 and 5 constitute together a full folio gathering of two conjugate leaves.

Leaf 6. recto—TS, p. 1—7½ × 8½ (right margin) or 9⅝ (left margin)

Leaf 6, verso—TS, p. 2

Leaf 7, recto—TS, p. 3—7⅜ × 12 (right margin) or 11¼ (left margin)

Leaf 7, verso—TS, p. 4. Leaves 6 and 7 also constitute together a full folio gathering of two conjugate leaves.

Leaf 8, recto—TS, p. 8—8 × 9 (trimmed)

Leaf 8, verso—TS, p. 9

Leaf 9, recto—TS, p. 11—7⅛ × 9

Leaf 9, verso—TS, p. 12

The other folio leaf belonging to the *Epistle to Dr. Arbuthnot* is at the Huntington Library in San Marino, California (here referred to as HLC). Its recto is TS, p. 5 and its verso, TS, p. 6. How this clearly indicated title-leaf of the poem as revised managed to become separated from the other leaves, and how and why the one extant leaf of the autograph of the *Epistle to Burlington* came to be inserted in its place remains as inexplicable as the quite arbitrary order of the various leaves and fragments in the Morgan manuscript. I have tried to simplify matters for the reader of this volume by presenting first the manuscript pages (with their corresponding transcripts) belonging to the original 260-line epistle addressed to Cleland, and, second, the several additions and revisions by means of which the poem became the *Epistle to Dr. Arbuthnot.* These additions and revisions I have arranged in the order in which, still further expanded and revised, they appear in the poem we know.

2. "Pope's Poetical Manuscripts" (Warton Lecture on English Poetry), *Proceedings of the British Academy* 40 (1956): 23–59. This should be compulsory reading for anyone who works with Pope's manuscripts.

3. But see below, p. 428.

4. Cleland wrote or at least lent his name to the *Letter to the Publisher, Occasion'd by the Present Edition of the Dunciad,* which prefaced the 1729 Variorum, and performed a similar function for the *Epistle to Burlington* by a letter printed in *The Daily Post-Boy* on 22 December 1731, and in *The Daily Journal* the next day, entitled "To J.[ohn] G.[ay] Esq. To be supportive of a poem containing palpable hits at the king and possibly at Walpole must have required some courage for one in Cleland's position.

5. For the history and several texts of the Atticus lines, see *TE,* 6:142–45, 283–86, and Norman Ault, *New Light on Pope* (London: Methuen, 1949), ch. 6.

6. *TE,* 6:338–40.

7. See *Correspondence,* 3:226. See also *TE,* 6:333–34. The "successful Youth" has been variously identified as George Lyttelton, later Lord Lyttelton, William Murray, later Lord Mansfield, and James Thomson the poet. Lyttelton, for reasons given by the *TE* editor, seems the likeliest candidate. The other "kind Hand" of the original reading is of course Bolingbroke's, but the revision (TS, 14:13) indicates that Pope toyed with the idea of assigning the hand to Hugh Bethel or Bathurst.

8. Pope to Caryll, 31 January 1733 (*Correspondence,* 3:345). See also Spence, Nos. 321–21a.

9. *An Epistle from a Nobleman to a Doctor of Divinity: In Answer to a Latin Letter in Verse. Written from H——n C——t,* Aug. 28, 1733.

10. For Hervey's own account of his favors from the queen, see his *Memoirs,* ed. Romney Sedgwick, 3 vols. (London: Cresset Press, 1931), 2:398–99.

11. Hervey to Henry Fox, 31 January 1734, in the Earl of Ilchester's *Lord Hervey and His Friends, 1726–38* (London: Murray, 1950), p. 189.

12. Hervey to Stephen Fox, 6 December 1733, *ibid.,* p. 183.

13. 17 July (*Correspondence,* 3:417).

14. Ibid., p. 423.

15. Ibid., p. 428.

16. Ibid., p. 431.

17. *TE,* 4:92–93.

And of myself too something must I say? &c.

Take then this Verse, the ~~Labor~~ [Trifle] of a Day;
And if it lives, it lives but to commend
The Man, ~~whose heart has never forgot a Friend~~ [of Friendship, but no boasting Friend;]
The man of Courage, ~~learned~~ but not prone to fight,
~~Or Head an Author, Critick, yet polite,~~
~~The man of~~
~~And Friend to~~ Learning, yet too wise to write.

(3)

The genuine Heart that ne'er forgot a friend
The Hand the valiant, never prone to fight
The Head the learned, yet too wise to write

that

3. Why did I write? what Sin to me unknown
Dipt me in Ink? my Parents, or my own?
As yet a Child, ~~and~~ [nor] yet ~~no~~ [the] Fool ~~to~~ [of] Fame,
I lisp'd in Numbers—For the numbers came.
I left no Calling for this idle Trade,
No Duty broke, no Father disobey'd; +
The Muse but eas'd some Friend, or Nurse, or Wife, (not. wife)
To help me thro' this long Disease, my Life.

qu. For fickle Fame I risqu'd no great good
& if men prais'd, it was because they would.

But why then publish? Granville the polite,
And knowing Walsh, ~~would~~ [would tell] me I c^d write;
Well-natur'd Garth inflam'd with early praise,
And unaffected Congreve lov'd my lays:
The courtly Talbot, lofty Sheffield, read;
Ev'n mitred Rochester would nod the head,
And St. John's self, great Dryden's Friend before,
With open arms receiv'd one Poet more.
Happy my Studies, when by these approv'd!
Happier their Author, when by these belov'd!
From these the world shall judge of Men & Books,
Not from the + Burnets, + Oldmixons, & + Cooks.

[Marginal note, partly illegible:] [A] Tender Poet [illegible] the my name &c. He afterwards went to prayers

If meagre Gildon drew his venal quill,
I wish'd the man a Dinner, & sate still:
If Dreadful Dennis rav'd in furious fret,
I never answer'd, I was not in debt.

'Twas

+ The Bp of Salisbury who writ ye History of his own times.

+ Author of ye scandalous History of ye Family of ye Stuarts

+ Author of a Party History intitled, The Detection of ye Reigns of Charles I. II. &c

&c <1>

And of myself too something must I say?

Triffle
Take then this Verse, the ~~labor~~ of a Day; ~~tr.~~

And if it lives, it lives but to commend

of Friendship, but no boasting Friend,
The Man ~~whose Heart has ner forgot a Friend~~,

The Man of Courage, Learned but not prone to fight,
~~Or Head an Author, Critick, yet polite,~~
stent
The Man of ~~writers Writing, but~~
~~And Friend to~~ Learning, yet too wise to write.

(3)

The gen'rous Heart that n'er forgot a friend
The Hand tho valiant, never prone to fight,
The Head tho learned, yet too wise to write

3. Why did I write? what Sin to me unknown
Dipt me in Ink? my Parents, or my own?

not the of
As yet a Child, ~~and~~ yet ~~no~~ Fool ~~to~~ Fame,
I lisp'd in Numbers -- For the numbers came.
I left no Calling for this idle Trade, ^
No Duty broke, no Father disobey'd; ^

qu. For fickle Fame I risqu'd no great^{r} good
& if men prais'd, it was because they woud.

(not Wife)
The Muse but eas'd some Friend, or Nurse, or Wife,
To help me thro' this long Disease, my Life.
But why then publish? Granville the polite,
woud tell
And knowing Walsh, ~~assur'd~~ me I c^{d} write;
Well-natur'd Garth inflamd with early praise,
And unaffected Congreve lov'd my lays:
The courtly Talbot, lofty Sheffield, read;
Ev'n mitred Rochester would nod the head,
And St. John's self, great Dryden's Friend before,
With open arms receivd one Poet more.
Happy my Studies, when by these approv'd!
Happier their Author, when by these belov'd!
From these the world shall judge of Men & Books,
Not from the +Burnets, +Oldmixons, & +Cooks.

[A modest Poet What tho my name &c.
&c after went to prayrs

If meagre Gildon drew his venal quill,
I wish'd the Man a Dinner, & sate still:
If Dreadful Dennis rav'd in furious fret,
I never answer'd, I was not in debt.

+The Bp of Salisbury who writ ye History of his own Times.

+Author of ye scandalous History of ye Family of ye Stuarts

+Author of a Party History intitled, The Detection of ye Reigns of Charles 1. 11. &c

Twas

And twere a Sin to rob them of their Mite.
In future ages how their fame will spread,
For routing Triplets, and restoring ed!
Yet ne'r one Sprig of Lawrel grac'd those Ribalds,
From sanguin Bentley down to pidling T—s;
The Wretch who reads not, but scans & spells,
The Word-catcher, that lives on Syllables!
Ev'n such small Criticks some regard may claim,
Preserv'd in Miltons & in Shakesp^rs name:
Pretty! in Amber to observe the forms
Of Hairs, or Straws, or Dirt, or Grubs, or worms;
not that The Things, we know, are neither rich nor rare,
But wonder how the devil they got there?
Were Others angry? I excus'd them too,
Well might they rage, I gave them but their Due.
Each man's true merit 'tis not hard to find;
But each man's secret Standard in his mind,
That Casting-weight, Pride adds to Emptiness;
This, who can gratify? for who can guess?
The Wight whom pilferd Pastorals renown,
Who turns a Persian Tale for half a crown,
Just writes to make his barrenness appear,
And strains, from hard-bound brains, six lines a year:
In Wit still wanting, tho he lives on Theft,
Steals much, spends little, yet has nothing left.
Johnson who now to Sense, now Nonsense leaning,
Means not, but blunders round ab^t a Meaning;
And He, whose Fustian's so sublimely bad,
It is not Poetry, but Prose run mad:
All these, my modest Satire bade Translate,
And own'd that nine such Poets made a Tate;
Well might they fume, & stamp, & roar & chafe!
Well might they swear, not Congreve's self was safe!

<Commas and Points they set exactly right,> <2>

And 'twere a Sin to rob them of their Mite.

In future ages how their fame will spread,

For routing Triplets, and restoring ed!

Yet ne'r one Sprig of Lawrel grac'd those Ribalds,

B —— y

From sanguin Milbourne down to pidling T —— s

and but

The wretch who not, ~~meerly~~

~~Who thinks he~~ ^ reads, ~~who only~~ scans & spells,

The

~~A~~ Word-catcher, that lives on Syllables!

Ev'n such small Criticks

~~Yet ev'n this Creature~~ some regard may claim,

Preserv'd in Miltons & in

~~Wrapt round, & sanctify'd with~~ Shakesp.rs name:

Pretty! in Amber to observe the forms

Of Hairs, or Straws, or Dirt, or Grubs, or Worms;

are ei or

Not that The Things, we know, is neither rich nor rare,

all ye is they

But ^ wonder, ^ how the devil ~~it~~ got there?

Were Others angry? I excus'd them too,

Well might they rage, I gave them but their Due:

A

Each man's true merit tis not hard to find;

But each man's secret standard in his mind,

That Casting-weight, Pride adds to Emptiness;

This, who can gratify? For who can guess?

Wight

The ~~Wretch~~ ^ whom pilferd Pastorals renown,

Who turns a Persian Tale for half a crown,

Nurse Namby—

~~Just~~ writes to make his barrenness appear,
Who

year;

And strains, from hard-bound brains, six lines a ^

1 He who ~~ever~~

~~In Wit~~ still wanting, tho he lives on Theft,

Steals

~~Steals~~ much, spends little, yet has nothing left.

1. Nurse Namby with a Song to sucking Child, The stiff Anacreon & the Pindar mild

~~Johnson~~ who now to Sense, now Nonsence leaning,
And He

Means not, but blunders round abt a Meaning;

And He, whose Fustian's so sublimely bad,

It is not Poetry, but Prose run mad:

All these, my bade,

~~When~~ ^ modest Satire ~~bids all these~~ ^ Translate,

'd

And own'd, that nine such Poets made a Tate;

might

Well ~~may~~ they fume, & stamp, & roar, & chafe!

might

Well ~~may~~ they swear, not Congreve's self was safe!

Peace to all such! but were there One, whose fires
True Genius kindles, and fair Fame inspires,
Blest with each Talent & each Art to please,
And born to write, converse, & live with ease;
Should such a Man, too fond to rule alone,
Bear like the Turk, no Brother near the Throne,
View him with scornful yet with fearful eyes,
And hate for arts that caus'd himself to rise;
Damn with faint praise, assent with civil leer,
And, without sneering, teach the rest to sneer;
Willing to wound, and yet afraid to strike,
Just hint a Fault, & hesitate Dislike;
Alike reserv'd to blame, or to commend,
A tim'rous Foe, and a suspicious Friend,
Dreading ev'n Fools; by Flatterers besieg'd,
And so obliging, that he ne'r oblig'd:
Who, if two Wits on rival Themes contest,
Approves of each, but likes the worst ye best;
Like Cato, gives his little Senate laws,
And sits attentive to his own applause;
While Wits & Templars ev'ry sentence raise,
And wonder with a foolish Face of Praise.
What pity, Heav'n! if such a man there be?
Who would not weep, if A——n were he?

— were he

If ere it make
honest
one worthy Man my foe.
Friendships from Youth I sought, & keep them still;
Fame, like the Wind, may breath where-e'er it will.
The world I knew, but made it not my School, And in a Course of Flattery liv'd no Fool.
What tho' my Name stood rubrick on ye walls,
Or plaister'd Posts, with Claps, in Capitals?
Known but by that to all the race ye write,
I kept like Asian Monarchs, from their sight;
But left to ... the whole Parnassian State.

— still, a Moral Fact.
This shall be my praise
who pleas'd ye Great but not
by servile ways
Who knew ye World, but

But all such babling
Coxcombs in his stead.
A moral Poet — who carry
Fame and keeps on still,

— Parnassian State.

[Proud, as Apollo on his forked Hill,
Sate full-blown Bubo, puft by ev'ry Quill;
Fed with soft Dedication all day long,
Horace and He went hand in hand in Song;
His Library (where Busts of Poets dead
& a true Pindar stood without his head)
Receiv'd of wits an undistinguish'd race,
Who first his Judgment ask'd, & then a Place;
Much they admir'd his Pictures, much his Seat,
Flatter'd ev'ry day, and some days eat;
He pay'd some Bards with Port, & some with praise;
To some a dry Rehearsall was assign'd,
& some ... he pay'd in Kind.

Planted, chatted, drank, & eat,
Whole years had past, since I had writ or read,
Or known if Dennis were alive or dead

Meat, kept high honors in reserve
... whom he held ...

Peace to all such! but were there One, whose fires
True Genius
~~Apollo~~ kindles, and fair Fame inspires,
Blest with each Talent & each Art to please,
And born to write, converse, & live with ease;
Should such a Man, too fond to rule alone,
Bear like the Turk, no Brother near the Throne,
View him with scornful yet with fearful eyes,
And hate for arts that causd himself to rise;
Damn with faint praise, assent with civil leer,
And, without sneering, teach the rest to sneer;
Willing to wound, and yet afraid to strike;
Just hint a Fault, & hesitate Dislike;
Alike reserv'd to blame, or to commend,
A tim'rous Foe, and a suspicious Friend,
Dreading ev'n Fools; by Flatterers besieg'd,
And so obliging, that he ne'r oblig'd:
if
Who ~~wh~~ two Wits on rival Themes contest,
Approves of each, but likes the worst ye best;
Like Cato, gives his little Senate laws,
And sits attentive to his own applause;
While Wits & Templars ev'ry Sentence raise,
And wonder with a foolish Face of Praise.
What pity, Heav'n! if such a man there be?
~~Atticus~~
Who would not weep, if A —— n were he?
~~[Nay, Cursd be the Fame with all its noise & show~~
~~I sigh'd; & curs'd in bitterness of Woe~~
If ~~That~~ ere it ~~shall~~ make honest
~~The Fame that made one worthy Man my foe:~~
If Bridgman while his head contrives a Maze
Good man, ~~mistakes~~ my Satyr from my Praise.
each good Man's love
them
Friendships from Youth I sought, & ~~seek it~~ still;
keep ^
~~The Friendships formd in Youth I cherish still~~
will
Fame, like the Wind, may breath where-e're it will
The World I knew, but made it not my School, And in a Course of Flatt'ry livd
no Fool
^ [What tho' my Name stood rubrick on ye Walls
Or plaister'd Posts, with Claps in Capitals?
Known but by that to all the race
~~Who says, I ruld <lead> the ragged Race~~ y^{t} write,
kept
I ~~keep~~ like Asian Monarchs from their sight;
~~I bore em all good will & wish'd em luck To Allen Ramsay & to~~
~~Stephen Duck:~~
~~But thinking Thought neither play --- worth~~ No Party
~~On Play or Poem never held~~ debate
With ⟷ Wits ⟷ no Party formd nor
held debate
~~To Bubo~~ But left to Bubo
~~But leave to B-b~~ the ~~whole~~ Parnassian State, θ
~~Meantime While peacefull I lay~~
~~A quiet Prince, I slumbring on my Seat~~
^
plant ~~but ne'r eat alone~~
Or planted, saunter'd, chatter'd, drank, & eat.
~~Preferrd my friends to Fame~~
~~neither nor~~
~~What years have pass'd~~ ~~or writ or read~~
Or kn dead?

Proud as Apollo &c
Throne

--were he
flow
[Cursd be ye Verse, how well so ere it
That tends ⟷ to
~~justly~~ ~~That ever shall~~ make one worthy ma<n>
my foe
Virtue Innocence ~~Decency~~ a
Give ~~ye Good~~ scandal, ~~or ye Guiltless~~ Fear,
from steal
Or ~~make~~ ye softeyd Virgin ~~shed~~ a Tear
But he who hurts a harmless neighb^{rs} Peace
~~Or steal frō softeyd Innocence a Tear~~
~~The Fop whose pride~~ ~~That more abusive~~
~~The Scribler y^{t} invades ye public peace~~
Insults faln worth or Beauty in distress
~~The woman's fool who~~ scandal helps about,
Who loves a Lye, lame
Who writes ye Libel, or who copies out
~~after--Wherer it will~~
defend
The Fop whose Pride &c ^ who to ye Dean
& saw - who - betray. Let never honest man
--will. A morall Poet But all such babling
coxcombs in his stead.
This shall be my Praise A modest Poet - fools
chose
who pleasd ye Great but not ~~Friendship~~ who early ~~formd~~
his friends and keeps em still,
by servile ways
Who knew y^{e}
Fame
World but θ After [What tho ~~Whose early'st friendsps are his~~

--Parnassiā State. his
[Proud, as Apollo on the forked Hill,
Sate fullblown Bubo, puft by ev'ry Quill;
Fed with soft Dedication all day long,
Horace
~~Virgil~~ and He went hand in hand in Song;
His Library (where Busts of Poets dead
& a true Pindar stood without his head)
Receivd of wits an undistinguishd race,
Who first his Judgment askd, & then a Place.
Much they admird his Pictures, much his Seat,
~~At all times they~~ ⟷ & flatterd ev'ry day, and
days
⟷ some ~~times~~ ~~y^{y}~~ eat
~~Not prouder Phoebus on ye forked hill~~

Till grown more wiser
~~But Bubo~~ frugal in his ~~latter~~ days,
^
He payd Some Bards ~~payd~~ with Port & some with
praise
a dry ~~on~~ was
To some Rehearsals ~~& gilt Stools~~ assignd,
^ ^ ^
some alas still
& ~~others~~ (worse ~~than all~~) he payd in Kind.
^
Mean ~~thoughtless~~ on Thamess brink in sweet
[~~I all the~~ [While ~~peaceful I lay slumbring in~~ Retreat,
I
~~Or~~ planted, saunterd, chatted, drank and eat,
Whole years had past, since I had writ or read
Or known if Dennis were alive or dead
others, kept high honors in reserve
to bury whom he help'd to <starve>

Let Johnston write, [illegible] in each line
E'en let him write, for me, till ninety nine
In faith, what matter if he miss or hit?
It lays to him a better friend than wit
Careless [illegible] sweet retreat
I sauntered, chatted, plunked, drank or eat

— out
What? this Skoll [illegible] of Real Kings
Or History of Bits & Leading strings?
For Pope 'tis certain [illegible] great Work
is done:
Ethic or Epic, I am sure tis one!
your Hymns & Heaven [illegible]
But something said of Charles, is too bold
Tis all in vain &c
Style

But authors, authors are a heavier curse!
Their anger [illegible]
Dreadful [illegible]
Their Friendship [illegible]
A dire Dilemma! either way I'm sped
[illegible]
My foes will write, my friends will read me dead
Seiz'd & ty'd down to judge, how wretched I!
I can't keep silence, & I will not lye
To laugh, were want of Goodness & of Grace
& to be grave, exceeds all Power of Face
[illegible]
Receive with sad Civility, & read
With honest anguish, & an aking head
& drop (thank Horace) in all authors ears
One saving counsel — Keep yr book 9 yrs.
Nine years! cries He who prints before Term ends
obliged by [illegible]
The Piece he owns, [illegible] correct; But take it
I'm all Submission — as you'd have it, make it.
Three things and then —
Plead Sickness, Visits, Journeys, all is vain —
[illegible] trusts his works to me & [illegible] again
[illegible] of my Health, asks if expected soon?
[illegible] Comes, at nights, & oftner still at noon.

before
in
initio

O that my [illegible] sweet retreat
I still had plantes, saunter'd drank & eat
Where years had past, [illegible]
Now all ye Race [illegible]
Set forth for Twitenam, [illegible]
No walls [illegible]

Meantime the Town imagined I must write
And ask'd, what Works were rising into light?
"I saw him walk with Swift — Indeed? no doubt
(Cries honest [illegible]) something will come out.
Tis all in vain, deny it as I will,
"No, such a Genius never can lye still.
Oh Sir, 'tis certain [illegible] great work's done / Ethic or Epic
And then for current as my Piece they take
The first dull thing, Sir Will. and Cibber make
Poor guiltless I! and can I chuse but smile
When ev'ry Coxcomb knows me by my Stile?
[illegible]
[illegible]
[illegible]
And, walk like Margrets Ghost at dead of night
No Walls can guard me, & no Shades can hide
They thrid my Thickets, thro' my Grot they glide
By Land, by Water, they renew the charge
They stop the Chariot, & they board the Barge
No place is sacred, not the Church is free,
Ev'n Sunday shines no Sabbath day to me;
Then from the Mint walks forth ye Man of Rhime
Happy to catch me
And gets to Twitnam — just at dinner time
Is there a Parson much be-mus'd in Beer
A maudlin Poetess, or rhyming Peer?
Is there, who kept from pen & paper scrawls
With desperate charcoal round his darken'd Walls
Is there a Bard in durance? Turn them free,
With all their brandish'd Reams, & they run to me.
Is there a Prentice, having seen two Plays
Who would do Something in his Sempstress' praise
Is there a Clerk, his Fathers soul to cross;
Who writes a Stanza when he should Ingross?
All fly to Twitnam, & in humble strain
Apply to me to keep them mad or vain.
Arthur, whose giddy Son neglects ye Laws,
Imputes to me & my damn'd works ye cause
Poor B—— [illegible] elope,
And.

too
Evn Johnston writ, ~~& happy in each~~ Line
Een let him write, for me, till ninety nine.
For Fame, what matter if he miss or hit?
Follys to him a better friend than Wit
On
Careless on ~~lay~~ Thames's bank in sweet retreat
I saunterd, chatted, planted, drank or eat

— out
But
What? What? His Short Acc^{t} of Real Kings,
Or History of Bibs & Leading Strings?
~~Apron~~

"Tis known for
~~For Pope~~, tis certain ~~his~~ great Work
some
is done,
Ethic or Epic, I am sure tis one:

Your Hymn to Heav'n, polite enough
~~His Thoughts on God & Gardens, good,~~ (I'm told)

But something said of Chartres, is too bold

Tis all in vain &c

—style

still are more a
But Authors, Authors are a heavier Curse!
Their anger ~~worse far worse~~

dreadful! ~~Yet worse the Race be-musd y^{t} walk by Night~~,

but ~~ere ye morning Light~~:
~~The Spectres haunt me with~~ ~~A famous~~
Friendship
their ~~Repentance~~ worse!

sped
A dire Dilemma, either way I'm ~~<Ballad>~~

~~They write or read me dead. How wretched I~~

I cant keep
⟷ ~~Silence I must not keep &~~
~~I will not Lye~~

My foes will write, my friends will read me dead

Seizd & tyd down to judge, how wretched I!

I can't keep silence, & I will not lye

To laugh, were want of Goodness & of Grace

& to be grave, exceeds all Powr of Face

~~yet~~ but not my school
Saw ye great world nor made it knavrys

& in a course of flattry, livd no fool

Receivd with sad Civility, & read

With honest anguish, & an aking head

I drop (thank Horace) in all authors ears

One saving Counsel — Keep y^{r} book 9 y^{rs}.

ends
Nine years! cries He who prints before Term

Obligd by

The not quite
~~His~~ Piece he owns, ~~is in~~correct; But take it

I am all submission — as youd have it, make it.

Three things anothers—

Plead Sickness, Visits, Journies, all is vain —

⟷ trusts his Works wth me & calls again all this

Asks of my Health, asks if expected soon?

oft
~~Oft~~ comes at night, & oftner still at noon.

before

in

initio

O that in Windsor groves in sweet retreat <4>
I still had planted, saunterd, drank & eat
Whole years had past, since — prayrs.
Now all ye Race bemusd y^{t} wake by night
Set forth for Twitnam with ye morning Light.
No walls can guard &c - to -

Meantime the Town imagin'd I must write
Why sh^{d}

were
And ask'd, what Work s ~~is~~ rising into light?

"I saw him walk with Swift — Indeed? no dou<bt>

prating K—l ~~busy V—n~~
(Cries ~~honest H — n~~) something will come out.
ay Sir (says
Upton <)>
some

Tis all in vain, deny it as I will,

"No, such a Genius never can lye still

some
⟷ Oh Sir, I'm certain ~~y^{e}~~ great work is done Ethic or epic I am

piece
And then for current as my ~~Work~~ they take

and
The first dull thing Sir Will ~~or~~ Cibber make

~~your~~ ~~poet~~ ~~he~~
Poor guiltless I! and can I chuse but smile

~~him~~
When ev'ry Coxcomb knows me by my Stile?

~~Trust me tis no Satire y^{t} I~~
~~all~~
~~The Fop whose pride~~ < ~~they need> dread~~ ~~But such~~ ⟷
~~Let never modest man my satire dread~~ ~~Coxcombs~~

~~Yet worse — vile Poets rise before ye Light~~
~~sleepless all~~

~~A Race be-mus'd y^{t} never sleep by night that Ghostlike walk by night~~
~~And walk like Margrets Ghost at dead of night~~

(2)

Alas!
No walls can guard me, & no shades can hide

They thrid my Thickets, thro' my Grot they glide

By Land, by Water, they renew the charge

the the
They stop ~~my~~ Chariot, & they board ~~my~~ Barge

No place is sacred, not the Church is free,

Ev'n Sunday shines no Sabbath day to me;

Then from the Mint walks forth ye Man of Rhime

Happy to catch me
~~And gets to Twitnam~~ — just at dinner time

much bemus'd
Is there a Parson ~~mad or steep'd~~ in Beer

a maudlin
~~An Irish~~ Poetess, or rhyming Peer?

Is there, who kept from pen & paper scrawls

desprate his
With ~~Skewrs &~~ charcoal round ~~y^{e}~~ darkend Wall<s>

2 Is there a Bard in durance? Turn them free,

With all their brandishd Reams run
~~Unlock those mortals~~, & they fly to me

δ ~~Is there a Prentice, having seen two Plays~~

Who would do Something in his Sempstress praise

ordaind
Is there a Clerk, his Fathers Soul to cross;
1
Who writes a Stanza when he shou'd Ingross?

fly
All ~~run~~ to Twit'nam, & in humble strain

keep or
Apply to me to make them mad & vain.

Arthur, whose giddy Son neglects ye Laws,

Imputes to me & my damn'd works ye cause

Poor B--- sees his frantic Wife elope,

And

Incipit. [EPISTLE to ARBUTHNOT.]

(1)

Shut, shut the door, good John! fatigu'd I said,
Tye up the Knocker, say I'm sick, I'm dead.
The Dogstar rages; nay tis past a doubt,
All Bedlam, or Parnassus, is let out:
Rags on their back, & Papers in their hand,
They rave, & beg, & madden round the land.

Obligd by Hunger, and Request of Friends.
The things, we own, are incorrect, but take them
[Good Sir] & just what you w^d have them make them.

To one, of Business, Sickness, I complain:
He leaves his Papers, & comes & comes again.
Three things another's modest wishes bound,
My Friendship — and a Prologue — & ten pound.
[then Welsted sends to me — You know his Grace
And I'm a Stranger — Ask him for a Place.

To plague Sir Robert, turn Divine.
Bless me! that Pacquet!
An Orphan Tragedy — a Virgin muse —
Enough: If I dislike it, Death & Rage!
If I approve, "Commend it to the Stage.
"There, thank my Stars, my whole commission ends,
"Cibber & I are (luckily) no friends.
Alas! the Players send it back.
"Printer! dull Rogue! will think the Price too much —
"Not Sir, if you revise it, & retouch.
All my Demurrs but double his Attacks,
At last he whispers, Do, & you go Snacks.
Glad of a Quarrel, strait I clap the door,
"Sir, let me see your works or you no more.

With Hymns to C— & Satyrs upon Pope.

Think you, these Peoples Anger is a Curse?
Ah Cleland! their Repentance is a worse.

(3)

Oblig'd — Term ends

Nine years? alas! we print before

x Ed. Bealowes, a Gentleman of Oxfordshire in ye time of Charles I. who patronized all ye bad Poets of that Reign. They anagrammatized his Name, Benevolus, wch cost him his Estate.

His Asses ears if Midas w^d not hide,
What could his Wife? She told it, or had dy'd.
And is not mine, my Friend, a selfsame Case.
If folks will thrust their Honors in my face?
Speak out then, Dunciad, let ye Secret pass,
That Secret to each Fool, that he's an Ass.
The truth once told, & wherefore sh^d we lye?
The ... & so may I.

(1)

Shut, shut the door, good John! fatigud I said,
Tye up the Knocker, say I'm sick, I m dead.
The Dogstar rages; nay tis past a doubt,
All Bedlam, or Parnassus, is let out:
Rags on their back, & Papers in their hand,
They rave, & beg, & madden round the land.
Alas! no Walls can guard, no Shades can hide &c.

this to Him who prints before Term
What's ~~one must publish ere~~ y[e] ~~Season~~ ends,
Obligd by Hunger, and Request of Friends.

The things we ~~owne~~ are But
~~His piece!~~ ~~say is~~ incorrect — ~~Then~~ take them
Good Sir
~~(He cries)~~ & just what you w[d] have thā, make them.

To one of Business, Sickness, I complain:
~~&~~ comes ~~to~~ and
He leaves his Papers, ~~& will~~ comes again.

Three things another's modest wishes bound,
My Friendship—and a Prologue—& ten pound.

Then sends to me—
[One Welsted ~~this Message sends~~—You know his Grace,
And I'm a Stranger--Ask him for a Place.
~~Who is the Man? One famous in Blackfryers:~~
~~Welsted has libelld me;—For that, this Letter~~
True
<Sure> ~~once he libel'd you~~ ~~<but>~~ ~~now admires.~~
~~Sir~~ Stet
~~Informs you, that as then they knew no better;~~

~~I know him not~~—
~~Refused by me~~ with Curl to dine:
~~If you refuse, He goes as Fates incline~~
Refuse them, and they re gone <&>
~~To plague~~ Sir Robert, ~~or to~~ turn Divine.
That serves this must turn~~s~~

S[r] a stranger sues
Bless me! that Pacquet! ~~Patience Sir~~—Excuse
An Orphan Tragedy—a Virgin Muse—
Furies
~~Enough~~: If I dislike it, Death & Rage!
If I approve, "Commend it to the Stage:
my stars
"There, thank~~s to fate~~, my whole commission ends,
"Cibber & I are (luckily) no friends.
players send it back. He'll
Alas! the ~~House reject, & he must~~ print it
And prove them Fools. Your Int'rest Sir with
To ~~show their Folly.~~ — ~~Sir, you'l speak to~~ Lintot—
Lintot Rogue! will
"~~He too is~~ dull, ~~&~~ think~~s~~ the Price too much—
"Not Sir, if you revise it, & retouch.
All my Demurrs but double his Attacks,
At last he whispers, Do, & you go Snacks:
Glad of a Quarrel, strait I clap the door,
"Sir, let me see your works or you no more.

One Welsted &c

~~Away he turns, O Curll! t'enrich~~ thy Shop,
~~With Hymns to C— & Satyrs upon Pope~~.

people's
Think you, these ~~Authors~~ Anger is a curse?
Ah Cleland!
~~Believe me~~, Their Repentance is a worse.

The Fop whose Pride—
Who cries Dear Pope! I love him—he's my friend—
Yet wants y[e] honor &c --
~~Let never modest Man my Satire dread, But all such~~

(3)

— they reach me, how distrest am I
[If once ~~I see them, how unhappy I!~~
I can't keep silence, & I <detest> will not
~~Silence I must not keep, & cannot~~ lye;
To sport with Mis'ry is to play y[e] knave;
& here y[e] gravest Judge could n'er be grave
I see I
~~Receivd~~ with sad Civility, ~~&~~ read
anguish and
With honest ~~pain & with~~ an aking head,

~~The selfsame counsel~~ ~~<evry>~~ author
~~At length I pass to Judgment~~ ~~&~~ ~~<harsh>~~ ~~words he~~ hears
~~<selfsame> counsel evry~~

~~Th advice of Horace~~, Let it lye nine years.
~~sleep~~
~~What's this &c~~
Nine years? alas, We print before
term ends
oblig'd

But y[e] grand Project Shaksp[r] to restore
That y[e] Wag hid. For w[t]? To get ten more
Bless me! that
<Pithy> & short! another brings Cook
~~Then~~ Hesiod a Peace offring ~~comes~~ frō
The most composing terms, his own
dull
<Embassage>
~~Then comes a n Message too frō Hesiod~~ Cook
~~Joind wth that dull Peace Offring, his own Book~~

but sir
These ~~men~~ have libelld you. ~~Alas, this letter~~
but heres a Let<ter>
Informs you Sir y[t] then y[y] knew no better:

~~Let~~ meet fit
Fools ~~find fit~~ Patrons still in ev'ry age,
Quarles had his+ Benlows, Tibald has his
Gage

Grub
~~make such large demands~~
~~How pleasd to see some Patron to each~~
~~Then takes off hands~~
~~Quarles had his Benlows, T has his B—~~

~~And one kind Knight~~, ~~<so>~~ ~~gen'rous Heavn coma<n>ds~~
~~Now takes~~
~~Has took a hundred Dunces off my hands~~
And Peers for Flattry make such large
[demands, They take a hundred Dunces off my hands

+Ed. Benlowes, a Gentleman of Oxfordshire in y[e] time of Charles 1. who patronized all y[e] Bad Poets of that Reign. They anagrammatizd his Name, Benevolus, w[ch] cost him his Estate.

—G-ge Oft as some Job requires
~~Whene'er~~ Corruption wants a days defence
As oft as
~~Whenever~~ Envy is at war wth Sense
Or Lordly
~~Whenever~~ Pride for flattry makes demands
~~They take a Tribe of Dunces off my hands~~
some
So oft a Dunce is taken
~~a scribling dunce~~
May fools find Patrons still in evry age! Gage
had so ~~has~~
As Quarles ~~has~~ his Benlows ~~<must not>~~ Tibb~~ald~~ ~~<shoud~~ have>
Gage

Some scrub Mecenas ~~for each Poet~~ Scrub
~~<to>~~ W—d
Ducket for Oldmixon for W--d, B--
a days
~~<Think>~~ For Whene~~ver~~ Job ~~a~~ requires defence
Whene~~ver~~ Envy makes short- War wth Sense / Some or other's
livd < > dunce <is >
Whenever Pride for flattry ~~Then still some scriblers~~ tak
Or Lordly en off my hands

[His Asses ears if Midas w[d] not hide
What could his Wife? She told it or had dyd.
And is not mine, my Friend, y[e] selfsame case
If folks will thrust those Honors in my face?
"Nothing: --their ears a God's name let em prick--
But is it nothing, if they bite & kick?
Speak out then, Dunciad! let y[e] secret pass
(That secret to each Fool) that he's an Ass
The truth once told, & wherfore shd we lye?
d slept--and
The ~~gentle Dame e sleep~~, ~~&~~ so may I.
Wife of Midas ~~rested~~

~~This One~~ Think you &c &c--to--stead
~~The Fop whose Pride~~

N A

One from all
That [illegible] Grubstreet will my fame
Some who have paid for 20 yrs [illegible] 220 let me see on now
[illegible]
[illegible] fairly Light—
[illegible] Swift — [illegible] no doubt
[illegible] some thing
[illegible]
Which a Epic, [illegible]
'Tis all in vain
[illegible]
And
The first
Poor guiltless authors, [illegible]
When every [illegible] knows [illegible]
Even to my person

One dedicates in high Heroic Prose,
[illegible]
And proves not all odd fellows are not all my foes.
[illegible]
One [illegible] & expects a Bribe:
Another [illegible] Subscribe, Subscribe!
[illegible] to my Person some make their Court
I cough like Horace, & am thick & short;
Ammon's great Son one Shoulder had too high;
Such Ovid's nose; but then, I have an Eye—
Go on obliging Sir! and make me joy to see
All that disgrac'd my Betters met in me:
Say for my comfort when I'm sick a-bed,
Just so immortal Maro held his head;
And when I dye, be sure to let me know,
That Homer dy'd, three thousand years ago.

But Friend! this Shape wch you & Curl admire
Came not from Ammon's Son, but from my Sire;
And very ill that Head-ake I could well excuse)
I sure inherit from a mother, not the Muse:
Happy! if I in whom their [illegible] joind
Had heird as well the virtues of their mind.
My Christian Father held it for a rule
It was a Sin to call our Brother Fool;
She, harmless matron, judg'd no wife a Whore;
Hear this, & spare my Family, James M—re!

And coudst thou think my honest Sire unknown
Meerly because thou dost not know thy own?
Known he shall be! & lov'd, and honor'd long,
If there be Force in Virtue or in Song.

Of gentle blood, part shed in Honor's Cause
(While yet in Albion Honor had applause)
The Good man sprung: his Fortunes all his own,
Well got, oblig'd to few, in debt to none:
Unlearn'd, his Morals never taught by Art;
One Language, but that Language of the Heart:
By Genius honest, & by Nature wise;
Healthy, by Temp'rance & by Exercise:

who

(Never [illegible] debt)

One from all
~~That ag~~st Grubstreet will my fame

< >Some who have raild for 20 yrs allow

~~<Scrib>~~ | Tis ⟷ Twas ~~<their>~~ mistake, and let me
| ~~<Youre>~~ wrongd never write serve em
1 Oh Sir A soon will it quickly now
~~When will~~ His ⟷ says U— see ye Light—

I saw him walk wth Swift--nay then no doubt

<Replies a wise man?> something
<sage>
Cries honest U--n
2 ~~O Sir tis certain <his great>~~
Tis known for certain his great

Ethick or Epic,

Tis all in vain

No

And for my Piece

The first

I
Poor guiltless Authors! can ~~they~~ chuse

me
When evry Coxcomb knows ~~<y^m>~~ by

Evn to my person

One high Heroic Prose,
~~This~~ dedicates in ~~blustring~~ ~~<pompous>~~ prose
~~One his dull Zeal in Dedication shows~~.

not all odd fellows are
And proves ~~the Dunces are not all~~ my foes.

~~That will in Verse my Character~~ defend, & (more abusive) calls himself my F<riend>

~~One brings wrong Praises~~, & expects a Bribe
One humbly flatters,

Another roars aloud, Subscribe, Subscribe!

~~One who has raild for 20 yrs descends To beg at last we may~~ be constant
To beg I'd think that he's ye best of Friends ~~friends~~

Ev'n will
~~Some~~ to my Person some ⟷ make their Cour<t>

I cough like Horace, & am thick, & short;

Ammon's great Son one shoulder had
~~The Son of Ammon had a Back~~ too high,

Such Ovid's Nose! but then, I have an Eye--

and make me
Go on, obliging Sir! ~~What Joy to~~ see

A ~~This~~ monstrous mixture of
~~All the defects of those great men~~, in me!
All that disgracd my Betters, met in me

Say, for my comfort, when Im sick a-bed,
~~Why not to comfort me w^n sick a-bed~~

Just ~~Say thus~~ immortal
So ~~Bacon yawnd~~; ~~so~~ Maro held his head;

~~Why not w^n dying kindly~~
And when I dye, be sure to let me know,

~~That~~
So Homer dy'd, three thousand years ago.

But Friend! this Shape wch you & Curl admire

Came not from Ammon's Son, but from my Sire;

Virgils ~~that curst~~ I could well
And ~~for my~~ Headake (~~you'l the truth~~ excuse)

a
Since ~~wch came~~ a mortal ~~frō any~~
~~I had it~~ from ~~my~~ Mother, not ~~the~~ Muse:

if He in whom their frailties joind
Happy! ~~thrice happy, had I heir'd as well~~

\+ Had heird as well y^e virtues of their mind
~~The Christian Kernel, as the crazy Shell~~

~~He meek~~ My christian Father
~~Meek was my Sire, &~~ held it for a rule

It was a Sin <u>to</u> <u>call</u> <u>our</u> <u>Brother</u> <u>Fool</u>;

She, harmless Matron, judgd no
~~My Mother judgd no wedded~~ Wife a <u>Whore</u>;

Hear this, & spare my Family, James M-re!

honest Sire unknown
And cou'dst thou think my ~~Father was un~~

Meerly because thou dost not knowe thy own?

Known he shall be! & lov'd, and honord long,

If there be Force in Virtue or in Song.

Of gentle blood, part shed in Honor's Cause

(While yet in Albion Honor had applause)

all
The Good man sprung: his Fortunes ~~were~~ his
own

Well-got, obligd to few, in debt to none.
~~And better gain'd than from th' ungrateful~~
~~Throne~~:

never
Unlearn'd, his Morals ~~were not~~ taught by
Art;

One Language, but that Language of the Heart:

By Genius honest, & by Nature wise;

Healthy, by Temp'rance & by Exercise:

Who

| never ow'd a debt |

(2)

~~Who Wine's mad~~ softer transports never deign'd to try;
~~Who never risqu'd an Oath, nor dar'd a Lye:~~
~~Who [illegible]~~ Who knew no Lawsuit, ~~or~~ no domestick Strife,
Religious Contest, ~~and~~ or mad Party-Life: [illegible] never in debt, & never in a Strife, [illegible] friend neighbor [illegible] great mens friendship try
~~Whose [illegible] days the [illegible]~~ Whose Life, tho long, to Sickness ~~[illegible]~~ was unknown; ~~Nor ever risk'd an Oath, or dar'd a Lye.~~
Whose Death was instant, & without a Groan:
Oh grant me thus to live, & thus to dye!
Who sprung from Kings shall ~~have less bliss than~~ not be blest as I.
~~taste~~ know less Joy than I.

~~false~~
~~Who Wine's mad transports never deignd to try~~;

~~Who never risqu'd an Oath, nor dar'd a Lye~~:

~~Stranger~~ to ~~to no~~|~~to~~
~~Stranger to~~ ~~no~~
~~Who n'er knew~~ Law Suit, ~~or~~ domestick Strife,
who knew no no

~~& and~~ or
Religious Contest, or mad Party-Life:

~~see~~ ~~Relations~~ ~~wou'd~~ he
~~Nor Courts wd know, no Great Mans Friendship try~~, Nor ever riskd an Oath, or dard a Lye.

Nor Courts w^d ⟷
see nor ~~armys wd he try~~

strife,
Never in debt, & never in a

Friend
W^{th} Church or State, wth neighbor
~~or Wife~~ ^
Great mans friend
ship try

~~Whose days, tho full~~, to Sickness ~~were~~ unknown;
Whose life, tho long, was

Whose
~~Whose~~ Death was instant, & without a Groan:

O grant me thus to live, & thus to dye!

not be blest as
Who sprung from Kings shall ~~know less~~^~~bliss than~~ I.
~~taste~~ less joy than I.
know

~~Approves of each, but likes the worst the best;~~ (A*)

Like Cato, gives his little Senate laws,
And sits attentive to his own applause;
While Wits and Templars ev'ry Sentence raise,
And wonder with a foolish Face of Praise.
What pity, Heav'n! if such a man there be?
Who would not weep, if A——n were he?

Stet [What tho' my Name stood rubrick on the walls,
Or plaister'd Posts, with Claps in Capitals?
~~Known, but by that to all~~
What tho' I rul'd the ragged Race that write;
I kept like Asian Monarchs, from their Sight;
not like a Puppy, daggled thro the Town, To fetch & carry Sonnets up & down;
Nor, at Rehearsals sweat, & mouth'd, & cry'd, With Hankerchiff & Orange at my side;
But sick of Fops, and Poetry, & Prate, To Bubo left the whole Parnassian State.
[Proud, as Apollo on his forked Hill,
Sate full-blown Bubo, puft by ev'ry Quill;
Fed with soft Dedication all day long,
Horace and He went hand in hand in Song;
To Bards reciting, he vouchsaf'd a nod, and snuff'd their Incense like a gracious God.
His Library (where Busts of Poets dead
And a true Pindar stood without a head)
Receiv'd of Wits an undistinguish'd race,
Who first his Judgement ask'd, and then a place,

~~Approves of each, but likes the worst the best~~;
Like Cato, gives his little Senate laws,
And sits attentive to his own applause;
While Wits and Templars ev'ry Sentence raise;
And wonder with a foolish Face of Praise.
What pity, Heav'n! if such a man there be?
Who would not weep, if A---n were he?
stet [What tho' my Name stood rubrick on the walls,
Or plaister'd Posts, with Claps in Capitals?
~~Now~~
~~But < >to all the giddy~~ ~~Known but by that to all~~
~~Known but by that to all the~~ Race that write?
What tho I rul'd the ragged ^
I kept, like Asian Monarchs, from their Sight;
Not, like a Puppy, daggled thro the Town, To fetch & carry Sonnets up & down;
~~Held with the Wits, nor Concert, nor debate~~,
Nor at Rehearsals sweat, & mouth'd, & cry'd, With Hankerchiff & Orange at my side;
But ~~left to Bubo the Parnassian State~~ .
sick of Fops, & Poetry, & Prate, To Bubo left the whole Parnassian State.
[Proud, as Apollo on his forked Hill,
Sate fullblown Bubo, puft by ev'ry Quill;
Fed with soft Dedication all day long,
Horace and He went hand in hand in Song;
To ~~The~~ Bards reciting, he vouchsafd a Nod, And snuffd their Incense like a gracious God.
His Library (where Busts of Poets dead
a
And a true Pindar stood without ~~his~~ head)
Receiv'd of Wits an undistinguish'd race,
Who first his Judgement ask'd, and then a place,

9

May Fools find Patrons still in ev'ry age!

As Quarles had Benlows, so may Tibbald G— yu:

Some kind Mecænas fall to ev'ry Scrub, Si

Ducket to Old~~mixon~~, to W—d B— del.

[And,] ~~For~~ when some Job requires a Day's defence,

Or Envy holds a whole weeks war with sence,

Or Lordly Pride for Flatt'ry makes demands;

[Dunce after] ~~So oft~~, ~~a~~ Dunce [be] ~~or~~ taken off my hands! ~~What fits not Others, may Bec~~

Give me[ ] On Thames's silver bank, in ~~sweet retreat~~ [in lib.] learned Ease

~~Oh let me~~ [To] ~~plant or~~ [write, or plant, or] saunter, [which I please;] ~~drink or eat~~!

Whole years ~~had~~ [have] pass'd, since I ha[ve] writ ~~or~~ [or] read,

Unknown if Dennis were alive or dead;

A vulgar Soul, not born to great affairs,

I ~~gravely~~ [I] payd my debts, ~~and [illegible]~~ [nor blush to say] ~~to~~ [my] prayers.

× ~~Payd every Groat I ow'd, and went to Prayers.~~

Why ill

~~Meantime~~

May Fools find Patrons still in ev'ry age! qu:
As Quarles had Benlows, so may Tibbald G--
Some kind Maecaenas fall to ev'ry Scrub, si
Du~~ck~~et to Old~~mix~~on, to W---d B--- del.
And,
~~For~~ when some Job requires a Day's defence,
Or Envy holds a whole weeks war with sence,
Or Lordly Pride for Flatt'ry makes demands;
Dunce after be What fits not Athens, may Boeo-
~~So oft, a~~ Dunce ~~is~~ taken off my hands!
tia fit.

Give me [On Thames's silver bank, in ~~sweet retreat~~, learned Ease
To write, or plant, or which I please;
~~Oh let me plant or~~ saunter, ~~drink or eat~~
have ve or
Whole years ~~had~~ pass'd, since I ha~~d~~ writ ~~or~~ read,
Or known if Dennis were alive or dead;
A vulgar Soul, not born to great affairs,
I nor blush to say my
~~I gravely~~ pay my debts, ~~and went to~~ prayers
~~Pay'd ev'ry Groat I ow'd, and went to Pray'rs.~~ Why will
~~Meantime~~

And now ye Town imagines
all ask.
I saw
Cries
Sir sure says U—n) his great
Ethic or Epic, I am
Tis all in vain
Who
Or then
The
Poor
When

"But why write Satyr? Bubo asks: 'Tis true
Bubo hates Satire, Satire hates him too.
"& why make Folly (cries Ld Frott) yr theme?
"Better by far to sing a purling stream.
[illegible] Bubo & Frott are eccho'd by each Sot:
But Z—ds gives B—y, Sir why should you not?
[illegible]
"You did so lately; was it understood?
[illegible]
Like trembling D—g or a Norfolk Hound,
[illegible]
[illegible]
[illegible] Amelia [illegible] nine,
[illegible]
No—the high task to lift up Kings to Gods,
Leave to Court Sermons & to Birthday Odes.
On themes like these superior far to thine,
Let laurell'd Cibber & great Arnall shine.
Why write at all? yet, silence if you keep,
"The Town, ye Court, ye vamp'd Dunciad weep?
Write then, but publish not; Be Vice yr Text
But keep this Age's Picture for ye next
Your Foes shall wish yr Life a longer date,
& every friend sleep lament yr fate
Agreed. Shall you who hurt a harmless Neighbors peace,
Insult fall'n worth, or Beauty in distress,
Who love a Lye, lame Slander help about
Who write a Libel, or who copy out
2 Fop whose Pride
Yet abuse
3 That more abusive
Yet wants ye Honor
Who courts ye name of wit at ye expence
1 Of Candor Decency Religion Sense
Who to ye Dean & silver Bell can swear
And sees at C—s what was never there
Who Wore I mean when I say
& if he lies not, must at least betray
Let never modest men my Satire dread
But all such babling blockheads in their stead

What if I sing augustus great & good?
You did so lately, was it understood?
You praise too nicely

Of any Rogue ye scape ye Law take note
For Sire who write, who judge, who chuse, who vote.

What if I
~~tis Better to~~ sing ~~ye great~~
Augustus great & good?

~~it nicely~~
~~You did so lately — was~~
y^{u} did so lately--was it understood

~~< > You w^{d} not open sure~~

~~Too nice y^{r} praise~~;~~<come>~~ extend y^{r}
~~Be nice no more~~ ~~<your>Notes with~~ mouth pro
but with a
You praise too nicely, ^

Of evry
~~Let then each~~ Rogue y^{t} scapes y^{e}
Law take note

For Hire who write, who judge~~s,~~ who chuse,
who vote

And now ye Town imagines
All ask,
I saw
Cries
Tis sure (says U--n) his great
Ethic or Epic, I am
Tis all in vain
"No
& then
The
Poor
When

asks?
'But why write Satyr? Bubo ~~cries~~: Tis true

Bubo hates Satire, Satire hates him too.

'& why make Folly (cries Ld Froth) y^{r} theme?

'Better by far to sing a purling stream.

~~<W^{t}> Fro~~ Bubo & Froth are echoed by each Sot:

But Z--ds cries B--y, Sir, Why should you not?

I'd rather praise Augustus
~~I'd write a Panegyric if y^{u} cd--~~

did so
"You ~~try'd it <once>~~ lately. Was it understood?

~~<Will you>~~ Speak out, Man, open in a
~~<Go then>~~ ~~with open Mouth~~'d ~~&&~~ Notes~~-~~ profound
as
~~Like~~ rumbling D — s or a Norfolk hound,

cramm the
~~Wth George & Fred'ric roughen evry Verse;~~

~~Then smooth up all, & Caroline reherse,~~

~~charm~~
Wth soft Amelia ~~sooth ye tuneful nine~~,

~~& sweetly flow thro all ye Royal Line.~~

No--the high task to lift up Kings to Gods,

Leave to Court Sermons & to Birthday Odes.

On themes like these superior far to thine,

Let ~~his~~ laurelld Cibber & great Arnall shine.

Why write at all? "Yes, silence if y^{u} keep,

very
~~How will~~ The Town, ye Court, ye dunciad weep?

Be
Write then, but publish not. ~~Make~~ Vice y^{r}. Text

~~& give~~ But keep this Age's Picture for ye next

Your Foes shall wish y^{r} Life a longer date,

& evry friend ~~shall~~ ye less lament y^{r} fate

all you! harmless
Agreed. ~~The Man~~ who hurt a neighbors peace,

Insult fal'n Worth, or Beauty in distress,

lame
Who love a Lye, ~~who <midwife>~~ slander ~~out~~ help about

or who copy
Who write a Libel, ~~copy or give~~ out

2 The ~~Man wh~~ Fop whose Pride

Yet absent

3 That more abusive

Yet wants ye Honor

1 Who courts ye name of Wit at ye expence

Of ~~Honor~~ Candor Decency Religion Sense

Who to ye dean & silver Bell can swear

And sees at C--s what was never there

who w^{t}ere I mean w^{t}ere I say

& if he lies not, must at least betray

Let never modest men my satire dread

But all such babling Blockheads in their stead

— Blockhead's (10) in his Head. (5) 10

[Let] ~~Who [illegible]~~ Sporus, [trembles] when his whispring breath

Would blast a Foe, & stinks a Friend to death;

~~When on th' Imperial~~ [where perch'd behind the] Car (a shamefull Load!)

Close at the Ear of Eve ~~I perch~~ [we spy] the Toad,

Spitting ~~his~~ [vile] Politicks, unmanly Lyes,

~~& Tales, Puns, & Bawdy, Lies~~ [& Tales & Smutt, & Puns,] & Blasphemies:

Or when ~~[illegible]~~ [that] florid Impotence of Style

Like his own Face, half Malice, half a Smile

~~[illegible]~~ [In windy Nonsence o'er the Se-nate breaks,]

~~In [illegible] of Buffoonry [illegible]~~

~~When [illegible]~~ [and what the Prompter breaths,] the Puppet squeaks:

His Wit meer See-saw, between that & this,

Now high, now low, now Master up, now Miss,

And he himself one poor Antithesis:

Who sillily immoral, pertly dull,

Profess'd a Knave, yet nothing but a Fool,

Tatler at Toiletts, Fop at C—l board,

Now trips a Lady, & now struts a Lord. [Eternal Smiles his emptiness betray]

Beauty, or Wit, his courtly hours employs, [As shallow streams run dimpling all the way.]

This he ne'r tastes, & that he ne'r enjoys;

So well-bred Spaniels civilly delight

In mumbling of the Game they dare not bite.

Satire & Sense are things he cannot feel,

Who breaks a Butterfly upon a Wheel?

Yet let me flap this Bug with silken wings,

This [painted] ~~glittring~~ Child of Dirt that stinks & stings;

This

[Margin:] Close at the Ear of Eve when sitts the Toad
& ~~spits~~ all his froathy Essence spits abroad
A Pun, a Tale a Joke a Bite a Lye
& Ryme & Smut & Spite & Blasphemy

[Margin, crossed out:] ~~The Monkey that [illegible] if a man but speaks, The Ape [illegible] flatters [illegible] [illegible] speaks.~~ [illegible] what —

--Blockheads in his stead.

[Let tremble,
~~Who hates not~~ Sporus ^ when his whispring ^ breath
Would blast a Foe, & stinks a Friend to death;

~~or when~~
When perchd behind the
~~When on th' Imperial~~ Car (a shameful Load!)

Close at the Ear
of Eve when sits y^e
Toad

we spy
Close at the Ear of Eve ~~is perchd~~ the Toad,

all
& ~~spits~~ his froathy
Essence spits abroad

vile
Sputt'ring ~~low~~ Politicks, unmanly Lyes,

A Pun, a Tale a Joke a
Bite a Lye

& Tales & Smutt & Puns,
~~& Tales, & Puns, & Bawdy, Puns~~ ^ & Blasphemies:

& Ryme & Smut & Spite
& Blasphemy

that
Or when ~~that~~ ^ florid Impotence of Style
(Like his own Face, half Malice, half a Smile)

~~From Pug in Robes the grave Buffoon'ry breaks~~
~~Ermine~~

~~The Monkey Chatters if a man but speaks.~~
~~The ape so chatters that you w^d think it he speaks.~~
< us > what

o In windy Nonsense o'er
~~In grave Buffonry begins to break~~ the Se-
-nate breaks,

~~As~~ and what the Prompter breaths,
~~When W---le blows, & bids~~ ^ the Puppet Squeak ^ s:

His Wit meer See-saw, between that & this,
Now high, now low, nor Master up, now Miss,
And he himself one poor Antithesis:
Who sillily immoral, pertly dull,
Profess'd a Knave, yet nothing but a Fool,
Tatler at Toiletts, Fop at C---l board,
Now trips a Lady, & now struts a Lord. ^

Eternal smiles his emptiness
betray
As shallow streams run dimpling
all ye way.

Beauty, or Wit, his courtly hours employs,
This he ne'r tastes, & that he ne'r enjoys;
So well-bred Spaniels civilly delight
In mumbling of the Game they dare not bite.
Satire & Sense are things he cannot feel,
Who breaks a Butterfly upon a Wheel?
Yet let me flap this Bug with silken wings,

painted
This ~~glittring~~ Child of Dirt that stinks & stings;

This

This Thing amphibious, acting either part,
A ~~the~~ trifling Head, or ~~the~~ a corrupted Heart:
A Pimp, yet Babler, Sycophant, yet Spy;
Did ever Smock-face hide such Villany?
Eve's Tempter thus by Rabbins is exprest,
A Cherub's Face, a Reptile all the rest;
Beauty that shocks you, Parts that none can trust,
Wit that can creep, & Pride that licks the Dust.

This Thing amphibious, acting either part,
A|~~The~~ triffling Head, or a ~~the~~ corrupted Heart:
A Pimp, yet Babler, Sycophant, yet Spy;
Did ever Smock-face hide such Villany?
Eve's Tempter thus by Rabbins is exprest,
A Cherub's Face, a Reptile all the rest;
Beauty that *shocks* you; Parts that none can *trust*,
Wit that can *creep*, & Pride that *licks the dust*.

Came not from Amm[on]

~~And Virgil's Headake~~ & Marot Megrim part ~~could~~

Since from a mortal Mother, not a

Happy! if He in whom their frailties join'd,

Had heir'd as well the Virtues of their mind. (2*)

My Christian Father held it for a rule

It was a Sin to call our Brother Fool;

The harmless Matron, judg'd no Wife a Whore;

Hear this, and spare ~~my Family~~, James M— re! Stet.

And couldst thou think my honest Sire unknown

Meerly because thou dost not know thy own?

Known he shall be, and lov'd and honor'd long,

If there be Force in Virtue or in Song.

Of gentle blood, part shed in Honor's Cause

(While yet in Albion Honor had applause)

The Good Man sprung: his Fortunes all his own

And better got than from th' ungrateful Throne.

Not Pope autog

Came not from Amon

& Maro's Megrim <——>
~~And Virgils Headake~~ I ~~could~~ ^

Since from a Mortal Mother, not <a>

Happy! if He in whom their frailties join'd, (2*)

Had heir'd as well the Virtues of their mind.

My Christian Father held it for a rule

It was a Sin to call our Brother Fool;

She, harmless Matron, judg'd no Wife a Whore;

<~~them-- D----s~~ and >
Hear this, and spare ~~my Family~~, James M-re! Stet.

And couldst thou think my honest Sire unknown

Meerly because thou dost not know thy own?

~~or envy'd~~
Known he shall be, & lov'd & honor'd long,

If there be Force in Virtue or in Song.

Of gentle blood, part shed in Honor's Cause

(While yet in Albion Honor had applause)

The Good Man sprung: his Fortunes all his own ^

And better got than from th' ungrateful Throne.
~~<Well-got, obligd to few, in debt to none>~~

...n not be blest as I.

... thine Joy be thine!

Be no unpleasing Melancholy mine;

me let the tender Office long

engage

To rock the Cradle of reposing Age,

With lenient Arts extend one Parents breath,

Make Languor smile, and smooth the Bed of Death!

And when the cares my better Years have shown

A Mother's age, shall hasten on my own;

Shall some kind Hand, like B— —'s or like thine,

Support my gentle, un-perceiv'd Decline?

In Wants or Sickness, shall a Friend be nigh,

Explore my thought, & watch my asking Eye?

Whither that Blessing be deny'd, or giv'n,

Thus far was right — the rest belongs to Heav'n.

not be blest as I.

<Domes>tic
~~livelier~~ Joy be thine!
^

Be no unpleasing Melancholy mine;

Me let the tender Office long
~~Mine the soft pleas<ure>~~ ingage

To rock the Cradle of reposing Age,

extend
With lenient Arts ~~prolong~~ one Parents breath,
^

Make Languor smile, and smooth the Bed of Death!

And when the cares my better Years have shown

+A Mother's age, shall hasten on my own;

~~Say~~ Shall kind like
~~Let~~ some ~~kind~~ Hand, like B--'s or thine,
^

Support my gentle, un-perceivd Decline?

shall
In Wants or Sickness, ~~let~~ a Friend be nigh,

Explore my thought, & watch my asking Eye?

Whether that Blessing be denyd, or giv'n,

Thus far was right -- The rest belongs to Heav'n.

Epistle to Dr. Arbuthnot

NOTES TO THE TRANSCRIPTS

Page:Line

1:7 The Man: *Pope's friend William Cleland: see Introduction.*

1:23 eas'd *overwrites an erasure, probably of* help'd.

2:6 B——y: *Bentley. See TE, 4:108.* T——s: *Tibbalds, i.e. Lewis Theobald. TE, 4:108, 389; 5:455–56.*

2:7 Milbourne: *the Rev. Luke Milbourne (1649–1720), who had severely attacked Dryden.*

2:10 who only *overwrites erasures, possibly of* but meerly.

2:13 small *overwrites an illegible word, possibly* mad.

2:27 secret *overwrites an erasure.*

2:29 *The transcript inadvertently omits the insertion* Knows <not?> *below and to the right of* guess.

2:33 Nurse Namby: *Ambrose Philips (1675?–1749) who is also the "Wight" of l. 30. See TE, 4:109, 377–78; 5:451–52.*

2:41 Steals *overwrites* Spends.

2:43 Johnson: *Charles Johnson (1679–1748). See TE, 5:446.*

2:46 He: *possibly Thomas Tickell, who with encouragement from Addison began a translation of the "Iliad" intended to outshine Pope's; more probably, Sir Richard Blackmore, whose epic writings Pope burlesqued for their "Tremendous Sound" in the "Epistle to Fortescue," ll. 23–26.*

2:51 own'd *is altered from* owns, made *from* make. Tate: *Nahum Tate, TE, 4:389. (Conceivably, with a pun on tate–a wisp of hair or fiber, or a small piece or particle.)*

2:55 was *overwrites* is.

3:3 kindles *is altered from* kindled.

3:8 fearful *overwrites an erased word, apparently* jealous.

3:12 Wi *of* Willing *seems to overwrite* Or.

3:18 ye *is altered from* yt.

3:21 ever *is altered from* e'er, make *from* made.

3:22 my foe *is to be read with l. 21.*

3:24 Give *is altered from* gave.

3:35 A——n: *Addison. TE, 4:109–11.*

3:37 the *is altered from* that.

3:38 sigh'd *and* curs'd *appear to be altered from* sigh *and* curse.

3:39 honest *overwrites* modest.

Page:Line

3:41 morall *overwrites an illegible word, possibly* modest.

3:42 Bridgman: *Charles Bridgman (d. 1738), landscape gardener, whom Pope had complimented in his "Epistle to Burlington," ll. 73–74.*

3:43 *The first and second* my *each seem to overwrite* a; modest *overwrites* Morall, *or vice-versa.*

3:48 keep *belongs with l. 47.*

3:49–51 *Much in these lines overwrites erasures.*

3:55 *Pope has canceled the bracket;* stood *overwrites* stand.

3:59 ruld *is altered from* rule; lead *overwrites* ruld *or vice-versa;* full-blown *overwrites an illegible word.* Bubo: *Bubb Dodington. (See also l. 69.) TE, 112–13, 337–38.*

3:63 Allen Ramsay: *Allan Ramsay (1686–1758), Scots poet.* Stephen Duck: *TE, 4:359.*

3:66 Or *and* never *are altered from* nor *and* ever.

3:72 While *overwrites an illegible word.*

3:73 slumbring *is altered from* slumbered.

3:75 Or planted, saunter'd, chatter'd, *and* drank *are altered from* I plant, I saunter, chatter, *and* drink.

3:79 What *overwrites an illegible word, possibly* Ten.

3:84 Bards *overwrites an illegible word, apparently* Poets.

3:91 Retreat *overwrites* my Seat.

3:93 Saunterd . . . and *overwrites several illegible words.*

3:94 had *is altered in both instances from* have.

3:95 if *possibly overwrites* yt.

4:2 Johnston: *above, 2:43.*

4:4 wake *overwrites* walk.

4:5 with *overwrites* in.

4:7 on *overwrites* I.

4:8, 11 imagin'd *and* ask'd *are altered from* imagines *and* asks.

4:14 K——l: *George Hay, seventh earl of Kinnoul. TE, 4:115 and 364–65.* V——n: *Thomas Vernon (d. 1726), Pope's grasping landlord at Twickenham, or possibly his wife (d. 1743).*

4:15 Bibbs & Leading Strings: *evidently a glance at the Queen's and Walpole's domination of George II.* Upton: *evidently the John Upton whom David Mallet describes as "the Center of all trifling Intelligence" (Mallet to Pope [January 1730], "Correspondence, 3:80).*

Page:Line	
4:18–19	known *overwrites an illegible word;* his *also overwrites an illegible word, possibly* ye.
4:21	is done *completes l. 19.*
4:24	Thoughts on God & Gardens: *presumably the "Essay on Man" and "Epistle to Burlington."*
4:25	Chartres: *Francis Chartres (1675–1732). TE, 3, 2:85–86; 4:353. A variant of this line found its way into the "Epistle to Fortescue," l. 4.*
4:29	Sir Will: *Above, p. 417. TS 25:34.*
4:41	Ballad *is possibly* Balked, *and in that case a reading replaced by* sped; *but Pope would more probably have written* balkd; *the capital* B *seems reasonably clear; and therefore I take the word to be* Ballad, *the poet's reminder to himself of situations to be developed in the passage below at right (l. 45).*
4:45	*The illegible words are possibly* want to give. Marg'ret's Ghost: *in David Mallet's ballad "William and Margaret" (1724), the ghost of the betrayed Margaret visits her faithless lover William at dead of night and invites him to her grave.*
4:64	Irish Poetess: *TE, 4:97.*
4:66	He *is altered from* he.
4a:86	Arthur: *Arthur Moore. TE, 4:97, 374.*
4a:89	B——: *This is probably William Bromley, son of the William Bromley who was Speaker of the House of Commons during the last years of Queen Anne. Young Bromley married Lucy Throckmorton on 2 July 1724, and according to Egmont ("Diary," 12 March 1737; 2:366–67), "in a short time" was "made a cuckold." In 1736 he "put her away" for an affair "with my Lord Lee's son." Ibid., 6 January 1736, 2:218.*
5:4	n *of* nay *overwrites an illegible letter or letters, possibly* st.
5:12	What's *overwrites* Here's.
5:13	could *overwrites* can.
5:17	he *overwrites* I; them *overwrites* it.
5:20	thē *and* them *each overwrite* it.
5:21	Business *and* Sickness *overwrite erasures.*
5:23	comes *overwrites* leaves.
5:24	will *overwrites* would; s *of* comes *is added.*
5:28	We *seems to overwrite* I.
5:29	Welsted: *Leonard Welsted. TE, 4:393;* this *seems to be altered from* his, Message *from* Verses.
5:36	Cook: *Thomas Cooke, who was sometimes called Hesiod Cook (l. 37) for his translation of Hesiod (1728). See also ll. 37, 42.*
5:37	they *is altered from* he.
5:39	Curl: *Edmund Curll. TE, 4:356–57; 5:436.*
5:41	them *is altered from* him, theyre *(inadvertently* they re *in the transcript) from* he's.
5:43	Sir Robert: *Walpole, who employed a good many hacks to write for his ministry.*
5:44	That *overwrites* This: this *overwrites* that; must *seems to overwrite* one.
5:51	I *of* If *overwrites* i.
5:54	Quarles: *Francis Quarles (1603–76). See below, ll. 73–77, and TE, 5:321 n.* Tibald: *above, 2:6.*
5:55	Gage: *probably Joseph Gage. See TE, 3. 2:130 n.*
5:58	dem *of* demands *is possibly overwritten by* Poet.
5:62	B——: *Bubb. Above, 3:59.*
5:63	Lintot: *Bernard Lintot. TE, 4:100, 370–71.*
5:65	One kind Knight: *evidently Walpole—above, l. 43.*
5:66	*Pope has canceled quotation marks before* Not.
5:76	They *is altered from* He.
5:80	C——; *Court?*
5:97	W——d: *Welsted. Above, 5:29.*
5:98	Ducket: *George Duckett (1684–1732). TE, 5:438–39.*
5:101	makes *seems to overwrite* is at.
5:113	told *overwrites* out.
6:3	One *overwrites* This.
6:8	humbly flatters *overwrites illegible words.*
6:10	U——; *(see also l. 15). Above, 4:15.*
6:15	some ↔ *overwrites illegible words, possibly* come to.
6:21	*Exclamation point seems to be altered from a comma.*
6:44	He *overwrites an illegible word, possibly* one.
6:46	Had *is perhaps altered from* Cd.
6:48	He *seems to be altered from* Her.
6:53	M——re: James Moore-Smythe. TE, 4:126; 385–86.
7:6, 9	domestic strife *and* Religious *overwrite erasures.*
7:12	*The second* Nor *may be altered from* Or; riskd *and* dard *are altered from* risk *and* dare, *which seem in turn to have been altered from an earlier* riskd *and* dard.
7:14, 15	Whose *is altered from* His.
9:16	O *of* On *overwrites* o.
9:19	have *is altered from* are.
9:21	Or known *is altered from* Unknown.
9:24	pay *is altered from* payd.
10:19	Bubo *seems to be altered from* Babo.
10:22	did so lately. *(See also l. 25.) Conceivably a reference to ll. 195–204 of the "Epistle to Burlington." The mock panegyric on the royal family in the "Epistle to Fortescue" (ll. 29–36) was still to be written, as this page shows. The* t *of* Augustus *seems to overwrite* I *(revising* yu *in l. 232).*
10:23	I'd *overwrites* You'd.
10:30	Norfolk hound: *alluding perhaps to the hunting (and drinking) jamborees that took place periodically at Robert Walpole's Houghton in Norfolk for the cementing of political ties, but more particularly, no doubt, to the "baying" of the ministerial writers—Walpole's "pack."*
10:32–35	*For these names see the "Epistle to Fortescue," TE, 4:7.*
10:40	Arnall: *William Arnall. TE, 4:102, 345; 5:428.*
10:43	The *overwrites* ye.
10:49	*After* Fo *of* Foes *Pope has struck out a letter. Perhaps he started to write* Friend.
10:58	The *overwrites* Who.
10:65	C——s: *Cannons, Chandos's estate. TE, 4:117; 3. 2:23 n.*
10:68	men *overwrites* man.

Page:Line	
10:69	their *is altered from* his.
11:7	When perchd *overwrites an illegible word or words, possibly* thron'd. *To left of this line Pope has obliterated a number indicating rearrangement, as also before ll. 20 and 32 below.*
11:30	the Prompter: *Walpole.*
11:37	C——l: *evidently "Civil," but one suspects there must be a cryptic allusion to account for the partial concealment.*
12:4	Pimp: *probably an allusion to Hervey's supposed role in arranging amours for the Prince of Wales, notably one with Anne Vane, who had been his own mistress.*

Page:Line	
13:2	*The truncated word may be* patiently.
13:10	*A name that may be* Dennis *overwrites* D——s.
14:5	*The* l *of* long *in l. 5 overwrites an obscure mark that may be a raised* r *on* pleasr *in l. 6.*
14:13	kind *appears to overwrite* Hand.
14:14	B——'s: *Bolingbroke's. But see above, Introduction, p. 420.*
14:15	*The question mark overwrites a semicolon.*

ADDENDA

1. Further Notes on the Transcripts: (a) *At 10:23,* write a *should probably read either* strive at *or* shine in; (b) *At 10:26,* Man *should probably read* then.

2. MS. Variants Recorded by Jonathan Richardson, Jr. *Richardson set down variants between the MS. text and that printed in the 1735 quarto "Works" on unbound sheets of the latter that are now preserved at the Huntington Library. His record shows clearly that he had access to some eight lines or half lines not found in the MS. leaves that we possess today: a loss possibly occasioned by the disappearance of a leaf or fragment at the time of the accident which divided the MS. of "Arbuthnot" between New York and California. The variants in question all appear in the margins of p. 71 of the quarto and read as follows:*

(a) *Cued apparently to follow TE, line 290, but with no rhyming line indicated:* To spread the Scandal wch *the Bilingsgate* he dare not own.

(b) *Cued to TS 3:43 in this volume; but where I have* Good man, mistakes, *JR has both this and* Knows not, Good Man.

(c) *Cued to follow TE, line 292:*

> Once, & but once, my heedless Youth was bit,
> And lik'd that dang'rous Thing, a Female Wit;
> Safe, as I thought, tho all ye Prudent chid;
> I writ no Libels, but my Lady did.
> Great odds! in Am'rous or Poetic Game,
> When Woman's was the Sin, & Man's the Shame.

In a number of instances, Richardson emends the quarto readings to later readings: in every instance, the readings of the text we habitually use, available in TE. These alterations represent, I believe, his updating of the quarto text from a revised printed text of later date and therefore are not found, nor could be expected to be found, in the MS. reproduced here. For what is probably a similar procedure by Pope himself, see above, p. 159, note 9.